The Old English Gloss to the Lindisfarne Gospels

Buchreihe der ANGLIA/ ANGLIA Book Series

Volume 51

The Old English Gloss to the Lindisfarne Gospels

Language, Author and Context

Edited by
Julia Fernández Cuesta
Sara M. Pons-Sanz

DE GRUYTER

For an overview of all books published in this series, please see
http://www.degruyter.com/view/serial/36292

ISBN 978-3-11-063529-4
e-ISBN (PDF) 978-3-11-044910-5
e-ISBN (EPUB) 978-3-11-044716-3
ISSN 0340-5435

Library of Congress Cataloging-in-Publication Data
A CIP catalog record for this book has been applied for at the Library of Congress.

Bibliographic information published by the Deutsche Nationalbibliothek
The Deutsche Nationalbibliothek lists this publication in the Deutsche Nationalbibliografie; detailed bibliographic data are available on the Internet at http://dnb.dnb.de.

This volume is text- and page-identical with the hardback published in 2016.
Cover image: Lonely/iStock/Thinkstock
Typesetting: PTP-Berlin, Protago-TEX-Production GmbH, Berlin
Printing and binding: CPI books GmbH, Leck

♾ Printed on acid-free paper
Printed in Germany

www.degruyter.com

Contents

Acknowledgements

We wish to express our gratitude to the colleagues who first encouraged us to undertake this project, and those who have helped us and supported us during the process, especially to Rolf Bremmer, Richard Dance, Robert D. Fulk, Susan Irvine, Charles Jones, Roger Lass, Kathryn Lowe, Gary Miller, Mª Nieves Rodríguez Ledesma and Mercedes Salvador Bello. We would also like to thank all the contributors and peer reviewers for all their hard work in making this book a reality, and all those who attended the workshop on the Lindisfarne gloss. In this respect, we are also indebted to the Society for the Study of Medieval Languages and Literature, and the Department of English, Linguistics and Cultural Studies of the University of Westminster for their financial contribution to the workshop. We are equally grateful to the 'Ministerio de Economía y Competitividad' of the Spanish government for the award of an I+D grant (FFI2011-28272), from which we have greatly benefitted.

Special thanks go to Lucia Kornexl and Ursula Lenker, the editors of the Anglia book series, for believing in our project and for their assistance throughout the process of editing; to Johann Schedlinski, the copy-editor, for the care and attention that he has put into the formatting and bibliography of the volume; and to Christopher Langmuir, for valuable comments and suggestions. The remaining errors and infelicities are of course our own.

Seville and London, March 2015
Julia Fernández Cuesta and Sara M. Pons-Sanz

Abbreviations

a left-hand column in a page
acc. accusative
act. active (voice)
Angl. Anglian
b right-hand column in a page
c. L *circa* 'around'
cent. century
cp. compare
caus. causative
dat. dative
e.g. L *exempli gratia* 'for example'
f. folio
ff. folios
fut. future
gen. genitive
Go. Gothic
Gr. Greek
i.e. L *id est* 'that is'
imp. imperative
ind. indicative
infl. inflection
intran. intransitive
L Latin
Li. Lindisfarne Gospels (Latin text or gloss)
lit. literally
ML Medieval Latin
MS manuscript
MSS manuscripts
n. footnote
no. number
nos. numbers
NP noun phrase
NSR Northern Subject Rule
OE Old English
OEN Old East Norse
OFris. Old Frisian
OHG Old High German
OIc Old Icelandic
OS Old Saxon
part. participle
pass. passive (voice)
PDE Present Day English
PGmc Proto-Germanic
perf. perfect

pl.	plural
pres.	present
PRO	pronoun
r	recto
refl.	reflexive
Ru.	Rushworth Gospels (Latin text or gloss)
Ru^1	Part of the gloss to the Rushworth Gospels attributed to Farman
Ru^2	Part of the gloss to the Rushworth Gospels attributed to Owun
sg.	singular
so.	someone
st.	strong
sth.	something
subj.	subjunctive
tran.	transitive
trans.	translation
v	verso
vs.	L *versus* 'against'
wk.	weak
WS	West Saxon

Editorial conventions

In order to make this volume as cohesive as possible, we have followed a number of editorial conventions with regard to various formatting and transcription issues:

1. Given that most papers make use of the *Dictionary of Old English Corpus*, we have adopted its practice of giving Latin words and longer structures in italics. Old English is quoted in Roman characters, although Old English dictionary forms are given in italics in order to differentiate them from particular forms in their paradigm.
2. On the basis of the *Anglia* stylesheet, we use ampersand for L *et* in Latin quotations and the Tironian sign for OE *and*, except in cases where the manuscript, and not an edition, is specifically quoted.
3. We use various special characters as follows:
   - ( ) indicate editorial expansions of abbreviated forms in a manuscript;
   - [ ] indicate authorial comments or phonetic transcriptions;
   - < > indicate that the matter under discussion has to do mainly with spelling;
   - \` ´ indicate that the character(s) appear(s) above the text line;
   - ´ \` indicate that the character(s) appear(s) below the text line;
   - ' indicates an abbreviated form.
4. Vowel length in dictionary forms is not marked.

Illustrations

The images from the Lindisfarne Gospels and the Durham Collectar have been reproduced by kind persmission of the British Library and the Dean of Durham Cathedral, respectively.

Julia Fernández Cuesta and Sara M. Pons-Sanz

Introduction

The present collection on the Old Northumbrian gloss to the Lindisfarne Gospels contains some of the papers presented at a workshop on the Lindisfarne gloss held at the University of Westminster, London, in April 2012, as well as various additional papers. The aim of the workshop was to bring together scholars working on the Lindisfarne gloss from different perspectives (palaeography, glossography, history, linguistics and philology) in the belief that it is not possible to solve the problems posed by the language of one of the most intriguing Old English texts that have come down to us without carefully exploring the socio-historical context and the cultural and intellectual milieu in which it was produced.

Some of the contributors to this volume have dedicated a great part of their professional lives to the study of the Lindisfarne Gospels and its Old English gloss, and are experts in the linguistic features of the text and its context, while others have recently completed doctoral theses which are themselves already important contributions to the field. All of us share a fascination with the Lindisfarne Gospels, although our methodological approaches vary considerably.

Aldred's Old English glosses to the Lindisfarne Gospels (London, British Library, MS Nero D.iv) and to the Durham Collectar or Ritual (Durham, Cathedral Library, MS A.iv.19), and Ru^2, Owun's interlinear gloss to most of the Rushworth or MacRegol Gospels (Oxford, Bodleian Library, MS Auct. D.2.19), are the most substantial representatives of what has been traditionally labelled 'Old Northumbrian', more particularly, 'northern late Old Northumbrian'.[1] Apart from a few brief runic inscriptions, the first records that have been preserved in English were written in varieties of northern English.[2]

As is well known, in the seventh and eighth centuries the kingdom of Northumbria was one of the most important centres of learning in Europe, producing scholars of the stature of Bede and Alcuin, and spiritual figures such as St. Cuthbert. As the result of Viking attacks, which started in the late eighth century, the monastic community of Lindisfarne was compelled to leave the island and undertake a journey that would take them to Chester-le-Street (and eventually to

---

1 Owun's gloss is commonly referred to as Ru^2 in order to distinguish it from Farman's Mercian gloss (Ru^1), which extends through all of Matthew's Gospel, Mark 1.1–2.15 and John 18.1–18.3.

2 Early witnesses of northern Old English include coin inscriptions, the runic inscriptions on the Franks Casket and the Ruthwell Cross, the northern versions of *Cædmon's Hymn*, the *Leiden Riddle*, *Bede's Death Song* and some 9,000 names contained in the early manuscripts of Bede's *Historia ecclesiastica* and in the Durham *Liber Vitae*, all from the seventh to the ninth centuries. The language in which they are written has been traditionally labelled 'early Old Northumbrian'.

Durham) in what has been described as a "move closer to the new seat of political power, which had shifted [...] to Viking-held territory and its power-base at York" (Brown, this volume: p. 21; see also Brown 2003: 85–90). It was at the community's new home in Chester-le-Street that in the tenth century a priest named Aldred furnished one their most valuable possessions, the Lindisfarne Gospels, with a continuous interlinear gloss in Old Northumbrian, producing the first extant translation of the Gospels into the vernacular and the most extensive text that has come down to us written in northern Old English. Given the scanty nature of the surviving texts, the Lindisfarne gloss is of inestimable value for the study of the language at a time when some of the most interesting changes in the grammar of English were taking place. Although the gloss has received a great deal of attention and has been widely studied in the past two centuries,[3] there are still numerous problems which remain unresolved. It was largely for this reason that the time seemed ripe for a new approach to the text from an interdisciplinary perspective, not only to revise and assess the work of our predecessors, but also because we believe that the application of modern methodologies (variationist approaches, quantitative analysis, statistics, linguistic archaeology) may shed new light on both the language of the text and its context.

The papers included in this collection have been organized into three parts. Those presented in the first section, "The Gloss in Context", aim to help us understand Aldred's goals and interests, as well as the cultural milieu he was working in. **Michelle Brown** offers further evidence in support of the idea, first put forward in Brown (2003), that the composition of the gloss must be understood against the background of the sociohistorical and political situation of tenth-century Northumbria, when the area was being integrated into the newly unified England and was also threatened by the ambition of the Viking kings of York. She offers a survey of the figure of Aldred the glossator in the context of the

3 The gloss was edited by Stevenson and Waring (1854–1865) and Skeat (1871–1887), and some excerpts are included in Sweet (1978). Various dissertations have been devoted to the study of individual Gospels: e.g. Foley (1903) on Matthew's Gospel; Lea (1894) on Mark's Gospel; Kellum (1906) on Luke's Gospel; and Füchsel (1901) on John's Gospel. Palaeographic studies of the text include Ker (1943) and Kendrick et al. (1960). With regard to the various levels of linguistic analysis, Foley (1903), Stolz (1908) and Hogg (2004) deal with the phonology of the gloss. The standard reference grammars of Old English (Campbell 1959, Brunner 1965 and Hogg 1992a) also refer to aspects of the phonology of the gloss, especially inasmuch as they differ from West Saxon; its morphology has been studied, amongst others, by Carpenter (1910), Kolbe (1912), Chadwick (1934), Ross (1934, 1937, 1960), Blakeley (1949–1950), Brunner (1947–1948), Berndt (1956), and Hogg and Fulk (2011); Bale (1907), Callaway (1918), Jones (1987) and Cole (2014) analyze its morphosyntactic features; Ross (1940, 1982), Thomson (1961), Wenisch (1979), Hill (1989) and Pons-Sanz (2000), amongst others, examine its lexis.

history of St. Cuthbert's community after their forced exile from Holy Island, followed by their negotiations with both the Danes and King Æthelstan in order to secure for themselves a new (and safer) home. In her view, Aldred, who joined the community one or two decades after Æthelstan's visit to Chester-le-Street in 934 and was later sent on a diplomatic mission to Wessex, played an important role in the reinforcement of the 'Englishness' and Christian character of the region. As regards the problem of the colophon, also discussed by Roberts (see below), Brown too reaffirms her belief in its historical reliability, arguing that the information offered (the names of the makers of the codex) is too accurate for it to have been invented by the glossator.

Jane Roberts's paper revisits previous work on Aldred's colophon in the light of recent research which has questioned its reliability as evidence for the connection of the manuscript with Lindisfarne (Newton et al. 2013: 133). She offers fresh arguments in favour of her discovery that the colophon makes use of a pre-existing poem, and of her translation of the hapax legomenon OE "gihamadi" as 'made himself at home', which she interprets as referring to Aldred's earning a place for himself in the monastic community of Chester-le-Street through the glossing of the first three gospels and generous gifts. She further argues in favour of interpreting OE *ora* as a 'monetary unit' rather than as 'border, edge, margin', as Newton et al. (2013) would have it. The second section of the article compares the use of some linguistic features such as runic letters and the possessive adjective *sin* in Aldred's glosses to the Lindisfarne Gospels and the Durham Collectar. The final section comments on other differences between the two glosses and speculates as to what books might have been available to Aldred in Chester-le-Street.

The following three papers share an interest in Aldred's connection with Southumbrian practices. **Philip Rusche**'s contribution addresses the influence of the tenth-century Benedictine Reform on Aldred's work. He compares the methods of glossing employed in Southumbrian manuscripts with Aldred's practice and concludes that there are very few similarities, suggesting that there is no evidence to believe that Aldred was trained in the south. The interlinear psalter glosses, which predate the Reform, appear to provide a better model for the Lindisfarne glossing technique, in Rusche's opinion. His work supports Brown's (2003) and Jolly's (2013) contention that Aldred may have been keen to maintain his northern identity in spite of his political contacts and negotiations with Southumbria.

Paul Cavill examines Aldred's marginalia on the Beatitudes in Matthew's Gospel. He argues that Aldred's comments, expressed in the form of maxims, clearly show that he shared some of the concerns of the Reform movement, regardless of where he was formally trained. According to Cavill, Aldred used the style of wisdom literature in order to encourage the members of his community to observe their religious obligations and conform to monastic ideals, laying special emphasis on material poverty and purity of heart.

In his analysis of the letter-forms in Aldred's interlinear gloss, **Stewart Brookes** suggests that the remarkable variation in script type is Aldred's creative response to variation in the Latin text of the Lindisfarne Gospels. Through study of Aldred's script choices and imitative tendencies, we are able to trace his deep connection to the manuscript's style and aesthetics. In addition, the paper challenges the prevailing notion that Aldred lived in a Northumbrian backwater, providing evidence that he was aware of the latest scribal fashions, including Square minuscule and Caroline minuscule.

From a linguistic perspective, the Lindisfarne gloss poses a series of problems concerning morphological simplification, such as the apparent confusion of the final unstressed vowels, which was eventually to lead to the merger of /æ/, /a/, /e/, /ɪ/, /o/, /u/ in one (or several) vowel(s) represented by <e>; the variation between verbal *-ð* and *-s* in the present indicative and imperative plural, and various processes of analogical extension, levelling and case syncretism; the analogical extension of *ð* to the nominative singular masculine of the determiner *se – seo – ðæt*; the extension of genitive singular *-es* and nominative and accusative plural *-as* from the masculine *a*-stems to other noun classes; the use of strong forms of the adjective in contexts that require a weak inflection; and the presence of etymologically masculine or neuter adjectival forms modifying feminine nouns. While all these processes have been amply studied, notably by Ross (1936, 1937) and the contributors to the Aldrediana series, many still await a satisfactory explanation. The gloss also presents examples of unetymological gender, thus anticipating the loss of grammatical gender, which took place in Middle English and which distinguishes English from the other Germanic languages.[4] Some of these problems have also been dealt with by past scholarship (see especially Ross 1936 and Jones 1987), but (again) no definitive solutions have been offered.[5]

4 Grammatical gender, for example, is kept in Ru^2, and analogical extension processes are more limited in this text. On the other hand, there are also some differences between the language of the Lindisfarne and Ritual glosses which might be attributable to the earlier date of the former.

5 Ross (1936) put forward his "neutralization theory", according to which the language of the gloss reflects the beginning of the change from grammatical to natural gender. Other instances of unetymological forms are explained as a result of the influence of the Latin original on the gloss. Jones (1987), in his extensive study of grammatical gender in Lindisfarne, adopts a completely different approach based on Anderson's (1975) case grammar. Although in some instances he appears to be in agreement with Ross (acknowledging the influence of the Latin original and the drift towards natural gender), his approach is much more comprehensive. He sets out to account for almost every instance of unhistorical grammatical gender found in the gloss and argues that,

A range of linguistic aspects are addressed specifically in the six papers that make up the second part of this volume, "The Language of the Gloss". **Robert McColl Millar** explores the simplification of the nominal morphology reflected in the language of the gloss within the context of the evolution of English. His contribution, which draws on previous work on the morphology of the determiners (Millar 2000), sets out to demonstrate that many linguistic developments found in early Middle English, such as the loss of grammatical gender, which is directly related to the collapse of the deictic paradigms, are already found, at least in embryo, in the language of the gloss.

Marcelle Cole's paper addresses the still vexed question of authorship. Based on the results of her recent work on verbal morphology in the gloss (Cole 2014), she offers further evidence in support of the view that Aldred, who on palaeographic grounds has been generally regarded as the sole author (Ker 1943), relied on other pre-existing Gospel glosses which have not survived. Her findings strengthen the hypothesis that the language of the gloss cannot be taken as representative of a homogeneous dialect, but rather reflects features of different varieties of northern Old English besides Aldred's own idiolect.

Derivational rather than inflectional morphology is the focus of **Luisa García García**'s paper. It contrasts the results from her previous work on morphological causatives in Old English with the data obtained from Lindisfarne in order to assess whether the gloss differs from other Old English texts as regards the use and morphological status of causative verbs. After identifying all deverbal *jan*-pairs in the Lindisfarne corpus, she establishes the semantic value of each member of the pair in all attestations. Her main conclusion is that the language of the gloss is not particularly innovative in the use of the causative formation. Derivational morphology appears to behave differently from inflectional morphology, as the latter is clearly more advanced in Old Northumbrian than in the other dialects of Old English.

Mª Nieves Rodríguez Ledesma's contribution studies the genitive constructions in the gloss. While she also analyzes the syntactic structure of the noun phrases where the genitive forms appear (*pre*position of the genitive, characteristic of Old English, versus *post*position, characteristic of Latin), she focuses mainly on some morphological issues, such as zero genitives, a linguistic feature which links the gloss to later northern texts. She concludes that, although the gloss tends to follow the Latin text closely in terms of word order, it also exhibits features which are characteristic of the Northumbrian dialect.

---

as a consequence of the loss of the lexical classification of nouns in terms of grammatical gender, the various forms of the determiners were "recycled" to indicate different discourse-internal relations between the nouns (anaphoric reference and case relationships).

Also in the field of morphosyntax, **George Walkden**'s paper claims that (with the appropriate caveats) the Lindisfarne gloss can be legitimately used as evidence for the study of Old English syntax. Although Aldred's attention is mainly fixed on the word unit (see also Jolly, this volume), Walkden shows that the gloss offers evidence for the analysis of syntax at the phrasal level. The omission of subject pronouns cannot be attributed simply to the influence of the Latin original, since null subjects only appear frequently in the third person. Walkden claims that the omission of subjects in the gloss is more likely to represent a genuine Northumbrian syntactic feature, as quantitative/statistical analysis reveals that the phenomenon is more frequent in Anglian or Anglian-influenced texts than in West Saxon. He concludes that Aldred's work may contribute to our understanding of the comparative syntax of Old English.

Finally, **Julia Fernández Cuesta** stresses the importance of returning to the original manuscript.[6] She shows that the collation of Skeat's edition with the Lindisfarne manuscript reveals aspects of his editorial practice (emendations, additions, and alteration of the manuscript, word-division and word-spacing) that can result in the loss of valuable material for linguistic analysis. These practices may also obscure possible cases of linguistic change in progress and linguistic variation, which are characteristic of the dialect of the gloss.

The final part, "Glossing Practice", brings together articles directed at exploring some of the (methodological) decisions facing Aldred and other fellow glossators when carrying out the task at hand. Two papers deal with the use of multiple glosses in the Lindisfarne text. **Christine Bolze**'s contribution analyzes the ordering principle underlying multiple glosses of present tense forms of OE *beon* and suggests that the various patterns reflect Aldred's attempts to convey both the grammar and the meaning of the Latin forms as precisely as possible in the English vernacular. **Sara Pons-Sanz** sets out more generally to identify what patterns, if any, underlie Aldred's ordering of double or multiple glosses. She demonstrates that the glossator has a preference for placing the interpretamenta which most frequently render the Latin lemmata in first position, although the practice is not fully consistent.

The aim of **Patrizia Lendinara**'s paper is to explore why some words are left unglossed, for the most part names of individuals, places and peoples, but also words for Jewish festivals, animals and everyday objects. She concludes that Aldred wanted to avoid overburdening his text with redundant glosses following consideration of both the page layout and the Latin text of the Gospel. The paper

---

6 The Lindisfarne Gospels are available online at <http://www.bl.uk/manuscripts/FullDisplay.aspx?ref=Cotton_MS_Nero_D_IV>. Those interested in the Rushworth Gospels can visit <http://bodley30.bodley.ox.ac.uk:8180/luna/servlet/s/4p8a54>.

points out that the number of unglossed words varies in the four Gospels, with Matthew's Gospel featuring the largest percentage of unglossed words and John's the lowest percentage. Another remarkable difference lies in the prefatory material and the *capitula*, where Aldred leaves a large number of words unglossed, possibly because he did not have another vernacular gloss to the biblical text at hand.

Karen Jolly's and Tadashi Kotake's papers link Aldred's gloss to the Lindisfarne Gospels with the two other major witnesses of late Old Northumbrian. **Karen Jolly** analyzes the process of glossing in Aldred's additions to the more modest (and less cohesive) Durham Collectar in order to explore the function of the gloss in this manuscript and potentially in the Lindisfarne Gospels. She offers compelling evidence in the form of Aldred's additions and corrections to the work of other scribes to show that Aldred's gloss to the Durham Collectar was a tool for reflection, communication, and instruction. His project was both a written and oral one, involving extensive conversation with members of the community about the interpretation of Latin words. Jolly argues that the written and oral, pedagogical and spiritual dimensions of Aldred's gloss cannot be separated from one another.

Jolly further suggests that the fact that the main purpose of the Durham Collectar gloss was bilingual reflection accounts for Aldred's preoccupation with individual word units (or even morphemes), as illustrated by examples of literal translations of the Latin terms, whose main aim seems to be to explain both the meaning of the words as well as their etymology. This last aspect is interesting because it reveals some of the differences between the two Aldredian glosses. The purpose of the additions to the Durham Collectar appears to have been more pedagogical; they were much more accessible to the community than the Lindisfarne gloss, which is not likely to have been used for study in the 'classroom'.

The relationship between the Lindisfarne gloss and Ru^2 is the focus of **Tadashi Kotake**'s contribution. Albeit possibly written in a more southerly variety of Old Northumbrian (but see Hogg 2004), Ru^2 has traditionally been assumed to be a direct copy of the Aldredian gloss. Through detailed analysis of the sections of Ru^2 which follow neither the Latin text of the Lindisfarne Gospels nor that of the MacRegol Gospels, Kotake suggests that, rather than Owun occasionally making use of other manuscripts, as received wisdom has it, both the Lindisfarne and the Ru^2 glosses could stem from a common (and now lost) source.

This brief summary introduces a number of salient themes running through the present volume. Aldred the priest (and later provost) emerges as a scholar and a teacher, as well as a diplomat and politician, who strove to maintain his Northumbrian identity and a heritage going back to Cædmon, Bede and St. Cuthbert in the face of both the Viking incursions and the pressures from the powerful

West Saxon monarchy. In this context, the Lindisfarne gloss could well represent, as Brown puts it, “a statement of local identity in the face of Scandinavian incursion against a backdrop of attempts to reassert an English identity throughout England” (2003: 100; see also Brown, this volume).

Palaeographic analysis of the gloss supports the above hypothesis. Brown (this volume: p. 35) only identifies occasional features in the Lindisfarne script which can be associated with “those working in ‘reforming’ circles in the mid-tenth century, prior to its fuller introduction as part of the Benedictine Reform of the 970s onwards” (see also Kendrick et al. 1960). In the same way, in her edition-cum-study of the Durham Collectar, Jolly (2013: 74–88) shows that the old-fashioned script employed is relatively free from southern influence and from the innovative features of later additions. However, it is important to emphasize that Brookes demonstrates that in his gloss to the Lindisfarne Gospels Aldred evinces some familiarity with innovative practices commonly associated with Southumbria.

Other contributions to this volume support the hypothesis that Aldred is relatively independent from southern practices and manages to adhere to his northern tradition. Although he shows clear concerns about some issues of contemporary monastic practice, which would associate him with the southern Benedictine Reform (as shown by Cavill’s analysis of the marginalia to the Beatitudes), Rusche’s study indicates that Aldred’s work shows no signs of him having been trained in the Southumbrian tradition (cp. Jolly 2013).

The grammatical and lexical aspects of the glosses also reveal independence from ‘standard’ West Saxon. The gloss’s language is Old Northumbrian, although its heterogeneity indicates that Aldred must have made use of other sources also written in varieties of northern English.[7] As shown by Millar (2000 and this volume) and Rodríguez Ledesma, the Old Northumbrian dialect represented in the Lindisfarne gloss is in the vanguard of linguistic processes of change which took place in more southern dialects much later, during the Middle English period. In the same way, Walkden’s and Cole’s contributions show that there are syntactic patterns of the gloss, such as zero subjects and the Northern Subject Rule, which appear to be characteristic of the grammar of Old Northumbrian.

As suggested in Jolly’s paper, one of the possible reasons for the ‘resilient’ use of the northern dialect in Lindisfarne is that Aldred was writing for a limited and local audience (see also Millar 2006: 61). Contact with Southumbria later in his life, as evidenced by his diplomatic mission to Wessex with bishop Ælfsige, could explain the southern/West Saxon influence observed in the Durham Collec-

7 The idea that there is a demarcation at the beginning of Mark’s Gospel (Brunner 1947–1948) has found support in van Bergen (2008) and Cole (2014).

tar (see Pons-Sanz 2013: 253–257, 265–269; and Fernández Cuesta, forthcoming). As is the case in the Early Modern English period, the spread of northern English verbal morphology southwards (and also the adoption of features of the London standard in the north during the same period) cannot be explained if the social and cultural context is not taken into account. Language drift and inherited tendencies (whatever is meant by those terms) cannot by themselves explain the direction of language change. It is people as agents (speakers/writers and listeners/readers) who make histories of languages, even though they are not aware of doing so.

With regard to the sources of the gloss, some of the contributions to this volume corroborate the existence of a demarcation at the beginning of Mark's Gospel already noted by previous studies (Brunner 1947–1948, van Bergen 2008, Kotake 2012, and Cole 2014). Rodríguez Ledesma argues that the section of the gloss corresponding to Matthew's Gospel stands apart from the others regarding the distribution of the genitive singular inflections of kinship and other proper nouns, which present variants that are not attested elsewhere in the gloss, while Lendinara shows that Matthew's Gospel also differs from the rest of the gloss in that it contains the largest percentage of unglossed words.

What finally remains is the question of the purpose of the continuous gloss. From the discussion above, it seems clear that Aldred's major preoccupation was the word (Jolly) or the phrase unit (Walkden), rather than sentential or textual levels (but see Pons-Sanz), which indicates the interest of the glossator in clarifying (to himself as well as to others) the sense of individual lexical items in the sacred text. In this sense, Aldred's is a work of scholarship (cp. Robinson 1973: 466). Aldred was aware of the significance of the fact that he was translating the Latin Vulgate into English, which in the mid-tenth century was beginning to be explored as a valid vehicle to transmit the sacred word to the Christian community. This is possibly why he strives to achieve a high level of precision in his glossing, with multiple glossing (Bolze and Pons-Sanz) and occasional comments (Cavill), which can be interpreted as an attempt to clarify the Gospel text and apply it to the needs of his community.

The aim of this collection then is to offer the reader a fresh approach to the Lindisfarne gloss, one that stresses the importance of interdisciplinary work in the field of Old English studies, the history of English, and linguistic change in general. It also emphasizes the need to return to the original manuscripts, and recognizes the dangers of relying exclusively on corpora of edited texts, without taking the 'physical' context into consideration. As Brown (2013: 31) rightly states, the forensic study of books, *l'archéologie du livre*, is useful and even necessary. The original manuscript cannot be replaced, as it may be (and often is) obscured and contaminated in the editorial process.

We hope that the present volume will represent a solid contribution to the study of the language and context of the Lindisfarne gloss. Nevertheless, we are well aware that there are many aspects which remain unexplored. Aldred's work continues to offer many intriguing avenues of research for scholars interested in the sociohistorical and cultural context of early Anglo-Saxon England, his language and his glossing practices.

Part I: **The Gloss in Context**

Michelle P. Brown

'A Good Woman's Son': Aspects of Aldred's Agenda in Glossing the Lindisfarne Gospels

Abstract: This paper examines Aldred's gloss and colophon from the perspective of how his work is to be situated in relation to the Lindisfarne Gospels' original manufacture and its subsequent role as a focal point of the cult of St. Cuthbert. Aldred's motivation in 'completing' the work and the cultural and political circumstances in which he was operating are discussed, as is his role in establishing the credentials and credibility of the English vernacular as a suitable medium for transmitting Scripture and consolidating cultural cohesion. Aldred, the community of St. Cuthbert, the cult and cult book emerge as key components in attempts to forge a united nation, whilst acknowledging the crucial role of northern England within it.

1 The making of the Lindisfarne Gospels, community tradition and Aldred's place within it

I have previously suggested that, at the time that the Lindisfarne Gospels was made, it was thought in ecclesiastical circles that the scribe could become a channel between God and humanity, like the evangelists themselves (Brown 2003 and 2011a). Writing and painting sacred texts were absorbing acts of meditation, during which the scribe might glimpse the divine. Our artist-scribe undertook his physically and intellectually demanding labours on behalf of all Creation as a hermit, the book becoming his 'desert', like Christ in the wilderness and Cuthbert on Inner Farne. Cassiodorus said that each word written was a wound on Satan's body. This was the spiritual front-line. Such was the tradition within which Aldred was placing himself when he glossed the Lindisfarne Gospels and commemorated his contribution, along with that of others who had laboured on the book previously, in a colophon.

Remarkably, the initial manufacture of this complex book was, essentially, the work of one outstandingly gifted, committed individual. For those dedicated to God's service, to be entrusted with the transmission of his Word, as preachers and scribes, was amongst the highest of callings. A few Insular Gospel books, notably the Lindisfarne and MacRegol Gospels, are remarkable amongst western tomes in being by single artist-scribes – a primarily eastern phenomenon (Brown 2003, 2006, 2011a and forthcoming a; Rapp 2007). Undertaking such an heroic feat of patience alongside the monastic duties of the Divine Office (celebrated eight times each day and night), prayer, study, and manual labour, suggests that making the Lindisfarne Gospels may have taken closer to five years, depending on how much exemption was granted from other duties, such as that accorded to anchorites. For if, as I have proposed, Bishop Eadfrith of Lindisfarne (698–722) both conceived the vision for its great Gospel book and physically made it himself around 715–720, overseeing one of the largest dioceses in Britain, embracing much of northern England and southern Scotland, would have made such work additionally challenging. Some of the back aching, eye straining work was probably undertaken on 'Cuddy's Isle', a windswept tidal islet near the monastery on Holy Island, where during Lent and Advent the bishop retired on retreat – a wild northern wilderness (Burns 1969; Cramp 1981; Brown 2003). Combining fasting, study and copying during Lent was a practice also favoured by Byzantine churchmen, as recounted in the *vitae* of Euthymius, patriarch of Constantinople (died 912), and patriarch Methodius (died 847), who copied a complete psalter during each of the seven weeks of Lent (Rapp 2007: 209).

I have suggested that such solitary scribal activity formed part of a distinctive 'Celtic' response to the eastern eremitic tradition in which the writing of Scripture could be undertaken as a living act of prayer, somewhat like icon writing (Brown 2000 and 2003). Whereas copying other texts was the communal work of the scriptorium, transmitting Scripture was entrusted only to the most senior community-members. The Irish saint Columba and his friend, the hermit St. Canice, were acclaimed as hero-scribes (Brown 2000 and 2003; Gameson 2001a), the latter writing a Gospel book single-handedly, in the manner of both male and female eastern precursors. In accordance with the teachings of Cassiodorus and others, such scribes became evangelists and, by study, contemplation, and meditation upon the text (*ruminatio, contemplatio* and *meditatio*), might actually glimpse the divine (*revelatio*; Brown 2003: 397–399).

This was a book to be seen, a shrine of sacred text and its role in the public prayer life of the Church, and a cult focus. It would have been seen on the altars, successively, of Lindisfarne, Norham, Chester-le-Street and Durham and used during important services (hardpoint crosses in the margins indicating its liturgical use during Christmas, Easter and the feast of St. Cuthbert). The monks presumably had access and guests were probably given privileged 'private views'. Ordinary people would have been able to see it in performative use at key points in the liturgical year and at other times on display, as pilgrims to the shrine. Glimpsing its candlelit pages or covers could change their lives, such relics being famed for their powers of healing body and soul. It symbolized hope and a colourful foretaste of a better existence to come amidst the coarse earthenware fabric of everyday life.

For this was a time when Christianity was a radical, transforming force. A time when warriors might be induced to adopt pacifism and kings to forgive enemies and free slaves, thereby risking assassination for reforming the fabric of society. The margins of some of the great Gospel books penned in England during the eighth century (such as the Lichfield Gospels) carry the earliest medieval written records of such manumissions (Brown 2007b). Christianity certainly helped to transform Anglo-Saxon society, but also preserved its traditions, and its books and their liminal spaces played a key part in inspiring, signalling and enacting both clerical and secular social transactions. Writing in the sacred space of Scripture, as Aldred would later do, was seldom undertaken lightly and placing oneself in the ongoing process of biblical transmission was an honour indeed.

The translation of St. Cuthbert's relics to the high altar of Lindisfarne in 698, eleven years after his death, marked the beginning of the creation of a cult that was to serve as a rallying point for the emerging identity of the North – which survives to this day. In the post-Whitby period there was a need for reconciliation between the various peoples and traditions that had prevailed and it was under Bishop Eadfrith, who came into office later that year, that the work of elevating Cuthbert as a social and spiritual role model began. During the twenty-three years of Eadfrith's leadership three lives of St. Cuthbert were written: one by an anonymous monk of Lindisfarne and two by Bede. The shrine on Holy Island became a focus for pilgrimage, featuring stations of the Cross marked by stone crosses at key points on the island and by the saint's coffin (resembling a painted Egyptian sarcophagus of the sort in which the eastern desert fathers might be enshrined) set adjacent to the high altar in the main church, upon which liturgical metalwork and relics were probably displayed, alongside the Word of God in the form of a Gospel book. This complemented the stone crosses in the Holy Island pilgrimage landscape by initials marking lections for the stational Good Friday liturgy, newly introduced into Roman liturgical books c. 715, a development which may have helped to spur production of the Lindisfarne Gospels (Brown 2003, 2011a and forthcoming a).

In my view, the spiritual, cultural and political agendas and strategies underpinning this complex book suggest that it was Bishop Eadfrith himself who was probably responsible for conceiving and making this focal cult book (perhaps to replace an earlier volume), which could rival the purple codex that graced St. Wilfrid's shrine in Ripon from c. 710. Lindisfarne's great book, by contrast, was to bring together not only elements from Rome and the Mediterranean (including a fine version of the Vulgate text copied from a Neapolitan book available as a model via Wearmouth/Jarrow) but visual motifs redolent of the range of local cultures and of those stretching across the Christian ecumen, as far as the Christian Orient. My recent research has indicated that, at one level, the Lindisfarne Gospels were intended to embody a statement of the conformity and a contribution of the Insular churches to the international orthodoxy of Chalcedon and to celebrate the reintegration of several schismatic (or potentially schismatic) parts (including Columban Iona) into this whole around 715–716 (Brown, forthcoming a).

St. Cuthbert's shrine soon became one of the most significant pilgrimage sites of medieval Britain and his relics found several resting places during their journey – not least the old Roman fort of Chester-le-Street, where they sojourned for a century (Jolly 2012). It was there that, around 950–970, the great cult book of St. Cuthbert was glossed in Old English by a monk who had newly joined named Aldred, who also added a colophon at the conclusion of John's Gospel associating his work with that of the original evangelists and with those who were thought to have made the book originally. It is assumed to have come there having accompanied the monks on their travels in search of a new home after they were forced to leave Lindisfarne because of Viking attacks. Aldred was working sometime before 970 when he glossed another book, the Durham Ritual, and had been promoted to the role of provost.[1] Aldred's colophon in the Lindisfarne Gospels occupies the remainder of a column that was largely left blank at the end of John's Gospel (f. 259r; this volume: p. 45) – the sort of blank yet significantly sited space in which manumissions and other important documents were added in the Lichfield Gospels, the Bodmin Gospels (London, British Library, MS Add. 9381) and London, British Library, MS Royal 1.B.vii earlier in the tenth century. It attributes the making of the volume to three figures: the writing (and by implication the decoration) to Eadfrith, bishop of Lindisfarne; the binding (sewing and covering) to Aethilwald, bishop of Lindisfarne (721–740); and the metalwork cover (a treasure binding or book-shrine) to Billfrith the Anchorite. This statement, and a subsequent version of it reiterated by Symeon of Durham in the twelfth century, cannot be taken at face value, however, and Aldred's methods and motives in writing it need to be assessed to determine its reliability. If the book's original manufacture was so bound up with the social and political realities of its day, and with spiritual aspirations for eternity, then might not Aldred's intervention have been similarly motivated?

Scholars would not usually accept an inscription added some 250 years after manufacture as reliable or conclusive evidence alone of origins, but those inclined to accept it have also argued, in different ways, in favour of contextual historical, palaeographical and archaeological evidence supporting a Lindisfarne origin (Kendrick et al. 1960; Brown 2003 and 2011a; Roberts, this volume). The reliability of Aldred's colophon statement about manufacture was first ques-

1 See, however, Roberts's paper (this volume) for a different interpretation of Aldred's status.

tioned by McAlister in 1913, when he claimed it as a ninth-century Irish work (McAlister 1913: 299). This was rebutted by Baldwin Brown and his acceptance of the colophon was repeated in the volume edited by Kendrick et al. (1960) and by most other commentators. It has subsequently been challenged again by O'Sullivan, Dumville and Nees (Brown 1903–1937: V, 337–341; O'Sullivan 1994; Dumville 1999; Nees 2003). Nees backs his comments with a proper discussion of the colophon as an historical document.[2] He suggests that Aldred manufactured the colophon in order to stress his own role as the fourth in a quartet of 'makers' of the book, as a reference to the four evangelists and to the continuing process of evangelistic transmission of the Gospels, this 'quadriga' also reflecting other symbolic quartets such as the four elements, the four rivers of Paradise, the four cardinal virtues, the ages of man and the four compass directions. His choice of the three other latter-day 'evangelists' who made the Gospel book was guided, so Nees maintains, by the references to the two bishops in the works of Bede and by the inclusion of Billfrith's name in the list of anchorites in the Durham *Liber Vitae* (London, British Library, MS Cotton Domitian A.vii, f. 18r).[3] This does not explain why a metalworker should have occurred to Aldred as one of the quartet, why a

2 See Nees (2003), where he states that the scholarly choices "are not simply between accepting or disregarding the evidence of Aldred's colophon. The evidence needs to be investigated". Prior to this he cites my statement in my Jarrow lecture (Brown 2000: 21): "To dismiss Aldred's colophon out of hand is to challenge the value of provenance evidence as a whole, something which may be done when there is good reason, but which is counter-productive as mere iconoclasm." (Nees 2003: 337). The context in which he cites me seems to suggest that I was tacitly accepting the colophon, which was not the case. Later in his own text he says: "In comparison to other important early manuscripts with impressive illumination, its [the Lindisfarne Gospels] early history is more secure than many [...]. The manuscript known as the Lindisfarne Gospels was in the possession of the community of St. Cuthbert by the mid-tenth century, as we know from Aldred's colophon, and that colophon's claims for its early history must have been thought at least credible, and support a view that the manuscript had already been in the possession of the community of St. Cuthbert for a considerable, if indeterminate time" (Nees 2003: 377). This is, of course, what I meant when I said that to discount the value of the colophon (regardless of its claims concerning the original production of the book) as provenance evidence, linking the book to the community of St. Cuthbert from quite an early stage, that is the tenth century, was not consistent with usual scholarly approaches.

3 At the end of his examination Nees concludes that "The story that Aldred tells of its early history could actually be true, could reflect a remarkably accurate oral tradition, although without the evidence of the colophon it seems to me that on grounds of script and decoration scholarship would put the manuscript later, not in the first but in the second quarter, even toward the middle of the eighth century" (Nees 2003: 377). Whilst agreeing with much of this conclusion I have presented my evidence (Brown 2003 and 2011a) for seeing the stylistic context, as well as the historical context, as favouring a dating for planning and manufacture somewhere between 710 and 725, with the lections marked suggesting that the layout may have been determined around 715.

'random' name for such should have been selected from a list of anchorites as opposed to another ecclesiastical category, or why this particular name should have been selected from the long list in which it occurs. Billfrith is 21st in the list of anchorites on f. 18r of the *Liber Vitae*, and is separated by 19 intervening names from that of Bishop Aethilwald, also an anchorite, who was thought to have commissioned him. Furthermore, if Aldred simply plucked a name from the community's book of life, why did he not preserve the spelling adopted in the *Liber Vitae*, using two 'l's rather than the one found in the name as it appears in the list? It is perhaps more likely that he encountered the name in another context. Jane Roberts's proposal that the colophon incorporates a vernacular poem would support this (Roberts 2006), as does the mixed use of Old English and Latin elements.

It therefore remains possible that Aldred was drawing upon an existing source (or sources) and incorporating material into his own colophon. This may have taken the form of an inscription upon a metalwork cover or shrine or an earlier written account which might even have been included in the volume itself.[4] Any such earlier nucleus for the contents of Aldred's colophon proper would not necessarily have come any closer to relating fact concerning the circumstances of the book's manufacture, but the likelihood of its existence does

4 Such an account of the book's makers may have been written into one of the community's books, rather like the anonymous account of its 'wanderings' which was included in Durham's 'Liber Magni Altaris'. The latter (or the 'liber de reliquiis' attached to St. Cuthbert's shrine, which some scholars think may have been the same volume) may even have been the Lindisfarne Gospels itself, which once included extraneous matter, to judge from the codicological evidence. Craster (1954: 177–199) identified the 'Liber Magni Altaris' with the 'liber de reliquiis', remarking that a notary writing at Durham in 1433 states that he was shown "various writings concerning the condition of the cathedral church" entered in an ancient hand near the middle of a book kept on the high altar (the 'Liber Magni Altaris') and that around the same time passages from the same book were copied into London, British Library, MS Cotton Claudius D.iv, notably those on ff. 94v, 95v and 96r–97v. It can be deduced thereby that the added matter within the 'Liber Magni Altaris' included the *Chronica monasterii Dunelmensis*, which extended the *Historia de sancto Cuthberto* to the reign of William I and attempted to place information concerning the community's possessions within an historical context. I am deeply indebted to Simon Keynes for drawing my attention to this information. The unlikelihood of such a substantial chronicle being entered into a Gospel book such as we know the 'liber de reliquiis' to have been, inclines him against identifying the references to this and the 'Liber Magni Altaris' as appertaining to the same book. It is worth adding, however, that marginal notes probably added to MS Cotton Claudius D.iv in the sixteenth century (such as that on f. 94v) say that grants made by Kings Edward the Elder and Æthelstan during the early tenth century were confirmed on the 'Liber Magni Altaris', indicating that this volume was of an earlier date. The parallels for the writing of documents into books to confirm their legitimacy, and for guaranteeing legality by swearing upon a book all point to such a book containing a sacred text. The likelihood is, therefore, that the 'Liber Magni Altaris' was a Gospel book which pre-dated 900. This could have been the Lindisfarne Gospels.

suggest that there was a pre-existing tradition of such within the community. Furthermore, the historical and contextual circumstances that I have advanced for the production of the Lindisfarne Gospels suggest that it is likely to have been made at Lindisfarne during the period of the floruits of the bishops whose names continued to be associated with the book (Brown 2003, 2011a and forthcoming a). Both Bishops Eadfrith and Aethilwald rapidly achieved saintly status within the community. Symeon tells us that their bones accompanied the community when it left Holy Island in 875 (Arnold 1882: 57). They were certainly reported to have joined Cuthbert in his coffin when it was opened in 1104 (Miracle 7, see Arnold 1882: 252, 255). A particularly enthusiastic custodian of the shrine, Alfred Westou, had acquired Billfrith's bones for Durham in the mid-eleventh century, along with those of Bede and Cuthbert's teacher, Boisil (Battiscombe 1956: 113–114).

As an anchorite, or hermit, Billfrith had less of a career structure and might be expected to have left little mark on the historical record, and this is indeed the case. His name occurs in a list of anchorites in the Durham *Liber Vitae* (London, British Library, MS Cotton Domitian A.vii, f. 18r), made initially at Lindisfarne or Norham (or less probably Wearmouth/Jarrow, although it includes material relating to all of these communities) around 840, by which time Billfrith was evidently deceased. Aldred's colophon gives no indication of when Billfrith may have contributed his metalwork to the adornment of the Lindisfarne Gospels, but Symeon, quoting a source probably other than the colophon itself says that he was commissioned by Bishop Aethilwald to produce it (Arnold 1882: 67–68). This implies that they were contemporaries, intent upon further honouring and embellishing a Book of St. Cuthbert (presumably the Lindisfarne Gospels) soon after its production by Bishop Eadfrith.

To my mind, these figures named in the colophon are indeed likely to have been involved in the making of the Lindisfarne Gospels, as the place and period of their activities accord well with other historical, textual and stylistic evidence for its manufacture. In the 1956–1960 facsimile commentary, and in much subsequent scholarship, it was argued that Eadfrith and Aethilwald could not have worked on the Lindisfarne Gospels in their busy mid-life, but rather before they achieved major ecclesiastical positions at the end of the seventh century (Brown and Bruce-Mitford 1960: 12–13, 19). I would suggest, however, that Eadfrith would have planned and undertaken the writing and illumination from around 715, spurred on by contemporary events which led him to incorporate the marking in the book of liturgical readings for Good Friday that were only then being absorbed into the liturgy in Rome's liturgical books. The artwork was left unfinished in places, a month or two short of the project's completion, and it may be that this was interrupted by Eadfrith's death in 721. As one of the *seniores*, a leading, experienced member of the community, this remarkable offering of labour and prayer would have formed his own particular *opus dei*, contributing to his own acclaim as a saint, in accordance with Columban and eastern eremitic tradition. It was evidently deemed inappropriate that others should finish it, for the colouring of the opening carpet-page's interlace and the laying on of gold was left unfinished, although another hand was entrusted with the tasks of adding the marginal numbers (or Eusebian sections) marking the passages referred to in the canon tables, in order to make this system for the celebration of the Gospel harmony work. Aethilwald, his successor as bishop and a skilled book producer in his own right, was entrusted with the task of binding the book and Billfrith was then, or sometime over the next century, instructed to adorn it with metalwork covers or plaques or to enshrine it in a *cumdach* 'book shrine'. Irish cumdachs of the late eighth century onwards provide a particularly good context and many of them carry inscriptions naming those responsible for making, commissioning and enshrining the books that they contained. If Billfrith did indeed supply metalwork embellishment (either a treasure binding or a cumdach) it may have carried a litany of names, including that of the metalworker (in accordance with contemporary Irish practice), to which Aldred added himself.

The names cited by Aldred in his colophon therefore correspond in terms of their floruits to the stylistic and historical context which I have proposed for the making of the Lindisfarne Gospels. The rubrication and correction of the volume post-dated the disappearance of the artist-scribe, Bishop Eadfrith, in the final stages of illumination and so would the act of binding and any metalwork adornment, which may have been added any time prior to c. 840, when Billfrith's name was inscribed in the *Liber Vitae*. The close stylistic relationship with the one dated artifact of the period, the coffin of St. Cuthbert, made at Lindisfarne for the translation of 698, would tend to pull the dating of the manuscript back towards 700 rather than propelling it further towards 750, as some scholars might wish. If Aldred concocted the account of the book's manufacture in his colophon he must have been either a good historian or a remarkably 'good guesser' to have hit upon names which mesh in their historical inter-relationships and which correlate with the likely stylistic and historical contexts for production.

The brethren of Lindisfarne do not seem to have been easily deterred in their attempts to preserve the early history of their foundation. Eadberht virtually enshrined the wooden church in sheets of lead and the original wooden church of Aidan, which may even have been itself enshrined within this larger church (like the Holy Sepulchre), was physically moved to Norham in the ninth century (Cramp 1989: 218). The sculpted cross erected by Bishop Aethilwald around 740 was also taken with the community, along with Cuthbert's coffin and associated relics, when it was displaced by Viking attacks later in the ninth century (Cramp 1989: 223–225, 228). Preserving the recollection of association with important figures within the history of such cult-orientated communities seems to have been an important feature and may have some bearing upon the ascription preserved in the colophon. Such relics and, as Rosemary Cramp has suggested, the distinctive nature of their Insular ornament, continued to serve as a rallying point for identity in the North East into the twelfth century (Cramp 1989: 220–221). Indeed, they continue to do so today.

2 Aldred, Chester-le-Street and the community's role in tenth-century England

In 793 Lindisfarne was the first victim of Viking raids. Cuthbert's shrine was desecrated and many monks killed. The community never fully recovered from the blow, and the number of monks within a progressively secular community remained as low as two or three until the Benedictine Reform of the later tenth century. In the 840s, as raids escalated, the monks and laypeople associated with the monastery ('the people of St. Cuthbert') moved temporarily northwards to Norham on Tweed. In 875 they quitted Lindisfarne as their principal house – although the assembly of ninth- and tenth-century sculptures on Holy Island indicate a continuing ecclesiastical presence there – and went walkabout, carrying Cuthbert's coffin, relics and the stone cross commemorating Bishop Aethilwald. The twelfth-century historian Symeon of Durham says they headed for Ireland but were prevented by the Book of St. Cuthbert 'jumping' overboard, thereby indicating that the community still had work to do in Britain (and avoiding the future academic assumption that the book was made in Ireland). Symeon records that one of the bearers of St. Cuthbert's coffin, Hunred, was shown the volume's whereabouts in a vision and the monks accordingly found it unharmed in the sands of the Solway Firth and went first to St. Ninian's foundation of Whithorn on the Galloway coast (with which they had traditionally had relations). They then turned south, travelling via Carlisle (where they were joined by members of their fellow monastery there) and into what is now County Durham and, for a while, into Yorkshire.

I have suggested that this 'flight', rather than being (as it is usually represented) the aimless wandering of refugee monks in search of sanctuary, in fact represented an astute move to avoid marginalization and move closer to the new seat of political power, which had shifted from Bamburgh, some ten miles from Holy Island, to Viking-held territory and its power-base at York. They confirmed old allegiances and authority as they went by displaying Cuthbert's relics – a recognized means of asserting legal ownership by processing the relics through a church's patrimony. Symeon's account is couched in a way that was probably intended to compare them to Moses (Cuthbert) and the Israelites (the People of St. Cuthbert) seeking the 'promised land' (in their case Durham, where the community eventually settled and where Symeon's own affiliations lay), with the book's survival of immersion in water symbolizing Moses's parting of the Red Sea (Brown 2003 and 2011a). The ability of books to survive 'trial by drowning', as a proof of their status as relics and of a saint's power, was well-known in early medieval Britain and Ireland: the cult of St. Columba boasted many such manuscripts during the Middle Ages.

The community headed straight for Viking territory – a strange thing to do if fleeing from them – moving to their daughter-house of Crayke, only a few miles from York. They then staged a bloodless coup, deposing the Viking leader in favour of a Dane, Guthred/Guthrith (see Cavill, this volume: n. 17), whom they had redeemed from slavery. The way was paved for King Alfred of Wessex to open negotiations with the more amenable Guthred and begin reclaiming England from Viking rule. Tradition concerning King Alfred's resistance movement even includes an account that around this time St. Cuthbert began appearing to him in a vision while he was hiding out in the Athelney marshes in Somerset. In accordance with the Gospel's injunction to be "wise as serpents and gentle as doves" (Matthew 10.16), the community of St. Cuthbert was perpetuating its role of intervening in politics in order to safeguard the survival and stability of Christian society, just as I have suggested its earlier bishops, such as Aidan, Cuthbert and Eadfrith, had (Brown 2003 and 2011a).

From the late ninth century the community of St. Cuthbert extended their authority in southern Northumbria, as well as the northern parts of the territory and southern Scotland, which they had come to administer when the kingship had been based at Bamburgh, near Lindisfarne. In 883 Guthred, presumably rewarding the community for its part in his rise to power, gave it the sizeable Roman fort of Chester-le-Street, lying upon a major Roman road, as its new caput, along with property formerly owned by Wearmouth/Jarrow. The community was now strategically placed to control access to the rivers Tyne and Wear and a part of a key overland route linking North and South. The wealth of sculpture in the Anker's House at Chester-le-Street bears witness to the importance of the shrine there, which was visited by Anglo-Saxon rulers, notably Alfred's grandson, King Æthelstan (924–939), who presented prestigious gifts, including books and embroidered vestments, to the saint during his visit in 934. I have raised the possibility that, rather than being closed and only occasionally opened to receive such prestigious gifts, Cuthbert's incorrupt body may have been more regularly made visible in its coffin – like Lenin's tomb or that of Padre Pio, whose intact body has recently been put on public devotional display some forty years after his death (Brown, forthcoming a).

Æthelstan's visit to the shrine formed part of his strategy for reintegrating the Danelaw into English England, under a single West Saxon monarchy. In this he recognized the role of the cult of St. Cuthbert and the enduring influence of his community in securing the allegiance of the North (Brown 2003, 2011a, and forthcoming a). This policy was evidently perpetuated after Æthelstan's reign. One of the tenth-century cross-shaft fragments at Chester-le-Street depicts a mounted warrior identified by an inscription as Edmund, perhaps recording continued royal West Saxon patronage by the king of that name who ruled from 939–946. By the time that we encounter Aldred as glossator of the Durham Ritual he is in Wessex, as a Cuthbertine representative at the negotiations to establish a border between the kingdoms of England and Scotland.

3 Aldred's background and the nature of his work

Within a decade or two of Æthelstan's visit, Aldred had joined the community as a monk and was accorded the tremendous privilege of translating its great cult-book into the English language to establish his credentials upon entering the community, dedicating his work of each of the Gospels to the saint, the bishop, the monks and the good of his own soul, with the accompaniment of a monetary dowry,[5] thereby securing his reception into the community.

Although the gloss is essentially a word-by-word translation in Northumbrian dialect composed in the fashion of a schoolroom exercise, rather than continuous prose, Aldred cannot resist occasionally adding comment on the text. These

5 I find the suggestion (Newton et al. 2013: 101–144) that the volume once contained silver borders implausible, for although there are signs that the Lindisfarne Gospels once contained additional documents and materials and was 'tidied up' in the post-medieval period, the tendency of silver to tarnish and bleed make it highly unlikely that such borders would have left no trace in the volume, even if they were trimmed off (see also Roberts, this volume). Another possibility might be that the silver mentioned in the colophon referred to silver used to cover or inlay the binding boards (rather than the borders of pages). This brings to mind the inscription in Old English added in the eleventh century to f. 4r of the Thorney Gospels (London, British Library, MS Add. 40000) referring to the former binding of the manuscript: "+ Aelfric ⁊ Wulfwine, Eadgife goldsmiðes geafen to broþerraedenne twegen orn weghenes goldes þæt is on þis ilce boc her foruten gewired" ('Ælfric and Wulfwine, goldsmiths of Eadgifu, gave for the confraternity two oras of weighed gold which is wired without upon this same book'). This would appear to refer to the external embellishment of the volume. But whatever his gift of silver was to be used for, it remains that Aldred's inscription records a donation for the good of his soul and recalls the Old English inscription commemorating the redemption of the Stockholm Codex Aureus from Vikings by Ealdorman Alfred and his wife in the mid-ninth century.

lengthier, more expansive passages of the gloss reveal a concern with monastic reform and abuses of clerical power of the sort espoused by the great reformers of the Anglo-Saxon Church at this time: St. Dunstan, St. Æthelwold and St. Oswald, and their supporter, King Edgar (959–975). This may reflect the ecclesiastical affiliations of the community per se, and/or Aldred's own concerns.

Might Aldred have been recruited from the North (given his use of the Northumbrian dialect), perhaps having studied in southern England or on the Continent (see Rusche, this volume), and have been placed in the influential community of St. Cuthbert by the West Saxon monarchy and its reforming ecclesiastics, where he practised his skills as a vernacular glossator as a visible and symbolic testimony to the reassertion of the 'Englishness' of the cult and the region? I shall return to this below, but any such backing might explain the extraordinary privilege of adding to the prized cult-book which was accorded by the community to a new member. Promoting English, which was not the first language of the Danish settlers, and affirming its statuts as one of the biblical 'sacred languages' (*linguae sacrae*) in succession to Hebrew, Greek and Latin, certainly would have assisted in the reunification of England and would have formed an assertion of a new English identity in which the Scandinavian presence was subsumed. By 970 Aldred's career had flourished and he had become provost of Chester-le-Street. It is in this capacity that we encounter him glossing in English the Durham Ritual, an early tenth-century West Saxon liturgical manuscript.[6] This gloss is datable to 970, when Aldred tells us that he was writing in a tent on Oakley Down, Wiltshire, where he was serving as a member of a diplomatic mission accompanying the king of Scotland in order to negotiate the Anglo-Scots border – the community of St. Cuthbert once more working to safeguard Christian continuity of life in the face of political tensions, and Aldred was evidently playing a significant part in this process.

The colophon and other inscriptions by Aldred on f. 259r are often termed collectively 'the colophon group', acknowledging that it is formed of several components.[7] Aldred is obviously struggling to fit everything he wishes to include into the ruled area into which the colophon is set, and has to add some components

6 A third example of Aldred's work as a glossator occurs in a mid-eighth-century copy, made at Wearmouth/Jarrow, of Bede's commentary on Proverbs (Oxford, Bodleian Library, MS Bodley 819).

7 See the excellent and full treatment of the language of the 'colophon group' by Ross et al. 1960). The following transcription varies somewhat from theirs, but only in small details, such as the possibility of a Caroline question mark (*punctus interrogativus*) following Aldred's statement of humility. For an insightful recent discussion see Roberts (2006). For a counter view, see Newton et al. (2013), whose arguments are addressed in Jane Roberts's contribution to this volume. Transcription of Aldred's Colophon (based on Brown 2003: 102–103):

of his text, including that concerning his lineage, in the margins. Adjacent to the display capitals of the original text's Explicit rubric, in the outer margin and preceded by a cross, are written the following Latin hexameters:

> + *Lit(er)a me pandat*
> *sermonis fida*
> *ministra*
> *Omnes alme*
> *meos fratres*
> *voce salvta*ꝛ

This may be translated as:

> 'May the letter, faithful servant of speech, reveal me; greet, O kindly [book], all my brothers with thy voice'.

The subject of these may be intended to be either the text of John's Gospel, Aldred's gloss, or both.

Embedded within the first part of the Old English colophon is the Latin text known as the 'Five Sentences', which is of uncertain origin but may derive in part from the *Plures fuisse* prologue, included in the Lindisfarne Gospels (commencing at f. 5v). These may be translated as:

ðe ðrifalde ⁊ ðe anfalde god ðis godspell/ aer vorvlda gisette + Trinus et unus d(eu)s evangelium hoc ante / saecula con stituit ærist avrat of mvðe crist(es) + Mathevs ex ore c(h)r(ist)i scripsit of mvðe petres avrat + Marcus ex ore Petri scrips(it) of mvðe paules avrat + Lvcas de ore Pavli ap' scrips(it) in deigilnisi ł i(n) f(ore)esaga siððа rocgetede ł gisprant + Ioh(annes) in prochemio deinde ervctavit pord mið gode gisalde ⁊ halges gastes 'ł mið godes geafa| ⁊ halges gastes verbum d(e)o donante et sp(irit)v s(an)c(t)o scrip(it) |mæht avrát ioh(annes)'

+ Eadfrið biscop/b lindisfearnensis æcclesiæ he ðis boc avrát æt frvma gode ⁊ s(an)c(t)e cvðberhte ⁊ allvm ðæm halgvm. ða. ðe `gimænelice´in eolonde sint. ⁊ eðilvald lindisfearneolondinga `bisc(op)´hit v́ta giðryde ⁊ gibélde sva hé vel cuðę. ⁊ billfrið se oncrę he gismioðade ða gihríno ða ðe vtan ón sint ⁊ hit gihrínade mið golde ⁊ mið gimmvm ęc mið svlfre' of(er)gylded faconleas feh:- ⁊ (ic) Aldred p(re)`s´b(yte)r indignus ⁊ misserim(us)? mið godes fvltv(m)mę ⁊ s(an)c(t)i cuðberhtes hit of(er)glóesade ón englisc. ⁊ hine gihamadi:. mið ðæm ðríim dælvm. Mathevs dǽl gode ⁊ s(an)c(t)e cvðberhti. Marc' dǽl. ðæm bisc(ope/um?). ⁊ lvcas dæl ðæm hiorode ⁊ æht `v´ ora seo`v´lfres mið tó inláde.ꝛ ⁊ sci ioh(annes) dæl f(or) hine seolfne `i(d est) f(or)e his savle´ ⁊ feover óra seo`v´lfres mið gode ⁊ s(an)c(t)i cvðberhti. þ(æt)te he hæbbe ondfong ðerh godes miltsæ on heofnv(m). séel ⁊ sibb on eorðo forðgeong ⁊ giðyngo visdóm ⁊ snyttro ðerh s(an)c(t)i cvðberhtes earnvnga:,

+ Eadfrið. oeðilvald. billfrið. Aldred. hoc evange(lium) d(e)o ⁊ cvðberhto constrvxer(vn)t:, ´ł ornavervnt`..

> God, three in one, these Gospels have since [the dawn of] the age consisted of:
> Matthew, who wrote what he heard from Christ;
>
> Mark who wrote what he heard from Peter;
> Luke, who wrote what he heard from the Apostle Paul;
> John who willingly thereupon proclaimed and wrote the Word given by God through the Holy Spirit.[8]

There then follows:

> (Sign of the Cross, followed in Old English by:)
> Eadfrith, Bishop of the Lindisfarne Church, originally wrote this book, for God and for St. Cuthbert and—jointly—for all the saints whose relics are in the island. And Aethilwald, Bishop of the Lindisfarne islanders, impressed it on the outside and covered it—as he well knew how to do.[9] And Billfrith, the anchorite, forged the ornaments which are on it on the outside and adorned it with gold and with gems and also with gilded-over silver—pure metal. And (I)[10] Aldred, unworthy and most miserable priest? [He] glossed it in English between the lines with the help of God and St. Cuthbert. And, by means of the three sections, he made a home for himself: the section of Matthew was for God and St. Cuthbert, the section of Mark for the bishop[/s], the section of Luke for the members of the community (in addition, eight ores of silver for his induction) and the section of St. John was for himself (in addition, four ores of silver for God and St. Cuthbert) so that, through the grace of God, he may gain acceptance into heaven; happiness and peace, and through the merits of St. Cuthbert, advancement and honour, wisdom and sagacity on earth.

The final element of the colophon (+ Eadfrið. oeðilvald. billfrið. Aldred. | *hoc evange(lium) d(e)o ⁊ cvðberhto constrvxer(vn)t:, ´ł ornavervnt`..)* mixes Old English and Latin elements and seems not to belong with the rest of the text, repeating the names of the 'makers' within a Latin infrastructure. If this was copied from an earlier source it would have been enough to have provided Aldred with the names to which he appended his own and to have formed the core of his text.

Against the mention of his own name (in the first line) Aldred tells us something of his parentage, asserting his legitimacy and good reputation, adding in

8 The following translation, closer to Aldred's own, has been proposed by Roberts (2006): '+ God, three and one, established this Gospelbook before the world.+ Matthew wrote from the words [lit. mouth] of Christ.+ Mark wrote from the words [lit. mouth] of Peter.+ Luke wrote from the words [lit. mouth] of Paul the apostle.+ John thereafter poured forth 'in the beginning'; he wrote the word given by God and the holy spirit'.

9 The wording is evocative of the decorative treatment of the binding of the St. Cuthbert Gospel and its unusual sophisticated 'Coptic' sewing technique.

10 The reference to the first person singular is erased, presumably to de-personalize the character of the inscription, or because it conflicted with the use of the third person singular in the remainder of the text.

the margin the rhythmic couplet: *Ælfredi natvs aldredvs uocor: bonæ mvlieris filivs eximivs loquor*, which I would translate as:

> 'Aldred, born of Alfred, is my name:
> a good woman's son, of distinguished fame'.

An inveterate fiddler, he then glosses the reference to his mother with the words "*i(d est)* til p'", "til wif" meaning 'good woman' (Ross 1943: 321; Ross et al. 1960: 10; Brown 1969: 24).

On f. 89v he added a related prayer in Old English, confirming his intent of associating his own contribution with the original project and its offering up to God: "Thou Living God, remember Eadfrith and Aethilwald and Billfrith and Aldred, a sinner; these four, with God, were concerned with this book."[11] Thus the four latter-day evangelists perpetuate the work of the Gospel writers in a line of transmission stemming from Christ, the Holy Spirit and the chief Apostles, Peter and Paul.

Nees asserts that the context of extant colophons and dedication inscriptions points to the ninth or tenth centuries being the time at which Aldred's colophon, or any original core text that it may have incorporated, is likely first to have been composed and highlights the possibility of the particular influence of dedications in books presented by King Æthelstan to the community of St. Cuthbert in the 930s (Nees 2003). The practice of applying such inscriptions to books certainly increased somewhat in that period, but is not unknown earlier. Ceolfrith's dedication inscription in the Codex Amiatinus is one such example, as is the colophon copied from an earlier exemplar into the Echternach Gospels.[12] Original colophons also occur prior to the ninth century, such as the behest to *ora pro uuigbaldo* 'pray for Wigbald' in the late eighth-century Barberini Gospels.[13] There is, however, no doubt that Aldred actually compiled the colophon as it now appears on f. 259r of the Lindisfarne Gospels, and he was probably doing so within a tradition of Carolingian and tenth-century English practice, but it remains possible that part of his text was based upon earlier material. The language and layout of Aldred's compilation would tend to suggest that this was indeed the case. Its layout is curiously erratic, with Aldred glossing his own text for the 'Five Sen-

---

11 A better sense of which may be 'were devoted to this book'.

12 Gameson (2002: 33).

13 F. Henry intriguingly proposed an identification with a contemporaneous Bishop Hygebald of Lindisfarne (Alexander 1978). I recently proposed an identification with Wigbald, archdeacon or anchorite of Peterborough, who attested charters there around 800 (Brown 2007a: 89–116). On colophons in general, see Gameson (2002).

tences' and adding marginal inscriptions (the *litera me pandat* and the verse concerning his parentage), and includes indentation of the lines mentioning the manufacturing team. Indentation was an established form of indicating a quotation (Lowe 1928: 43–62). Another prominent feature of the inscription is that its major component parts, the clauses of the 'Five Sentences' and the incipit of the colophon proper, are marked by large crosses of the sort that often mark the beginnings of inscriptions on metalwork and stone, which could reflect a source. A linguistic feature might also suggest that the colophon was not a single, new composition. The name of Bishop Aethilwald is given in different orthographical forms: <Eðilvald> and <Oeðilvald>, and on f. 89v it takes the form <Æðilwald>, with an *e* caudata and a *wynn*. This might indicate that Aldred copied the name from various sources as well as using the form with which he was familiar. Likewise, as we have seen, the name Billfrith differs from the <Bilfrith> in the Durham *Liber Vitae*, whence Nees argues that he derived the name, and Eadfrith also occurs therein with the spelling <Eatfrith>. The inclusion of Latin elements within the Old English text (*hoc evange(lium) d(e)o, lindisfearnensis æcclesiæ* and *constrvxerv(nt)*:, ˊ*ł ornavervnt*ˋ ..) might also reflect the copying of parts of the text from another source. Furthermore, Jane Roberts has advanced the important suggestion that there may be a previously unnoticed poetic verse embedded within the part of Aldred's 'colophon group' concerning the manufacturing team. It is as if he were reworking an earlier verse, amplifying and extending it to include the passage relating to himself and thereby corrupting the poetic form.[14] On balance the evidence conspires to suggest that Aldred was adapting an earlier source or sources for his statements concerning the 'makers' of the Lindisfarne Gospels as part of his intent to associate his own contribution with theirs.

Aldred may have thereby effectively corrupted an earlier vernacular verse naming the makers of the Lindisfarne Gospels. He did, however, preserve or possibly compose some Latin verse as part of the 'colophon group'. Next to the original explicit to the Gospel of St. John on f. 259r he has written a Latin verse (+ *Lit(er) a me pandat* ...) which may be translated as: 'May the letter, faithful servant of speech, reveal me; greet, O kindly [book], all my brothers with thy voice'. In this verse writing is acclaimed as the servant of speech. The statement concerning

14 This previously unnoticed feature was first pointed out to me in 2003, when I was writing the commentary to accompany the facsimile of the Lindisfarne Gospels issued that year (Brown 2003), by Jane Roberts, to whom I am deeply indebted for sharing her thoughts and preliminary text. If she is correct only one word needs to be altered in order to make an original meter scan (Roberts 2005 and 2006). For Jane Roberts's further thoughts on the subject, and her response to subsequent comment, see her significant contribution to the present volume.

Aldred's parentage likewise takes the form of a Latin rhyming couplet indicating that Aldred himself harboured aspirations as a poet.

Aldred's continuous interlinear gloss is written in the Northumbrian dialect. A further Anglo-Saxon translation is preserved in the form of later (twelfth-century) manuscript copies and is known as the West Saxon or Wessex Gospels, being written in the West Saxon dialect.[15] Another gloss, added during the tenth century to an early ninth-century Irish Latin Gospel book, the MacRegol Gospels, by Farman, a priest from Harewood (either that lying in West Yorkshire or that near Ross-on-Wye or Lichfield),[16] relies upon Aldred's gloss, or a shared source, and is in the Mercian dialect.[17]

The Lindisfarne Gospels may contain the earliest extant translation of the Gospels into English, but we know that work on disseminating the biblical texts in the English vernacular had commenced earlier. Bede was engaged in translating John's Gospel, for the good of his soul and those of all people, on his deathbed (dictating to an assistant) in 735. The Vespasian Psalter (London, British Library, MS Cotton Vespasian A.i), a Kentish work of around 730, was also given an interlinear Old English gloss during the second quarter of the ninth century (probably at Canterbury by one of the scribes who also worked on the Royal Bible, London, British Library, MS Royal 1.E.vi, some time between 820 and 840 – perhaps under the reforming archbishop Wulfred; Brown 2005; Budny 1985). The spirit of evangelization that engendered such an openness to spreading the Word by any means was very different to the official intolerance encountered by Wycliffe and Tyndale in the late Middle Ages. There was, of course, a background of glossing as part of the learning experience as practised, for example, in the Canterbury school established by Theodore and Hadrian. And around the time that the Vespasian Psalter was translated, the Book of Cerne (Cambridge, University Library, MS Ll.1.10) also received a planned interlinear Old English gloss to one of its prayers, the Lorica of Laidcenn/Loding, in the hand of the book's scribe who wrote the book for Bishop Æthelwald of Lichfield (818–830; Brown 1996 and 2011b). This pre-exist-

---

15 Brown (2003: 96).

16 Proximity to Chester-le-Street would favour the former location and the use of the Mercian dialect the latter. Farman was assisted, or more probably sponsored, by one Owun who is also named in inscription. See also Coates, who argues for a location for Harewood near Lichfield (Coates 1997: 453–458).

17 A synoptic edition of both glosses and of the Latin text of the Lindisfarne Gospels is given by Skeat (1871–1887). Skeat considered that Farman's gloss was based upon the Latin version of the Vulgate in the Lindisfarne Gospels as well as the original text of the Irish Gospel book he was glossing, implying that he was consulting the Lindisfarne Gospels itself. This hypothesis might repay closer investigation and testing. Aldred's gloss may, in any case, have been available in another form. See further Kotake's paper in this volume.

ing Insular tradition, along with the Carolingian scholarly use of glossed texts, provide something of a background to the community of St. Cuthbert's decision to permit Aldred to gloss their prized cult-book.

This work may have been Aldred's way of establishing his credentials and making a contribution to the community which he seems only recently to have joined, his work being sponsored by the community and perhaps by the monastic reformers associated with the West Saxon court and its rulers. Aldred glossed Matthew, Mark, Luke and the beginning of John in a neat, tiny pointed cursive hand using black ink. From 5.10, and in mid verse, John's Gospel is glossed in the same hand, but using red ink. The Prefaces are also in red, up to the beginning of the *Plures fuisse*, as are some further glosses added to Matthew. There are also a few additional glosses in red on f. 140v (Luke 1). The change in ink may simply have resulted from some unpredictable change in Aldred's circumstances, or it may be that he decided to accord John's Gospel the particular distinction that it often seems to have attracted, especially in the context of the cult of St. Cuthbert (who studied it with his master, Boisil, and who was interred with a copy of it), by glossing it in a higher grade ink. It is tempting to wonder whether Aldred's model for the gloss on John might even have been indebted, if only in part, to the translation to which Bede devoted his last days on earth and that the red ink might honour such a source. Boyd (1975a) outlined the sources to which Aldred may have had access,[18] including Bede's Old and New Testament commentaries and his homilies upon the Gospels. However, in his 'gloss 62' (to John 19.38) Boyd (1975a: 52) notes that Aldred glossed the passage "*post* / .i. *est* in die examinis iudicii. Districti iudicis. ðus beda ðe bróema bóecere cućð"[19] ('thus said Bede, the famous scribe'), and states that

18 See Boyd (1975a: 56–57), where he lists Aldred's possible sources as Jerome's *Liber interpretationis hebraicorum nominum*, his *Commentarii in Esaiam, in Ezechielem, in euangelium Matthaei, in iv epistulas Paulinas (ad Galatas, ad Ephesios, ad Titum, ad Philonem)*, his homilies and perhaps his correspondence; Pseudo-Jerome, *Interpretatio alphabeti hebraeorum*, and *Commentarius in euangelium secundum Marcum*; Augustine's exegesis on the Gospels, such as his *De sermone Domini in monte, Tractatus in euangelium Ioannis* and his De *consensu euangelistarum*; Isidore's encyclopaedia, *Etymologiarum sive originum*, and perhaps his De *ortu et obitu patrum*; Gregory the Great's *Moralia sive expositio in Iob, Homiliae in Ezechielem, Homiliae in euangelia* and his *Registrum epistularum*; Pseudo-Chrysostom, *Opus imperfectum in Matthaeum*; Bede's Old Testament commentaries, including his *In Samuelem prophetam allegorica expositio, In Esdram et Nehemiam prophetas allegorica expositio, In librum patris Tobiae allegorica expositio* and his New Testament *In Marcum et Lucam expositio, Super Acta Apostolorum expositio, Explanatio apocalypsis* and *Homeliarum euangelii libri ii*.

19 The *Dictionary of Old English Web Corpus* has "cuæð" as the final word here, which is to be preferred.

> it has proved impossible to pin down the precise reference in Bede. Aldred may have derived his explanation from Bede's *Explanatio Apocalypsis*.[20] The great value of this marginal explanation is that Aldred confirms Bede as one of the sources of his scholarship.

Might this, alternatively, represent a Bedan gloss on his otherwise lost translation of John's Gospel, signified by the use of red ink? Later in the Middle Ages *de luxe* volumes would often be ruled in red or purple ink as a sign of status, and the popular expression *red-letter day* derives from the practice of grading liturgical feast-days by the use of different coloured inks in calendars; might Bede's contribution to the gloss be signalled here by the use of the higher grade red ink? Aldred might then have gone on to gloss the ancillary, prefatory texts and have decided to make a few additions to Matthew and Luke, correcting/supplementing his initial gloss and still using his red ink.[21]

Aldred seems to have been building a reputation as a glossator/translator and his hand can also be observed in the Durham Ritual (Durham, Cathedral Library, MS A.iv.19; Brown 1969; Ker 1943; Temple 1976: no. 3), where he glossed some of the collects interlinearly and added red initials to the text, and in Latin glosses to Oxford, Bodleian Library, MS Bodley 819, a late-eighth-century copy of Bede's commentary on the Proverbs of Solomon written at Wearmouth/Jarrow (which probably passed to the community as part of its absorption of Wearmouth/Jarrow's properties in the late ninth century; *CLA*: II, 235). He emerges as something of a champion of the written English vernacular in northern England at a time when it was being reintegrated into the new, unified England. This process had been initiated by Alfred and considerably forwarded by his successors, Æthelstan effectively reclaiming the North. It was not, however, an inevitable one and encountered much opposition. At around the time that Aldred was glossing the Lindisfarne Gospels Eric Bloodaxe (died 954), ruler of Viking York, was advancing his 'kingdom' in Northumbria. Alba (Scotland) and Strathclyde also posed a threat to English control of the North. The community of St. Cuthbert seems to have been 'doing its bit' to keep the region 'English' and the promotion of Old English may have been part of this. The use of the vernacular would also, of course, have served to further enhance the popularity and accessibility of the cult of St. Cuthbert and to have strengthened Christianity in the region. The visits

---

20 In which Bede on Revelation 1.7 writes: *In eadem illum forma videntes judicem potentem, in qua velut minimum judicaverunt, sera semetipsos poenitentia lamentabunt.* This is translated by Weinrich as 'When they see him as a powerful judge in the same form in which they had judged him as someone insignificant, they will lament for themselves with a repentance that will be too late'; see Weinrich (2011: 115).

21 Such a possibility is also implied in Elliott and Ross (1972: 49–72).

of Kings Æthelstan and Edmund to the shrine of St. Cuthbert over the preceding decades can also be viewed in the light of fostering the process of reintegration and may have helped to stimulate Aldred to perpetuate King Alfred's agenda of translation as an essential adjunct to unification and national spiritual wellbeing and an earlier Insular tradition of glossing texts. This may subsequently have been reinforced by Aldred's own visit to southern England as a scribal notary in the train of his bishop in 970, during which time they may have obtained the Durham Ritual, made in southern England earlier in the century, for the community (Brown 1969; Ker 1943). Indeed, the visit may have been partly motivated by diplomacy to ensure the stability of the North, Bishop Ælfsige and Aldred accompanying Kenneth, King of Alba, to Wessex, perhaps as diplomatic mediators and presumably with the intention of safeguarding the community of St. Cuthbert's interests in negotiations concerning the English/Scottish frontier zone (Miles 1898: 247–250).[22]

Aldred's explanatory glossing of certain passages evinces a concern with celibacy and simony, which may suggest an interest in a reforming celibate monastic agenda.[23] Like most English monasteries at the time, that at Chester-le-Street would have been largely secular (Boyd suggested that it may have contained as few as two or three monks, and pointed out that its abbots were not monks from the time following the flight from Holy Island until the early eleventh century). According to Boyd, Aldred's 'colophon group' and parts of his gloss indicate that he may have had to purchase his ordination into the community, paying eight ores of silver for his induction (and glossing Luke's Gospel for the community), whilst he is at pains to point out that his other qualifications – his reputable, legitimate parentage, his humility, his priestly status, his scholarship and his

22 King Edgar appears to have ceded Lothian to Kenneth, perhaps to ensure an amenable balance of power in the North.

23 See Boyd (1975a: 4–5). See also pp. 8–10 (gloss to Matthew 1.18, concerning celibacy): 'to take care of, by no means to have as wife' and 'Abiathar the leader (?) was at that time High Priest in Jerusalem. He entrusted Mary to Joseph to take care of, and to deal with in purity'; pp. 22–23 (gloss to Matthew 7.6, concerning abuse and reform): 'those are the pearls, those are the commandments of the Gospel. *Ante porcos* before swine, those are the fatted swine, those are the men in holy orders and the good men and the proud men. They despise the commandment of God and the Gospel'; pp. 24–31 (glosses to Matthew 10.8 and 10.14, concerning simony): 'He said to the apostles and bishops foremost after him. You received orders gratis; give [them] gratis without any price to those who are worthy in learning and in habits and in purity and in virtues and in health of body. For the bishop must test and teach the priest eagerly, unless he has learnt beforehand' and 'A bishop is commanded to receive a newly-arrived priest, and to consecrate him quickly. Let him teach him first and eagerly prove him and ask those who know him what kind of a man he is ... [and] examine his doctrine unless he have a good person who will bear witness for him'.

dedication to *opus dei* in the labour of glossing the Gospels – are in accordance with the Church's teaching which demanded that the Bishop ordain, freely, the worthy candidate. The additional, voluntary payment of four ores of silver which he makes, accompanying the glossing of John for his own soul's sake, along with the labour, perhaps served to demonstrate that he was transcending the simoniacal demands of the contemporary episcopacy. This raises the question of Aldred's background. Where had he acquired such high monastic ideals and the learning to back them (see Rusche, this volume)?

His command of the Northumbrian dialect of Old English would tend to suggest that Aldred had a northern birthplace and/or training, and Millar has pointed to mistakes and variants in the gloss which he takes as indicative of a "seepage up of originally low status usages", which he interprets as exhibiting a familiarity with more recent, local linguistic trends (Millar 2000: 61). He goes on to say that

> before the Norman Conquest, the position of late West Saxon as *Schriftsprache* led to the at least partial submersion of most other written dialects at the time, except, as with the glosses to the Lindisfarne and Rushworth Gospels and the Durham Ritual, where the primary purpose of the written product appears either to be for personal use only, or at the very least for a limited group.

Brunner (1947–1948: 32), however, in a discussion of the frequent occurrence of variant linguistic forms in the Lindisfarne gloss, outlined two explanatory views. The first, favoured by Bouterwek 1858, Waring 1854–1865 and Skeat 1871–1887, was that the gloss was by two or more scribes who spoke different dialects, a theory belied by the palaeography, which indicates only one hand. The second view, favoured by the palaeographers (including Thompson 1873–1883; Warner 1873–1883; Ker 1943; and Brown 1969), that it was written by one scribe who spoke 'a language admitting many variants in its morphology' (Brunner 1947–1948: 32). This supports the possibility that, although Aldred's gloss is essentially his own composition, written directly into the Lindisfarne Gospels and based upon its text, he also consulted one or more pre-existing translations and preserved their linguistic and orthographic forms alongside those of his own sections (see also Cole, this volume). Aldred's approach to language and its variant forms was as fluid as his approach to script, his hand, as analysed by Ker, exhibiting an exceptionally wide range of letter-forms and styles, again perhaps reflecting in part the influence of his exemplars.

So, it would appear that Aldred's gloss was the work of someone from Northumbria for local use, composed directly for the Lindisfarne Gospels and written in it by one hand (Aldred's) which was familiar with writing both Old English and

Latin in both Cursive minuscule and Half-uncial,[24] but perhaps with reference to some previously translated matter. It represents a statement of local identity in the face of Scandinavian incursion against a backdrop of attempts to reassert an English identity throughout England. As Millar (2000: 47 n.17) states,

> it is unfortunate that because of the unsettled environment of the North of England at this time, our first inklings that something 'odd' was happening to the nature of English comes from texts, such as the gloss to the Lindisfarne Gospels, which originates in a part of the North which exhibits both then and now a lesser Scandinavian influence (to the extent of being readily classified as a Secondary Contact dialect), and which were written by older, probably conservative, men who had a considerable grounding in the South-Western Schriftsprache.

4 Conclusion: Aldred's work in context

Aldred thus emerges as a scholar who was familiar and in tune with the aims and linguistic background of the West Saxon educational and religious revival, and who was applying it to the needs and traditions of his native Northumbria. The community of St. Cuthbert, with its key role in the ecclesiastical and political life of the area, was an obvious base from which to pursue such an agenda. Another indication of Aldred's background is gained, as Ross (1958: 38–52) noted, from the disagreement of proper names in the original text of the Lindisfarne Gospels and its gloss, leading him to conclude that Aldred was consulting one or more other texts as well, these exhibiting affinities with forms in manuscripts of the 'Celtic' family, of the sort that the community of St. Cuthbert would originally have used. Another possibility is that Aldred was consulting other pre-existing translations of the Gospels into the vernacular (such as that already mentioned, by Bede) which, like Farman's gloss to the MacRegol Gospels, had been based upon other Insular texts of the Latin Gospels (see also Kotake, this volume). In any case, Ker (1957) was of the opinion that Aldred's work in the Lindisfarne Gospels was essentially his own composition and that this was his first attempt to write it down as he went through the manuscript, as certain errors have occurred specifically because of the layout of the original Latin text in Lindisfarne.[25]

24 For Aldred's cursive, see, for example, the foot of f. 248v between the columns, and for his Latin in a higher grade script, see the foot of f. 251r and the 'Five Sentences' component of the colophon on f. 259r.

25 Ker writes: "that the gloss was actually composed by Aldred and copied directly into this manuscript is suggested by such an eye-error as 'ðaðe' glossing *quinque*, f. 174 (where *quin* is at the end of a line), which has been corrected to 'fifo'" (Ker 1957: 216).

If standards at a house as important as Chester-le-Street were so lax by the time that Aldred glossed the Lindisfarne Gospels, where else might he have trained beforehand? At the period in question the most likely options are outside of Northumbria and the Danelaw in southern or western England, or on the Continent. Might Aldred have travelled South to receive his training, or even to the Continent, as had that arch-reformer Archbishop Dunstan himself? Another example of an English scribe working on the Continent during the second half of the tenth century is the Ramsey Psalter artist-scribe who was active in England and in several Continental houses including Abbo's Fleury (Brown, forthcoming b).

Aldred's work on Lindisfarne has been conducted with tremendous care and is presented both stylistically, and in the colophon, as a formal contribution. His hand is an elegant, pointed Anglo-Saxon minuscule, occasionally exhibiting Half-uncial features (especially when he adds words in Latin, as on the colophon page, where the 'Five Sentences' give the impression of having been copied from an Insular Half-uncial model, and when he seems to be copying some of the original scribe's letters as a pen-trial on f. 121r). It exhibits limited influence of Caroline minuscule and its confident cursive nature supports the conclusion that Aldred's is a hand that was probably used to penning documents and which was adapting itself for the purposes of glossing. The Half-uncial elements may simply reflect the visual influence of the Lindisfarne Gospels itself upon Aldred's hand during his work in glossing it, or may indicate that he was also used to writing a more formal 'old fashioned' book hand to which he nonetheless introduced 'modern' Caroline features (see further Brookes, this volume).

The importance of spoken language (the vernacular) is emphazised in the opening phrase of the colophon, where writing is acclaimed as the servant of speech and where Latin interacts with Old English, a reference to the oral/scribal processes of Gospel transmisson and also to Alfred's educational agenda and its emphasis upon the vernacular. Yet, although he is primarily writing Old English, rather than Latin, Aldred's hand occasionally admits features of Caroline minuscule, such as the Caroline *a* in the "allvm" of the third line of the part of the colophon naming the manufacturing team and the previously unnoticed possible Caroline question mark (*punctus interrogativus*) ending its tenth line, "and (I) Aldred, unworthy and miserable priest?". Such features are in accordance with the early influence of Caroline on the hands of those working in 'reforming' circles in the mid-tenth century, prior to its fuller introduction as part of the Benedictine Reform of the 970s onwards (Dumville 1993). Boyd saw him as joining the community in the 960s, during the reign of the pro-monastic reform monarch, King Edgar (959–975) and this may have been the case. It may be that Aldred was recruited from and 'planted' specifically back into his native region as part of an attempt to address such issues of reform in one of the most powerful houses in the North, in which case he may even have been 'sponsored' by one of the great tenth-century reformers, or, as already suggested above, have been encouraged by contact with one of the West Saxon royal visitations of the North from Æthelstan's time onwards. Ker's palaeographical assessment of the development of Aldred's hand is persuasive, and his work on the Lindisfarne Gospels at the time of his entry into the community was certainly conducted some time before he became its provost, by 970. Even if he undertook his gloss during the 960s as opposed to the 950s he could still have been in the front ranks of the monastic reform movement and a valuable northern ally for the reforming Church and Monarchy.[26] If this were the case, a West Saxon sensitivity to the historically independent cultural identity of Northumbria may have led to the reassertion of its own dialect, rather than the imposition of the West Saxon, as part of an attempt to win hearts and minds in the North, as well as political integration into the new 'England'.

In conclusion, the colophon which Aldred adds, recording names of others associated with what must have been a greatly treasured and venerated relic in its own right, would not have been undertaken lightly and should probably be viewed in the nature of an official statement by the community of St. Cuthbert on the presumed origins of the Lindisfarne Gospels – a tradition in which Aldred carefully situates himself and his community, thereby helping it to continue to play an important, formative role in the development of a new, unified England,[27] just as those who originally contributed to the making of this remarkable book had done in an earlier age.[28]

26 The impact of the Continental Benedictine reform movement appears to have begun to exert a limited influence upon some individual English ecclesiastics from the 930s onwards. Glastonbury and Abingdon witnessed the establishment of regular monastic communities during the 940s–950s, and Winchester, Canterbury and Worcester retained traditions of learning even prior to their reform. Might such a centre have nurtured the vocation and education of Aldred during his priesthood?

27 This need not preclude Nees's (2003) suggestion that Aldred has composed his colophon with a view to incorporating points of contemporary relevance, placing himself in the line of evangelistic transmission.

28 My current affiliations are: Professor Emerita, SAS, University of London; Visiting Professor, University College London; Visiting Professor and Senior Research Fellow, Baylor University; Senior Scholar and Editor, Green Scholars Initiative; and Senior Researcher, University of Oslo. I should like, in particular, to thank the University of Oslo for kindly supporting me in this work.

Jane Roberts

Aldred: Glossator and Book Historian

Abstract: Aldred of Chester-le-Street, in furnishing two manuscripts with vernacular glosses, provides the central evidence for northern English in the tenth century. The first part of this paper centres on Aldred's colophon, worked into the final page of the Lindisfarne Gospels (London, British Library, MS Cotton Nero D.iv), in which he reflects authoritatively on the book's history, making use of information handed down in verse. Discussion in the second part examines some lesser-known linguistic features found in his glosses, in particular his use of runes and of the reflexive form *sin*, both in the Lindisfarne Gospels and in the Durham Collectar (Durham, Cathedral Library, MS A.iv.19). A further short section considers Aldred's part in the tenth-century Latin additions to the Durham Collectar and on books that were perhaps available at Chester-le-Street in Aldred's day.

1 Introduction

Two books in particular allow us to create a picture of Aldred, a tenth-century northerner and member of the community of St. Cuthbert at Chester-le-Street, in County Durham. The first is the Durham Collectar (Durham, Cathedral Library, MS A.iv.19), into which "aldred se p(ro)fast" inserted a memorandum which gives us a time fix for him: he records that he wrote four collects down for Ælfsige, bishop of Chester-le-Street (968–990), at Oakley Down in Dorset on "Wednesday, Lawrence's feast day (the moon being five nights old), before terce" – the 10th August 970 (Brown 1969: 24). In a colophon added into the second book, the Lindisfarne Gospels (London, British Library, MS Cotton Nero D.iv), Aldred tells us a little about himself and the task he had just finished – glossing the Gospels in English – along with the history of the book itself. His hand is identified in a third book, in which his interventions, this time only in Latin, are sporadic (Oxford, Bodleian Library, MS Bodley 819). All we know about him stems from these three manuscripts. As long ago as 1943, Neil Ker disentangled for us the range of scripts represented by Aldred's hand, and Julian Brown has mapped out, in the 1969 Durham Collectar facsimile volume, the context not only for Aldred's run-of-the-mill glossing script but also for the wider array of scripts he essayed.

The Collectar to which Aldred added vernacular glosses came to Durham from the south of England: copied c. 900 from a volume imported from the Continent, it stems, according to Pfaff, from the "Alfredian book programme" and is "an attempt to supply the distinctive prayers and other formulae needed by the officiant at the daily office" (Pfaff 2012: 452). In script and decoration therefore the Collectar comes from the context epitomized by Oxford, Bodleian Library, MS Hatton 20, the earliest manuscript containing Alfred's translation of the *Cura Pastoralis*. Even so, in the words of Julian Brown, its scribe "belonged to a far more up-to-date milieu" than Aldred and the five others who glossed and added to the manuscript some seventy years later (Brown 1969: 15). Brown notes in particular that the script of Aldred and two of his contemporaries gives the impression "of an ancient and unbroken Northumbrian tradition, preserved in isolation from developments elsewhere in England" (Brown 1969: 41). With the Lindisfarne Gospels, Aldred, like the glossators of the Vespasian Psalter (London, British Library, MS Cotton Vespasian A.i) and the Blickling Psalter (New York, Pierpont Morgan Library, MS 776), worked his way through an old treasured manuscript. He is very much in their tradition, except that he reveals, in his colophon to the Lindisfarne Gospels gloss, his identity and his pride in having entered into the book's history. So too, Farman and Owun record their role in adding to the MacRegol (or Rushworth or Birr) Gospels (Oxford, Bodleian Library, MS Auct. D.2.19). Oddly, there is no manuscript witness extant of an earlier tradition of continuous interlinear vernacular glossing in Gospel books in England; and, strikingly, the Lindisfarne and Rushworth glosses were made at a time when the entering of running glosses into old treasure books had become a lot more discreet or altogether ceased. The Blickling Psalter, already carrying early vernacular glosses, received an additional layer of glossing in the late tenth or early eleventh century (Pulsiano 2001), but at much the same time the glosses that cluster in one particular section of a fine imported Gospel book, London, British Library, MS Add. 40000 (Kotake 2013), do not obtrude because they are scratched rather than in ink.

Aldred of Chester-le-Street has received a lot of attention in the twenty-first century. In particular his interventions in the Lindisfarne Gospels have been subjected to repeated scrutiny, not only in the descriptive volume published with the splendid new facsimile (Brown 2002–2003), but also in two substantial monographs as well as in articles and notes and other publications. I should like therefore to preface this article by singling out a book published since the paper I gave at the workshop on the Old English Gloss to the Lindisfarne Gospels held on the 17th–18th April 2012 in the University of Westminster. An important monograph by another of those who attended the workshop, Karen Jolly, appeared later that year, and I could wish it had been available to me earlier. In effect, it complements Michelle Brown's *The Lindisfarne Gospels: Society, Spirituality and the Scribe* (2003). Although focused on the additions Aldred and others made to the second manuscript into which Aldred wrote vernacular glosses, Jolly's book, *The Community of St. Cuthbert in the Late Tenth Century*, a searching analysis of Aldred and his context, includes a full transcription and translation of his colophon to his Lindisfarne Gospels gloss, which is central to her argument (2012: 41–60). Anyone who wants to find out about Aldred and Chester-le-Street in his day should begin by reading this book.

2 Aldred's history of the Lindisfarne Gospels

The final page of the Lindisfarne Gospels affords us a glimpse of Aldred actually writing English rather than using English to gloss Latin, which is why I selected it to represent the Lindisfarne Gospels in my *Guide to Scripts Used in English Writings up to 1500*. Although the final page had often been pored over, I decided to transcribe and describe it as a whole, giving special attention to lay-out (Roberts 2005: plate 5; 15–16, 34–37; and the coloured plate that accompanies this paper). As I returned again and again to reading the words from a xeroxed page, to my surprise, late one evening, these twelve verses leapt out in sequence:

Eadfrið biscop/b   ðis boc avrát
allvm ðæm halgvm   ðe in eolonde sint
eðilvald bisc(ob)   hit v́ta giðryde
gibélde sva hé vel cuðę   billfrið se oncrę
hit gihrínade mið golde   ⁊ mið gimmvm ęc
mið svlfre of(er)gylded   faconleas feh

'Bishop Eadfrith wrote this book in honour of all the saints who are in the island. Bishop Aethilwald compressed it from the outside, strengthened it as he well knew how to. Billfrith the hermit adorned it with gold and also with jewels, covered it with silver – a flawless treasure'.[1]

I discussed the discovery in a paper given at the 2003 MANCASS conference in Manchester (Roberts 2006). In the *Guide to Scripts* (2005: 36) I noted briefly that Aldred "used as nucleus an older poem available to him" for "the original book's history"; and Michelle Brown made a glancing reference to the relevance of my discovery to the case for Aldred's having had access to "earlier material" (Brown 2003: 95 and n. 33). Now, years later, it comes as a relief to find that the verses identified as embedded within Aldred's account of the book's early history are gaining recognition. Jolly, for example, describes them as "an Old English poem embedded in the text" (2012: 54), and Gameson as "an undatable Old English poem preserved within a later prose account" (2012: 8; also Gameson 2013: 17–18, 91–94).

1 Translations from Old English, unless otherwise indicated, are my own.

The doubts cast upon the reliability of the narrative Aldred transmitted had begun to gather momentum with Dumville's assessment that its evidence for the making of the book is "inadmissable" (1999: 78), and the case against Aldred was re-examined and developed in great detail by Nees: "Without the evidence of Aldred's colophon, attribution of the Lindisfarne Gospels to Lindisfarne is a plausible hypothesis, but no more certain than that, not a reliable fixed point" (2003: 373; see also Brown, this volume: pp. 16–18). Central to the stand taken recently in an article by Newton and colleagues is the view that the Gospel book glossed by Aldred came to him without evidence for "a connection with Lindisfarne or St. Cuthbert, or even with Northumbria" (2013: 133). Following Nees, they hold that the details of Eadfrith, Aethilwald and Billfrith are to be ascribed to Aldred's invention and that for them he consulted Bede's *Historia* and the Durham *Liber Vitae* together with both the anonymous and Bedan Cuthbert *vitae* (Newton et al. 2013: 130 and n. 89). As a result they strongly resist the suggestion that six lines of Old English poetry are buried within Aldred's colophon, slating me for discarding what is outside the putative poem as "merely Aldred's spin" (their use of the adverb *merely* (p. 127) confers a negative feel that is absent from my own argument). Had they chosen to consult the discussion and transcription of f. 259r published by me in 2005, they would have seen that I there deal with the page as a whole and, in taking pains to show how its contents may be fitted together, discard no part of Aldred's additions. It was never my concern to exclude parts of Aldred's colophon, rather to highlight within it twelve phrases fished out sequentially, paired verses with the contours of Old English poetry.

In response to Nees's call for examination of Aldred's sources, Newton et al. (2013: 112) argue for "the high culture of Aldred and his circle". Quite where to position the brief Latin inscription to the right of the Explicit for John's Gospel I had found problematic, noting that it could be placed either before the five sentences with which Aldred's colophon opens (the choice of Jolly 2012: 43 and of Newton et al. 2013: 140) or at its end: + *Lit(er)a me pandat* | *sermonis fida* | *ministra* | *Omnes alme* | *meos fratres* | *voce salvta* ⁘ ('Let the letter, the word's true servant, speak for me. Greet with friendly voice all my brothers').[2] As Brown points out (2003: 103), "[t]he subject may be intended to be either the text of John's Gospel, Aldred's gloss, or both"; and parallel passages are interestingly sifted by Jolly (2012: 48–52). The recognition within this inscription of resonances from Ovid's *Tristia* is important (Newton et al. 2013: 111); yet the use of similar wording within a letter written in Alcuin's circle need indicate only that the topos was available. Was Aldred necessarily indebted to "the *envoi* tradition not only in Ovid but also

2 The translation is free; "alme" should be construed as a vocative, perhaps 'O holy [book]'. For discussion, see Ross et al. (1960: 5), Brown (2003: 96, 145), Nees (2003: 341), and Jolly (2012: 56).

in the world of Carolingian poetry" (Newton et al. 2013: 111) or was he drawing on collocations that had established currency? According to the *Fontes Anglo-Saxonici* database, there are two traces of Ovid's *Tristia* in Bede's *De die iudicii* and Aldhelm had access to Ovid, making a longer inheritance possible. Again, whether emendation is required so that the second line becomes a hexameter is open to question. If the agenda is to add to Aldred's access to "high-status culture", the addition of *ex* before *uoce* is attractive, but sense can be made of the words as they stand. The couplet is further *tweaked* into dialogue (the words around the scribal portrait in the Eadwine Psalter are compared), with the first line spoken by St. John and second by Aldred's gloss (Newton et al. 2013: 109). The riff which moves from Ovid as an exile among speakers of foreign languages segues into a St. John "alone at the outermost fringes of Christendom – he is therefore *hamleas* in Aldred's tongue", with Aldred as enabler of John "to speak a Germanic language"; and the Gospel book itself is termed *hlafordleas* (Newton et al. 2013: 133). The trail of sources – it is argued – Aldred used is impressive, except that all seem designed to contribute to what may be their erroneous image of "Carolingian sophistication".

On balance, Aldred's reliability as historian of the book to which he added glosses is buttressed by his incorporation of twelve older English verses. Aldred was not the fabricator of the book's story, but its inheritor. This is evidenced not only in his brief account of the book's history but also in the prayer that marks his completion of glossing Matthew's Gospel (f. 89v):[3] "ð(-ẹ\`u´) lifigiende god | gemyne ðu | eadfrið ⁊ | ęðilwald ⁊ | billfrið ⁊ | aldred peccator(em) | ðas feowero | mið gode ymb|w`o´eson ðas bóc" ('O living God, remember Eadfrith and Aethilwald and Billfrith and Aldred, a sinner: with God these four engaged in [making] this book'). The prayer added to f. 89v is paralleled in two lines at the foot of Aldred's colophon: + Eadfrið . oeðilvald . billfrið . Aldred . | *hoc evange(lium) d(e)o ⁊ cvðberhto constrvxerv(nt):, ´ƚ ornavervnt`..* ('+ Eadfrith, Aethilwald, Billfrith, Aldred | made `or adorned this Gospel´ book for God and Cuthbert').

One explanation of these lists might be to assume that the three names of the book's first makers were in the splendid binding Symeon describes in his account of the miraculous recovery of the book after it had fallen into the sea (Rollason 2000: 118–119): *ipsum sanctum euangeliorum codicem reperiunt, qui sicut forinsecus gemmis et auro sui decorem, ita intrinsecus litteris et foliis priorem preferebat pulchritudinem, ac si ab aqua minime tactus fuisset* ('they found that same holy book of the Gospels, which retained its enrichment of gems and gold on the outside, as on the inside it showed the former beauty of its letters and pages, as if

3 The first *e* is subpuncted; the *r* of *pecator(em)* is not wholly visible; and *s* is perhaps a mistake for *r* in "ymb|w`o´eson".

it had not been touched by the water at all'). There is no mention of a miraculously undamaged Gospel book in an earlier account of the community's interrupted flight to Ireland, to be found in the anonymous *Historia de sancto Cuthberto*, § 20 (South 2002) and known to Symeon.[4] Nevertheless, this life does have its own reference to a Gospel book (§ 16): St. Cuthbert, in King Alfred's vision of him the night before a significant battle, is [...] *senex sacerdos infulatus nigris quidem capillis, habens in dextera manu euangelii textum auro gemmisque ornatum* ('[...] an old priest wearing a bishop's insignia and with black hair, holding in his right hand a Gospel book ornamented with gold and gems'). One would like to think that this richly ornamented Gospel-book associated with the saint is an image of the workmanship of Billfrith.

The listing of the names of the makers of the Lindisfarne Gospels is paralleled in the three names scrawled into the Codex Aureus (Stockholm, Kungliga Biblioteket, MS A.135, f. 1; Gameson 2001–2002): + *Orate p(ro) ceolheard pr(esbyter) inclas ⁊ ealhun ⁊ wulfhelm aurifex* ('+ Pray for Ceolheard, priest [and] hermit and for Ealhun and for Wulfhelm, goldsmith'). But only a few actual examples remain from Anglo-Saxon England of the names of makers or commissioners of precious objects worked in precious metal other than on rings. From the early period there is the Mortain Casket inscription, the runic inscription on the back of its lid reading (Okasha 1971: no. 93): "+ GOOD HELPE : ÆADAN ÞIIOSNE CIISMEEL GEWARAHTÆ" ('God, help. Aidan made this chrismal'). Later inscriptions to consider include the gold letters set in a panel around the Alfred jewel (Okasha 1971 no. 4): "+ AELFRED M|ECH|EHTGEVVYRCAN" ('Alfred had me made'); and the incised words on the Brussels Cross: "ÞAS RODE HET ÆÞLMÆR WYRICAN ⁊ AÐELWOLD HYS BEROÞOR CRISTE TO LOFE FOR ÆLFRICES SAULE HYRA BEROÞOR :-" ('Æthelmær had this cross made and his brother Æthelwold in Christ's honour for their brother Ælfric's soul'), together with the craftsman's identity "+ DRAHMAL ME WORHTE" ('Drahmal made me') on its back (Okasha 1971: no. 17). From outside the Anglo-Saxon period proper there was lettering on the cover of a tenth-century Gospel book, Oxford, Bodleian Library, MS Auct. D.2.16, one of two "mycele cristes bec gebonede" ('large ornamented Gospels') recorded at Exeter among the gifts of Leofric (d. 1072) and still there in 1506, when it was described (Ker 1957: no. 291) as:

> *Textus argenteus et deauratus cum Crucifixo, Maria, et Iohanne, cum 4 Evangelistis in 4 angulis, cum 1 olla subtus pedem crucifixi, cum hac scriptura subtus eandem romanis literis sculptam 'Hic textus est ornatus ex communi erario Leofrici episcopi curialiumque ejus'*

4 South (2002: 16) reports Gullick's identification of the first copy extant of the three manuscripts as in Symeon's hand.

> 'A silver-and-gold-bound book with the Crucifixion-scene, including Mary, and John, with the Four Evangelists in the four corners, with one vessel underneath the foot of the cross with this writing engraved underneath it in Roman letters: "This book was ornamented with funds from the general treasury of Bishop Leofric and his curia"'.

This at least is evidence of an inscription, shortish and in Latin, giving information about the binding's origin. You can get a fair bit of such text on to a book cover one way or another.[5] There is evidence as well of donors who wanted their generosity to be remembered in a late eleventh-century inscription in London, British Library, MS Add. 40000, f. 4r, quite pleasingly laid out in three lines on the originally blank recto of the first leaf of the preliminary quire (ff. 4–10, containing tables of the Eusebian Canons): "+ Ælfrici ⁊ wulfwine. Eadgife goldsmiðes geafen to broþer|rædenne twegen órn weghenes goldes þ(æ)t is on þis ilce | bóc her forúten gewíred·" ('Ælfric and Wulfwine, Eadgife's goldsmiths, gave to the brothers' community two ores of weighed gold which is twisted here on the outside of this book'). The book's present binding is eighteenth-century, and but for this note of its former binding we would not know these donors' names.

The names Eadfrith, Aethilwald and Billfrith could well have been memorialized in the rich binding made by Billfrith. In the absence of the binding, we cannot tell. But what of the verse lines? On reflection, I surmise that they were to be read not on the outside of the Lindisfarne Gospels but in pages that at one time travelled with the book and are now lost. Across time Gospel books and psalters were refurbished, and often they were topped or tailed with additional pages or even quires in which inscriptions might appear. Michelle Brown identifies, among the descriptions of eight books containing Gospels at Durham in 1383, three as possibly "applicable to the Lindisfarne Gospels" (2003: 118). Although she is, very properly, reluctant to press the issue, she does single out one description as worthy of reappraisal: "iv) Item a Gospelbook adorned with gold with a gilded crucifixion with many evidences and monuments" (*cum multis evidenciis et monumentis* in Fowler 1898: 432). We cannot know what preliminary and/or closing pages the Lindisfarne Gospels once had, space into which documents might have been written, but, as Brown (2003: 118–121) points out, additional inscriptions could have included "a tradition concerning the original circumstances of the manufacture of the Lindisfarne Gospels and the names of its makers/commissioners". Earlier, Gameson had suggested that Aldred had access to "the words of a now lost earlier record" (2001b: 47). Is it too fanciful to think that some time before Aldred's day someone had added a vernacular book poem into a blank

5 I should like to thank Rebecca Rushforth for this reference. Cp. also Bishop Bernward's Gospels: Hildesheim, Dom-Museum MS 18 (c. 1015): Rosenthal (2011: 244 fig. 12).

page then still part of Nero D.iv? Just as with the inscription at the foot of f. 89v, Aldred could have had access to information then part of the book on which he worked. Alternatively, he knew and used a poem handed down orally.

Whatever way the book poem had come down to him, Aldred has added little to what it preserves, say twenty words apart from the frequent conjunctions. Perhaps he had it in his head as he wrote and as he added snippets of explanation. He tells us that Eadfrith was bishop of the community of the people of Lindisfarne, *lindisfearnensis æcclesiæ*, and that "he" at its beginning wrote the book for God and St. Cuthbert and all, in common, on the island, "æt frvma gode ⁊ s(an)c*te* cvðberhte ⁊ allvm ðæm halgvm . ða . ðe \`gimænelice´ in eolonde sint". Next, the book was bound by Aethilwald, bishop of the people of Lindisfarne, "lindisfearneo londinga", a phrase which, straying clumsily into Aldred's rather fluid right margin, throws up the nonce word *londing*. The finishing touches were put by Billfrith, a hermit, who forged the metal ornaments that are on its outside: "he gismioðade ða gihríno ða ðe v́tan ón sint". To my mind, these explanatory details are, so to say, added off the cuff, as Aldred began on his history of the book. For Gameson (2001a: 14) in his discussion of why Eadfrith wrote the Lindisfarne Gospels, Aldred's use of English raised the questions: did Aldred "express himself more readily in the vernacular"; or would he even have thought "that he would be more easily understood in Old English" than in Latin? But it could just have been that Aldred, equipped with a source of information in English, in order to use it switched to the vernacular. What he had to say, with additions and second thoughts added in, overflowed the enticing space available. The content comes from the strange animal that is the occasional book poem, an uneasy mix of prayer and panegyric, and, despite his expansions, this block of material is demarcated from what follows by heavy punctuation to mark its end. These nine lines of writing give us the fullest account extant of the making of an early Anglo-Saxon book.

In the account of himself that follows, Aldred positions himself for a second time as the fourth maker of the Lindisfarne Gospels in modern times,[6] just as he had done at the end of Matthew's Gospel, but adding a new story. Again the mode is prayer: the *peccator* of f. 89v now confesses himself to be *indignus ⁊ misserim(u)s*. In line with the preceding section, he begins in English: "⁊ (-ic) Aldred p(re)\`s´b(yte)r" (a feeling for symmetry may have led to his cancellation of *ic*, to better align himself with the three makers of the book back when it was at Lindisfarne). He returns to English to explain his own part in the making of the book. In a marginal flourish he tells us proudly who he is, in jingling Latin:

6 Nees (2003: 345–46, 365–69) explores the importance of fours in Aldred's colophon, as do Newton et al. (2013).

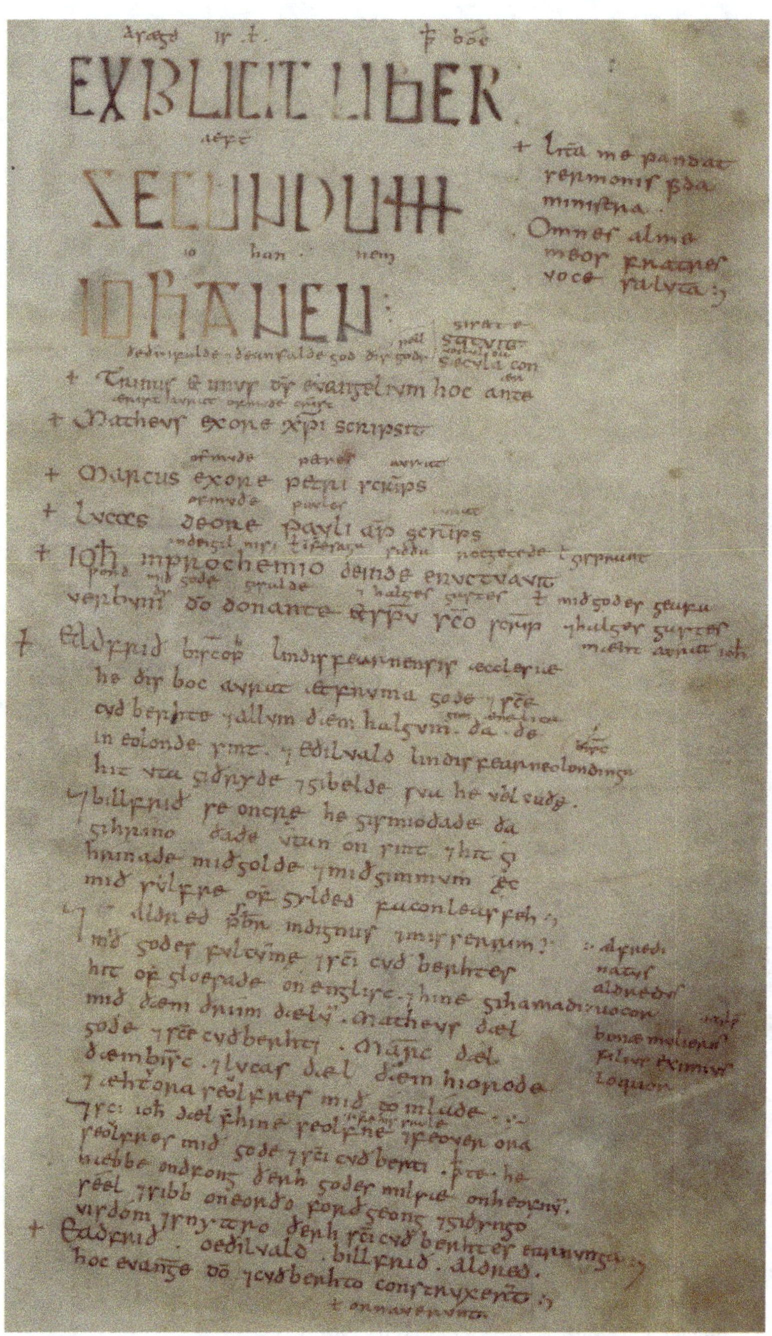

Figure 1. London, British Library, MS Cotton Nero D.iv, f. 259r col. b

ælfredi | *natvs* | *aldredvs* | *uocor* | *bonæ mvlieris* | *filivs eximivs* | *loquor*, appositely translated by Michelle Brown (2003: 104) as "Aldred, born of Alfred, is my name: a good woman's son, of distinguished fame". He even makes a half-hearted attempt to gloss this jingle in English, with "*i*(*d est*) til p'" jotted in to explain *bonæ mvlieris*. Generously he allows himself twelve lines for his own part in the history of the book, though within the larger structure of the new main text he has created, not disproportionately. In the five preliminary sentences of his additions he distinguishes between the three synoptic Gospels and John, and in this final part heavy punctuation divides his role in the book's making into two sections:

> 'And Aldred, an unworthy and most wretched priest, with the help of God and St. Cuthbert, he glossed it in English and made himself at home ["gihamadi"] with these three divisions, Matthew's section for God and St. Cuthbert, Mark's section for the bishop and Luke's section for the community, together with eight silver ores for its use ["tó inláde"]; and St. John's section for himself, i.e. for his soul, together with four pieces of silver for God and Saint Cuthbert, so that through God's mercy he may have in heaven acceptance, on earth well-being and peace, death and mediation, learning and wisdom through the intercession of Saint Cuthbert.'

The meaning of the verb form "gihamadi", paralleled only by the infrequent *hamettan*, is hard to gauge, but the drift is clear.[7] The labour of love on which Aldred has engaged in the first three Gospels is dedicated, together with eight ores of silver to God, St. Cuthbert, the bishop and the community. Aldred is often accused of having bought his way into the community at Chester-le-Street because the phrase "tó inláde" is customarily translated 'for his induction', as in the 1956 and 1960 facsimile edition by Kendrick et al. (Ross et al. 1960: 10). A more generous interpretation of the phrase is adopted in the translation given above, reflecting the interpretation for 'traffic [in the book]' (Roberts 2006: 35–36 and n. 39).[8] In the five lines about glossing the fourth Gospel Aldred makes an interesting distinction between his labour and his gift of silver – the former, the task of glossing St. John's Gospel, the Gospel traditionally read for and by the dying, is presented as undertaken for the needs of his own soul, and the latter as a further offering to God and St. Cuthbert, but both these gifts carry with them his prayer for his future and trust in St. Cuthbert (the force here of *earnung*, extending both to 'merit' and 'intercession', is not easy to convey in modern English). A final two lines of Latin, in script approaching the formality of the introductory five sentences of his colo-

7 *Pace* Newton et al. (2013: 120–121), who translate "homed him"/"domiciled him" as making St. John "a native speaker and thus 'homed' [...] or domiciled in Anglo-Saxon England. Or, to be more precise, he 'homed him along with the [other] three parts [...]'".

8 Newton et al. (2013: 126 n. 73) do grudgingly admit "There has, to be sure, been a protest against this baseless cynicism; see Roberts (2006: 35 n. 39) on 'ungenerous interpretation'".

phon, bring together and complete Aldred's history of the book. Again, as at the end of the Gospel of Matthew, he aligns himself with the three original makers of the Gospel book on which he has worked lovingly and doubtless long.

For the two occurrences of *ora* in the Aldred colophon, Newton et al. (2013: 121–126) put forward a new interpretation, arguing that it is "the word for 'border, edge, margin'", "from Latin *ora, orae*, with this meaning (as in 'the border of a garment')". But Old English *ore* 'border, edge, margin' applies to landscape features (see Cavill, this volume: p. 81, n. 3). The only evidence for its use of the border of a garment got into the first volume of the Bosworth-Toller dictionary from Spelman's edition of the Stowe Psalter, where it is a form that has not found its way into the *Dictionary of Old English Web Corpus* (hereafter *DOEC*). Consultation of the Stowe Psalter edition by Kimmens (1979: 316) indicates that the earlier edition had mistakenly recorded as Old English an alternative reading above the line for the Latin. So the evidence for the border of a garment is dubious, let alone a border surrounding a block of writing. Nevertheless, *ora* is made to bear the weight of an argument that Aldred gave twelve silver borders to the book but that these have all been trimmed away. (We may ask what happened to the silver from the inner margins when the borders were entirely trimmed away: do they envisage three-sided borders?). While Newton et al. provide references to borders in other manuscripts, these are a part of the original making of the manuscripts and generally near the writing. In addition, they interpret *inlad* as the 'beginning' of a new Gospel or new section, i.e. an opening or incipit pages bordered in silver privileging such introductory pages. Never mind that the grand count to twelve has to take in some end pages as well as incipits (Newton et al. 2013: 124). Rather they argue: "We understand that 'to inlade' might imply, by shorthand, closing pages ('utlada') as well as opening ones, as in the Sanaa Qur'an and the MacRegol Gospels" (Newton et al. 2013: 125 n. 69). They pile in more learned references, which do not really help, and they oppose less ingenious interpretations of *inlad* as impugning "Aldred's integrity" (Newton et al. 2013: 122). Not only is *ora* asigned an unattested meaning, but *inlad* and *utlad* as well. Surely it is simpler to recognize here the *ora* of the Danelaw (for Aldred maybe a measure of weight rather than the monetary unit of the Danes in their parts of England). These meanings are not recorded in earlier Old English, which did have a cognate word for 'metal'. The twelve ores of silver mentioned on the last page of St. John's Gospel are paralleled by Aldred's use once of the same word in LkGl (Li) 19.13: "ðæm tea ora i(*d est*) libras".[9] A few verses later, at Luke 19.18, he may have avoided *ora*; unlike Owun, he does not use it again when rendering Luke 19.18.

9 The short titles used for Old English texts in this paper are those of the *DOEC*.

In twenty-one lines of English prose Aldred gives his history of the Lindisfarne Gospels. He begins with the book's first makers, using (*pace* Newton et al. 2013) information available to him in verse form, details Symeon of Durham also later recalls, and then he writes himself into the book's history. How he amassed so much silver we do not know, but what is evident is that he wished to honour St. Cuthbert and his community. Grateful for the privilege of having become a part of the book's making and adornment, he gives generously.

3 Some aspects of Aldred's English

On the last page of the Lindisfarne Gospels Aldred introduces himself as "Aldred p(re)`s´b(yte)r", much as does Farman in the Rushworth Gospels, f. 50v, "far*man* pres*b(yte)r þas boc þus gleosede *dimittet ei dominus omnia peccata sua si fieri po(t)est apud deum:/*" ('Farman, priest, glossed this book thus. The Lord forgives him all his sins if he can be with God'),[10] or as Brand is described on the Kirkdale sun-dial in the middle of the eleventh century, "+ ⁊ HAWARÐ ME WROHTE : ⁊ BRAND PR(E)S(BYTER)" ('And Hawarth made me: and Brand, priest') (Okasha 1971: no. 64), and as Eadhyse is remembered on a cross from Ripon, "+ ADH[Y]SE [PR(ES)] B(YTER)" (Okasha 1971: no. 102). The label *presbyter* does not often slip into Old English contexts. Where it does, it follows names in identifying phrases. It turns up twice in the Anglo-Saxon Chronicle, but only in the C version: ChronC (O'Brien O'Keeffe) 565.1: "Her Columba presbiter com of Scottum on Brittas Peohtas to lærenne ⁊ on Hii þam ealande minster worhte" ('In this year Columba, priest, came from Ireland into Britain to teach the Picts and founded a monastery on the island of Iona'); 666.1: "⁊ Eoppa presbiter be Wilferþes worde ⁊ Wulfhere cing brohte Wihtwaran fulwiht ærest manna" ('and according to Wilfred's account Eoppa, priest, Wulfhere, king of the people, first brought Christianity to the Isle of Wight'). The first of these instances directly reflects one of the annals that follow Bede's *Historia ecclesiastica*: [ANNO DLXV] *Columba presbyter de Scottia uernit Brittaniam ad docendos Pictos, et in insula Hii monasterium fecit* ('The priest Columba came from Ireland to Britain to teach the Picts and established a monastery at Iona'; Colgrave and Mynors 1969: 562–563). For the other, there is no underlying Bedan annal, but, as pointed out by Plummer (1892–1899: II, 27), the chronicle annal contains misinformation about the conversion of the Isle of Wight shared with the spurious charter (Sawyer 1968: no. 72) recorded in the Peterborough Chronicle under 656, so some early source must lie behind both.

10 See <http://bodley30.bodley.ox.ac.uk:8180/luna/servlet/s/5m4332> for direct link to f. 50v.

Again, the C redactor, from whatever wording to which he had access, chose to retain *presbyter* in his English annal. There is one instance only in the Old English Bede: "be þam Fortunatus pre(sbyter) (Miller 1890–1898: I, 34), translating *de quo presbyter Fortunatus* (Colgrave and Mynors 1969: 28), as if prompted by the Latin. A curious nonce word occurs in the Lauderdale *Orosius*: "On ðæm dægum Arrius se mæssepr(es)b(yter) wearþ on gedwolan ymb þone ryhtan geleafan" ('In those days the priest Arrius fell into error concerning the true faith', Bately 1980: 149, ll.10–11), where the later manuscript reads "mæssepreost". Otherwise the form appears in a vernacular context in a late-eleventh-century list of sureties in the last six leaves of the York Gospels manuscript, describing six priests: "Gamal presbyter [...] Cetel presbyter [...] Ulfcetel presbyter [...] Ulf presbyter [...] [l]dolf presbyter, Auðcetel presbyter" (Rec 24.4 (Stevenson) 1–12). It would seem possible, therefore, to recognize *presbyter* as a loanword of limited frequency in Old English, occurring for the most part in northerly texts (but cp. Feulner 2000: 311–313). For Ælfric, *presbyter* is a Latin term, the highest of the seven ranks in the church: ÆLet 1 (Wulfsige a) 29 "Seofon hadas syndon gesette on cyrcan: an is hostiarius, oðer is lector, þridda is exorcista, feorða acolitus, fifta subdiaconus, sixta diaconus, seofoða presbiter" – a term that later in this same pastoral letter needs explanation in English, ÆLet 1 (Wulfsige X a) 40–41: "Presbiter is mæssepreost oððe ealdwita. Na þæt ælc eald sy, ac þæt he eald sy on wisdome" ('Presbiter is a priest or a man old or eminent in wisdom; by no means that each is old, but that he is old in wisdom'). As Hill has recently observed: "there is no intrinsic difference between priests and bishops, since both are within the seventh order of the church" (2012: 151).

It is the term *preost* that is omnipresent in vernacular contexts except, curiously, in these few instances. Yet we persist in talking about Aldred the priest and provost and assuming that when he worked on the Lindisfarne Gospels he had not yet been promoted to a senior position. Should we? Of one thing I am sure, Aldred was very aware of rank. After all, there is an elaborated list of church ranks, *De gradibus æcclessiæ* (DurRitGlCom (Thomp-Lind) 193.19), among the assorted notes and records in the final folios of Durham, Ms A.iv.19, running from *hostarius* up to *papa*. This is no simple list like Ælfric's, but a set of explanations of the meanings of widely used terms vis à vis biblical and Greek equivalents. For Aldred, the Greek term *presbyter* denotes a senior grade: *Præsbyter grecum est quia seniores aetate greci presbyteri uocant* ("meas p'eost crecisc is f'ðon aeldro from ældo crecas measa p'stas geceigað"; DurRitGlCom (Thomp-Lind) 194.9). And there is a bit of plain speaking about what a bishop is: *Ępiscopus græcum est nomen operis non honoris inde dictum est epi super scopus inspector ideo episcopi superinspectores nominantur ('Episcopus* in Greek is the name of an office, not an honour; hence it is *epi* "over", *scopus* "observer, supervisor"; thus bishops are called “overseers”’), “bisc' crecisc is noma voerces no worðvnges of ðon acvoeden is ofer insceawre f'ðon bisco' of’insceawras genomado biðon” (DurRitGlCom (Thomp-Lind) 194.11). Etymologically, a bishop is an overseer – a job name, not necessarily a description of honour achieved. Another list follows, *Interpretatio nominis sacerdotvm* (DurRitGlCom (Thomp-Lind) 195.1), one entry explaining the term *sacerdos*: *Sacerdos huic nomine tum functus est melchisedech et aaron primus in lege sacerdotalem nomen accipit et liberi eius sacerdos nominatur qui et presbiteri nuncupati factum est quod presbyteri et episcopi sacerdotes nomnatur* (‘*Sacerdos:* under this name then Melchisedech, and Aaron, first carried out office according to the Law; on account of his being noble he receives the priestly title and is called *sacerdos*; and those who [are] are named priests, it is because priests and bishops are called sacerdotes’) and glossed “sacerd ðissvm nome gebrycsade væs melchi' ⁊ aaron ærist in æ sacerdlichad nome onfeng ⁊ freo his sac' genomad bið ða ða æc meas' genomad aworden is þæt meas' ⁊ bisco' sac' biðon genomado” (DurRitGlCom (Thomp-Lind) 195.2). Indebted Aldred may be ultimately to Isidore, but the selection is his own.

As with Ælfric’s pastoral letters for priests, we are in teaching territory, and Aldred is listing information about which he can ask questions. Compare from the *Adrian and Ritheus* dialogue (Cross and Hill 1982: 36):

13 Saga me hwilc bisceop wære ærest on þare ealdan æ ær cristes tokyme. Ic þe secge, Melchisedech and Aaron.
14 Saga me hwilc bisceop wære on þære niwan æ.
Ic þe secge, petrus *and* iacobus.

13 ‘Tell me, which bishop was first in the Old Testament, before the coming of Christ? I’ll tell you, Melchisedech and Aaron.
14 Tell me, which bishop was in the New Testament? I’ll tell you, Peter and James’.

Two of Aldred’s short entries actually begin with *Dic mihi* (DurRitGlCom (Thomp-Lind) 192.13, 192.17). But Aldred ranks *presbyteri* and *episcopi* together as the successors of the *sacerdotes* of old. (In our terms, Aldred is dean alongside Chester-le-Street’s bishop.) It is well to remember that, although the community of St. Cuthbert was in contact with the southern and reforming church of Edgar’s reign, it must still, in Aldred’s day, have operated much as in the pre-Alfredian world so well described by Sarah Foot, a past encapsulated in her statement “There was nothing ‘regular’ about English monasticism before *c.* 900” (2006: 346).[11] The Benedictine Reform was not to hit the community until 1083 (Law-

11 Cf. Jolly (2012: 10 *et passim*). Her monograph was not available when the paper from which this article is drawn was delivered, and for the most part I refrain from comment where our views

rence-Mathers 2003: ch. 1). We know little about the circumstances of the *congregatio* at Chester-le-Street across the years 883–995, but the later Benedictine community of Durham, looking back from their vantage point, described their predecessors as a group consisting of "a provost or dean and seven clerks, who with their families held designated portions of the land of their church; associated with them was an unspecified number of priests and clerks who participated in the life of the church and the shrine" (Foster 1994: 53). Aldred lived in a context where there was no binary division between minster churches and enclosed monasteries (Foot 2006: 11), where as often as not the knowledge of Latin was rudimentary.

3.1 Aldred's use of runic letters

One of the most striking oddities of Aldred's glossing in the Durham Collectar is his use of the *dæg* and *mann* runes (42x and 10x times respectively). As Derolez points out, they are used "in a more or less systematic way", and he argues that "Here we find a still greater degree of integration than in those cases where the rune (i.e. the rune-name for which it stood) was part of a compound: in the Durham Collectar we even come across **d**es = *dæges* or **d**e = *dæge*" (1954: 401–402). Runes written for their names, i.e. as ideographs, are otherwise, according to Derolez, infrequent in Old English writings. Most famously they occur in the Cynewulf signatures of the Vercelli and Exeter books, occasionally elsewhere in these two manuscripts, and in the *Rune Poem*, for which we are dependent on Hickes's transcript because its manuscript was lost in the Cottonian fire. Other instances are infrequent. The rune for *eðel* occurs 3x in *Beowulf*, 1x in *Waldere* and 1x in the Lauderdale *Orosius*. Eric Stanley suggests the use of *eðel* in *Beowulf* could be regarded as a provincialism, and he points out that some have suggested a Northumbrian origin for *Waldere*, but that the Lauderdale *Orosius* is "non-provincial" (Stanley 1981: 229). For Fleming (2004: 181–182), observing that the three *Beowulf* instances are in the first scribe's hand and in the "context of things Germanic", they could have been introduced "as a sort of archaism". Interestingly, there is a single example of the *wynn* rune as a word in the Junius Psalter (Ps 99.2 "**w**sumiaþ"), a manuscript thought closely related in script to the Lauderdale *Orosius*. And in the Cambridge, Corpus Christi College, MS 41 *Solomon and Saturn*, lines 39 and 63, where the name *Salomon* ends with the **m** rune, the scribe seems to hedge his bets by supplying an overline above the rune; Derolez suggests

are in agreement.

he was probably "not fully aware of the ideographic value of the rune" (Derolez 1954: 401). This oddity allows us, momentarily, to align Aldred with Old English writings mainly from before the period dominated by Ælfric and Wulfstan, but it gives rise also to the observation that occasional runes also crop up among the Lindisfarne Gospel glosses. Runes as ideographs are not, as far as I know, to be found in the glosses added to the MacRegol Gospels, although the name of one of the MacRegol glossators, Far**m**, ends in the rune for *mann* (f. 50v, in the colophon cited above on p. 48). There has been much speculation as to why Aldred should have moved towards the use of pointed *u* (*v*) rather than the runic letter-form for *w* used in glossing the Gospels, with Bede's putative choice in his reported translation of John seen as contributory (Elliott and Ross 1972: 65). Keefer, noting Aldred's use of the *mann* and *dæg* runes, points also to his frequent use of *v* rather than *wynn* as a letter-form when initial (Keefer 2007: 95). Might it not just be that he was beginning to avoid *wynn* as open to interpretation as a full word?

3.2 Confusion of *forþ* and *soþ*

A noteworthy spelling oddity that seems not to have received attention is the Durham Collectar's distribution of *forþ* forms with the spelling <soð>: eight in all, all of them in DurRitGl 1 (Thomp-Lind): *forþcuman* 3x and single instances each for *forþclipian*, *forþlædan*, *forþfylgan*, *forþgestriend* and *forþtacen*. By contrast, there are only two such forms among the Lindisfarne Gospels glosses, both *forþsecgan*. All these forms can be found in the *DOEC*, but none among the entries edited for *F* in the *Dictionary of Old English* (hereafter *DOE*). The three instances of *forþcuman* (DurRitGl 1 (Thomp-Lind) 2.17 <soðcuom>, 12.13 <soðcyme>, 57.2 <soðcuom>) stand above forms of *praevenire* or *procedere*; this is a word that lasts into later English, and it is to be found in the *OED* (s.v. *forthcome*). Other verbs that last into later English are *forþclipian*, in the separated DurRitGl 1 (Thomp-Lind) 42.7 <soð ue cliopiað> above *provocare*, and *forþlædan*, as DurRitGl 1 (Thomp-Lind) 108.19 <soðlæde> above *producere* (see *OED*: s.vv. *forthclepe* and *forthlead*, respectively). For the fourth of these Collectar verbs, *forþfylgan* (DurRitGl 1 (Thomp-Lind) 29.17 <soðfylga>), the *DOEC* has a single representative, a *Regularis concordia* gloss (RegCGl (Kornexl) 65.1574 <forþfylige>, also above *prosequi*), so the Durham Collectar phrase supplies a second attestation. Neither of the two nouns appears in *DOE*, nor do they have a later history in English: DurRitGl 1 (Thomp-Lind) 29.13 <soð gistrynd> above *progeniem*, and DurRitGl 1 (Thomp-Lind) 43.19 <soð taceno> above *prodigia*. The former may be compared with the poetic hapax legomenon MSol 330 "eormenstrynde", the latter with the frequently occurring noun "foretaken" (see *OED:* s.v. *foretoken*, n.). Both Lindisfarne forms are in the preliminaries to John's Gospel: JnHeadGl (Li) 11 and 31 <soðsæges> above *pronuntiat* (i.e. in material not universally in all early Gospel manuscripts). The *DOE* editors record 24 psalter glosses for *forþsecgan* from the relatively early Vespasian and Junius Psalters and the old-fashioned Cambridge Psalter; there are no *OED* citations, whereas OE *foresecgan* with approximately 350 occurrences is better established (and see also *OED*: s.v. *foresay*). From our perspective, where the letter-forms *f* and *s* are very different in shape, it is easy to lose sight of these forms. Given the similarity of their Insular shapes, the substitution of *soþ* for *forþ* has all the looks of simple error. Then there is the problem of the omission of *r*. Tadashi Kotake tells me that Farman sometimes omits *r*, for example writing *for* as *fo* in MtGl (Ru) 4.20 <foletende> and 6.14 <forleteþ>, which has a caret mark below *o*. More obviously, *f*-*s* substitution may have led to lexical confusion between *forþ* and *soþ*. The distribution of these few aberrant *soþ* forms remains to tantalize. Is their presence in the Lindisfarne Gospels gloss only in the preliminaries to John's Gospel significant? Does the fact of there being appreciably more instances among the Collectar glosses attest to the lesser degree of care with which that task was undertaken?

3.3 Use of the possessive adjective *sin*

How far did Aldred himself create the glosses we attribute to him? With Bede's Commentary on Proverbs in MS Bodley 819, for the fifty or so pages glossed he mostly fills in biblical verses absent from Bede's commentary or adds the occasional *id est* explanation, so there he was principally a copyist, and his mainly explanatory glosses are in Latin, for himself. As Mark Faulkner has pointed out, "someone who had poor Latin was unlikely to be reading it, and could more profitably be studying the relatively easy Latin of the Gospel text" (2008: 99). With the Lindisfarne Gospels, just how far Aldred made use of an exemplar or exemplars is still to be resolved (see Cole, this volume). There is the question as to whether the qualitative differences between his practice in the three synoptic Gospels and in John sets the fourth Gospel apart, as inheriting something of Bede's deathbed translation or as in some way more original. An enormous amount has been written on the language of the Lindisfarne Gospels glosses, and comparatively little on the Collectar glosses. The facsimile volume (Brown 1969) has a glossary "founded on work done by Constance O. Elliott", with a remarkably slim introduction in which we are told magisterially that "the two glosses are very similar, but not identical", that Aldred's phonology is "perhaps best ascertained from a perusal of" Campbell's *Grammar* (1959) and his grammar as set out in the Lindisfarne volume and in Ross (1937); and that much of the work done on the vocabulary “can be extracted from the relevant entries” in Holthausen (1934); and that the Aldrediana series of papers is to be consulted (Ross and Stanley 1969: 53). The reader is left to decide for himself how closely the Collectar glosses resemble those in the Lindisfarne Gospels.

Whether or not Aldred had an exemplar for his Lindisfarne glosses continues to be debated. Two long-recognized Scandinavian loans in the glosses to John’s Gospel, *floege* and *ðir*, are considerable flies in the ointment for the theory that vocabulary independent of the other three Gospels points to Aldred’s use of Bede’s translation of John (Elliott and Ross 1972). Pons-Sanz has sifted the evidence for Scandinavian loans in the Lindisfarne Gospels gloss scrupulously, flushing out a goodly number of loans overall. Yet she finds no clear morphological influence from Old Norse in Aldred’s usage, and she points out that no structure words are borrowed (2004: 188; see also Pons-Sanz 2000 and 2013). The trouble with the glosses to John’s Gospel is that every time someone tries to be specific, there prove not to be hard and fast differences. A further anomaly is the use once only of the possessive adjective *sin*, in the phrase “sinum ambehtum” which stands above JnGl (Li) 21.14 *discipulis*. JnGl (Ru) 21.14 reads *discipulis suis* with “ðegnum his” above. It could therefore be argued that Aldred uses *sin* in John’s Gospel but not in the glosses to the three Gospels for which some argue he was copying earlier glosses (Elliott and Ross 1972), an absence which could have constrained him in his solitary use of the form while glossing the fourth Gospel. Overall I find the distribution of *sin* in the two books to which Aldred added English glosses surprising. It occurs once only in Lindisfarne, where Aldred, perhaps expecting a possessive form, added “sinum” with little thought, but pervasively in the Durham Collectar, where for the most part the instances of *sin* correspond to *suus* forms. Quite how the form *sin* is to be viewed presents difficulties. Ross (1978: 198), comparing the differences in glossing Matthew 22.2–14 between Lindisfarne and the Durham Collectar, describes the contrasting phrases MtGl (Li) 22.5 “in lond his” and DurRitGl 1 (Thomp-Lind) 107.13 “in londe sinvm” as a difference in syntax, but whether he is commenting on the noun inflection or the rendering of *suam* is hard to tell.

My assumption is that *sin* was in Aldred’s idiolect alongside the genitive forms of *he* and could be triggered by Latin *suus*, but that it was not his inveterate response to *suus* forms even in passages where *sin* appears. Possessive adjective and genitive pronoun may occur in linked phrases, each answering to Latin *suus* forms, for example: DurRitGl 1 (Thomp-Lind) 4.7 “in his giręste ł sinvm” above *in accubitu suo*; and DurRitGl 1 (Thomp-Lind) 77.17 “gibedde sinvm ⁊ broðer his” above *conjugem suum ualerianum affinemque suum*; or in parallel phrases, as in DurRitGl 1 (Thomp-Lind) 107. 13 “foerdon oðer in londe sinvm oðer to cepinge his” above *habierunt alius in uillam suam alius ad negotionem suam*. More often they occur farther apart, as in DurRitGl 1 (Thomp-Lind) 109.21 "noht in ðær of dedvm sinvm he frvmwyrhta gyltincges gispilla gicnyht to lvfe bibodvm æc ðerhwvnia anvm brydsceam' gifoegedo cunnvnga ða vnclænlico gifliie afæstnia vntrymnisse hire mægne ðeatscipes" above *Nihil in ea ex actibus suis ille auctor preuaricationis usurpet nexa fidei mandatisque permaneat uni toro iuncta conactus inlicitos fugiat muniat infirmitatem suam robore discipline*. The orthodox view of *sin* is that it is "a lost reflexive" which "occurs mostly in poetry, rarely in prose, and it does not survive into ME" (Mustanoja 1960: 156). Bauer (1963), like Mustanoja, also sees *sin* forms as archaizing and traditional. Mitchell (1985: I, § 290) rules that *sin* is largely replaced by the genitive forms of *he*: observing that it is "spasmodic" in poetry of all periods and occurs as late as the Death of Edward poem in ChronC (O'Brien O'Keefe) 1065 and ChronD (Cubbin) 1065, he (1985: I, § 291) argues that it is archaic and retained for metrical reasons. Oddly, *sin* occurs only twice in Old English prose, in the Kentish Laws of the early twelfth-century *Textus Roffensis*: LawAbt 82 "Gif man mægþmon nede genimeþ: ðam agende l scillinga ⁊ eft æt þam agende sinne willan ætgebicge" ('If a man forcibly carries off a maiden, [he shall pay] 50 shillings to her owner, and afterwards buy from the owner his consent'); and LawWi 10 "Gif esne deþ his rade þæs dæges, vi se wið dryhten gebete oþþe sine hyd" ('If a servant makes a journey of his own [on horseback] on that day, he shall pay 6 [shillings] compensation to his lord or undergo the lash'). Here is the adjectival possessive *sin* being copied in the early Middle English period – though how trustworthy these seventh-century law-codes are linguistically is sometimes questioned (Lendinara 1997). A very few instances of *sin* crop up in glosses in three southern psalters – not in the earliest psalters that bear Old English glosses but in eleventh-century glossed Gallicanum psalters (London, British Library, MS Cotton Vitellius E.xviii; London, British Library, MS Arundel 60; and London, Lambeth Palace Library, MS 427), all with strong Winchester connections (Roberts 2011). Fossilized traces of early glosses? Who can say? But it is worth bearing in mind that this further curious coincidence with the Collectar glosses is restricted to the glossing of John's Gospel.

Overall, Aldred's Lindisfarne Gospel and Durham Collectar glosses together furnish the main evidence for northern English in the tenth century, along with the Rushworth Gospel glosses, especially those by Owun, insofar as they relate to the Lindisfarne glosses and wherever they were written. As Chester-le-Street, where Aldred, *presbyter* and *profast*, had his base, was beyond the great belt of Scandinavian settlement, his form of English displays the effects of secondary contact with Scandinavian. His dialect must have sounded strange to southern churchmen at Oakley Down, accustomed to the conservative grammatical and lexical norms that were becoming widespread in West Saxon; but no matter – the shared language of worship and learning was Latin. The absence of earlier

Anglian literature demonstrably from this area means that we have little idea of any northern English writings Aldred might have read or of what written vernacular sources were available to him. When working on the Lindisfarne Gospels, he could have had an earlier glossed text as exemplar, but probably without the preliminaries to John's Gospel. If so, the changes in practice in the introduction to John could have come about because he had no exemplar to which to cling. It is, however, unlikely that there was an earlier glossed version of the Collectar. If he was without an exemplar for the Collectar, did he, I wonder, draft his intended glosses on tablets? If so, the substitutions of *soþ-* for *forþ-* could have come about through his miscopying his own rough work.

4 Aldred, scribe

Whatever comparisons may be made tenuously between Aldred's English and original writings and translations being made or copied in his day, we can agree he had not been trained to write English according to more southerly norms and he was not a speaker of late West Saxon. The make-up alone of his vocabulary makes that very clear: in addition to Scandinavian borrowings (Pons-Sanz 2000), there are words from Irish and Welsh (Ross 1982: 197–198). Again, although some of his contemporaries in the community were experimenting with Caroline minuscule, he seems to have kept fairly clear of its letter-forms;[12] generally indeed his glossing hand shows little influence from Square minuscule. His input into the final quires that follow the Collectar is often overestimated, most recently by Pfaff, who describes them as "three quires of further, largely liturgical, material, written at Chester-le-Street by Aldred, the celebrated scribe who glossed the Lindisfarne Gospels" (2012: 452). Whereas in the Lindisfarne Gospels Aldred's is the only hand responsible for its late-tenth-century glosses, in A.iv.19 five other hands made additions c. 970 (Brown 1969; and more recently Jolly 2012: ch. 3).[13] The five other hands appear in quires VIII–XI: in ff. 61r11–65 of quire VIII, the empty pages at the end of the Collectar, A [= Aldred], B, C, D, F account for few Old English glosses; in quire X (7 folios, of which f. 69 is a singleton) further additions by A, C and F, and in quire IX (two bifolia) A responsible for the main text of the opening two folios and glosses; and quire XI or ff. 77–88 six bifolia

12 But see Stewart Brookes's new analysis of the scripts used by Aldred (this volume).

13 Also see Jolly (2006) for discussion of the field prayers in Aldred's hand in the opening pages of the Further Additions booklet, Jolly (2012: 155–162) for analysis of Aldred's input to Scribe B's prayer against poison, ff. 61r 11–22, and Jolly (2013 and this volume).

to which E contributed as well as A. Overall these added materials have been described as "disorderly and various" (Corrêa 1995: 49). Yet, quire XI on its own (ff. 77–88) strikes me as sensibly put together; as Jolly (2012: 82) puts it, Aldred was "in full control" in this quire. The attention given to the placing of materials and the helpful gradations in script make it easy to follow and to understand major junctures in the liturgical materials presented. This is especially the case if you begin reading from the top of f. 78 and disregard the additions in E's hand. Ff. 78–83 contain the full order for a service, for which f. 77 has the five hymns that are not written out in full in the order of service. The present ff. 78–87 form a five-folio quire in which f. 77 together with its conjoined f. 88 might have been supplementary; ff. 77 + 88 could as easily stand after an eight-folio quire. Aldred left a blank verso (f. 84v, after the Cuthbert page and before the four folios filled with useful information), into which Scribe E crams an incomplete list of antiphons and respond incipits for the four Sundays of Advent (Billett 2010: 454); and a later scribe scavenges the end-page gap on f. 77v, lines 19–25. There is a pleasing tidiness about ff. 77 + 88 when read continuously, with the hymns on f. 77, on f. 88r the names of the resting-paces of the apostles, and on f. 88v an alphabet poem followed by a summary canon table tucked neatly into remaining space. Whereas on the last page of the Lindisfarne Gospels we recognize Aldred's clever deployment of the space available in a part-written page, in these pages we see him as a scribe at work.

Apart from the three manuscripts in which we see Aldred's hand, we know of some other books that could have been available to him (Ross 1981; Lawrence-Mathers 2003: 18–26; Gameson 2010). Best attested are books given by Æthelstan when he visited Chester-le-Street in 934. The life of St. Cuthbert written in verse and prose he gave to the shrine of St. Cuthbert would seem to be Cambridge, Corpus Christi College, MS 183, although it has been suggested that the first real evidence for this book's presence in Durham dates to 1071–1080 (Rollason 2000). Æthelstan also gave the community a couple of Gospel books, ornamented in gold and silver, one of them a Breton Gospel book, London, British Library, MS Cotton Otho B.ix, destroyed in the Cotton fire (Keynes 1985: 177–178), and a service book of some sort – has anyone ever suggested that is when the Durham Collectar could have travelled to the north? Some of the earliest manuscripts in Durham today could have been among books known to Aldred (Gameson 2010). The Stonyhurst Gospel of St. John must have been there, if unseen, in Cuthbert's coffin, and a Gospel book that reputedly Boisil had used in teaching Cuthbert. He must have had a psalter, and indeed "a long list of Psalters" was recorded as at Durham in the mid-twelfth century (Lawrence-Mathers 2003: 23 n. 52), but like so much else, it has vanished. The earliest extant witness to a psalter in Durham is from after his time: Muniments of Dean and Chapter, Misc. Cht. 5670, a leaf in a good hand of the early eleventh century (Mynors 1939: 29). What we do not have is any evidence for the dissemination of books in English as far north as Chester-le-Street (Lawrence-Mathers 2003: 22–23, 37) at this time. The vernacular inscriptions written in the tenth and eleventh centuries into some of these great books are in more conventional English than Aldred manages in his glosses, and he must have known the short passages of early West Saxon to be found in the Collectar. It is sobering to reflect that Aldred, "indignus ⁊ misserrimus" ('unworthy and most wretched'), belongs to much the same time-span as the Vercelli and Exeter books. Later a copy of Ælfric's *Catholic Homilies*, the only complete copy of the second series (Cambridge, University Library, MS Gg.3.28) was in Durham, and a copy of his *Grammar* (bound with a Latin hymnal, Durham, Cathedral Library, MS B.iii.32), but there is nothing to indicate that books in early West Saxon and Mercian were available in Aldred's Chester-le-Street.

5 Conclusion

Enticingly, Aldred has a name, but it is a common one. His father's name too is among the most frequent recorded from Anglo-Saxon England. We know nothing of him before his entry into the community of St. Cuthbert at Chester-le-Street. In a memorandum from his hand we glimpse him at a meeting in Wessex in 970. Twice he describes himself: as priest in the Lindisfarne Gospels, as provost on his 970 visit to Oakley Down. More importantly, he tells us about the history of the great Gospel book into which he wrote vernacular glosses. He had details of the separate tasks undertaken by the three men responsible for making the treasured Gospel book and whose work he sought to complement. His vernacular glosses provide the most important witness to northern English in the latter part of the tenth century: in the Collectar, very much, it would seem, his own words; though perhaps for the Lindisfarne Gospels he drew upon glosses already in circulation (Ross et al. 1960: 11; Kotake 2012: 19). Above all, the impression left is of a man who wanted to explain and to teach, and to help others to understand what they read. Of course he got some things wrong (for example, Lindelöf's 1927: lxv–lxx list of glosses that show misunderstanding of the Latin of the Collectar makes fascinating reading). For his use of English, there remain to us only two books, and even they present a contrast: the Collectar glosses smaller and more cursive, the Lindisfarne glosses more formal, larger and better spaced. With the Lindisfarne Gospels he may well have seen himself as opening up the metaphorical "sacred building" (Newton et al. 2013: 134) he glossed.[14] As Michelle Brown has observed, and before her Carl Nordenfalk, the book's first quire of canon tables may be thought of "as an architectural atrium through which the mystery of Scripture could be accessed" (Brown 2003: 304). One thing is certain: at its end Aldred thought deeply about the task he had undertaken of glossing a book treasured in the community's history and by doing so wrote himself in, irrevocably, to the history of one of greatest treasures from the insular past, MS Nero D.iv.

14 But when I read "The *palatium* has at least four parts or chambers edged or bordered in silver at the entrance ("inlad"), and in each one of these parts or chambers, an Evangelist has been 'homed' or 'domiciled' ("gihamadi") as a native speaker", I find myself reflecting on just how hard the forms "inláde" and "gihamadi" are worked by Newton et al., and I am unconvinced that Aldred actually had a "poetic concept of four altars, each dedicated to a saint or saints, as the whole building is dedicated to God and St. Cuthbert" (2013: 135 – the "perhaps" of p. 118 is forgotten).

Philip G. Rusche

The Glosses to the Lindisfarne Gospels and the Benedictine Reform: Was Aldred Trained in the Southumbrian Glossing Tradition?

Abstract: Since Aldred glossed the Lindisfarne Gospels in the second half of the tenth century, the height of the Benedictine Reform in southern English churches, some scholars have connected him to this movement. It has even been suggested that he was trained in the south to carry reform ideals to the northern churches. Unfortunately, no evidence has been adduced for these suggestions. In this article I look at the methods of glossing in Southumbrian manuscripts and compare them to the methods seen at work in the Lindisfarne Gospels. In general, there are very few similarities, suggesting that Aldred was not trained in the south. Instead, his method of glossing seems much closer to what we find in the interlinear psalter glosses, the origins of which predate the Reform. It is likely that the psalter glosses provided the model for the style of glossing in Lindisfarne.

1 Aldred and Southumbria

One of the unanswered questions in the study of the glosses to the Lindisfarne Gospels is where Aldred was trained. Although he has left two long and somewhat informative colophons in the Gospels and in the Durham Ritual (see Gameson 2001a; Nees 2003; Roberts 2006; Newton et al. 2013; Roberts, this volume), we are still very much in the dark about what led him to add these glosses and where or how he acquired the necessary techniques to provide a thorough interlinear translation to the Gospels. In the last several decades there have been suggestions that Aldred must have been influenced by, perhaps even trained by, the monastic reformers then in charge of the southern churches. If such training could be demonstrated, it would be rare evidence that the ideals of the Benedictine Reform had spread beyond Southumbria and were effective in the north of England. Vernacular glossing of Latin texts was one of the most prevalent intellectual activities of the southern church in the tenth century, and if Aldred had come under the influence or training of these churches he could have learned a wealth of techniques for adding a gloss to a manuscript. Thus, as one way to evaluate whether Aldred may have been exposed to southern training, I will compare his glossing techniques with those prevalent in Southumbria.

The first major connection of Aldred with the Benedictine Reform came in two 1975 papers by W. J. P. Boyd. He (1975a: 4) prefaced his work on the marginalia in the Lindisfarne Gospels with the statement that Aldred's "context is that of the vigorous reform of the monastic houses and the general revival of Church life and of learning in the reign of the West Saxon monarch Edgar (959–75), which we have come to know as 'the Benedictine Renaissance'". In his article of the same year on the Hebraica in Aldred's glosses in the Durham Ritual, Boyd (1975b: 56) describes "the revival of English scholarship attested by Aldred and the *familia* of St. Cuthbert" as a "felicitous result" of the efforts of Edgar, Dunstan, Oswald and Æthelwold to reinvigorate English learning, which was "struggling up from the murky ignorance caused by the incessant waves of Scandinavian attack and settlement". Boyd, however, left it to others to explain in more detail how the glosses in the Lindisfarne Gospels were a "felicitous result" of the work going on in the south of England, giving only a few suggestions here and there in his commentary on the glosses (e.g. Boyd 1975a: 22).

A major problem in making this connection between Aldred's glosses and the reform of the monasteries is that the reform movement is usually considered to be a Southumbrian phenomenon with little influence in the north (see, for instance, Farmer 1975: 14). The slim evidence for manuscripts, liturgical or otherwise, owned by the community of St. Cuthbert does not contradict this view (see Dumville 1992: 98; Lawrence-Mathers 2003: 16–26). Nevertheless, Boyd's suggestion has been picked up by a number of other scholars. Michelle Brown (2003: 98) notes that Boyd pointed to Aldred's concern with celibacy and simony as testimony that "he was joining the community with a reforming celibate monastic agenda in mind". Karen Jolly (2012: 11) has also pointed to the Durham Ritual's liturgy, updated by Aldred and the community at Chester-le-Street "with some of the reform innovations noted in the *Regularis concordia*". If this is so, then we must ask where he could have developed such a reforming mindset. Dumville (1992: 98 n. 13) has suggested that he was trained at an unknown centre in Northumbria, and this would accord well with his use of the Northumbrian dialect and his decision to use an older style of writing, in spite of the availability of Square minuscule models at Chester-le-Street (see Jolly 2012: 75). Ker (1943: 11–12) has noted that it is unlikely that there was a scriptorium in the north in the tenth century that was teaching a standard form of writing and that the few scraps of contemporary writing produced at Chester-le-Street "bear no resemblance" to Aldred's script; however, he (1943: 8) also remarked upon his use of "an *a* which resembles Caroline *a*", and Brown (2003: 101) has suggested that the Caroline features might indicate some training either in the south, where Caroline was becoming influential in reform circles, or on the Continent.[1] She (2003: 101) has even suggested the possibility that "Aldred was 'planted' specifically in his native region as part of an attempt to address such issues of reform in one of the most powerful houses in the north, in which case he may even have been 'sponsored' by one of the great tenth-century reformers". The south was certainly interested in promoting Cuthbert as a national English saint in the tenth century, and planting a reformer in his community would have helped to spread the new monastic ideals (see Rollason 1989; Simpson 1989; South 2002). Was that Aldred's role? Having briefly mentioned this somewhat contradictory, or at least inconclusive, evidence concerning Aldred's training, I would like to turn to some of Aldred's glossing techniques to see what light, if any, they can shed on where Aldred may have learned how to gloss a text. It is somewhat difficult to compare the Lindisfarne glosses with the glosses produced or at least copied in Southumbria in the tenth century, since there are no interlinear Gospel glosses other than Rushworth, whose connection with Lindisfarne is complex (see Kotake, this volume). Nevertheless, glossing was a major component of the monastic efforts at revitalizing education throughout the century, and many of the glosses in southern manuscripts share similar features with each other even though they are for different texts. By comparing these common features with the glosses in Lindisfarne, it may be possible to see if the latter reveal any influence in glossing techniques from those from the south.

For comparison I have used the following texts produced in southern centres. First, there are the early, pre-Reform glossaries from the school of Canterbury, primarily the Leiden Glossary (Hessels 1906), the Épinal-Erfurt Glossary (Goetz 1888–1923; Pheifer 1974), and the Corpus Glossary (Lindsay 1921). The primary material in Leiden and Épinal-Erfurt seems to have been gathered together originally in the Canterbury school of Theodore and Hadrian in the late seventh century, and the Corpus Glossary presents a late eighth- or early ninth-century adaptation of this material.[2] From the later period, roughly contemporary with the Lindisfarne glosses, there are glossaries as well as glosses in manuscripts of Latin texts. The main glossaries are the Cleopatra Glossaries (Rusche 1996), the Brussels Glossary (Rusche 1996: 554–566), the Harley Glossary (Oliphant 1966),

1 The evidence for Caroline influence has so far been considered to be relatively weak: a Caroline *a* in "allvm" in the colophon and a possible Caroline *punctus interrogativus* (see Brown 2003: 101). Dumville has said that "Anglo-Caroline does not seem to have penetrated northern England before the eleventh century" (Dumville 1993: 156). See, however, Brookes's paper (this volume) for a different view.

2 Although these glossaries are earlier than the tenth century, I mention them because they were heavily used as source material for the later glossaries and provide insight into the development of several techniques found in tenth-century glossing.

and the Antwerp-London Glossary (Porter 2011). The manuscripts with glosses in Old English are primarily of Aldhelm's prose and verse *De virginitate* (Gwara 2001; Goossens 1974; Rusche 1994), but there are numerous glosses to authors such as Sedulius, Prudentius, and Bede (see, for instance, Napier 1900; Meritt 1945 and 1959). Finally, I have used the glossed psalters, relying mostly on the edition of psalms 1–50 by Pulsiano (2001). As complete interlinear versions of biblical texts, these perhaps provide the most promising comparisons to the Lindisfarne glosses. Although the interlinear psalters are not originally products of the Reform, they were largely copied and disseminated in reform circles throughout the tenth and eleventh centuries (see Gretsch 1999).

This collection is of course a huge and disparate group of works, and I have doubts that coherent sense can be made out of looking at them as a unified whole and identifying features of glossing that are pertinent to them all. In fact, it seems best to divide these works into three groups. The first will consist of the glossaries, which are either pre-Reform or based mostly on pre-Reform scholarship; second is the set of occasional glosses in manuscripts of school texts that proliferated in the reform period; the final group will consist of the psalter glosses, which differ from the second group in being complete interlinear glosses. This division may seem somewhat artificial, and given the similarity in format of the Lindisfarne glosses to the complete interlinear vernacular gloss in the psalters, it would seem to weigh the comparison against the school texts. Nevertheless, I think there is merit in dividing the glosses this way, since both the glossaries and the 'occasional' glosses would still be influential on anyone educated or trained in that tradition, and signs of their influence would show up regardless of the medium.

2 Features of Southumbrian glosses

There are five features I have often noticed in working with these glosses over the years:[3]

1. heavy reliance on older English glossaries or previously existing glosses as a source;
2. heavy reliance on reference works, especially Isidore's *Etymologiae*, for definitions of Latin terms (mostly but not limited to those that we might call technical terms);

3 Compare this list with the eight characteristics Page (1982: 151) identified in the Latin glosses in London, British Library, MS Harley 110. The two lists are for different purposes, but it is instructive that several of his characteristics, especially nos. 5 and 6, are similar to those given here.

3. gradual replacement of Latin glosses with Old English glosses;
4. use of specific grammatical indicators (such as prepositions, pronouns, and periphrastic tenses) to handle inflectional and morphological differences between Old English and Latin;
5. close attention to glossing individual morphemes rather than whole words.

Each of these features builds on the concepts inherent in the others and reveals a certain philosophy behind glossing. Glosses in Southumbrian manuscripts not only provided a simple lexical translation but also a thorough linguistic and etymological commentary on the Latin texts. I will take these features in order.

2.1 Reliance on early English glossaries

The first of the features given above, the reliance on previous English scholarship, is especially important to stress given the amount of recent discussion of the influence of the Frankish church on the intellectual endeavours of the tenth century (see, for example, Gretsch 1999 and the studies discussed in Cubitt 1997: 78–81). In spite of the influence from the Continent, much of the educational component of the reform was thoroughly English. Most of the tenth-century glossaries, such as Cleopatra, Brussels and Antwerp-London, consist of large amounts of materials from the seventh- and eighth-century English glossaries, with only a few signs of updating to include new efforts by Frankish scholars. Glosses in manuscripts of Latin texts also depend heavily on the work of previous scholars (Lapidge 1982). To take one of the most prominent examples, the glosses in manuscripts of Aldhelm's prose *De virginitate* originate in a core that was available at least as early as the ninth century and probably prior to that (see, for instance, Gwara 2001: I, 276–306), and manuscripts like Brussels, Bibliothèque Royale, MS 1650 and Oxford, Bodleian Library, MS Digby 146 seem in some ways to be attempts to record all available previous English scholarship on Aldhelm. The glosses to the psalters are also based on pre-Reform English scholarship. The earliest English psalter manuscript containing glosses is the Vespasian Psalter, with its interlinear gloss added in the early- to mid-ninth century; it has even been suggested that these glosses ultimately originate in the same milieu as the Épinal-Erfurt Glossary, i.e., the late-seventh-century school at Canterbury (Kitson 2002: 481). The glosses in Vespasian, known today as A-type glosses, are found in several other psalters, but in the mid-tenth century, a second tradition of psalter glosses, known as the D-type, was copied into the Regius Psalter. The origin of the D-type glosses, which were transmitted in numerous tenth- and eleventh-century manuscripts, is debated, but it is likely that they are a reworking of the earlier

A-type glosses rather than a completely new production (Gretsch 1999: 36; Kitson 2002).

When we turn to the glosses in Lindisfarne, it is difficult to evaluate whether, or to what extent, Aldred based his work on earlier English materials. There is no earlier surviving Northumbrian gloss to the Gospels, nor does the gloss show any correspondence with the near-contemporary West-Saxon translation or with the southern Gospel glosses such as those in the Second Cleopatra Glossary. Precisely what manuscript resources would have been available to the community at Chester-le-Street is uncertain, though it was presumably limited (Ross 1981: 7; see also Jolly 2012: 150–199), and Aldred may well have had to rely on his own knowledge to provide the gloss. Ker (1957: 216) pointed out an error suggesting that Aldred was composing the gloss as he wrote it in the manuscript: he wrote "ðaðe" as a gloss to *quin* at the end of a line, only correcting it to "fifo" after realizing that the Latin word continued on the next line to make *quinque*. Countering this suggestion are the numerous examples of errors found by Ross (1932a: 392–394) that reveal that Aldred was following the text of at least one different manuscript, and he later (1981) shows that Aldred made use of Latin readings in Rushworth. Aldred's use of the Latin text of Rushworth led Ross to suggest hesitatingly that the glossing of Rushworth and Lindisfarne occurred at the same time and that some of the glosses in Lindisfarne may have been copied from the glosses in Rushworth. Although Ross (1981: 11) concludes that there is "not sufficient evidence to show that Lindisfarne was influenced by Rushworth in this way", it remains quite possible that at least one of the Latin manuscripts used by Aldred was already glossed in Old English and that he made use of these glosses.

Perhaps of most relevance here is the unverifiable suggestion that Aldred based some of his glosses in John's Gospel on the lost translation that Bede was working on before his death (see Ross 1969; Elliott and Ross 1972). Such a reliance on a much older and authoritative translation from a revered predecessor would be in keeping with what we see in southern circles in the tenth century and emphasizes the Reform as a renewal of the past. Nevertheless, Aldred's possible reliance on Bede or on other lost Northumbrian translations and his apparent avoidance or ignorance of the large Canterbury tradition of glosses, especially of those on the Bible, do not lend support to the suggestion that he was trained in the South; on the contrary, it suggests that he was trained somewhere in the north, which had access to scholarly traditions distinct from those in the south. In fact, Aldred's work seems more thoroughly situated in a Northumbrian-Irish milieu than in a southern one (Jolly 2012: 10–14).

2.2 Reliance on Isidore

The second feature is the use of Isidore, especially the *Etymologiae*, as a source to explicate the meaning of Latin words. Isidore's influence in the glossing tradition of Southumbria is vast, extends through all periods, and reflects a keen interest in understanding and elucidating the morphemic elements that underlie Latin words and their relationship to the external world (Di Sciacca 2007 and 2011). The clearest place to look for the use of Isidore in glosses is in the 'technical' vocabulary of the Roman Empire – names of people, places, objects of daily life, or the religious, political, social, and military world –, knowledge of which was transmitted to England largely through the *Etymologiae*. Such terminology is often explained in long, so-called encyclopedic glosses (see Wieland 1983: 168–185), often quoted directly from Isidore.

We would expect to see signs of Isidorian influence in the marginal commentaries Aldred added to Lindisfarne, where he had more space to explain the meanings of the Latin terms, and in his interlinear translations of the names and places of the Bible. These have been thoroughly analyzed by Boyd (1975a) and Pons-Sanz (2001), but it is rare that they find evidence of Isidore as a possible source for Aldred. In fact, in the few places where Boyd mentions Isidore, Aldred's commentary suggests that he was entirely ignorant of Isidore's definitions. For example, to explain the word *legio*, Aldred comments: "here ł xij ðus(end) þæt is legio [...] wæs diowla legio" ('army or twelve thousand, that is, a legion [...] it was a legion of demons'; Boyd 1975a: 38). Isidore (*Etym*. IX.iii.46), however, specifically defines a *legio* as *sex milium armatorum* ('6000 armed men'; Lindsay 1911: I, 367).[4]

Another likely place to check for signs of Isidorian influence is in the interlinear glosses to technical terminology and proper names. It may seem unfair to expect to find signs of the use of Isidore's *Etymologiae* in what is largely an Old English translation, but the use of Isidore can be found in vernacular glosses just as in Latin ones. As a brief example, which I have discussed elsewhere, the Latin word *venabulum*, a type of hunting spear, is given glosses such as "eofursperum" or "barsperum" ('boar-spears') in manuscripts of Aldhelm's prose *De virginitate* (Rusche 2005: 448–449). The glosses are not translations of the Latin word *venabulum* but rather of Isidore's definition of the spear as used for catch-

4 Boyd's statement that "Aldred would know this [i.e., that a legion numbered 6000 soldiers] from reading Isidore's encyclopedia" makes an assumption of Aldred's reading that does not currently seem sustainable. Boyd also mentions Isidore on Aldred's gloss on myrrh, which, however, also shows no knowledge on Aldred's part of the Isidorian definition (Boyd 1975a: 52–53). Other places where Aldred reveals ignorance of Isidore could be multiplied, such as his marginal gloss of *tribunus* at Mark 6.21 (cp. *Etym*. IX.iii.29).

ing boar (*Etym.* XVIII.vii.4), which was probably an original Latin gloss in earlier manuscripts of the text. I have been able to find no similar examples in the interlinear glosses in Lindisfarne. Instead, he seems to have relied mostly on church fathers, especially Jerome and Bede, as shown by Pons-Sanz (2001) in her study of Aldred's glosses on proper names. In other words, Aldred shows no clear sign that he is familiar with such an indispensible encyclopedia on Latin vocabulary and Roman culture, in sharp contrast to what we might expect from someone trained in glossing in one of the southern monasteries.[5]

2.3 Replacement of Latin glosses with Old English

Old English glosses derived from Isidore as found in Southumbrian manuscripts provide an illustration of my third feature above – that Old English glosses are often translations of previous Latin glosses and not of the words of the primary Latin text. Similar Latin glosses may underlie at least some of the Old English of the Lindisfarne glosses. This does not necessarily mean that Aldred, or the original composer of the Old English glosses, was translating an interlinear Latin gloss to the Gospels. Instead, it suggests that their knowledge of the meaning of Latin words comes from a tradition of Latin exegesis, and as they provide vernacular glossing to a Latin text, they are relying on that Latin tradition for their interpretation of the text and the words in it. In this way, the gloss is less a vernacular rendering of the Latin text than a vernacular rendering of the scholarly traditions and commentary on that text.[6]

One example of this type of gloss in Lindisfarne is in the Old English translation of *parasceve*, the day before the sabbath (i.e., Friday), at Luke 23.54 and John 19.14. The word is glossed several times as "foregearuung". OE *foregearwung*, however, is not a direct gloss on *parasceve* but rather a loan-translation of *praeparatio*, which is the usual Latin rendering of *parasceve*. Both the Latin and the Old English words are included in the gloss to JnGl (Li) 19.14: "metes foregearuung *i. est praeparatio cibi*" ('preparation of food, that is, preparation of food').[7] This gloss explains the somewhat nonsensical gloss at MtGl (Li) 27.62, where

---

5 It is possible that, by the time Aldred was making additions to the Durham Ritual, he had access to the *Etymologiae* and perhaps other Isidorian texts like *De ecclesiasticis officiis* (see Jolly 2012: 186–188), but his knowledge of these texts at first hand is not clear.

6 For a few examples of Old English glosses that are translations of Latin glosses, see Brussels 1650, nos. 861, 928, 930, 988, 990, etc. (see Goossens 1974).

7 The abbreviations of books of the Bible when citing glosses in the Lindisfarne Gospels are those employed in the *Dictionary of Old English Web Corpus* (hereafter *DOEC*). Unless otherwise noted, all quotations of the Lindisfarne Gospel glosses are taken from Skeat (1871–1887).

altera autem die quae est parasceuen conuenerunt principes sacerdotum is rendered “oðero ðonne doege ðiu is mettes gearwing gesomnadon ða aldor sacerdas” (‘then on the next day, that is, the preparation of food, the leaders of the priests gathered’). Glosses like this suggest that providing a clear and readable running translation, such as one might find in the prose translation of the Gospels, was not the principal aim of such interlinear glosses. Instead, the glosses should be taken individually, as comments on each Latin word.[8] Other examples can be found as well, such as the gloss to *beelzebub* at MtGl (Li) 10.25 “ðæt is diowla foruost” (‘that is, chief of devils’), which is a translation of the phrase *princeps daemonium* found elsewhere in the text itself of the Gospels (Matthew 12.24; Luke 11.15). Similar examples abound through the Latin manuscript glosses in Southumbria and reveal an effort on the part of the glossators to provide in English the type of detailed lexical commentary that had been available only in Latin. To date I have only found a few of them in Aldred’s Lindisfarne glosses, suggesting that the translation of Latin commentary in the Old English glosses was not a major technique of his glossing.

2.4 Grammatical glossing

The final two features to be discussed deal with some of the difficulties in translating from Latin into English while taking into account the morphological and inflectional differences between the two languages. For example, Latin and Old English have different methods of signifying and using the different cases of nouns and adjectives. I will give a few examples of these from Southumbrian manuscripts in order to illustrate the various types of approaches that are common in the tenth-century glosses. Perhaps the simplest of these are the glosses that merely provide the name of the case in Latin with no lexical information.

> *apum* : *genetiuus pluralis* (Rusche 1996: CleoI A154, Aldhelm)[9]
> *luce* : *ablatiuus* (Rusche forthcoming: MS Bodley 49, l. 213, Aldhelm’s *Carmen*)

8 See, for example, Jolly (2012: 162), who says, “[h]is Northumbrian Old English gloss is word-for-word, not a readable syntactic gloss, suggesting a focus on language itself”.

9 In the citations of glosses from editions not used in the *DOEC*, I cite the edition, an abbreviated reference to the text or manuscript from which they are taken, and the name of the author of the Latin text; fuller information will be found in the relevant editions. ‘Aldhelm’ refers to the prose *De virginitate* unless otherwise specified. The three Cleopatra glossaries are distinguished as CleoI, CleoII, and CleoIII.

In other places, however, the case is indicated by the inclusion of a definite article in Old English where there is no corresponding word in Latin, especially when the Latin form alone could be ambiguous. For example, the ablative case in Latin is often signified by a definite article in the dative case in Old English. The article can either be included with the appropriate noun or adjective, as in:

bombosa : þære rarigendan (Rusche 1996: CleoIII 1109, Aldhelm);

or the gloss can consist of solely the definite article:

impetu : þære (Rusche 1996: CleoII 1028, Matthew 8.32).

Finally, there are also glosses where the case is explained through a preposition, where no preposition was used in the Latin. Again these may occur where the preposition is simply added to the translation of the noun or adjective, as in:

lacrimosis singultibus : mid woplicum siccitungum (AldV 1 (Goossens) 4070–4071);

or more rarely, a preposition may be used alone with no corresponding lexical gloss, simply as an indication of case. In these instances the preposition is often written directly above the inflectional ending of the Latin word:

gurgustio : æt (Rusche 1994: 47, Aldhelm).

In glosses to verbs, there are frequently pronoun subjects that are unexpressed in Latin but given in the Old English. These are usually included along with a translation of the verb:

componat : heo gesette (AldV 1 (Goossens) 961).

Sometimes, however, only a pronoun is given to clarify the subject, especially if the subject of the verb is feminine or neuter:

curauit : heo (AldV 1 (Goossens) 4375)
rubescit : hit (Stork 1990: 94.1, Aldhelm, *Aenigmata*).

More common are glosses which take into account the different tense formations of Latin and English. For example, glosses to Latin verbs in the passive voice often include a form of *beon*:

tendor : ic eom tobrædd (AldÆ (Nap) 1.47)
asstipulatur : is geseþed (AldV 13.1 (Nap) 217).

Latin participles are sometimes glossed simply with the English participial ending to indicate their grammatical forms:

concrepans : ende (AldV 2.3.1 (Nap) 146).

One place where southern glosses fail to take into account differences between Latin and Old English is in distinguishing between imperfect, pluperfect and perfect cases; these are most often translated by a simple preterite in Old English. Far rarer are examples where the imperfect tense is marked in the gloss by a form of *beon* with a present participle:

animaduerteret : ða he ongitende wæs (Rusche 1996: CleoI A92, Aldhelm).

The examples given above require a brief comment before continuing. There is nothing particularly surprising about them, and most students of glosses have come across them often enough for singling them out here to seem superfluous. Yet an important point to notice about them is that their usage is in fact much more restricted than one might expect. If we look through the earliest glossaries such as Leiden and Épinal-Erfurt, it is quite common to find the Latin headwords in lemmatized form. There are also many entries in which the forms remain inflected, with glosses that mirror that inflection as close as possible, but it is quite rare to find grammatical information handled in the way described above with the use of prepositions, demonstratives or pronouns. In the Old English glosses in Épinal-Erfurt, for example, a definite article before the noun is extremely rare, as is a preposition clarifying the function of the Latin inflectional ending. There are no pronouns clarifying the subject of verbs. These features appear somewhat more often in the Corpus Glossary, but it is not until the tenth century that they become common, though still hardly ubiquitous. Even in the tenth-century manuscript glosses, there are still many instances in which lemmatized forms of the Latin words are given in the margins, accompanied by the appropriate gloss.[10] While the use of pronouns to provide the subject and person for verbs and of prepositions to explain the case of nouns becomes somewhat more common, Latin verb tenses are still most often translated simply by the Old English present or preter-

10 For example, in Brussels 1650, by the word *fatescens* we find "*fatesco* ic acwince" written in the margin (AldV 1 (Goossens) 3951) and by *molimina* we find "*Molimen* searecræft" (AldV 1 (Goossens) 3975).

ite tense. It is unclear whether the increase in grammatical information is a reaction to a growing ignorance of Latin grammar in the ninth and tenth centuries, but it would seem to be in line with the efforts to provide a vernacular explication of the Latin grammar and not just the lexicon; it is also in the tenth century that syntactical construe marks become quite popular in Anglo-Saxon manuscripts (see Robinson 1973; Korhammer 1980).

Since Aldred was writing a complete interlinear gloss, it should be no surprise that he adds much necessary grammatical information to his glosses, far more than is found in the southern glossaries and glosses. Aldred is quite conscientious in translating the grammatical information of the Bible by means of pronouns, prepositions, case endings, and demonstratives, examples of which can be found in almost every line. In fact, Aldred often provides multiple grammatical translations by supplying double or even triple glosses (Curme 1912: 181; Kotake 2006a; Pons-Sanz, this volume). For example, to gloss the Latin imperfect *sedebat* (MtGl (Li) 13.1), he gives first a lexical translation "gesætt", but then adds "ł wæs sittende" as a grammatical variant, which may have been a closer grammatical approximation of the imperfect than the simple Old English preterite (Kotake 2006a: 38–39).[11] As we saw above, distinguishing the imperfect from other past tenses is not a common feature of the later tenth- and eleventh-century southern glossators, although such distinctions are made throughout Aldred's glosses.

2.5 Morphemic glossing

The final feature to be discussed, the glossing of individual morphemes, has received much attention in the comments on Aldred's glosses. Therefore, I will review only briefly the Lindisfarne material before moving on to consider the Southumbrian glosses. Ross (1933b: 112–13 and 1982: 196) refers to this technique as the 'artificial' use of prefixes, but it is perhaps better considered under Gneuss's (1955: 31–33) category of 'loan-translation'. In these glosses each element of the Latin word, each morpheme, receives an individual gloss, often creating new words in Old English, presumably words that did not exist outside of the gloss itself. We have already seen one instance of this in the gloss to *parasceve*, where *prae-para-tio* is glossed by *fore-sceaw-ung*. The technique is most easily seen in

11 Kotake here considers the simplex forms as "morpheme-by-morpheme" glosses whereas the periphrastic examples are "more morphologically marked". I do not see this distinction, since the *BE*-verb with the participle is itself a gloss on the imperfect morphological suffix; it should be noted that the precise function of the periphrastic here is still uncertain (Mitchell 1985: 272–277).

the glossing of prefixes, and Ross (1933b) has supplied a list of the most common ones. I give a few examples here, excerpted and adapted from his fuller list:

Table 1. Common prefix glosses in Lindisfarne

Latin	OE	Examples
ad-	*to-*	*admirabantur* : togewundradun hia (MkGl (Li) 7.37)
anti-, ante-	*before-, fore-*	*anticristos* : before ł anticrist (LiProlMt (Skeat) 12); *antecedebat* : foregeeade (MtGl (Li) 2.9)
com-	*efne-*	*concurrerunt* : efnegeuurnun (MkGl (Li) 6.33); *consurget* : efnearisas (MtGl (Li) 24.7)
de-	*a-, dune-, from-, of-*	*descendat* : adunestigeð (MkGl (Li) 15.32); *describens* : of ł fromawrat (LiProlMt (Skeat) 10); *deprehensam* : ofnumen ł befoen (JnGl (Li) 8.3)
in-	*in-, on-*	*inquirunt* : insoecas ł befraignes (MtGl (Li) 6.32); *instabant* : onstodon (LkGl (Li) 23.23)
prae-	*befora-, fore-*	*praeibis* : beforefæres (LkGl (Li) 1.76); *praecurrens* : forearn (LkGl (Li) 19.4)
re-	*eft-*	*resurrectionem* : efterest (MtGl (Li) 22.23) *recurres* : eftgeiorn (LiEpis (Skeat) 22); *residens* : eftsæt (MkGl (Li) 9.35)
sub-	*dune-, under-*	*summiserunt* : dunasendon (LkGl (Li) 5.19); *subductis* : underlæded woeron (LkGl (Li) 5.11)

Many of these words are what Ross would call ‘abnormal’, that is, they only appear in ‘artificial’ settings such as glosses to Latin texts. Artificial they may be, but this term should not be seen as a condemnation; as we have seen, glosses function as explications of the Latin more than simply as translations, and glossing by morpheme clarifies the structure of the Latin word and makes plain its etymological origins, thus revealing the true meaning of the word.

When one looks through the range of glosses produced in Southumbria for similar examples of morphemic glossing, several interesting features become clear. First, as with the grammatical glosses discussed above, this type of gloss is rarely found in the early glossaries Épinal-Erfurt, Leiden, Corpus and the like. Even in a tenth-century glossary like the Cleopatra Glossary most glosses do not show this type of attention to the morphemic structure of the Latin. The exception is found in the Cleopatra glosses on Aldhelm. The following chart, in which all but one of the examples come from the Aldhelm glosses in the First and Third Cleopatra Glossaries, illustrates some of the common translations of prefixes:

Table 2. Prefix glosses in the Cleopatra Glossaries

Latin	OE	Examples
ad-	*to-*	*attonitis* : tohircniendum (CleoI A64); *adgrederetur* : he togeeode (CleoI A122)
ante-	*fore-*	*antecessor* : foreiernend (CleoI A18)
com-	*efen-*, *somod-*	*commanipularibus* : efenheapum (CleoI C536); *concordia* : somodðyrlice (Symphosius) (CleoI C666); *concretione* : somodwell-unge (CleoI C750); *concertatio* : somodgeflit (CleoI C829); *cooperante* : somodwyrcendum (CleoI C884)
de-	*be-*, *from-*	*detracta* : framatoge (CleoI D276)
in-	*in-*, *on-*	*ingerebat* : ongebrohte (CleoI I38)
prae-	*fore-*	*praestare* : forestandan (CleoI P10); *prescius* : forewis (CleoI P25)
re-	*eft-*	*repetante* : eftsiðgendum (CleoIII 217); *recapitulatio* : eftspellung (CleoIII 222)
sub-	*under-*	none in Cleopatra

This list is similar in some ways to that for the Lindisfarne glosses, but it should be emphasized that the number of examples is much lower in Cleopatra. Furthermore, as already noted, they are restricted almost exclusively to the glosses taken from the works of Aldhelm, which may suggest that these glosses are more recent than others in Cleopatra. In fact, a few of the glosses seem to be adaptations of earlier glosses found in the Corpus Glossary. For example, the two glosses given above, "*attonitis* : tohircniendum" and "*adgrederetur* : he togeeode" may be updated versions based on the Corpus entries: A228 "*adtonitus* : hlysnende" and A217 "*adgrediuntur* : geeodun". If so, it is instructive that the older, Corpus versions do not yet have the prefix *to-* added.

Although the amount of morphemic glossing is much scantier in Cleopatra than in Lindisfarne, it is instructive to observe where they agree and where they disagree in their choices of Old English equivalents to Latin prefixes. Aldred's glosses agree with those in Cleopatra by translating *to-* for *ad-* and *in-*/*on-* for *in-*, but neither *dune-* nor *of-* occurs as a translation of *de-* in Cleopatra, which prefers *be-* and *from-*. Cleopatra has no examples of an Old English prefix used to translate *sub-*. In Lindisfarne, *efen-* is the standard gloss for *com-*, but in Cleopatra it only appears in the glosses to *commanipulares*, twice glossed "efenheap" and once "efenwerod". It may be that the prefix *efen-* had become standardized in the glosses to this one word, or these glosses were copied from some earlier use, but much more common as a translation of *com-* in Cleopatra is *somod-*, which occurs five times and with different words each time; this prefix is never used in Lindisfarne. Also rare in Cleopatra is the use of *eft-* for *re-*, occurring only in the two examples given above. It is found in numerous places throughout Lindisfarne, however (see Cook 1894: 47–50).

If we extend our search through other glosses found in manuscripts of the later tenth and eleventh centuries, we find a great increase from Cleopatra in the use of morphemic glossing, generally along the same lines seen in Lindisfarne. I present here a very brief list of examples from glosses on school texts like those by Prudentius, Aldhelm, Sedulius, as well as works by Isidore and Bede:

Table 3. Prefix glosses in Southumbrian manuscripts

Latin	OE	Examples
ad-	*to-*	*aduentum* : tocyme (IsGl 2); *adherescat* : he togeþeode (AldV 13.1 (Nap) 2355)
ante-	*fore-*	*antecessor* : forgencga, forstæp (AldV 13.1 (Nap) 619); *anticipatur* : beo forehradod (AldV 13.1 (Nap) 1232)
com-	*efen-, samod-, tosomne-*	*consortibus* : efenhlyttum (AldV 1 (Goossens) 4158); *coheres* : samodgesiþ (PrudGl 1 (Meritt) 910); *confluentibus* : *.i. conuenientibus* samodcumendum (AldV 13.1 (Nap) 2095); *coeunte* : tosomnegeganre (PrudGl 9 (Nap) 4); *confluebant* : tosomnebecomon (OccGl 45.1.2 (Meritt) 86)
de-	*a-, be-, froma-*	*descripta* : ascrifenum (OccGl 45.1.2 (Meritt) 255); *dissimulare* : bemiþan, bedyrnan (AldV 13.1 (Nap) 983); *degenerent* : fromacnyslien (SedGl 3 (Meritt) 105); *defluxerant* : toflowan (AldV 13.1 (Nap) 2857)
in-	*in-, on-*	*irrumpit* : inbræc (PrudGl 1 (Meritt) 330); *inferat* : ongelæde (PrudGl 1 (Meritt) 32)
prae-	*fore-*	*precedo* : ic forestæppe (PrudGl 1 (Meritt) 508)
re-	*eft-*	*fontis redundantia* : eftflowende wætere (AldV 1 (Goossens) 589)
sub-	*under-*	*subire* : underhni(gan) (AldV 1 (Goossens) 2943); *subductus* : underðeod (PrudGl 6 (Nap-Ker) 53)

This list could be greatly extended, with numerous other prefixes and translations added. In other words, this type of morphemic glossing or loan translation is a common feature of late tenth-century glossing, both in Southumbria and in Lindisfarne.

The question then becomes one of influence. Where did the southern glossators learn to gloss morpheme by morpheme in the relatively short time between Cleopatra in the first half of the century and these other glosses in the second half? Did the growing trend towards this type of glossing in the south influence Aldred? I think the most likely answer to this question can be found in the psalter glosses. These glosses show a very clear use of both the same type of grammatical glosses discussed above and of morphemic glossing that is seen in both the Lindisfarne glosses and in the Southumbrian glosses, but the psalter glosses are much older in their use of such techniques. The Vespasian, or A-type, psalter glosses, added into the Vespasian manuscript in the ninth century, show a highly developed use of grammatical and morphemic glossing (see Mertens-Fonck 1960: 13; Wiesenekker 1991: 100–104), and the choices made in these psalters are much closer to what we find in Lindisfarne than to the glosses in the school texts. Just a few examples from the Vespasian Psalter should make this clear. For instance, Vespasian agrees with Lindisfarne in using *eft-* to gloss *re-*, *efen-* to gloss *con-*, both rare in the other glosses, and even *dune-* and *ofdune-* to gloss *de-*, not found at all in the southern glossaries or manuscript glosses. These same glosses appear in most of the later psalter glosses as well. Aldred also frequently alters the order of the Old English glosses to give a more natural Old English word order than a strict word-for-word gloss of the Latin would give, a feature seen in some psalters as well (Ogura 2006; Kotake 2008a).

3 Conclusion

When we look for influence on and sources for Aldred's glosses to Lindisfarne, we should look at the psalter glossing traditions. It may seem that I have come to this conclusion the long way around, since I suggested at the start that interlinear psalter glosses were the obvious comparison to make with Lindisfarne, but a sense of obviousness without examination is what led Boyd to the supposition that Aldred was working in the context of the Southumbrian monastic revival. We should be somewhat hesitant, however, to ascribe too much influence from the intellectual efforts of the Benedictine Reform on Aldred's training, at least in terms of his style of glossing. If we consider again the five features of Southumbrian glossing I listed above, Aldred is lacking in the first three. He apparently had no access to or was not interested in using the older Canterbury materials which seem to have been available in multiple southern centres. He also shows no signs of having been trained in a centre that approached its understanding of Latin through Isidore's etymological explanations, nor do the glosses betray much evidence of an earlier Latin gloss. For the fourth and fifth features, Aldred goes far beyond what is found in southern glosses: not only does he use specific grammatical indicators like pronouns and demonstratives to gloss the inflectional endings of Latin nouns and verbs, but he is far more conscientious in adding forms to clarify, for example, the Latin passive or imperfect. In the final feature, both Aldred and the later southern glossators pay attention to individual morphemes in their glosses, shown here primarily in their glosses on prefixes, but the individual translations often differ between the two.

The growing use of interlinear psalter glosses in the tenth century seems to have had a twofold influence, that is, on both the glosses found in Southumbrian school text manuscripts and on Aldred's gloss to the Lindisfarne Gospels. This may well be the chief influence that the Benedictine Reform had on Aldred's glossing, supplied through a copy of a Southumbrian glossed psalter, one of the most important books of the reformers (see, for example, Gretsch 1999).[12] Although we cannot say for certain where Aldred came across a copy of a glossed psalter, the importation of such a text to the community of St. Cuthbert, or even some other northern centre where Aldred may have been trained, can be seen along the lines of the importation of the Durham Ritual itself, and may have been all the inspiration Aldred needed to supply glosses to both the Gospels and the Ritual. It may be that further research into the specific conventions of psalter glossing that Aldred uses could allow us to be more specific in tying his work to one of the psalter types and could reveal to us more information about the spread of manuscripts from Southumbria into the north.[13]

12 There may, of course, have been copies of psalters in the north that pre-date the Reform and that survived the Viking invasions, but with no extant copies to examine, it is impossible to know what type of glossing, if any, these may have had. Suffice it to say, Aldred's glosses show similarities with those that survive from Southumbria.

13 I would very much like to thank Sara Pons-Sanz and Julia Fernández Cuesta for hosting the workshop on the Lindisfarne Gospel glosses and the attendees for their advice and comments on ways to improve this paper.

Paul Cavill

Maxims in Aldred's Marginalia to the Lindisfarne Gospels

Abstract: Much of the commentary on Aldred's glosses to the Lindisfarne Gospels quite rightly focuses on his language and on the way he translates the Latin text. His gloss is mostly literal and tied to the Latin words and syntax on the page before him. But he adds comments in the margins, and these are the focus of the discussion here.

This paper draws attention particularly to the cluster of additional material occurring in the context of the Beatitudes at the beginning of the Sermon on the Mount in Matthew 5, and the longer annotation in Matthew 10. The marginalia are in the form of maxims and are deliberately shaped for literary and rhetorical effect. It is suggested that Aldred was concerned with monastic reform, and that he appreciated wisdom literature. So he took the opportunity offered by the gospel text to elaborate particularly relevant passages for his Church and community in the authoritative style of maxims in order to enforce the teaching. This is a literary intervention in an essentially practical work.

1 Introduction

The glosses and marginalia in the justly famous Lindisfarne Gospels (London, British Library, MS Cotton Nero D.iv) are, so far as the hand is concerned, the product of one man.[1] He identifies himself in the colophon (f. 259r) as *Aldred p(re)sb(yte)r indignus ⁊ misserrim(us)* 'Aldred, unworthy and most miserable priest', a rhetorical flourish of humility which he goes some way to adjusting in

1 This is at least the generally accepted view at the present time, and reflects the view of Ker (1957: 216), who identified the glossator of both the Durham Collectar and Lindisfarne as Aldred, though in the latter "the writing varies much in appearance, except in the first gospel". Ross et al. (1960) confirmed this view. However, there have been other perspectives: Waring (Stevenson and Waring 1854–1865: IV, xlvi) states, "Two scribes have been employed on our Gospels; the first portion was written by some person deputed by Aldred, and probably under his dictation; the second hand in red ink, which we know to be Aldred's autograph, is distinguished [...] by certain orthographical peculiarities"; and Skeat (1878: ix–x) concludes that Aldred's remark in the colophon relating to the glossing of John "for hine seolfne" 'for himself' suggests that "the glosses to this gospel are in his own handwriting, whilst those to the other gospels (in a different hand) were merely made under his superintendence". This view is no longer widely accepted.

the rest of the colophon, where he gives more of his biography and, according to Nees, at least, aligns himself with, and identifies himself as a second John, Evangelist and writer of the fourth Gospel (Nees 2003). Apart from information in the colophon and the glossing in the Lindisfarne manuscript, and a further colophon and glossing in Aldred's hand in the Durham Collectar (Durham Cathedral Library, MS A.iv.19) and Latin glossing in a manuscript of Bede's commentary on the Proverbs of Solomon (Oxford, Bodleian Library, MS Bodley 819), we know relatively little about Aldred. The consensus is that he joined the Cuthbertine community at Chester-le-Street sometime after 950 and became prior in 970, and that between the two dates he completed the work on the Gospels.

Aldred's glosses tell us a good deal about his Latin learning and the range of vernacular linguistic material and interpretative strategies he had at his command. In addition to the glosses, however, there are seventy-one distinct marginal annotations in the Lindisfarne manuscript according to Boyd's study (1975a). Boyd concerns himself primarily with exploring the theology and sources of Aldred's commentary, and this augments our knowledge of the kind of works Aldred knew. The glosses are functional: once Aldred had set himself (or had been commissioned) to the task of a continuous literal gloss on the Gospels, he could not properly miss passages out. Sometimes he shows remarkable lexical range in his glossing, sometimes he makes mistakes (Ross 1932a); but the glossing is thorough. By contrast, the marginalia are optional and occasional, and reveal Aldred's reading, his habits of interpretation, and his understanding of the needs of his community. The marginalia, in other words, are different from the glosses in that they might give us a novel perspective on the man and his concerns.

They are not all uniform however. The marginalia before and after the Beatitudes are clearly informative. Matthew 1.18 reads, "abiathar ðe aldormon wæs in ðæm tid in hierusalem. forebiscob [...]" 'Abiathar the leader (?) was at that time High Priest in Jerusalem' (Boyd 1975a: 9 no. 5; Boyd's translation); and Matthew 6.24, "mamon. þ(æ)t is gidsunges hlaferd ðe diowl [...]" 'Mammon's; that is, the lord of avarice, the devil' (Boyd 1975a: 15 no. 11; Boyd's translation). There is essential information in these additions, which contrasts with the slight adjustments that characterize the marginalia on the Beatitudes (Boyd 1975a: 10–14 nos. 6–10), which will be the major focus of discussion below. For various reasons, I do not believe Aldred's main concern in the marginalia relating to the Beatitudes is with theology, not least because the additions here have less theological content than those elsewhere, and are hortatory rather than informative: Ker (1957: 215) remarks that "[t]he glossator sometimes places a less literal rendering of the text in the margin". They, like the additions on simony and the role of the bishop (Boyd 1975a: 23–24 nos. 16–17), relate more intimately to the concerns of Aldred himself and his vision of the community.

This paper will argue that Aldred's additions to the manuscript show him to have two discernible concerns: first, with wisdom and second, with applying that wisdom to his community by relevant and pointed teaching. It will show that these two preoccupations come together in the maxims he uses in the marginalia. The first part of the paper explores Aldred's context and establishes his interest in wisdom and use of maxims; the second part discusses the maxims in the marginalia themselves and shows how they indicate Aldred's preoccupations.

2 Aldred and the community at Chester-le-Street

The information we have about Aldred, though meagre, is remarkably interesting. According to the Lindisfarne Gospels colophon, he paid eight ores of silver for his induction to the priesthood and to the community and this apparently links to his denunciation of simony in one of the marginalia in the Gospels (Matthew 10.8; Boyd 1975a: 24–31 no. 18; Brown 2003: 98–99; and see further below).[2] Another marginal note on the same page, f. 45r, comments on a bishop's responsibility not to delay consecration of a newly arrived priest. It is suggested that the plain statement in the colophon relates to Aldred's own experience, and in the addition to the Gospel text he was outlining the precepts that he felt were not followed in his case (Boyd 1975a: 26–28). If this is true, it indicates that the Church in Northumbria around the middle of the tenth century was in some particulars not in a good state.[3]

2 The long-running question as to whether the colophon is trustworthy relates principally to the details given by Aldred concerning the original makers of the book, not especially to Aldred's claims about himself. Gameson sees the rationale given by Aldred for the book's creation as "purely spiritual and altruistic" (2001b: 47), intended to "elevate a whole foundation spiritually" (2001b: 57); and while these comments relate to the original creation of the volume by Eadfrith, Aethilwald and Billfrith, they might also reflect the intentions of Aldred himself.

3 A recent article (Newton et al. 2013) proposes a new interpretation of the colophon and, in particular, OE *ora*. It is suggested that *ora* should be rendered as 'border', and might refer to the kind of decorative border that appears around the text in some pages of the MacRegol Gospels. A significant difficulty with this interpretation (apart from the fact that these borders are no longer present in the Lindisfarne manuscript, and cannot be demonstrated ever to have been present) is that *ora* does not securely mean 'border'. The word occurs predominantly in southern place-names where it means 'bank'; elsewhere, as Gelling and Cole (2000: 203) remark, "[t]here appear to be two literary occurrences [...]. One of these is poetic: a cuckoo is heard calling from a grove *on hlithes oran*. This can fairly be translated 'on the edge of the slope', though a more specific sense for **hlith** [Gelling and Cole's emphasis] can be deduced from place-names. The second is a translation of a Latin phrase, *in oram vestimenti eius*, by *on oran his hrægles*: this may indicate

The community of St. Cuthbert at Chester-le-Street to which Aldred made such notable contributions had certainly declined from its original monastic purity at Lindisfarne before the Viking attacks and settlements of the ninth and early tenth centuries. It was predominantly clerical early in the second half of the tenth century. The main evidence for any continuing monastic observance during the years at Chester-le-Street derives from Symeon of Durham (Rollason 2000: 102–105), who makes reference to those,

> *qui inter eos ab etate infantili in habitu clericali fuerant nutriti atque eruditi, quocunque sancti patris corpus ferebatur secuti sunt, moremque sibi a monachis doctoribus traditum in officiis – dumtaxat diurne uel nocturne laudis – semper seruarunt. Vnde tota nepotum suorum successio magis secundum instituta monachorum quam clericorum consuetudinem canendi horas [...]*
>
> 'who had been brought up and educated among the monks from childhood, albeit in the habit of clerks, followed the body of the holy father wherever it was carried, and they always preserved the custom – which had been handed down to them by their teachers the monks – of singing the day and night offices. As a result all their descendants who succeeded them [...] followed their fathers in the custom of singing the hours according to the regimen of the monks rather than that of the clerks'.

There is some discussion about these claims: Rollason (1992: 185–186) refers to the idea that the community and its bishops were anything other than lay clerks, except for Bishop Eadred, as "implausible and surely propagandist". And in the nature of the case it is difficult (for modern scholars, at least – Symeon might have had reliable sources) to generalize accurately about the circumstances and observance of the community for the period 883–995 (Bonner 1989). Karen Jolly suggests that some of Aldred's additions to the Durham Collectar, Durham Cathedral Library, MS A.iv.19, indicate that "a small group of monks may have conducted services exclusive to the body of St. Cuthbert, which would account for the collects for the saint that Aldred copied into Quire XI" (2012: 208). But these additions might be in hopes of revitalizing monastic life rather than of continuing it; as Jolly also notes, "the vast majority of the rest of the office materials could have been used by both secular and monastic clergy, separately or together" (2012: 208). Alicia Corrêa (1992: 76–80) by contrast takes the view that the manuscript was probably "a commonplace book" (1992: 76), and that "it may well be that the original portion ... was never used, directly or indirectly, in the office liturgy at Chester-le-Street" (1992: 80).

---

that OE *ora* meant something like 'hem', but the choice of word may be an echoing of the Latin rather than common usage". See further Roberts's response in this volume.

Michelle Brown (2003: 101), working from the Caroline features of Aldred's handwriting, characteristic of the monastic reform movement of the second half of the tenth century, suggests,

> It may be that Aldred was 'planted' specifically in his native region as part of an attempt to address such issues of reform in one of the most powerful houses in the north, in which case he may even have been 'sponsored' by one of the great tenth-century reformers, such as Dunstan [...], Aethelwold [...] or Oswald, or [...] encouraged by contact with one of the West Saxon royal visitations of the north from Athelstan's time onwards.

Aldred's visit to Wessex in 970 with Bishop Ælfsige, recorded in the former's colophon in the Durham Collectar, reinforces the notion that he had contacts with the reform movement, though it might not have been to the reforming council that produced the *Regularis concordia* that he was going (Bonner 1989: 394–395; Jolly 2012: 10–11); and his concerns to educate and promote literacy, to expand the liturgical resources available, and to correct abuses, evident in the glosses and additions to manuscripts belonging to Cuthbert's community at Chester-le-Street, reflect many of the preoccupations of the Benedictine Reform movement.[4] Much more cannot be said with certainty, but that there was some need for reform in the Church and Cuthbert's community in northern Northumbria, and that Aldred had both connections with the reform movement and a concern for reform himself, is evident.

3 Aldred and wisdom

One of the less obvious things about Aldred that might be noted is his concern with wisdom. In the Lindisfarne Gospels colophon on f. 259r, following his account of glossing the Gospels, Matthew "for God and St. Cuthbert", Mark "for the bishop", Luke "for the community", and John "for himself", he writes:

> Þ(æt)te he hæbbe ondfong ðerh godes miltsæ on heofnv(m). séel ⁊ sibb on eorðo forðgeong ⁊ giðyngo visdóm ⁊ snyttro ðerh s(an)c(t)i cvðberhtes earnvnga

> '[...] so that he might have through the grace of God acceptance in heaven; happiness and peace on earth, success and promotion, knowledge and wisdom through the merits of St. Cuthbert'.[5]

4 See Rusche (this volume).

5 Translations of Old English are my own except where otherwise stated.

There is a distinct echo in the third doublet here ("visdóm ⁊ snyttro") of Solomon's prayer on his accession to the throne of Israel after the death of David. Solomon prays to God in his dream, *Da mihi sapientiam et intelligentiam* 'Give me wisdom and knowledge' (II Paralipomenon 1.10),[6] and in response God twice promises to give him *sapientiam et scientiam* 'wisdom and knowledge' (II Paralipomenon 1.11, 12), the same things that Aldred prays for. Aldred consistently translates L *scientia* with OE *wisdom* (LkGl (Li) 1.77, 11.52), and *sapientia* with OE *snyt(t)ro* (MtGl (Li) 12.42, 13.54; MkGl (Li) 6.2; LkGl (Li) 2.40, 2.47, 2.52, 6.11, 7.35, 11.31, 11.49, 21.15),[7] and thus he effectively seeks *scientia et sapientia* on earth through the merits of St. Cuthbert.[8] The association with Solomon is somewhat obscured by the translation favoured by Gameson (2001b: 45 n. 2), Nees (2003: 341), Brown (2003: 104) and Newton et al. (2013) of 'wisdom and sagacity' for this doublet.

In addition to this, it is notable that while Aldred glosses in English two of the books that might have been used in the liturgical life of the community, namely the Gospels and the Collectar, when he might have had unfettered choice he annotated in Latin Bede's commentary on the Proverbs of Solomon, which is a collection of wisdom sayings attributed to the Old Testament exemplar of wisdom. Solomon also appears in a text on the "Ecclesiastical Grades" in the encyclopedic material copied by Aldred into the folios at the end of the Durham Collectar (at the top of f. 87r; Jolly 2012: 347). Jolly observes that the associations of these rather curious texts are with the "glossaries, colloquies, and pedagogical dialogues derived from older encyclopedic works by Isidore of Seville, Raban Maur, Amalarius of Metz, Alcuin, and Bede [...] or in the popular insular versions of the Dialogue of Solomon and Saturn" (2012: 172). In particular, closest of all the analogues to the text *De octo pondera de quibus factus est Adam* 'The eight pounds from which Adam was created' on ff. 86r–87v of the Collectar is that in the later Old English *Prose Solomon and Saturn*, as noted in Brown (1969: 51) and Jolly (2012: 172 n. 80, 342). Here we have a wisdom text associated with Solomon. Aldred's work shows a remarkable interest in the Old Testament model of the wise man, Solomon, and in wisdom literature more generally.

6 Translations from the Vulgate are from the *Douay-Rheims Bible*.

7 The title abbreviation and editions of the Old English texts mentioned in this paper are those employed by the *Dictionary of Old English Web Corpus* (hereafter *DOEC*) except where otherwise stated.

8 Aldred's consistency of translation in this respect extends to his glosses in the Durham Collectar, where *snyttro* (and variants) glosses *sapientia* (and variants) ten times, and *wisdom* glosses *scientia* three times: see Ross and Stanley's glossary (Brown 1969: 53–92, at 83 and 89 respectively). Seebold (1974: 294–305) shows that *snyttro* glossing *sapientia* is distinctively Anglian: in southern dialects the term is translated by *wisdom*.

4 Aldred and maxims

It has not before been noticed that some of Aldred's marginalia are expressed in the traditional Anglo-Saxon form of wisdom sayings, maxims. These include the annotations to the Beatitudes of Matthew chapter 5 (numbered 6–10 by Boyd 1975a), and also the passage on simony in Matthew 10.8 (numbered 17 by Boyd 1975a). Before I analyze the maxims in the margins of the Gospels, I will briefly discuss the form and style of maxims.

4.1 Maxims: form and style

Scholars have variously commented on the characteristics of maxims. Early studies attempted to categorize maxims into types (Chadwick and Chadwick 1932–1940: I, 377–403), but this was widely found to fail on the grounds of inconsistency (Cavill 1999: 42–43). A series of articles considered the characteristic "gnomic" verbs used in maxims, *sceal* and *bið*: Greenfield and Evert (1975) in their article on the Old English poem *Maxims II* noted that no single sense could consistently be applied to either of the verbs even in that one poem; Nelson (1981) took the question further, but came to a similar conclusion. Recent book-length studies which range more widely over the wisdom mode, and editions of wisdom texts, have included Shippey (1976), *Poems of Wisdom and Learning in Old English*; Cross and Hill (1982), *The Prose* Solomon and Saturn *and* Adrian and Ritheus; Howe (1985), *The Old English Catalogue Poems*; Hansen (1988), *The Solomon Complex*; Larrington (1993), *A Store of Common Sense*; Cavill (1999), *Maxims in Old English Poetry*; and Anlezark (2009), *The Old English Dialogues of Solomon and Saturn*, among others. All of these to some extent attempt to characterize the forms and properties of maxims and wisdom literature and reinstate them as important in enabling us to have a better understanding of medieval worldviews.

Hansen's summary of wisdom in *Beowulf* (1988: 57) is helpful in isolating characteristic features of maxims (or "gnomes", as she refers to them):

> It has long been thought that many of the two dozen or so gnomic sayings in *Beowulf* come from a traditional Old English gnome-hoard with numerous analogues in Old English, Old Norse, Old Welsh, and Old Irish, and all of the gnomic passages are readily identifiable by those formal and thematic characteristics which, in accord with what we know from other extant works, conventionally signal the gnomic mode. Formally the sayings in *Beowulf* depend on a conventional gnomic vocabulary and syntax: the specialized use of the verb forms *sceal*, *bið* and *mæg*, organizing experience into what is and what ought to be; [...] and the *se þe* or *se þæm* construction, used to invoke the unspecified and representative indi-

> vidual. [...] Underlying the gnomic world view in *Beowulf* is the centrality of difference – as in grammar, the existence of binary pairs – to the construction of a moral universe [...].

Even though Hansen is referring to *Beowulf*, it will be immediately apparent that this description applies to those of Aldred's marginalia I have isolated. Those on the Beatitudes (Boyd's 6–10) consistently use the *bið* verb form and often the *se þe* construction in the plural (*biðon* and *ða* (*ðe*)): "eadge biðon ða ðaerfe(ndo), eadge biðon ða ðe hyncgrað ⁊ ðyrstas soðfæstnisse" 'blessed are the poor, blessed are those who hunger and thirst after righteousness', and so on. These also consistently use the adjective headword *eadig* 'blessed', which has twelve verse parallels in maxims from the Old English *Metrical Psalms*, four from other, secular, verse, and innumerable parallels in glossed and translated psalters (Cavill 1999: 91–94). These expressions also employ the binaries of "here and now *versus* there and then" and "this without that". The maxim at Matthew 10.8 (Boyd 1975a: 24–31 no. 17) uses the verb *sceal*, and in outlining the bishop's duty, conforms to the "trade rules" type of maxim: once again, this has numerous parallels in the works of Ælfric, Old English laws and the tract *Gerefa*, as well as Old English verse (Cavill 1999: 14–17).

4.2 Maxims in clusters

There is a tendency for maxims to accrete in collections, either because of some thematic or verbal linking, or because they are perceived as fundamentally similar to each other, in style or (presumably educative) purpose. A string of poems in the Exeter Book of Old English poetry follows related themes referred to in the titles, like the *Gifts* and *Fortunes of Men*, or the poem *Maxims I* in three parts which cover a vast range of human experiences and observation, not all very obviously related to each other (Krapp and Dobbie 1936; Muir 1994). The *Durham Proverbs* (Arngart 1981) and the Old English *Dicts of Cato* (Cox 1972) similarly unite disparate proverbial ideas under the form and style of maxims (among other features).

One striking example of an *ad hoc* collection of wisdom material, containing generalizations in the form of maxims from both Latin and Old English, is in the hand of Archbishop Wulfstan, a near-contemporary of Aldred, in Copenhagen, Kongelige Bibliotek, MS Gl. Kgl. Sam. 1595, f. 66v (Cross and Tunberg 1993; Cavill 2012). On a space following a copy of one of Wulfstan's homilies, he wrote a series of sentences: "Ælc man behofað gastlices fosters" 'Everyone needs spiritual sustenance' is linked through *signes de renvoi* to the thematically related but linguistically distinct verse from Matthew 4.4, *Non in sola pane. uiuit homo. sed in omni uerbo quod procedit de ore dei* 'Not in bread alone doth man live, but in every word that proceedeth from the mouth of God';[9] other expressions of similar type were also written in, apparently at different times (Ker 1971: 320). In a rather similar fashion, Aldred's wisdom literature additions (the Adam dialogue, lists and encyclopedic material mentioned above) to the Durham Collectar fill the vacant folios at the end of that manuscript. In a very similar fashion to Wulfstan's additions to the Copenhagen manuscript, Aldred's marginalia relating to the Beatitudes in the Lindisfarne Gospels are clearly linked to the biblical text, but they also extrapolate from it, and are all collected in the right-hand margin of the single folio, 34r. They are clearly clustered in this location.

4.3 Maxims: rhetorical effect

Overall, on the basis of these distinguishable formulaic, stylistc and even palaeographical or codicological features, there is clear and sufficient reason to believe that Aldred was consciously invoking the maxim form and presenting his maxims in a way that would be recognizable as characteristic of wisdom literature. The Sermon on the Mount itself is a wisdom discourse and the Beatitudes here have the same basic linguistic features in Greek and Latin as they do in Old English. But maxims in Old English are used for particular effects and for specific purposes in both secular and religious texts. An ambiguous feature is that they are habitually expressed in present-tense verbs, which makes it difficult to know whether they have present or future sense; and of course part of the purpose in people using maxims is often to blur that temporal distinction. Aldred exploits this feature in his augmented version of the Beatitudes. Maxims are expressed in general terms about specific types of person or creature, so they have the appearance of observable fact even if, in some cases, it is doubtful the phenomenon could have been observed. For example, dragons inhabiting burial mounds were well-known in Germanic stories, noted in place-names[10] and categorized in a maxim in Max II 26b–27a, "draca sceal on hlæwe / frod frætwum wlonc" 'a dragon belongs in a mound, old and proud of its treasures'; but dragons may not have been empirically observed exhibiting this behaviour.

For the most part, maxims invoke the predictable or desirable behaviour of people, and the properties of classes of animals or things. They have the authority of the truism, the obvious, or an implied consensus view of life. In Old English

9 The syntax, spelling and punctuation is that of the manuscript; the Vulgate has *non in pane solo vivet homo sed in omni verbo quod procedit de ore Dei.*

10 Smith (1956: I, s.v. *draca*) records Drakelow ('dragon's mound', *draca + hlaw*) names in Bedfordshire, Derbyshire and Worcestershire, among other dragon place-names.

poetry, in particular, they articulate a distinctive worldview, one that insists, for example, that shame is a fate worse than death, or that it is better to avenge than to mourn. So when in *Beowulf* Wiglaf says "Deað bið sella / eorla gehwylcum þonne edwitlif" 'death is better for every warrior than a life of shame' (Beo 2890b–2891a), it would be clear to those listening (in the imagined world of the text) that this was not his own idea, a merely personal ideal, but one of the bases on which his society functioned. It is what everybody believed, even if in a moment of crisis some might fail to react in the appropriate way. The truth of the maxim is tested but not negated by those who run away in *Beowulf*: they cease to be *eorlas* 'warriors' in the sense articulated in the formula. There is an implied "We all know that ..." about maxims: they are what Michael Polanyi calls "fiduciary acts" (1958: 28). So maxims frame an ideal or an aspiration or a conception which is real for the person articulating the expression and believed to be real by the audience addressed in the immediate context.

Maxims have this effect because of their formulaic generality of expression. As with the maxims collected by Wulfstan mentioned above, these kinds of wisdom expressions can be used in homilies and for exhortation, but in their formal structure and generalization of expression they are not directly didactic or "homiletic" in the negative sense that critics often use. They engage the imagination and invite listeners and readers to envision an ordered and meaningful universe where phenomena and roles are predictable and properly hierarchical; and by describing and promoting – even promising – this kind of ideal, they invite an audience to imagine an alternative to the present. They create a sense of community by implicitly articulating what everyone believes. And they persuade by using traditional and proverbial forms of expression without the intrusion of directly personal assertion.[11] Maxims, then, have a rhetoric which is at once imaginative, memorable and powerful, whether in verse or prose.

5 The Beatitudes and the Sermon on the Mount

Aldred would, of course, have recognized the Latin Beatitudes themselves as wisdom literature. The structure that the Beatitudes take is well-evidenced not only in Old Germanic and Old Celtic languages, as well as in Hebrew literature,

11 Wulfstan exploits the duality of personal and impersonal address consistently: he uses all kinds of formulas to reinforce his personal voice, e.g. "soð is þæt ic secge" 'it is true what I say', followed almost immediately by the impersonal maxim "Se gefærð gesællice þe godcundre lare. oftost gehyreð ⁊ geornlicost gymeð" 'He travels well who most often and most earnestly hears and attends to religious teaching' (see further Cavill 2012).

particularly the Psalms, as has already been noted, but also in biblical Greek and Latin tradition. The commentary in Barton and Muddiman (2001: 853) observes:

> The form, 'blessed' (*makarios*) + subject + 'that' (*hoti*) clause, is attested elsewhere (cf. Gen 30:13; Tob 13:16), as are the eschatological orientation (cf. Dan 12:12; *1 Enoch* 58:2–3), the grouping together of several beatitudes (cf. [...] *2 Enoch* 52:1–14), and the third person plural address (cf. *Pss Sol.* [Psalms of Solomon] 17:44; Tob 13:14 [Tobit 13.18 Vulgate]) [italics of titles from the Apocrypha those of Barton and Muddiman].

As a thoughtful biblical scholar, Aldred was sensitive to the purpose and context of the original Beatitudes. The Sermon on the Mount (Matthew 5–7) is recognized by scholars as a wisdom discourse, a unit with themes running through its various sections (Barton and Muddiman 2001: 852). The Matthean discourse of the Sermon on the Mount collects together stories, exempla and direct instruction in pithy form, as well as the Beatitudes. There is a parallel block of teaching in Luke 6.17–6.49, sometimes known as the Sermon on the Plain. The Beatitudes of Matthew 5 are expressed in the generalized form of maxims, "blessed are the poor, the merciful" and others. The parallel Lucan expressions are addressed directly and specifically to the audience, "blessed are [you] poor for yours is the kingdom of God", rather than characterizing types of people generally and impersonally as is diagnostic for maxims. Though there is a good deal of overlap between the Beatitudes of Matthew 5 and those of Luke 6, there are fewer in Luke, and indeed the teaching is structured around a stark contrast with the woes that follow, "woe to you who are rich" and others, in Luke 6.24–6.26.

Although Old English poetry takes up the contrast of blessing and woe as exhibited in Luke's Gospel in several paired maxims (*wa–wel* in Beo 183b–189 and Pr 13b–20; *eadig–earm* in Max I 37; see Cavill 1999: 82–105), the Lucan Beatitudes are not maxims. A distinction is implicitly recognized by Aldred in his additions to the Lindisfarne manuscript because he expands the Matthean maxims with marginal commentary while leaving the Lucan expressions without. Some sort of distinction is made in Eadfrith's Latin text, too: while both sets of Beatitudes are picked out with alternating green and yellow infilling of the bowl of the initial *b*, the initials of the Beatitudes in Matthew (ff. 34r and 34v) are significantly larger than those of Luke (f. 154r); and all the initials *b* in Matthew are picked out with dots outlining the letter, while only the two green-bowled *b*s of Luke (*beati pauperes* and *beati qui nunc fletis*) are. The cluster of marginal additions in Matthew is also unusual: this page (f. 34r) contains the densest collection of marginalia in the entire manuscript. This indicates that the Beatitudes in Matthew were of immediate interest to Aldred, that he wanted to use them in some way, not merely to gloss them, and that they appealed to him as the Lucan ones did not. Aldred was, however, aware of the similarity in the Gospel passages, and his marginal maxims bring the Matthew and Luke passages to bear on each other and act as commentary on both.

The Beatitudes in Matthew presuppose a counter-cultural community living by different rules from those that apply in ordinary circumstances:

> The first half of each beatitude depicts the community's present; the second half foretells the community's future; and the juxtaposition of the two radically different situations permits the trials of everyday life to be muted by contemplation of the world to come. This hardly excludes the implicit moral demand [...]. But Matthew's beatitudes are not formally imperatives. Like the eschatological blessings in 13:16 and Rev 19:9 and 22:14, they offer hope and indeed function as a practical theodicy. Although there is no explanation of evil, the imagination, through contemplation of God's future, engenders hope and makes the present tolerable (Barton and Muddiman 2001: 853).

The point that the Beatitudes are not imperatives is important: they ask people to identify themselves with the eschatological community, the Kingdom of God. Aldred's marginalia show that he understood and appreciated the rhetoric of the Beatitudes, but also that he had something to add for the benefit of his own community.

6 Analysis of Aldred's maxims

It has been assumed so far that the marginal additions in the Lindisfarne Gospels in Aldred's hand are, in fact, Aldred's own. There is little evidence to prove or disprove this, but no clear source has yet been found for the marginalia as a whole, nor indeed for the glosses. Owun's and Farman's glosses to the MacRegol (Rushworth) Gospels (Oxford, Bodleian Library, MS Auct. D.2.19) might rely on Aldred's work or a common source (Brown 2003: 96; Jolly 2012: 164; and Kotake, this volume), but they do not exhibit the marginalia, even though it is thought the scribes worked closely with the Lindisfarne manuscript, and Aldred himself might have used the MacRegol Gospels in his turn too (Ross 1981, Kotake 2012).[12] This suggests either that the marginalia were not present in the Lindisfarne manuscript (or any common source) at the time of the collaboration (that is, they might have been added later), or that Owun and Farman ignored them. Either way, this evidence would seem to suggest that the marginalia were Aldred's additions and

---

12 Ross (1981: 11) remarks that "There is at least one case where he [Owun] has incorporated a Lindisfarne marginal gloss into his text: *treé heard* (margin *.i. gelíc ficbeame*) 'arborem sicomorum' / *treo heord onlic ficbeome* L 19, 4." The expansion is on f. 186v of Lindisfarne, and is not properly a marginale, being written at the end of the left-hand column largely under *ascendit*.

probably his own ideas, not integral to the enterprise on which the glossators were focused.

I propose to examine the maxims in Aldred's marginalia firstly on the Beatitudes and then on the role of the bishop to see what they tell us about the situations Aldred was addressing. For each Beatitude passage, I give first the Latin text, then the gloss followed by my translation of the Old English, then the marginale read from the high-definition manuscript photographs,[13] with Boyd's (1975a) translation of the marginal Old English.

(1) Matthew 5.3

L	*Beati pauperes spiritu quoniam ipsorum est regnum caelorum*
MtGl (Li) 5.3	eadge biðon ða ðorfendo [corrected from ðærfendo] of ł from gaste f(or)ðon hiora is ric heofna
Trans. (gloss)	'blessed are the needy in/of spirit for theirs is the kingdom of the heavens'
Margin	eadge biðon ða ðaerfe(ndo) þ(æ)t is unspoedge menn ł unsinnige f(or)ðon hia agan godes r(ic)
Trans.	'blessed are the poor, that is unwealthy or sinless men, for they shall possess God's [...]'

The most obvious thing about this marginale is that it realigns the textual gloss by omitting *spiritu*. The marginal comment focuses on what we might call real, physical poverty in addition to the spiritual poverty of the original. The "ðorfendo" here might indeed be, as Boyd (1975a: 10) suggests, "generally pious people who are not wealthy because they care more for obeying God's will than for amassing wealth" in a biblical context, but that much would be clear from the gloss itself. The expansion in the marginale of "ðorfendo" 'poor, needy' with "unspoedge ł unsinnige" 'indigent and/or innocent' makes explicit the two dimensions of physical poverty and spiritual innocence which would be of particular relevance to a community like that at Chester-le-Street.[14] The community had great property and some political influence, but it is not clear that it was properly monastic. Indeed if Aldred had to pay for his admission to the community as the colophon seems to suggest, he might well have seen this as an indication of neither physical nor spiritual poverty, in which case this marginale has particular point.

This focus on real poverty is characteristic of the Lucan parallel to this Beatitude, Luke 6.20, which has no direct reference to spiritual poverty, omitting *spiritu*, as does Aldred's addition to Matthew:

13 See note 6 in the Introduction.

14 ł (L *vel*) is ambiguous: it could mean 'and' as well as 'or'.

Luke 6.20

L	*Beati pauperes quia uestrum est regnum dei*
LkGl (Li) 6.20	eadgo ða ðorfendo forðon iuer is ric godes
Trans. (gloss)	'blessed are the poor for yours is the kingdom of God'

What the recent high-definition photographs of the manuscript show is that the last word of the Matthean marginale has disappeared into the binding of the manuscript, as does the *-a* of "hlifgiendr-" in the marginale to Matthew 5.5. The descender of a letter is clearly visible after "godes", and a short word has been lost. The descender is compatible with that of Aldred's *r* or *s*, and from the context, the missing word is overwhelmingly likely to be "ric".[15] Thus the Matthean passage is not "unfinished" as Boyd believed (1975a: 10), but rather assimilated to the Luke passage: "f(or)ðon hia agan godes r(ic)" 'for they shall possess God's kingdom' in Matthew, "forðon iuer is ric godes" 'for yours is God's kingdom' in Luke.

The two main changes Aldred made in his commentary, omitting the word *spiritu* and using "godes r(ic)" instead of "ric heofna" (the more characteristic Matthean idiom), show that Aldred wanted to align the Beatitudes in Matthew and Luke, to focus on fundamentally similar ideas:[16] real and present physical poverty, as well as spiritual poverty and innocence. Thus his purpose might have been to encourage his community to believe that they would indeed possess the kingdom of God if they kept to, or adopted, a fully monastic vocation. A story related in the *Historia de sancto Cuthberto* (Johnson South 2002: 52) and Symeon of Durham (Rollason 2000: 122–126) shows that they might have had a hand in making Guthred king,[17] they might have influenced his policies and benefited from his generosity in their early years at Chester-le-Street – and indeed that of Kings Æthelstan, Edmund and Eadred somewhat later – but Aldred's additions remind them that the real kingdom, the Kingdom of God, is promised to the poor and humble.

(2) Matthew 5.5

L	*Beati mites quoniam ipsi posidebunt terram*
MtGl (Li) 5.5	eadge biðon ða milde forðon ða agnegað eorðo

15 The *r* of "r(ic)" was visible to Stevenson (1854–1865: I, 57 n. 6), though the *a* of "hlifgiendr(a)" was apparently not (I, 57 n. 7).

16 Bowden (2005: 690) observes, "the Gospel of Matthew always speaks of the kingdom of heaven, to avoid mentioning the divine name"; this is widely understood to be a reflex of the Jewishness of Matthew and/or his primary audience, and is a reflection of Old Testament usage.

17 Bonner (1989) and Rollason (2000: 122–125 n. 78) identify Guthred with the historical Guthfrith who died in 894.

Trans. (gloss)	'blessed are the meek for they will possess the earth'
Margin	[...] f(or)ðon ða milde g(e)byes hlifgiendr(a) eorðo
Trans.	'[...] for the meek shall possess the land of the living'

Aldred adds "hlifgiendr(a)"[18] 'of the living' to the original text here about the meek possessing the earth. Boyd explains how the Fathers interpreted the Old Testament expression "the land of the living" as having an eschatological dimension. Boyd quotes Pseudo-Chrysostom (1975a: 11),

> This earth [...], as long as it is in its present state, is the land of the dead, because it is subject to vanity; when on the other hand, it shall be freed from the slavery of corruption into the glorious freedom of the sons of God it becomes the land of the living, that the immortal may inherit an immortal country.

However, in the context established by the previous marginale, it seems possible that this one might have immediate reference to Aldred's audience and community. Here the land of the living might well be the here and now, as it customarily is in the Psalms (Boyd 1975a: 12); and this is where the collocation of *lifigend* and *eorðe* mainly occurs in Old English. *The Seafarer* (Gordon 1979), lines 65b–66a, speaks of "þis deade lif / læne on londe" 'this dead life, ephemeral on land', echoing the Pseudo-Chrysostom passage, but contrasting the 'dead life' with the joys of the Lord to be sought in the dedicated life of voluntary exile and pilgrimage. The expression in Old English usage is less eschatological than might appear from the comments of theological writers. Aldred might, then, have understood the Beatitude as teaching that the meek will possess the land of the living both in the earthly life as well as in the eschatological future.

This focus might be thought to be reinforced by the addition of *nunc* in the main text of the next Beatitude, *beati qui lugunt [nunc] quoniam ipsi consolabuntur* 'blessed are they that mourn [now]; for they shall be comforted', which explicitly contrasts the present and the future. The word *nunc* is added after *lugunt* to the original text in lighter ink, in slightly smaller Half-uncials to match the main Latin text.[19] The idea of the Beatitude is expressed slightly differently (and with

18 Aldred occasionally gives syllable-initial liquids an inorganic *h*- (e.g. here and "gehriorded" in LkGl (Li) 6.21, mentioned below); see further Foley (1903: 71) and Scragg (1970: 182–185).

19 The extended horizontal stroke on the *t* of *lugunt* (here, but elsewhere on other letters such as the *r* of *consolabuntur* below on the same folio of the manuscript) indicates the end of a line in Eadfrith's text. The addition of *nunc* to the text here is found in the Stockholm Codex Aureus (at f. 15r; Stockholm, Kungliga Biblioteket, MS A.135), a mid-eighth-century Kentish production, according to Jülicher (1938: 20). Wordsworth and White (1889–1898: 54) add: the Book of Armagh (Dublin, Trinity College Dublin, MS 52), the Egerton Gospels (London, British Library,

the deictic *nunc*) in Luke 6.21: *Beati qui nunc fletis quia ridebitis* 'Blessed are ye that weep now; for you shall laugh'. The two perspectives, difficulty now (represented by mourning) and consolation to come (future, but not necessarily eschatological) may be carried through from the previous Beatitude. Aldred glosses the text, but does not add anything to it.

The next Beatitude is more clearly eschatological. The marginal comment reorders the elements and adds only in "ece lif" 'in eternal life' to the ideas.

(3) Matthew 5.6

L	*Beati qui esuriunt et sitiunt iustitiam quoniam ipsi saturabuntur*
MtGl (Li) 5.6	eadge biðon ða ðe hyncgrað ⁊ ðyrstas soðfæstnisse forðon ða ilco gefylled biðon ł geriorded
Trans. (gloss)	'blessed are those who hunger and thirst for righteousness for the same will be filled or feasted'
Margin	eadge biðon ða ðe ðyrstas ⁊ hyncgras æfter soðfæstnisse f(or)ðon ða gefylled biðon in ece lif
Trans.	'blessed are those who thirst and hunger after righteousness for they will be filled in eternal life'

In the Latin the tenses are perfectly clear, but in Old English they are not, so this addition serves to contextually disambiguate the meaning. In this Beatitude Aldred wishes to make clear that the hunger and thirst is spiritual in nature and the feasting likewise will be spiritual in nature. He wishes to avoid the confusion that might arise in hearers from the Lucan Beatitude, which omits all reference to righteousness. In Luke 6.21, the physical deprivation of hunger and thirst has physical recompense: "eadgo ðaðe nu gehyncres f(or)ðon gie biðon gehriorded" 'blessed are those who hunger now for they will be feasted'. Aldred not only adds "in ece life" 'in eternal life' but also omits the specifically physical metaphor of feasting (in both glosses: Matthew "geriorded", Luke "gehriorded"), thus focusing on the spiritual message here, and quite possibly reinforcing the necessity of fasting. Aldred does not wish his audience to be distracted from the point by the thought of food; the marginal comment focuses resolutely on the spiritual interpretation, and the desire and quest for righteousness which can only be met and fulfilled in eternal life.

MS Egerton 609), the Codex Epternachensis (Paris, Bibliothèque Nationale, MS Lat. 9389), the Lichfield Gospels and the MacRegol Gospels; all are dated between the seventh and ninth centuries. The addition was made in the Lindisfarne manuscript before Aldred (or less likely, by Aldred), since he glosses it, as does Farman, and the reading is standard in the West Saxon Gospels (Skeat 1887: 44; Liuzza 1994: I, 8).

Eternity remains the focus for the last marginal additions in the set, relating to purity of heart and peace. The interesting feature of these two additions is that they both contain a "bute" clause with two alternative faults to be avoided.

(4) Matthew 5.8

L	*Beati mundo corde quoniam ipsi deum uidebunt*
MtGl (Li) 5.8	eadge biðon clæne of ł from hearte forðon ða god geseas
Trans. (gloss)	'blessed are the pure of/from the heart for they will see God'
Margin	eadge biðon clæne hearte bute esuice ⁊ eghwoelcum facne f(or)ðon hia geseas god in ecnisse
Trans.	'blessed are the pure in heart, without treachery or any crime, for they shall look on God in eternity'

Purity of heart excludes "esuic" and "facen", which Boyd (1975a: 13) translates 'treachery and crime'. This translation is rather too "heroic", I think, for Aldred's "esuic" and "facen". One might compare his gloss to Luke 20.23, where nearly the same doublet is used: *considerans autem dolum* 'considering then [their] guile' is glossed "sceauade ł beheald ða facen ł esuicnise hiora" 'He perceived or saw their hypocrisy or deceit'. Similarly, in the Durham Collectar 25.12, *omnem dolum et simulationes* 'all guile and pretence' is glossed "aelc facon ⁊ esuico".

The examples of the words "esuic" and "facen" in the Old English corpus and as defined in the *Dictionary of Old English* (hereafter *DOE*; s.vv. *ǣ-swic* and *fācen*), are much more to do with hypocrisy and deviousness or deception than overt crime. In particular, there is a repeated religious sense of hypocrisy in Aldred's use of "esuic" and its variants (glossing *hypocrita* in MtGl (Li) 6.16, 7.5, and *hypocrisis* in LkGl (Li) 12.1) and of deceit and lies about "facen" (glossing *fraus* 'deceit' in MkGl (Li) 10.19, and *dolus* 'deception' in MkGl (Li) 14.1). Also to be noted is the usage in the Lindisfarne colophon, where Aldred mentions the "faconleas" gilding of Billfrith's binding to the book, where "faconleas" seems to refer to the purity of the metal (Brown 2003: 104; *DOE*: s.v. *fācen-lēas*; Jolly 2012: 53). I suggest that Aldred's concern in this Beatitude is not very dissimilar from that of Archbishop Wulfstan some thirty or forty years later: both sense a creeping hypocrisy and insincerity, a residual but debilitating accommodation with secular values and worldliness in the Christian community, and both want to stamp it out. There is no beatific vision for the compromised.

(5) Matthew 5.9

L	*Beati pacifici quoniam ipsi filii dei uocabuntur*
MtGl (Li) 5.9	eadge biðon sibsume ł friðgeorne forðon ða suna godes biðon geceigd ł genemned

Trans. (gloss) 'blessed are the peaceable/those who yearn for peace for they will be called/named sons of God'
Margin eadge biðon ða friðgeorne ða ðe hea buta eghwoelcum flita ⁊ toge behalda(s) ða sint godes sun(u)[20] genemned
Trans. 'blessed are the eager for peace, those who keep themselves without any quarrel or strife[:] they are called sons of God'

The final marginal comment on the Beatitudes brings the message home. In the biblical text, the peaceable will be called sons of God. In Aldred's addition, the peace that is sought is focused on the community. The change from the "biðon" 'will be' of the interlinear gloss to the "sint" 'are' of the margin is marked. The noun *(ge)flit* 'dispute' and the related verb are used by Aldred to gloss terms for contention, noise and disagreement (MtGl (Li) 5.40, 12.19, 27.24; LkGl (Li) 22.24; JnGl (Li) 9.16, 10.19), particularly in the context of communities.[21] The role of the community is to live in peace and to keep peace among themselves and so merit the name *filii dei* 'sons of God' in the present. And, as he did at the beginning of the marginal commentary on the Beatitudes, Aldred brings the focus back onto the here-and-now of the community. He started with their real poverty and ends with their real peaceableness, refusing to keep these spiritual and eschatological as they are in Matthew's text and making them defining characteristics of the community as it is or should be.

The remaining marginal maxim occurs at Matthew 10.8, prompted by *gratis accipistis gratis date* 'freely have you received; freely give':

(6) Matthew 10.8
Margin cueð to ðæm apostolum. ⁊ bisceopum æft(er) him f(or)ðmest. unboht ge hád fengon ⁊ unboht ł unceap buta eghuelcum worðe seallás ðæm ðe sie wyrðe ł worð bið in lare ⁊ in ðæwu(m) ⁊ in clænnisse ⁊ in cystum : ⁊ in lichoma hælo f(or)ðon bisc(op) scæl cunnege ⁊ leornege ðone preost georne buta ær geleornade
Trans. 'He said to the apostles and bishops foremost after him. You received orders gratis; give [them] gratis without any price to those who are worthy in learning and in habits and in purity

20 Stevenson and Waring (1854–1865), Skeat (1871–1887) and Boyd (1975a: 14) supply the letter *a* here. The initial stroke of the letter is visible in the manuscript photograph, and it is vertical and seriffed, so very unlike that of an *a* or *o*. Ross (1937: 79) has "sunu" for the nominative/accusative plural of *sunu* in the Lindisfarne Gospels 17 times, "suno" 36 times, "suna" nine times. The letter shape makes *u* the most plausible choice here.
21 The word also occurs in place-names relating to disputed land (Smith 1956: I, s.v.).

and in virtues and in health of body. For the bishop must test and teach the priest eagerly, unless he has learnt beforehand'.

Boyd (1975a: 24–31) has explored the context and background to this passage (and the marginale towards the head of the right column on the same page, f. 45r), and how it relates to the colophon in helpful detail:

> In the colophon he [Aldred] emphasizes that he is worthy in learning and in habits, for he had glossed Matthew for God and St. Cuthbert, Mark for the bishop, Luke for members of the community – which showed concentration and persistence as well as devoted scholarship (1975: 26).

Boyd shows the personal nature of this passage, but he does not notice its rhetoric or precise contemporary context.

The marginale begins in the top margin, which demonstrates that Aldred intended to make a long comment from the beginning. The passage itself begins with reporting the dominical saying to the apostles, and applying it to bishops, the successors to the apostles; he also adds "the standard requirement of western canon law" (Boyd 1975a: 31) for the bishops to teach, examine and judge the physical suitability of candidates for the priesthood. He then concludes with the maxim, summarizing what the role of any bishop is in relation to ordinands: to test, teach and ordain promptly. The passage goes from instruction, to application, to summarizing statement of accepted fact; from Scripture, to canon law, to maxim. These are equally authoritative statements, but enforce the anti-simoniac message in different ways.[22]

While Aldred most likely thought of himself in the category of someone who had "ær geleornade" 'learnt beforehand', the maxim is impersonal. It provides a way for Aldred to instruct the bishop in his duties without presumption. The maxim allows Aldred to imply that it has always and everywhere been the duty of a bishop to test and teach and admit swiftly to the priesthood. A simoniac bishop

22 Somewhat later, Wulfstan uses the same technique in his homilies and notes (Cavill 2012), and even uses some of the same vocabulary, *georne* especially. The rhetoric of the context is important here, but one might observe the curious maxim in St. Petersburg, National Library of Russia, MS Lat. O.v.XVI.1, f. 15r, "A scæl gelæred smið swa he gelicost mæg be bisne wyrcan butan he bet cunne" 'the learned smith must always follow his exemplar as closely as possible, unless he knows better' (Ker 1976: 127 item 145; Cavill 1999: 16–17), which has no obvious context, but shows how a scribe might want to preserve a wisdom saying because of its intrinsic value. Note too the condition clause with "butan", where a single exception is allowed to the general rule, and Aldred's condition clause with "buta".

might feel uncomfortable reading the annotation, but could not refute the ideas.[23] There is evidence of just such a bishop in the mid-940s at Chester-le-Street.[24] Symeon of Durham in his *Libellus de exordio*, ii. 19, tells of Bishop Seaxhelm, who was expelled by St. Cuthbert for avarice:

> *Cum enim a uia predecessorum suorum aberrans, populum ipsius sancti et eos qui in ecclesia seruiebant, auaritia succensus affligeret, exterritus a sancto per somnium iussus est quantotius abscedere.*
>
> 'When, turning aside from the ways of his predecessors and consumed with avarice, he had brought ruin to the people of the saint and those who served in his church, he was terrified by the saint in a dream and ordered to depart summarily' (Rollason 2000: 140–141).

Since Seaxhelm was unwilling to leave the bishopric, the saint threatened him with punishment and finally death in successive dreams. When he began to grow ill as the saint had threatened, he fled to York and there recovered. While simony is not specified as the particular form that Seaxhelm's avarice took, this passage records that Seaxhelm departed from "the ways of his predecessors", and suggests that the scandal was remembered in the community.[25] It is tempting to imagine that Aldred's payment mentioned in the colophon might have been part of the scandal, and the dates are not irreconcilable, but this is speculation.[26]

---

23 This passage goes some way to casting doubt on the reinterpretation of the colophon proposed by Newton et al. They (2013: 122) argue that in the colophon "Aldred's words are focused upon the manuscript, its creation and what he has done to enhance the book", and thus the traditional interpretation that Aldred paid money to be admitted to the community is a "gratuitous factoid" that is "an offence against the colophon's integrity". But there is a dual focus in the colophon: the manuscript and Aldred himself; and the marginale at Matthew 10.8 shows the glossator to be passionately concerned about simony in a way that might, under unsympathetic eyes, be thought to be an offence against the integrity of the Gospel text. But Aldred carefully and deliberately put the comment in; he intended the message to be taken seriously.

24 The precise dates of Seaxhelm's episcopacy are unknown (Rollason 2000: 141 n. 110), but this story is told before the death of King Edmund is recorded (dated in the text 948, *rectius* 946). Simon Keynes (2014: 565) places Seaxhelm's brief episcopacy between the accessions of Uhtred "?942" and Ealdred "before 946".

25 Bernard Meehan (1998: 129) suggests that Seaxhelm is the simoniac referred to by Symeon of Durham in the *Libellus* i. 2 and iii. 18, but Rollason (2000: 22 n. 12, 195 n. 69, and see also iii. 9) notes that the references here are to Eadred, c. 1040, not Seaxhelm.

26 Newton et al. (2013: 122) argue that mention of simony in the colophon "constitutes an offence against the colophon's integrity" on the basis that it was a "moral solecism". But if Aldred's payment of money and part-payment by glossing was part of the scandal, then Aldred could hardly avoid referring to it, not because "simony was so common in the church in Aldred's day" (as Newton et al. 2013: 122 suppose defenders of this interpretation to be arguing), but because for Symeon, at least, it was rare. Such a reference would chime with the marginale to Matthew 10.8

Aldred's marginale is nevertheless clearly part of the process by which Scripture and wisdom were brought to bear on the contemporary troubles and difficulties of the community and Church.

7 Aldred's purpose

An obvious question to ask is what Aldred's purpose was in adding these marginal comments. Boyd's general approach is to suggest that Aldred was trying to elucidate the Beatitudes by summarizing ideas from the Fathers. Clearly Aldred does that on occasion, but there are two main reasons why I think that is not his primary purpose here. The first reason is that of all the passages in the Gospels, the Beatitudes are probably the least obscure. These passages need little explanation, and are perennially at the heart of the monastic and Christian counter-culture. And the second reason is that the marginalia actually use predominantly the wording and structure of the original Latin and the interlinear gloss. The adjustments made are small (though significant), and very much less like commentary than they are exposition: they make clear the relevance of the teaching to the community and the Church, applying these generalizations powerfully in a form they would recognize as doubly authoritative, being both biblical and in the form of maxims. While Aldred's marginale on the role of the bishop is more clearly commentary, it too uses Scripture and maxim to enforce the point.

We might imagine two related intentions in this set of annotations, then. The first is that Aldred was adding notes for a sermon or series of sermons on the Beatitudes, adding ideas to focus the minds of his audience on the relevance of the teaching to people in their situation. He wanted those who had voluntarily entered clerical life to think at least of the monastic vow of poverty, and to look forward to the kingdom of God, and to thirst and hunger for righteousness, and to seek God with constant focus without wavering or contention. He certainly opposed simony and delay in ordination and saw this as contrary to the teaching

here discussed. Moreover, it would bring together themes in the colophon, which when read differently has a different kind of integrity. Aldred's reference to himself as *indignus et misserrimus* 'unworthy and wretched' was perhaps not a flourish of humility, and the situation also required reference to his good parentage in the colophon. Reference to the payment, and obliquely to the possible scandal, redounds to the glory of St. Cuthbert, who resolved the issue by dismissing Seaxhelm. And the idea that the payment of work and money, while gaining Aldred's admission to the community, was not ultimately for that purpose but for his admission to heaven, is consistent with Aldred's perspectives on the Beatitudes discussed above. On this reading, the colophon might be thought to deal sensitively with a difficult issue.

of the Bible and to the bishop's calling. But he also had ambitions for the community in the world. He wanted them to be a community of the blessed who possessed the land of the living, who lived in peace, and were known as sons of God. Committed to pages of the community's treasured Gospel book, Aldred's work became part of the teaching resources of the community, and his ideas might well have been picked up and used time and time again as teachers in the community read the book and its marginalia.

A second intention of these annotations might have been to present Aldred's vision and aspirations. The gloss shows his learning and general understanding of Latin and biblical theology. The marginal additions augment that with comments on matters of urgency and relevance that preoccupied Aldred. His comments on hypocrites in the addendum to Matthew 7.6 show much the same concern as his comments on Matthew 5.8 above. In these marginal additions his vision is for the growing power, prosperity, purity and impact of his community and Church in syncretistic and fractious times, but such effectiveness could not be gained by underhand means, only by returning to Gospel teaching and monastic devotion. If the glossing of the manuscript was "part of the payment for joining" the community (Jolly 2012: 39), and his additional payments of eight ores of silver for induction and four ores additionally as a gift, then Aldred took the opportunity of making it clear that he did not approve of such payments in general, and that he personally had not failed in generosity, giving much more than was required.

I do not believe that these marginalia are detached and merely annotatory. They are selective, omitting two of the Beatitudes,[27] and making the others a mini-catalogue fitting a pattern of dual focus on the physical and present as well as the spiritual and future. They use the form and style of the maxim (and indeed other structuring devices such as "buta" with a clause of condition) to assert powerfully the worldview that Aldred believed should shape his community and Church. They are persuasive and rhetorical, outlining the two worlds in which the community lived, the here-and-now and the eternal world of God's kingdom. If the community and the Church heeded the teaching of the Beatitudes and Aldred's insights in the margins, they would cease to be marginal and would be blessed and prosper.

---

27 "Blessed are the merciful" (Matthew 5.7) and "blessed are the persecuted" (Matthew 5.10) are omitted, perhaps because at this stage they were less directly relevant to the community.

8 Conclusion

There can be little doubt that Aldred's project of glossing the Lindisfarne Gospels was one to which he committed himself wholeheartedly. The glossing, colophon and marginalia together reveal a great deal about the man, his commitment, his preoccupations and his learning. This discussion has shown that he had a profound concern with wisdom, seeing himself as a successor to Solomon in the colophon, using the traditional forms of Anglo-Saxon wisdom literature, maxims, in the marginalia, and augmenting by means of the marginalia the most important wisdom discourse of Christianity, the Sermon on the Mount.

In previous discussion of the marginalia, the theological and patristic teaching they contain has been carefully outlined (Boyd 1975a). This article has suggested that Aldred had a less abstract and more practical purpose in writing the marginalia. He was a reformer himself, and very likely was associated in some way with the Benedictine Reform of Edgar's reign. He lived in difficult times and there is some evidence that there were or had been abuses in the community of St. Cuthbert at Chester-le-Street and in the diocese of which it was a part. His purpose in the marginalia analyzed above was to assert biblical teaching and apply it to the community forcefully through maxims, addressing contemporary and perennial issues. It was natural for him to use, as part of his rhetoric, a recognizable wisdom form, the maxim, to present his teaching. This enabled him to draw lessons from the Gospel text and apply them to his community without presenting the ideas as idiosyncratic and personal but rather as obvious truth. The use of an impersonal mode of address nevertheless shows what was of deepest importance to Aldred: the well-being of his Church and community.

Stewart Brookes

The Shape of Things to Come? Variation and Intervention in Aldred's Gloss to the Lindisfarne Gospels

Abstract: This paper examines Aldred's response to the gospel text he was glossing through close analysis of his choices of script. The focus is on Aldred's experimentation with different types of letter-forms and the resultant variation in the realization of the letters. I suggest that these point to Aldred's deep engagement with the manuscript, prompting him to produce a response to its script and layout that positions him as a scribe working in the Northumbrian artistic tradition. The paper also argues, however, that Aldred's script offers evidence of his familiarity with Caroline minuscule and Square minuscule and thus of his awareness of the scribal fashions previously assigned exclusively to scribes working in southern England.

1 Introduction

In his polemical essay *Areopagitica*, John Milton asserted that "[b]ooks are not absolutely dead things, but doe contain a potencie of life in them to be as active as that soule was whose progeny they are; nay, they do preserve as in a violl the purest efficacie and extraction of the living intellect that bred them" (Wolfe 1959: 492). This notion seems particularly apposite in the case of Aldred and his tenth-century gloss to the Lindisfarne Gospels (London, British Library, MS Cotton Nero D.iv). The Old English words that Aldred wrote between and around the Latin lines of the four gospels represent more than a simple act of explication, translation and occasional commentary. They are his personal meditation on the gospels and bear witness to his spiritual and scholarly engagement with a text that lies at the heart of Christian belief. If anything preserves his "living intellect", it is this. A second and interrelated story is that of the physical act of his writing the gloss. It must have been a daunting task for Aldred to write alongside the elaborate carpet pages, decorative letters and Half-uncial Latin text of what has been described as one of the "great monuments of human endeavour" (Brown 2002–2003: I, 187). The manuscript had a particular religious significance also, being a volume dedicated to Cuthbert, the special saint of the community among whom Aldred lived. In this paper, I examine Aldred's response to the text through analysis of his choices of script, focusing on his experimentation with different types of letter-forms and the resultant variation in the realization of the letters. I suggest that the motive behind this variation is style: in the scripts he chose for his gloss, Aldred offers a creative response to the variation in letter-shapes in the decorative script and main Latin text of the Lindisfarne Gospels, one which evolves from the Northumbrian artistic tradition in which he was steeped. I argue that the variations in the letter-forms afford us insight into Aldred's intentions in glossing the Lindisfarne Gospels, serving as a visual articulation of his self-positioning as a scribe in dialogue with the manuscript and as a priest responsible for translating the Gospels.

2 Variation in the gloss

Written in the years following the mid-tenth century, Aldred's gloss to the Lindisfarne Gospels has frequently been described as old-fashioned, a throwback to an eighth- or ninth-century way of writing (Brown 1969: 39; Roberts 2005: 15; Jolly 2012: 76). For T. J. Brown (1969: 15), Aldred's choice of Anglo-Saxon pointed minuscule marked him out as a relic from the distant past and as a "backward, but not necessarily an incompetent, provincial". Brown (1969: 39) argues that because Aldred was located in Northumbria, he was unaware of the style of writing current in southern England and thus does not write in the "square" style found in glossed manuscripts more or less contemporary with his own. While it is not in doubt that Aldred often writes in a Cursive minuscule that owes much to the Northumbrian scribal habits and styles of at least a century earlier, there is reason to challenge the notion of his isolation from the scribal fashions that swept the south.[1] In this paper, I present evidence which suggests that Aldred was aware of both Square minuscule and Caroline minuscule and that this is reflected in his choice of letter-forms in his gloss. Beyond this, however, is the question of the significance of variation in the style of Aldred's writing. Right from the start Aldred signals his intention to use alternative forms of letters, with a straight-backed *d* (gesturing towards Half-uncial) alongside a round-backed minuscule form on f. 3r4 (2.45).[2] When Aldred adds a pen trial in the top right corner of f. 122r, he does so using the "oc" form characteristic of Half-uncial *a* (4.49), rather

1 The terminology used in this paper to describe the various grades, hierarchies and types of script, including Insular Half-uncial, Hybrid minuscule and Caroline minuscule, is discussed with illustrative figures and plates in M. P. Brown (1990: 48–71), Roberts (2005: 13–103) and Rumble (2009: 37–49).

2 See the first part of Appendix 2 below for explanatory references, and the second part of the appendix for images of the letter-forms discussed in this paper. A version of Appendix 2 which

than the minuscule in which he mostly wrote. And, most tellingly of all, his pen trial of the Tironian symbol in the middle margin of f. 193v shows two quite different forms (1.34). It would seem that his reflex was to experiment with varying forms. Only with an awareness of this variation can we understand the creative energies that Aldred put into the visual presentation of his gloss.

It would be difficult to overstate the impact of variation in the gloss. It is everywhere: from the range of alternative letter-forms that Aldred deploys to the size of his letters, which varies considerably. Some words are written neatly, others scratched hastily on to the vellum. On the same folio, minims may be formed slowly with frequent pen lifts and feet and wedges added, or they may be written hurriedly in the style of the lowest grade of cursive script. And, most surprisingly, different types of script are mixed together in the same sentences. In 1.1 and 1.6, for example, there are three forms of *a* (1.1 has Caroline, Square and open forms of *a*; 1.6 has open, pointed and Square forms of *a*) and in 1.8 there are two forms of *g* in the same passage. The variation extends beyond word-to-word differences: it is very common to find different forms of letters within the same word, as we see in 1.2 and 1.3 (Caroline and open *a* in "ana" and "sacerdas"), 1.11 (pointed and open *a* in "aras") and 1.7 (two types of *g* in "getreowfæstnig"). It is, of course, unusual to find this range of letters from different scripts being used alongside each other as interchangeable alternatives. The consequence is that letter-types that are not usually found in a cursive context start to be adapted to the underlying script type; for example, the Caroline *a* in "ðara" (1.5) is joined with the *r* which follows it.

3 Methodology

Although the above examples give some sense of the range of letter-forms in the gloss, a wider sample is required in order to demonstrate the extent of the variation. I have, therefore, 'cut out' individual letter-forms (or "graphs" to use the terminology adopted for the DigiPal project) from across the manuscript.[3] When selecting graphs for inclusion, I have attempted to present a spectrum of the forms that Aldred uses, placing the graphs in groupings according to shared features and characteristics. For example, graphs of open *a* are grouped from

---

is linked to the relevant pages of the Lindisfarne Gospels on the British Library digitized manuscripts site can be found here:<http://www.digipal.eu/blog/aldred/>.

3 The 'Digital Resource and Database for Palaeography, Manuscript Studies and Diplomatic' (DigiPal), available at <http://www.digipal.eu>.

4.1–4.8, the majority of graphs of *g* which have a closed tail from 8.45–8.76 and *2*-shaped *r* from 9.49–9.53. This arrangement also offers the opportunity for comparison of various of the component features of the letter-forms; for example, 6.2–6.18 shows the tongue of *e* at various lengths, curved, rising and horizontal, and 10.1–10.6 gives a sense of the split ascenders which are typical for *s*. This also helps to provide a context for forms which otherwise might seem atypical. For example, the long, upright body of the *g* in "geworht" (1.12) is markedly different from the other *g* in that detail, but it seems less of an anomaly once it is placed next to similar instances (8.71–8.76). It is important to remember that the graphs are selected from across the complete manuscript, and do not necessarily occur on the same folio. In addition, although viewing the letters like this suggests a sort of evolution of script, the reality is that variant forms are used alongside each other in most sections of the gloss and that overall there is not a progression from one type to another.

4 Examples of *a* and *g*

Although it is not new to say that Aldred's handwriting is subject to variation, the extent to which this is the case has been underestimated. A useful example of the range of letter-forms that Aldred employs can be seen by looking at the variants for *a* in examples 4.1–5.11. The graphs offer instances of virtually every possible type of *a* that was used in the Old English period. Amongst them is the "oc" *a* of Half-uncial (4.46–4.49); open *a* (4.1–4.8); the decorative enlarged *a* of Anglo-Saxon minuscule (4.87); the point-topped bowl of Anglo-Saxon pointed minuscule (4.53, 4.56, 4.57), with a tendency for the back to rise high above the bowl (4.50, 4.54); square and lozenge-shaped forms that are clearly influenced by Square minuscule (4.14–4.20, 4.37–4.39); and Caroline *a* (4.76–4.78). In addition, there are forms of *a* that demonstrate a calligraphic flourish (4.89), or an attempt to produce a higher grade of script (e.g. 4.43) and round forms (5.9–5.11) that may have emerged naturally when writing cursively. Aldred, it is clear, had a magpie's scribal repertoire.

That this multiplicity of forms is typical of Aldred's writing can be seen from the images accompanying this paper. With *g*, for example, he uses a *3*-shape (8.1, 8.65), a *5*-shape (8.4, 8.20, 8.31); the tail may be open (8.2–8.40), three-quarters closed (8.41-8.44) and closed (8.45–8.50). The body hangs from the left (8.18), from the right (8.1, 8.2), and from the middle (8.53). At times, he creates his *g* from five separate strokes, as can been seen when he neglects to add the bottom curve in "bigencga" (1.21, 8.66). One feature to which it is worth drawing attention is Aldred's addition of a stroke to close the tail of the *g* (8.59–8.64). This is unusual for an Anglo-Saxon minuscule script and it seems almost certain that he borrowed this from the *g* in the Latin text where it is ubiquitous (see 16.32–16.34 and particularly 16.35, which shows Aldred's *g* in close proximity to its Latin equivalent).

5 Ascenders and feet

The way that Aldred treats his ascenders varies considerably also. They may be tall and comparatively straight (2.3), sway-backed (2.24), compressed (2.5–2.6) or even squat (2.11, 2.14, 2.16). Some have approach strokes (2.11–2.13), others are unadorned (2.1, 2.3) or they may have wedges (2.17–2.22) or flags (2.24, 2.46). The ascenders appear forked in a few cases (2.35, 2.36) while in others a decorative hairline has been added (2.40–2.45). As so often, some variation in appearance is due to the care in execution, with the blob-like additions (2.5, 2.7, 2.14) most likely a poorly implemented attempt to add wedges to these letters. In similar manner, the minims of letters cover the full range of what one might expect to find across different types of script. What one would not expect is to find them together on the same page, executed by a single scribe. *n* may be narrow and tapered to give a claw-like appearance (7.24), thickly made and short (7.22) or have a pronounced wedge on the minim (7.20). The arch of *h*, *m* and *n* may descend below the line, curving inwards to the left (1.20, 7.8–7.10, 7.25), sometimes finished with a thick horizontal stroke (7.9, 7.25). At times, Aldred is careful to add feet to minims (7.21, 1.17, 1.19), but often does not (1.4, 1.7, 1.14, 1.28, 1.29). What is remarkable is that the varying forms are found in close proximity to each other, as we see in 1.18 with wedges on some minims and not on others.

The wish to vary letter-shapes seems to run in Aldred's scribal blood. He just cannot write them the same way each time. A clear demonstration of this variety can be seen in his treatment of *u*. As Ross et al. (1960: 23) note, Aldred makes a "sharp and unmistakable" switch away from the use of <u> to <v> after f. 203v. Having made that decision, Aldred then begins to vary his *v*, sometimes adding wedges, altering the angle at which it is written, and even adding a tail (7.38–7.46)[4].

4 "While *v* is the predominant form from f. 203v onwards, Aldred does still deploy *u* on occasion, often it would seem for the purpose of variation alongside *v*. See for example, "uv`u´nden" (7.46), "suindriga" (f. 204ra10), "fvluande" (f. 204rb20–21), "throvung" (f. 207va12) and "ðvruuardæ" (f. 251va4). The *v* form can also be found on early folios because Aldred began a second campaign of glossing, in red ink, after he switched to *v*; see, for example, "gisomnvng" (f. 5va6).

Aldred also seems to have delighted in trying out unusual letter-forms that he had seen elsewhere, as we see in the *k* that he uses in the word "stenk" (10.80) which, for all its distinctiveness, is not unique.[5]

6 Aldred's minuscule

As noted earlier, Aldred's writing owes much to an older tradition. It exhibits many of the features one might expect to find in Anglo-Saxon pointed minuscule of the ninth or very early tenth century, and also betrays the influence of Phase II Insular Cursive minuscule which had fallen into disuse by the early ninth century (though Roberts (2005: 14) suggests that Phase II Insular minuscule had a longer life in the north of England than it did in the south). Examples of Aldred's indebtedness to these older styles of minuscule include occasional low-slung *l*, the lower curve of which swings below the line (2.56–2.59, with a particularly graceful example at 2.60); *f*-shaped *y* (7.64–7.66); the arch of *m* and *n* descending below the line, curving inwards to the left (7.8–7.10, 7.25), sometimes finished with a thick horizontal stroke; and elongated *i* at the beginning of words, either standing on the line, rising to the height of the ascenders of other letters (2.63, 2.64) or dropping far below it (2.65).[6] Another tell-tale feature of early Insular Cursive minuscules is the placing of subscript vowels below the line in ligature (3.29, 3.35, 3.38). Indeed, throughout the gloss there is a frequent use of ligature forms, including the distinctive reversed ductus *e*, with its *8*-shape (6.63, 6.66, 6.68) that Lindsay (1921: 17) notes is *par excellence* the Insular Cursive form (for recent discussion of *8*-shaped *e*, see Sparks 2013: 30). At first glance, Aldred's use of letters in ligature seems typical of older Cursive minuscules. For example, the tongue of *e* is often drawn out to form the top stroke of *g* (3.1–3.9) and *t* (3.12–3.15); and *i* may hang from the tongue of *f* (3.29), the top stroke of *g* (3.17 and 3.18), the lower curve of *t* (3.20) and the top stroke of *t* formed from the tongue of *e* (3.12). Aldred goes further, however, constructing a range of idiosyncratic ligatures, including *o* formed in ligature with the top stroke of *g* (3.19); ligatures between *b* and *r* (3.22 and 3.23); the tongue of *e* forming the top of the bowl of *d* (3.16); and the calligraphic yet curiously constructed use of the tongue of *e* to form the arch

5 I am grateful to Elaine Treharne for bringing to my attention the analogous instances of *k* in the Parker Chronicle (Cambridge, Corpus Christi College, MS 173), f. 26r (10.82) which probably dates from a few decades before Aldred, and to those in the twelfth century London, British Library, MS Cotton Vitellius A.xv, f. 49v (10.81). In editions of the gloss, and in Ross et al. (1960), Aldred's *k* has been read as an *nc* ligature.

6 Unconventionally, Aldred also uses elongated *i* in a medial position.

of *h* (3.21). His subscript ligatures are noteworthy because in many cases they have become stylistic and are no longer really ligatures in the true sense where the stroke of one letter serves as part of another (as, for instance, the tongue of *e* does for the top stroke of *g* (3.2)). So, while Aldred uses the classic subscript real ligature of *m* with open *a* (3.39) – which Jane Roberts (2005: 39) describes as a "relic of earlier practices" in the context of the usage by the first hand of the Parker Chronicle – many more of his subscript letters are false ligatures, pushed up against, but not joined to, the letter above (3.34, 3.36–3.37, 3.41). Aldred sometimes manages to create true ligatures for traditional combinations such as *nt* and *ht* (3.26), but on closer inspection there are many that turn out to be lookalikes (3.24, 3.25). In some cases, it is possible that Aldred deliberately allows the second element of the ligature to break free in order to create visual impact (compare the true ligature of *fi* in 3.29 with the subscript *i* in 3.32). This stylistic effect is most fully developed in Aldred's playful *hi* ligature with its appended *a* (3.31) and his suprascript *l* rising above *d* (3.27), both of which seem to be his own invention. Another example of Aldred apparently extending the traditional model for subscript ligatures, false or otherwise, is in the combinations *bi* (3.30), *di* (3.33), *mo* (3.40) and *æ* (3.44, 3.45). Striking also is his decision to drop *e* below the line, which is purely for visual effect (3.46), and combined with the reverse ductus *e* (3.43) is almost certainly Aldred's innovation. The reverse ductus *e* is itself of much interest for understanding Aldred's method: its practical purpose was to save scribes time as part of a ligature combination, but he creates a standalone version (6.71–6.79) which is unlike anything I have seen elsewhere; presumably this is to add another form to his repertoire for the purposes of variation.[7] Similarly, we may note the placing of looped cursive *y* (7.49–7.51) at the end of words when in genuinely cursive hands it would be found in a medial position where it serves as a means to link letters without lifting the pen. While Aldred does use the looped *y* medially (7.47), economy of effort is not his main concern and more often he introduces this form as a feature of style, lending his writing a cursive appearance.

Examples of actual cursivity can be seen in the *rn* of "carchern" (1.26), where Aldred clearly did not lift his pen between minims; the *is* of "israhela" (1.27); and the rapidly written *ym* of "cymeð" (1.25). As is typical in a cursive script, *n* and *r* (9.10) can look very similar. Another feature of Cursive minuscule is that the letters *f*, *p*, *r* and *s* frequently have a *v*-shaped "split". This is the result of Aldred moving his pen away from the base of the descender after the initial downward

7 Due to the idiosyncrasy of this letter-form, Ross et al. (1960: 14) do not recognize this as a form of *e*, describing it as "no more than a change from *o* to *e*". The frequency with which it occurs means that they cannot, however, be correct about this.

stroke. See, for instance, the split ascenders in *f*, *r* and *s* in "getreowfæstnig" (1.7) and in *p* in "papa" (1.7). The split is often deep and very noticeable, of the sort seen in *r* (9.12, 9.16, 9.17) and *s* (10.1, 10.4, 10.9). Such splitting is a consequence of rapid writing as it takes longer to return up the descender with the second stroke and is a feature typical of Aldred's writing. He was capable of minimizing the split, as we see in the *s* of 10.32, and the Hybrid minuscule on the first page (1.35), but speed of writing seems often to have been more important to him than care of execution. When he does make efforts to avoid the split, the difference is particularly apparent. A good example of this can be seen in the proto-Square minuscule of 1.17: the square-ish letters are formed carefully and evenly and are the result of frequent pen-lifts between minims.

Another letter-form typical of early Anglo-Saxon Cursive minuscule that we find with great frequency in Aldred's gloss is open *a*, made up of a bowl and *c*-shaped back (4.1–4.5, 4.7–4.8). Clemoes (1995: 33 n. 77) observes that the use of this form of *a* is an old-fashioned trait of Aldred's writing and that open-headed *a* was not used for documents after the middle of the ninth century and "killed off in non-documentary contexts south of the Humber" by the creation of Square minuscule in the early tenth century (1995: 32). The form seems never to have been in widespread use in a vernacular context, as is made clear from Ker's (1957: xxviii) description of it as an "unusual" form which appears only in five manuscripts. In all of Ker's examples, open *a* is used very sparingly, sometimes featuring only once, whereas for Aldred it is a standard form used throughout his gloss.[8] Antiquity and scarcity aside, an issue with open *a* is that it is easily confused with *u*, as can been seen in, for instance, "gebecnades" (1.1), "apostola" (1.5), "vallað" (1.6) and "papa" (1.7). Lindsay (1922: 8–9) remarks that this potential for mistaking the two letter-forms was an issue even in early minuscule and that scribes often added small touches to differentiate between them. This is the case with Aldred who responds to the problem by adding small wedges on the lower curve and the minim of *u*. Even so, it can be difficult to distinguish between the two letters, and there are occasions on which one has to look twice, such as "gearuas" (1.9).[9]

8 The five are Cambridge, Corpus Christi College, MS 144, which seems only to have one example, the interlinear gloss "aþryid" (f. 26vb24); St. Petersburg, National Library of Russia, MS Lat. Q.v.I.18, f. 107r, where it occurs in the three lines of *Cædmon's Hymn* added in the bottom margin; London, British Library, MS Add. 23211, f. 2r, in the word "hiora" on line 1; London, British Library, MS Cotton Domitian A.ix, f. 11r, which has a few examples; and Paris, Bibliothèque Nationale, MS Lat. 8824, which has only one instance on f. 19rb26.

9 Newton et al. (2013: 107, 113, 140) fall foul of this, offering "gisulde" instead of "gisalde" in their transcription of Aldred's colophon.

Aldred's familiarity with older styles of writing may also be seen in his use of the runes for "monn" (13.1–13.4) and "dæg" (13.5–13.7). The introduction of these ideographs cannot simply be to save time because he occasionally adds them as alternatives to support a word (13.5–13.6). Example 13.2 is particularly intriguing because Aldred first wrote the word "monn" and then erased it, writing the rune on top of the erasure. Perhaps here we see more than a penchant for variation: the use of the runes could be an expression of cultural identity, pointing to the ancient Lindisfarne and Northumbrian heritage with which the community at Chester-le-Street was associated. With this in mind, we might notice the angularity of many of Aldred's forms for *thorn* (11.1–11.12) and *wynn* (12.7–12.12). Several of these appear more epigraphic than designed for a bookhand, and he even seems to attempt majuscule forms (11.1, 12.1, 12.6) which might point to a familiarity with runes and the runic letters in a carved context.

7 Square and English Caroline minuscule

In contrast to the variety of letter-forms found within Aldred's Cursive minuscule, the founding principle of both Square minuscule and English Caroline minuscule was one of simplicity. Accordingly, these scripts moved toward discarding the myriad abbreviations, interchangeable letter-form equivalents, elaborate conjoined letters and subscript ligatures that were salient characteristics of Insular minuscule (Dumville 1987: 153). Both Square minuscule and English Caroline minuscule have been claimed by scholarship to have originated in the south of England. The assumption has been that Square minuscule was written exclusively in the south: as Ganz (2012: 188) puts it, "south of a line running from the Thames to the Severn". Similarly, Dumville (1987: 143) is "practically certain that almost all the surviving specimens were written in Southumbrian England". Although Dumville (1987: 148) remarks that "there is some evidence for its penetration of Northumbria in the third quarter of the tenth century", he adds the caveat that "if one were to judge by the scanty specimens of tenth-century Northumbrian writing, it would have to be said that Square minuscule had few practitioners in that region".

As we have seen, however, Aldred's gloss to the Lindisfarne Gospels (not considered in this context by Ganz or Dumville) does include instances of letter-forms drawn from Square minuscule. In fact, the numbers of Square (and square-ish) forms in Aldred's writing suggest that he was familiar with the latest styles, as well as slightly older fashions. For example, 1.17 is arguably an example of Aldred writing what Dumville (1987: 163) terms proto-Square minuscule, a transitional script which shares some of the features of Square minuscule. There is a square-ish aspect to Aldred's letter-forms here, and an even height to minims which have feet and wedge-like serifs, creating an appearance radically different from, say, the Cursive minuscule of 1.14. What this demonstrates is a familiarity with a reformed minuscule, antecedent to Square minuscule, which has some of the proportions but not all of the characteristics which identify that script. While 1.17 suggests a script style that anticipates Square minuscule, Aldred frequently uses a form of *a* which meets the distinctive and defining characteristics of Square minuscule, an open *a* closed by a top stroke which may be horizontal (4.10, 4.16) or rising from left to right (4.26–4.30). There are many examples of the lozenge-shaped *a* (4.37–4.39), another form within the spectrum of Square minuscule. There are examples of "horned" *e* (6.22–6.38) which also seem to be influenced by Square minuscule, looking very much like what Dumville (1994: 145) identifies as Phase III Square minuscule. The dates Dumville assigns for this, c. 940–959, coincide with precisely when Aldred is thought to have glossed the Lindisfarne Gospels; Aldred's use, I argue, is an early instance.

The above indicates that Aldred was well aware of the latest fashions, and that he assimilated some of the features of Square minuscule into his script. This is not to say that he wrote what would be termed Square minuscule, but it certainly demonstrates Aldred's familiarity with the southern move to create a new English minuscule. A point worth noting is that while palaeographers have identified a progression from Insular minuscule to Square minuscule, that trajectory might well not have been apparent to Aldred.

8 Influence of Caroline minuscule

When considering Aldred's awareness of contemporary scribal practice, one of the most significant pieces of evidence is his frequent use of the Caroline form of *a* (4.74–4.78). Ker (1943: 8) was the first to comment upon this, but stopped short of calling it Caroline; instead, he said that it "resembles" the Caroline form. Ross et al. (1960: 13) were more confident in making the association, noting that amongst the variant forms that Aldred uses is one which is "the same as the standard Carolingian *a*". More recently, Roberts (2005: 36) returned to the issue in her study of the colophon page, arguing that what has been termed the Caroline-like *a* of Aldred is [...] more likely to have been an inherited feature within his hand". There are, indeed, many examples in Aldred's writing of the Anglo-Saxon pointed minuscule *a* with a high back of the sort that Roberts cites from Oxford, Bodleian Library, MS Hatton 20, the first hand of the Parker Chronicle (Cambridge,

Corpus Christi College, MS 173) and London, British Library, Add. Cht. 19791 (4.40, 4.41, 4.61, 4.64, 4.88). When one looks beyond the colophon page, however, a different picture emerges of a distinctive Caroline *a* that is noteworthy both for Aldred's confident fluency with the form and his use of it initially, medially and in final position. On ff. 5r–5v, for instance, there are 60 occurrences of unmistakably Caroline *a*. The next most common form is the open *a*, of which there are 28 instances; as is usual in Aldred's gloss, there are also examples of several other types of *a*, which I have not recorded. (See Appendix 1 for the distribution of Caroline *a* and open *a* on these folios.[10]) While the frequency of the Caroline form at this point in the gloss is not typical of its distribution in the manuscript as a whole, it was clearly an established part of Aldred's scribal repertoire. It is surprising, therefore, to discover that his use of the form seems not to have continued beyond his work on the Lindisfarne Gospels. Judging by the description of Oxford, Bodleian Library, MS Bodley 819 by Ross et al. (1960: 32–33), Aldred did not use Caroline *a* in what is taken to be his next project. Nor, it seems, did he use it in his extensive glosses to the Durham Ritual: Brown (1969: 25 n. 11) notes only four occurrences of Caroline *a* in the Ritual, and from what I can see in the facsimile edition, the examples look like the high-backed forms of *a* found in the first hand of the Parker Chronicle and do not seem Caroline. It is possible that it was an experiment introduced for the purpose of variation, but his confidence with it is in contrast to his attempts at Hybrid minuscule "oc" *a* (4.46–4.49), suggesting that he had experience with it prior to the Lindisfarne Gospels. Perhaps he saw it as a higher grade of script, not suited to the task of glossing less grand manuscripts than the Lindisfarne Gospels.

At any rate, Aldred's use of Caroline *a* is not the only indication of his familiarity with Caroline minuscule. For example, he often writes *s* in a way suggestive of Caroline influence, with the downstroke more or less on the base-line and a small wedge half-way up the downstroke (10.41, 10.43, 10.50). Another pointer in this direction is the distinctive *st* ligatures Aldred uses (10.66–10.70), which are likely to have been informed by Caroline models. Finally, Aldred occasionally deploys a *2*-shaped *r* ligature in both his Old English gloss and occasional Latin notes (9.40–9.44).[11] The *or* ligature is not common in an Old English context, and

---

10 The forms listed in Appendix 1 are those which seem to have been part of Aldred's first pass at glossing the Gospels, and do not include the later additions that he made. There seems to be no pattern or preference for using individual forms with particular words; for example, in this sample Aldred uses both Caroline and open *a* for "regula" and writes both forms alongside each other in "aehteða" (1.8).

11 Ross et al. (1960: 15) record fifteen instances of this ligature between ff. 19ra14 and 189ra5.

more unusual still is Aldred's use of the *4*-shaped *-um* abbreviation (9.45–9.46).[12] These two ligatures were a borrowing from Latin manuscripts, and were typical of Caroline minuscule.

In light of the above, there seems to be enough evidence to argue that Aldred was familiar with Caroline minuscule, had a willingness to experiment with some of its letter-forms, and had access to resources which would have provided a model (whether in the form of manuscripts or other scribes). The implications of this argument are significant. Aldred is thought to have written his gloss in the middle of the tenth century, or a little afterwards, a time-frame that corresponds closely with the earliest dated examples of English Caroline minuscule, which would place Aldred's use of Caroline letter-forms very early on in this chronology. His usage would thus be contemporary with the single sheet charters that are the earliest datable witnesses to Caroline minuscule in an English context (Rushforth 2012: 198–199).

9 Variability in the quality of the writing

While I have focused until now mainly on deliberate experimentation in script type, another aspect of the variation is the inconsistency in the quality of the writing. The difference between, say, 1.17 and 1.23 is marked and this has led to an often contradictory response to the gloss. For Ker (1943: 12) "Aldred's skill is apparent in the Gospels", whereas Gameson (2013: 83) sees Aldred's handwriting as "functional and variable rather than elegant and constant". Newton et al. (2013: 106) describe the gloss as "discreet and orderly throughout", whereas Horobin (2013: 45) classes it as scruffy. G. Baldwin Brown (1903–1937: V, 337) comments that the "neatly written interlinear gloss really does no harm to the manuscript", while Gilbert (1990: 154 n. 13) decries it as "an aesthetic disaster unparalleled in insular manuscripts". Aside from the last, all of these comments might be judged appropriate to particular stints by Aldred, even if none of them, aside from perhaps that of Gameson, is applicable for the gloss in its totality. What the differing responses point to is the lack of consistency. There is evidence to suggest that the glossing process was not a linear one, and that Aldred moved back and forth, adding additional glosses to earlier sections of the manuscript on different days. This can be seen most noticeably in the appearance of glosses in red on the earlier folios (for example, f. 5va6). While this accounts for a small part of the

12 Roberts (2005: 50) notes the use in the first hand of the Parker Chronicle (Cambridge, Corpus Christi College, MS 173, f. 15r).

inconsistency, much more of this is down to care and attention in preparation of the writing materials. When Aldred's pen is freshly-cut and the gloss written carefully and evenly, his hand is well deserving of the description "neat" (1.17, 1.19). In many other places though his pen is worn or poorly cut, which gives the gloss a rough, scratchy appearance (1.13–1.14, 1.24, 2.54, 4.84, 4.85) and leads to letters getting filled in or poorly made (4.92–4.97, 6.52–6.53, 6.57–6.62, 8.6, 8.7). The way that Aldred trimmed his quill also had some effect on the size of his writing, which differs markedly from folio to folio. What the cut of the quill does not account for though are the significant differences in letter-size from line to line on the same folio. A clear example of this can be seen on f. 242v (2.49–2.52), where the abbreviation sign used for *vel* – or most likely *oððe* in a vernacular context – exhibits marked differences in height, width and weight (this in addition to the stylistic variations, such as treatment of the ascenders and the application of points either side of the abbreviation). While some variation in the size of the writing might, perhaps, be expected between early and later folios over the course of glossing such a large volume, the frequent occurrence of differences in the size of individual letters on the same folio is unusual. (For a sense of how significant the differences in the size of letter-forms can be, see *a*: 4.43, 4.92; *f*: 7.1, 7.2; *g*: 8.9, 8.76; and *wynn*: 12.6, 12.26.) When he wants to, Aldred is quite capable of writing letters of an even size (1.15, 1.17, 1.19). That he does not always write like this suggests that uniformity was not his main priority.

Another highly noticeable variation in the gloss is in the colour of the ink. Nominally, the ink that Aldred uses is black, but the colour often drifts from black to a brownish hue and may appear washed out before the writing resumes in a blacker colour. (See, for example, the sudden ink change at 160rb19.) As has often been noted, Aldred switches to a reddish ink for the closing pages of the manuscript. Despite this deliberate change, there is as wide a variation in the vividness of his red ink as there is with his black (235r, 237v). As with the variation in size, it seems likely that Aldred was not particularly concerned about this, and certainly not enough to expend the considerable effort in careful mixing of the ink and making sure his pen was dipped in ink between words.

That it is possible for a scribe to maintain size and ink colour is clear from the enviable and impressive model Aldred had before him. The writing of Eadfrith, the artist-scribe who created the Lindisfarne Gospels, is even and disciplined, the result of time-consuming attention to detail. Judging by the regularity of the writing, Eadfrith was careful to cut his pen to a consistent width and must have been diligent in supplying it with ink because the richness of the black is remarkably constant over what Gameson (2013: 29) estimates as a line-length of nearly two kilometres. If anything demonstrates the craft of the experienced scribe, it is this. At his most sedate, with frequent pen lifts and attention to spacing, Aldred achieves a neat and consistent handwriting. More often, though, haste appears to have won out over quality of execution.

Of course, what lies behind all of this is the question of presentation. To Eadfrith, a balanced visual appearance was paramount and so he wrote in a disciplined manner, keeping his words parallel to the twin guidelines that he had carefully scored into the vellum. Even a brief look at Aldred's style of glossing indicates that he did not have the same intention. His words are often jumbled around each other (1.14, 1.23, 1.30, 1.31) or written at an angle, flying away from the Latin in a way that suggests the manuscript had not been positioned carefully (1.22). The occasional passages of explanatory commentary that Aldred adds are sometimes written with an awareness of the visual balance of the page, but just as often are squashed around the Latin text. Examples of both of these approaches can be seen on f. 45r (14.1) where Aldred squeezes his commentary at an angle into the gap between the two columns and yet across the page arranges it carefully to the right of the second column (where it has suffered at the hand of the post-medieval binder who trimmed the manuscript). When considering Aldred's attitude to presentation, a significant piece of evidence is provided by the colophon and additional material on f. 259r (18.1). Although Aldred put both thought and preparation into this, even ruling the section in hard-point, he was not able to fit it all into the layout he had planned. We see this on the very first line of the new text that he added, with his Latin and its Old English glosses crashing into each other, meaning that Aldred had to write *sæcvla constitvit* (18.1, line 4) in two stages above the line in order to preserve the single column width modelled on Eadfrith's layout (Roberts 2005: 36). One has to be careful, of course, not to impose a modern aesthetic on Aldred's work, assuming that what might look careless, ill-planned, or untidy to us would have been viewed in the same way by Aldred or his contemporaries. We might also consider the possibility that this treatment of the line, and Aldred's more general practices of layout in his gloss, reflects the design of manuscripts that he had seen. In particular, it is possible that he was familiar with the writing habits found in some Irish manuscripts where, as Parkes (1991: 112) puts it, the "finish of the book" was less important than preserving the information and this led to an appearance of "comparative untidiness". Lowe (*CLA*: II, xvi) notes that Irish scribes often treated the line as if it were "something elastic, not a fixed and determined space which has to be filled in a particular way". That description has much resonance for Aldred's approach. Nevertheless, one does not need to go in search of Irish manuscripts for a model of glossing. Cambridge, Trinity College, MS B.10.5 has an interlinear gloss in Latin that spills into the margins in a manner not dissimilar to Aldred's practices. That Aldred might have known this manuscript is suggested by his use of a system of abbreviations in the Durham Ritual that are, as T. J. Brown (1969: 40) notes, found only in this and one other extant Northumbrian volume.

10 Artistic variation in the decorative capitals

If we are seeking a paradigm for Aldred's variation in letter-forms, we need only look at the Lindisfarne Gospels. Everywhere, there are twists and turns: stylistic reimaginings, elongations of strokes, inventive ligatures, flourishes and, above all, elegant variation in the letter-forms. And yet this variation is subtle and nuanced: one both sees and does not see the differences. Eadfrith switching between Uncial, Half-uncial, Roman capitals, and minuscule is not the equivalent of eighteen computer fonts on the same page, with Comic Sans alongside Garamond, Zapf Chancery, and Chalkduster. Rather, he weaves his letter-forms with their arching backs and reaching feet into the atmosphere of the page with a lithe congruity, variant forms embracing each other both physically and stylistically. Close study brings the subtleties to the surface, something which would not have been lost on Aldred both as a scribe curious about interpreting letter-forms and someone who demonstrably examined the artistic realization of the manuscript in detail. Evidence of this is Aldred's sketching of Eadfrith's geometric patterns (f. 202v), his Uncial pen trial in the top right of f. 122r, his alteration of Eadfrith's Uncial *g*s (see below), and his tracing of the lamb image on f. 137r. These are examples of interventions we can detect; most of his study is, of course, hidden from us. In the following lines I will explore examples of variation in the letter-forms, starting with the decorative capitals, then moving on to the main Latin text.

As an example of the style of letter-form variation in the Lindisfarne Gospels, we can begin by discussing the decorative capitals on f. 29r5–6 (15.1).[13] The letter-forms in the six words (*esset*, *desponsata*, *mater*, *eius*, *maria*, and *ioseph*) vary both from word to word and within individual words. We can see, for example, two variations on the angular form of *s*: the first is constructed of three strokes (like a *z* in modern type, reflected in the *x*-axis) and is found in *esset*, the first *s* of *desponsata*, and *ioseph*. The second has an additional two strokes towards the stem and is filled with a yellow flower motif. Eadfrith elsewhere experiments with this further, creating a seven-stroke s (15.2). A third type of *s*, this time Uncial, is to be found in *eius*, with the round upper and lower curves curling in towards

13 It should be noted that the variation I discuss is typical of the decorative capitals and that there a number of alternative folios which I might have chosen.

the back of the *s* to create an oval proportion, the lower half larger than the top. (Compare this to the elongated shape and symmetry of the *s* in *plures* (15.3).) There are three types of *e*: a Roman capital form in the first *e* of *esset*, *desponsata*, and *ioseph*, with a diamond-shaped tongue; the square second *e* in *esset* is a variant on the Roman capital form, with additional strokes to create balance and a long tongue rising upward forming the top stroke of the *t* with which the *e* is in ligature; and a round Uncial form of *e* in *mater*. In addition, the hook of the *e* in *eius* curves down to meet the tongue of the *e*, giving it a Half-uncial appearance. Finally, there are three different types of *a*. The first of these, the first *a* in *desponsata*, is derived from Roman capitals, and has a wide cross bar on top and an angular connecting stroke which meets the base-line.[14] The second *a* is the Uncial form found in the second *a* of *desponsata*, with its long straight back and connecting stroke angled towards the base-line, and in the first *a* in *maria* with a straight connecting stroke and a curved back with a head that curls down towards the left, ending in a serif. The third type of *a* is the Half-uncial *a* found in *mater* and the second *a* of *maria*. While these two Half-uncial forms look similar, there are subtle differences: the hook at the top of the *c*-shaped back of the *a* in *mater* is flattened out almost to a right-angle and pressed so close to the *t* which follows that it creates the appearance of a ligature-like join, while the hook at the top of the *c*-shaped back of the second *a* in *maria* curves downwards, ending in a serif which both embellishes its appearance and aligns it with the curved heads and tails which finish many of the other letters.

Consideration of the small sample of letter-forms on f. 29r is enough to grasp both the variety and individuality of the letters created by Eadfrith. It is worth looking elsewhere in the manuscript, however, to get a fuller sense of the range of influences behind his style. For instance, the varied forms of *g* in the decorative capitals, include examples of letter-forms derived from Uncial (15.11, 15.12); from Insular Half-uncial (15.13); an angular stylization of Half-uncial (15.14); and Rustic capitals (15.15). To this list I would add the point that Eadfrith creates decorative capitals derived from minuscule forms; for example, a form of *a* with a back that curves to the right, and a lower curve that joins with the border (15.7); a straight back with serifs at either end and a curved connecting stroke (15.8) or a straight connecting stroke (15.9); and in ligature with *n* (15.10). The range of forms for *g* and *a* are enlarged majuscule (Uncial, Half-uncial and Rustic capitals) and minuscule forms; angular forms of the majuscule and minuscule which owe something to the Anglo-Saxon runic letters carved into wood and stone; and

14 For stylistic variants on this, see *a* with a straight connecting stroke (f. 136va3, 15.4); with a serif where the connecting stroke touches the base line (f. 3r3, 15.5); and with a triangular head in place of the crossbar which is typical of *a* in Eadfrith's Roman capitals (f. 27r5, 15.6).

Roman capitals, which are, like the rune-like forms, ultimately derived from an epigraphic context.

11 Letter-form variation in the Latin text of the Gospels

While the decorative capitals make the case for variation well, Eadfrith's main Latin text is, of course, of the greatest significance when looking for immediate influences on Aldred's handwriting. Here too there is a great deal of variation, and while Half-uncial forms predominate, Eadfrith frequently uses letter-forms drawn from Uncial and even minuscule. Such variation is, of course, to be expected in an Insular Half-uncial manuscript. Lowe (*CLA*: II, xvi) notes that the interchangeable use of *d*, *n*, *r* and *s* is a salient characteristic of Insular majuscule manuscripts, commenting that "[t]hey are handled in a diversity of ways in which it is hard to see a design". The final comment resonates with what we saw earlier in Aldred's usage – that there is diversity without detectable design beyond the desire for variation itself. We can see this by looking at Eadfrith's *a*, a letter that, as we saw, exhibits much variation in Aldred's gloss. There are three types of *a* in Eadfrith's main Latin text: Half-uncial, minuscule and Uncial. Half-uncial *a* is the most common type, with the characteristic "oc" shape (16.1–16.4). Minuscule *a* occurs much less frequently than the Half-uncial form; the back is either upright (16.10) or slanting to the left (16.8, 16.12). The top of the back may be level with the bowl (16.6), though often extends to form a distinct head rising well above the bowl (16.12, 16.15). The Uncial form is the least common type of *a* found in Eadfrith's Latin text; the back of the *a* slants to the left, and the bottom of the back stroke often does not descend much or at all beyond the connecting stroke (16.17–16.20). With mixed results, Aldred attempts to copy the Half-uncial *a* (4.46–4.49) and it is possible that Eadfrith's minuscule *a* also had some impact on Aldred's own minuscule (4.50, 4.51). The most significant influence though is not the letter-forms themselves, but the way that Eadfrith mixes them together on a line or a single word; see *mandata* (16.23), which has the three versions of *a* in the same word in a manner comparable to Aldred's practice. (Similarly, one might compare *receperunt* (16.39), which has two different forms of *r* in close proximity.)

The possibility that variation in the Latin letter-forms provided Aldred with a creative model seems a strong one. Beyond this, the Latin seems to have influenced Aldred in other ways also. We know that he studied closely the construction of Eadfrith's letter-forms because there are frequent signs of his adding strokes to the Latin text. Partly his interventions seem to be aimed at removing ambiguity, as is the case with the wedges he adds to Eadfrith's Uncial *g* to differentiate it from *c* (16.29–16.32, 17.9). Another measure he takes to increase legibility is to draw a lower curve to create a *t* where Eadfrith has only a top stroke to represent the letter in final position (17.7, 17.16). Once we watch for Aldred's interventions, there are many, including his splitting up the words of *scriptura continua* on f. 3r and isolating easily confused Latin words elsewhere (17.12); adding abbreviation marks to identify the *nomina sacra* (17.8); and introducing apex signs, again to assist reading (17.13). This in addition to his constant revisions to the Latin text, either by striking out letters (17.14) or inserting those that were missing (17.15). Some of his other alterations seem to be motivated by stylistic interests, such as his addition of a triangular wedge to the leg of *r* (17.9), the wedges he adds to *y* (17.3, 17.4), the short stroke he attaches to the back of *a* (17.6) and a long, curved stroke to another *a* (17.5). On many occasions Aldred attempts to replicate the Half-uncial of the Latin, for example when he inserts a missing word or letter to correct the text (17.10, 2.24). With this close study in mind, it is perhaps not surprising that some of the variants we find in Aldred's gloss appear to be borrowings from, or at least influenced by, Eadfrith's text. Aldred's *f*, for example, occasionally seems to be modelled on the Latin (compare 7.3, 7.4, 17.2); at least one instance of *f*-shaped *y* looks remarkably like Eadfrith's (cp. 7.66, 7.67), as does the finish of the lower-left branch of *x* in 17.1. The attention that Aldred paid to Eadfrith's *y* results in a round *y* in the gloss that echoes that of the Latin (cp. 7.61, 7.62). The Half-uncial *n* which occasionally appears in Aldred's gloss (7.11–7.15) has much in common with the form found in the Latin (7.16) and there are telling examples of imitative behaviour to be seen in 7.17, where Aldred offers a version of Eadfrith's *i* and *n*, and 7.18 where Aldred attempts Half-uncial *n* to supply a letter omitted from the main text. Aldred's low-slung *l* may well betray a similar influence (cp. 2.60, 2.61). The subscript *i*-ligatures in the Latin may also have been suggestive (cp. 3.38, 3.47). Finally, on many occasions, Aldred modelled his layout upon that devised by Eadfrith, as can be seen in 14.2–14.8, where his spacing, vertical writing and splitting of words provides a creative engagement with the text he is glossing.

12 Non-scribal interventions

If we are to fully understand Aldred's interaction with the manuscript he was glossing, it is important to note that his efforts extend beyond those expected of a glossator and towards those of an artist. Thus, Aldred adds a rough line drawing in the top-left margin of f. 202v (17.17), copying what could be seen through the page of the decorative initial *I* of *Iohannes* on f. 203v (17.19). He goes much further than this, however, introducing a sketch on f. 137r of the calf iconographically associated with the evangelist Luke. Aldred's calf is loosely traced from Eadfrith's portrait of Luke on the other side of the folio and, as is apparent from a comparison of 19.1 and 19.2, it is much simpler than its model. Placing the two representations alongside each other as I have done does not favour Aldred's line-drawing. Eadfrith's portrait is alive with colour, from the bright mustard-flower yellow of the nimbi of Luke and the calf to the rust red of the cushion on which Luke sits. The wings of the calf are washed with blue pigment, and the book the calf holds is green with yellow edging. In contrast, Aldred's version of the calf is simplistic: the image is reduced to strokes, with no shading or colour, and Aldred makes basic errors of anatomy, drawing only three legs and misplacing the calf's right ear behind its head. He does not draw the book or the haloes, seemingly using technology of the page to have these present in the form of a show-through. The differences in detail and execution led R. L. S. Bruce-Mitford (1960: 126 no. 1) to observe that Aldred's calf is "drawn in rather uneven and shaky lines and is not the work of a practised artist". Rather than focus on Aldred's lack of artistic flair, we would do better to recognize the sketch for what it is, a scribe's interpretation of the aesthetic element. Aldred hints at this by placing the left foot of the calf on the enlarged letter *h* of *haec*, pointing to the letters which make up the words of the Gospel, thereby drawing attention to the craft of the scribe. Adding the picture in the blank space in the manuscript is another act of completion of something which only Aldred saw as not yet done. In doing so, he brings himself closer to the domain of the original artist-scribe, Eadfrith.

13 Conclusion

In his study of the development of Square minuscule, Ganz (2012: 190) observes that it is scribes, and not scripts, who are at the heart of the story. As I hope to have shown, this notion could not be more appropriate in the case of Aldred. In his gloss we see ninth-century letter-forms, runes and the latest scribal innovations placed alongside each other, seemingly all in the service of variation and an imaginative scribal response to the artistry of the Lindisfarne Gospels. The variation in Aldred's writing that I have discussed here illuminates Aldred's relationship with the manuscript he glossed. Aldred's deep connection to the manuscript's style and aesthetic can be traced in his altering of the Latin letter-forms, his juxtapositioning of the glosses in response to Eadfrith's organization and layout of the text and, even more significantly, in his imitative behaviour with regard to the variation he saw in Eadfrith's writing. As a consequence of immersing himself in the patterning of the manuscript, Aldred is taken back to a much older time, imbibing the Insular impulse for creativity. As much as he is a glossator, he is also an interpreter of that visual tradition.

Within Aldred's script, we witness a clear refutation of the notion that he was a rustic, living in a backwater far removed from the shifts in scribal fashions. My close analysis of the letter-forms shows that Aldred was familiar with both Square minuscule and Caroline minuscule and we see evidence of writing which approaches both in his gloss. This finding is particularly significant in light of the general scholarly agreement that Aldred's script is our most important evidence for Northumbrian handwriting in the mid-tenth century. With so much variation and flirting with other styles, his writing cannot be taken as typical of Northumbria. It is, perhaps, typical only of Aldred, and even then only of Aldred when he is glossing the Lindisfarne Gospels.

The Lindisfarne Gospels was not just Aldred's training ground, it was also his playground, as his experimentation with features of style and variant letter-forms makes clear. When we next see his work, it is in a Latin gloss to Bede's commentary on the biblical Book of Proverbs found in Oxford, Bodleian Library, MS Bodley 819 (see Roberts, this volume: p. 53) and his writing is more restrained, with the most noteworthy variation being the addition of feet to minims about half-way through his interlinear additions. Later in his career, when he came to gloss and write in the Durham Ritual, Aldred was more expert, as is witnessed in his decorative Anglo-Saxon minuscule,[15] but possibly less creatively engaged with the manuscript than he had been with the Lindisfarne Gospels.[16]

15 Examples of Aldred's script in the three different manuscripts may be seen on the DigiPal website at <http://goo.gl/mm5Ejv>.

16 I am grateful to Francisco J. Álvarez López, Marc Michael Epstein, Jane Roberts, Peter Stokes and Louise Sylvester for their encouragement, support and advice at various stages of this paper. In addition, I thank Stella Wisdom at the British Library who kindly helped with image permissions at a crucial juncture. I also acknowledge the financial support of the European Research Council: I was able to pursue this research due to funding of the DigiPal (digipal.eu) project by the European Union Seventh Framework Programme (FP7) under grant agreement no. 263751. Finally, I express my deep gratitude to Sara Pons-Sanz for her patience and kindness throughout the editorial process.

Appendix 1[17]

Distribution of Caroline *a* and open *a* on ff. 5r–5v

Caroline *a*	Open *a*	Caroline *a*	Open *a*
"arun", 5ra2, 5ra5	"alra", 5ra7	"aehteða", 5rb3	"aanu(m)", 5rb11
"fearða", 5ra20	"æfterra", 5ra1, 5ra14	"forma", 5rb20	"aehteða", 5rb3
"fifta", 5ra23	"gelicra", 5ra6	"habbas", 5rb9	"aerest", 5rb20
"forma", 5ra10	"regula", 5ra14	"nioða", 5rb5	"án", 5rb8
"gegead", 5ra10	"ðrea", 5ra15	"regula", 5rb3	"blaccu(m)", 5rb14
"gegeadriges", 5ra10–11		"seofunda", 5rb1	"regula", 5rb7, 5rb21
"regulas", 5ra3–4		"tal", 5rb1, 5rb5, 5rb13, 5rb17, 5rb20	
"sceomaes", 5ra5		"ða", 5rb1, 5rb5, 5rb7	
"seista", 5ra25		"ðara", 5rb13	
"sua", 5ra8			
"tal", 5ra10, 5ra17, 5ra23			
"ða", 5ra1, 5ra3, 5ra4, 5ra17, 5ra20, 5ra23, 5ra25			
"ðrea", 5ra17, 5ra20			
"buta", 5va19	"æfterra", 5va23	"æteawdon", 5vb21	"eadga", 5vb2
"gearn", 5va4	"ceasa", 5va24	"frumma", 5vb16	"fæstnunga", 5v20
"gefundena", 5va20	"gebecnades", 5va21	"geembihtatun", 5vb17–18	"gecunnate", 5vb11
"gesceaden", 5va6	"gemerca", 5va17	"sago", 5vb12	"gemyndga", 5vb1
"gesomna", 5va6	"habas", 5va16	"ða", 5vb13, 5vb16, 5vb16, 5vb21	"hia", 5vb16
"ilca", 5va7, 5va10	"talo", 5va15	"ðinga", 5vb13	"larwum", 5vb22
"sona", 5va7			"papa", 5vb2

17 An electronic version of Appendix 1 and Appendix 2 may be found at <http://www.digipal.eu/blog/aldred/>.

Caroline *a*	**Open *a***	**Caroline *a***	**Open *a***
"stowa", 5va22			"ða", 5vb6
"tacon", 5va8			"ðerhwunadun", 5vb18–19
"talum", 5va5			
"tuia", 5va20			
"ða", 5va22			

Appendix 2

Folio and Line Numbers for the Images

1.1: 5va20–21
1.2: 6ra11
1.3: 125vb7
1.4: 196va20
1.5: 6ra7
1.6: 226ra7
1.7: 5vb1–2
1.8: 5rb3
1.9: 95va3
1.10: 224ra20
1.11: 125vb22
1.12: 7ra24–25
1.13: 176rb21
1.14: 134vb22–24
1.15: 225rb4
1.16: 223ra9
1.17: 222r63–5
1.18: 171ra4–5
1.19: 7vb4
1.20: 225vb20
1.21: 174vb9
1.22: 52ra1
1.23: 85va4–5
1.24: 193vb2
1.25: 171rb18
1.26: 106vb21
1.27: 239vb12
1.28: 86rb21
1.29: 254va3
1.30: 238va17
1.31: 5vb16
1.32: 207rb22–24
1.33: 259ra9
1.34: 193vb9
1.35: 3r7

2.1: 249rb9: ælces
2.2: 7va10: his
2.3: 8ra1: hia
2.4: 171ra6: huoego
2.5: 236rb4: martha
2.6: 99rb19: hæfde
2.7: 220vb8: ł
2.8: 224va1: villo
2.9: 236rb12: gebecnas
2.10: 8rb18: but`te´an
2.11: 99rb24: hæbbende
2.12: 70vb1: his
2.13: 19vb16: hates
2.14: 123vb3: hwidder
2.15: 222va4: hvv
2.16: 7vb9: getal
2.17: 99rb22: hueðer
2.18: 19vb17: lichoma
2.19: 236rb10: hire
2.20: 8ra2: nabbas
2.21: 236rb15: heono
2.22: 20rb5: rehtlic
2.23: 7vb13: lomb
2.24: 7vb14: *fu`l´gora*
2.25: 105ra3: hal
2.26: 20rb4: læras
2.27: 236rb21: vldre
2.28: 249rb2: vnderhebendvm
2.29: 236rb11: broðer
2.30: 232vb21: his
2.31: 259ra11: villo
2.32: 161rb23: blodes
2.33: 259rb13: lindisfearnensis
2.34: 96ra4: leaf
2.35: 200va17: his
2.36: 144rb5: his
2.37: 99rb21: behealdon
2.38: 249rb2: vnderhebendvm
2.39: 99rb21: hine
2.40: 45rb17: bið
2.41: 45ra13: his
2.42: 73ra1: in
2.43: 194ra1: iuh
2.44: 33va7: hælend
2.45: 3r4: neddes
2.46: 4va6: gelæded
2.47: 174vb9: ðæm

2.48: 5rb12: wið
2.49: 242va4: ł
2.50: 242va1: ł
2.51: 242vb19: ł
2.52: 242vb5: ł
2.53: 222rb1: cvðe
2.54: 193vb3: aldormon(num)
2.55: 201vb16: laf
2.56: 156rb16: geleafo
2.57: 123va6: lichoma
2.58: 236rb12: latzar
2.59: 229va14: lichoma
2.60: 70vb3: locadon
2.61: 146vb24: *populo*
2.62: 7vb16: ymbiornas
2.63: 45rb10: iu`e´ra
2.64: 73vb21: is
2.65: 41rb2: in
2.66: 244rb23: ilca
2.67: 20ra13: is

3.1: 34va9: eghwelc
3.2: 44vb10: uoeg
3.3: 37vb1: legeras
3.4: 33vb4: tuoege
3.5: 258ra21: gesegon
3.6: 139vb7: boege
3.7: 108ra7: gesegon
3.8: 110va14: tueg
3.9: 191va19: tuoeg
3.10: 5rb8: eghwelc
3.11: 238ra18: egvm
3.12: 200ra22: su`u´eti
3.13: 20rb1: mettes
3.14: 73va14: settas
3.15: 232va14: gesette
3.16: 121ra10: sedla
3.17: 235vb16: gie
3.18: 178rb8: gif
3.19: 73ra9: god
3.20: 249rb4: tid
3.21: 103vb14: hæl(end)
3.22: 72va13: broeðer
3.23: 72va6: broeðer
3.24: 20rb19: sint
3.25: 34vb1: sint
3.26: 72ra22: penningslæht
3.27: 99rb23: gete`l´don
3.28: 46vb7: findes
3.29: 39vb2: fic beamas
3.30: 169ra10: bið
3.31: 91vb1: hia
3.32: 117rb8: hierusal(em)
3.33: 8ra14: hlifiendiu(m)
3.34: 251rb16: eorodmonna
3.35: 252ra1: anna
3.36: 8rb13: gewordena
3.37: 49rb22: ðona
3.38: 242vb22: mið
3.39: 255rb21: broema
3.40: 259ra24: doemo
3.41: 203va7: gemana
3.42: 175vb17: untyn
3.43: 93ra5: ðone
3.44: 35va4: gesellæ
3.45: 90va3: ðæs
3.46: 221rb1: ðone
3.47: 147va1: *mihi*
3.48: 164ra12: wo`s´anne
3.49: 72rb24: *mo`y´ses*

4.1: 5va24: ceasa
4.2: 142va18: witgena
4.3: 34ra13: moniga
4.4: 61rb14: nallas
4.5: 5rb11: aanu(m)
4.6: 255ra12: groefa
4.7: 161rb1: noma
4.8: 161rb3: aldormon
4.9: 5va20: rimas
4.10: 244rb12: fader
4.11: 174vb20: hia
4.12: 161rb21: fasne
4.13: 201vb9: wuna
4.14: 199vb1: gast
4.15: 199vb3: aworden
4.16: 174va13: gefeall
4.17: 259rb33: earnvnga
4.18: 207vb8: ðegla
4.19: 8va1: hamcuða
4.20: 100va11: wiðerwearda
4.21: 135vb18: f(a/o?)la

4.22: 221rb25: aec
4.23: 105rb5: inhlogan
4.24: 95vb8: andoa/undoa?
4.25: 174va16: ðailco
4.26: 39va16: behaldas
4.27: 3r1: canona
4.28: 259rb8: *mathevs*
4.29: 4va1: ana
4.30: 3va19: sceawað
4.31: 244rb6: la
4.32: 128vb21: aldor(men)
4.33: 8vb18: bocana
4.34: 4ra8: aldrum
4.35: 4ra3: arun
4.36: 223rb11: avorden
4.37: 4va1: ana
4.38: 44va12: hia
4.39: 3r1: ðara
4.40: 3va2: fagas
4.41: 3r5: aefter
4.42: 3r5: alde
4.43: 3r6: bissena
4.44: 99rb14: hlafard
4.45: 186vb19: abrahames
4.46: 117rb19: hua
4.47: 158rb9: ad
4.48: 259rb10: lvcas
4.49: 122r (top right margin)
4.50: 148ra12: ab(raham)
4.51: 122va6: ilca
4.52: 259rb29: ora
4.53: 70rb24: dalf
4.54: 167vb23: aworden
4.55: 9ra13: anra
4.56: 214va1: astag
4.57: 95r9: esaia
4.58: 68rb4: sona
4.59: 207va16: aron
4.60: 174va10: alle
4.61: 191va24: alle
4.62: 5rb20: tal
4.63: 4ra23: apostol
4.64: 125vb22: aras
4.65: 259rb22: aldred
4.66: 259rA28: aldred
4.67: 89vb2: heafud
4.68: 207va13: gebiotate
4.69: 253rb22: ae
4.70: 113ra10: an
4.71: 120va3: alra
4.72: 145vb2: awundrade
4.73: 6vb15: awrat
4.74: 127va4: all
4.75: 6vb1: aet
4.76: 5ra2: arun
4.77: 5rb3: ða
4.78: 5rb3: regula
4.79: 259rb15: allvm
4.80: 125vb1: alle
4.81: 126va19: arð
4.82: 128vb1: astigon
4.83: 204ra10: suindriga
4.84: 157vb12: aeldeuutu(m)
4.85: 214va1: æft(er)
4.86: 97va25: (bottom left margin) að
4.87: 259rA7: eadfrið
4.88: 213vb23: aec
4.89: 254va3: cempa
4.90: 174va9: ah
4.91: 135rb17: f(or)esaga
4.92: 61ra23: ða
4.93: 20rb2: ah
4.94: 102ra11: walana
4.95: 36vb22: singa
4.96: 35ra24: haaldum
4.97: 204rb20: fvluande
4.98: 74va18: onduarde
4.99: 215b4: vserna

5.1: 191va11: mara
5.2: 51r2: arises
5.3: 106vb13: að
5.4: 177ra6: afor
5.5: 167vb16: astyred
5.6: 5va2: sona
5.7: 161rb22: sona
5.8: 245va9: aldormonn
5.9: 190vb1: buta
5.10: 245va19: hiona
5.11: 184va24: monna

6.1: 162ra11: tuoelfo
6.2: 205vb14: f(or)doemendvm
6.3: 86va19 : wedo
6.4: 211vb10: hine
6.5: 201vb5: hine
6.6: 39va11: suiðe
6.7: 207vb23: hine
6.8: 211va10: ne
6.9: 259ra4: me
6.10: 20ra9: lufianne
6.11: 174va23: alle
6.12: 6vb1: aet
6.13: 215vb5: onfoas
6.14: 39va7: rumwelle
6.15: 207vb23: onsoce
6.16: 128vb8: seðe
6.17: 30rb24: me
6.18: 223vb8: hine
6.19: 3r2: niwe
6.20: 3r4: neddes
6.21: 213vb11: gesegn
6.22: 23vb3: ðegna
6.23: 235vb23: genaelle
6.24: 37ra24: heara
6.25: 5vb11: gecunnate
6.26: 33ra1: bebead
6.27: 34vb11: lehteð
6.28: 207vb17: tiberiaðes
6.29: 235vb17: ebolsongas
6.30: 212va17: begeonda
6.31: 222va19: eastro
6.32: 219rb8: earde
6.33: 205ra5: ðe
6.34: 21ra15: hine
6.35: 105va7: haligdoeg
6.36: 85vb13: fæste
6.37: 207vb2: lecvord
6.38: 207va8: brenise
6.39: 212rb8: gefrvgnon
6.40: 97rb5: ec
6.41: 41rb23: onfoeng
6.42: 107rb26: geseað
6.43: 45rb18: eorðe
6.44: 199vb24: iudeæ
6.45: 19vb6: caeseres
6.46: 82vb21: menigo
6.47: 53va7: gewæxe
6.48: 199vb9: aworden
6.49: 39va12: bogehte
6.50: 215vb10: heofne
6.51: 7vb1: eft
6.52: 215rb10: geondsværade
6.53: 35ra23: acueden
6.54: 83va14: feorra
6.55: 68rb3: ego
6.56: 68rb11: sende
6.57: 258ra20: eorðv
6.58: 235vb1: ne
6.59: 34rb24: oehtnisse
6.60: 75ra10: witnese
6.61: 37va16: ec
6.62: 216ra2: hæfeð
6.63: 213vb17: monnes
6.64: 86va16: acueden
6.65: 232va14: gesette
6.66: 240vb6: engel
6.67: 34va9: eghwelc
6.68: 19va21: ðeignas
6.69: 105va10: gewundrade
6.70: 19ra4: enne
6.71: 18vb8: sie
6.72: 215vb16: gefeage
6.73: 205va21: f(or)eðon
6.74: 208ra1: ðirde
6.75: 45rb10: iu`e´ra
6.76: 93ra5: ðone
6.77: 34vb23: cueðo
6.78: 35ra23: acueden
6.79: 34ra20: geneolecedon
6.80: 259rA7: eadfrið

7.1: 4vb22: eft
7.2: 235va20: from
7.3: 222ra4: stefne
7.4: 29vb11: *filium*
7.5: 215rb10: hæl(end)
7.6: 49ra8: hehsynne
7.7: 223va6: am
7.8: 174va19: monnum
7.9: 73va21: monnum
7.10: 241rb12: egvm
7.11: 3r2: niwe
7.12: 222rb14: ane

7.13: 70rb14: hreonise
7.14: 102va14: ðorn
7.15: 109vb18: on
7.16: 100va9: *non*
7.17: 47va14: in
7.18: 151vb7: era`n´t
7.19: 73vb14: nallas
7.20: 122va8: ne
7.21: 244va13: noma
7.22: 73vb8: nalleð
7.23: 143vb22: binna
7.24: 52ra24: ne
7.25: 214rb13: biðon
7.26: 9rb5: tal
7.27: 119vb3: uut(edlice)
7.28: 34vb10: sint
7.29: 217vb7: to
7.30: 3r6: w`u´ritta
7.31: 207vb20: ðriu
7.32: 7vb4: middum
7.33: 19ra22: wundres
7.34: 35rb8: unuis
7.35: 73vb8: uut(edlice)
7.36: 34va6: cuoeðas
7.37: 249ra11: cuom
7.38: 240vb14: avorpen
7.39: 243va19: bitvih
7.40: 214rb3: gevorden
7.41: 207ra12: svæ
7.42: 240vb6: cvoedon
7.43: 240vb14: vt
7.44: 259ra20: svnt
7.45: 252ra8: ðegnvm
7.46: 253ra11: uv`u´nden
7.47: 135ra16: tocymende
7.48: 109ra15: wyrcas
7.49: 179va21: miððy
7.50: 200rb16: miððy
7.51: 200rb22: miððy
7.52: 259ra4: fyl`i´gdvme
7.53: 173ra4: gegyrdedo
7.54: 200va8: miððy
7.55: 173ra10: cymeð
7.56: 222vb24: styd
7.57: 202vb18: byrig
7.58: 202vb5: syn(na)
7.59: 173ra17: gegyrdeð
7.60: 259ra3: ðy
7.61: 6va15: shya
7.62: 204vb20: *mystice*
7.63: 166ra1: wyrðe
7.64: 135rb21: gefyldon
7.65: 256va5: miððy
7.66: 216rb5: cymmeð
7.67: 147vb14: *symeon*

8.1: 96ra2: geworden
8.2: 39ra18: berg
8.3: 106vb1 giuge
8.4: 239vb12: cynig
8.5: 249vb17: æni`g´h
8.6: 102rb8: gedegled
8.7: 44ra18: geeadon
8.8: 4va16: reglas
8.9: 204vb9: fvl`g´uge
8.10: 137r3: gegearuad
8.11: 127vb19: intinges
8.12: 106vb1: giuge
8.13: 157rb20: witge
8.14: 34rb19: god
8.15: 49rb4: gefræpgedon
8.16: 8ra5: god
8.17: 34va14: monigfalde
8.18: 181rb3: hlogon
8.19: 34rb4: gbyes
8.20: 207vb9: gebecnað
8.21: 87va10: halga
8.22: 207va14: ðrovvnges
8.23: 256ra8: byrgenne
8.24: 248vb5: geddv(m)
8.25: 207va10: longvnga
8.26: 179vb11: f(or)abreng
8.27: 35ra17: geworðe
8.28: 253r11: gewvndvn
8.29: 5va12: writting
8.30: 240rb8: gesea
8.31: 259rb24: gloesade
8.32: 226vb21: geliornade
8.33: 83ra8: geongende
8.34: 5rb18: ungelices
8.35: 72ra2: geceigdo
8.36: 4va13: gemendum
8.37: 214va8: astag

8.38:	68vb2: menigo
8.39:	95r4: godspelles
8.40:	85vb1: getreudon
8.41:	135rb1: ænig
8.42:	95vb9: ðuongas
8.43:	107rb26: geseað
8.44:	83va22: somnung
8.45:	65va14: ingeonga
8.46:	99rb25: drygi
8.47:	131ra11: byrig
8.48:	147vb22: nathaning
8.49:	53rb12: dæg
8.50:	88vb2: ge
8.51:	147vb1: sorobabeling
8.52:	35ra17: monigfald
8.53:	35ra21: ingaes
8.54:	3vb24: girihtæ
8.55:	131ra3: fostring
8.56:	88va1: astag
8.57:	34rb1: gaste
8.58:	34rb1: unspoedge
8.59:	136ra24: tuoge
8.60:	103vb24: geflugon
8.61:	54va14: gæs
8.62:	132vb4: ceping
8.63:	199vb4: god
8.64:	199vb1: ofgæf
8.65:	225rb24: gesende
8.66:	174vb9: bigencga
8.67:	157va18: wege
8.68:	63va4: synngiga
8.69:	160ra1: astag
8.70:	173rb20: sgiire(monn)
8.71:	34ra11: geboeta
8.72:	181rb3: hlogon
8.73:	75rb3: gesomnungum
8.74:	50va15: monigfaldnisse
8.75:	80ra5: gie
8.76:	7ra25: geworht
8.77:	95r1: godspell
8.78:	19ra23: georne
8.79:	122va19: gecoreno

9.1:	3r3: werc
9.2:	259rb7: *trinus*
9.3:	113ra1: *sc`r´ibas*
9.4:	121ra11: farmum
9.5:	7va9: gearwas
9.6:	3r4: wyrce
9.7:	131vb10: *desc`r´ibturu*(*m*)
9.8:	259rb8: *scripsit*
9.9:	243vb21: fadores
9.10:	34va15: forðon
9.11:	99rb13: ræstdæge
9.12:	103rb14: recone
9.13:	226vb17: lærde
9.14:	222vb23: gærs
9.15:	222vb15: broðer
9.16:	135vb2: unrod
9.17:	226vb18: wvndradon
9.18:	214ra5: wvndar
9.19:	95va3: gearuas
9.20:	73vb15: eorðu
9.21:	85va10: crist
9.22:	61ra3: mor
9.23:	5rb14: her
9.24:	3vb22: gihverfde
9.25:	202rb13: grapað
9.26:	106vb21: carchern
9.27:	258ra22: veron
9.28:	91rb14: geðreatnum
9.29:	103ra10: færende
9.30:	73vb9: laruas
9.21:	3vb19: grecisc
9.32:	35rb22: broðre
9.33:	255rb24: arimaðia
9.34:	61va1: gefrugnun
9.35:	85va5: carcern
9.36:	8vb8: mercunga
9.37:	238va2: forðon
9.38:	46va17: forðor
9.39:	161rb23: hire
9.40:	35ra18: suiðor
9.41:	38va18: suiðor
9.42:	46va17: forðor
9.43:	110ra22: suiðor
9.44:	39ra20: *porcos*
9.45:	103rb12: gerasenor(um)
9.46:	234ra21: *singvlor*(*um*)

10.1:	153rb16: symbeldæg
10.2:	108ra9: gesprecend

10.3: 259rb23: cvðberhtes
10.4: 113rb6: sona
10.5: 135vb13: losade
10.6: 178vb14: scip
10.7: 135vb18: asales
10.8: 73vb17: is
10.9: 191va10: ðas
10.10: 137r10: lucas
10.11: 3vb16: swa
10.12: 102ra11: loswist
10.13: 73vb16: is
10.14: 252vb7: ðis
10.15: 213ra18: sie
10.16: 34rb1: unspoedge
10.17: 259rb16: sint
10.18: 240rb21: vvnas
10.19: 19vb1: salt
10.20: 134vb22: soecane
10.21: 259rb31: milsæ
10.22: 221rb22: salde
10.23: 73rb18: gidyrstig
10.24: 34rb18: esuice
10.25: 7ra18: saego
10.26: 113vb20: soð
10.27: 109rb7: bissen
10.28: 196ra3: se
10.29: 242vb15: soð
10.30: 191va10: cursung
10.31: 121ra19: hierusal(em)
10.32: 44ra19: gemersadon
10.33: 240va17: gesæh
10.34: 259rb12: *scrip(sit)*
10.35: 191rb17: his
10.36: 108ra1: gesegon
10.37: 37rb15: nallas
10.38: 34rb11: soðfæstnisse
10.39: 207vb17: seofanv(m)
10.40: 249vb2: sint
10.41: 85va4: *misus*
10.42: 108va9: sie
10.43: 134vb6: sinapis
10.44: 259rb28: seo`v´lfres
10.45: 137r8: godspelles
10.46: 223ra11: his
10.47: 19ra14: geleornas
10.48: 119vb15: us
10.49: 242vb17: onfoas
10.50: 122va19: his
10.51: 246ra17: ðegnas
10.52: 182rb1: his
10.53: 242vb2: wyrcas
10.54: 195rb16: his
10.55: 211vb4: væs
10.56: 224ra18: is
10.57: 222rb22: moisi
10.58: 68rb11: sende
10.59: 46va14: husa
10.60: 174rb13: seleð
10.61: 40rb16: huse
10.62: 68rb11: sende
10.63: 113vb24: saet
10.64: 259rb10: *scripsit*
10.65: 259rb8: *scripsit*
10.66: 191va11: maasto
10.67: 18va10: cristes
10.68: 108va9: ðingstow
10.69: 19rb7: crist
10.70: 7va4: cristes
10.71: 145rb17: stigendu(m)
10.72: 34rb1: ofgaste
10.73: 7va8: stefn
10.74: 212vb21: gesiist
10.75: 97vb2: spræc
10.76: 190vb19: ðisses
10.77: 241vb4: sprecend
10.78: 241ra18: spreccend
10.79: 9ra14: f(or)esprecon
10.80: 216ra7: *mundus*

11.1: 239v17
11.2: 97va1
11.3: 109vb3
11.4: 135ra22
11.5: 146rb2
11.6: 142ra18
11.7: 159rb12
11.8: 159rb4
11.9: 7ra18
11.10: 253rb1
11.11: 242vb12
11.12: 259ra2
11.13: 4rb19
11.14: 145rb1

11.15: 259ra6
11.16: 99ra3
11.17: 243vb3
11.18: 108va1

12.1: 125rb8: wæs
12.2: 4rb16: eftniwige
12.3 7ra24: geworden
12.4: 37rb15: wosa
12.5: 88va11: aworden
12.6: 3r6: w`u´ritta
12.7: 3r4: wyrce
12.8: 3r2: niwe
12.9: 86va20: wede
12.10: 74ra3: wæ
12.11: 74va5: wæ
12.12: 157vb1: win
12.13: 86va19: wedo
12.14: 73va3: wuðuto
12.15: 70vb15: wyflo
12.16: 214vb1: gewyrce
12.17: 259ra21: worht
12.18: 6vb15: awrat
12.19: 7va6: woestern
12.20: 159ra1: wæs
12.21: 113vb4: walde
12.22: 222rb16: woenæ
12.23: 241rb3: hwa
12.24: 215vb3: we
12.25: 230va1: worde
12.26: 30ra8: cwomun
12.27: 157va3: weron
12.28: 194ra1: iw
12.29: 238va3: wyrces

13.1: 232va23
13.2: 117vb20
13.3: 215ra19
13.4: 229rb10
13.5: 193rb16
13.6: 200rb3
13.7: 200ra24

14.1: 45r
14.2: 101rb24
14.3: 89va9
14.4: 27r7
14.5: 237rb25
14.6: 90ra1
14.7: 19rb24
14.8: 84rb24

15.1: 29r5–6
15.2: 27r6
15.3: 5vb5
15.4: 136va3
15.5: 3r3
15.6: 27r5
15.7: 27r7
15.8: 136va3
15.9: 95r9
15.10: 95r5
15.11: 27r5
15.12: 27r5
15.13: 19r3
15.14: 3r4
15.15: 29r4
15.16: 203r11
15.17: 137v2

16.1: 101vb17: *petrosa*
16.2: 101vb9: *circa*
16.3: 89rb5: *iudaeos*
16.4: 89va7: *saeculi*
16.5: 19va5: *columba*
16.6: 101vb12: *satanas*
16.7: 257va24: *erat*
16.8: 97ra11: *ianua*(*m*)
16.9: 43ra19: *pharisaei*
16.10: 183va13: *intrauit*
16.11: 180rb23: *erat*
16.12: 195a23: *mea*
16.13: 4ra1–2: *librariis*
16.14: 75rb21: *prophetas*
16.15: 3vb12: *exemplarib*(*us*)
16.16: 211va3: *facta*
16.17: 99ra12: *spicas*
16.18: 43ra11: *misericordia*(*m*)

16.19: 258vb5: *tuas*
16.20: 19va1: *iordane*
16.21: 92va24: *ficulneae*
16.22: 196ra23: *uenerant*
16.23: 65va14: *serua mandata*
16.24: 245ra20: *diligit*
16.25: 90rb4–5: *euangelicae*
16.26: 42ra19: *grgem*
16.27: 81va10: *singuli*
16.28: 90rb25: *intellegendum*
16.29: 20ra9: *diligendos*
16.30: 245ra16: *diliget*
16.31: 245ra2: *diligam*
16.32: 70rb5: *regno*
16.33: 211vb23: *gloriam*
16.34: 169va13: *generationis*
16.35: 160vb1: *ingredi*
16.36: 90rb21–22: *congregationem*
16.37: 131rb2: *graecis*
16.38: 19vb5: *glorificandum*
16.39: 211vb8: *receperunt*
16.40: 133rb24

17.1: 175rb1: *sex*
17.2: 174vb3: ficbeames
17.3: 239vb4: *hierosolyma*
17.4: 227rb23: *hierosolymis*
17.5: 212ra12: *gratia*
17.6: 177va10: *illa*
17.7: 221ra24: *honorificent*
17.8: 95r6
17.9: 223rb8: *regem*
17.10: 234vb8
17.11: 103rb2: hwæt
17.12: 72rb5
17.13: 206vb12
17.14: 178rb15
17.15: 237rb25
17.16: 240va11: *ministrabit*
17.17: 202v
17.18: 203r
17.19: 203v

18.1: 259r (detail)

19.1: 137r (detail)
19.2: 137v (detail)

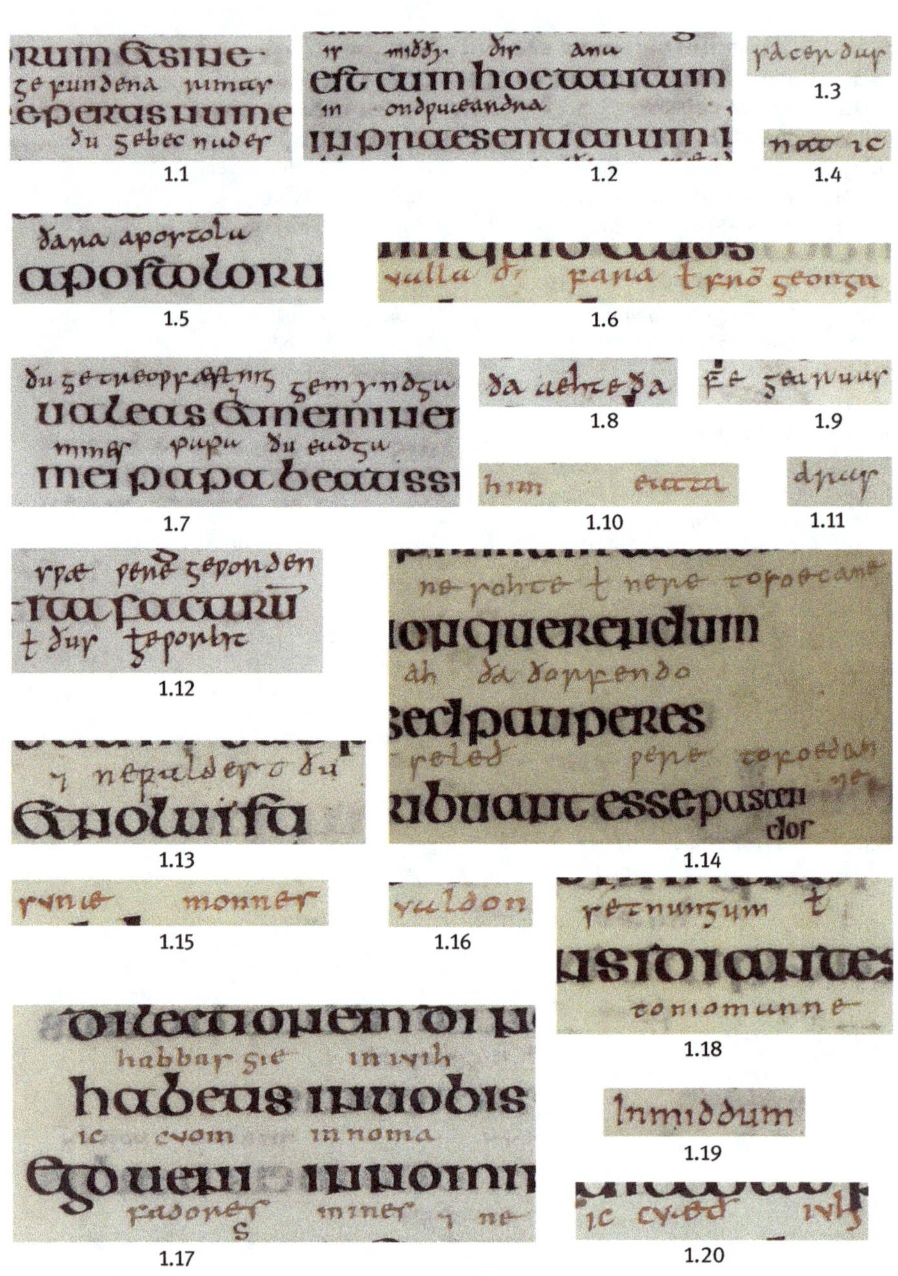

Images are from London, British Library, MS Cotton Nero D.iv © The British Library Board

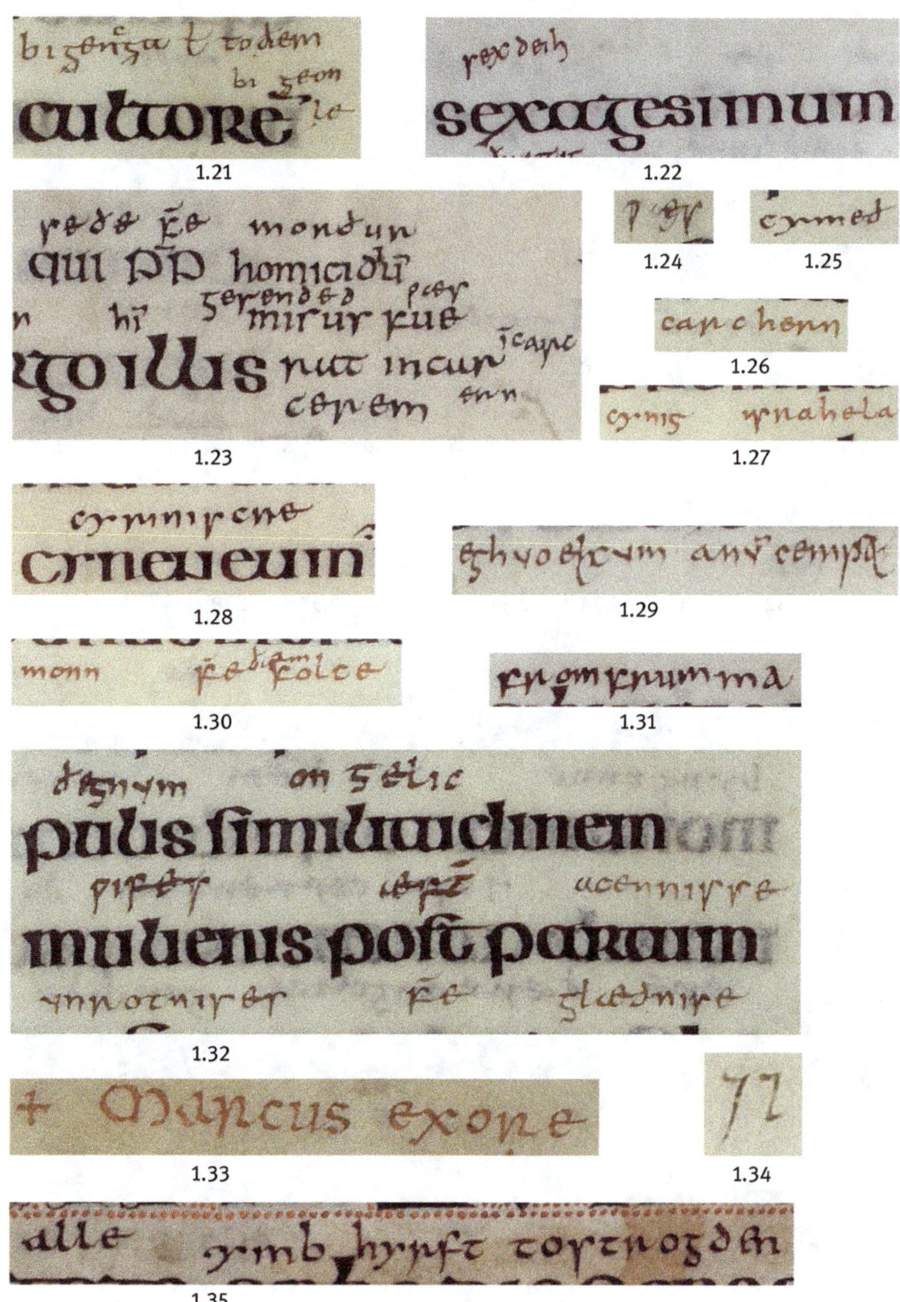

1.21 1.22 1.23 1.24 1.25 1.26 1.27 1.28 1.29 1.30 1.31 1.32 1.33 1.34 1.35

3.1 3.2 3.3 3.4 3.5 3.6 3.7 3.8 3.9 3.10
3.11 3.12 3.13 3.14 3.15 3.16 3.17 3.18 3.19 3.20
3.21 3.22 3.23 3.24 3.25 3.26 3.27
3.28 3.29 3.30 3.31 3.32 3.33
3.34 3.35 3.36 3.37 3.38 3.39 3.40 3.41
3.42 3.43 3.44 3.45 3.46 3.47*
3.48 3.49

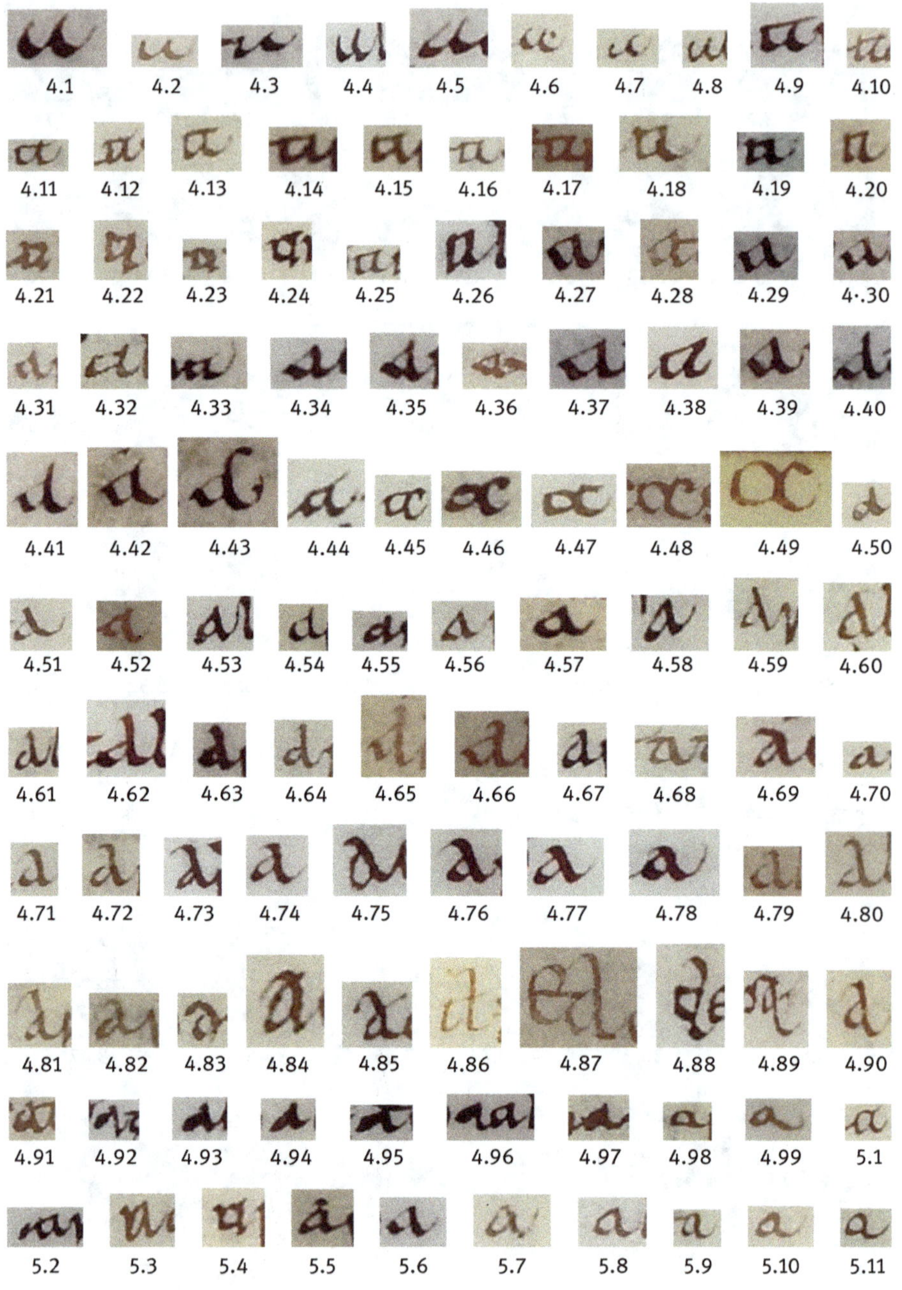
4.1 4.2 4.3 4.4 4.5 4.6 4.7 4.8 4.9 4.10
4.11 4.12 4.13 4.14 4.15 4.16 4.17 4.18 4.19 4.20
4.21 4.22 4.23 4.24 4.25 4.26 4.27 4.28 4.29 4.30
4.31 4.32 4.33 4.34 4.35 4.36 4.37 4.38 4.39 4.40
4.41 4.42 4.43 4.44 4.45 4.46 4.47 4.48 4.49 4.50
4.51 4.52 4.53 4.54 4.55 4.56 4.57 4.58 4.59 4.60
4.61 4.62 4.63 4.64 4.65 4.66 4.67 4.68 4.69 4.70
4.71 4.72 4.73 4.74 4.75 4.76 4.77 4.78 4.79 4.80
4.81 4.82 4.83 4.84 4.85 4.86 4.87 4.88 4.89 4.90
4.91 4.92 4.93 4.94 4.95 4.96 4.97 4.98 4.99 5.1
5.2 5.3 5.4 5.5 5.6 5.7 5.8 5.9 5.10 5.11

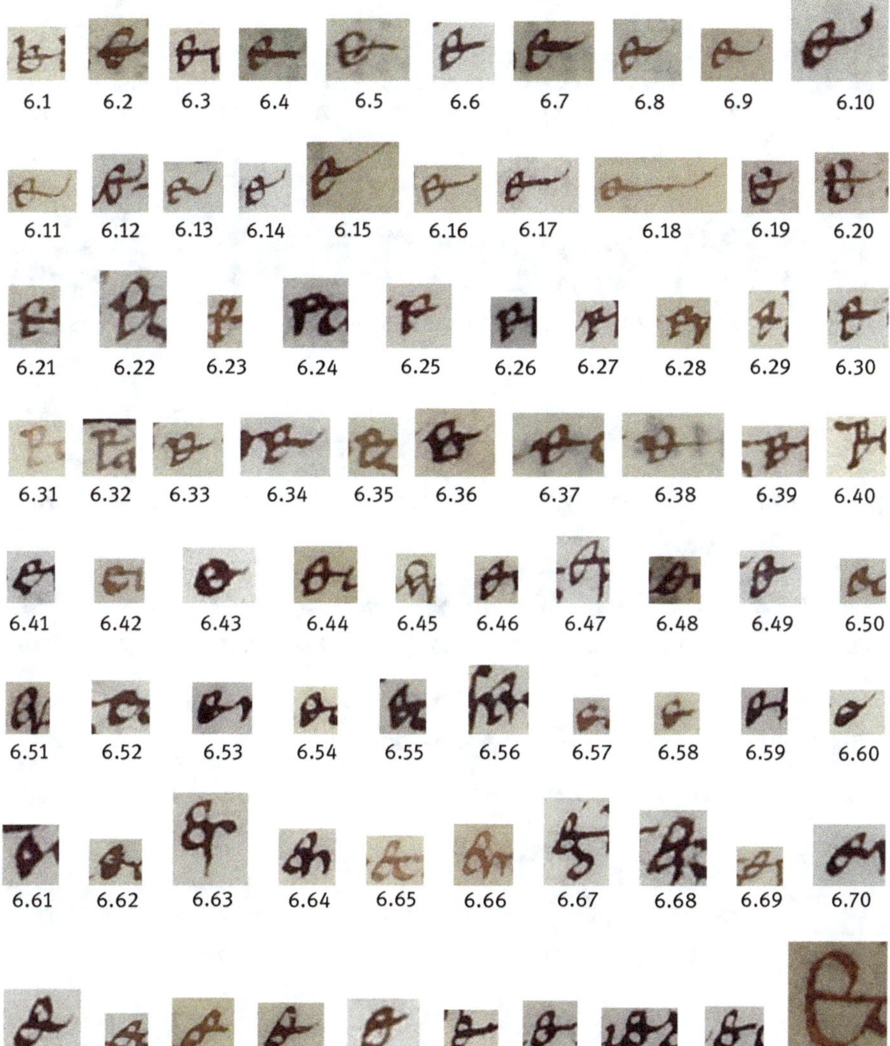
6.1 6.2 6.3 6.4 6.5 6.6 6.7 6.8 6.9 6.10
6.11 6.12 6.13 6.14 6.15 6.16 6.17 6.18 6.19 6.20
6.21 6.22 6.23 6.24 6.25 6.26 6.27 6.28 6.29 6.30
6.31 6.32 6.33 6.34 6.35 6.36 6.37 6.38 6.39 6.40
6.41 6.42 6.43 6.44 6.45 6.46 6.47 6.48 6.49 6.50
6.51 6.52 6.53 6.54 6.55 6.56 6.57 6.58 6.59 6.60
6.61 6.62 6.63 6.64 6.65 6.66 6.67 6.68 6.69 6.70
6.71 6.72 6.73 6.74 6.75 6.76 6.77 6.78 6.79 6.80

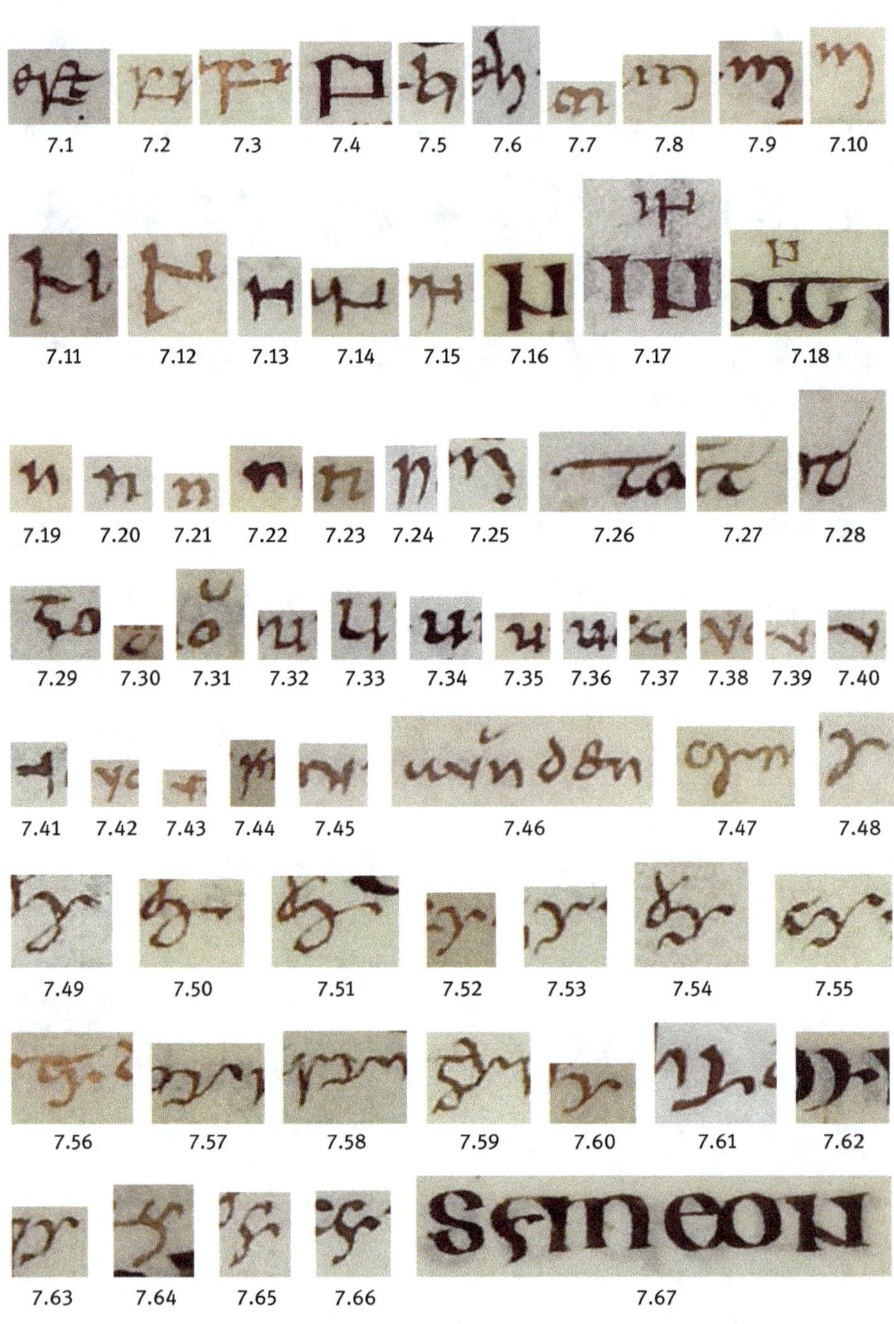
7.1 7.2 7.3 7.4 7.5 7.6 7.7 7.8 7.9 7.10
7.11 7.12 7.13 7.14 7.15 7.16 7.17 7.18
7.19 7.20 7.21 7.22 7.23 7.24 7.25 7.26 7.27 7.28
7.29 7.30 7.31 7.32 7.33 7.34 7.35 7.36 7.37 7.38 7.39 7.40
7.41 7.42 7.43 7.44 7.45 7.46 7.47 7.48
7.49 7.50 7.51 7.52 7.53 7.54 7.55
7.56 7.57 7.58 7.59 7.60 7.61 7.62
7.63 7.64 7.65 7.66 7.67

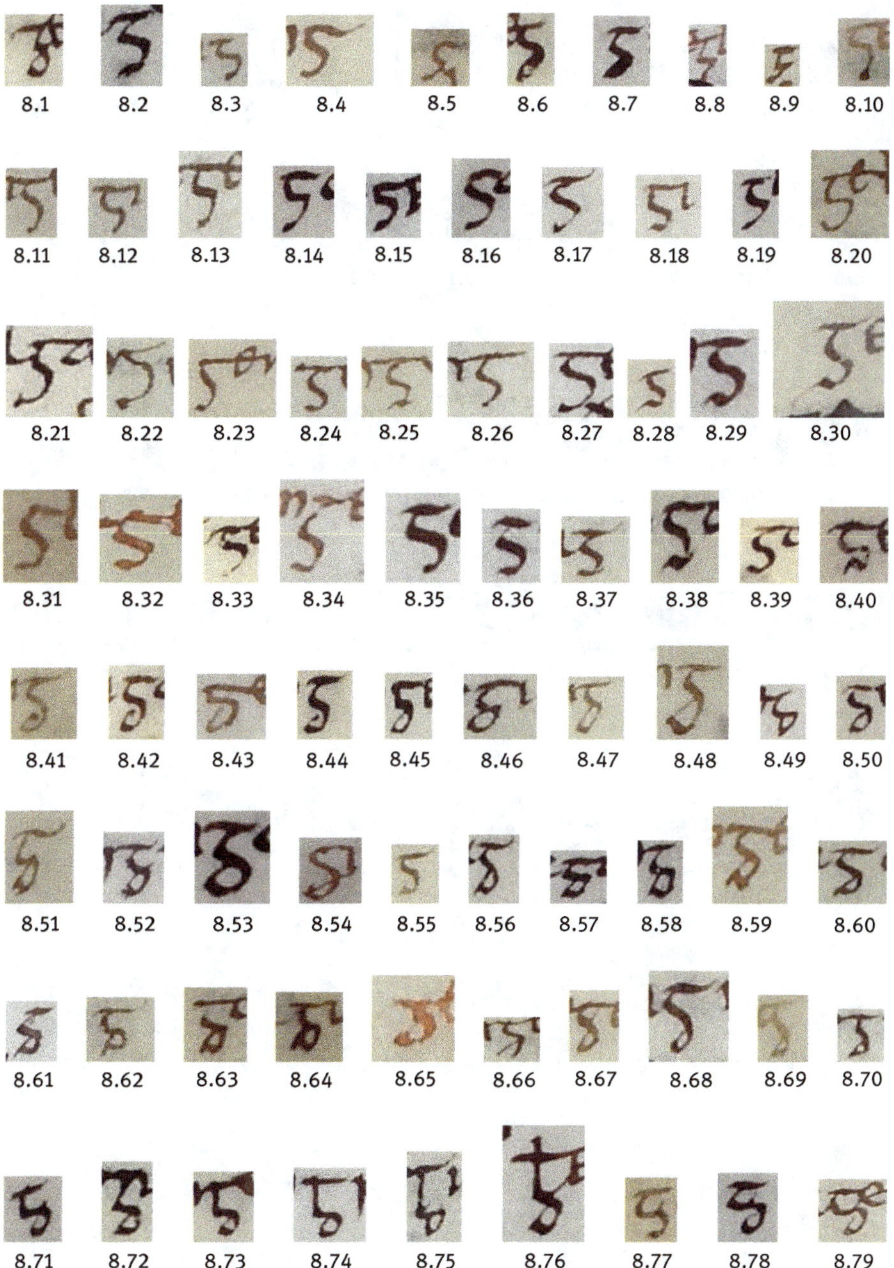
8.1 8.2 8.3 8.4 8.5 8.6 8.7 8.8 8.9 8.10
8.11 8.12 8.13 8.14 8.15 8.16 8.17 8.18 8.19 8.20
8.21 8.22 8.23 8.24 8.25 8.26 8.27 8.28 8.29 8.30
8.31 8.32 8.33 8.34 8.35 8.36 8.37 8.38 8.39 8.40
8.41 8.42 8.43 8.44 8.45 8.46 8.47 8.48 8.49 8.50
8.51 8.52 8.53 8.54 8.55 8.56 8.57 8.58 8.59 8.60
8.61 8.62 8.63 8.64 8.65 8.66 8.67 8.68 8.69 8.70
8.71 8.72 8.73 8.74 8.75 8.76 8.77 8.78 8.79

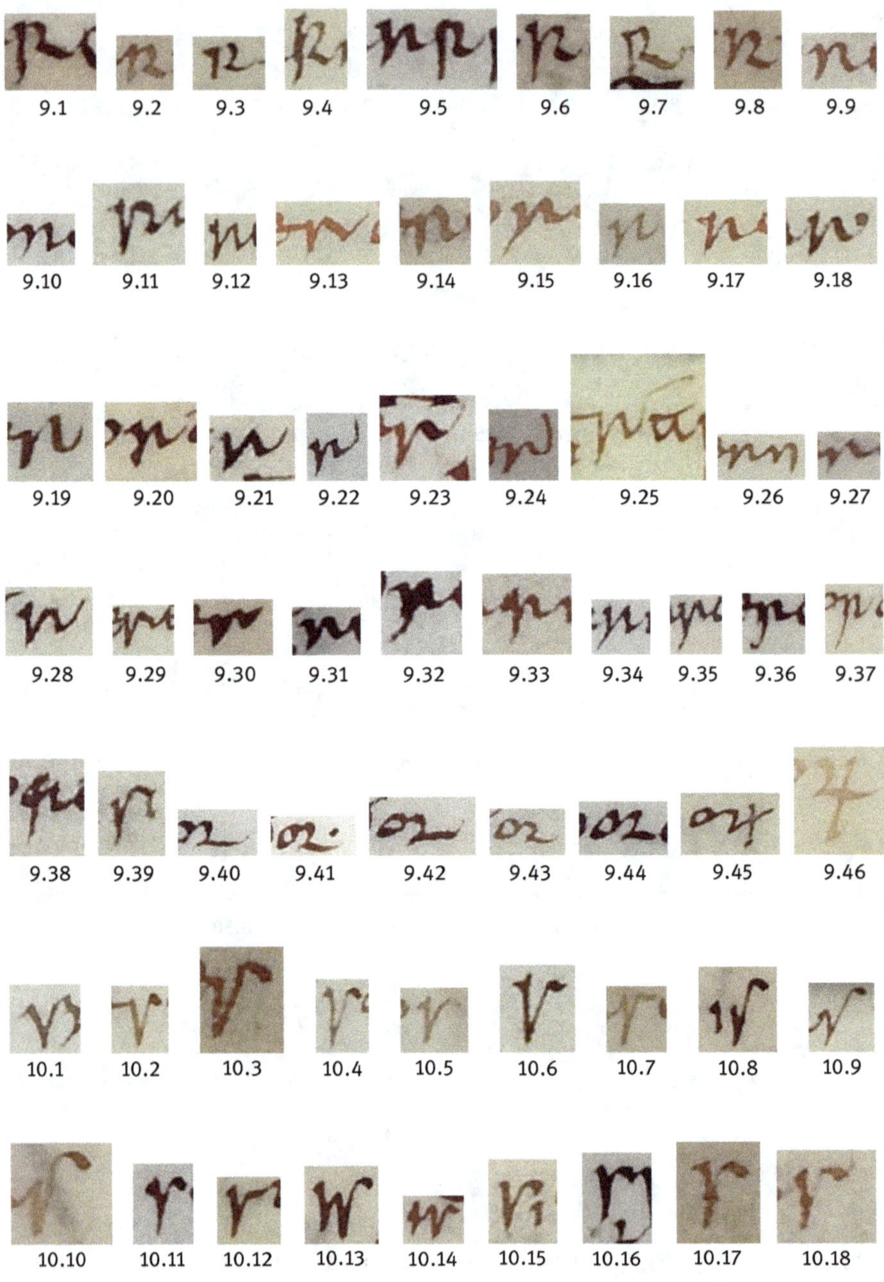
9.1
9.2
9.3
9.4
9.5
9.6
9.7
9.8
9.9
9.10
9.11
9.12
9.13
9.14
9.15
9.16
9.17
9.18
9.19
9.20
9.21
9.22
9.23
9.24
9.25
9.26
9.27
9.28
9.29
9.30
9.31
9.32
9.33
9.34
9.35
9.36
9.37
9.38
9.39
9.40
9.41
9.42
9.43
9.44
9.45
9.46
10.1
10.2
10.3
10.4
10.5
10.6
10.7
10.8
10.9
10.10
10.11
10.12
10.13
10.14
10.15
10.16
10.17
10.18

10.19 10.20 10.21 10.22 10.23 10.24 10.25 10.26 10.27 10.28

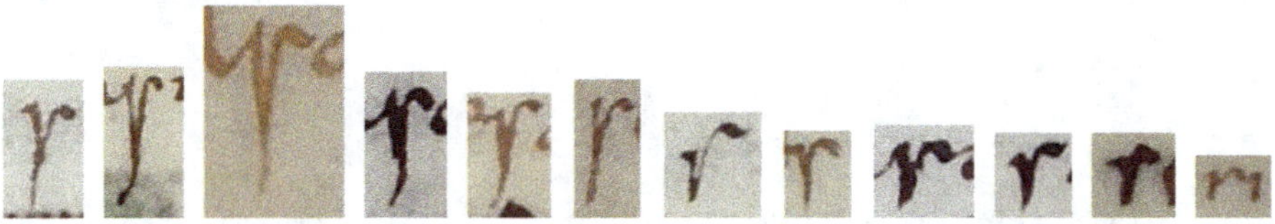

10.29 10.30 10.31 10.32 10.33 10.34 10.35 10.36 10.37 10.38 10.39 10.40

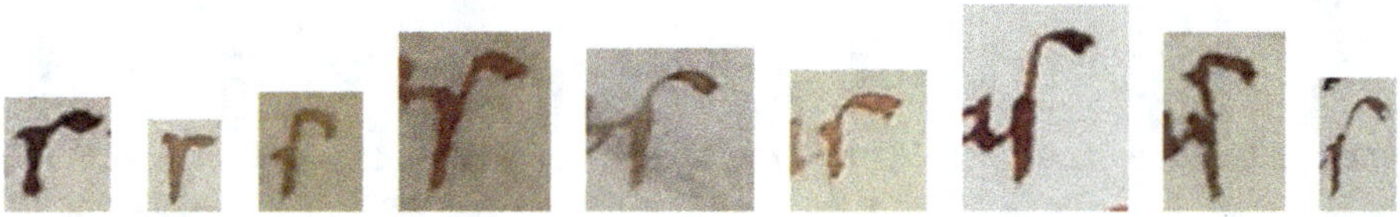

10.41 10.42 10.43 10.44 10.45 10.46 10.47 10.48 10.49

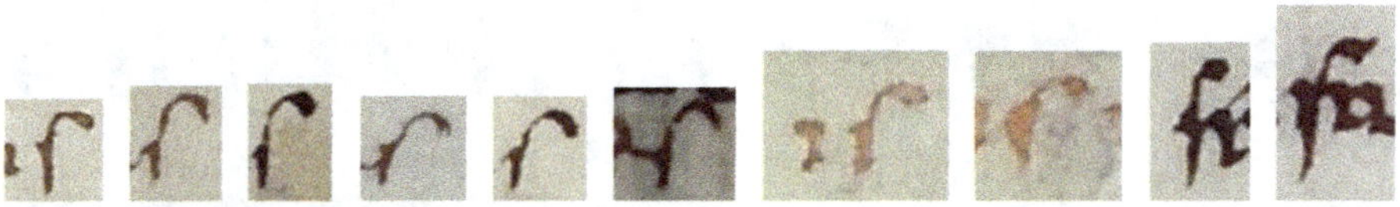

10.50 10.51 10.52 10.53 10.54 10.55 10.56 10.57 10.58 10.59

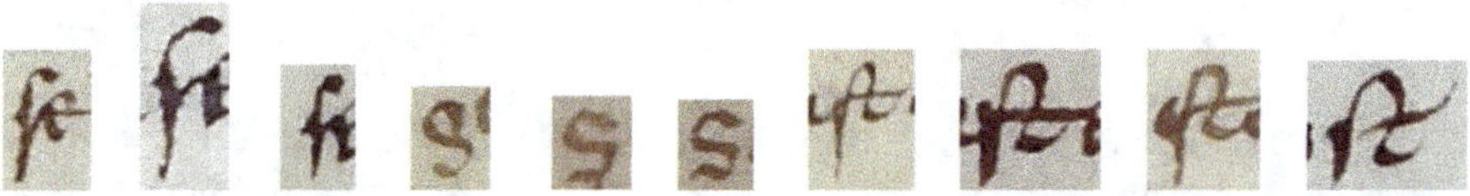

10.60 10.61 10.62 10.63 10.64 10.65 10.66 10.67 10.68 10.69

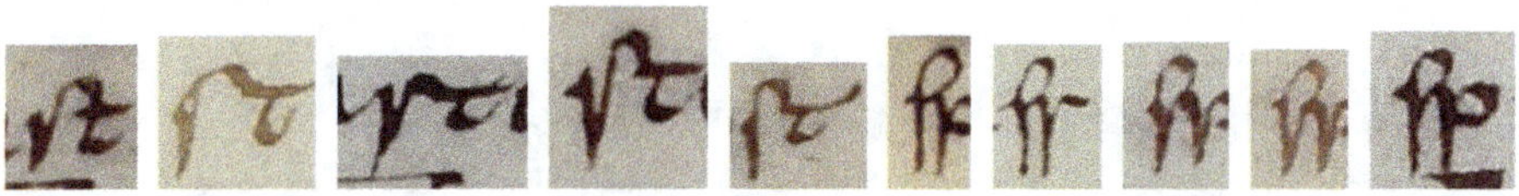

10.70 10.71 10.72 10.73 10.74 10.75 10.76 10.77 10.78 10.79

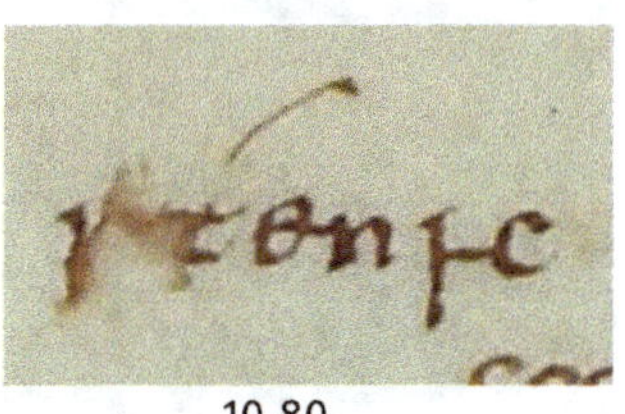

10.80

10.81

BL, MS Cotton Vitellius A. xv, f. 49v

10.82

CCCC, MS 173, f. 26r

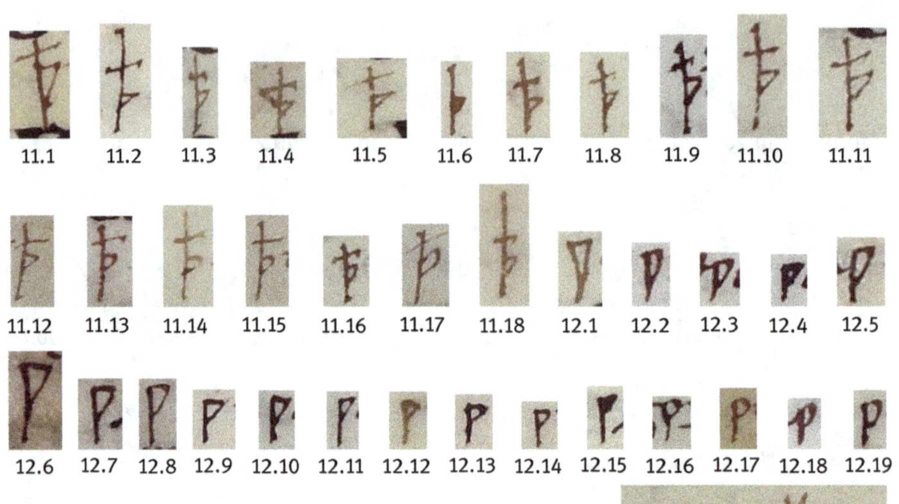

11.1 11.2 11.3 11.4 11.5 11.6 11.7 11.8 11.9 11.10 11.11

11.12 11.13 11.14 11.15 11.16 11.17 11.18 12.1 12.2 12.3 12.4 12.5

12.6 12.7 12.8 12.9 12.10 12.11 12.12 12.13 12.14 12.15 12.16 12.17 12.18 12.19

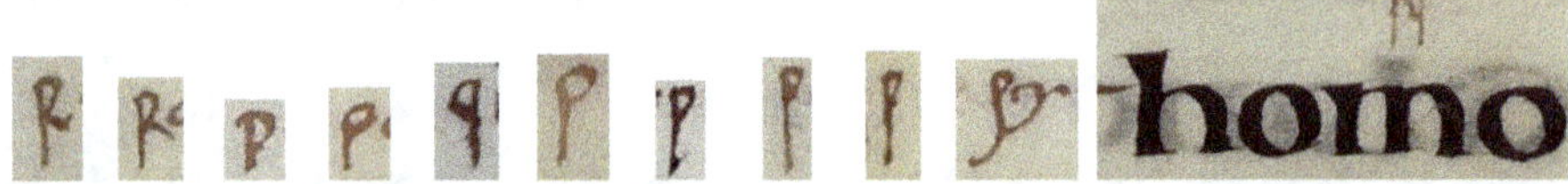

12.20 12.21 12.22 12.23 12.24 12.25 12.26 12.27 12.28 12.29 13.1

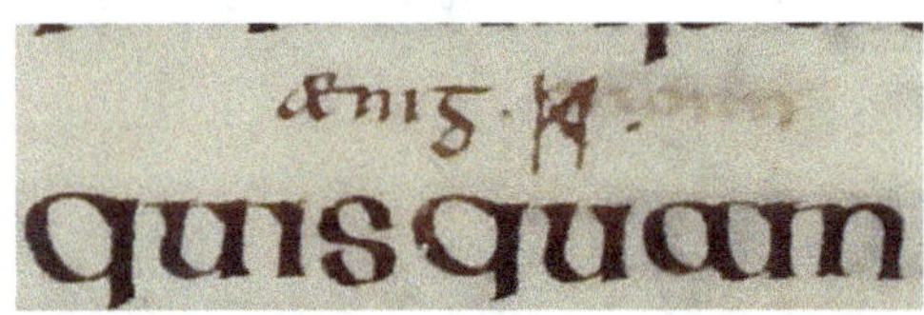

13.2 13.3

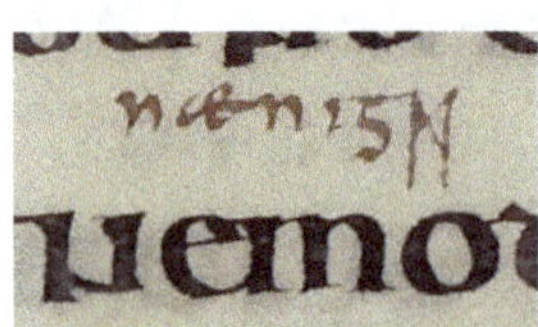

13.4 13.5

13.6

13.7

14.1

14.2 14.3 14.4 14.5 14.6 14.7 14.8

15.1

15.2  15.3  15.4  15.5  15.6  15.7

15.8 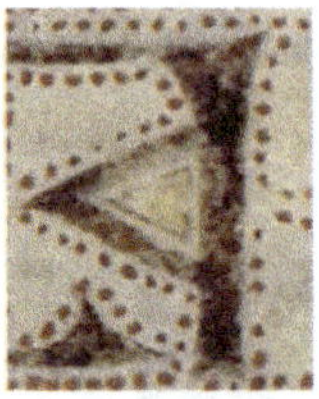 15.9  15.10  15.11 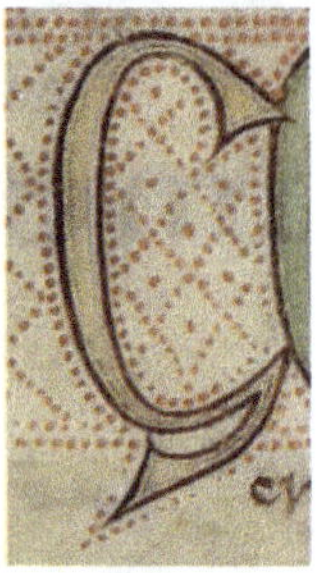 15.12

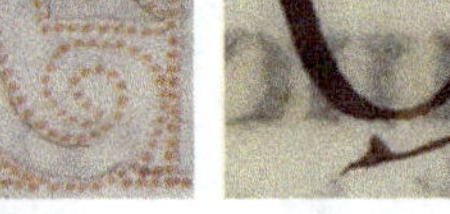

15.13  15.14 15.15 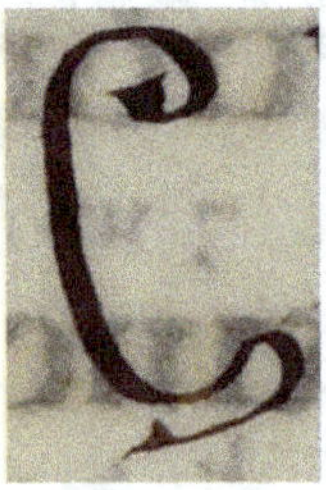 15.16 15.17

16.1 16.2 16.3 16.4 16.5 16.6 16.7

16.8 16.9 16.10 16.11 16.12 16.13 16.14 16.15

16.16 16.17 16.18 16.19 16.20 16.21 16.22

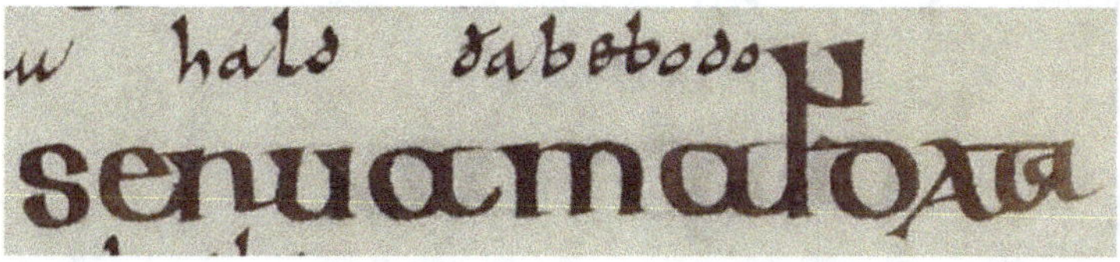

16.23

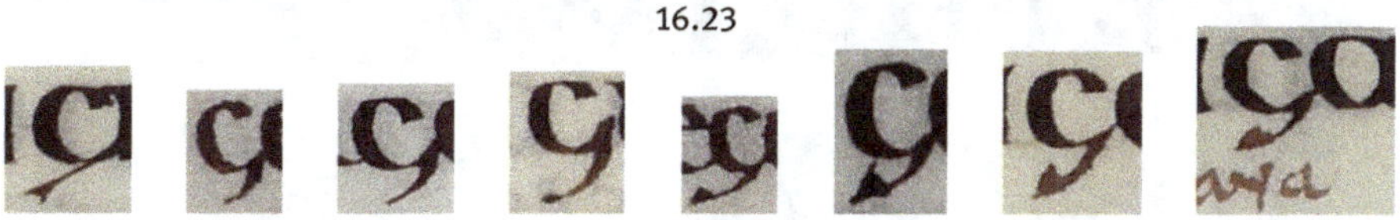

16.24 16.25 16.26 16.27 16.28 16.29 16.30 16.31

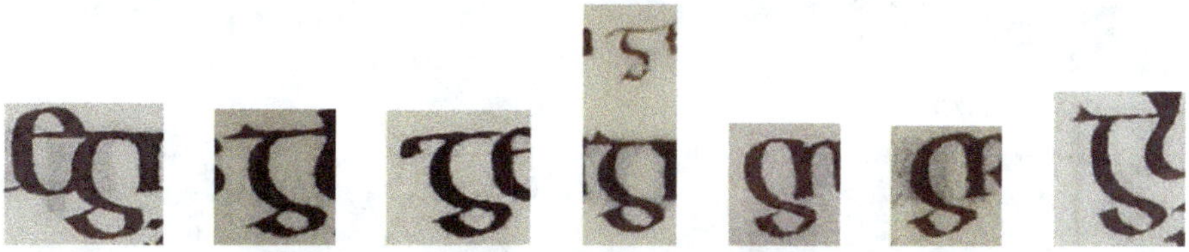

16.32 16.33 16.34 16.35 16.36 16.37 16.38

16.39

16.40

17.1 17.2 17.3 17.4

17.5 17.6 17.7

17.8 17.9

17.10 17.11

17.12 17.13

17.14 17.15 17.16

17.17 17.18 17.19

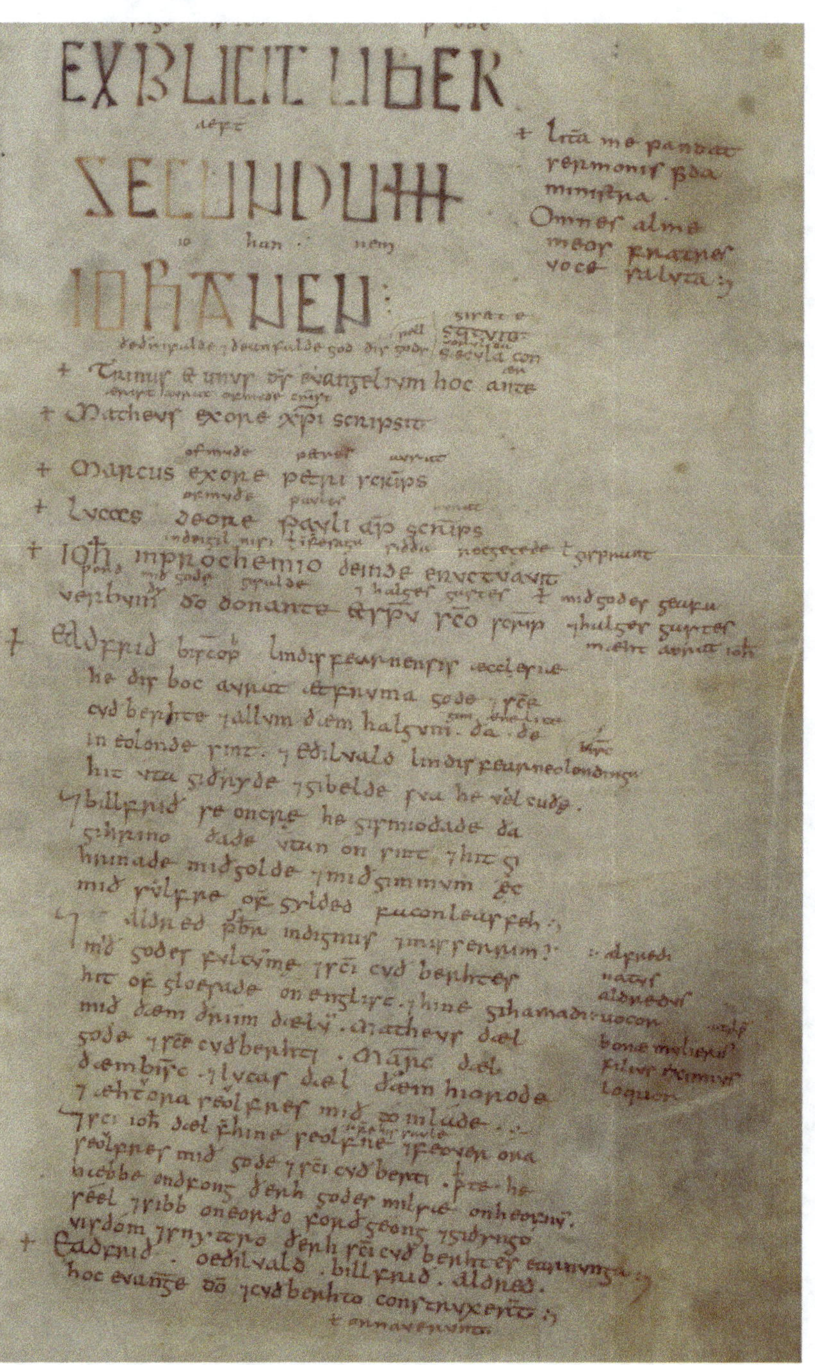

18.1: detail of f. 259r: Aldred's colophon

19.1: detail of f. 137r: Aldred's tracing of Luke's calf

19.2: detail of f. 137v: portrait of the Evangelist Luke (reversed in vertical axis)

Part II: **The Language of the Gloss**

Robert McColl Millar

At the Forefront of Linguistic Change: The Noun Phrase Morphology of the Lindisfarne Gospels

Abstract: This paper considers the major typological changes which affected late Old English and early Middle English, with particular reference to noun phrase inflectional morphology. It demonstrates that many of the large scale linguistic developments found in the inherited system in early Middle English texts were already present in the English gloss to the Lindisfarne Gospels.

1 The determiner systems of the English gloss to the Lindisfarne Gospels: evidence for change

It will be the contention of this paper that the noun phrase morphology realized in the English gloss to the Lindisfarne Gospels represents an early stage in a series of developments which would alter the typological associations of the language over the next four hundred years. The paper will illustrate these changes both in that text and in early Middle English materials.[1]

It could, for instance, be argued that the grammatical gender-assignment patterns of the English gloss to the Lindisfarne Gospels are more complex than those of its contemporary southern equivalents, a point which, paradoxically, provides early evidence for simplification of the inherited system (a point recognized as early as Carpenter's analysis of 1910). While most of the time nouns are assigned the "correct" gender-expressing morphology and determiners, on a minority of occasions other relationships are realized which historically would not normally be expressed in that way in those contexts. This paper will consider these apparent "infelicities" in relation to both the inflectional system of the text itself and the history of the English language as a whole; particular interest will be taken in the use of the "simple demonstrative" paradigm.[2]

---

1 Some parts of these changes are covered with considerable success by van Kemenade (1987), Allen (1999) and most recently van Gelderen (2011). Their findings are not immediately different from those discussed here, although their focus may be more general than is found in this paper.

2 For discussion of these features in relation to the collapse of the grammatical gender system see Jones (1967a, 1967b, 1983, and 1987). Curzan (2003) provides a fascinating portrayal of

This distribution of new usage is not random, however; patterns are discernible. Some feminine nouns are occasionally found in dative case singular contexts with (in the gloss) "ðæm", historically associated with neuter or masculine nouns. Examples of this change in associations can be found in

(1) Matthew 21.24

L	*respondens iesus dixit eis interrogabo uos et ego unum sermonem quem si dixeritis mihi et ego uobis dicam in qua potestate haec facio*
MtGl (Li) 21.24	geonduearde ðe hælend cueð ðæm ł him ic fregno iuih ⁊ ic an word ðone gie cueden me ⁊ ic iuh sægo in **ðæm** mæht ł in huelc mæht ðas ic doa
Trans.	'Jesus answering, said to them: I also will ask you one word, which if you shall tell me, I will also tell you by what authority I do these things'[3]

as well as

(2) Luke 17.34

L	*Dico uobis illa nocte erunt duo in tecto uno unus assumetur et alter relinquetur*
LkGl (Li) 17.34	ic cuoeðo iuh **ðæm næht** biðon tuoege in hrofe anum an genumen bið ⁊ oðer forleten bið
Trans.	'I say to you: in that night there shall be two men in one bed; the one shall be taken, and the other shall be left'.

Two nouns dominate this apparent change. These are OE *tid* 'time', as found in

(3) Matthew 15.28

L	*tunc respondens iesus ait illi o mulier magna est fides tua fiat tibi sicut uis et sanata est filia illius ex illa hora*
MtGl (Li) 15.28	ða onduearde ðe hælend cueð him la wif micil is leafa ł lufa ðin sie ðe suæ ðu wilt ⁊ gehæled wæs dohter ðæs ł hire **of ðæm tid**

change in gender systems across the history of English which might be claimed to be flawed since it equates grammatical gender distinctions with natural, sex triggered differences.

3 The title abbreviations and editions of the Old English texts mentioned in this paper are those employed by the *Dictionary of Old English Web Corpus* (hereafter *DOEC*). The translations are from the *Douay-Rheims* translation.

Trans. ‘Then Jesus answering, said to her: O woman, great is thy faith: be it done to thee as thou wilt: and her daughter was cured from that hour’

and

(4) Mark 13.11

L *Et cum duxerint uos tradentes nolite praecogitare quid loquamini sed quod datum uobis fuerit in illa hora id loquimini non enim estis uos loquentes sed spiritus sanctus*

MkGl (Li) 13.11 ⁊ miððy hia gelædas iuih sellende nælle gie foreðence huæt gie spreca ah ł hwoeðre þæt gesald iuh bið **on ðæm tid** þæt gie sprecca ne forðon biðon iuih spreccendo ah gaas halig

Trans. ‘And when they shall lead you and deliver you up, be not thoughtful beforehand what you shall speak; but whatsoever shall be given you in that hour, that speak ye. For it is not you that speak, but the Holy Ghost’

as well as OE *byrgen* ‘burial place, tomb’, as found in

(5) Mark 16.8

L *At illae exeuntes fugerunt de monumento inuaserat enim eas tremor et pauor et nemini quicquam dixerunt timebant enim*

MkGl (Li) 16.8 soð ða ilco ðona foerdo flugon **of ðæm byrgen** forcuom forðon hia ondo ł ⁊ fyrhto ł ⁊ ne ænigum menn gecuoedon ondreardon forðon

Trans. ‘But they going out, fled from the sepulchre. For a trembling and fear had seized them: and they said nothing to any man; for they were afraid’

and

(6) John 20.1

L *Una autem sabbati maria magdalene uenit mane cum athuc tenebrae essent ad monumentum et uidet lapidem sublatum a monumento*

JnGl (Li) 20.1 an uutedlice ðara dagana ł <synnadagana>< ł ><sunnadagana> maria ðio magðalenisca cuom armorgen miððy ða gett ł ðiostro uerun **to ðæm byrgenn** ⁊ gesaeh ł þæt stan genumen ł auęled **of ðæm byrgenne** ł from ðæm

Trans. 'And on the first day of the week, Mary Magdalen cometh early, when it was yet dark, unto the sepulchre; and she saw the stone taken away from the sepulchre'.

Until the 1960s, when Charles Jones began to publish ground-breaking work on the breakdown of grammatical gender during the late Old English period, scholars often interpreted usage of this type as *Genuswechsel* 'gender change', rather than *Genusverlust* 'gender loss' (for an intelligent use of this type of argument, see Ross 1936 and 1937). In other words, rather than seeing examples of this type as inherently anomalous or as evidence for the spread of a system where gender was ceasing to have a meaningful position within the rules of English morphological concord, scholars who favoured this position perceived evidence of an evolving but still intact gender system.

There are problems with such a viewpoint, however. The first is teleological: we know that grammatical gender *did* cease to be a viable noun classification feature in the (not too distant) future history of the language. Usage of this type appears to represent the beginnings of such a process. More importantly, there is evidence that the glossator himself might have struggled with formal assignment of gender- and case-sensitive morphology:

(7) Matthew 9.22

L *at iesus conuersus et uidens eam dixit confide filia fides tua te saluam fecit et salua facta est mulier ex illa hora*

MtGl (Li) 9.22 soð ðe hælend gecerde ⁊ gesæh ða ł hia cueð getriu ł gelef dohter gleafo ðin ðec hal dyde ⁊ hal geworden wæs wif **of ðæm ł ðær tið**

Trans. 'But Jesus turning and seeing her, said: Be of good heart, daughter, thy faith hath made thee whole. And the woman was made whole from that hour'.

On this occasion both the historical and innovative determiners are realized. Does this distribution mean that Aldred had two competing systems in his head? Was the historical system derived primarily from his written models?

A further significant feature in the gloss revolves around the use of *þæt* beyond nominative and accusative contexts with members of the historical neuter gender-class. Thus while *þæt* is regularly employed in these historical contexts, it can now also be used with masculine nouns, as with

(8) Mark 11.13

L *cumque uidisset a longe ficum habentem folia uenit si quid forte inueniret in ea et cum uenisset ad eam nihil inuenit praeter folia non enim erat tempus ficorum*

MkGl (Li) 11.13 ⁊ miððy gesæh fearra **þæt ficbeam** hæbbende leafo cuom gif huæt eaða ł woenunga gemitte in ðær ł on ðæm ⁊ miððy gemitte ł gecuome to ðær ilca noht infand buta leafo ne forðon wæs tid ðara ficbeama

Trans. 'And when he had seen afar off a fig tree having leaves, he came if perhaps he might find any thing on it. And when he was come to it, he found nothing but leaves. For it was not the time for figs'

or

(9) Luke 8.24

L *accedentes autem suscitauerunt eum dicentes praeceptor perimus at ille surgens increpauit uentum et tempestatem aquae et cessauit et facta est tranquillitas*

LkGl (Li) 8.24 geneolecton uutedlice awoehton hine cuoeðende ł cwoedon la haesere we losaiað soðlice he aras geðreade **þæt wind** ⁊ hroeðnise ł unwoeder ðæs wætres ⁊ geblann ⁊ aworden wæs ðio smyltnise

Trans. 'And they came and awaked him, saying: Master, we perish. But he arising, rebuked the wind and the rage of the water; and it ceased, and there was a calm'

as well as

(10) John 21.9

L *Ut ergo discenderunt in terram uiderunt prunas positas et piscem superpositum et panem*

JnGl (Li) 21.9 þætte ł miððy uutedlice ofstigun on eorðu gesegon gloedi asettedo ueron ⁊ **ðone** fisc ofersetted ⁊ **þæt laf**

Trans. 'As soon then as they came to land, they saw hot coals lying, and a fish laid thereon, and bread'.

It is noteworthy that while the Lindisfarne gloss has *þæt* with *(h)laf*, *fisc* in the same phrase triggers the "correct" determiner, thus demonstrating how variable the system had become.

Þæt can also be used with members of the historical feminine gender class, such as

(11) Matthew 18.30

L *ille autem noluit sed abiit et misit eum in carcerem donec redderet debitum*

MtGl (Li) 18.30 ðe ł he uutetlice nalde ah geeade ⁊ sende hine in carcern wið he gulde **þæt scyld**

Trans. 'And he would not: but went and cast him into prison, till he paid the debt'

or

(12) John 11.6

L *ut ergo audiuit quod infirmabatur tunc quidem mansit in eodem loco duobus diebus*

JnGl (Li) 11.6 þætte uutedlice ł geherde forðon ł þætte uuntrymig uæs ða ł ðonne fæstlice geunade **in ðæt ilca stoue** ł **styde** twæm dagum

Trans. 'When he had heard therefore that he was sick, he still remained in the same place two days'

where, interestingly, members of both the feminine and masculine gender classes appear to be modified (as alternates) by the same non-historical determiner.

In the past there have been attempts either to apply a *Genuswechsel* interpretation for this set of changes or one based on *neutralization* (see, in particular, Ross 1936, and 1937). This second position – essentially a development of the former – assumes that there was a general drift of inanimate or nonhuman entities towards the neuter gender as part of an ongoing replacement of grammatical gender associations with those connected with natural sex divisions. More likely, however, is Jones's interpretation (given most fully in his 1987 book) of these apparent aberrations as a fundamental shift in the grammatical and pragmatic functions of the ancestor of *that* in texts of the period, foreshadowing its present function as distal demonstrative. Much of this grammatical gender-based variation is, as we have seen, most readily observed in the use of the simple demonstrative pronoun.

Other patterns can be described in the demonstrative use of the gloss, all associated with those members of the simple demonstrative paradigm where distinction in function is supplied largely by a word-final vowel. In "classical" Old English this part of the paradigm involved a distinction between the *sV* (*V* =

'plus indeterminate vowel') forms *se*, associated with masculine nouns in nominative singular contexts, and *seo*, associated with feminine nouns in the same contexts, as against the *þV* form *þa*, associated with feminine nouns in accusative singular contexts (as well as with all nouns in nominative and accusative plural contexts). In the gloss to the Lindisfarne Gospels, however, while the *sV* forms do survive, they occupy the same place as, and apparently compete with, new analogical *þV* forms such as "ðe" and "ðio". While it is difficult to say which pattern is winning out in the gloss, the fact that eventually the *sV* forms would be replaced throughout the language by the innovation at the very least suggests the direction of change. The forms produced by analogy put added pressure on the vowels to deliver functional information in particular in a situation where the forms themselves are regularly given minimal stress, if any at all.

There are a number of occasions where "ðio" is found with masculine nouns, such as

(13) Mark 14.38

L	*Uigilate et orate ut non intretis in temtationem spiritus quidem promtus caro uero infirma*
MkGl (Li) 14.38	wæccas ⁊ gebiddas þætte ne ingae in costunge se gaast uutedlice is gearuu **ðio lichoma** ðonne untrymig
Trans.	Watch ye, and pray that you enter not into temptation. The spirit indeed is willing, but the flesh is weak'

and one example of "se" being used with a feminine noun:

(14) Luke 12.23

L	*anima plus est quam esca et corpus quam uestimentum*
LkGl (Li) 12.23	**se sauel** mara is ðon mett ⁊ lichoma ðon woede
Trans.	'The life is more than the meat, and the body is more than the raiment'.

There are also occasions where *þV* forms are used with members of the neuter gender class, whether that be with "ðe":

(15) Matthew 23.17

L	*stulti et caeci quid enim maius est aurum an templum quod sanctificat aurum*

MtGl (Li) 23.17	⁊ blindas[4] huæt forðon mara is þæt gold ł **ðe tempel** þæt gehalgas þæt gold
Trans.	'Ye foolish and blind; for whether is greater, the gold, or the temple that sanctifieth the gold?'

where the immediate proximity to the use of "þæt" with OE *gold* should be noted; with "ða":

(16) Matthew 7.27

L	*et descendit pluuia et uenerunt flumina et flauerunt uenti et inruerunt in domum illam et cecidit et fuit ruina eius magna*
MtGl (Li) 7.27	⁊ ofdune astag regn ⁊ cuomon streamas ⁊ gebleuun windas ⁊ inręsdon **in huse ða ilco** ⁊ gefeall ⁊ wæs fæll his micel
Trans.	'And the rain fell, and the floods came, and the winds blew, and they beat upon that house, and it fell, and great was the fall thereof'

and with "ðio":

(17) Mark 15.28

L	*Et adimpleta est scribtura quae dicit et cum iniquis reputatus est*
MkGl (Li) 15.28	⁊ gefylled wæs **ðio gewrit** ðio cuoeðes ⁊ mið unrehtuisum ł wohfullum getaled wæs[5]
Trans.	'And the scripture was fulfilled, which saith: And with the wicked he was reputed'.

With each of these patterns we can claim that the inherited morphosyntactic system appears in danger. If this were a matter of only one text, the apparent change might be an anomaly. This does not appear to be the case, however. In the following section we will see whether any of these patterns can be found in later forms of English in order to see how these match up with the Lindisfarne material.

4 The glossator apparently did not provide a translation for *stulti*.

5 On this occasion and that immediately preceding it could be argued that the feminine grammatical gender of L *illam* or *scribtura* has affected the outward expression of gender in the English equivalent. There may be something in this; it would be very surprising if there were no influence of Latin upon English in a text fundamentally focussed on the former language and its interpretation. That such an explanation cannot be used on the regular occasions when Latin and English disagree over gender attribution, and there still appears to be a 'shift' in gender-assignment brings such an interpretation dangerously close to special pleading, however.

2 Diachronic change in the English noun phrase

In work on change in the demonstrative pronoun paradigms in late Old English and early Middle English (see, in particular, Millar 2000), I have proposed a number of tendencies in which changes in these paradigms are expressed. On these occasions, however, the "classical" model has not regularly been maintained as an alternative with these texts, except for some writers where it perhaps represented a minority variant derived from textual experience.

The first of these patterns is *ambiguity in function*, where the descendant of OE *þæt*, historically associated with neuter nouns in nominative and accusative contexts, is found in other contexts, such as:

(18) Peterborough Chronicle, Second Continuation (mid twelfth century) 1127.28: "for **þet** micele unsibbe" ('on account of that/the great betrayal')[6]

(19) *South English Legendary* (late thirteenth century) 130.63: "And **þat** muche del aȝen wille" ('and wished to own that/the great part).[7]

As Millar (2000) suggests, this represents the process of the functional split between *the* (as definite article) and *that* (as distal demonstrative), where previously both functions were carried by the same simple demonstrative functions.

Secondly, *ambiguity in ending* is used to refer to, in the first instance, where descendants of OE *þæm* are used when descendants of OE *þone* would be expected:[8]

---

6 Throughout this paper, reference is made to the text of the Peterborough Chronicle as edited and presented in Clark (1970). Reference is made to the annal and the line reference following Clark's edition; the annals for 1122–1131 as the 'First Continuation'. The annals for 1132–1154 are generally referred to as the 'Second Continuation'. Both Continuations are written in a form of language which is heavily indebted to the late West Saxon written in earlier parts of the manuscript. It also carries evidence for the provenance of the scribes in the (south-)east Midlands of England (Clark 1970: in particular xxii–xxv).

7 The edition used here is that of D'Evelyn and Mill (1956), a composite edition of a range of manuscript witnesses. Reference is to page of the edition and line reference on that page. The manuscripts used derive from the south-west Midlands or south-west of England; they are generally dated to the late thirteenth century (Laing 1993: 22, 23, 95–6, 123).

8 It could be argued that *þVn* in accusative contexts is actually a descendant of *þVne* rather than *þVm*, meaning that the change posited does not have significant repercussions. This ignores the fact that, in early Middle English, the *þVm* form has become *þVn* almost universally, thus neutralizing any distinction between originally distinct accusative and dative forms when no *–e* is realized.

(20) *The Owl and the Nightingale* (third quarter thirteenth century) 741–742 C: "þan bidde þat hi moten iseche/**ðan** ilche sang þat euer is eche" ('then order that they must seek out that/the very song which always is eternal')[9]

(21) *Vices and Virtues* (early thirteenth century) 13.30–31: "Ʒewiss hafð godd forworpen **ðan** ilche man" ('indeed God has cast out that/the very man')[10]

(22) *South English Legendary* (late thirteenth century), *Oswald the Bishop* 167–168: "as seint Oswold com/And **þen** wey from Euerwik to Wircestre nom" ('as Saint Oswald came and took that/the way from York to Worcester').

This second pattern can also be associated with the opposite phenomenon, where formal descendants of OE *þone* are used where descendants of OE *þæm* would be expected:

(23) Peterborough Chronicle, First Continuation (first half twelfth century) 1129.25–26: "Se kyng Henri geaf þone biscoprice æfter Micheles messe **þone** abbot Henri" ('The King Henry gave the bishopric to the abbot Henry after Michaelmas')

(24) Laȝamon's *Brut* (third quarter thirteenth century) 1359 O: "þohte Gorgwind **þane** king" ('it seemed to Gorgwind the king').[11]

9 The edition used in this paper for this text is that of Atkins (1922), with further reference to Stanley (1960). Line references are to Atkins's edition (a common line numbering is given for both manuscripts). The text is found in two manuscript versions: London, British Library, MS Cotton Caligula A.ix (here termed C) and Oxford, Jesus College, MS 29 (here termed J). Both manuscripts date from the third quarter of the thirteenth century. They are written in language varieties associated with the south-west Midlands of England (Ker 1963: ix; Laing 1993: 70, 145).

10 The edition used in this paper for this text is Holthausen (1888). References are to pages and lines on individual pages. Its unique manuscript witness (London, British Library, MS Stowe 34) is dated to the beginning of the thirteenth century; its provenance is Essex (Laing 1993: 106).

11 The edition used in this paper for this text is that of Brook and Leslie (1963 and 1972); reference is to the line assignment of that edition throughout. Line references are to the common numbering system used for both texts by Brook and Leslie. The text of the *Brut* was probably written in the early thirteenth century, but the surviving manuscripts – London, British Library, MS Cotton Caligula A.ix (here termed C) and London, British Library, MS Cotton Otho C.xiii (here termed O) – both date from the third quarter of that century and were written in the south-west Midlands of England (Laing 1993: 70, 79). The O manuscript was seriously damaged in the Cottonian Fire of 1731. Quotations from that manuscript recognize this damaged state, as transcribed by Brook and Leslie.

Thirdly, this ambiguity can refer to situations where forms appear interchangeable, as with the following example from a text with a range of manuscripts deriving from essentially the same place and time:

(25) *Seinte Katerine* (first half thirteenth century)
B 433–434: "he bichearde **þene** feont ant schrencte **þen** alde deouel"
R 547–548: "he bi-cherde **þene** feont. and schrencte **þen** alde deouel"
T 801–802: "he bicherde **þene** feond. 7 schrencte **þen** alde deouel"
('he deceived the fiend and tricked the old devil').[12]

Fourthly, ambiguity can exist between *þe* (and variants) and either *þone* or *þæm*, as with

(26) *Seinte Iuliene* (first half thirteenth century)
R 316–317: "binime ham **þene** wil"
B 406–407: "bineo(-)me ham **þe** wil"
('take the will from them').[13]

The apparent end stage of this ambiguity can be seen in the use of *þe* along with its variants where *þone* or *þæm* would have been expected:

(27) *Seinte Katerine* (first half thirteenth century)
B 68–69: "and wrat on hire breoste [...] **þe** hali rode-taken"
R 87–89: "7 wrat on hire breoste [...] **þe** hali rode taken"
T 138–140: "7 wrat on hire breoste [...] **þe** ha(-)li taken"
('and wrote on her breast the holy sign of the cross').

---

12 The edition used in this paper for this text is that of d'Ardenne and Dobson (1985). The work probably dates from the late twelfth or early thirteenth centuries. Three manuscript witnesses are available – Oxford, Bodleian Library, MS Bodley 34 (here termed B), dated between 1220 and 1225; London, British Library, MS Royal 17.A.xxvii (here termed R), dated between 1220 and 1230; and London, British Library, MS Cotton Titus D.xviii (here termed T), written around 1250. All have their origin in the 'AB dialect' of the south-west Midlands (d'Ardenne and Dobson 1981: xliii, xlvi–xlix), although T demonstrates some influence from the language of the north-east Midlands of England (d'Ardenne and Dobson 1981: lii).

13 The edition used in this paper for this text is that of d'Ardenne (1961). The work probably dates from the late twelfth or early thirteenth centuries. Two manuscript witnesses are available – Oxford, Bodleian Library, MS Bodley 34 (here termed B), dated between 1220 and 1225; and London, British Library, MS Royal 17.A.xxvii (here termed R), dated between 1220 and 1230. Both have their origin in the "AB dialect" of the south-west Midlands of England (d'Ardenne 1961: xv, xxvii).

It is important to note that each of these apparent stages can be found in the same text, often in close proximity. This must lead us to question further the extent to which many of the original distinctions truly survive as markers of grammatical categories.

The corollary to this process involves confusion between the various demonstrative pronouns of the type *þV*, as was already seen for the Lindisfarne material. In the early Middle English period, much confusion between forms is apparent, due to what I have termed *ambiguity in form*. In the first instance, these features can be expressed where the "incorrect" form is used where another manuscript witness has *þe*:

(28) Laȝamon's *Brut* (third quarter thirteenth century) 219
C: "muchel wes **þa** neode"
O: "mochel was **þe** neode"
('great was the need')

(29) Laȝamon's *Brut* (third quarter thirteenth century) 4256
C: "**þeo** wile hefede þe king : Cassibellaune . ȝeond al his kinelond : isomned ferde stronge"
O: "**.e** wile adde þe king Cassibilane . ouer al his kine-lond : hii-somned ferde strong"
('for this period the king Cassibellaune had brought together a strong force across his kingdom').

Secondly, *þe* is often used in accusative feminine contexts, where *þa* would historically be expected:

(30) Peterborough Chronicle, Second Continuation (mid twelfth century) 1137.47–48: "⁊ brenden sythen **þe** cyrce" ('and afterwards burned the church')

(31) Laȝamon's *Brut* (third quarter thirteenth century) l. 2954
C: "Biwunnen heo Rome : **þe** riche burh wel i-done"
O: "þus hii biwonne Rome : **þe** riche borh wel idone"
('They conquered Rome, that well-appointed city')

(32) *Vices and Virtues* (late thirteenth century) 127.20: "hie hafden **ðe** heiȝere hand ouer me" ('they had the upper hand over me')

(33) Kentish Sermons (early thirteenth century), *Sermo in Die Epiphanie* 64: "stor sigifieth **þe** herte" ('incense signifies the heart').[14]

Finally, there are several occasions where *þe* is used in plural contexts, sometimes in apparent variation with *þa* and its descendants:

(34) *Vices and Virtues* (early thirteenth century) 75.33–34: "Ac clepe **ðo** wrecches and *to* unmihti, **ðe** blinde, **ðe** dumbe, **ðe** deaue, **ðe** halte" ('but call the wretches and the unmighty, the blind, the dumb, the deaf, the lame').

Again, these apparent alternations can occur in the same manuscript, often within a circumscribed textual space.

Naturally, what I have described here is a schematization of an often seemingly chaotic situation. Nevertheless, its features can be taken as representing the central means by which concord broke down in the English noun phrase. It is striking that many of these phenomena are already present in the English gloss to the Lindisfarne Gospels, with the exception of *ambiguity in ending*, possibly because unstressed vowels had not as yet been 'weakened' as they would be in the succeeding centuries (although Blakeley 1948–1949 does document a range of examples of accusative-dative syncretism), and the spread of *ambiguity in form* into plural contexts. A common chain of development appears to run through late Old English and early Middle English.

3 Changes in the noun phrase in the late Old English and early Middle English periods: an analysis

A narrative can be constructed for the nature and spread of changes in noun phrase inflectional morphology from the late Old English to the early Middle English periods. Essentially, during the period the English noun phrase (and English as a whole) changed from having *synthetic* tendencies to having *analytic*

14 The edition used in this paper for this text is that of Morris (1872). The sole manuscript (Oxford, Bodleian Library, MS Laud Misc. 471) is dated to the final quarter of the thirteenth century, written in the dialect of Kent (Laing 1993: 138). References are to the individual sermons following the line numbering of Morris's edition.

tendencies (an alternative typological transit would be from *fusional* towards *isolating*). On neither occasions can this journey be said to be complete. Moreover, the nature and extent of change in Old English appears regionally triggered. We are, of course, at the mercy of a sometimes tenuous record of use and change, made opaque by the omnipresence of West Saxon throughout England before 1066–1067 and the decline in status of written English after the Conquest. Nevertheless, it is still possible to say that, starting in ninth- to tenth-century northern England, a move away from the use of grammatical gender and case as a means of marking function within the clause developed and spread, with its replacement by an essentially rigid word order pattern where function was expressed through clause position rather than form. These changes appear to have passed first into the east Midlands of England. The *Ormulum* (second half of the twelfth century), for instance, displays little or none of the case- or gender-associations the ancestral variety had (Palmatier 1969), while the more southerly First Continuation of the Peterborough Chronicle (first half of the twelfth century) demonstrates a relationship to the Old English system, but with the same "issues" the gloss to the Lindisfarne Gospels and other late Northumbrian varieties demonstrate, albeit of a more general nature. The Second Continuation, written by someone at most two generations younger than the First, demonstrates no such survival. In essence its noun phrase relations are the same as those of Modern English (for further discussion, see Millar 2000 and 2012: 115–118).

Evidence, as sifted by Millar (2000), suggests that the south-west Midlands of England were next affected. In many of the works of the Katherine group (and in the "AB dialect" as a whole) elements of the inherited case- and gender-sensitive morphology continued, but not in a systemically coherent way. At around the same time (or slightly later) these changes become noticeable in south-western texts. The most conservative morphological usage can be found in south-east England (in particular Kentish). Essex works, such as *Vices and Virtues*, are considerably ahead of Kent, but exhibit the same set of changes. In all the cases where we can observe the process a generation which uses a 'halfway house' system with elements of both the inherited and new patterns is followed by one where (virtually) no elements of the original system are still present. The former is arguably the case with the Lindisfarne material.

In a sense this reflects emphatically the paths of linguistic change across England in the medieval period described by Samuels (1989a), northern features being mediated through the Midlands before reaching London. The 'leap' west found in our typology may be more perception than reality, at least in relation to London usage, which, from what extended early Middle English material we possess, suggests a city open to influence from the north, especially in comparison with Kent (Millar 2012: 57–59).

Samuels emphasizes that these northern innovations did not pass through the Midlands *en bloc*. Certain features – perhaps those most unlike more conservative varieties – are likely to have taken longer to incorporate, unless change made their adoption necessary. Equally inevitably, some features of the language would have been maintained long after they had ceased to be useful. For instance, in the English employed by Chaucer in the last decades of the fourteenth century, elements of the 'strong vs. weak' distinction in the adjective were maintained, as well as number concord between noun and adjective (Samuels 1989b). The former survival in particular is surprising, since the purpose it had (in carrying case and gender information when not provided by a definer) had long since ceased to be meaningful in any English variety.

4 Conclusion

The English gloss to the Lindisfarne Gospels represents a unique window into the early stages of changes which would eventually affect all varieties of English and help alter the typological nature of the language. In relation to noun phrase morphology – in particular the simple demonstrative paradigm – patterns of non-historical usage can be found in the Lindisfarne materials, which are very similar to those realized later in the history of the language in more southern texts. The gloss to the Lindisfarne Gospels can therefore be said to be at the forefront of linguistic change.

Marcelle Cole

Identifying the Author(s) of the Lindisfarne Gloss: Linguistic Variation as a Diagnostic for Determining Authorship

Abstract: This article aims to contribute to the small, yet growing, body of research that has explored the distribution of linguistic variants in the Lindisfarne gloss as a diagnostic for determining to what extent the composition of the gloss was a fully independent achievement by the glossator Aldred. The results corroborate earlier findings (Brunner 1947–1948; Blakeley 1949–1950; van Bergen 2008) which indicate that it is highly unlikely that Aldred did not rely on pre-existing, now lost, translations of the Gospels. This, of course, has important implications for our understanding of the language of the gloss.

1 Introduction

The interlinear Old Northumbrian gloss to the Latin text of the Lindisfarne Gospels (London, British Library, MS Cotton Nero D.iv) has traditionally been attributed to Aldred, a member of the St. Cuthbert community, who is commonly believed to be the same "Aldred the Provost" whose name appears in the Latin collectar known as the Durham Ritual (Durham, Cathedral Library, MS A.iv.19).[1] The issue of whether Aldred was the only hand involved in writing the gloss has been widely commented on in the earlier literature.[2] Since Ross et al.'s (1960) palaeographical and philological study, the widely accepted view is that, if a change in hand did occur in the Lindisfarne Gospels, as the striking linguistic variation in the gloss would suggest, it must have occurred in the exemplar or source material rather than in Lindisfarne itself.

While much attention has been paid to the possible reliance of Farman and Owun, the authors of the gloss in the Rushworth Gospels, on Aldred's gloss, the issue of whether Aldred used pre-existing sources remains understudied.[3] In

1 See Ker (1943: 215–226), Ross et al. (1960: 24); cp. Skeat (1871–1887: III, ix). This article draws from Cole (2014).

2 See Skeat (1871–1887: III, ix; IV, vii).

3 The gloss added to the Rushworth Gospels (Oxford, Bodleian Library, MS Auct. D.ii.19) was written by two glossators: a scribe by the name of Farman wrote MtGl (Ru), MkGl (Ru) 1.1–2.15, and JnGl (Ru) 18.1–3 in a Mercian dialect (Ru[1]) and Owun glossed the remainder

what follows, I detail a review of the available colophonic and palaeographical evidence in favour of considering Aldred the sole glossator of Lindisfarne and explore how this evidence interacts with the linguistic evidence, which suggests that there must have been a change in hand, if not in the gloss itself, then in the source material Aldred used. My main concern will be to explore the distribution of linguistic variants in Lindisfarne as a diagnostic for determining to what extent Aldred relied on other sources in the composition of the gloss. To this end, I will discuss new evidence that corroborates the view that there must have been at least two changes in the source material (Brunner 1947–1948; Blakeley 1949–1950; van Bergen 2008).

1.1 Non-linguistic evidence

The traditional basis for asserting that Aldred wrote the tenth-century interlinear Old Northumbrian gloss to Lindisfarne rests upon the evidence of a colophon text, added to f. 259r of the manuscript. In the colophon Aldred appears to take credit for having written the gloss and associates his work with other members of the community, whose involvement in the original production of the Latin gospel book is also briefly described. The colophon credits Eadfrith, bishop of Lindisfarne (698–721), with having written the text. His successor, Bishop Aethilwald, is said to have bound the volume and an anchorite by the name of Billfrith forged the metalwork covering.

The difficulties posed by the translation and interpretation of the portion of the colophon where Aldred discusses the glossing process, and draws a distinction between the glossing of the first three Gospels ("sections") and that of John's Gospel, have led to considerable debate as to whether Aldred does indeed claim

in Old Northumbrian (Ru[2]). Up until recently, commonalties between the interlinear glosses to the Lindisfarne Gospels and the Rushworth Gospels were believed to be the result of Farman and Owun's reliance on Aldred's gloss as an exemplar (Morrell 1965: 177; Ross 1979). Recent research, however, challenges the traditional view on the direction of influence between the Gospels (Kotake 2008a, 2008b, 2012 and this volume). Kotake (2012) convincingly shows that Farman, the author of Ru[1], did not copy from Aldred when glossing Matthew 26–28; if anything, it was Aldred that relied on Farman's gloss or both glosses relied on independent translations of Matthew 26–28 that are known to have circulated independently as a Passion text. Similarly, Kotake (2008a, 2008b) has also proved that Owun's glossing activity did not rely exclusively on Lindisfarne, and was in all likelihood reliant on a number of other sources. The abbreviations used in this paper to refer to the glosses are those employed by the *Dictionary of Old English Web Corpus* (hereafter *DOEC*).

sole responsibility for writing the entire gloss. Consider Brown's (Brown 2003: 104) translation of this part of the colophon text:

> ⁊ (ic) Aldred p(re)`s´b(yte)r indignus ⁊ misserim(us)? mið godes fvltv(m)mę ⁊ s(an)c(t)i cuðberhtes hit of(er)glóesade ón englisc. ⁊ hine gihamadi:. mið ðæm ðríim dælvm. Mathevs dǽl gode ⁊ s(an)c(t)e cvðberhti. Marc' dǽl. ðæm bisc(ope/um?). ⁊ lvcas dæl ðæm hiorode ⁊ æht `v´ ora seo`v´lfres mið tó inláde.:~ ⁊ sci ioh(annes) dæl f(er) hine seolfne `i(d est) f(or)e his savle´ ⁊ feover óra s(eo)`v´lfres mið gode ⁊ s(an)c(t)i cvðberhti. þ(æt)te he hæbbe ondfong ðerh godes miltsæ on heofnv(m).
>
> 'And (I) Aldred, unworthy and most miserable priest? [He] glossed it in English between the lines with the help of God and St. Cuthbert. And, by means of the three sections, he made a home for himself – the section of Matthew was for God and St. Cuthbert, the section of Mark for the bishop[/s], the section of Luke for the members of the community [in addition, eight ores of silver for his induction] and the section of John was for himself [in addition, four ores of silver for God and St. Cuthbert] so that, through the grace of God, he may gain acceptance into heaven'.

The difficulty lies in translating the phrase "hine gihamadi mið ðæm ðriim dælvm", which is complicated by the fact that the verb "gihamadi" is not recorded elsewhere in Old English (Ross et al. 1960: 8). Ross et al. render the phrase 'by means of the three sections, he made a home for himself'. In other words, Aldred translated the first three Gospels with the intention of earning a home within the community and he translated John's Gospel with the intent of securing for himself a place in heaven. This interpretation is in line with that of Maunde Thompson's translation of "hine gihamadi" as 'got for himself a home [in the monastery]' (cited by Skeat 1887: vii). Contrastively, Skeat translates the phrase as 'made himself at home with the three parts', which he interprets as meaning that Aldred familiarized himself with the three parts, i.e. revised the gloss to the first three Gospels, which had been written by others, and glossed the last one, that of John, himself (Skeat 1878: ix). Skeat was later to concede, however, that Maunde Thompson's translation was probably a more accurate rendering of the intended meaning (Skeat 1887: vii). A recent reconsideration of the colophon (Newton et al. 2013) endorses Maunde Thompson's view in suggesting that the troublesome hapax legomenon, "gihamadi", is a competing form of the denominative verb OE *gehamettan* 'to home or domicile (someone)'.

Given that it was unusual for colophons to accompany glosses (Erik Kwakkel, personal communication), one may well ask what motivation lay behind Aldred's insertion of a colophon. He appears to have been driven by a desire to prove his worth and commitment and thereby facilitate his entry into the community of St. Cuthbert, as posited by Brown (2003: 96). Aldred's description of his glossing activity alongside reference to the eight ores of silver he paid for his induction further suggests that the elaboration of the gloss was an *opus dei*, carried out with the specific intention of securing a place for himself within the community (Brown 2003: 99). There is evidence to suggest that such practice was not uncommon, although the other two instances recorded in the tenth century involved only a monetary contribution (Stanton 2002: 50).[4]

Skeat's suggestion that Aldred could have carried out a supervisory role of part of the glosses finds support in the change from brown ink to red ink in John from f. 220va2 onwards. The use of red ink is not confined to John's Gospel, but also occurs in isolated glosses elsewhere in the gloss, namely between ff. 3v–5v and at f. 141va3 (Ross et al. 1960: 24). In these cases, the entries made in red ink involve alterations and corrections that appear to be the result of a general revision carried out once the gloss to John had been completed (Ross et al. 1960: 24). Skeat suggests that these red corrections indicate that "Aldred [...] seems merely to have superintended the glossing of the first three gospels, but to have glossed the fourth gospel himself for the most part" (Skeat 1874: vii). This view is borne out by an orthographical peculiarity shared by the red corrections and much of the gloss to John. The abbreviation <· ł ·> as opposed to <ł> occurs for *vel* in these red corrections (Ross et al. 1960: 24). This variant makes its appearance for the first time in the main body of the gloss around f. 224r, and coincides with the occurrence of other orthographical and palaeographical peculiarities found in the gloss to John, such as the change in ink colour, the use of <v> instead of <u> and *wynn*, and of prefixal <gi-> instead of <ge->. If Aldred was also responsible for glossing the Durham Ritual, as is generally assumed (Ker 1943: 215–226; Ross et al. 1960: 24), then the use of <v> and of prefixal <gi-> may actually be a weightier argument than first appears in favour of the hypothesis that Aldred restricted his glossing activities to John, given that these forms are equally characteristic of the Durham Ritual (Skeat 1871–1887: III, x).

Even if Ross et al.'s interpretation of the colophon, which attributes the entire gloss to Aldred, is accurate, we still need to consider to what extent the colophon should actually be taken at face value. In recent years, scholars have started to question the assumption that the colophon is a reliable historical document (Gilbert 1990; Dumville 1999: 78; see the discussion in Brown 2003: 92–95; Nees 2003; Roberts's and Brown's papers, this volume). Gilbert proposes the hypothe-

4 Newton et al. (2013: 121–122) question the traditional interpretation of OE *ora* as 'ores of silver' (cf. Ross et al. 1960: 10; Brown 2003: 99). They argue that such an overt reference to Aldred's supposed simony is at odds with his condemnation of the practice in a marginal note at f. 45r. Instead, they suggest that OE *ora* here means 'border, margin' and Aldred added edges of silver to selected pages of the gospels, which have long since disappeared due to over-zealous cropping (Newton et al. 2013: 123–126). See Roberts's and Cavill's responses in this volume.

sis that the original production of the codex was in fact a team effort that involved many more individuals than Aldred mentions. Several factors inform his view; firstly, the sheer enormity of the endeavour would have required a considerable amount of manpower. Productions of this nature would have been characterized by the "communal and cooperative ethos of monasticism in general and of the scriptorium in particular" (Gilbert 1990: 155). The names included in the colophon should not therefore be taken as an exhaustive list of the artists involved. Significant in this regard is the fact that no mention is made of the rubricator, who unquestionably participated in the production of the codex (Gilbert 1990: 153 n. 7). Gilbert attributes Aldred's economical reference to only the most important names involved in the manuscript's production to the young priest's ambition. The colophon is essentially a fine piece of self-promotion on Aldred's part, intended to associate him with some of the most prestigious names in Lindisfarne's "hall of fame" (Gilbert 1990: 154). In a similar vein, Nees (2003) has also noted that Aldred presents his contribution as the culmination of work initiated by other important members of the Lindisfarne community. Just as it appears likely that less illustrious names involved in the production of the codex were omitted, it is not implausible that Aldred applied the same criteria in naming only himself, possibly in the role of master scribe, in relation to the gloss (Gilbert 1990: 155).

Given the possible unreliability of the colophon as a historical document and the difficulty of interpreting its text with any absolute certainty, considerable palaeographical and linguistic debate has also arisen as to whether the Old Northumbrian gloss was the work of a single hand. In the introductions to their respective editions of Lindisfarne in the nineteenth century, early commentators posited that the gloss was the work of two or more scribes speaking different dialects (see Stevenson and Waring 1854–1865; Bouterwek 1857; and Skeat 1871–1887). Only this in their opinion would account for the wealth of variant forms in the gloss.

The palaeographical and philological team working on the gloss in the late 1950s regarded the whole gloss as the work of the same man, who they took to be Aldred, based on the assumption that the colophon proper is a reliable autobiographical statement by Aldred (Ross et al. 1960). Nevertheless, based on orthographical differences and discrepancies in the general appearance of the gloss, Ross et al. divided the text into two main parts with a break at ff. 203r–203v, i.e. at the end of Luke. This demarcation effectively distinguishes John from the other three Gospels, and, as it happens, parallels the distinction drawn by Aldred himself in the colophon between the glossing of the first three Gospels and the glossing of the fourth (Ross et al. 1960: 23):

> [there is] some evidence that the Gloss falls into two main parts, dividing at ff. 203r–203v, that is, at the end of St. Luke's Gospel. Here <v> supplants <u>, and at this point also the hand becomes neat and compact [...] in contrast to the rather untidy, thin look of the pages immediately before [...]. The Colophon, too, suggest that the glossing of St. John's Gospel was in fact a distinct operation from the glossing of the other three.

The same scholars observe the "considerable" contrast between the first and last pages of the first main section up to ff. 203r–203v (end of Luke) and also suggest that there are "slight indications" of a break around the beginning of Mark at ff. 93r–95r and at f. 160v, i.e. around LkGl (Li) 8.30 (Ross et al. 1960: 24). The outset of the first sub-section of the first main part (ff. 3r–93r), which essentially comprises Matthew, is characterized by a "bold, vigorous" hand that becomes notably smaller and less vigorous around the beginning of Mark (ff. 93r–95r). The second main section (from f. 203v to the end of the text) essentially comprises John's Gospel and is distinguished by neat, compact writing. This latter section is also characterized by a series of orthographical quirks that only occur in John, as previously mentioned.

In spite of marked differences in general appearance between parts of the gloss, such as differences in the size and neatness of the handwriting or changes in ink colour, the formation of the individual letters is nonetheless consistent enough throughout the gloss for Ross et al. to conclude that not even the writing of two scribes formed in the same school would be so similar as to "reproduce with precision all the minor details of execution" (Ross et al. 1960: 20). The scholars are not unaware of the problems posed for their 'one hand' hypothesis by the remarkable linguistic variation found in the glosses. They suggest the possibility that Aldred wrote the gloss singlehandedly, but was not necessarily entirely responsible for its composition and may have copied parts of the gloss from other sources (Ross et al. 1960: 11, 22).[5] The view that Aldred was solely responsible

5 In later work, Ross (1969) was to argue that Bede translated John's Gospel and Aldred's gloss to John may have relied on Bede's translation (see also Elliott and Ross 1972: 65). Boyd (1975a: 56–57) includes Bede's commentaries on the Old and New Testaments and his Gospel homilies among the sources Aldred might have had access to. Additions in Aldred's hand occur in Bede's commentary on the Book of Proverbs (Oxford, Bodleian Library, MS Bodley 819) written in the second half of the eighth century at the Wearmouth/Jarrow scriptorium (Backhouse 1981: 16). Boyd (1975a: 56–57) also draws attention to a marginal note inserted by Aldred at f. 255rb22 (JnGl (Li) 19.37) which reads *post /.i. est in die examinis iudicii. Districti iudicis* followed by "ðus beda ðe broema boecere cueð" ('thus said Bede the famous scribe'). The source of this particular reference has not been located, but such marginalia appear to confirm that Bede's work was available to the glossator of Lindisfarne. If Bede did indeed translate John's Gospel into English, it is reasonable to suppose that Aldred would have had access to the text. The pocket size John's Gospel found in St. Cuthbert's coffin (London, British Library, MS Loan 74) indicates that Latin versions

for writing the gloss, but relied on pre-existing vernacular translations of the Gospels, has gained much currency in recent years. It is a view borne out by the distribution of linguistic variants in Lindisfarne.

1.2 Linguistic evidence

As long ago as 1947, Alice Brunner highlighted the importance of assessing the distribution of linguistic variants in Lindisfarne as a diagnostic for establishing demarcations in the script. Earlier stages of written English clearly tolerated a higher degree of morphological variation than that permitted by the highly codified nature of standardized Modern English. However, the manner in which certain variant forms are confined to particular sections of the text in Lindisfarne needs to be accounted for.

Brunner's survey of several variant forms in Lindisfarne shows that certain variants are either confined to, or are dominant in, specific parts of the text, with a clear demarcation at MkGl (Li) 5.40 and around the beginning of John (Brunner 1947–1948). With regard to the use of <he(o)no> as opposed to <he(o)nu> 'behold', Brunner finds that, whereas <he(o)no> occurs throughout the gloss, <he(o)nu> ceases to appear after MkGl (Li) 3.34. Similarly, the nominative/accusative singular feminine demonstrative forms <ðy, ðyu> are used throughout Matthew and the first five chapters of Mark, at which point they are entirely replaced by <ðio, ðiu>.

Other variant forms occur throughout the glosses, but predominate in certain parts of the gloss. This is the case of the variant stem forms of the verbs OE *wesan* 'to be' and *cweðan* 'to say', which show variation between the rounded and unrounded mid-front vowel. Unrounded forms of *wesan* (<e>) predominate throughout Matthew and the first five chapters of Mark, whereas rounded (<oe>) forms gain in currency in the remainder of the text. Both rounded and unrounded stem variants of *cweðan* (<cuoeð-> and <cueð->) occur in roughly equal measure up to MkGl (Li) 5.40, but at this point <cueð-> becomes infrequent and the rounded variant (<cuoeð->) predominates. In the last four chapters of John, however, forms with <e> rather than <oe> once again occur more frequently.[6] The observed pat-

---

of individual Gospels existed, making it reasonable to suppose that translations or glossed versions of individual Gospels may also have been in circulation.

6 The predominance of unrounded stem variant forms of OE *cweðan* in John's Gospel has also been put forward as a corroborating argument in favour of viewing Bede's hypothesized translation of this Gospel as one of Aldred's sources. Ross (1969: 494) points out that <cueð-> is precisely the form that Bede would have used. Yet Ross's argument is flawed in assuming that late Old Northumbrian was a homogeneous variety. While it is true that rounding of [we(:)] to [wø(:)] is not found in early Old Northumbrian, but is common in late Old Northumbrian, this is only true of

terning of variant forms leads Brunner (whose study is prior to that of Ross et al.'s palaeographical study of the gloss) to conclude that either there was a change of hand in the exemplar, or more than one scribe was involved in writing the gloss (1947–1948: 52).

Blakeley (1949–1950) considers the effect of person and number on the distribution of *-s* and *-ð* present-tense markings in Lindisfarne. The study establishes demarcations at MtGl (Li) 26.16, MkGl (Li) 5.40, and LkArgGl (Li). In line with Brunner, Blakeley postulates that either the gloss was written by one scribe at different stages of his life or – more probably – different scribes from the same scriptorium wrote the gloss (1949–1950: 27).

In recent years Brunner's and Blakeley's findings have been supplemented by further studies that have considered the distribution of variants in the gloss. Van Bergen's survey of negative contraction in Old English dialects indicates that there are parts of the gloss where contracted negative forms, such as OE "nis" (< "ne is") 'is not', "nolde" (< "ne wolde") 'did not want' and "nallas" (< "ne wallas") 'do not want' occur more frequently than in others (van Bergen 2008). The section from MkGl (Li) 5.40 through to the end of Luke shows an increased use of uncontracted forms, although, as van Bergen points out, the data are too scarce for the first five chapters of Mark to determine whether there is actually a neat "before and after" division at MkGl (Li) 5.40 (van Bergen 2008: 291). Nevertheless, the higher rates of uncontracted negative forms in Luke give way to a notable increased incidence of contracted forms in John, a change in linguistic properties that coincides with the main division stipulated by Ross et al. on palaeographical grounds and once again distinguishes John from the first three Gospels. The distribution of uncontracted negative forms in the gloss also points in the same direction as Brunner's study. In view of the palaeographical evidence, van Bergen does not suggest a change of hands in Lindisfarne itself, but posits that Aldred's translation was informed by several sources or relied on an exemplar in which various scribes had been involved.

The uniqueness of John's Gospel has been observed on other occasions in the literature. Elliott and Ross (1972) found that the meaning or the form of certain Anglo-Saxon words is often restricted to John's Gospel. More recently, Kotake's (2008a) survey of element order in the gloss shows that John differs in its syn-

the northern variety of late Old Northumbrian. In the southern variety of late Old Northumbrian, as possibly attested in Ru^2, rounding of the mid-front vowel after [w] appears to be restricted to <woeg> (Hogg 2004: 248). This difference between varieties of late Old Northumbrian does not rule out the possibility of Aldred having relied on an early Old Northumbrian exemplar, such as a hypothesized Bedan translation, but it also suggests that Aldred could just as plausibly have used a source written in a southern variety of late Old Northumbrian.

tactic choices from the other Gospels, further highlighting the gloss's lack of linguistic unity.

The tendency in the literature to overlook the manner in which linguistic variants are restricted to certain parts of the gloss has further propagated the assumption that the language of Lindisfarne reflects the idiolect of a particular scribe, namely Aldred. Thus, Ross (1970: 363–366) discusses certain linguistic features of the language of the Durham Ritual, in which Aldred's language is more conservative than in Lindisfarne. With regard to the *-ð* and *-s* endings, Ross (1970: 365) points out that "in Lindisfarne, the forms occur in nearly equal proportions", whereas *-s* forms are relatively infrequent in the Durham Ritual. While this observation is valid in so far as the *overall* average of *-ð* and *-s* forms in Lindisfarne is roughly equal, Ross ignores the fact that the distribution of the endings is far from uniform throughout Lindisfarne, even though the results of Blakeley's (1949–1950) study on present-tense markings in Lindisfarne point in this direction. Similarly, Ross (1970: 364) further states that the late demonstrative form <ðy> "is found in Lindisfarne, but it does not occur in Ritual". Once again, Ross's wording would suggest that <ðy> occurs uniformly throughout Lindisfarne, which it does not. As discussed above, Brunner (1947–1948) shows that the occurrence of <ðy> is confined to Matthew and the first five chapters of Mark. If the distribution of linguistic variants in Lindisfarne is borne in mind, the Durham Ritual is not as conservative with respect to Lindisfarne as Ross claims. The language of the gloss to the Durham Ritual *is* conservative compared with that of Matthew's Gospel in Lindisfarne, but with regard to the aforementioned features, so too is the language of the other three Gospels in Lindisfarne itself.

The results of studies that have considered the distribution of linguistic variants in the glosses, discussed above, point tentatively in the direction of an emerging pattern of demarcation, but these studies are too scarce in number for their results to be conclusive. The linguistic evidence also appears to interact in an insightful way with the palaeographical and colophonic evidence. The palaeographical evidence points to the gloss being the work of one hand, but it also identifies breaks in the script at the beginning of John and possibly around the beginning of Mark. These breaks not only partly parallel the distinction drawn by Aldred himself between the glossing process of the first three Gospels and that of John in the colophon, but also replicate the demarcations established to date by studies that have focused on the distribution of linguistic forms. The present study aims to further explore the role of linguistic variation as a diagnostic for determining to what extent the composition of the Lindisfarne gloss was a fully independent achievement by Aldred. In what follows, I consider how the distribution of a Type-of-Subject Constraint on the selection of present tense verbal morphology in the interlinear gloss parallels the distribution of variant forms observed in previous studies and strengthens the argument for considering the glosses to Matthew and John to be linguistically divergent from both each other and from the glosses of the other Gospels.

2 The present study

2.1 Preliminaries

Old and Middle English verbal morphology in the northern dialects diverged most remarkably from that of the southern dialects in two main regards. Crucially, the tenth-century Northumbrian texts bear witness to the replacement of the inherited present indicative and imperative *-ð* suffixes with *-s* forms. In addition to plural and third person singular forms in *-ð*, such as "wyrcað" 'work(s)', forms in *-s* of the type "wyrcas" also occur.[7] Furthermore, by the Middle English period, present indicative plural verbal morphology in northern dialects was governed by a grammatical constraint commonly referred to as the Northern Subject Rule (NSR) that conditioned verbal morphology according to the type and position of the subject. The plural marker was *-s* unless the verb had an immediately adjacent personal pronoun subject in which case the marker was *-e* or the zero morpheme, giving a system whereby *þai sai* 'they say' occurred in juxtaposition to *storis sais* 'stories say', *ye þat sais* 'you that say' and *þai tel and sais* 'they tell and say'. The constraint in Middle English was also operative in the north-west and east Midlands and exhibited a degree of morphological variation, with *-th* occurring as a variant of *-s*, and *-n* as a variant of *-e/-Ø* (McIntosh 1989; de Haas 2008, 2011).

In a 'pure' categorical NSR system, the crucial environment for determining morphological differentiation involves pronominal adjacency: the present-tense plural marker is *-s* (as opposed to *-e/-Ø*), unless the verb is in immediate proximity with the pronoun subject. The Position-of-Subject Constraint is not, however, a consistent feature of later varieties of northern dialects and does not exhibit the same remarkable diachronic stability as the Type-of-Subject Constraint (Pietsch 2005; Cole 2008). The Type-of-Subject Constraint involves a broad NP/

7 The vowel distinction that differentiated third person singular from plural forms in Old English had already been lost in Old Northumbrian by the late Old English period, so that *-es/-eð* and *-as/-að* occurred indiscriminately in both plural and third singular environments. Hence, inflectional *-e-* often replaces *-a-* in plural forms ("hia spittes" 'they spit', MkGl (Li) 10.34; "hia gedrifes", 'they cast out', MtGl (Li) 12.27), just as *-a-* occurs for *-e-* in singular forms ("he wyrcað", 'he works', JnGl (Li) 5.20; "he syngias", 'he sins', MtGl (Li) 19.9).

PRO[8] constraint whereby the verbal morphology triggered by personal pronoun subjects differs to that of non-pronominal subjects regardless of adjacency, e.g. *thay droupun and daren* 'they droop and tremble' versus *byernes bannes the tyme* 'nobles curse the time' (de Haas 2011: 102). Even in northern Middle English the effect of subject type is generally found to be more robust than that of adjacency, although this would hardly be surmised from the categorical tone of the dialect descriptions. Recent quantitative studies show that in northern Middle English the adjacency constraint does not appear to be as categorical as previously assumed (de Haas 2008, 2011; Fernández Cuesta 2011: 106–107).[9]

In an exhaustive study of the replacement of *-ð* by *-s* in Old Northumbrian, I have demonstrated that the distribution of competing present-tense markings in Lindisfarne shows the workings of the NSR in Old Northumbrian, but with different morphological material (Cole 2012a, 2014). Subject type has a statistically significant effect on the distribution of *-s* and *-ð* ($p < .001$), as does adjacency ($p < .05$); pronominal subjects favour verbal forms ending in *-s*, while non-adjacent pronoun subjects and nominal subjects prefer *-ð*. This pattern is exemplified in (1–3):[10]

(1) f. 130ra2
MkGl (Li) 16.18 nedro hia niomas
L *serpentes tollent*
Trans. 'They shall take up serpents'

(2) f. 98va25
MkGl (Li) 2.18 ðine uut(edlice) ðegnas ne fæstað
L *tui autem discipuli non ieiunant*
Trans. 'But your disciples do not fast'

(3) f. 235rb18
JnGl (Li) 10.26 giene gelefeð
L *vos non creditis*
Trans. 'You do not believe'.

8 PRO is used throughout this paper simply as an abbreviation for 'pronoun'.

9 There is evidence to suggest that the Position-of-Subject Constraint may have reached a high degree of regularity in Older Scots. Montgomery (1994) reports a near categorical adjacency effect with *I*, *we* and *they* in the fourteenth- to seventeenth-century texts he surveys that only starts to wane notably from around the mid-seventeenth century, presumably under the pressure of Anglicization. Rodríguez Ledesma's (2013) survey of Older Scots also finds that the Position-of-Subject Constraint is as robust as the Type-of-Subject Constraint.

10 Biblical translations follow the *Douay-Rheims Bible*.

The identification of subject and adjacency effects in Old Northumbrian belies the early Middle English dating commonly attributed to the emergence of the morphosyntactic constraints at the crux of the NSR. It also challenges the assumption that the NSR necessarily involves syntactically constrained variation between *-e/-Ø* and *-s* (cp. Pietsch 2005; de Haas 2008).

While the discovery of an agreement system reliant on subject type is interesting for what it tells us about later northern developments such as the NSR and related processes, the aim of the present study was to establish what insight the distribution of *-s* and the Type-of-Subject Constraint in the gloss might provide into the Lindisfarne authorship debate. More concretely, it set out to explore whether the distribution of *-s* and the Type-of-Subject Constraint remained constant throughout the gloss, and was thus indicative of the kind of linguistic uniformity we would expect of the same hand, or whether there were fluctuations in its occurrence that would be more in line with a change of hand in the source material.

2.2 Data analysis

The study relied for its data on the standard edition of Lindisfarne (Skeat 1871–1887) collated with the facsimile edition of the manuscript (Kendrick et al. 1956). An important methodological issue in Lindisfarne is whether to treat the text of the gloss as a continuous narrative or to divide it according to Gospel. Older studies on Lindisfarne have tended to divide the data taken from the gloss strictly according to Gospel (Holmqvist 1922; Ross 1934; Berndt 1956). Since Brunner (1947–1948), however, the custom has been to divide the whole gloss arbitrarily into sections of equal length (cp. Blakeley 1949–1950) or to subdivide the data at the point where Brunner found a marked change in linguistic properties around MkGl (Li) 5.40 (cp. van Bergen 2008).

The distribution of *-s* and *-ð* across the different sections of the gloss was first examined by Blakeley (1949–1950), whose methodological point of departure was Brunner's division of the gloss. As previously mentioned, Blakeley's consideration of the effect of person and number on the distribution of *-s* and *-ð* across these sub-sections leads him to divide the gloss into four sections: Section 1 LiEpis (1)–MtGl (Li) 26.16, Section 2 MtGl (Li) 26.17–MkGl (Li) 5.40, Section 3 MkGl (Li) 5.41–LkArgGl (Li), and Section 4 LkArgGl (Li)–end. Blakeley considers the following person and number categories: third singular, third plural, and second plural. No consideration is given to the effect of subject type and the first plural environment is excluded from the analysis.

For the data analysis in the present study, every instance of a plural and third singular present form with an *-s* or *-ð* ending was extracted from all four Gospels, including the forms found in the prefaces. The corpus consisted of 3053 present indicative and imperative tokens with *-s* or *-ð* endings. Following Brunner's (1947–1948) methodology, the data were divided into 64 (arbitrarily determined) equal sections to determine the general distribution of *-s* and *-ð* across the text. My findings parallel those of Blakeley but with one crucial difference: they also identify a break around JnGl (Li) 3.14–4.47, which justifies a five-way partitioning of the data. Differences in the occurrence of *-s* across these five sections are statistically significant at the < .001 level.

Section 1 LiEpis (1)–MtGl (Li) 26.16	(*N* = 794/975: 81 % *-s*)
Section 2 MtGl (Li) 26.17–MkGl (Li) 5.40	(*N* = 55/194: 28 % *-s*)
Section 3 MkGl (Li) 5.41–LkArgGl (Li)	(*N* = 185/318: 58 % *-s*)
Section 4 Lk ArgGl (Li)–JnGl (Li) 3.13	(*N* = 209/947: 22 % *-s*)
Section 5 JnGl (Li) 3.14–end	(*N* = 261/619: 42 % *-s*)

The general distribution of *-s* across the whole gloss indicates that section 1 stands out as having notably higher rates of *-s* than the other sections. The high occurrence of *-s* usage (81 %) found throughout most of Matthew drops sharply between MtGl (Li) 26.17–MkGl (Li) 5.40. There is then a rise in the rate of *-s* between MkGl (Li) 5.41–LkArgGl (Li), followed by a further drop, and an increase once again in the last part of the gloss from JnGl (Li) 3.14 onwards.

For the analysis focusing on the influence exerted by subject type, tokens were coded according to the subject type with which the verb form occurred:

- Personal pronoun: "we getrymes", cp. L *testamur* 'we testify' (f. 215vb1, JnGl (Li) 3.11);
- Indefinite pronoun: "gif hua uord min gehaldað", cp. L *si quis sermonem meum seruauerit* 'if any man keep my word' (f. 231rb22, JnGl (Li) 8.51);
- Demonstrative pronoun: "cuæðes ðes", cp. L *dicit hic* 'this says' (f. 224va23, JnGl (Li) 6.42);
- Full NP: "ða scipo stefn his geheras", cp. L *oues uocem eius audiunt* 'the sheep hear his voice' (f. 234ra17, JnGl (Li) 10.3);[11]

---

11 An anonymous reviewer questioned the accuracy of *Full NP* as a single category given that NPs may have different weights according to the presence/absence and type of complements and/or modifiers. Separating NPs according to weight has not been deemed necessary, however, as the NSR attested in Middle English involved a broad NP/PRO contrast whereby light and heavy NPs did not trigger differentiated verbal morphology.

- Relative pronoun:[12] “seðe gelefeð in sunu”, cp. L *qui credit in filium* ‘he that believes in the Son’ (f. 217ra3, JnGl (Li) 3.36);
- Null subject co-occurring with a present indicative form: “heono eauunge sprecað”, cp. L *ecce palam loquitur* ‘behold, [he] speaks openly’ (f. 227va1, JnGl (Li) 7.26);
- Null plural imperative: “gaeð ł faereð”, cp. L *ite* ‘go!’ (f. 42ra 21, MtGl (Li) 8.32).

Unlike the Middle English NSR system, this preliminary analysis demonstrates that the effect of subject type in Lindisfarne extends outside the plural environment to the third person singular (see Cole 2014 for a detailed discussion). The analysis therefore includes both third person singular and plural personal pronouns, and noun phrase subjects, as well as first and second person plural subjects. Overall rates of *-s* have been calculated for each subject type with the aim of providing a detailed breakdown of the influence exerted by subject type on the occurrence of *-s* across the five sections of the gloss. The results are provided in Table 1 and represented pictorially in Figure 1.

Table 1. Present tense *-s* markings in Lindisfarne according to SUBJECT TYPE

Subject Type	Section 1 LiEpis (1)–MtGl (Li) 26.16	Section 2 MtGl (Li) 26.17–MkGl (Li) 5.40	Section 3 MkGl (Li) 5.41–LkArgGl (Li)	Section 4 LkArgGl (Li)–JnGl (Li) 3.13	Section 5 JnGl (Li) 3.14–end
Null subject	124/158 (79 %)	9/50 (18 %)	26/52 (50 %)	30/235 (13 %)	25/96 (26 %)
Demonstrative	12/14 (86 %)	3/4 (75 %)	1/3 (33 %)	3/7 (43 %)	4/10 (40 %)
Personal PRO	211/255 (83 %)	14/35 (40 %)	56/95 (59 %)	59/191 (31 %)	110/184 (60 %)
Indefinite PRO	6/12 (50 %)	0/4 (0 %)	8/9 (89 %)	11/29 (38 %)	17/30 (57 %)
Full NP	186/236 (79 %)	5 /40 (13 %)	23/52 (44 %)	34/197 (17 %)	33/117 (28 %)
Relative PRO	161/194 (83 %)	9/29 (31 %)	29/51 (57 %)	31/160 (19 %)	58/147 (40 %)
Null imp.	94/106 (89 %)	15/32 (47 %)	42/56 (75 %)	41/128 (32 %)	14/35 (40 %)
***-s*/total (% *-s*)**	794/975 (81 %)	55/194 (28 %)	185/318 (58 %)	209/947 (22 %)	261/619 (42 %)

12 The code *Relative PRO* includes both indefinite relative pronouns of the type illustrated above and definite relative pronouns as in “uðuutum ðaðe wallas in stolum geonga”, cp. L *scribis qui uolunt in stolis ambulare* ‘scribes who love to go in long garments’ (MkGl (Li) 12.38). Relativization in Lindisfarne generally involves relative pronouns of the demonstrative *se þe* type rather than the invariable relative marker *þe* (see Suárez Gómez 2009).

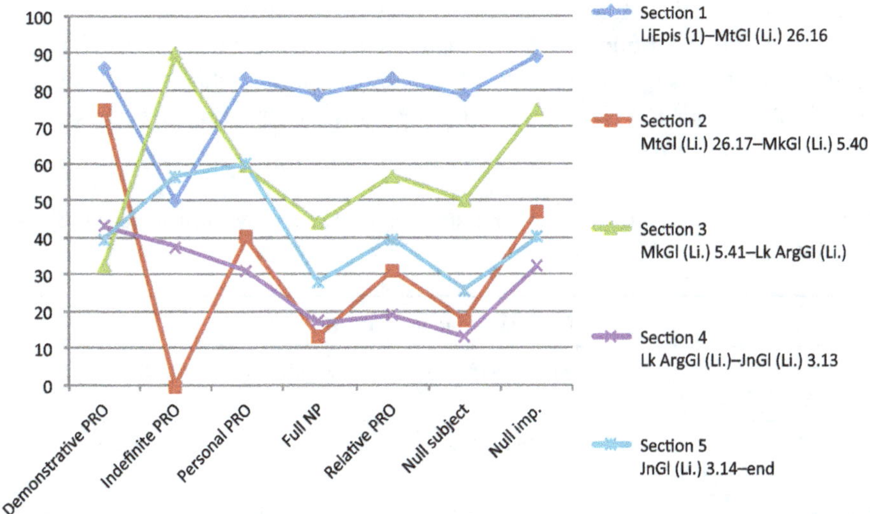

Figure 1. Present tense *-s* markings in Lindisfarne according to SUBJECT TYPE

The effect of subject type is readily observable across sections 2–5. Conversely, the influence exerted by subject type appears to neutralize in section 1, where rates of *-s* for each subject type are practically identical across the board with only indefinite pronoun subjects exhibiting a notably much lower incidence of *-s*. The high rate of *-s* found throughout section 1 and the lack of a Type-of-Subject Constraint in the data suggests that the effect of subject type is lost as the levelling process nears completion.

The erratic behaviour of indefinite and demonstrative pronouns, which varies between prominent peaks and dips across sections, is in all likelihood due to low counts for these subject types in each section. Logistic regression analyses in which sections 2–5 were collapsed in order to test for subject effects that might not emerge in smaller data samples suggest that, in the NSR system operative in Lindisfarne, the morphosyntactic behaviour of indefinite and demonstrative pronouns concurs with that of personal pronouns in contrast to nominal subjects (see Cole 2014: 106).

With regard to the contrastive morphological behaviour of personal pronoun and full NP subjects, the traditional core of the NSR, a consistent pattern emerges across sections 2–5: personal pronoun subjects favour *-s*, notably more so than full NP subjects. The pairwise chi-square evaluations of these environments, summarized in Table 2, show that a subject effect does not operate in the first section that comprises MtGl (Li) up to MtGl (Li) 26.16, but is solidly in evidence in the other sections. The NP/PRO constraint is not statistically significant in section 3, although the distribution of *-s* nevertheless conforms to the same pattern with personal pronouns favouring *-s* (*N* = 56/95: 59 %) more so than full NP subjects (*N* = 23/52: 44 %).[13] The NP/PRO constraint is particularly robust in section 5 from JnGl (Li) 3.14 onwards.

Table 2. Distribution of present tense *-s* markings with full NP and personal pronoun subjects in Lindisfarne

	Personal pronoun	Full NP	
Section 1 LiEpis (1)–MtGl (Li) 26.16	211/255 (83 %)	186/236 (79 %)	χ^2 1.224, p = 0.268
Section 2 MtGl (Li) 26.17–MkGl (Li) 5.40	14/35 (40 %)	5/40 (13 %)	χ^2 7.463, p < 0.01
Section 3 MkGl (Li) 5.41–Lk ArgGl(Li)	56/95 (59 %)	23/52 (44 %)	χ^2 2.928, p = 0.087
Section 4 Lk ArgGl (Li)–JnGl (Li) 3.13	59/191 (31 %)	34/197 (17 %)	χ^2 9.888, p < 0.01
Section 5 JnGl (Li) 3.14–end	110/184 (60 %)	33/117 (28 %)	χ^2 28.570, p < 0.0001

The evidence of the Type-of-Subject Constraint appears to distinguish the language of Matthew's Gospel up to MtGl (Li) 26.16 from the other Gospels and to indicate that the language of John's Gospel is distinctive as well. This corroborates the hypothesis that there must have been at least two changes of scribe in the exemplar or source material – in Mark's Gospel and another around the beginning of John's Gospel – and that Aldred changes his glossing practice in the last few chapters of Matthew's Gospel. The drop in *-s* usage at MtGl (Li) 26.16 corroborates Kotake's (2012) hypothesis that Aldred changes his glossing practice in the last few chapters of Matthew's Gospel, possibly due to his reliance on independent translations of Matthew 26–28 (cp. n. 3). The general distribution of *-s* in the glosses also indicates a break at MkGl (Li) 5.40 and at the start of Luke in line with Brunner's findings and those of Blakeley, respectively. There is also evidence

13 A chi-square (χ2) test calculates the statistical significance of a cross-tabulation involving an independent variable and a dependent variable, in this case, subject type and verb ending, respectively. The χ2 procedure tests whether the difference between the expected frequencies of the various verb endings for each subject type and the observed frequencies is statistically significant.

of a break around the beginning of John, which further confirms the linguistic uniqueness of John's Gospel (cp. Elliott and Ross 1972; Kotake 2008a; van Bergen 2008). The findings of this study, when considered collectively alongside those of Brunner (1947–1948), Blakeley (1949–1950), van Bergen (2008) and Kotake (2012) indicate that it is highly unlikely that Aldred did not use pre-existing translations or glosses of the Gospels.

The difficulty, as van Bergen points out, lies in interpreting what the differences between different parts of the gloss mean. Is the linguistic variation prevalent in Lindisfarne indicative of a change of scribe (either in the exemplar, or in Lindisfarne itself) or simply of a change in the glossator's practice? Not all of the changes identified manifest themselves in the same way. Abrupt changes would suggest a change of scribes, while a gradual transition from one variant to another would be more in line with a change in the same scribe's practice (van Bergen 2008: 291).[14]

With respect to the distribution of the *-s* ending and the subject effects that constrain the occurrence of *-s* and *-ð*, there are statistically significant differences in the robustness of the Type-of-Subject Constraint and a sharp quantitative difference in the use of *-s* across the gloss, which suggests that the language of the gloss does not reflect the speech of an individual speaker. Variation between *-s* and *-ð* in the gloss records a generational change in progress, which, historical records show, goes to completion in the north (except in contexts constrained by the NSR). Modern sociolinguistic theory would therefore predict that we are dealing with 'change from below', linguistic change which avoids stigmatization and is pushed to completion by successive cohorts (Labov 2006, 1994). The replacement of *-th* by *-s* in Early Modern English has been shown to conform to such pervasive sociolinguistic tendencies, with *-s* entering the grammar via speakers of lower status and being pushed forward by women (Nevalainen and Raumolin-Brunberg 2003: 195). The distribution of *-s* would be subject to the same internal constraints across the generations, but would differ notably in how often it occurred. In fact, the linguistic constraints governing the competing variants would be constant factors across the entire course of the change, with the only change being in the increased probability of use of the innovative grammar over time (Kroch 1989). While individual speakers might change their speech to some extent in the direction of the change as

14 A case in point, discussed by van Bergen (2008: 291–292), is that of the use of <v> instead of <u> and *wynn* in John's Gospel, which Elliott and Ross (1972: 65) consider a gradual change that is therefore likely to have been an innovation adopted by Aldred himself. Skeat also accounts for the occurrence of prefixal <gi-> instead of <ge-> towards the end of John's Gospel as indicative of a change in scribal practice (Skeat 1878: x).

they age (Sankoff 2006), a drastic drop in the use of the innovative form in the same speaker would be highly unexpected.

If this interpretation of the replacement of *-ð* by *-s* is correct, we would expect the higher levels of the innovative form found in Matthew's Gospel to be the product of a younger hand. This view is substantiated by Bouterwek (1857), who calls attention to the use of "biað", a plural form of *beon* 'to be', and the demonstrative form "ðasser" in the last chapters of Matthew's Gospel, both of which he regards as late forms. Brunner's aforementioned finding that the late forms of the feminine demonstrative <ðy> and <ðyu> (instead of <ðio> and <ðiu>) are restricted to Matthew's Gospel and the beginning of Mark's also appears to corroborate the view that the language of Matthew's Gospel is less conservative. Nevertheless, archaic forms such as "heonu" also occur (Brunner 1947–1948: 34), although, as Millar (2000: 64) observes, it is not uncommon to find instances of anachronistic features in the same hand in written material at this time. In fact, in a situation of rapid change of this sort where there is no standard variety against which the emerging new variety might be judged, we would expect such variety and change to be the rule rather than the exception (Millar 2000: 64).

Great care clearly needs to be taken when dealing with historical material of this nature. The observed variation in Lindisfarne cannot be explained simply by attributing the drastic quantitative differences in *-s* usage prevalent across the glosses to different aged scribes. It would be a mistake to assume that a speech community in the Labovian sense might be inferred from the language of the gloss. Northern scribes such as Aldred would have been well-versed in the West Saxon semi-standard, making it debatable to what extent the written language they employed would actually have reflected the vernacular of the glossator(s) or an attempt to emulate a conventionalized form (Millar 2000: 47 n. 17). Aldred's reliance on unidentified pre-existing vernacular translations further complicates the picture, as Aldred undoubtedly preserved the linguistic forms found in these sources, while incorporating his own. It is striking, nonetheless, that Aldred consistently filtered the present tense markings at his disposal through a Type-of-Subject Constraint. The glossator's reliance on differing dialectal sources may also explain the higher rates of *-ð* found in some sections of the gloss, such as Luke's Gospel, or indeed the higher rates of *-s* found in Matthew's Gospel. From this perspective, the drastic quantitative differences in the occurrence of *-s* could indicate the influence of varying degrees of conservatism across the Old English dialects, as opposed to varying degrees of conservatism across generations speaking the same dialect. This, of course, has very important implications for our understanding of the language of the Lindisfarne gloss. There would appear to be little basis for asserting that the language recorded in the gloss is exclusively of late North Northumbrian extraction; in all likelihood, it also reflects features of early North Northumbrian, as well as aspects of South Northumbrian and other dialectal influences, including West Saxon.

3 Conclusion

Conclusive evidence clearly proves elusive, but as Gilbert so eloquently states with respect to the inevitable vacuum of certainty that revolves around scholarship on Lindisfarne, "the inevitable absence of conclusive proof does not invalidate reasoned speculation" (Gilbert 1990: 155). The evidence provided by the distribution of both the *s*-forms and the NP/PRO constraint suggests that most of Matthew's Gospel stands as a single linguistic unit in contrast to the rest of the text and that John's may also be considered distinctive. The sharp differentiation in the use of the *s*-forms across the gloss makes it highly unlikely that the language of the gloss represents the speech of an individual speaker and even begs the question of to what extent the language of the gloss represents the features of a particular dialect. The distribution of the variant under discussion lends credence to the hypothesis that Aldred relied on a variety of different sources from which he copied the variant forms as well as incorporating his own forms. Given the palaeographical evidence in favour of viewing the handwriting of the gloss as that of a single hand, despite marked differences between the different parts, scholarly opinion has generally veered away from suggesting a change of hand in Lindisfarne itself. Nevertheless, it is striking that the changes in linguistic properties that occur throughout the gloss coincide with the patterning of palaeographical variation outlined by Ross et al. (1960), and discussed above. Recall that the bold, vigorous hand of the outset becomes smaller at the beginning of Mark's Gospel, at ff. 93r–99v. Similarly at f. 203v, i.e. the beginning of John's Gospel, the writing becomes neat and compact and the dilapidation that characterizes the last parts of Luke's Gospel becomes less common (Ross et al. 1960: 23–24). These palaeographical breaks, which essentially involve differences in the size and neatness of the handwriting, rather than in the formation of the individual letters, are also suggestive of different "stints" in the glossing activity of a single scribe, instigated by a break in the source material upon which he relied (Erik Kwakkel, personal communication). Yet, the commonalities between the linguistic and palaeographical demarcations could indicate that the involvement of other hands in writing the gloss remains a possibility, a view substantiated by the fact that the linguistic and palaeographical demarcations partly replicate the distinction drawn by Aldred himself in the colophon between the glossing process of the first three Gospels and that of John.[15]

15 Earlier versions of this paper were delivered at the 33rd Symposium on Old English, Middle English and Historical Linguistics in the Low Countries, Leiden University, 2011, and at the 17th International Conference of English Historical Linguistics (ICEHL 17), University of Zurich, 2012. I am grateful to the audiences at these presentations for discussion that has greatly improved the quality of this article and to the anonymous reviewers and the editors of this volume for their valuable comments. I am also very thankful to the Spanish Ministry of Science and Technology (project FFI2011-28272) for its financial support.

Luisa García García

Simplification in Derivational Morphology in the Lindisfarne Gloss

Abstract: The language of the English gloss to the Lindisfarne Gospels bears witness to early morphological simplification in the late Northumbrian dialect compared to other Old English varieties. Cases of merger in the nominal inflection have already been widely noted. Morphological syncretism in the area of derivation has attracted less attention, although here too variation with respect to other Old English dialects is to be expected. The aim of this paper is to establish how the language of the Lindisfarne gloss differs from that of other Old English texts concerning the degree of syncretism of the causative *jan*-formation. To that end, all deverbal *jan*-pairs (base and derivative) in the gloss have been identified, and the syntactic valency and meaning of each member of the pair have been assessed by studying each attestation individually. The main conclusion reached is that the language of the Lindisfarne gloss does not show more innovative traits than that of other Old English texts in the use of the causative formation. This points to derivational morphology behaving differently from inflectional morphology with respect to morphological loss in Old Northumbrian.

1 Introduction: the *jan*-formation in early Germanic languages

In this section, the Germanic causative formation will be briefly described, differences in the lexicalization stage of causatives among West Germanic languages will be pointed out and the aim of this paper will be more precisely defined against that background. Section 2 focuses on Old English causatives and their processes of semantic and morpho-syntactic change. Section 3 explains the methodology followed in this study, its sources and the process of data collection. Section 4 presents the data and the results obtained. Section 5 summarizes the conclusions of the study and suggests some questions which deserve further research. An appendix contains a list of all the *jan*-causatives and their derivational bases attested in the Lindisfarne gloss, with an indication of their meaning and syntactic use in the gloss as well as in 'general' Old English (for this term see note to section 2 below). A label indicates the relationship between *jan*- and strong verb in Lindisfarne, general Old English, and Germanic. The selection of items in the list and the information contained there have resulted from research conducted for this paper and from previous work (see García García 2012a). All *jan*-pairs discussed below may be found in the Appendix.

In the Germanic proto-language there existed a productive word-formation mechanism for deriving causative verbs from non-causative verbal bases by means of the suffix *-*(i)ja*, subject to Siever's Law. It is the most common deverbal word-formation pattern in this language, where deverbal *jan*-pairs constitute a significant portion of the verbal lexicon, with roughly a third of all Germanic strong verbs (about 640 listed by Seebold 1970) having a *jan*-derivate attested in one or another Germanic language. This mechanism, which goes back to Indo-European, consists of the addition of the aforementioned suffix to a primary verbal root in the Indo-European *o*-grade (Germanic *a*-grade). One example is:

(1) PGmc

**seta*- 'to sit, be seated'	strong base
**sat-ja*- 'to place, set, sit (sth.)'	weak derivative.

Although this pattern had ceased to be productive by the time of the first Germanic texts, *jan*-causatives constitute a substantial part of the verbal lexicon of early Germanic languages and are still recognizable in Present-Day English; cp. *sit* ~ *set*; *fall* ~ *fell*; *rise* ~ *rear*; *drink* ~ *drench*; *lie* ~ *lay*.

As has been pointed out in previous research (García García 2012b, 2013), the formal relationship between the base verb and its *jan*-derivative is rather opaque in all Germanic languages except Gothic, and is further obscured by semantic and syntactic changes associated with a process of lexicalization understood literally as a shift from grammar to lexicon.[1] As an example of semantic change undergone by both members of the *jan*-pair, in this case metaphorization, consider:

(2) a. non-causative base OE *weallan* 'to bubble forth, flow; well (with); exist in large numbers'
b. causative derivate OE *wyllan* 'to boil (sth.); torment, agitate (so.)'.

The causative *jan*-pair PGmc **melta*- 'to melt' (non-caus./intran.) ~ **maltija*- 'to melt' (caus./tran.) provides a good example of syntactic change. Whereas in Germanic the causative and non-causative senses of the verb *melt* are distinguished morphologically, in Present-Day English both senses are expressed by the same

1 See for instance Brinton and Traugott (2005: 54), quoting Ramat (1992: 557): "today's grammar may become tomorrow's lexicon". Incidentally, Brinton and Traugott refer repeatedly to Germanic causatives as instances of lexicalization (see pp. 54, 87, 105, 153 among others).

form, in what is known as a 'labile causative opposition' (Haspelmath 1993: 91, and n. 7):

(3) The ice melts (non-causative)
The sun melts the ice (causative).

Note that causativization is a valency-increasing word-formation mechanism, and that the causative derivatives of intransitive verbs differ from their transitive counterparts only in syntactic valency, as in, for example, *fall* ~ *fell*.[2]

Old English represents a transition between Proto-Germanic and Present-Day English, as in the following example:

(4) a. causative OE *myltan* (wk. I) 'to melt' (tran. and intran.) < PGmc **maltija-* 'to melt' (tran.)
b. non-causative OE *meltan* (st. 3) 'to melt' (mostly intran.) < PGmc **melta-* 'to melt' (intran.).

The weak verb, originally causative, is labile, that is to say, it can be used in both a causative and an intransitive sense in Old English. However, the intransitive use was originally reserved for the non-causative strong base. It is a case of 'syntactic merger' in that the valency frames of the causative and its base are no longer kept apart, and the morphological alternation *myltan* (wk.) ~ *meltan* (st.) is functionally empty (see García García 2012a: 137–139). Predictably, once syntactic merger has begun, one (or both) of the members of the causative opposition will disappear or change its (their) meaning. The loss of the distinctions formerly expressed by a given word-formation pattern, in this case the causative *jan*-formation, constitutes an instance of morphological simplification at the derivational level.

As a result of the lexicalization process of *jan*-causatives, the causative sense might ultimately become barely recognizable, as in *singe*, the *jan*-causative derived from *sing*, or disappear entirely, as in OE *onegan* 'to fear', *jan*-derivative to *og* 'fear'; cp. Go. *jan*-verb *ogjan* 'to scare (so.)'.[3]

As explained in García García (2013: 253–256), *jan*-causatives are affected by semantic and syntactic changes to a greater extent in Old English than in other Germanic and even West Germanic languages. Old English causatives exhibit a

2 For a detailed description of valency-changing morphological mechanisms cross-linguistically, see Haspelmath and Müller-Bardey (2000: 1130–1145).

3 Not all *jan*-verbs are causative. For a description of the functions of the Germanic -(*i*)*ja*-suffix, see Ringe (2006: 252–254).

higher degree of lexicalization. Thus, for instance, Go. *ogjan* 'to scare (so.)' above preserves its causative sense, but OE *onegan* 'to fear' does not.

By comparing their nominal and verbal paradigms it is apparent that Old English is inflectionally less rich than other West Germanic languages, with the exception of Old Frisian. A well-known example is the plural present inflection, with three different personal endings in Old High German as against one in Old English (Old Saxon and Old Frisian coincide with Old English in this). The nominal inflection provides further examples, as detailed in García García (2000). In addition, note that Old Saxon seems to occupy an intermediate position between Old High German and Old English, with, for instance, overt instrumental case in *a*-, *i*- and *u*-stems, like Old High German.

The causative formation provides an example of the comparatively greater syncretism of Old English in the area of derivational morphology. Compare the reflexes of the Germanic causative pair **-leiba-* 'to remain' ~ **-laibija-* 'to leave' in Old High German, Old Frisian, Old Saxon, and Old English:

(5)	OHG *biliban* 'to stay'	OHG *leiben* 'to leave, leave unfinished'
	OFris. *biliva* 'to stay'	OFris. *leva* 'to leave, let'
	OS *bilivan* 'to remain'	OS *farlevian* 'to leave (over)'
	OE *belifan* 'to be left over, remain'	OE *læfan, belæfan* 'to leave; remain'.

The causative opposition expressed by this *jan*-pair has remained intact in all West Germanic languages except Old English. Both OE *belifan* and *belæfan* can express the (non-causative) meaning 'to remain', with OE *belæfan* adopting the valency frame of the non-causative verb OE *belifan*. This is, as mentioned above, a process of syntactic merger that leads to morphological indistinctiveness, as the same meaning (in this case 'remain') can be expressed by both the strong and the *jan*-verb. The example illustrates a process that is often alluded to, though there has been no systematic study of it to date. The morphological behaviour of Old Northumbrian with respect to other Old English varieties seems to replicate that of Old English – even at its most inflectionally complex, early West Saxon – with respect to other early Germanic languages. The early inflectional syncretism undergone by Northumbrian has been widely acknowledged (see Ross 1937: 119–124; and standard Old English grammars, especially Brunner 1965).[4] To mention just two examples, consider the disintegration of the gender system (Brunner 1965: 195 n.; Fernández Cuesta et al. 2008: 139) and analogical levelling towards the most common noun inflectional pattern, masculine

4 Toon (1992), in his survey of Old English dialects for the first volume of *The Cambridge History of the English Language*, does not deal with it.

a-stems (see Fernández Cuesta and Rodríguez Ledesma 2001a: 480–481).[5] The aim of this paper is to determine whether the equation holds for derivational morphology too, as illustrated by the causative formation in the Old English gloss to the Lindisfarne Gospels (hereafter Lindisfarne). The meaning and valency of the *jan*-causatives and their bases attested in Lindisfarne will be established and contrasted with those found in other Old English varieties. The latter are drawn from a previous study on Old English causatives and will be summarized in the following section.

2 Old English causatives and their lexicalization process

As pointed out in García García (2012a), the extant Old English lexicon contains 106 deverbal *jan*-verbs with potential causative meaning with respect to their strong bases.[6] In that article the meaning and syntactic use or valency of both the non-causative bases and the *jan*-derivatives (a total of 212 verbs) were determined in order to ascertain the current relationship between the base and its potentially causative derivative in Old English. The *Dictionary of Old English* (hereafter *DOE*), complete up to letter *G*, and the nineteenth-century but still indispensable Old English dictionaries by Bosworth and Toller (1882–1898 and 1908–1921) and Clark Hall (1960; first edition in 1894) were consulted for every item. In cases where the meaning or valency of a formation is not sufficiently clear or different dictionaries supply conflicting versions, primary sources were collated via the *Dictionary of Old English Web Corpus* (hereafter *DOEC*).

Once the meaning and use of Old English *jan*-verbs with respect to their verbal bases were established, they were compared with those of their cognates in other Germanic languages, with the aim of determining the original derivational meaning of each pair in Proto-Germanic as the starting point from which that extant in Old English developed. The reconstruction of Proto-Germanic *jan*-pairs derives partly from previous work (García García 2005).

---

5 Extension of the endings of the *n*-declension to strong nouns does also occur in Old Northumbrian to a greater extent than in other varieties (Ross 1937: 101; Brunner 1965: 196).

6 In this paper, and in subsequent sections in particular, the term 'Old English' refers to 'undifferentiated' or 'general' Old English, including Old Northumbrian and the language of the Lindisfarne gloss. In the citation of infinitive forms, (general) Old English is skewed towards the late West Saxon variety. However, in the meaning and syntactic description of verbs, all areas and periods of Old English are represented.

As a result of the analysis, a basic list was compiled of Old English deverbal *jan*-verbs that were most probably causative in origin (including one which was intensive/iterative). The relationship between each *jan*-verb and its base, so far as it is attested, was analyzed and labelled, both in Old English and in Proto-Germanic, when the *jan*-formations were coined. By comparing the function of *jan*-verbs in the two languages it is possible to assess the changes that these verbs have undergone in Old English and identify some tendencies in their evolution, which were summarized in the previous section of the present paper.

Table 1 below presents numerically the results of the development of all 106 deverbal *jan*-verbs in Old English. Fifty-seven of them have a causative sense with respect to their bases in Old English, as against 71 in Proto-Germanic. These have evolved into Old English as follows: 56 Germanic causative pairs remain causative in Old English, three are doubtful, four develop idiosyncratic semantic relationships, five show no difference between the members of the pair and three Proto-Germanic causative pairs are clearly not causative in Old English.

Table 1. Old English deverbal *jan*-verbs according to function with respect to their base[7]

Function	Old English verbs	Germanic verbs
Causative	57	(56 causative in Germanic)
Causative?	12	(3 causative in Germanic)
Idiosyncratic	4	(4 causative in Germanic)
No difference	20	(5 causative in Germanic)
Non-causative	9	(3 causative in Germanic)
Not identifiable	3	
Intensive?	1	
TOTAL	106	(71 causative in Germanic)

Notice that of the 57 secure causative pairs attested in Old English (first line), nine show semantic deviation in one or both of their members; they are labelled 'C+IDI' (causative with idiosyncratic semantic development) and 'C+SPE' (causative with specialized meaning) in the aforementioned article. Thirteen have

7 The number of verbs in each group that has causative function in Germanic is presented in brackets (adapted from García García 2012a: 135).

changed their valency frame, and are labelled 'ColC' (collapsing causative opposition). This labelling convention is maintained in the final list in the Appendix.

The results of the study described above are global, that is, do not reflect textual, temporal or dialectal variation. This means that the deverbal *jan*-verbs that appear in Lindisfarne are obviously included, but they are not considered separately from those in other Old English texts. The next step is thus to contrast those global results against the textual data in Lindisfarne, as a representative of Old Northumbrian. The methodology of the study will be described next.

3 Methodology, sources and data collection process

For the present study, all occurrences of the 106 Old English deverbal *jan*-verbs and their strong bases attested in Lindisfarne were collected and analyzed to begin with. The exact meaning and syntactic use of the relevant verbs were determined and the relationship between each *jan*-verb and its base was classified according to the types listed in Table 1 above. The results obtained for the *jan*-verbs attested in Lindisfarne were then contrasted with those obtained for the whole Old English period.

For the purposes of the study (degree of morphological syncretism in Lindisfarne causatives), only those 57 verb-pairs for which a causative relation holds in Old English (see Table 1) were found relevant. They will be included in the final list attached. All the clauses in which they are attested in Lindisfarne, together with their Latin original, were analyzed. The relationship between the members of the *jan*-pairs is labelled 'Causative', 'Causative+SPE', 'Causative+IDI' and 'ColCausative', depending on whether they are straightforward causatives or display any semantic and/or syntactic (valency) changes (see above). In addition, one of the 12 instances registered in Table 1 of 'Causative?' (that is, where a causative relation is suspected but impossible to confirm) was clarified thanks to the present study.

Concerning the sources of the primary data for the study, the localization of *jan*-derivatives and their basic strong verbs was carried out by means of comprehensive searches in the *DOEC*; the task was facilitated by Cook's (1894) glossary and the *DOE*. Skeat's edition of the glosses to the Lindisfarne Gospels was used primarily (Skeat 1871–1887), mainly via the *DOEC*. However, the facsimile of the original manuscript was routinely consulted in the digitized version of the British Library webpage in all less than straightforward cases.

For the purposes of the study both the *jan*-verb and its strong base are equally relevant. That is, if the *jan*-member of an Old English causative pair is not attested in Lindisfarne but its base is, the semantic and syntactic behaviour of the latter has to be analyzed in order to determine whether it is additionally used in a causative sense (as a labile verb), in lieu of its *jan*-counterpart.

Simple formations were chosen as primary data to avoid semantic interference by prefixes. If these were not attested for a given verb, all its prefixed formations were considered, starting with *ge*-formations, which are least likely to carry substantial additional meaning. This is the case for instance of Li. *-drenca*, the *jan*-derivative to *drinca* 'to drink', only attested as *gedrenca* (*demergere*) 'to drown, sink', as *ofgedrenca* 'to drown, sink' (cp. L *demergere*) or as *underdrenca* 'to throttle' (cp. L *suffocare*). This example touches upon two other points which need clarifying with respect to the treatment of data. One is that if the verb is attested only in the past participle, no firm conclusion about its valency can be drawn. All formations with *-drenca* are attested in the past participle. See for instance f. 166rb17 (Luke 10.15) under (6). The Lindisfarne text is from the digitized facsimile of the manuscript in the British Library webpage, cited by folio, page, column and line in that order (see n. 6 in the Introduction); the relevant verbs are in bold; all English translations have been adapted from the *Douay-Rheims Bible*; the one below reflects the Latin verb in question, not the Old English one:

(6) (f. 166rb17; Luke 10.15)
et tu capharnaum usque in caelum exaltata usque ad infernum **demergeris**
⁊ ðu þæt is burg oðð heofon ahefen oðð to helle **gedrencged**
'and you, Capharnaum, which are exalted to heaven, shall be submerged into hell'.

L *demergeris* is in the passive voice and L *demergere* is a transitive-causative verb, but this need not be the case with Li. *gedrenca*, attested in the past participle *gedrencged* in the excerpt above. A past participle, even in a perfect construction with auxiliary verb, can have a transitive reading (*he was captured by bandits*), an intransitive one (*she was gone*) and even both (*he/the bottle was drunk*). Of course, comparison with the use of *drencan* elsewhere in Old English heavily suggests that it should be transitive-causative in Lindisfarne too, but caution has to be exercized in every case.

The other point to make explicit is that the translations of the verbs in this paper (see Appendix) are contextual; etymological translations are avoided, as far as possible. In the above example Li. *gedrenca* means roughly 'to submerge', even though its etymological translation would be 'to give to drink' or 'to drench'. Similarly, Li. *lecga*, *jan*-causative to Li. *licga* 'to lie', translates L *sternere*, *substernere* only, and contextually means 'to spread, strew', not 'lay', which would be its etymological translation.

Finally, the lemmatization of the attested forms has to be addressed. Present tense forms cannot always be classified as belonging to a strong verb or its weak *jan*-counterpart. The root vowel should provide information as to whether a particular present form is a reflex of the *jan*-verb or the strong verb, but given the sound changes affecting particularly diphthongs and long vowels in Old Northumbrian, this is not always the case (Campbell 1959: esp. 110–112; Brunner 1965: 38–51, 106–119). In fact, dictionaries tend to interpret the forms differently. By way of illustration, "(leht fato) beornendo" 'burning (candles)' (f. 134va 2; Luke 7.17; cp. L (*lucernas*) *ardentes*) appears under *berna* (wk.) in Cook (1894) and under *byrnan* (st.) in the *DOE*. This is a particularly intricate *jan*-pair, in which even the normalized infinitive forms are disputable. For the purposes of this study, however, the correct ascription of the form "beornendo" is not decisive, since its meaning and function are found in other forms that clearly belong either to the strong verb or the weak *jan*-verb. A more significant case is Li. *reca* 'to fumigate', as will be explained in the following section.

The data relevant for the study have been collected in the final list attached. The list is the result of both an etymological and a textual study of the verbs involved. The former determines the selection of items and the historical classifications proposed; the latter brings about a new assessment of their meaning and syntactic usage.

4 Data analysis

This section presents the results obtained from the analysis of the deverbal *jan*-verbs and their derivational bases attested in Lindisfarne. Their exact meaning and valency in the gloss will be established, classified and contrasted with those found in other Old English texts. The basic assumption is that those instances where Lindisfarne diverges significantly from other texts point to general directions of linguistic change in Old Northumbrian derivational morphology. In the first subsection (4.1), those Old English *jan*-verbs unattested in Lindisfarne will be dealt with; those attested will be the concern of the second subsection (4.2)

4.1 Old English *jan*-causatives unattested in Lindisfarne

Thirty-five *jan*-verbs out of 57 are not attested in Lindisfarne. They are:

(7) *(a)bylgan* 'to anger, offend', *acwencan* 'to extinguish (fire, lamp); snuff out (a candle)', *ahryran* 'to destroy, cause to fall', *astyrfan* 'to cause to die, kill', *aþrytan* 'to weary, tire out (so.)', *beryfan* 'to deprive (so. + acc.)', *beswemman* 'to make to swim', *bætan* 'to bridle and saddle; bait (so. + acc./dat.)', *cennan* 'to make known, declare', *dwellan* 'to lead into error (so. + acc.); err (intran.)', *dyrfan* 'to bring into danger, afflict; engage in (sth.)', *flygan* 'to put to flight, disperse (so., sth.)', *fyllan* 'to cause to fall, fell, kill', *gremman* 'to enrage, provoke', *leccan* 'to moisten, wet (sth.)', *hnægan* 'to cause to bow; humiliate', *litan* 'to incline (sth.)', *myltan* 'to melt (caus.; intran.); digest', *ræran* 'to cause to rise, rear, raise', *slypan* 'to put, slip (sth. + acc.)', *scremman* 'to cause to stumble', *sencan* 'to sink (sth.), submerge, drown', *slætan* 'to incite (a beast + acc.) in order to cause damage', *smican* 'to emit smoke (intran.); smoke, fumigate (sth.)', *sprengan* 'to scatter; burst (sth.); cause to spring; apply a clyster', *stæþþan* 'to support', *stepan* 'to cause to take a step', *swebban* 'to put to sleep; kill', *swengan* 'to cause to swing; swing, fling, strike', *sycan* 'to suckle, give suck', *wyrdan* 'injure, annoy; hinder', *þwænan* 'to reduce the size, cause to dwindle', *þyrran* 'to render dry', *wecgan* 'to move, shake (sth.)', *wyllan* 'to boil (sth.); torment, agitate (so.)'.

Most of these verbs are only scantily attested even outside Lindisfarne, but there are two conspicuous absences in the gloss. One is OE *myltan,* the causative corresponding to the strong verb OE *meltan,* also unattested in Lindisfarne. The reason probably lies in the lack of context for it in the original text. L *fundere*, which would most closely correspond to OE *myltan,* is used in the sense of 'to pour' (not 'to melt') in Lindisfarne and more accurately glossed with OE *ageotan*. The other notable absence is OE *ræran* 'to cause to rise, rear, raise', causative to OE *risan* 'to rise', which is attested in Lindisfarne only in the elsewhere rarer sense 'to be fitting, becoming' (L *debere*, *licere*). For the sense 'to rise', the prefixed formation OE *arisan* is mostly used, glossing L *surgere*, *oriri*, *ascendere* and others. The sense 'to cause to rise, raise' is frequent in Lindisfarne, where L *tollere* is glossed mostly as Li. *ahebba*. The absence of OE *ræran* seems therefore to be a genuine gap in the Old Northumbrian lexicon.[8]

8 For a detailed summary of dialectal differences in vocabulary in Old English see Fernández Cuesta and Rodríguez Ledesma (2001b).

After studying all the attestations of the relevant verbs in the gloss, we are entitled to conclude that none of the *jan*-verbs in the above list has been functionally replaced by its strong counterpart in Lindisfarne. That is, none of the strong verbs that serve as bases for any of the *jan*-formations absent in the gloss (see (7)) shows causative meaning in Lindisfarne in addition to its original non-causative sense. This is the case, however, in other Old English texts. Consider for example the strong verb Li. *smeca*, used only as intransitive 'to emit smoke' (L *fumigare*), whereas OE *smeocan* can be used both as intransitive 'to emit smoke' and transitive 'to smoke; fumigate (sth.)'. This verb serves as the base to the *jan*-formation OE *smican* 'to emit smoke (intran.); smoke, fumigate (sth.)', not attested in Lindisfarne as shown above. Thus, with respect to *jan*-verbs not attested in Lindisfarne, the preservation of original non-causative meaning and valency in their strong bases in the gloss is a conservative feature in comparison with other dialects.

4.2 Old English *jan*-causatives attested in the Lindisfarne gloss

Twenty-three out of 57 secure Old English causatives are attested in Lindisfarne. The meaning and function of 17 of them do not diverge from those in other Old English texts. They are:

(8) Li. *bega* 'to humiliate', *berna* 'to burn', *gecæla* 'to cool (sth.), *cwœlla* 'to destroy', *gedrenca* 'to drown', *græta* 'to greet', *hwerfa* 'to convert', *læda* 'to lead', *læra* 'to teach', *lecga* 'to spread', *generiga* 'to deliver', *reca* 'to smoke', *setta* 'to set', *geswœnca* 'to afflict', *wæcca* 'to watch', *towælta* 'to roll (sth.)', *wœnda* 'to turn'.

Little of interest can be gleaned from similarities in a contrastive study, beyond ascertaining their existence, determining the extent of overlap (in this case, roughly three quarters of the verbs show no difference in their usage in Lindisfarne with respect to other varieties) and some more detailed observations, which follow.

Li. *reca* 'to send forth smoke' cannot be clearly classified as strong or weak. Its sole attestation is the present participle "recende" 'smoking (flax)' (cp. (*linum*) *fumigans*; f. 49vb5, Matthew 12.20). The form might reflect (non-northern) OE *reocan* 'to reek, send forth smoke' with Anglian smoothing, or the weak verb OE *recan* 'to smoke (sth.), fumigate (sth.)'. Both the meaning and intransitive use of Li. *reca* in this attestation support its interpretation as strong verb.

The elsewhere rather common simplex OE *nerian* is not attested in Lindisfarne. L *salvare* is glossed with Li. (*ge*)*haela*, *gehalgiga*. For L *eruere*, which in other texts is also sometimes glossed with OE *nerian*, Lindisfarne uses *generiga* and *genioma*.

Occasionally, the absence of a verb in a causative opposition can be put in relationship with the existence of a frequently attested synonym. This applies to the strong verb OE *cwelan* 'to die', base to the causative OE *cwellan* 'to kill' (cp. Li. *cwœlla*). The former is not attested in Lindisfarne, where verbal derivatives of the adjective OE *dead* (Li. *deadiga* and others) and the verb Li. (*ge*)*swelta* are used instead.

Furthermore, Lindisfarne preserves the original meaning of the *jan*-verb *gretan* (cp. Li. *græta*). This is the *jan*-causative to the strong verb OE *gretan* 'to bemoan, weep for', not attested in Lindisfarne. The usual meaning of the *jan*-verb OE *gretan* is 'to approach, visit, address, greet'. In Lindisfarne it translates L *salutare* 'to greet'. The original causative sense of the *jan*-verb OE *gretan* is appreciable in the meanings 'to insult', 'to attack' and the like, which are attested in Old English, but much less frequently than the senses 'to approach, greet'. Not so in the Lindisfarne text, where they are pervasive in the prefixed formations Li. *agræta* 'to throw down' (cp. L *elidere*), or even more telling, Li. *gegræta* 'to torment' (cp. L *torquere*). Again in this instance the Lindisfarne gloss preserves inherited material to a higher degree than other Old English texts. Finally, for one of the *jan*-verbs attested in the gloss, Li. *besenca*, an alternative reading has been proposed; this will be addressed in more detail below.

Five of the 23 causatives attested in Lindisfarne show a different meaning or function from other texts in Old English. They are:

(9) Li. *depa* 'to dip', *feriga* 'to carry', *læfa* 'to leave', *gescrenca* 'to cause to dry', *stenca* 'to stink'.

The diverging instances have varying degrees of significance depending on the robustness of attestation among other factors. They will be dealt with individually. The *jan*-verb Li. *læfa* is attested twice in Lindisfarne (Mark 12.9 and Mark 12.22) with the meaning 'to leave (sth.)' (L *relinquere*), causative to the strong verb OE *belifan* 'to be left over, remain', unattested in the gloss. The *jan*-verb is attested in other Old English texts mainly with causative sense ('to leave (sth.)'), but also, though seldom, as non-causative 'to remain' (e.g. in Ælfric's *Catholic Homilies*, ÆCHom II, 3 21.79, following the *DOEC* citation system), having incorporated the meaning of the strong verbal base OE *belifan*. This innovation is not found in the gloss in the simplex. The prefixed formations Li. *gelæfa* and *oferlæfa* do have the intransitive sense 'to remain', glossing L *manere* and *superesse*, respectively; on Li. *gelæfa*, see below.

Two other *jan*-verbs remain faithful to their original causative meaning in Lindisfarne, namely Li. *depa* and *gescrenca*. The first is attested only once (Matthew 23.26), translating L *intingere* 'to dip, lower into or immerse in liquid', causative to a strong verb OE *dufan* 'to dive, plunge, sink (intran.)', unattested in the gloss.[9] The *jan*-verb has developed the specialized metaphorical meaning 'to baptize' outside Lindisfarne, where it is well-attested (normalized as OE *dypan*) in this sense. In the gloss, however, L *baptizare* is rendered by Li. *clænsiga*, *fulwiga*, *gefulwiga* and *ingefulwiga*, never by Li. *depa*.

As for Li. *gescrenca* 'to dry (sth.)' (strong base Li. *gescrinca* 'to wither away, dry up'), it is only in Lindisfarne that the straightforward causative meaning appears. Its only occurrence follows, with the English translation:

(10) (f. 51vb16; Matthew 13.6)
sole autem orto aestuauerunt et quia non habebant radicem ***aruerunt***
sunna uutedlice miððy arras weron forbernedł besenced ⁊ forðon ne hæfdon ł næbbend wyrtrumme gescriungon ł **weron gescrencde**
'And when the sun was up they were scorched: and because they had not root, they withered away'.

Outside Lindisfarne the fairly well-attested OE (*ge*)*screncan* has the meaning 'to cause to stumble, ensnare' (L *supplantare*). Given the semantic divergence, it is a fair question whether L (*ge*)*screncan* 'to cause to dry' and 'to cause to stumble, ensnare' represents one or two different formations. The *Oxford English Dictionary* (*OED*: s.vv. *shrench*, v.1, and *shrench*, v.2) gives two different entries for *shrench*, reflexes of OE *screncan* and Li. *gescrenca*, respectively. In assuming homonymy, the authors circumvent the difficulty of harmonizing the meanings 'to dry (sth.)' and 'to put a stumbling block on the way of'. In this, they follow Bosworth and Toller, who separate OE *screncan* 'to lay a stumbling block in a person's way, trip up, ensnare' from OE *gescrencan* 'to cause to shrink', for which they provide the Lindisfarne citation. For the purposes of this study, the argument is of little relevance: whether OE *screncan* is a single verb with two related senses or two homonymous verbs, the original causative sense is attested in Lindisfarne only. The *jan*-opposition OE *screncan* 'to cause to stumble' ~ *scrincan* 'to wither away, dry up' was defined as 'C+IDI?' in García García (2012a), that is, doubtful causative with idiosyncratic lexical development. A close reading of its only attestation in Lindisfarne yields the meaning 'to cause to dry', causative to 'to dry', and allows us to confirm the interpretation of OE *gescrencan* as causative. Thus, the number of causative oppositions attested in Old English has to be increased from 57 to 58.

A semantic hapax is also provided by the only attestation of the *jan*-verb Li. *stenca* in Lindisfarne. This verb has the meaning 'to stink' (L *foetere*) in John 11.39,

9 For the ultimately unexplained sound relationships in this verbal root see Seebold (1970: 155–156), Heidermanns (1993: 153–154) and García García (2005: 102–103).

whereas OE *stencan* means 'to scatter; emit breath with effort' in other texts.[10] The verb is in a collapsing causative opposition with OE *stincan* 'to spring, leap; emit a smell', which is not attested in Lindisfarne.

The last of the *jan*-verbs whose function in Lindisfarne diverges from other Old English texts is OE *feriga*, OE *ferian*, causative to OE *faran* 'to go, travel', widely attested throughout Old English texts, including Lindisfarne. The entry of OE *ferian* in the *DOE* supplies the information that this verb is attested around 200 times, with the transitive-causative meaning 'to carry, transport'. The *DOE* lists only one occurrence of *ferian* as an intransitive verb of movement 'to go, travel, depart', namely Mald 175 (their abbreviation). Because of the exceptionality of this usage, it is tagged with a question mark in the *DOE* entry, and a possible mistake for OE *feran* is suggested.

The *jan*-verb Li. *feriga* is attested twice in Lindisfarne, in both instances as a gloss for L *ferre*. However, the syntax of the constructions is dissimilar. In f. 97vb4 (Mark 2.3), "feredon" glosses L *ferentes* in a paratactic verbal construction (in bold) with "brengende" as second gloss:

(11) *et* ***uenerunt ferentes*** *ad eum paraliticum qui a quatuor portabatur*
⁊ **cuomon feredon** vel brengende to him ðone eorðcrypel se ðe from feowrum wæs geboren
'And they came to him, bringing one sick of the palsy, who was carried by four'.

In f. 156va4–5 (Luke 7.12) the Latin verb in the passive voice *efferebatur* 'was being carried' is rendered with the active participial construction "wæs ferende" 'was going past':

(12) *et ecce defunctus* ***efferebatur*** *filius unicus matris suae*
⁊ heono dead **wæs ferende** sunu ancende moderes his
'behold a dead man was carried out, the only son of his mother'.[11]

The Lindisfarne manuscript reads clearly "wæs ferende", and not "wæs ferede", which would normally be expected if Li. *feriga* was used in a transitive sense 'to carry'. The fact that the subject of "wæs ferende" is not animate is not an obstacle for the interpretation of the verb as active 'going past', OE *feran* 'to go', for which Li. *feriga* has been suggested to stand (see above), is consistently attested with

10 The noun OE *stenc* can mean both 'fragrance' and 'stench', as well as neutral 'odour'. The sense 'stench' might have influenced the meaning of Li. *stenca*.

11 The West Saxon version of the Gospels, which reads "geboren", is consistent with this translation.

inanimate subjects (see *DOE* s.v. *feran*). Therefore we could conclude, with all due caveats because of poor attestation, that the causative verb Li. *feriga* is in a process of syntactic merger in the language of the Lindisfarne text. In this case, the transitive-causative verb *feriga* adds to its original valency pattern that of its intransitive counterpart in the causative opposition Li. *fara* 'to go, travel, depart' (L *ire*, *abire*, *exire* etc.). This may be interpreted as an innovative trend in Lindisfarne with respect to other Old English texts, where, as has been pointed out, the intransitive use is virtually absent in OE *ferian*.[12]

The process of syntactic merger has been detected in 13 causative pairs in Old English so far, including for instance OE *bærnan* 'to burn (caus.; intran. (-))', and its strong base OE *byrnan* 'to burn (intran.; caus. (-))' (García García 2013). In Lindisfarne the following causative pairs with a collapsing opposition showing syntactic merger are attested:

Table 2. Causative pairs with syntactic merger in the Lindisfarne gloss

***jan*-causative in Lindisfarne and (general) Old English**	**non-causative base in Lindisfarne and (general) Old English**
Li. *bega* 'to humiliate' (tran.); bend (the knees)' (only past part.) (cp. L *humiliare*, *flectere*) OE *bigan* 'to bend (tran.; intran. (-)); turn (caus.; intran.); 'humiliate'	Li. *gebuga* 'to bow, bend; cut down' (tran.) (cp. L *caedere*, *inclinare*) OE *bugan* 'to bow, bend (intran.; tran.?); turn (intran.)'
Li. *berna* 'to burn, light' (tran. and intran.) (cp. L *accendere*, *ardere*, *comburere*) OE *bærnan* 'to burn' (tran.; intran. (-))	Li. *bearna* 'to burn' (intran.) (cp. L *ardere*) OE *byrnan* 'to burn (intran.; tran.(-))'
Li. *hwerfa* 'to convert (intran.); borrow' (L *convertere*, *mutuari*) OE *hwyrfan* 'to go, return; turn, change (caus.; intran.); exchange'	Not in Li. OE *hweorfan* 'to go; turn, change (intran.; caus. (-))'
Li. *wæcca* 'watch, be awake; raise, provoke' (cp. L *vigilare*, *suscitare*) OE *weccan* 'to waken, arise, spring (intran.; caus. (-))'	Not in Li. OE *wæcnan* 'come into being, be born, spring'
Li. *wœnda* 'to turn' (intran.) (cp. L *verti*, *reverti*) OE *wendan* 'to turn (round), change (caus.; intran.); go (refl.; intran.)'	Li. *winda* 'to plat (sth.)' (cp. L *plectere*) OE *windan* 'to spring (intran.); roll (intran.; caus.); weave (sth.)'

12 As one of the reviewers has aptly pointed out, "wæs fregend" glosses L *interrogatus* in Luke 9.9. Whether both instances of a present participle glossing a Latin past participle respond to the same underlying causes is unclear.

The above examples illustrate the kind of meanings which are amenable to double valency (causative and non-causative) in one and the same form, that is, for which expression through a labile verb might be expected. Briefly, these are verbs that denote a change of state (more rarely, a process) that can be conceived of as either happening spontaneously or induced by an agent, such as for instance 'to melt', 'to turn', 'to change', 'to cool', 'to fold' (Haspelmath 1993: 90). The meaning of Li. *feriga* 'to carry' does not belong to this group, as it inevitably involves an agent. In verbs with this and similar meanings an intermediate stage between causative and intransitive usage is often attested in which a reflexive pronoun is used to express intransitive 'to go' (in this case, *feriga hine*; see Hermodsson 1952: *passim* for numerous examples in West Germanic languages). This predictable stage is not attested in Lindisfarne, although there is context for it glossing the very frequent L *ire* and verbs of similar meaning. The *DOE* gives only one instance of OE *ferian* used with reflexive pronoun, for which the translation 'to convey oneself by walking, walk' is given. The occurrence follows, with the verb construction and reflexive pronoun in bold and a translation:

(13) (ÆCHom II, 10 82.36)
ic wolde ðine ðenunge sylf nu gearcian. gif **ic me** mid feðunge **ferian mihte**
'I would now prepare your refection myself, if I could walk (literally 'convey myself by walking')'.

In summary, Li. *feriga* ~ *fara* stand in a 'collapsing causative opposition', with the *jan*-causative adopting the valency of its intransitive base. This is on the one hand typologically rare for this type of meaning, and on the other it constitutes an innovation with respect to most other Old English texts, where OE *ferian* is almost exclusively transitive.

With respect to the last of the *jan*-verbs to be addressed, Li. *besenca*, there are sufficient grounds for interpreting the manuscript reading <besenced> as an alternative spelling for <besenged>, from the OE *jan*-verb *besengan* 'to singe, burn slightly'.[13] Its only occurrence follows:

(14) (f. 51vb14; Matthew 13.6)
[sole autem orto] aestuaverunt: weron forberned ł besenced
'[And when the sun was up] they were burned or scorched'.

13 This is assumed by the *DOE*, too, where Li. <besenced> is listed under the entry for OE *besengan*.

In the first place, the context requires a meaning closer to OE *besengan* 'to singe, burn slightly' than to OE *besencan* 'to cause to sink, submerge, drown'. Further, variation between <nc>, <ng(c)> and <nc(g)> in the same phonetic environment, i.e. nasal and velar plosive originally followed by palatal semivowel, is found elsewhere in the gloss. Notice the following instances belonging to the paradigms of Li. *-drenca* and *ge-screnca*:

(15) *-drenca*: <gedrencged> (f. 166rb17; Luke 10.15), <ofgedrenced> (f. 62vb16; Matthew 18.6)
gescrenca: <gescrengc> (f. 153va4; Luke 6.8), <gescrencde> (f. 51vb16; Matthew 13.6).[14]

Finally, during the data collection process and analysis several questions have arisen that might be worth further study. In some verbal derivational paradigms the prefix *ge-*, rather than the suffix *-jan*, seems to function as causativizer. This is the case with the strong verb Li. *luta* 'to fall down, bend forward', an intransitive verb glossing L *procidere*, the *jan*-formation of which is not attested in Lindisfarne; its semantic causative pendant is the prefixed formation Li. *geluta* 'to lay', glossing L *reclinare*. Another example is the strong verb Li. *bearna* attested only once as intransitive 'to burn', whereas the prefixed Li. *gebearna* is transitive 'to burn' in its four occurrences (Matthew 22.7, Luke 3.17, Luke 8.16 and Luke 11.33); the *jan*-formation Li. *berna* 'to burn' is used both as transitive and intransitive. Finally, the *jan*-verb Li. *hwerfa* 'to convert; borrow' is intransitive in its first and original meaning, whereas Li. *gehwerfa* 'to convert' is transitive-causative in its only conclusive occurrence, viz. the imperative singular "gehuerf", cp. L *converte* (f. 83rb2; Matthew 26.52; it is also attested in the past participle). In other verbal paradigms, however, the *ge*-formation seems to have exactly the opposite function; this is the case with Li. *læfa* 'to leave', transitive-causative, and Li. *gelæfa* 'to remain', intransitive. That the verbal prefix *ge-* had in its origin a transitivizing function has been considered and rejected by a few authors previously (see for instance Hiltunen 1983: 49). The question here is whether the suffix *ge-* stood in competition with the *jan*-formation as a causativizer during the Old English period itself.[15]

14 To my knowledge, the causes of this variation remain to be established. At any rate, it cannot be solely explained by assibilation (or lack of it) of palatalized velars, as described in Luick (1964: 907 § 689).

15 See Martín Arista (2012) for a recent evaluation of the morphological status of the prefix *ge-* in Old English.

Another issue that deserves attention is the weakening of strong verbs in the Lindisfarne gloss. The shift to the weak inflection is present in all Old English varieties, but it seems to be more frequent in the Lindisfarne text in the wake of morphological, or more precisely, inflectional levelling in this variety (thus e.g. Hogg 1992b: 90). Ross (1937: 153–154) lists some instances of weak forms of strong verbs in Lindisfarne. To these the case of OE *sweltan* 'to die' should be added. This is an ablauting verb in other Old English varieties. In Lindisfarne it is attested in the past singular as "suoelte" (f. 237vb24; John 11.37), non-ablauting and with final *-e* by analogy with weak pasts (compare, with the same root-vowel combination, the present participle form "suoeltende" in f. 238va23; John 11.51). The past tense to the *jan*-causative to a strong verb Li. *swelta* would probably be Li. *swælte*, in accordance to the attested past tense of the deverbal *jan*-causative Li. *-wælta*, namely Li. *-wælte* (see e.g. "to wælte" in f. 129ra5; Mark 15.46); the derivative base of Li. *-wælta* is not attested in Old English, but can be reconstructed as PGmc **welta-* on account of OIc *velta* 'to roll (intran.)', a strong verb with the same phonetic structure as OE *sweltan*.[16]

Summing up the results obtained from the data analysis, in the first place the initial list of secure Old English causative *jan*-pairs has to be increased by one item (viz. (*ge*)*screncan*). Twenty-three out of those now 58 causative pairs are attested in the Lindisfarne gloss. There is some information to be gained from unattested causative *jan*-verbs. All of their strong bases attested in the gloss show non-causative meaning exclusively, whereas some of them have adopted additional causative meaning in other texts. The evidence suggests that the variety of which the Lindisfarne text is witness has not taken part in this innovation. The vast majority (17) of the 23 *jan*-verbs attested in the gloss do not diverge in meaning and/or valency from other Old English texts. Their label in the attached list is the same as that in (general) Old English. One of these verbs, Li. *græta* 'to greet', retains the original causative meaning to the strong verb OE *gretan* 'to weep' in its prefixed formations Li. *agræta* 'to throw down' and Li. *gegræta* 'to torment'. This is not the case in other Old English texts, where the first formation is not attested[17] and the second (OE *gegretan*) almost universally has the meanings 'to visit, address, greet'. Again, the Lindisfarne text preserves rather than innovates. The form "besenced" must be ascribed to an infinite Li. *besenga* 'to

16 Seebold (1970: 491) proposes, on the strength of the attestation of this verb in Lindisfarne, a deverbal *jan*-formation from the strong verb OE *sweltan* and sets the infinitive form as OE *swæltan*. The alternation in the root vowel is not supported by the attestation. This is rather an instance of pure weakening, with no word-formation process involved.

17 The *jan*-verb *agræta* 'to throw down' is only attested in the Northumbrian gloss to the Rushworth Gospels, besides Lindisfarne.

scorch' (L *aestuare*) rather than Li. *besenca*, and agrees in meaning and valency with *besengan* in other Old English texts. Five out of 23 *jan*-verbs present diverging meaning and/or valency in the gloss. Allowing for distortions due to the limitations and arbitrariness of attestation, the behaviour of three of them (Li. *læfa*, *depa*, *gescrenca*) can be read as conservative, whereas Li. *stenca* and *feriga* show rather innovative traits. In a nutshell, the Lindisfarne gloss does not diverge substantially from other Old English texts in its use of causative *jan*-verbs. There are a few divergences, which point both in the direction of preservation and innovation, with a tendency to the former. There are no signs that the Lindisfarne gloss is more innovative than other Old English varieties with respect to derivational morphology, as opposed to inflectional.

5 Conclusions and questions for further study

In this paper all the attestations of the deverbal *jan*-verbs in the Old English glosses to the Lindisfarne Gospels have been analyzed in context from the point of view of their meaning and morphosyntax. The main aim was to find out whether the Lindisfarne text showed signs of greater morphological syncretism than other Old English varieties in this area of derivational morphology. The results obtained for the Lindisfarne gloss have thus been contrasted with those obtained for general Old English in a previous study on the topic (García García 2012a).

The most relevant conclusion of this study is that the Lindisfarne text does not show greater syncretism in the use of the word-formation pattern of deverbal *jan*-verbs than other Old English varieties; if anything, it is rather conservative with respect to the preservation of their causative meaning and valency compared to other texts. This stands in contrast to the proportionally abundant cases of merger and loss of inflectional markers evident in the Lindisfarne gloss (see the papers by Millar, Cole and Rodríguez Ledesdma in this volume). Clearly, derivational morphology has to be separated from inflectional morphology in this regard.

A further contribution is the etymological, lexicological and syntactic reassessment of the verbs on which the study is based, specified in the attached list. The inclusion of a verb in the list is a statement of its etymology. The meanings and usages proposed for each verb follow the textual analysis of all their respective occurrences in the gloss. Moreover, the list has both diatopic and historical depth as the general Old English correspondence of each of the *jan*-causatives attested in Lindisfarne is provided and their function in those two variants and in their Germanic ancestor tagged. The data collected in the Appendix afford information that can be useful for other researches.

The present analysis confirms, for those verbs attested in the Lindisfarne gloss, the etymological, semantic and syntactic classification set out in García García (2012a), with a single exception. The verb OE *screncan* 'to cause to dry' has clearly causative meaning in the gloss, but had been labelled 'doubtful' in the earlier study. The number of secure causatives in Old English thus rises from 57 to 58.

One of the questions for further study addressed by the paper is the possible encroachment of the prefix *ge-* in the function of the *jan*-formation as expression of the causative pendant to a non-causative base. One such example is Li. *luta* 'to fall down, bend forward' and *geluta* 'to lay (sth.)' (see previous section). Another issue worth pursuing is the use of weak for strong forms in Lindisfarne, as in Li. *swelta* 'to die'.[18]

Appendix

Deverbal *jan*-verbs with possible causative meaning attested in the Lindisfarne gloss

The following alphabetical list includes all potentially causative *jan*-pairs attested in Lindisfarne and their function in the Lindisfarne gloss (Li.), general Old English (OE; see n. 6) and Germanic (PGmc). In the first column of the table the *jan*-verb is given in its (conjectured) Lindisfarne infinitive form with Present-Day English translation and Latin original in italics. This is followed by the normalized Old English form together with its meaning (revised from García García 2012a: 143–148). In the second column, the corresponding strong verbal bases in Lindisfarne (if attested) and Old English are listed. The third, fourth and fifth columns label the relationship between *jan*-verb and base in Li., OE and PGmc. The following labels describe the function of the *jan*-formation or the semantic relationship between *jan*-verb and strong base, as the case may be:

C = causative
Col C = collapsing causative opposition, with one or both members adopting new valency values (see section 1)

18 This research has been financially supported by the Spanish Ministry of Science and Technology (project FFI2011-28272). I am very grateful to the editors of the volume, my colleague Christopher Langmuir and anonymous reviewers for their helpful comments and suggestions, too many to be acknowledged individually. Of course, the remaining errors are only mine.

IDI = a Germanic causative relationship has undergone idiosyncratic semantic changes
SPE = semantic specialization in either member of the *jan*-opposition.

Jan-verb	Base	Func. in Li.	Func. in OE	Func. in PGmc
Li. *bega* 'to humiliate' (tran.); 'bend (the knees)' (only past part.) (cp. L *humiliare, flectere*) OE *bigan* 'to bend (tran.; intran. (-)); turn (caus.; intran.)'; 'humiliate'	Li. *gebuga* 'to bow, bend; cut down' (tran.) (cp. L *caedere, inclinare*) OE *bugan* 'to bow, bend (intran.; tran.?); turn (intran.)'	Col C+IDI	Col C+IDI	C
Li. *berna* 'to burn; light' (tran.; intran.) (cp. L *accendere, ardere, comburere*) OE *bærnan* 'to burn' (tran.; intran. (-))	Li. *bearna* 'to burn' (intran.) (cp. L *ardere*) OE *byrnan* 'to burn (intran.; tran.(-))'	Col C	Col C	C
Li. *gecœla* 'to cool (sth.)' (cp. L *refrigerare*) OE *celan* 'to cool or chill (sth.), make cold; quench (thirst)	Not in Li. OE *calan* 'to be or become cold'	C	Col C	C
Li. *cwœlla* 'to destroy, kill' (cp. L *interficere*) OE *cwellan* 'to kill'	Not in Li. OE *cwelan* 'to die'	C	C	C
Li. *depa* 'to dip, lower into, or immerse in liquid' (tran.) (cp. L *intingere*) OE *dypan* 'to dip, immerse in liquid (sth.); baptize'	Not in Li. OE *dufan* 'to dive, plunge, sink (intran.)'[19]	C	C+SPE	C
Li. *gedrenca* 'to drown, sink', tran.? (only *ge-* + past part.) (cp. L *demergere*) OE *drencan* 'to give drink to; drench, saturate'	Li. *drinca* 'to drink' (cp. L *bibere*) OE *drincan* 'to drink (sth. + acc)'	C	C	C

19 On *p/f* variation in this verb see Seebold (1970: 155–156).

Jan-verb	Base	Func. in Li.	Func. in OE	Func. in PGmc
Li. *feriga* 'to carry; go, pass' (cp. L *ferre*) OE *ferian* 'to carry, transport'	Li. *fara* 'to go, travel' (cp. L *ire*, etc.) OE *faran* 'to go, travel'	Col C	C	SPE (by ship)
Li. *grœta* 'to greet' (cp. L *salutare*); Li. *gegrœta* 'to torment' (cp. L *torquere*) OE *gretan* 'to approach, touch; damage, attack; address (so. + acc.); greet'	Not in Li. OE *gretan*, *greotan* 'to bemoan, weep for'	C+IDI	C+IDI	C
Li. *hwerfa* 'to convert (intran.); borrow' (cp. L *convertere, mutuari*) OE *hwyrfan* 'to go, return; turn, change (caus.; intran.); exchange'	Not in Li. OE *hweorfan* 'to go; turn, change (intran.; caus. (-))'	Col C	Col C	C
Li. *læda* 'to lead, carry' (cp. L *ducere, adducere, educere, tollere, ferre, conferre*) OE *lædan* 'to lead; take, carry, bring; produce'	Not in Li. OE *liþan* 'to go, sail'	C	C	C
Li. *læfa* 'leave (sth.)' (cp. L *relinquere*) OE *læfan* 'to leave; remain (-)'	Not in Li. OE *belifan* 'to be left over, remain'	C	Col C	C
Li. *læra* 'to teach, instruct' (cp. L *docere, instruere, admonere*) OE *læran* 'to teach; preach; persuade, suggest'	not in OE; Go. *lais* 'knows'	C	C	C
Li. *lecga* 'to spread, strew (sth.)' (cp. L *sternere, substernere*) OE *lecgan* 'to cause to lie, lay; slay'	Li. *licga* 'to lie, be at rest, lie down' (cp. L *jacere, discumbere*) OE *licgan* 'to lie, be at rest; lie dead'	C	C	C

Jan-verb	Base	Func. in Li.	Func. in OE	Func. in PGmc
Li. *generiga* 'to deliver, pluck out' (cp. L *eruere*) OE *nerian* 'to save'	Not in Li. OE *nesan* 'to be saved from, escape from'	C+IDI	C	C
Li. *reca* 'to smoke' (intran.) (cp. L *fumigare*) OE *recan* 'to smoke (sth.); fumigate'	Not in Li.?[20] OE *reocan* 'to reek, send forth smoke'	?	C	C
Li. *gescrenca* 'to cause to dry' (cp. L *arere*) OE *screncan* 'to cause to stumble, ensnare'	Li. *gescrinca* 'to wither away, dry up' OE *scrincan* 'to wither away, dry up; become weak; shrink'	C	C+IDI?	C?
Li. *besenca* 'to scorch' (cp. L *aestuare*) OE *sengan* 'to singe, burn slightly; afflict'	Li. *singa* 'to sing' (cp. *cantare, canere*) OE *singan* 'to sing'	C	C	C
Li. *setta* 'to set, place, put, settle' (cp. L *imponere, ponere, statuere, instituere, constituere*) OE *settan* 'to set, place, put; settle; subside (intran.) (-)'	Li. *sitta* 'to sit, be seated, sit down' (cp. L *sedere, discumbere*) OE *sittan* 'to sit, be seated; occupy (a seat)'	C	C	C
Li. *stenca* 'to stink' (cp. L *foetere*) OE *stencan* 'to scatter; emit breath with effort; stink'	Not in Li. OE *stincan* 'to spring, leap; emit a smell'	SPE	Col C +SPE	C
Li. *geswœnca* 'to afflict' (cp. L *vexare*) OE *swencan* 'to cause a person to labour; harass, afflict'	Not in Li. OE *swincan* 'to toil, labour, work with effort'	C	C	C

20 The occurrence in Lindisfarne might be an attestation of the strong verb OE *reocan* (see section 4).

Jan-Verb	Base	Func. in Li.	Func. in OE	Func. in PGmc
Li. *wæcca* 'to watch, be awake; raise; provoke' (cp. L *vigilare, suscitare*) OE *weccan* 'to waken; arise, spring (intran.; caus. (-))'	Not in Li. OE *wæcnan* 'to come into being, be born; spring'	Col C	Col C	C
Li. *to/ge/a/efta/fro-mawælta* 'to roll (sth.)' (cp. L *advolvere, revolvere*) OE *wyltan* 'roll (sth.)'	Not attested in OE; OIc *velta* 'to roll (intran.)'	C	C	C
Li. *wœnda* 'to turn' (intran.) (cp. L *verti, reverti*) OE *wendan* 'to turn (round), change (caus.; intran.); go (refl.; intran.)'	Li. *winda* 'to plat' (cp. L *plectere*) OE *windan* 'to spring (intran.); roll (intran.; caus.); weave (sth.)'	Col C +SPE	Col C +SPE	C

Mª Nieves Rodríguez Ledesma

Dauides sunu vs. *filii david*: The Genitive in the Gloss to the Lindisfarne Gospels

Abstract: This paper offers a quantitative study of the genitive singular inflection in adnominal constructions in the gloss to the Lindisfarne Gospels. It focuses, on the one hand, on zero genitives, and on the other, on the word order of adnominal genitives in the gloss. The present study shows that the gloss is innovative at the morphological level, as shown in the extension of genitive singular *-es* from the *a*-stems to all noun classes, including proper nouns, which tend to add the native inflection regardless of the Latin ending. Despite the generalization of genitive singular *-es*, however, the gloss also illustrates the omission of this case inflection, which will become one of the characteristic features of the northern dialects in later periods. With regard to word order, the gloss follows the Latin pattern (postposed genitives) in most cases. However, although very few in number, preposed genitives seem to illustrate the 'natural' word order in the dialect of the glossator, since they occur in the gloss independently from the original.

The present article offers a quantitative study of the genitive singular inflection in adnominal constructions in the gloss to the Lindisfarne Gospels. Previous research on the genitive in the gloss includes Bale (1907), which analyzes the variety of relations between nouns denoted by the genitive case, such as the partitive genitive, the genitive of possession, description and definition, or the subjective and objective genitives. The genitive as object of verbs and adjectives is also dealt with, together with the development of prepositional constructions as alternatives to the genitive case. Sections on the genitive are also found in works analyzing the language of the Northumbrian gloss to some of the Gospels, such as Lea (1894), focused on Mark's Gospel, or Füchsel (1901) on John's. More general remarks, based on the language of the gloss as a whole, are found in Ross (1960) and especially Ross (1937), among others.

In contrast with previous works, the present article focuses on the genitive singular inflection in adnominal constructions in the gloss.[1] It studies, on the one hand, zero genitives, in order to determine whether this feature, which is characteristic of northern dialects in later periods, is also present in the dialect of the gloss. For this purpose, a detailed quantitative analysis of the genitive singular of both common and proper nouns is carried out, taking into account those

1 The genitive as object of verbs and prepositions in the gloss lies outside the scope of the present paper.

factors which may condition the presence or omission of the inflection, such as the extension of *a*-stems to other noun classes or the ending of the genitive in the Latin original.

The second objective of the present paper is the study of the word order of adnominal genitives in the gloss (preposition vs. postposition) in order to determine the degree of influence exerted by the Latin word order and the extent to which Aldred innovates and deviates from the original in order to show the native pattern. Finally, in line with works such as Brunner (1947–1948), van Bergen (2008), Kotake (2012) or Cole (2014, and this volume), which have studied the distribution of linguistic variants in the gloss and have established a demarcation at Mark 5.40 and around the beginning of John, the present article aims to determine whether the distribution of the different variants found for the genitive of the nouns which form the basis of the present study remains stable throughout the gloss, or certain variants are confined to or predominate in certain sections of the text.

The *Dictionary of Old English Web Corpus* (hereafter *DOEC*), based on Skeat's (1871–1887) edition, has been used to collect the data, but all the tokens have been collated with the facsimile copy of the manuscript (Kendrick et al. 1956), which has revealed examples of poor editorial practice, mainly inconsistencies as regards abbreviations. In the case of *drihten*, for example, glossing L *domini*, an abbreviated form is often used: "drih'". Skeat has expanded it to "drihten" (with zero inflection) in LkGl (Li) 3.2,[2] but to "drihtnes" (with syncope and inflection *-es*) in LkGl (Li) 3.4, 10.39, 12.47, 13.35 and 19.38. By relying exclusively on the *DOEC*, therefore, one would posit the existence of both inflected and uninflected forms for the genitive of this noun, whereas in fact no instance of zero genitive is attested in the gloss. Something similar happens with the proper noun *Joseph*. Two abbreviated forms are used to gloss the indeclinable Latin genitive *ioseph*: "iosep'", which has been expanded to "iosepes" in LkGl (Li) 3.23 (suggesting an inflected form) and "ios'", expanded to "ioseph" in LkGl (Li) 4.22 (suggesting an uninflected genitive). This inconsistency regarding abbreviations makes it impossible, therefore, to give an accurate picture of the frequency and distribution of the different inflections used for the genitive in the gloss by relying exclusively on Skeat's edition or the *DOEC* (see further Fernández Cuesta, this volume).

With regard to the methodology, and because of the wealth of spelling and morphological variants attested in the gloss, the *DOEC* was searched for the Latin genitive form of both the common and the proper nouns which form the basis of the present study. Thus, for the kinship nouns ending in *-r* or *r-stems*, the terms of

2 The title abbreviations and editions of the Old English texts mentioned in this paper are those employed by the *DOEC*.

search were Latin *patris*, *matris*, *fratris*, *sororis* and *filiae*. In those cases in which the Latin noun is indeclinable (*Israel*) or has the same form in nominative and genitive (*domus*), a careful collation of all the examples obtained by searching for the base form was necessary in order to identify the genitive forms. Following the *DOEC*, the examples given throughout the article offer both the Latin text and the Northumbrian gloss, to which a modern English translation, taken from the *Douay-Rheims* version of the Bible, has been added.

The article is organized as follows: section 1 provides a quantitative analysis of zero genitives in the gloss. Common nouns are studied in section 1.1, in the following order: kinship *r*-stems, which had zero inflection in the genitive singular in early West Saxon; nouns used to gloss Latin nouns which had the same form in nominative and genitive (such as *hus* glossing L *domus*); and other common nouns whose uninflected forms cannot be accounted for by claiming Latin influence. Section 1.2 examines proper nouns, and a distinction is again established depending on the morphology of the Latin noun (indeclinable or not). Section 2 analyzes the word order of adnominal genitives (preposition vs. postposition) in order to determine to what extent Aldred is influenced by Latin or innovates and deviates from the original. Finally, section 3 provides conclusions.

1 Zero genitives in the gloss: a detailed quantitative analysis

1.1 Common nouns

1.1.1 Kinship *r*-stems

As claimed by Ross (1937: 99), the genitive singular inflection -*es* is extended to practically all declensions in the gloss, though older forms are often preserved as well. This is the situation found with kinship *r*-stems, although not all nouns belonging to this class behave in the same way, as happens also in West Saxon. Thus, according to Hogg and Fulk (2011: § 3.130), the five kinship nouns can be divided into three morphological types. The first type consists of *fæder*, "which during the period gradually assumes all the inflections of the *as*-declension, most reluctantly so in the gen./dat. sg."; the second consists of *sweostor*, "which is characterized by zero-inflection except in the gen./ dat. pl."; and the third type consists of the remaining three nouns.

As shown in Table 1, the gloss exhibits widespread generalization of the inflection *-es* to all nouns belonging to this declension, the only exception being *sweostor*, which takes zero inflection in the only example attested in the gloss:

(1) JnGl (Li) 11.1
Erat autem quidam languens lazarus a bethania de castello mariae et marthę sororis eius
uæs uutedlice sum adligne latzarus of beðania ðær byrig of ceastra maries ⁊ martha **suoester**[3] ðæs ł
'Now there was a certain man sick, named Lazarus, of Bethania, of the town of Mary and Martha her sister'.

The following are other examples of zero genitives with these nouns:

(2) JnGl (Li) 6.40
haec est enim uoluntas patris mei qui misit me
ðios is forðon uillo **fador** mines seðe sende mec
'And this is the will of my Father that sent me'

(3) MkGl (Li) 6.17
Ipse enim herodes misit ac tenuit iohannen et uinxit eum in carcere propter herodiadam uxorem philippi fratris sui quia duxerat eum
se forðon herodes sende ⁊ geheald iohannen ⁊ geband hine in carcern fore herodiades hlaf philipes **broðer** his forðon lædde hine
'For Herod himself had sent and apprehended John, and bound him in prison for the sake of Herodias the wife of Philip his brother, because he had married her'.

3 In all the examples throughout the article the nouns in genitive have been marked in bold.

Table 1. Genitive singular of kinship *r*-stems

	0	-S	Total
fæder	3[4]	30	36[5]
modor	0	5[6]	5
sweoster	1	0	1
broþor	2	8	10
dohtor	–	–	–
Total	6	43	52

Lindisfarne, therefore, is more advanced than other texts, anticipating the situation which will be found later in English, with the extension of *-es* to all nouns. By contrast, Ru^2 is more conservative, with *broþor* and *modor* always uninflected, and *fæder* usually uninflected in Matthew's and Mark's Gospels, and normally inflected in Luke's and John's.

Although forms ending in *-es* are the norm for the genitive singular of these nouns in the gloss, there are variants depending on the quality of the vowel of the unstressed syllable, some of which are confined to certain Gospels. In the case of *fæder*, for example, Mark's, Luke's and John's Gospels always have the same inflected form: "fadores" (2x in Mark, 7x in Luke and 9x in John). Although this form is frequent in Matthew's Gospel (5x), the variants "faderes" (4x) and syncopated "fadres" (3x) are also found. This confirms Hogg and Fulk's (2011) claim that in northern Northumbrian the usual form of the genitive singular of *fæder*

4 In two of them, MtGl (Li) 20.1 and JnGl (Li) 14.2, *fadores* has been altered to *fador*.

5 There are also three cases of abbreviated or contracted forms. About that found in MkGl (Li) 15.21, Ross (1943: 313) remarks that "*faeder*' is probably to be taken as gen. sg. *faederes*, the scribe having construed it wrongly". As Ross argues, the scribe must have made a mistake when writing the mark of abbreviation. Latin has acc. *patrem* (object complement) agreeing with *simonem* (the object), and therefore the expected form would be "faeder", without any mark of abbreviation:

(i) *et angariauerunt praetereuntem quempiam simonem cyreneum uenientem de uilla patrem alexandri et rufi ut tolleret crucem eius*
⁊ geneddon bigeongende ł bifærende sumne simon cyrenesce cummende of lond **faeder**'
⁊ þætte genome his his
'And they forced one Simon a Cyrenian who passed by, coming out of the country, the father of Alexander and of Rufus, to take up his cross'.

6 In one of these instances, superscript letters are used: <moder`es´> (f. 215rb20; John 3.4), probably indicating that both "moder" and "moderes" are alternative forms for the genitive singular of *modor* in the dialect of the glossator (see Fernández Cuesta, this volume).

is “fadores”, “with occasional syncopated forms and a few forms without inflection” (2011: § 3.68 n. 3). Similar variation is found with the other kinship nouns. In the case of *broþor*, the usual form of the genitive singular is “broþres” (7x), but “broþeres” is found once in Matthew’s Gospel. Finally, for *modor*, the usual form is “moderes” (4x), but the syncopated form “modres” is found once in Matthew. So this Gospel seems to stand apart from the others with regard to the genitive singular of three of the five kinship nouns: *fæder*, *modor* and *broþor*, using variants which are not attested in the other Gospels.

1.1.2 Other common nouns

In this group I deal first with nouns used to gloss words which had the same form in nominative and genitive in Latin, such as *domus*, and secondly with other nouns whose uninflected forms cannot be accounted for by claiming Latin influence.

The noun *hus* is used by Aldred to gloss L *domus*, which belongs to the fourth declension and has therefore the same form for nominative and genitive. As a neuter *a*-stem noun, *hus* etymologically adds the inflection *-es* in the genitive singular. Four uninflected forms, however, are attested in the gloss, probably because of influence of the Latin form:[7]

(4) MtGl (Li) 10.6
sed potius ite ad oues quae perierunt domus israhel
ah is rehtra gaes to scipum ða losodun **hus** israhel[8]
‘But go ye rather to the lost sheep of the house of Israel’

(5) MtGl (Li) 15.24
Ipse autem respondens ait non sum missus nisi ad oues quae perierunt domus israhel
ðe ł he soðlice onduearde cueð nam ic gesended buta to scipum ða ðe deade weron **hus** israheles[9]
‘And he answering, said: I was not sent but to the sheep that are lost of the house of Israel’

7 Cook (1894: 119), however, does not regard any of these instances of *hus* as genitive singular, but as nominative singular. These forms are also listed as nominative singular by Ross and Stanley (1960: 101).
8 MtGl (Ru) 10.6 has the inflected form: “huses israhela”.
9 MtGl (Ru) 15.24 has the inflected form: “huses israheles”.

(6) MkGl (Li) 14.14
et quocumque introierit dicite domino domus quia magister dicit
⁊ swa huidder inngeongæ cuoeðas drihtne **hus** forðon ðe laruu cuoeð[10]
'And whithersoever he shall go in, say to the master of the house, The master saith'

(7) LkGl (Li) 22.11
et dicetis patrifamelias domus dicet tibi magister ubi est diuersorium ubi pascha cum discipulis meis manducem
⁊ cuoeðas gie ðæm fædir hiuuisc ł hiorodes **hus** he coeðes ðe laruu huer is þæt gestern ł ðer eostro mið ðegnum minum ic brucco[11]
'And you shall say to the goodman of the house: The master saith to thee, Where is the guest chamber, where I may eat the pasch with my disciples?'.

In the remaining instances, however, the etymological form with *-es* is found:

(8) LkGl (Li) 6.49
qui autem audiuit et non fecit similis est homini aedificanti domum suam supra petram sine fundamento in qua inlisus est fluuius et continuo cecidit et facta est ruina domus illius magna
seðe ðonne geherde ⁊ ne dyde gelic is ðæm menn timbrende hus his onufa stan buta grund on ðon toslitten wæs þæt stream ⁊ sona gefeall ⁊ aworden wæs faell **huses** ðæs micel
'But he that heareth, and doth not, is like to a man building his house upon the earth without a foundation: against which the stream beat vehemently, and immediately it fell, and the ruin of that house was great'

(9) JnGl (Li) 2.17
Recordati uero sunt discipuli eius quia scribtum est zelus domus tuae comedit me
eftgemyndigo forðon ueron ðegnas his þætte auritten uæs elnung ł æfista **huses** ðines geet mec
'And his disciples remembered, that it was written: The zeal of thy house hath eaten me up'

10 The noun is also uninflected in MkGl (Ru) 14.14.
11 The noun is also uninflected in LkGl (Ru) 22.11.

(10) JnGl (Li) 10.22
facta sunt autem encenia in hierosolymis et hiemps erat
auorden sint uutedlice niuaes **huses** halgung ł cirica halgung in ðær byrig ⁊ uinter uæs
'And it was the feast of the dedication at Jerusalem: and it was winter'.

In examples (8) and (9) the noun in Latin is followed by an inflected demonstrative or possessive, indicating that the form *domus* is genitive, and not nominative, and that is probably the reason why *hus* adds the inflection *-es* in these cases. In example (10), on the other hand, *hus* is not glossing L *domus*, but explaining the Latin form *encenia*, using a paraphrase in a double gloss. In this context, therefore, free from the influence of the original, Aldred is assumed to be using the 'usual' genitive singular form of the noun. These examples show Aldred as a careful glossator, taking into account the phrase unit rather than the word unit.[12]

Other common nouns are also attested occasionally with zero genitives in the gloss independently of the Latin original. This is the case of *gebed* 'prayer', *wif* 'woman' and *domern*. The noun *gebed* is found four times glossing L *orationis*. As a neuter *a*-stem noun, it etymologically adds the inflection *-es* in the genitive singular. Two uninflected forms, however, are found in two parallel instances in Matthew's and Mark's Gospels:[13]

(11) MtGl (Li) 21.13
et dicit eis scribtum est domus mea domus orationis uocabitur uos autem fecistis illam speluncam latronum
⁊ cueð him awritten is hus min hus **gebed** geceiged gie uutedlice gie worhton ða ilca cofa ł græfe ðeafana
'And he saith to them: It is written, My house shall be called the house of prayer; but you have made it a den of thieves'

(12) MkGl (Li) 11.17
et docebat dicens eis nonne scribtum est quia domus mea domus orationis uocabitur omnibus gentibus uos autem fecistis eam speluncam latronum
⁊ lærde cuoeðende him ah ne auritten is þætte hus min hus **gebedd** geceiged allum cynnum gie uutedlice geworhton ł dydon hia ł ða ilca cofa ðeafana
'And he taught, saying to them: Is it not written, My house shall be called the house of prayer to all nations? But you have made it a den of thieves'.

12 In the case of mechanical glossing, the uninflected form would have been used in all cases.
13 In both cases the ending *-es* has been expuncted: f. 69ra6 and f. 118ra12.

In this same context in Luke's Gospel, however, the etymological form with *-es* is found:

(13) LkGl (Li) 19.46
dicens illis scribtum est quia domus mea domus orationis est uos autem fecistis illam speluncam latronum
cuoeð ðaem awritten is forðon ł þætte hus min hus **gebeddes** is gie uutedlice gedydon hia cofa hreafera
'Saying to them: It is written: My house is the house of prayer. But you have made it a den of thieves'.

In the remaining instance, the noun also adds the etymological inflection:
(14) MkGl (Li) 12.40
Qui deuorant domos uiduarum sub obtentu prolixae orationis hi accipient prolixius iudicium
ða ðe offreattas huso widwuana under sceawung longunga ł longes **gebeddes** ðas onfoað uneðlic ł lengra dom
'Who devour the houses of widows under the pretence of long prayer: these shall receive greater judgment'.

The uninflected forms of this noun in (11) and (12) cannot be accounted for by claiming Latin influence, since the noun is inflected in the original: *orationis.* The fact that both of them occur in the same collocation ("hus gebed") may indicate that this phrase is regarded as a compound.[14] Another possibility is that they show the first signs of the northern tendency to omit the genitive inflection, which will continue in later periods.

In the case of *wif*, this noun, as another neuter *a*-stem noun, etymologically adds the inflection *-es* in the genitive singular. Two instances of this form are attested in the gloss:

(15) MtGl (Li) 8.14
Et cum uenisset iesus in domum petri uidit socrum eius iacentem et febricitantem
⁊ miððy gecuom ðe hælend in hus petres gesaeh suer his ł his **wifes** moder liccende ⁊ cuacende ł <bifigende>
'And when Jesus was come into Peter's house, he saw his wife's mother lying, and sick of a fever'

14 In fact there exists the compound *gebed-hus* with the meaning 'oratory, chapel'; cp. Ross and Stanley (1960: 101).

(16) JnGl (Li) 4.39
ex ciuitate autem illa multi crediderunt in eum samaritanorum propter uerbum mulieris testimonium perhibentis quia dixit mihi omnia quaecumque feci
of ðær byrig uutedlice menigo gelefdon in hine ðara samaritaniscena fore word ðæs **uifes** cyðnise getrymmedes ł forðon cuęð to me alle ðaðe ł suæhuæd ic uorhte
'Now of that city many of the Samaritans believed in him, for the word of the woman giving testimony: He told me all things whatsoever I have done'.

In example (17), however, where *wif* is the object of the adjective "gemyndigo", the uninflected form is found:

(17) LkGl (Li) 17.32
Memores estote uxoris loth
gemyndigo wosað **wif** lothes[15]
'Remember [be mindful of] Lot's wife'.

As in the case of *gebed*, the uninflected form cannot be due to Latin influence, but may illustrate the northern tendency to omit the genitive inflection.

Another isolated occurrence of zero genitive is noticed by Lea (1894: 185) with the noun *domern*, used to gloss L *praetorii*:

15 Adjectives of remembering, such as "gemyndigo", take the genitive case. Bale (1907: 37) gives several examples of this adjective taken from Lindisfarne (this one included), and all of them except for one take a genitive. In the only exception the adjective takes a prepositional phrase with *to*:

MtGl (Li) 26.75
et recordatus est petrus uerbi iesu...
⁊ gemyste ł eftgemyndig wæs **to word** hælendes
'And Peter remembered the word of Jesus'.

Bale (1907: 37) comments that "the Latin here employs the genitive throughout. The construction *to word* is therefore not due to the original but indicates the development of a new construction with *gemyndig*", and adds that OIc *minnigr*, of the same meaning, occurs with a similar construction.

(18) MkGl (Li) 15.16
Milites autem duxerunt eum in atrium praetorii et conuocant totam cohortem
ða cempo ðonne læddon hine on wuorð ðæs **domern** ⁊ efneceigdon all[16]
'And the soldiers led him away into the court of the palace, and they called together the whole band'.

Table 2 summarizes the results found with common nouns other than kinship *r*-stems. In general, it can be said that very few examples of zero genitives are attested in the gloss with nouns which etymologically add *-es* in the genitive singular. Although in the case of *hus* the uninflected forms are probably due to Latin influence, in the others they seem to show the first signs of the northern tendency to omit the genitive inflection, which will continue in later periods.

Table 2. Genitive singular of other common nouns

	0	-S	Total
hus	4	3	8[17]
gebed	2	2	4
wif	1	2	3
domern	1	0	1

Although not exactly the same as the previous nouns, *mægden* is also included here. Being a neuter *a*-stem noun, it etymologically adds the inflection *-es* in the genitive singular. No occurrence of this form, however, is attested in the gloss. Variants ending in *-e* are found instead for the genitive singular of this noun:

16 MkGl (Ru) 15.16 has the inflected form of the genitive: "ða cempu læddun hine on worð ðæs domernes".

17 There is also one token of the form "huse" glossing L *domus*:
MkGl (Li) 13.35
Uigilate ergo nescitis enim quando dominus domus ueniat sero an media nocte an galli cantu an mane
gewaccas forðon nuuto gie forðon huoenne se hlaferd **huse** cymes on efrntid ł on middumnæht ł on uhtetid ł on honcroed ł on æring.
'Watch ye therefore, for you know not when the lord of the house cometh: at even, or at midnight, or at the cockcrowing, or in the morning'.
Cook (1894: 119) regards this form as dative singular as do Ross and Stanley (1960: 101). MkGl (Ru) 13.35 has "huses".

(19) MkGl (Li) 5.40
et inridebant eum ipse uero eiectis omnibus adsumit patrem et matrem puellae et qui secum erant et ingreditur ubi erat puella iacens
⁊ inhlogan hine he hueðre miððy fordrifenum allum ł miððy alle ute fordraf genom ðone fader ⁊ moder ðæra **maedne** ⁊ ðaðe mið him weron ⁊ infoerde ðer wæs ðæt mæden licende
'And they laughed him to scorn. But he having put them all out, taketh the father and the mother of the damsel, and them that were with him, and entereth in where the damsel was lying'

(20) MkGl (Li) 5.41
et tenens manum puellae ait illi talitha cumi quod est interpraetatum puella tibi dico surge
⁊ geheald hond dære **mægdne** cuoeð to hir <talitha> ðis is ebrisc word þæt is getrahtad in latin la dohter ł la mægden ðe ic sægo aris
'And taking the damsel by the hand [the hand of the damsel], he saith to her: Talitha cumi, which is, being interpreted: Damsel (I say to thee) arise'

(21) LkGl (Li) 8.50
iesus autem audito hoc uerbo respondit patri puellae noli timere crede tantum et salua erit
se hælend ða miððy geherde ðis word geondsuarede feder ðæræ **mædne** nælle ðu ðe ondrede gelef ana ⁊ hal hio bið
'And Jesus hearing this word, answered the father of the maid: Fear not; believe only, and she shall be safe'

(22) LkGl (Li) 8.51
et cum uenisset domum non permisit intrare secum quemquam nisi petrum iacobum et iohannem et patrem et matrem puellae
⁊ miððy gecuome to hame ne gelefde ingeonga mið ænig buta ⁊ ⁊ ⁊ fader ⁊ moder ðærę **mægdne**
'And when he was come to the house, he suffered not any man to go in with him, but Peter and James and John, and the father and mother of the maiden'.

As illustrated in the above examples, in the genitive singular, *mægden* is declined as a feminine, rather than as a neuter noun, adding *-e* instead of etymological *-es*, and is modified by the feminine form of the demonstrative.[18] The reason may be partly influence from the Latin original (*puella* is a feminine noun belonging to the first declension), but also partly the result of the conflict between the grammatical and the natural gender of the noun in Old English. A similar situation is found in the dative singular of this noun, as illustrated in example (23):[19]

(23) MtGl (Li) 14.11
et allatum est caput eius in disco et datum est puellae et tulit matri suae
⁊ gebroht ł gefered wæs heafud his in disc ⁊ gesald wæs ðær **mædne** ⁊ brohte moder hire
'And his head was brought in a dish: and it was given to the damsel, and she brought it to her mother'.

In the nominative singular, however, the etymological gender of the noun is preserved in all cases (6x), as illustrated in (24):

(24) MtGl (Li) 9.24
dicebat recedite non est enim mortua puella sed dormit et deridebant eum
he gecueð cerras ł eft gewoendas ne is forðon dead **ðy maiden ł þæt maiden** ah slepes ⁊ gehlogun ł smerdon hine
'He said: Give place, for the girl is not dead, but sleepeth. And they laughed him to scorn'.

In this first example of the occurrence of the noun, both the feminine and the neuter forms of the demonstrative are given as variants: "ðy maiden ł þæt maiden". In the remaining five instances, however, the neuter form of the demonstrative precedes the noun.

The noun *mægden*, therefore, runs against the widespread generalization of the genitive singular inflection *-es* in the gloss, illustrated, among others, by the kinship *r*-stems.

---

18 In MkGl (Ru) 5.41, LkGl (Ru) 8.50 and LkGl (Ru) 8.51, however, the noun adds etymological *-es* and is preceded by the neuter form of the demonstrative: "ðæs mægdnes".

19 There are another two occurrences of the dative singular of this noun in the gloss. In MkGl (Li) 6.22 it is regarded as a neuter noun, being preceded by the neuter form of the demonstrative: "ðæm mægdne". In MkGl (Li) 6.28, however, it is modified by the feminine form of the demonstrative: "ðæm mægdne".

1.2 Proper nouns

Proper nouns are frequently uninflected in northern dialects of Middle English.[20] Examples of this tendency are attested already in late Northumbrian:

(25) Kirkdale (North Yorkshire) (11th c.) [21]
IN:**EA*D*WARD**:DAGVM:CNG | ⁊N**TOS*TI***[:]DAGVM:EORL+ |
in : eadward : dagvm : cng ⁊ n tosti [:] dagvm : eorl +
'in the days of King Edward, and in the days of Earl Tosti'.

In Lindisfarne, proper nouns in the genitive case are glossed in an overwhelming number of cases, and therefore this text offers a substantial corpus for the study of the omission of the inflection in this context.[22] In fact, proper nouns in genitive tend to be more frequently glossed than in other cases, such as nominative or accusative. To prove this point, I have selected those personal names which occur more frequently in genitive in the gloss: *David*, *Iacob*, *Abraham*, etc. There are 14 names, with a total number of occurrences in the genitive case of 112 tokens. As can be seen in Table 3, only 14 are left unglossed, which amounts to 12.50 %, the percentage, therefore, being considerably lower than that given by Pons-Sanz (2001: 180) for personal names in general: approx. 22 %.[23] Thus, statements such as those by Lendinara in the present volume (p. 335 n. 25) do not apply to this case. According to her, "[t]he names *Johannes* (John the Baptist), *Maria*, and *Petrus* are frequently left unglossed". As can be seen in Table 3, both *Maria* and *Peter* are always glossed when occurring in the genitive case (*Mariae*, *Petri*).

20 Mustanoja (1960: 72) mentions this as one of the features of these varieties: "the use of the *s*-less genitive in many proper names and other personal nouns is mainly northern".
21 Cp. Fernández Cuesta et al. (2008: 155). Herold (1968: 32) reports some examples of uninflected proper nouns in the Old English *Orosius*, but all of them are foreign proper nouns which are supposed to show Latin inflections. With regard to native or Germanic proper names, however, he states that "for the most part they occur with the regular OE strong suffixes" (1968: 30).
22 Cp. Thomson's (1961: 35 n. 5) comment, quoted by Jolly (2012: 166): "One cannot but admire the conscientiousness of a glossator who should not merely insist on glossing something so eminently unglossable as proper names, but take counsel with other manuscripts for the purpose!".
23 According to her, "some names are left completely unglossed (approx. 22 %); among the rest, 90.3 % are glossed by a personal name (either anglicized, in its Latin form, or abbreviated), 8.2 % are glossed by a generic noun, and 1.44 % are rendered by a personal name and a generic noun together" (Pons-Sanz 2001: 180).

Table 3. Glossing of personal names in the genitive case in the gloss

	Glossed	Not glossed	Total	% Glossed
David	24	0	24	100
Iacob	10	3	13[24]	76.92
Abraham	12	0	12	100
Simon	8	3	11	72.72
Herod	6	2	8	75
Christ	7	0	7	100
Ioseph	5	2	7	71.42
Moses	4	2	6	66.66
Mary	4	0	4	100
Peter	4	0	4	100
Zachariah	3	1	4	75
Esaiah	3	1	4	75
Jonah	4	0	4	100
Salomon	4	0	4	100
Total	98	14	112	87.50

1.2.1 Proper nouns which are indeclinable in Latin

As with common nouns, I deal first with proper nouns used to gloss names which have the same form in nominative and genitive in Latin, such as *David*, *Israel*, *Abraham*, etc., and secondly with names whose uninflected forms cannot be accounted for by claiming Latin influence.

24 The total number of tokens corresponds to two forms in Latin: indeclinable *Iacob* 'Jacob' (5x) and *Iacobus, -i* 'James' (8x).

Table 4. Genitive singular of proper nouns glossing indeclinable names in Latin

	0	-S	Other infl.	Abbreviat.	Total
David	1	21		2	24
Israel	6	6	5	1	18[25]
Abraham	1	10		1	12
Jacob		5			5
Joseph		3		2[26]	5
Moses		3		1	4
Isaac		3			3
Abel		2			2
Loth		2			2
Zabulon		2			2
Total	8	57	5	7	77

As can be seen in Table 4, even though these proper nouns are used to gloss names which are indeclinable in Latin, they do not show influence from Latin, but consistently add the genitive inflection *-es*. Sporadic examples of uninflected forms are found for those names which occur more frequently in the gloss: *David* (1x out of 24x), and *Abraham* (1x out of 12x).

The name *Israel*, on the other hand, stands apart from the other proper nouns, with 6x out of 18x tokens of zero genitive. *Israel* is very frequently abbreviated in the gloss, which may account for the high number of occurrences of the uninflected form: in fact, four out of the six instances of zero genitives are abbreviated or contracted forms: "isr'l" (3x), "isra'l" (1x). This proper noun also stands out because of the variety of forms attested for the genitive singular in the gloss: "israheles", "israhelis", "israeles", "israhela", "israel", "isræle", "israhe'", "isr'les", "i'r'la", "isr'la", "isra'l", "isr'l". Although this variety of forms is found in all gospels, Matthew's stands apart, being the only Gospel where *-es* (4x) and the zero inflection (3x) are more frequent than the ending *-a* (1x). In the other Gospels, either *-a* is the only ending (Mark, with 1x), or as frequent as the others

25 Six of these tokens are listed as nominative singular by Ross and Stanley (1960: 108), but as genitive singular by Cook (1894: 127).

26 These two examples are listed as nominative singular by Ross and Stanley (1960: 105), but as genitive singular by Cook (1894: 126): LkGl (Li) 3.23 and LkGl (Li) 4.22.

(Luke, with 2x of *-a*, 1x of *-es* and 2x of zero inflection; John, with 1x of *-a*, 1x of *-is* and 1x of zero inflection).

1.2.2 Proper nouns which are declined in Latin

As shown in Table 5, an inflection ending in *-s* is added in most cases to proper nouns used to gloss Latin names in the genitive singular. Although in the majority of cases the inflection is native *-es*, extended from the *a*-stems to other noun classes, occasionally the quality of the unstressed vowel seems to be influenced by the Latin ending: cp. "simonis" (1x), "sidonis" (1x), "heroðis" (1x), "mariaes" (1x). Also found are sporadic examples of genitive singular ending in a vowel on the model of the Latin original: "zachariæ" (1x), "esaie" (1x).

The genitive, however, stands quite clearly apart from the other cases, such as nominative or accusative, where the influence of the Latin inflection is much more evident. Thus, the accusative of the names *Maria* and *Martha* in the gloss often has the same form as in Latin: "mariam", "martham". A similar situation is found in the nominative case: for the name *Peter*, for example, the form "petrus" is found 43x glossing Latin nominative *petrus*, as against sporadic examples of the anglicized forms "petre" (1x) and "peter" (1x).[27]

Table 5 also shows occasional examples of zero genitives ("crist", "martha") illustrating the northern tendency to omit the inflection of the genitive singular, which, as noted above, will become one of the features of these varieties in later periods.

Summing up this section, the Latin genitive inflection of proper nouns is normally not copied in the gloss, but rendered as native *-es*. Aldred, therefore, is innovative at the morphological level, as shown in the addition of native *-es* to proper nouns used to gloss names which are either uninflected, or have a different inflection in Latin.

27 Compare Pons-Sanz's comment to this respect: "In Luke 22.61, *Petrum* is glossed by *petrum*, whereas *Petri* is rendered as *petres*, with the OE. gen.sg. morpheme instead of the Latin one, in the explanation of the contents of the gospel according to St Mark, I" (2001: 180 n. 37).

Table 5. Genitive singular of proper nouns glossing inflected names in Latin

	0	-S	Other infl.	Abbreviat.	Total
Simon		8[28]			8
Christ	1	5		1	7
Herod		5[29]		1	6
Mary		4[30]			4
Salomon		2		2	4
Jonah		4			4
Peter		3			3
Zachariah		2[31]	1		3
Esaiah		2	1[32]		3
Sidon		2[33]			2
Martha	1				1
Total	2	37	2	4	45

2 Study of the word order of adnominal genitives: preposition vs. postposition

The second objective of this article is the study of the word order of adnominal genitives in order to determine to what extent Aldred follows the Latin original or innovates and deviates from Latin, as he does with regard to the genitive inflection. The corpus used is that compiled for the study of zero genitive. So kinship nouns are studied first, since their high number of occurrences makes it possible to draw conclusions from them, and secondly those proper nouns which occur more frequently in the gloss.

28 The ending -*es* is found 7x and -*is* (as in Latin) 1x.
29 The ending -*es* is found 4x and -*is* (as in Latin) 1x.
30 The ending -*es* is found 3x and -*æs* (cp. L *Mariae*) 1x.
31 The ending -*es* is found once and -*æs* (cp. L *Zachariae*) 1x.
32 The form "esaie" is found in Luke, probably because of influence of the Latin form *esaiae*.
33 Both the ending -*es* and -*is* (as in Latin) are found 1x.

2.1 Kinship *r*-stems

Table 6 summarizes the results found in the corpus studied. It does not simply show the position of the genitive in the NP, but compares the pattern found in the gloss with that of the Latin original. It also includes those cases in which the noun is not glossing a Latin genitive, as in example (26), where an explanation of the proper noun "herodiaðes" is found in the margin:

(26) MtGl (Li) 14.6
.i. ðæs cyninges **broðer** láf
'the king's brother's wife'.

Table 6. Word order of adnominal genitives in the gloss compared with Latin. Kinship *r*-stems

	Preposed Latin prep.	Preposed Latin postp.	Preposed No Latin	Postposed Latin postp.	Postposed Latin prep.	Total[34]
fæder	1	0	0	29	0	30
modor	1	0	0	4	0	5
broþor	0	0	1	7	0	8
sweoster	0	0	0	1	0	1
Total	2	0	1	41	0	44

As shown in the table, in all those cases in which the kinship noun is glossing a Latin genitive (43x), the word order follows the original. In most cases (41x: 95.34 %) the genitive is postposed, as in Latin:

34 The reason why the total number of tokens does not always agree with that given in Table 1 is that in some examples the head noun is omitted, and therefore they cannot be taken into account for the study of word order:

JnGl (Li) 14.24
qui non diligit me sermones meos non seruat et sermonem quem audistis non est meus sed eius qui me misit patris
seðe ne lufas mec worda mino ne gehaldas ⁊ þæt uord ðone gie geherdon ne is min ah ðæs seðe mec sende **fadores**
'He that loveth me not keepeth not my sayings: and the word which ye hear is not mine, but the Father's which sent me'.

(27) LkGl (Li) 1.15
erit enim magnus coram domino et uinum et sicera non bibet et spiritu sancto replebitur athuc ex utero matris suę
bið forðon micel befora drihtno ⁊ win ⁊ bear ne drinceð ⁊ gaaste halge gefylled bið ða gett wæs in inna **moderes** his
'For he shall be great before the Lord; and shall drink no wine nor strong drink: and he shall be filled with the Holy Ghost, even from his mother's womb'.

Sporadically (2x: 4.65 %), the genitive is preposed, following Latin:

(28) MtGl (Li) 19.12
sunt enim eunuchi qui de matris utero sic nati sunt
aron forðon cuoenhiordo ł ða ðe of **modres** hrif sua boren weron
'For there are eunuchs, who were born so from their mother's womb'.

As shown in examples (27)–(28), different word order is found in parallel noun phrases, thus confirming Nagucka's statement that

> Aldred does not seem to follow any methodologically consistent pattern, even in the structurally and lexically identical phrases [...]. The author of the English version felt at ease with Latin and translated it according to his own preferences at a given moment. (1997: 180)

As explained above, in (26) "broðer" is not glossing a Latin genitive, but is added in the margin to explain a personal name (*Herodias*). In this case, the genitive, which is preposed to the noun, is supposed to follow the 'natural' word order in the dialect of the glossator, since it is not influenced by the Latin original.

2.2 Personal names

A total of seven personal names (those which occur more frequently in the genitive case in the gloss) have been selected for the study of word order. Table 7 summarizes the results. As in the previous case, it shows the position of the genitive in the NP in comparison with the original, and includes those cases in which the noun is not glossing a Latin genitive.

As shown in the table, there are 65 personal names in the genitive case glossing a Latin genitive. Of these, 62x (95.38 %) follow the Latin word order, and only 3x (4.61 %) deviate from Latin and have a preposed genitive glossing a postposed one: 2x occur in Matthew's Gospel and 1x in John's:

Table 7. Word order of adnominal genitives in the gloss compared with Latin. Personal names

	Preposed Latin prep.	Preposed Latin postp.	Preposed No Latin	Postposed Latin postp.	Postposed Latin prep.	Total
David	0	2	0	21	0	23
Jacob	1	0	0	8	0	9
Abraham	0	1	0	11	0	12
Simon	0	0	0	7	0	7
Herod	1	0	1	4	0	6
Christ	1	0	0	3	0	4
Ioseph	0	0	0	5	0	5
n Total	3	3	1	59	0	66

(29) MtGl (Li) 1.1
Liber generationis iesu christi filii david fili abraham
boc cneurise haelendes cristes **dauides** sunu **abrahames** sunu
'The book of the generation of Jesus Christ, the son of David, the son of Abraham'[35]

(30) JnGl (Li) 7.42
nonne scribtura dicit quia ex semine dauid et de bethleem castelo ubi erat dauid uenit christus
ahne þæt uritt cueð þætte of **dauides** sed ⁊ of bethlem byrig ł ceastre ðer uæs dauid cuom crist
'Doth not the scripture say: That Christ cometh of the seed of David, and from Bethlehem the town where David was?'.[36]

No example is found in the corpus, however, of the opposite pattern: a postposed genitive in English glossing a preposed one in Latin.

As was the case with kinship nouns, in most cases the genitive is postposed, following Latin: 59x (95.16 %). Only sporadically (3x: 4.83 %) is it preposed, as in (31):

35 In MtGl (Ru) 1.1 the genitives are also preposed.
36 In JnGl (Ru) 7.42, however, the genitive follows the Latin word order and is postposed.

(31) MkGl (Li) 15.40
Erant autem et mulieres de longe aspicientes inter quas et maria magdalenae et maria iacobi minoris et ioseph mater et salomae
woeron uutedlice æc ða wifo fearra behealdon bituih ðæm æc maria magdalenisce ⁊ ðæs **iacobes** leasse ⁊ moder ⁊
'And there were also women looking on afar off: among whom was Mary Magdalen, and Mary the mother of James the less and of Joseph, and Salome'.

As shown in Table 7, there is also one genitive which has no parallel in Latin, but occurs in a NP which has been added in the gloss to explain a proper noun (32). As in (26), the genitive, which is preposed to the noun, is supposed to follow the 'natural' word order in the dialect of the glossator, since it is not influenced by the Latin original:

(32) MtGl (Li) 2.22
audiens autem quia archelaus regnaret in iudaea pro herode patre suo timuit illuc ire et admonitus in somnis secessit in partes galilaeae
geherde soðlice forðon ðe cynig **heroðes** sunu rixade in iudea fore herodes fæder his ondreard ðider fara ł to færenne ⁊ gelæred wæs in soefnum gewoende ðona in dalum geliornesse
'But hearing that Archelaus [king Herod's son] reigned in Judea in the room of Herod his father, he was afraid to go thither: and being warned in sleep retired into the quarters of Galilee'.

Especially significant in this respect is the behaviour of the proper noun *Zebedee* in the phrase 'son of Zebedee'. As in (26) and (32), in those cases in which Latin has just the proper noun in the genitive case (*zebedaei* (*iacobum zebedaei*)) and the NP 'son of' is added in English to gloss it, the genitive is preposed: "zebedes sunu".[37] Examples (33)–(36) illustrate this situation:

(33) MtGl (Li) 4.21
Et procedens inde uidit alios duos fratres iacobum zebedaei et iohannem fratrem eius in naue
⁊ gefoerde ðona gesæh oðer tuoege broðer iacob **zebeðes sunu** ⁊ broðer his in scip
'And going on from thence, he saw other two brethren, James the son of Zebedee, and John his brother, in a ship'

37 The same situation is found in Rushworth.

(34) MtGl (Li) 10.2
Duodecim autem apostolorum nomina sunt haec primus simon qui dicitur petrus et andreas frater eius iacobus zebedaei et iohannes frater eius
tuelfe uutedlice ðara apostolorum noma sint ðas ærist seðe acueden is ⁊ broðer his **zebeðies suna** ⁊ broðer his
'And the names of the twelve apostles are these: The first, Simon who is called Peter, and Andrew his brother, James the son of Zebedee, and John his brother'

(35) MkGl (Li) 1.19
Et progressus inde pusillum uidit iacobum zebedęi et iohannen fratrem eius et ipsos in naui componentes retia
⁊ foerde ðona lytel huon gesæh iacob **zebeðies sunu** ⁊ ðone iohannem ðone broðer his ⁊ ða ilco ł hia in scip gesetton ða netto
'And going on from thence a little farther, he saw James the son of Zebedee, and John his brother, who also were mending their nets in the ship'

(36) MkGl (Li) 3.17
et iacobum zebedęi et iohannem fratrem iacobi et imposuit eis nomina boanerges quod est filii tonitrui
⁊ iacob **yebeðies sunu** ⁊ iohannem broðer iacobes ⁊ gesette him þæt is suno ðunres
'And James the son of Zebedee, and John the brother of James; and he named them Boanerges, which is, the sons of thunder'.

However, when the NP 'son(s) of Zebedee' is found in Latin (*filii zebedaei*), the gloss follows the Latin word order and has the genitive postposed, as in examples (37)–(40):

(37) MtGl (Li) 20.20
Tunc accessit ad eum mater filiorum zebedaei cum filiis suis adorans et petens aliquid ab eo
ða cuom ł geneolecde to him moder **suno zebedies** mið sunum hire tobæd ł worðade ⁊ giwude huelchuoegu from him
'Then came to him the mother of the sons of Zebedee with her sons, adoring and asking something of him'

(38) MtGl (Li) 26.37
et assumto petro et duobus filiis zebedaei coepit contristari et maestus esse
⁊ ða genimmende ⁊ tuoege ł tuæm **sunum zebeðies** ongann unrotsiga ⁊ unbliðe moede wosa
'And taking with him Peter and the two sons of Zebedee, he began to grow sorrowful and to be sad'

(39) MkGl (Li) 10.35
Et accedunt ad eum iacobus et iohannes filii zebedaei dicentes magister uolumus quodcumque petierimus facias nobis
⁊ geneolecdon to him iacob ⁊ iohannes **suno zebeðies** cuoeðende la larua woe wallað þætte suae huæt we willniað ðu doe us
'And James and John the sons of Zebedee, come to him, saying: Master, we desire that whatsoever we shall ask, thou wouldst do it for us'

(40) JnGl (Li) 21.2
erant simul simon petrus et thomas qui dicitur didymus et nathanahel qui erat a cana galilaeae et filii zebedaei et alii ex discipulis eius duo
ueron aedgeadre simon petrus ⁊ se ðegn seðe is acuoeden on grecisc ⁊ ðe ðegn seðe uæs of ðæm tuune on galilees megð ⁊ **sunu zabedei** *id est* iacob ⁊ iohannes ⁊ oðro tuoge of his ðegnum
'There were together Simon Peter, and Thomas, who is called Didymus, and Nathanael, who was of Cana of Galilee, and the sons of Zebedee, and two others of his disciples'.

Table 8 summarizes the results found with both kinship and proper nouns. As can be seen, most of the adnominal genitives are postposed (100x out of 110x), but all of them follow the word order of the Latin original. By contrast, only 10x are preposed, but half are independent of the original, which would suggest that preposition of the genitive is the 'natural' word order for Aldred. This is reinforced by the behaviour of the proper noun *Zebedee* in the phrase 'son of Zebedee', as explained above, and by negative evidence: there are no examples in the corpus of a postposed genitive glossing a preposed one, or of a postposed genitive when there is no genitive in Latin.

Latin influence is evident in the word order of adnominal genitives in the gloss. As shown in Table 8, 105x out of 108x examples follow the Latin word order. Only in three cases does the pattern deviate from the original, with a preposed genitive glossing a postposed genitive in Latin, which confirms Ross's claim that "[o]nly in very rare instances has the order of the OE words been normalized so that it no longer corresponds with that of the Latin" (1933b: 111). Although innovative with regard to morphology, as shown above in the addition of native *-es* to proper nouns used to gloss names which are either indeclinable or have a different inflection in Latin, Aldred is conservative as regards syntax. This is in line with Nagucka's comment: "[g]enerally speaking, most of Aldred's 'innovations' with regard to the Latin original are connected to the lexical (semantic) and morphological aspects, the syntactic ones being few in number" (1997: 179).

Table 8. Word order of adnominal genitives in the gloss compared with Latin. Personal names and kinship nouns

	English preposed	English postposed
Latin preposed	5	0
Latin postposed	3	100
No Latin genitive	2	0
Total	10	100

3 Conclusions

Several conclusions can be drawn from this study. First, the gloss shows widespread extension of genitive singular *-es* from the *a*-stems to nouns belonging originally to other declensions, such as the kinship *r*-stems. Lindisfarne, therefore, is more advanced than other texts, anticipating the situation which will be found later in English, with the extension of *-es* to all noun classes.

This generalization can also be seen as far as proper nouns are concerned, both personal and place names, which tend to add the native inflection in the genitive singular regardless of the Latin ending. The genitive, therefore, behaves differently from the other cases, such as the nominative or accusative, which are often influenced by the Latin original.

In spite of the generalization of the *-es* ending, there are examples of zero genitives in the gloss, both with common and proper nouns. Zero genitives are found not only with nouns which did not add an inflection in early Old English (*fæder*, *modor*, *broþor*, etc.), or those used to gloss Latin nouns with the same form in the nominative and genitive (*hus* glossing *domus*), but also with nouns which etymologically added *-es*, such as *gebed*, *wif*, or *domern*. The same applies to proper nouns, and zero genitives are sporadically found with names such as *Christ*, *Abraham*, *Israel*, etc. Therefore, although *-es* is the norm for the genitive singular in Lindisfarne, the gloss also illustrates the omission of this case inflection, which will become one of the characteristic features of the northern dialects in later periods.

It is also notable that proper nouns in the genitive tend to be more frequently glossed than names in other cases, such as the nominative or accusative. As illustrated in Table 3 above, 98x out of a total of 112x tokens of personal names in the genitive case are glossed (87.50 %), the percentage of unglossed names (12.50 %) being considerably lower than for personal names in general: 22 % (Pons-Sanz 2001: 180).

With regard to the word order of adnominal genitives, the Latin pattern is followed in most cases, and therefore the genitive is normally postposed in the gloss. Preposed genitives are found sporadically in three different contexts: a) when Latin has a preposed genitive; b) when Aldred does not follow slavishly the original, but adds an explanation or commentary to gloss a word; and c) in cases where Aldred deviates from the Latin pattern. Therefore, although very few in number, preposed genitives seem to illustrate the 'natural' word order in the dialect of the glossator, since they occur in the gloss independently of the original.

Aldred, therefore, is innovative with regard to morphology, as shown in the extension of genitive singular *-es* from the *a*-stems to all noun classes, including proper nouns, but conservative at the syntactic level, following Latin word order in most cases. The present study also shows Aldred as a careful glossator, taking into account the phrase unit rather than the word unit, as illustrated in the distribution of "hus"/"huses" glossing L *domus*.

Finally, with regard to possible demarcations in the gloss, Matthew's Gospel seems to stand apart from the others regarding the genitive singular of three of the five kinship nouns: *fæder*, *modor* and *broþor*, using variants which are not attested elsewhere in the gloss. Similarly, this Gospel stands apart from the others concerning the distribution and frequency of the various inflections used for the genitive singular of the proper noun *Israel*. This is in line with studies such as Cole (2014), which point out the special nature of this Gospel with regard to the distribution of the *-s*/*-ð* endings in the present indicative.[38]

38 I would like to express my gratitude to Jeremy Smith for his invitation to the University of Glasgow and the Spanish Ministry of Science and Technology for the grant which financed the stay at the University (FFI2011-28272).

George Walkden

Null Subjects in the Lindisfarne Gospels as Evidence for Syntactic Variation in Old English

Abstract: This paper assesses the evidence for null subjects in Old English, demonstrating that in the Old English gloss to the Lindisfarne Gospels subjects are omitted in a way not found in classical West Saxon texts. The obvious hypothesis – that this difference is simply due to the nature of the text as a gloss of a Latin original, and thus tells us nothing about the syntax of Old English – is unlikely to be correct, since null subjects occur frequently only in the third person, not in the first and second persons. In Latin null subjects are permitted and occur in all of these contexts without restriction. The omitted subjects in the Lindisfarne gloss thus seem to represent a genuine (Northumbrian) Old English syntactic possibility; support for this conclusion is drawn from a new quantitative study of the Gospel of John. The results of the study therefore indicate that a text such as Aldred's gloss to the Lindisfarne Gospels, despite its glossal nature, can contribute to our understanding of the comparative syntax of Old English dialects if appropriate caution is employed.

1 Introduction: glosses and syntax

It would not be unreasonable to assume that studying the syntax of the Old English gloss to the Lindisfarne Gospels would be a complete waste of time. If the glossator's strategy was merely glossing in its simplest sense – proceeding on a word-by-word basis, considering and rendering each word only in isolation, without regard for its syntactic context – then one would not expect the Lindisfarne gloss to have any independent syntax at all. This is presumably what Callaway (1918: iii) had in mind when he referred to the text as "merely an interlinear gloss, and in many respects a faulty one"; Cole (2014: 87) also cautions against using the gloss as evidence for word order. Even if the glossing technique did take syntactic context into account, operating on the clausal level rather than solely on the word level, one might expect the syntax of the glosses to be heavily influenced by that of the Latin original.

The extent to which either of these expectations is met can only be assessed by investigating the text itself. Insofar as we can unearth syntactic generalizations about the glosses that have no obvious explanation in terms of the Latin original, we have evidence for an independent syntactic system that may well represent the competence of a native speaker of (a variety of) Old English – evidence that can then be supplemented by placing it in the context of the syntax of other Old English texts. Other studies which have demonstrated the validity of glosses of Latin for the study of Old English syntactic phenomena in this way are Ingham (2006), on negative concord, and Taylor (2008), on word order within prepositional phrases.

A few studies to date have provided evidence of this kind for the Lindisfarne Gospels. Nagucka (1997), for example, adduces a number of syntactic phenomena in the gloss of the Gospel of Matthew that, she argues, demonstrate independence and a certain amount of creativity on the part of the glossator: these include word order discrepancies (e.g. "dauides sunu" 'David's son' for *filii david*, MtGl (Li) 1.1; see Rodríguez Ledesma, this volume), negative concord ('double negation', as in "þte nan nyte" 'that no man see to it' for *ne quis sciat*, MtGl (Li) 9.30), and the rendering of participial constructions with finite clauses. Nagucka therefore suggests that the practice of referring to the Old English Lindisfarne Gospels as a gloss should be abandoned, and some intermediate term such as 'glossal translation' adopted (1997: 180). Callaway (1918: 199–200), in his study of non-finite clauses in the text, concludes among other things that, though the absolute participle construction is likely a Latin borrowing, the choice between accusative and nominative case is conditioned by factors native to the Northumbrian dialect itself. More recently, Cole (2012a, 2012b, 2014) has shown on the basis of the Gospels of John and Mark that the choice of present indicative plural verbal inflection, *-s* vs. *-ð*, was conditioned to a large extent by subject type (pronominal vs. non-pronominal) and by subject-verb adjacency.

This short paper presents another instance of the Lindisfarne glossal translation displaying features that can only be due to a genuine Old English syntactic possibility. Building on Berndt (1956), I show that the glossator omitted pronominal subjects under certain conditions, and systematically inserted them in others: the data is laid out in section 2. Section 3 broadens the focus by situating this text in a comparative perspective, contrasting it with other Old English texts as well as texts in other early Germanic languages. Section 4 summarizes and concludes. The aim of the paper is to demonstrate that, if used with care, the Old English Lindisfarne Gospels can indeed contribute to a better understanding of the diatopic morphosyntactic variation found within the language.

2 Null subjects in the Lindisfarne Gospels

In Present-Day English it is not possible to omit a referential pronominal subject under most conditions:

(1) *Speaks Italian (Intended meaning: 'He speaks Italian').

However, in many other languages of the world, such as Italian and Spanish, the pronominal subject is not required, as illustrated in (2) from Italian.

(2) Parla italiano
speak-3 SG. Italian
'He speaks Italian'.

In such languages, pronominal subjects are only used in marked contexts, for instance when focused. The Latin of the Vulgate was this type of language, and personal pronouns in the text are correspondingly rare. In some languages, the richness of verbal agreement morphology appears to be relevant in 'identifying' the intended subject of subjectless sentences; in others, such as Chinese, subject pronouns can be omitted despite an almost complete lack of such morphology. For overviews of research on null subject languages, see Huang (2000) and Holmberg and Roberts (2010).

What about the Old English glossal translation of the Lindisfarne Gospels? The glossator[1] can be seen to insert personal pronouns that correspond to nothing overt in the Latin, as in (3). In such cases, the pronoun is inserted along with the Old English verb, above the Latin verbal form.

(3) JnGl (Li) 6.36 ah **ic** cuæð iuh ðaðe **gie** gesegon mec ⁊
but I said you.DAT who you saw me and
negelefeð **gie**
NEG-believe you
L *sed dixi uobis quae* [sic] *uidistis me et non creditis*
Trans. 'But I have said unto you, that you also have seen me, and you believe not'

1 I refer to the glossator(s) throughout this paper as 'the glossator' or 'Aldred' in the singular for simplicity's sake, recognizing that the actual question of authorship is by no means a settled or straightforward one, and that other Old English exemplars may have existed: see Ross et al. (1960), Brown (2003) and Cole (this volume). Biblical translations follow the *Douay-Rheims Bible.*

From a functionalist point of view in which rich verbal morphology enables pronominal subjects to be recoverably omitted, this is not surprising given that Latin verbal endings are so much richer than those of Northumbrian Old English. However, pronouns are also frequently omitted in the Old English glossal translation in a way that would not be possible in modern English, as in (4) and (5).

(4)	MkGl (Li) 9.21	⁊	gefrægn	fæder	his
		and	asked	father	his
	L	*et interrogauit patrem eius*			
	Trans.	'And **he (Jesus)** asked his father'			
	Mk (WSCp) 9.21	And þa ahsode **he** his fæder			

(5)	MkGl (Li) 10.1	⁊	suæ	þe	he	gewuna	wæs	eftersona	lærde	hia
		and	so	that	he	used	was	after-soon	taught	them
	L	*et sicut consueuerat iterum docebat illos*								
	Trans.	'And as he was accustomed, he taught them again'								
	Mk (WSCp) 10.1	& swa swa he gewunode **he** hi lærde eft sona								

Example (5) illustrates both insertion of a pronoun counter to the source Latin, in the subordinate clause "suæ þe he gewuna wæs", and omission of a subject pronoun in a context in which omission would not be possible in modern English: although (4) and (5) are conjoined clauses, the subject of the previous conjunct is not co-referential in either example. Notably, the West Saxon version of the Gospels contains a pronoun in all instances.

The aim of this section is to gain a better understanding of the linguistic factors conditioning when the subject pronoun is inserted and when it is omitted in the glossal translation.[2] Nagucka (1997: 187) comments on the variation, though does not undertake a detailed study. Steps in this direction were already taken by Berndt (1956: 65–68), in a study of pronominal subjects by person and number in the Lindisfarne and Rushworth texts. Berndt's data is presented in Table 1; cp. also van Gelderen's (2000: 133) Table 3.1.[3]

---

2 Kroch and Taylor (1997) investigate the placement of the pronoun when it is inserted adjacent to the verb, and find that clause type conditions whether it is postverbal or preverbal. I do not address these word order issues here.

3 Berndt's division of the Lindisfarne Gospels into two parts is directly based on the division of the Rushworth glosses according to which parts were written by Farman (MtGl (Ru), MkGl (Ru) 1–2.15, JnGl (Ru) 18.1–3; i.e. Ru[1]) and Owun (the rest; i.e. Ru[2]), to ensure comparability.

Table 1. Pronominal subjects in finite indicative clauses in the Lindisfarne Gospels and the Rushworth Gospels, by person and number (based on Berndt 1956: 65–68)

Text	Person	N	Overt		Null		Total
Ru[1]	1	sg.	191	(97.0 %)	6	(3.0 %)	197
		pl.	44	(97.8 %)	1	(2.2 %)	45
	2	sg.	90	(88.2 %)	12	(11.8 %)	102
		pl.	168	(89.4 %)	20	(10.6 %)	188
	3	sg.	246	(58.2 %)	177	(41.8 %)	423
		pl.	141	(58.0 %)	102	(42.0 %)	243
	Totals		880		318		1198
Lindisfarne Gospels, part 1	1	sg.	212	(96.4 %)	8	(3.6 %)	220
		pl.	53	(100.0 %)	0	(0.0 %)	53
	2	sg.	103	(87.3 %)	15	(12.7 %)	118
		pl.	206	(95.8 %)	9	(4.2 %)	215
	3	sg.	116	(26.3 %)	325	(73.7 %)	441
		pl.	108	(36.9 %)	185	(63.1 %)	293
	Totals		798		542		1340
Lindisfarne Gospels, part 2	1	sg.	656	(98.6 %)	9	(1.4 %)	665
		pl.	120	(99.2 %)	1	(0.8 %)	121
	2	sg.	308	(93.3 %)	22	(6.7 %)	330
		pl.	428	(95.7 %)	19	(4.3 %)	447
	3	sg.	225	(18.3 %)	1003	(81.7 %)	1228
		pl.	154	(24.5 %)	475	(75.5 %)	629
	Totals		1891		1529		3420
Ru[2]	1	sg.	528	(96.5 %)	19	(3.5 %)	547
		pl.	100	(98.0 %)	2	(2.0 %)	102
	2	sg.	226	(91.1 %)	22	(8.9 %)	248
		pl.	302	(83.7 %)	59	(16.3 %)	361
	3	sg.	186	(19.0 %)	795	(81.0 %)	981
		pl.	124	(22.8 %)	420	(77.2 %)	544
	Totals		1466		1317		2783

Berndt's data reveal a striking asymmetry between the third person, in which (at least in the Lindisfarne Gospels) omission is the norm, and the first and second persons, in which insertion is the norm and omission very rare. Performing Fisher's (1922) exact tests reveals that this asymmetry is clearly statistically significant ($p < 0.0001$) for both parts of each text.[4] The effect of number, on the other hand, is not significant for Ru^1 ($p = 0.6885$) or Ru^2 ($p = 0.7520$), but is significant for Lindisfarne part 1 ($p = 0.0002$) and part 2 ($p = 0.0039$), with insertion being preferred in the plural.

I supplemented Berndt's data with an investigation of my own based on the Gospel of John. The aim was to replicate Berndt's findings with regard to person and number, and to discover whether other factors such as clause type also played a role in conditioning the alternation. The edition used was the standard one (Skeat 1878), collated and checked against the manuscript images made available online by the British Library. This step is important because Skeat's edition contains numerous errors and questionable editorial decisions: see Fernández Cuesta (2009), Fernández Cuesta (this volume) and Cole (2014: 88–93).[5] While these problems are likely to be of more concern to those interested in phonological and morphological variables rather than syntactic and lexical ones, they are also relevant to the issue of null subjects. Cole (2012b: 99) notes that in his edition of Matthew, Skeat (1887) omits the pronoun "hia" from the manuscript sequences "ða ondueardas ł hiaondsuerigað him" (JnGl (Li) 25.37) and "ða ðe ne suppas hia deað" (JnGl (Li)16.28). Skeat justifies this by noting in the margin that the pronouns have been under- or overlined by the glossator, which he interprets as deletion; however, as Cole notes (2012b: 99), there is no particular reason to believe that deletion was the glossator's intention, especially given the prevalence of subject doubling elsewhere in the text (see the discussion of (9) and (10) above, as well as Cole 2014: 201–202). Similarly, in my investigation I found that the first-person plural pronoun "we" is omitted by Skeat from the manuscript sequence "cuoeð him to we gemoetton" (1.41), for no discernible reason. A few other examples of this type were also uncovered.[6]

4 Fisher's exact tests are standard for small samples when dealing with a two-valued categorical dependent variable, as here – providing an exact p-value rather than an approximation. See, for instance, Stefanowitsch and Gries (2003) for discussion in a linguistic context.

5 The problem is potentially widespread: Skeat's edition is the one included in the *Dictionary of Old English Corpus* (hereafter *DOEC*), and is the one relied upon by Callaway (1918), Nagucka (1997), and Kroch and Taylor (1997).

6 Other palaeographical facts may be of relevance to the issue at hand. For instance, in the manuscript sequence "þte `hiá gesea mægeo" (JnGl (Li) 17.24), the third-person pronoun "hia" is in superscript (not rendered by Skeat). Following the view of Ross and Squires (1980: 490) that forms in superscript were "alternatives", this may indicate a perception on the part of the scribe

Tokens of both inserted and omitted subjects were collected manually in a spreadsheet, and marked for four factors: i) their grammatical person (1st, 2nd, 3rd); ii) their number (singular or plural); iii) their clause type (main, subordinate or conjunct); and iv) whether they corresponded to an overt or null subject in the Latin. Clause type was included as this has been shown to have an effect on subject expression in other early Germanic texts (see section 3); the effect of the Latin original was also included in order to see whether this interacted with other factors. Only finite clauses were considered. Contexts in which a null subject is possible in Present-Day English – for instance in conjunct clauses with a shared subject as in *I went to London and Ø attended the workshop*, and (arguably) in subject relative clauses such as *The man who Ø saw me* – were excluded.[7] Instances of non-referential arbitrary or expletive subjects, as in Present-Day English *It is raining* or *It is true that* ..., were also excluded, as they lie outside the focus of this investigation, which aims to determine whether omission of referential pronominal subjects was a possibility in the Lindisfarne Gospels and in what linguistic contexts. Examples of enclitic pronominal subjects, as in (6), and pronominal subjects included in only one of two glosses, as in (7), were treated as examples of insertion. The results by person and number are given in Table 2.

(6)	JnGl (Li) 1.22	huæd	cuoeðes**tu**	fro'	ðe	seolfum	
		what	say-you	from	you	self	
	L	*quid dicis de te ipso*					
	Trans.	'What sayest thou of thyself?'					

(7)	JnGl (Li) 3.10	ðas	**ðu**	nast	ł	ðas	ðe	sint
		those.ACC	you	NEG-know		those.NOM	you.DAT	are
		unncuðo						
		unknown						
	L	*haec ignoras*						
	Trans.	'and (you) knowest not these things'						

that the pronoun was optional; however, as this is an isolated example, little can be concluded from it.

7 The consensus in syntactic theory is that the relative pronoun *who* is not in subject position in the relative clause, but, like other relative pronouns, is a clause-introducer which combines with a gap in the relative clause.

Table 2. Pronominal subjects in the Gospel of John, by person and number

Person	N	Overt		Null		Total
1	sg.	428	96.8 %	14	3.2 %	442
	pl.	71	100.0 %	0	0.0 %	71
2	sg.	161	93.1 %	12	6.9 %	173
	pl.	226	95.8 %	10	4.2 %	236
3	sg.	76	18.4 %	337	81.6 %	413
	pl.	34	19.2 %	143	80.8 %	177
Totals		996		516		1512

In light of Berndt's (1956) findings as presented in Table 1, these figures are unsurprising. Once again, there is a significant effect of person (1st/2nd vs. 3rd; $p < 0.0001$): whereas first and second person subjects are almost always inserted, third person subjects are inserted only around 19 % of the time. Number is not significant either across the whole dataset ($p = 0.1632$) or within the third person ($p = 0.8183$).

Table 3 presents the results by clause type. Conjunct clauses are those introduced by a co-ordinating conjunction (mostly ⁊ 'and', and sometimes *ah* 'but'); these were included because the behaviour of conjunct clauses demonstrably differs from that of other main clauses in other respects, for example with regard to verb position (Campbell 1970: 93 n. 4; Mitchell 1985: 694; Bech 2001: 86–93). As previously mentioned, conjunct clauses where the subject is coreferential with that of the first conjunct (main clause) have been discounted for the purposes of this study. Subordinate clauses in this text are not always easy to distinguish due to the dual use of words such as *miððy* and *forðon* as adverbials as well as subordinators; an ambiguous example is given in (8).

(8) JnGl (Li) 4.40 miððy cuomon forðon to him ða samaritanisco gebedon hine
when/then came therefore to him the S. asked him
L *cum uenissent ergo ad illum samaritani rogauerunt eum*
Trans. 'So when the Samaritans were come to him, they desired' (*Douay-Rheims*)
OR
'Then the Samaritans were come to him, (and) they desired'
Jn (WSCp) 4.40 Ða þa samaritanisscen comon to hym. hyo ge-bæden hine

As the two alternative translations illustrate, this example could be analyzed as involving either subordination or co-ordination. Nevertheless, an attempt was made to distinguish subordinate clauses even in ambiguous cases, though this introduces a small element of subjectivity into the analysis. When in doubt, disambiguation was carried out on the basis of the parallel Latin and West Saxon versions in Skeat; in (8), the Latin original, introduced by the complementizer *cum*, suggests that a subordinate structure is likely to have been intended by Aldred.

Table 3. Pronominal subjects in the Gospel of John, by clause type

Clause type	Overt		Null		Total
Main	447	69.5 %	196	30.5 %	643
Subordinate	389	59.8 %	262	40.2 %	651
Conjunct	160	73.4 %	58	26.6 %	218
Totals	996		516		1512

As can be seen from Table 3, there is no significant difference between main and conjunct clauses (p = 0.3029), but subjects are more likely to be inserted in main clauses (p = 0.0002) and conjunct clauses (p = 0.0003) than in subordinate clauses. In a Germanic context this result is surprising; I will return to this in section 3.

The effect of the Latin original is essentially categorical: the subject is never omitted in the Old English unless it is omitted in the Latin. In 347 examples, an Old English personal pronoun was used to translate an element in the Latin, usually a nominative personal pronoun itself (*ego, nos, tu, vos, ille, ipse, illi*). Personal pronouns may be inserted in the Old English when there is no Latin model, but they may never be omitted when a Latin model is present.

In some instances, a first or second person pronoun is inserted even when another nominative pronoun (corresponding to the Latin) already exists in the same clause, as in (9) and (10). There are 36 such examples in John.

(9)	JnGl (Li) 8.46	forhuon	**gie**	ne	gelefeð	**gie**	me
		why	you	NEG	believe	you	me
	L	*quare uos non creditis mihi*					
	Trans.	'Why do **you** not believe me?'					

(10) JnGl (Li) 8.38	**ic** þ ic gesæh æt ðæm fæder **.ic**. spreco
	I what I saw at the father I speak
L	*ego quod uidi apud patrem loquor*
Trans.	'**I** speak that which I have seen with my father'

These examples of 'pronoun doubling' are intriguing, and suggest that the glossator's strategy sometimes involved rendering first- and second-person verb forms with the corresponding pronoun automatically, even if the clause already contained a pronominal subject on the model of the Latin. Rather than being a linguistic feature per se, this could simply reflect the glossator's narrow scope of vision in rendering successive elements of the gloss (see Jolly, this volume), or potentially a concern to disambiguate certain verbal forms without person distinction. On the other hand, in most examples of clauses containing a pronominal subject corresponding to the Latin, there is no doubling, even when the Latin pronoun and verb are non-adjacent: see (11) and (12).[8] Of 347 examples of pronouns inserted following the Latin model, only 36 examples (less than 10 %) also involve pronoun doubling.

(11) JnGl (Li) 8.55	**ic** uutudlice conn ł wat hine
	I truly know him
L	*ego autem noui eum*
Trans.	'I know him'

(12) JnGl (Li) 1.19	**ðu** huelc ł huæd arst ł arð
	you which/what are
L	*tu quis es*
Trans.	'Who art thou?'

Since the numbers are so small, whether pronoun doubling can be considered to be a native or a common feature of Northumbrian Old English cannot be conclusively established; Berndt (1956: 85–87) observes that it is found only rarely in the Rushworth and West Saxon Gospels. Pronoun doubling may well be an artefact of glossarial practice rather than a dialect feature.

Finally, in order to ascertain whether there were any significant interactions between the factors I considered above – for instance whether the effect of person was stronger in main clauses – I carried out a step-down logistic regres-

8 Example (12) is unusual in that a word for 'what'/'which' is used, rather than 'who'. For some discussion of the variation in interrogatives in Old English and of the polysemy of *hwæt* 'what', see Walkden (2014: ch. 4).

sion analysis on the data using Rbrul (Johnson 2009). All of the variables given above (person, number, clause type, presence vs. absence of Latin) were entered into the analysis, as well as all possible interactions between these variables. The results are given in Table 4.

Table 4. Results of multivariate analysis, effects in log odds

Variable	Factor	Log odds
Person	1st	2.384
	2nd	1.245
	3rd	-3.630
Number	Singular	-0.641
	Plural	0.641
Latin counterpart	Yes	10.688
	No	-10.688

The log odds values, if negative, indicate a disfavouring effect on pronominal subject insertion, and, if positive, indicate a favouring effect on pronominal subject insertion with respect to the mean. Thus, for instance, the presence of a Latin counterpart (e.g. a subject pronoun *ego* or *vos*) favours insertion, and the absence of such a counterpart favours omission. Similarly, first and (to a lesser extent) second person favours insertion, while third person favours omission.[9]

The best model, as can be seen from Table 4, incorporates no interactions and does not include the effect of clause type; removing these variables from the model does not make it significantly less effective at covering the data. Log odds values incorporate effect strength as well as likelihood of significance of effects; this explains why number is included as having a significant effect despite this not emerging from the Fisher's exact test, and why clause type is not included despite emerging as significant in the Fisher's exact test. Specifically, the step-down procedure has analyzed the model that includes clause type and compared it to the model that does not, and found that the model that includes clause type is no more effective.

This analysis therefore demonstrates statistically what is intuitive from the results presented in Berndt (1956) and earlier in this section: the effect of grammatical person on pronoun expression in the Old English glossal translation is

9 The Nagelkerke pseudo-R^2 value for the model is 0.832, roughly indicating that the factors included in the model explain 83 % of the variation attested in the data.

independent of the effect of the Latin. The preference for first- and second-person subject pronoun insertion in the text, then, is most likely to be ascribed to a genuine syntactic possibility in the grammar of North Northumbrian Old English.

A caveat must be mentioned, however: I have not taken sequential dependencies – e.g. morphosyntactic priming or persistence effects – into consideration. This is important, as it has been demonstrated that priming can affect subject pronoun expression in languages such as Spanish (cp., for instance, Travis 2007). Future work could check whether there is an effect in this text.

3 Null subjects in early Germanic beyond the Lindisfarne Gospels

The most striking feature of null subjects in the text is the person split: insertion is heavily favoured in the first and second persons, but not in the third person. From the traditional functionalist perspective that identification of the null subject rests on the presence of rich verbal agreement, this presents a problem, since agreement in late Northumbrian was extremely limited. Table 5 illustrates this.

Table 5. Present indicative verbal agreement endings in Northumbrian Old English (from Cole 2014: 24; based on Ross 1960: 39)

Person and number		Strong, Weak I	Weak II
sg.	1	*-o, -a*	*-iga, -igo*
	2	*-as, -es*	-(*ig*)*as*, -(*ig*)*es*
	3	*-að, -as, -eð, -es*	-(*ig*)*að*, -(*ig*)*as*, -(*ig*)*eð*, -(*ig*)*es*
pl./pl. imp.		*-að, -as, -eð, -es*	-(*ig*)*að*, -(*ig*)*as*, -(*ig*)*eð*, -(*ig*)*es*

The paradox is this: distinctive verbal endings are only found in the first person singular, yet in this context (among others) null subjects are extremely rare. Instead null subjects are found primarily in the third person, which cannot be distinguished from first or second person plural, or sometimes even from second person singular.

The idea behind the rich agreement approach to identifying null subjects has a long pedigree: Householder (1981) traces it back to Apollonius Dyscolus in the second century AD. In some languages it may have a role to play; however, as the existence of languages such as Chinese demonstrates, null subjects may be present even in languages without rich verbal morphology. As we have seen, in the case of Northumbrian Old English it does not seem plausible to assume that verbal morphology played a role.

Berndt (1956: 82–85) offers a historical explanation for the person split found in Northumbrian Old English. Noting that in the West Saxon Gospels null subjects are not found, and that in the Rushworth gloss they are found to a lesser extent than in Lindisfarne, he considers the possibility that null subjects are a Northumbrian dialect feature, ultimately rejecting it for reasons that are unclear. Instead Berndt (1956: 82) hypothesizes that the relevant criterion is register (*Schriftsprache* vs. *Umgangssprache*), and that the West Saxon Gospels are the closest to the 'standard' of the time, with the Lindisfarne Gospels being the furthest from it. He further hypothesizes that in Proto-Germanic null subjects were the rule across the board, and that while the use of the first and second person pronouns in Old English is a colloquial innovation, the use of the third person pronoun is a prescriptive rule imposed by the standard. Building on Benveniste's (1946) argument that the third person is logically and cross-linguistically distinct from the other two, he argues that first and second person pronouns were originally introduced for reasons of emphasis, and that in the third person this role could be fulfilled by demonstratives rather than personal pronouns. The consistent use of third person pronouns is then introduced as part of a conscious standardization effort for reasons of symmetry across the paradigm (Berndt 1956: 84).

Table 6. Pronominal subjects in early Northwest Germanic texts, by person and number (based on Walkden 2014: ch. 5)

Text	Person	N	Overt		Null		Total
Old Icelandic: *Morkinskinna* (Wallenberg et al. 2011)	1	sg.	269	99.3 %	2	0.7 %	271
		pl.	79	95.2 %	4	4.8 %	83
	2	sg.	185	99.5 %	1	0.5 %	186
		pl.	13	100.0 %	0	0.0 %	13
	3	sg.	562	90.1 %	62	9.9 %	624
		pl.	183	89.3 %	22	10.7 %	205
	Totals		1291		91		1382

Table 6. (continued)

Text	Person	N	Overt		Null		Total
Old English: *Beowulf* (Pintzuk and Plug 2001)	1	sg.	75	97.4 %	2	2.6 %	77
		pl.	21	100.0 %	0	0.0 %	21
	2	sg.	26	96.3 %	1	3.7 %	27
		pl.	10	100.0 %	0	0.0 %	10
	3	sg.	172	80.4 %	42	19.6 %	214
		pl.	49	71.0 %	20	29.0 %	69
	Totals		353		65		418
Old English: *Bald's Leechbook* (Taylor et al. 2003)	1	sg.	1	100.0 %	0	0.0 %	1
		pl.	11	100.0 %	0	0.0 %	11
	2	sg.	52	100.0 %	0	0.0 %	52
		pl.	0	–	0	–	0
	3	sg.	108	77.1 %	32	22.9 %	140
		pl.	35	71.4 %	14	28.6 %	49
	Totals		207		46		253
Old Saxon: *Heliand* (Behaghel and Taeger 1996)	1	sg.	262	100.0 %	0	0.0 %	262
		pl.	61	100.0 %	0	0.0 %	61
	2	sg.	247	99.2 %	2	0.8 %	249
		pl.	230	99.1 %	2	0.9 %	232
	3	sg.	1089	94.5 %	63	5.5 %	1152
		pl.	454	91.5 %	42	8.5 %	496
	Totals		2343		109		2452
Old High German: *Isidor* (based on Axel 2007: 315, Table 3; data from Eggenberger 1961; main and conjunct clauses only)	1	sg.	36	94.7 %	2	5.3 %	38
		pl.	2	40.0 %	3	60.0 %	5
	2	sg.	3	60.0 %	2	40.0 %	5
		pl.	1	100.0 %	0	0.0 %	1
	3	sg.	15	34.1 %	29	65.9 %	44
		pl.	4	25.0 %	12	75.0 %	16
	Totals		61		48		109

Whether or not Berndt's sociolinguistic scenario holds water, the use of first and second person pronouns cannot have been an Old English innovation. In work on other early Germanic texts (Walkden 2013 and 2014: 157–195) I have found that the same asymmetry is found all across Northwest Germanic. Table 6 gives figures for a selection of texts.

The overall percentages of null subjects vary from language to language and text to text, but in each case Fisher's exact tests show the difference between 3rd and non-3rd person to be statistically significant ($p < 0.0001$). The person split is therefore almost certainly an innovation that predates the fission of North and West Germanic.[10]

Beyond Germanic, languages which permit null subjects only in certain persons are not unattested. In Finnish and Hebrew, for instance, null subjects are possible only in the first and second persons (Vainikka and Levy 1999): this is the mirror image of what we find in Northumbrian Old English and elsewhere in early Northwest Germanic. Shipibo, an indigenous American language, is reported to allow null subjects only in the third person (Camacho and Elías-Ulloa 2010), essentially as in the Lindisfarne Gospels. How these patterns originate historically, and how to analyze them synchronically, is still a matter of debate: see Walkden (2014: 209–215) for one proposal, building on Holmberg (2010).

Within the context of Old English more generally, the Lindisfarne glossal translation occupies a special position, as null subjects are more common proportionally in this text than in any other. The effect of the Latin original likely favoured null subjects; nevertheless, the person split shows that this effect, if it existed, can only have served to amplify a natively existing pattern in Northumbrian Old English.[11] Previous studies of null subjects in Old English have reached different conclusions: Hulk and van Kemenade (1995), for instance, state that Old English is not a null subject language, while van Gelderen (2000) argues that null subjects can be found, partly based on Berndt's (1956) data. Mitchell

---

10 Gothic seems to behave differently: see Mossé (1956: 171), Abraham (1991), Fertig (2000), Ferraresi (2005: 47–49) and Walkden (2014: 158–164). The evidence from Runic Northwest Germanic, meanwhile, is not unequivocal: of 14 complete inscriptions containing first person singular verbs, two contain no corresponding pronoun (Antonsen 2002: 188–189), while, elsewhere, full pronouns are found, either *ek* or the enclitic *-eka*/*-ika*. This sort of distribution is to be expected if it was possible but rare for first person pronouns to be omitted in Northwest Germanic. Unfortunately, but unsurprisingly, contexts for second and third person subject pronouns are entirely unattested in the corpus of early inscriptions.

11 It is difficult to corroborate this using other texts, as the Lindisfarne Gospels are by far the most extensive text written in the Northumbrian dialect. However, Berndt's (1965: 69) data on the Durham Ritual – also a gloss by Aldred – show that this text also has a large majority of null subjects in the third person.

(1985: 633), building on Pogatscher (1901), states that the possibility of null subjects "occurs (or survives) only spasmodically" in Old English. Walkden (2013; 2014: 171–184) presents the results of a new quantitative study based on the York-Toronto-Helsinki Corpus of Old English Prose (Taylor et al. 2003), which shows that the numbers of null subjects found vary dramatically between texts (cp. also Rusten 2013, 2015): in classical West Saxon prose such as the works of Ælfric and Wulfstan, and in the *Cura Pastoralis*, for instance, null subjects are essentially not found, but in the Old English *Bede*, in *Bald's Leechbook* and in the C, D and E manuscripts of the Chronicle they are found with some frequency. In addition, they are frequently found in *Beowulf*, as seen in Table 6.[12]

Walkden (2013 and 2014: 183) argues that the correct generalization is that all those texts which robustly exhibit null subjects have been independently argued to be Anglian or Anglian-influenced rather than purely West Saxon. For instance, Fulk (2008: 96) observes that the Old English *Bede* and *Bald's Leechbook*, as well as the D and E Chronicle manuscripts, though traditionally classed as West Saxon, display Anglian features. Though it is agreed that *Bald's Leechbook* in its transmitted form was composed in Winchester (Meaney 1984: 236), Wenisch (1979: 54) argues on a lexical basis that an Anglian (probably Mercian) original must have existed. As for *Beowulf*, Fulk (1992: 309–325; 2007) notes a number of Anglian lexical and morphological features.

Since West Saxon was the Old English standard (to the extent that such a standard existed; see Smith 2000 on issues of standardization in early English), it is difficult to disentangle my hypothesis of dialectal variation from Berndt's (1956: 82–85) hypothesis of register variation. However, there are a few indications that the Anglian hypothesis is the one that is on the right track. For instance, historical texts such as the Chronicle and Bede's *History of the English Church* might be expected to conform closely to any standard, yet these texts still exhibit null subjects. Furthermore, under the register variation hypothesis, versions of the same text in different dialects would not be expected to display substantial variation, yet this is exactly what we find: the D manuscript of the Chronicle displays the most null subjects, and the C manuscript displays the fewest. Finally, the register

12 Two reviewers object that the metrical requirements of poetry will affect the expression of pronominal subjects, and this is certainly true; see Rusten (2015) for a clear demonstration of this. However, the fact that the person asymmetry is found very strongly in *Beowulf* suggests that this cannot be the whole story: pronominal subjects are typically unstressed monosyllables regardless of person, and so there is no *metrical* reason to omit third person pronouns more than first and second person pronouns. As in the glosses, then, null subjects in *Beowulf* can only be a native phenomenon. See Walkden (2013) and Rusten (2015) for more detail.

variation hypothesis must stipulate that the effect of the standard was felt in the Rushworth gloss by Farman but not by Owun.

Other comparative questions arise to which I have no firm answer. For instance, in all of the Old English texts investigated in Walkden (2013, 2014) that exhibited significant numbers of null subjects, these null subjects were also significantly more common in main clauses than in subordinate clauses; this also holds true for Old Saxon, Old High German and Old Swedish (Håkansson 2008). In the Lindisfarne glossal translation, on the other hand, null subjects were significantly more common in subordinate clauses than in main clauses (though this effect did not make it into the logistic regression model presented in section 2). Of the early Germanic texts investigated in Walkden (2014), only certain Old Icelandic texts behaved in this way. This might suggest that the distribution we see in the Lindisfarne Gospels is the result of syntactic transfer from Scandinavian; however, Thomason and Kaufman (1988: § 9.8.6.10) claim to find only lexical borrowings from Scandinavian in Old Northumbrian, and not structural transfer. Miller (2012: 134–145) presents several structural features of English for which a case for Norse influence can be made; these are mainly shared innovations rather than borrowings from earlier Scandinavian, and mainly surface during the Middle English period. Under a contact-based approach it also seems odd that null subjects in Old Northumbrian would pattern in terms of clause type with those in Old Icelandic rather than those we see in East Norse (at least on the basis of the Old Swedish evidence). The distribution across clause types we see in the Lindisfarne Gospels could just as well be an artefact of the glossing process, which may not have fully taken clause type into account – though, as mentioned earlier, the glossing process alone is not obviously able to account for the person split.

4 Conclusion: new hope for Old English dialect syntax

In their work *The Syntax of Early English*, Fischer et al. (2000: 37) are pessimistic about the prospects for discovering anything about the dialectal distribution of syntactic variables in Old English:

> There is little scope for work on dialect syntax in Old English; almost all the texts are in the West Saxon dialect, while those works of any length that were not written in West Saxon consist mostly of interlinear glosses on parts of the Vulgate bible, and are therefore of limited use for syntactic purposes.

However, recent work (Kroch and Taylor 1997 on pronoun position; Nagucka 1997 on various features; Ingham 2006 on negative concord; van Bergen 2008 on negative contraction; and Cole 2012a, 2012b, 2014 on the Northern Subject Rule) has shown that this position is in need of qualification: syntactic dialect differences within Old English can be identified, provided that the (admittedly limited) non-West Saxon material is used with care.

The present chapter adds another such study to the list: a new quantitative study shows that in all clause types in the Lindisfarne glossal translation, null subjects could be found, frequently in the third person but only rarely in the first and second. This distribution is not predictable on the basis of the Latin original. The study complements the findings of Berndt (1956), who already observed the person split, by demonstrating that clause type does not play a clear role in conditioning null subjects, and by assessing the strength of the effect of the presence or absence of a pronoun in the Latin original. The distribution found in the Lindisfarne Gospels also stands in stark contrast to that found in West Saxon Old English texts, in which null subjects are not robustly attested at all; from a wider perspective, however, it makes perfect sense, as the retention of a common Northwest Germanic syntactic feature.[13]

13 This work stems from a larger project on null subjects in early Germanic as part of my PhD, funded by AHRC grant AH/H026924/1. For comments and advice on this topic I am grateful to Elly van Gelderen, Susan Pintzuk, Kristian Rusten, Ann Taylor, my supervisor David Willis, and of course the audience at the workshop on the Old English Gloss to the Lindisfarne Gospels at Westminster; thanks also to Benedikt Szmrecsányi, two anonymous reviewers, and the editors of this volume for their comments on an earlier draft.

Julia Fernández Cuesta

Revisiting the Manuscript of the Lindisfarne Gospels

Abstract: The aim of this article is to demonstrate that Skeat's nineteenth-century edition of the gloss to the Lindisfarne Gospels, the most substantial Old Northumbrian witness that has been preserved, is not reliable for linguistic analysis. It will be shown that collation of the edition with the facsimile of the original manuscript (Kendrick et al. 1956) reveals a number of aspects of Skeat's editorial practice (emendations, additions, and alteration of the manuscript, word-division and word-spacing) that often result in the loss of valuable material for linguistic analysis and obscure, to some extent, the characteristics of the dialect of the gloss and possible cases of linguistic change in progress.

1 Introduction

This article will try to demonstrate the importance of returning to the original manuscript of the Lindisfarne Gospels (London, British Library, Cotton MS Nero D.iv, henceforth Li.) and the need for a revision of Skeat's standard edition, which has been (and still remains) the basis for linguistic and literary studies of the text. As is well known, one of the main problems in the study of Old English dialects is the paucity of the texts that have come down to us. In the case of northern Old English (generally referred to as 'Old Northumbrian'), the only records (aside from place- and personal names) that have survived are three short poems, about thirty runic inscriptions from the eighth and ninth centuries, which are difficult to date and impossible to locate with precision, and three interlinear glosses from the late tenth century: the gloss to the Lindisfarne Gospels, the Old Northumbrian gloss to part of the Rushworth Gospels (Ru^2; Oxford, Bodleian Library, Auct. D.ii.19) and the gloss to the Durham Collectar (Durham Cathedral Library, MS A.iv.19). All these texts have been edited and widely studied during the last two centuries. However, while some editions have been thoroughly revised (cp. Page's standard book on Anglo-Saxon runic inscriptions, fully revised and updated in 1999, and Tamoto's 2013 edition of the Rushworth Gospels), for the Lindisfarne gloss we are still dependent on a nineteenth-century edition.[1]

1 In Tamoto's edition (2013) scribal errors are emended and the reasons for emendation are given in footnotes. In the same way, additions and alterations are also included in the text and ex-

The standard edition of Li., together with the West Saxon Gospels and the gloss to the Rushworth Gospels, was published in the last quarter of the nineteenth century by Walter Skeat.[2] In his introduction to Mark's Gospel, Skeat mentions the deficiencies of previous editions (Bouterwek 1857; and Stevenson and Waring 1854–1865) and states that his aim is to present the reader with a text that reflects as nearly as possible "the *exact* peculiarities of the MSS" (Skeat 1871: xxiv, italics in the original). He warns about the possibly deliberate corrections made by previous editors and states that he intends to offer "the uncorrected readings of the MSS themselves, from a conviction that in many instances students not only prefer to correct them for themselves, but may be better able to correct them than [he is]" (1871: xxi). He also admits that his volume may contain "a few errors", but that "they can hardly be numerous" (1871: xxi). Nevertheless, it has been shown (Blakeley 1949–1950: 15–16) that the transcription of the manuscript does indeed contain a significant number of errors (1,200 according to Chadwick's 1934 collation), which effectively render his transcription useless for linguistic analysis. Benskin (2011) has recently argued that a new edition, fully collated with the manuscript, is needed for statistical analysis and, although it might be argued that 1,200 errors in an edition comprising some 75,000 words surely do not make statistical analyses based on it completely worthless, I believe that the need for a new edition of Li. is fully justified.[3] Errors of transcription are not the only problem that Skeat's edition presents. Some of his editorial criteria are (at the very least) questionable. He is not always consistent as regards abbreviations, sometimes expanding them, by his own admission, "as required by the grammar": "Near the beginning of the book, I have left the word hæł as written in the MS., but I have found it better to expand it into hæl*end*, hæl*ende* or hæl*endes*, as required by grammar" (Skeat 1871: xxviii). It is clear from his method that the grammar Skeat has in mind is the 'standard' West Saxon and not the grammar of the Old Northumbrian dialect, which he describes as "anomalous": "The noun-

plained in footnotes. As regards editorial procedure, abbreviations are generally expanded with the expanded part of the abbreviation italicized, except for the abbreviations '⁊' and '&' (for OE *and* and Latin *et* respectively), OE "ꝥ" and "ꝥte" for OE *þæt* and *þætte* respectively and "ł" for Old English *oþþe*. No punctuation has been added and letters are capitalized at the beginning of a verse, sentence or clause, especially when decorated (Tamoto 2013: cxii). However, there is no mention of how scribal word-division and word-spacing have been dealt with in the edition.

2 The four Gospels were edited between 1871 and 1887: Mark in 1871, Luke in 1874, John in 1878, and Matthew in 1887.

3 When referring to Holmqvist's (1992) statistics, based on Skeat's editions, on the distribution of verbal *-s*/*-ð* in the present indicative paradigm, Blakely states: "His statistics, erroneous as they are, yet enable him to place the frequency of the *-s* forms in the correct order" (Blakely 1949–1950: 23).

endings in L. are rather anomalous and inconsistent" (Skeat 1871: xxx).[4] In the section on inflections, Skeat comments on the "peculiarities of the dialect", but chooses, nevertheless, to expand the abbreviations according to the West Saxon standard dialect. Therefore, although he is critical of previous editors who normalized the language of the gloss, Skeat's own editorial practice obscures, to some extent, the variability of the language of Li. and for this reason alone his edition cannot be considered completely reliable.

In what follows I will illustrate the various aspects of Skeat's edition that are not faithful to the Li. text in one way or another and that justify the need to go back to the facsimile of the original manuscript. Apart from the errors in the transcription, the collation of a selection of excerpts of the edition with the facsimile of the Li. manuscript has revealed the following cases of questionable editorial practice:

1. Regularization. Skeat's practice of normalizing texts often results in the loss of valuable material for linguistic analysis, as will be shown below.
2. Alteration of manuscript word-division, word-spacing and punctuation.[5] This deprives us of valuable information on the prosody of the text.

For the present work I have collated and analyzed the first five chapters of Skeat's editions of the four Northumbrian Gospels against the facsimile copy of the manuscript (Kendrick et al. 1956).[6]

2 Transcription errors

As has already been mentioned, Skeat's edition of Li. contains errors, as is only to be expected in such an extensive work.[7] In the excerpt analyzed here the number

4 It should also be borne in mind that West Saxon is not a homogeneous variety, either from a diachronic or diatopic point of view.

5 In the colophon and a number of explanatory marginalia (cp. Ross et al. 1960: 19).

6 When I started to work on Li. the online facsimile of the gloss was still not available. It can be now consulted online (see n. 6 in the Introduction). Although editions are always of great help and a new edition of the gloss is certainly a *desideratum*, for linguistic purposes, return to the original manuscript is always advisable.

7 In the entry dedicated to Skeat in the *Oxford Dictionary of National Biography*, Sisam and Brewer state that "At a critical moment in English studies he saw the wisdom of Furnivall's doctrine, that the essential thing was to attract workers, and to make available for them quickly a great quantity of materials, edited as well as possible, but always with a time limit in view rather than perfection and minutiae". This could explain some of the errors found in the edition.

of errors detected is very low, especially if compared with the inconsistencies found in the representation of scribal "corrections" and word-division.

An example of a clear error is the omission of the personal pronoun on f. 140rb12; Luke 1.18 (see Figure 1). The manuscript reads <ic ƿitto>, but Skeat does not transcribe the pronoun <ic> and renders only <ƿitto> (Skeat 1874: 17). The same can be said about the omission of the preposition that introduces the second noun in two double glosses: <in oeðel ł in lond>, which is transcribed as <in oeðel ł lond> (f. 30vb4; Matthew 2.12; Skeat 1887: 33), and <to noƿihte ł tonænihte> (L *nihilum*), which is transcribed as <to nowihte ł nænihte> (f. 34va21; Matthew 5.13; Skeat 1887: 45).[8]

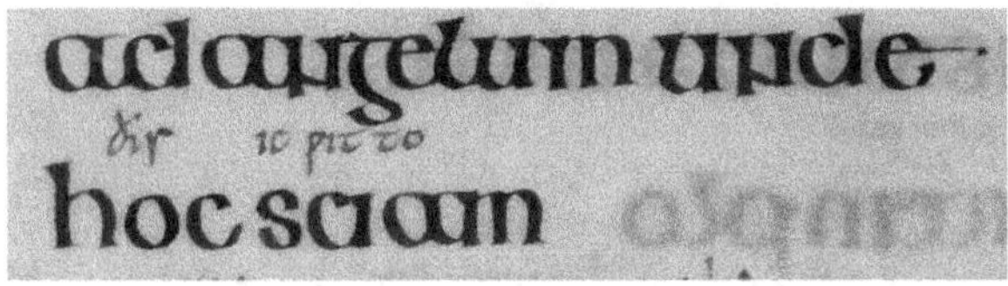

Figure 1. <ic ƿitto> (L *sciam*; f. 140rb12; Luke 1.18)

It might be argued that the above errors are a problem only for purist philologists. Nevertheless, at least two of these errors originating in Skeat's edition have been replicated in the most widely used standard grammars of Old English (Campbell 1959; Hogg 1992a; and Hogg and Fulk 2011) and in the *DOEC*. They might also have made their way into *A Corpus of Narrative Etymologies* (CoNE), if they had not been detected by Roger Lass, who drew my attention to two unusual forms of the second person plural pronoun in Li., <gæ> and <giæ>, for which it seemed difficult to offer an etymology which could explain them:

(1) (f. 125ra22–24; Mark 14.42; Skeat 1871: 117)

Li.	arisað **gæ ƿe** ł putu(n) geonga heono seðe mec selleð neh is
L	*surgite eamus ecce qui me tradit prope est*
Trans.	'Rise up, let us go. Behold, he that will betray me is at hand'[9]

8 In the *Dictionary of Old English Web Corpus* (hereafter *DOEC*) the preposition *to* in the second gloss has been transcribed.

9 All the translations of the Gospels are taken from the *Douay-Rheims Bible*.

(2) (f. 170rb5–7; Luke 11.42; Skeat 1874: 123)[10]

Li.	ah pæ iuh æl*dum* forðon **giæ teigðas** meric ł ⁊ cunela ł
L	*Sed uáe uobis pharisaei quia decimatis mentam et rutam*
Trans.	'But woe to you, Pharisees, because you tithe mint and rue'.

Hogg (1992a: 111–112, § 5.54) states that the forms <giæ> and <gæ> show a purely orthographic substitution of <æ> for <e>. The *OED* online gave until recently OE *giæ* under *ye* as "rare" in Old Northumbrian and argued that that OE *ge* apparently underwent raising (or possibly diphthongization) due to the preceding palatal and referred further to Hogg (1992a: 111–112, § 5.54).[11]

Once the "rare" forms in Skeat's edition were checked against the facsimile of the manuscript, I found that neither of them occurred in the gloss as a personal pronoun. The form <gæ> in example (1) is not a second person plural pronoun, but a reduced form of the first person plural subjunctive of OE *gan* ('to go'), which is followed by the first person plural pronoun <pe> and forms part of the double gloss "gæ pe ł putu(n) geonga" (L *eamus* 'let us go'). The verbal form "arisað" is a plural imperative with a null subject. In the manuscript <gæ> appears perfectly aligned above L *eamus* whereas in Skeat's edition the double gloss is not exactly centrally aligned over the Latin verb, giving the impression that <gæ> is the subject of "arisað". This error, if it is such, seems to have been what originated the misreading (cp. "arisað **gæ pe** ł putu(n) geonga heono seðe mec selleð neh is" in f. 125ra22–24; Mark 14.42).[12]

10 The *DOEC* gives the erroneous form in its transcription of LkGl (Li) 11.42:

Sed uae uobis pharisaei quia decimatis mentam et rutam et omne holus et praeteritis iudicium et caritatem dei haec autem oportuit facere et illa non omittere

ah wæ iuh ældum forðon **giæ teigðas** meric ł ⁊ cunela ł ⁊ ælc wyrt & biwærlas þæt dom ⁊ lufo ł broðerscip godes ðas uutedlice geras to wyrcanne ⁊ ða ilco ne to forhycganne (emphasis mine).

The editors of the *DOEC* assure me that the erroneous form had been detected in 2013, and that the corrected reading will appear in the next release of the *DOEC* and *DOE*.

11 After checking my findings, the editors of the *OED* have removed the erroneous form from the online version of the *OED*.

12 Cp. f. 97rb2 (Mark 1.38), which has the identical gloss "gæ pe ł putu(n) geonga" for L *eamus*.

Figure 2. <arisað gæ pe ł putu(n) geonga heono seðe mec selleð> (L *surgite eamus ecce qui me tradit*; f. 125ra22–24, Mark 14.42)

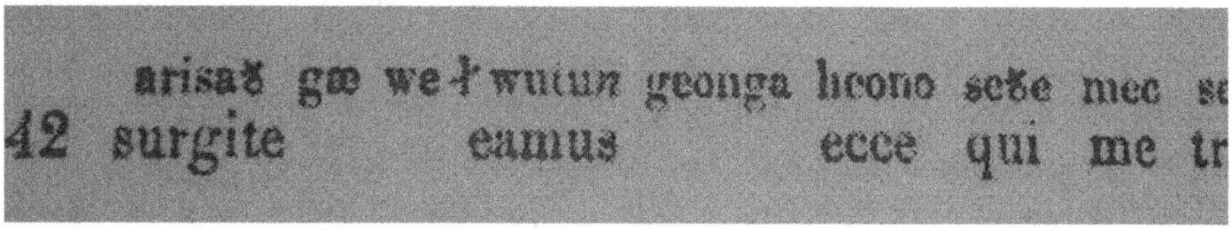

arisað gæ we ł wutun geonga heono seðe mec se
42 surgite eamus ecce qui me tr

Figure 3. Skeat (1871: 117)

As regards example (2) (Skeat 1874: 123), the form that appears in the manuscript is clearly the usual <gie>, showing palatal diphthongisation, not <giæ> (cp. "ah pæ iuh æl(dum) f(or)ðon **gie teigðas** meric ł ⁊ cunela ł" in f. 170rb5–7; Luke 11.42). Whether or not Campbell and Hogg also misread the text or simply relied on Skeat's edition, which is more likely, the problem is that the original error has not only been replicated but also subject to an explanation in standard reference grammars.[13] The mistake could have been easily corrected by checking the odd forms found in Skeat against the facsimile copy of the original manuscript. Cook (1894: 197) also appears to have relied on Skeat's edition as he includes the two forms in the entry for the second person pronoun in his glossary. However, in the *Index Verborum*, based on Chadwick's work (1934), Ross and Stanley (1960: 151) correctly list the form found under *gie* in the entry for the second personal pronoun.

13 Brunner (1965: 259, § 332.4) also gives these two forms for the second person plural pronoun, besides <gie>, <ge> and <gee>.

3 Emendations

It is not always easy to distinguish between transcription errors or lapses and conscious emendations. For instance, on f. 141va1–2 (Luke 1.42), the manuscript reads <stefne mið micla> (L *uoce magna* 'with a loud voice'), but Skeat (1874: 23) transcribes <stefn>. In the grammar of Li. there is variation between the *-e* inflection and the zero ending in the dative singular in nouns belonging to the Type α declension (Ross 1960: 38)[14]. Nevertheless, in the case of *stefn*, the *-e* ending of the dative singular is always preserved. The form "stefn" with zero ending only appears glossing L *vox* (nominative singular) and *vocem* (accusative singular), but not as a dative singular form.[15]

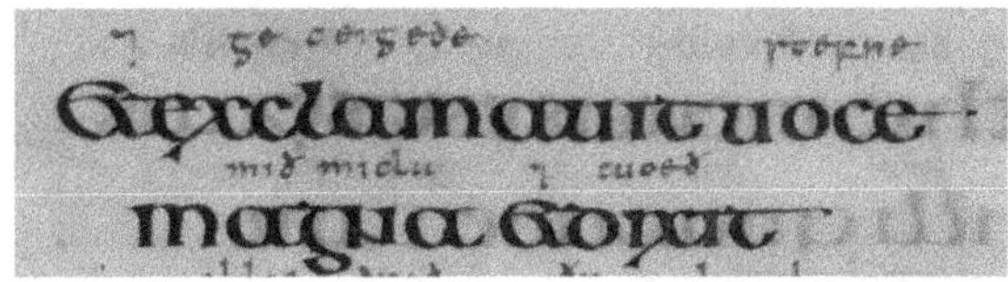

Figure 4. <stefne mið micla> (f. 141va1–2, Luke 1.42)

Another example is <ðec̣> on f. 36rb10 (Matthew 5.39). In the manuscript *c* has been expuncted, but Skeat (1887: 51) transcribes <ðec>, thus obscuring the scribe's correction or representation of a possible alternative form (see discussion below).

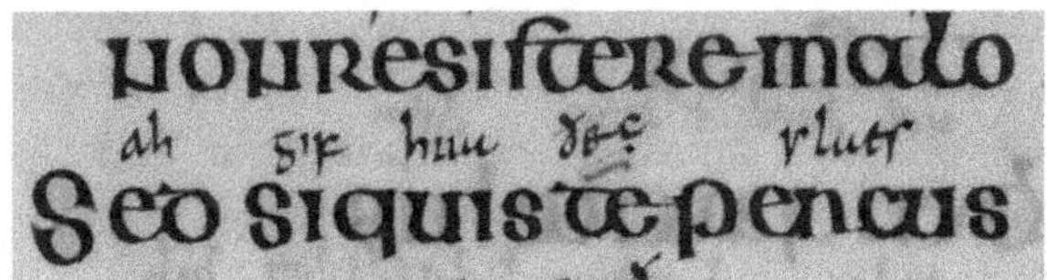

Figure 5. <ðec̣> (f. 36rb10; Matthew 5.39)

In the excerpt analyzed there are numerous occurrences of the prefix *ge-* without the vowel, which Skeat renders as <g[e]>. The scribal practice might represent an

14 The nouns that are declined according to what Ross (1960: 39) calls "α declension" are essentially *o*-stems, short *jo*-stems, long *ā*-stems, long and short *ja*-stems, long *i*-stems, non-abstract short masc. *i*-stems, long *u*-stems and *nt*-stems.

15 In the *DOEC* the form <stefne> is correctly transcribed.

abbreviation, as Skeat seems to interpret it, but could also indicate the weakening of the prefix. On f. 251ra4 (John 18.8; Skeat 1878: 157), *ge-* in <ġė gáa> (glossing L *abire* 'to go') is expuncted as a correction or as a way to indicate a variant form; however, Skeat transcribes <ge-gáa> (the hyphen also hides the fact that the prefix is separated from the verb in the manuscript). A similar example is found on f. 214vb1 (John 2.16; see Figure 4), where the vowel *e* has been added by the editor: <g[e]wyrce>, glossing L *facere* (Skeat 1878: 25). The absence of the vowel in the *ge*-prefix may indicate change in progress. Skeat generally indicates that there is an emendation by the use of the square brackets. Wojtyś (2008) has carried out a study on past participle marking in medieval English which advances the hypothesis that the prefix *ge-* was beginning to be lost in Old Northumbrian. She records examples in which the prefix does not appear in the language of Li. The presence of these possibly reduced forms in the gloss, which can be only detected by examination of the original manuscript, could strengthen this hypothesis.

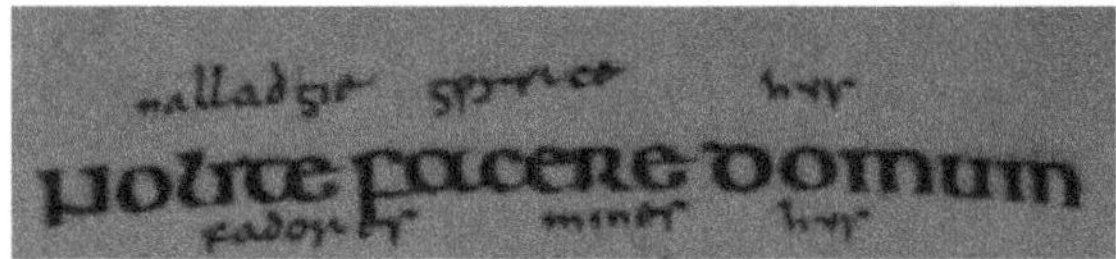

Figure 6. <gpyrce> (f. 214vb1; John 2.16)

Another example of an emendation that might be obscuring phonological change in progress, in this case the incipient weakening of mid unstressed vowels in the language of Li., is found in <ancenndes> (glossing L *unigeniti*; f. 211vb24; John 1.14). Skeat (1878: 15) transcribes <ancenn[e]des>. Despite indicating an inserted *e*, which does not appear in the original manuscript, he fails to signal that *d* is placed above and between *n* and *e* in the manuscript. This possible scribal self-correction is relevant for the study of glossing practice.

Figure 7. <ancenndes> (f. 211vb24 ; John 1.14)

In the following example Skeat also inserts *t* and marks it as an emendation: <soðfæsnisse>, (glossing L *iustitiam*; f. 32va4; Matthew 3.15), which he (1887: 39) renders as <soðfæs[t]nisse> .[16] See Figure 6.

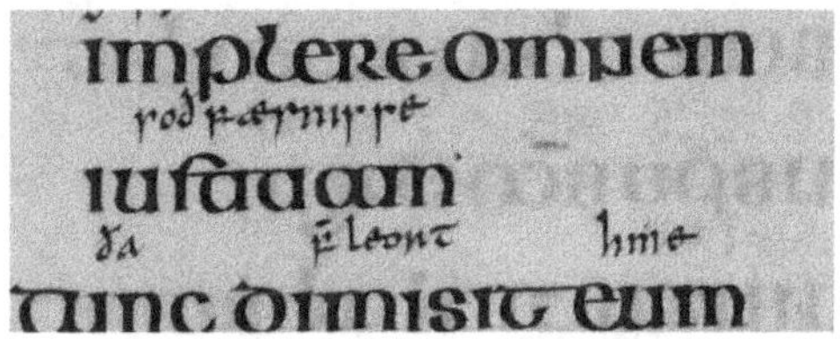

Figure 8. <soðfæsnisse> (f. 32va4 ; Matthew 3.15)

The form <soðfæsnisse> could be interpreted as an instance of final stop deletion (simplification of the consonantal cluster /st/). Lea (1894: 125) reports a similar example in the gloss to Mark's Gospel, in which final t has been omitted: <gaas> (L *spiritus*; f. 122ra3; Mark 13.11; Skeat 1871: 105), and there is also another instance in <gaas seðe liffæstas lichoma ne f(or)stondes> for L *spiritus est qui uiuificat caro non prodest* (f. 225vb6; John 6.63; Skeat 1978: 65). In both cases Skeat correctly transcribes <gaas>.[17]

Skeat sometimes omits the abbreviation sign for *vel* when there is no second gloss following it. In the fragment analyzed I have found two examples: <clænsvnge ł> (glossing L *purificationem*; f. 214ra13; John 2.6; cp. Skeat 1878: 23) and <geporhte ł > (glossing L *fecisset*; f. 214va15; John 2.15; cp. Skeat 1878: 25). Recovering this information is important as it may indicate that Aldred left an empty slot for synonyms to be filled in later, a practice which could shed light on the function of the gloss as a study aid. On the other hand, Skeat sometimes inserts the abbreviation for *vel* in square brackets to separate alternative glosses where there is no abbreviation sign in the gloss: <acende [ł] gebær> (glossing L *concepit*; Skeat 1874: 19; cp. f. 140va18–19; Luke 1.24). However, he is not always consistent, and in his transcription of <him ðæm> (glossing L *illis*; f. 139vb4; Luke 1.7), he

---

16 The transcription in the *DOEC* for MtGl (Li) 3.15 is <soðfæstnisse>. Skeat's emendation (in brackets) is not given.

17 There are other examples of possible simplification of the /st/ consonantal cluster in final position. One is <⁊ monn ðes **soðfæs**>, glossing L *et homo iste iustus* (f. 144rb23, Luke 2.25, Skeat 1874: 33). The loss of /t/ in this context also appears in <maas> instead of *maast*, which is recorded six times glossing L *maior*: <seðe heist ł **maas** is iuer bið ł sie embihtmonn iuer> (L *Qui maior est uestrum erit minister uester*; f. 73vb21, Matthew 23.11, Skeat 1887: 187).

(1874: 15) adds the abbreviation sign for *vel*, without any indication that it is an insertion: <him ł ðæm>.

Other examples of emendations found in the fragment analyzed are:

Li.	**Skeat**
<s angel> (L *angelus*; f. 140vb3; Luke 1.26)	<s[e] angel> (Skeat 1874: 19)
<sod> (L *stetit*; f. 143va6; Luke 2.9)	<s[t]od> (Skeat 1874: 29)
<gpunede> (L *mansit*; f. 212vb15; John 1.32)	<g[e]wunede> (Skeat 1878: 19)
<gpyrce> (L *facere*; f. 214vb1; John 2.16)	<g[e]wyrce> (Skeat 1878: 25)
<gsceoe> (L *calciamenta*; f. 32rb2; Matthew 3.11)	<g[e]sceoe> (Skeat 1887: 37)
<gbyes hlifgiendr>[18] (f. 34rb4 margin; Matthew 5.5)	<g[e]byes hlifgiendr[a]> (Skeat 1887: 45)
<ehvelc> (L *omnis*; f. 216ra1; John 3.16)	<e[g]hnelc> (Skeat 1878: 29)

Except for <s[t]od]>, which seems to be a lapse on the part of the scribe, the remaining cases appear to be, as has been pointed out before, conscious attempts on the part of the editor to correct what to him were defective forms. Yet these emendations may obscure phonological change in progress (i.e. the weakening of the *ge-* prefix). In the above cases Skeat does indicate that there is an emendation but his practice is not always consistent.

4 Skeat's treatment of scribal diacritic symbols indicating corrections or/and variant forms

Aldred makes alterations in the gloss by dotting and writing under and over the line. Ross et al. (1960: 18–19) make a clear distinction between corrections and what they call "alternative forms". According to them, scribal corrections are indicated by various procedures: points above and/or below the line, lines above and/ or below the line and, in a few cases, by a long vertical stroke (Ross et al. 1960: 18). On the other hand, Aldred indicates alternative forms

> by writing a letter (or letters) above the line; in doing this he employs two different methods: (i) the superscript letter(s) directly above letter(s) in the line; thus directly over the *a* of *broðra* Mt. 12,47 ([f. 51rb21] there appears an *o*; this we may indicate by the notation *broðra/*^{o}; (ii) the superscript letter(s) appear between, not directly above, letters in the line; thus *fad*^{e}*ro* J 6,31 [f. 224ra15] (Ross et al. 1960: 19).

In these two cases (as opposed to dotting) the scribe did not intend to indicate corrections, but simply to show variant forms. Thus, "*broðra/*^{o} should be read as *broðra*

18 The *f* has been added later and appears above and between the *i* and the *g*.

ł broðro and *fad*^{e}*ro* as *fadero ł fadro*" (Ross et al. 1960: 19). Despite this distinction, they sound a note of caution, stating that "the forms that have been altered are not necessarily erroneous [...]. [O]nly in some 200 cases is the alteration one that removes a form which is certainly erroneous [...]. In the remaining cases the alteration is merely from one (correct) variant form to another" (Ross et al. 1960: 19). As will be shown below, the strict dichotomy established between corrections and alterations does not hold water. There are many instances in which the scribal habit of dotting (writing a point above or below the line, or both) may indicate that both forms were acceptable.

4.1 The Li. scribal practice of dotting and under- and over-lining

As regards the scribal practice of dotting, Skeat does not generally transcribe the expuncted letter(s), but rather reproduces what he interprets to be the corrected form, as the examples in Table 1 show.[19] However, he sometimes also gives the alternative letter(s) without indicating that they are expuncted in the manuscript, as in <stiga/o>[20] (cp. Table 1, example 2). Elsewhere Skeat indicates that a particular form has been altered, but he does not explain the procedure employed by the scribe. For instance in <geherdọeṇ ge> (cp. f. 35ra23; Matthew 5.21) both *o* and *n* have been expuncted, which might indicate that the reduced form <geherde ge> is a variant. Skeat (1887: 47) transcribes <geherde ge> and comments in the margin: "geherdon, alt. to geherde".[21] Other instances of scribal alteration by dotting are found in Table 1.

---

19 In the fragments transcribed by Sweet (1978) this information is given.

20 I use </> to indicate that in the manuscript the letter after the slash is above the letter preceding it.

21 Another instance of the same practice is <svnuạ> (f. 213vb17; John 1.51). Skeat (1878: 23) transcribes <sunu> and adds in the margin: "suna alt. to sunu". In the same way, for <sunẏo> (f. 211vb11; John 1.12), Skeat (1878: 15) transcribes <suno>, indicating in the margin that *u* has been altered to *o*.

Table 1. The Li. scribal practice of dotting and under- and over-lining

	Li.	Skeat
1	<me tẹ/**o** cuæð> (L *mihi dixit*; f. 212vb20; John 1.33)	<me to cuæð> (Skeat 1878: 19)
2	<stigạ/**o**> (L *semitas*; f. 95va7; Mark 1.3)	<stigao> (Skeat 1871: 9)
3	<ð̣ẹ vitga> (L *propheta*; f. 212rb20; John 1.21)	<witga> (Skeat 1878: 17)
4	<æd eauḍnise> (L *ostensionis*; f. 143ra10; Luke 1.80)	<ædeaunise> (Skeat 1874: 27)
5	<suno israeleṩ> (L *filiorum israel*; f. 140ra22; Luke 1.16)	<suno israele> (Skeat 1874: 17)
6	<anglaṩ> (L *angelos*; f. 213vb15; John 1.51)	<angla> (Skeat 1878: 23)
7	<puniẹ̇gende> (L *manentem*; f. 95vb24; Mark 1.10)	<wunigende> (Skeat 1871: 11)
8	<ða iḷ̇ca> (L *eas*; f. 214ra20; John 2.7)	<ða ilca> (Skeat 1878: 23)
9	<ðaculỵ̇fero> (L *columbas*; f. 214va22; John 2.16)	<ða culfero> (Skeat 1878: 25)
10	<nẹ ænigmonn> (L *nemo enim*; f. 215rb7; John 3.2)	<nænigmonn> (Skeat 1878: 27)
11	<vọ̇er> (L *uir*; f. 212vb3; John 1.30)	<uer> (Skeat 1878: 17)
12	<in carcḥern> (L *in carcere*; f. 216rb21; John 3.24)	<in carcern> (Skeat 1878: 31)
13	<f(or)ðoṅ> (L *quia*; f. 142ra11; Luke 1.58)	<f(or)ðon> (Skeat 1874: 25)

With respect to the interpretation of this scribal practice of dotting, it has already been pointed out that it does not necessarily indicate self-correction, although there are instances in which this seems to be the case. For example, <pvniẹ̇gende> (present participle of OE *wunian*) could be an error for "wun(g)iende" (cp. <pvniende> on f. 245rb4; John 14.25; and <pungiende> on f. 48rb10; Matthew 11.23). In the same way, in example 4 the dotted <ḍ> in <æd eauḍnise> (L *ostensionis*) could represent a scribal error. Skeat renders it as <ædeaunise>, removing the expuncted consonant and attaching the prefix to the noun (cp. *DOE*: s.c. *eawisness* 'manifestness, openness'). The scribal error may have been induced by the proximity of the prefix <æd>. The form "ædeaunise" is recorded three times in Li., together with the verb Li. *ædeaua* on f. 48va13 (L *revelare*, *manifestare*; cp. Matthew 11.27). Nevertheless, in other cases there is no reason to think that the expuncted letters represent scribal corrections intended to eliminate erroneous forms. They could indicate mere variation (both forms were possible in the dialect of the scribe or of his exemplars). For example, the double *l* in <iḷ̇ca> (Table 1, example 8) is recorded 19 times in the *DOEC* and appears once more in Li. in the preface to John's Gospel (f. 206va4; John xxviii; Skeat 1878: 6).[22] It could be speculated that the instances of *ilca* with double *l* are backspellings, and indicate degemination of /ll/ in early English.[23] Similarly, the letter *v* in the second syllable of accusative plural <culỵ̇fero> (OE *culfer* 'pidgeon') (example 9) does not necessarily have to represent a scribal error. It could be a *svarabhakti* vowel, which is recorded ten times in the *DOEC*.[24] In the same way, the form <poer> (glossing L *vir*) (example 11) is attested once elsewhere in Li.: <poer> (f. 161ra9; Luke 8.38), which Skeat (1874: 91) silently emends to <weor>, but which is correctly cited in Cook (1894: 206).[25] Forms with *oe* are also frequent as a variant of OE *weorc* 'work' and the past of OE *wesan* 'to be' (cp. Cook 1894: 212, 214–215).

As has been previously mentioned, Aldred also marks alterations by writing only one dot, either above or below the letter(s). In some cases the alternative form is written above the letter, as in examples 1 and 2 in Table 1. While example 1 <me **tẹ/o** cpæð> probably reflects a lapse on the part of the scribe, and the dot under the *e* is probably a correction, the dot below the *a* of <stig**ạ/o**> and the superscript *o* (example 2) may indicate two alternative forms in the dialect of the gloss. The form <stiga> is found in exactly the same context in Matthew's Gospel: <stefn cliopende in poestern ge`a´ruas poeg drihtnes ræhta doeð ł pyrcas **stiga** his>, glossing L *vox clamantis in deserto parate uiam domini rectas facite semitas eius* 'A voice of one crying in the desert, Prepare ye the way of the Lord, make straight his paths' (f. 31va20–23; Matthew 3.3; Skeat 1887: 35).

---

22 This instance of OE *ilca* with double *l* is recorded in the *Index Verborum Glossematicus* (Ross and Stanley 1960: 103). Other forms with double *l* are also found in the *DOEC*. For instance the form <illcvm> is recorded once in the Durham Ritual (DurRitGlCom (Thomp-Lind) 192.13) and <illcan> appears nine times in the eleventh-century manuscript London, British Library, MS Cotton Tiberius B.iv (one in the D version of the Anglo-Saxon Chronicle and eight in Alfred's *Cura Pastoralis*: ChronD (Cubbin) 1065.40 and CP 14.83.1, 17.121.9, 17.125.23, 23.173.21, 27.187.20, 30.203.19, 36.257.1, 51.399.33).

23 OE *lytel* with double *t* is also frequent in Li. (it occurs 24 times). The *OED* attributes these forms (and ME *luttel*, *little*) to the fact that the vowel /y/ may have been short in some dialects, and perhaps generally in the syncopated inflected forms. Yet most of the instances of OE *lytel* with double *t* in Li. are found in the nominative singular <lyttel>, whereas inflected forms always have one *t* (<litle>). In the same way, the nominative singular of Li. *all* invariably appears with double *l* (<all>), whereas the oblique forms often present only one, as in <alra>, which is found together with <allra>. What is more, lightly stressed words tend to appear with only one *l*: all instances of the adverb *well* (27 in total) have a single *l* in Li.

24 Some of the forms attested in the *DOEC* are <culufre> (GenA,B 1464; LS 20 (AssumptMor) 341), <culufran> (GenA,B 1476) and <culufra> (MkGl (Ru) 11.15). It also appears with epenthetic *e*: <culefran> in PsGlI (Lindelöf) 67.14.

25 However, <poer> on f. 164rb14 (Luke 9.39) is correctly transcribed (cp. Skeat 1974: 101).

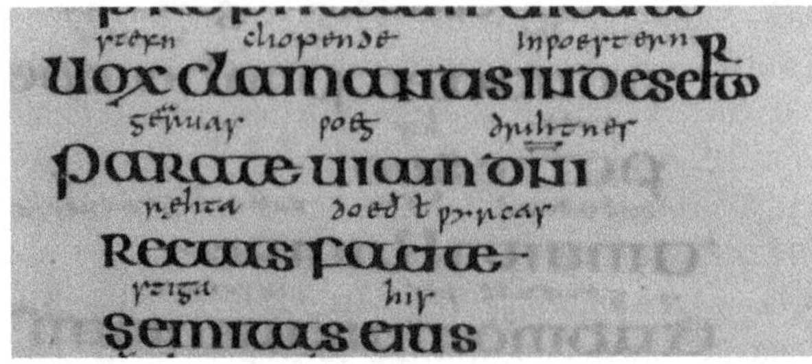

Figure 9. <stefn cliopende inpoestern ge`a´ruas poeg drihtnes ræhta doeð ł pyrcas stiga his> (f. 31va20–23; Matthew 3.3)

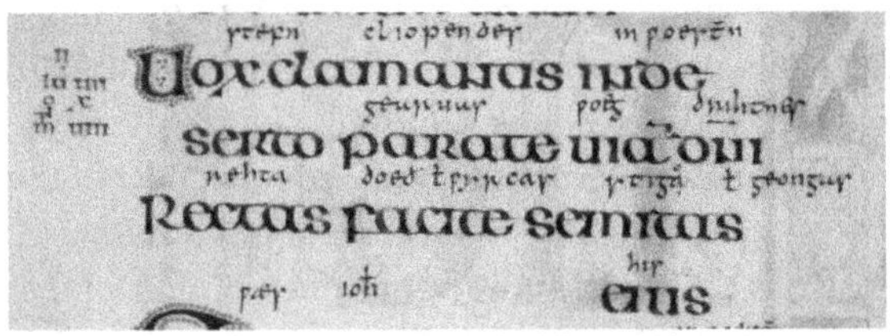

Figure 10. <stefn cliopendes in poest(er)n. gearuas poeg drihtnes rehta doeð ł pyrcas stigạ/o geongas his> (f. 95va7; Mark 1.3)

Similarly, the form <carchern> (with *h*) in example 12 is also found on f. 106vb21 (<in carchern>, glossing L *in carcere*; Mark 6.27; Skeat 1871: 47) and also on f. 132rb9 <herod(es) to caercherne seles ioh(annem)> (glossing L *Herodes carceri dat iohannem*; Preface to the Luke's Gospel; Skeat 1874: 4). This could indicate that *ch* is not necessarily an error of the glossator, but rather an alternative spelling, as in the previous instances. The spelling *ch* is also recorded, besides <c>, for the adjective *micel*: cp. <michelo> (f. 41vb3; Matthew 8.24; Skeat 1887: 71), <michelo> (f. 103ra9; Mark 4.37; Skeat 1871: 33) and as part of a double gloss: <miclo ł michelo> (f. 103rb1; Mark 4.39; Skeat 1871: 33). Finally, in example 3 the scribe has dotted the *e* of demonstrative <ðe> in <ðẹ uitga>, glossing L *propheta*.[26]

I have found two cases where there is dotting above the letter *s*: <israeleṡ> and <anglaṡ> (examples 5 and 6 in Table 1). As in the previous examples, both can be regarded as variants rather than corrections. The form <anglaṡ> is nominative plural. In Li. the usual form for nominative plural is *englas* (glossing L

26 Research is needed in order to assess the glossator's criteria for rendering (or not) the demonstratives in the gloss.

angeli or *angelos*). The form *engla* always appears as genitive plural, glossing L *angelorum*.[27] Therefore, there is no apparent reason why the scribe should have considered <anglas>, glossing L *angelos* (also with the *-s* ending), as an error to be removed. The same can be said about <isrælesṡ> (glossing L *israel*; f. 140ra22; Luke 1.16). In Li. the genitive singular of *israel* is sometimes abbreviated (cp. f. 44vb17; Matthew 10.6; and f. 195ra6; Luke 22.30),[28] and there is also one instance of zero genitive: <sunum israhel>, glossing L *filiis israhel* (f. 85ra21; Matthew 27.9; Skeat 1887: 229),[29] but there is no reason to think that the form with *-s* is erroneous.[30] In fact, genitive singular <*israeles*> is recorded twice in Li. (cp. f. 31rb10; Matthew 2.20; Skeat 1887: 35; and f. 31rb17; Matthew 2.21; Skeat 1887: 36).

As regards the cases where the scribe writes a line above or below certain forms, Skeat sometimes interprets this practice as if it were an erasure.[31] However, he is not consistent. For instance, on f. 140va16 (Luke 1.23) <ða dagas> (glossing L *dies*), the demonstrative <ða> is underlined, but Skeat (1871: 19) does not indicate it and transcribes <ða dagas>. However, in <sio tid> (f. 213rb3; John 1.39) there is a line above <sio>, and in this case Skeat (1878: 19) silently omits the demonstrative.

There are also cases in which the scribe deleted a particular form, but the partially ereased form is still legible, probably because it was made before the ink had dried. These erasures are not mentioned in Skeat's edition either. For instance, on f. 214ra2 (John 2.3; cp. Skeat 1878: 23) the determiner <ðio> in <cvoeð ðio moder hælendes> has been erased by the scribe but it is still legible in the middle of a stain. The same is true of <maslen>, glossing L *aes*, on f. 214va20 (John 2.15; cp. Skeat 1878: 25). The erased form of the demonstrative <þ> is still legible, but Skeat does not mention it in his edition.[32] By not indicating that there has been a correction, we lose information about the use of the demonstratives in the gloss.

27 Cp. Ross and Stanley (1960: 80). See also Cook (1894: 51).

28 The first one is transcribed by Skeat as <isr(ahe)l> (Skeat 1887: 83) and the second is expanded as <israhel> (Skeat 1874: 211).

29 The reason for this uninflected form could be the influence of the Latin word: *Israel* is indeclinable in Latin.

30 Cook (1894: 127) and Ross and Stanley (1960: 108) do not give this form in their glossaries.

31 See also Ross et al. (1960: 18–19).

32 <& ðaera mynetra ofgæt **mæslen** & ða discas ymbcerde> (Skeat 1878: 25).

4.2 The Li. scribal practice of writing superscript letters

There are cases in which the Li. scribe writes letters above the line, without any dotting or under- or overlining. As has already been stated (see above), for Ross et al. (1960: 19) this usage indicates variant forms which would be equivalent to double glosses. The examples found in the excerpts analyzed are listed in the Appendix. Skeat interprets this kind of alteration in different ways. Sometimes he reads them as scribal corrections. For instance <beby`c´gendo> (L *uedentes*; f. 214va11; John 2.14) is transcribed as <bebycgendo> (Skeat 1878: 25). Nevertheless in Li. the present participle of OE *(be)bycgan* (< PGmc *bugjanan 'to buy, sell') appears both with *c* and with *cg*: <ðæm biby**c**endu*m*> (L *uendentes*; f. 78va8; Matthew 25.9; Skeat 1887: 203) and <beby**cg**endra> (L *uendentium*; f. 118ra5; Mark 11.15; Skeat 1871: 89). It also occurs with *g* on f. 69ra1 (Matthew 21.12; Skeat 1887: 169) and, what is more, both forms (with *c* and *g*) are found side by side on f. 118ra1–2 (Mark 11.15; Skeat 1871: 89): <ða beby**c**endo & ða by**cg**endo> (L *uendentes et ementes*).[33] In the same way, *cg*, *c* and *g* alternate as variants in the plural present indicative and imperative, where the expected form would be *cg* indicating affrication (Campbell 1959: § 438). In Skeat's edition we find present indicative plural <by**cg**es>, glossing L *emant* (Skeat 1871: 4) and plural imperative <beby**cg**eð> glossing L *uendite* (Skeat 1874: 133). However, collation of the edition with the facsimile reveals that the *c* is in both cases superscript, which may indicate that both variants were acceptable to the glossator: <bi**`c´g**es> (f. 107rb16; Mark 6.36) and <beby**`c´g**eð> (f. 172vb16; Luke 12.33), respectively. What is more, there are examples with the <g> spelling in the same contexts: present indicative plural <by**g**es ue> (L *ememus*; f. 222vb2; John 6.5; Skeat 1878: 55) and imperative plural <by**g**eð iuh> (L *emite*; f. 78va9; Matthew 25.9; Skeat 1887: 203). In the same way, in the singular present indicative both *cg* and etymologically correct *g* are found side by side:[34] <seðe ne hæfeð **bebycgeð** ł cyrtel his & **bygeð** ł suord> (L *qui non* ***habet*** *uendat tunicam suam et* ***emat*** *gladium*; f. 195rb15–17; Luke 22.36; Skeat 1874: 211).[35] This may indicate that *g*, *c* are used as alternative spellings for the affricate consonant, as suggested by Cole (2014: 128), who argues that "these forms suggest that affrication may not have been restricted to the first-person singular, infinitive and plural present-indicative contexts as has generally been believed."

---

33 <. ł. ceapemenn> in margin, following <bebycendo>.

34 See Campbell (1959: 331, § 753.9).

35 There is a space between <ł> and the following words <cyrtel> and <suord>. The glossator appears to have left an empty slot for the possible addition of another gloss to the verbs. This is frequent in Li.

Another instance of the use of superscript forms occurs in <cvæð him`to´> (L *dicit ei*; f. 213va2; John 1.43). Skeat does not indicate that the preposition <to> is superscript and transcribes <cuæð him to> (Skeat 1878: 21). Both the postposition and preposition *to* are frequent in this context,[36] but a construction of OE *cweðan* directly followed by the personal pronoun is equally common: <**cveð him** se hæl(end)> (L *dicit eis iesus*; f. 219va17; John 4.50; Skeat 1878: 43). Therefore, there is no reason to believe with Skeat that the superscript preposition on f. 213va2 above is meant as a scribal correction.

The same can be said about <n`e´am> (glossing L *non sum*; f. 212rb7; John 1.20; and f. 212va13; John 1.27). Skeat (1878: 15, 17) transcribes <ne am> in both cases. Again the superscript letter may indicate variation rather than correction. The contracted form *nam* shows the tendency of the negative particle to cliticize to the verb as in <nam ic pyrðe> (L *non sum dignus*; f. 95vb7; Mark 1.7; Skeat 1871: 9). Another example is <moder`es´> (L *matris*; f. 215rb20; John 3.4), which is transcribed by Skeat (1878: 27) as <moderes>. In this case the superscript letters may indicate that both forms, the zero and *-es* inflection, coexisted for the noun *moder* (a feminine *r*-stem) in the dialect of the glossator/his exemplars. In the Preface to Luke's Gospel, which is not transcribed by Skeat, <moder> glosses L *matris* (f. 133ra4). The form <moderes> indicates the extension of genitive singular *-s* from the masculine and neuter *a*-stem nouns to other noun classes, which is characteristic of the grammar of Li. (see Ross 1960: 38–39).

I agree with Ross et al. (1960: 19) that most of the above alterations represent alternative forms. There are times, however, when this does not seem to be the case. In the following cases it is likely that they represent scribal corrections:

<froe`f´ra> (L *consulari*; f. 31rb2, Matthew 2.18)	<froefra> (Skeat 1887: 33)
<fep`o´rum> (L *quattuor*; f. 97vb6; Mark 2.3)	<feowrum > (Skeat 1871: 17)
<bi/rleð> (L *haurite*; f. 214ra22 ; John 2.8)	<birleð> (Skeat 1878: 23)

The same can be said about the use of superscript word in <of.`dune.´stigende> (L *descendentem*; f. 32va11; Matthew 3.16). In this case <dune> appears superscript and expuncted. Skeat (1887: 39) transcribes <of-dune stigende>.

36 Cp. <cvoeð **hi/mto** petrus> (L *dicit ei petrus*; f. 242rb5; John 13.8; Skeat 1878: 125); and <cveð **tohir** se hæl(end)> (L *dicit ei iesus mulier*; f. 218ra2; John 4.21; Skeat 1878: 37).

5 Punctuation

Skeat reproduces the manuscript accentuation and simplifies the conventions used by the scribe in his transcription of punctuation. For instance in the explanatory marginalia (cp. f. 27vb3; Matthew 1.6), he (1887: 25) does not make a distinction between lighter and heavier pauses, which in the manuscript are indicated respectively by a point and a pair of points arranged as in a colon followed by a horizontal stroke sweeping upwards (cp. Ross et al. 1960: 19).[37]

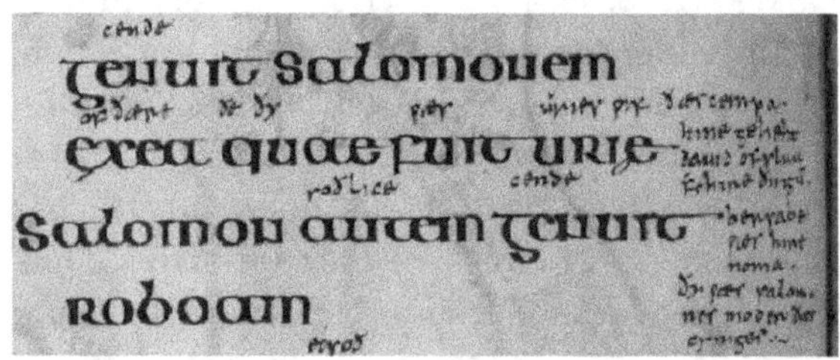

Figure 11. <ðæs cempa. / hine geheht / dauid of slaa / f(or)ehire ðingu(m). / bersabe / pæs hire / noma. / ðy pæs salomo / nes moder ðæs / cyniges.:~> (f. 27vb3; Matthew 1.7)

Skeat (1887: 25)	<ðæs cempa. hine / geheht dauid/of-slaa f(or)e / hire ðingum./ bersabe wæs / hire noma./ ðy wæs salomones/ moder ðæs cyniges. >
Literal trans.	'of the soldier. him ordered david to kill for her things. bersabe was her name. she was king Solomon's mother.'
Trans.	'of the soldier. David ordered him to be killed on account of her condition. Bathsheba was her name. She was King Solomon's mother.'

The same type of punctuation is found in one of the marginalia on f. 29r, a kind of footnote to the Latin text on the virgin birth of Jesus: *Cum esset desponsata Maria Ioseph*: <abiathar ðe aldormon pæs in ðæm tíd in hierusalem .fore biscop. he bebeod maria iosephe to gemenne ⁊ to begọeonganne mið claenisse:,> (literal translation: 'Ealdorman Abiatar was at that time in Jerusalem. high-priest. He commanded Maria to live with Joseph and serve him with purity'; Matthew 1.18; cp. Skeat 1887: 27).

37 The same applies to the colophon at the end of John's Gospel (f. 259r; Skeat 1878: 187–188).

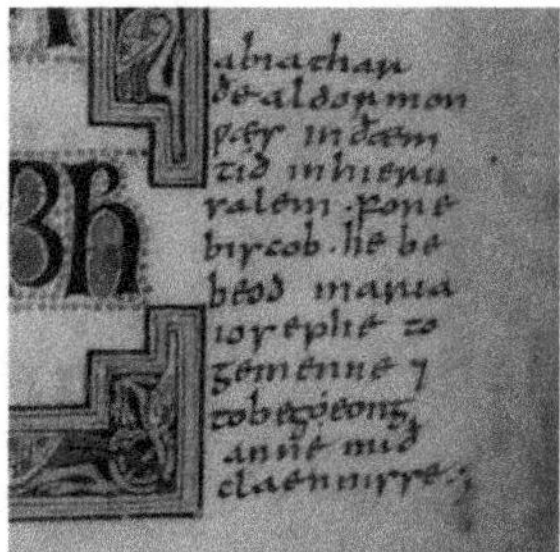

Figure 12. f. 29r (Matthew 1.18)

The reason why it is important to recover the original punctuation is that it may offer significant information about syntactic structures as well as prosodic and suprasegmental features (cp. Robinson 1973).

6 Scribal word-division and word-spacing

In Li., as with other Old English manuscripts, the scribe has the tendency to attach demonstratives to nouns (e.g. <seman>, cp. *se mann*), personal pronouns and negative adverbs to verbs (e.g. <secom>, cp. *se com*; <nam>, cp. *ne am*), and prepositions to prepositional objects (e.g. <cueð tohir>, cp. *cueð to hir*). Skeat modernizes the space division, as most editors do, and he frequently prints as compounds elements which are generally written separately in the manuscript (see Table 2 below). By failing to reproduce the word-division and spacing of the manuscript, the editor prevents us from having access to the scribe's intuitions about syntax, word grouping and prosody. As Lass aptly puts it:

> By modernising, the editor is forcing particular parses on the reader, and at the same time removing what the scribe apparently thought were prosodic details worth indicating. And some of these may have historical significance as well: does the fact that compounds are nearly always written with a word-separation-size space between the two elements say anything? Well it could say that compound nouns were not felt by certain tenth-century writers to be fully 'uni-verbated', but still sufficiently motivated to count as strings of lexical items, not 'words'. I do not know if this is *really* the case or not; but the question cannot even be asked if the evidence is removed before it can be processed (Lass 2004: 35, italics in the original).

I am not advocating that the word-division and -spacing of the manuscripts should be kept in literary editions addressed to a more general readership (see

Gneuss 1998: 136). However, I agree with Lass (1997: 44–68, and 2004) that for linguistic analysis it is indispensable to return to the original sources. This does not mean of course that literary editions *per se* cannot be useful for linguists, or that they should not be taken seriously and consulted, as they may provide us with valuable interpretations and insights about problematic aspects of the texts.[38]

Table 2. Scribal word-division and word-spacing

1. 'Compound' nouns[39]

Li.	Skeat
<burg paras> (L *ciuitas*; f. 97ra10; Mark 1.33)	<burgwaras> (Skeat 1871: 13)
<líc ðroper> (L *leprosus*; f. 97rb12; Mark 1.40)	<lícðrower> (Skeat 1871: 15)
<god spell> (L *euangelio*; f. 96rb1; Mark 1.15)	<godspell> (Skeat 1871: 11)
<soð fæstnise> (L *ueritatem*; f. 139va13; Luke 1.4)	<soðfæstnise> (Skeat 1871: 15)

2. Noun phrases: demonstrative followed by noun

Li.	Skeat
<sehælend> (L *ihesus*; f. 96va21; Mark 1.25)	<se hælend> (Skeat 1871: 13)
<ðaceastre> (L *ciuitates*; f. 97rb4; Mark 1.38)	<ða ceastre> (Skeat 1871: 15)

38 Gneuss (1998: 136) also acknowledges that the original punctuation can reveal that the scribes' grammar categories were not necessarily those of modern English: "For a long time editors who may have been regarded by some as conservative took modern punctuation in printed Old English prose and poetry for granted, and I still strongly believe that this practice provides very essential help for readers, even if we suspect that Anglo-Saxon authors, and especially poets, did not always think and write in terms of the categories and structures of our modern 'traditional' grammar". He (1998: 136) also admits that it is possible (as demonstrated in modern editions) to "adopt, without alteration, the punctuation of an Anglo-Saxon manuscript in which the pointing is intelligently and consistently devised and used, as in certain manuscripts of Ælfric's *Catholic Homilies*".

39 Sometimes words that appear spaced in the manuscript are hyphenated in Skeat's edition: e.g. <eorð-crypel> (L *paraliticum*; Skeat 1871: 17; cp. <eorð crypel> on f. 97vb5; Mark 2.3).

Table 2. (continued)

3. Verb phrases: verbs adjacent to a personal pronoun subject

Li.	Skeat
<cpomeðu> (L *uenisti*; f. 96va18; Mark 1.24)	<cwome ðu> (Skeat 1871: 13)
<ðumæht> (L *potes*; f. 97rb14; Mark 1.40)	<ðu mæht> (Skeat 1871: 15)

4. Prepositional phrases (preposition followed by noun)

Li.	Skeat
<ingalilea> (L *in galilaeam*; f. 96ra18; Mark 1.14)	<in galilea> (Skeat 1871: 11)
<tosomnung> (L *synagogam*; f. 96va4; Mark 1.21)	<to somnung> (Skeat 1871: 13)

5. Relativizers (demonstratives followed by *ðe*)

Li.	Skeat
<ðaðe> (L *quae*; f. 97va6; Mark 1.44)	<ða ðe> (Skeat 1871: 15)

6. Prepositional conjunctions

Li.	Skeat
<mið ðy> (L *cum*; f. 97ra5; Mark 1.32)	<miððy> (Skeat 1871: 13)

7. Infinitive marker *to* followed by an infinitive

Li.	Skeat
<tolosane> (L *perdere*; f. 96va18; Mark 1.24)	<to losane> (Skeat 1871: 13)

Table 2. (continued)

8. Affixes[40]

8.1 Prefix + adjective

Li.	Skeat
<ún claene> (L *inmundo*; f. 96va14; Mark 1.23)	<únclæne> (Skeat 1871: 13)

8.2 Prefix + verb

Li.	Skeat
<f(or)e hlutende> (L *procumbens*; f. 95vb8; Mark 1.7)	<f(or)e-hlutende> (Skeat 1871: 9)
<of stigende> (L *descendentem*; f. 95vb24; Mark 1.10)	<of-stigende> (Skeat 1871: 11)
<of clioppende> (L *exclamans*; f. 96vb1; Mark 1.26)	<of-clioppende> (Skeat 1871: 13)
<ge sæh> (L *uidit*; f. 95vb22; Mark 1.16)	<ge-sæh> (Skeat 1871: 11)
<ge do> (L *faciam*; f. 96rb10; Mark 1.17)	<ge-do> (Skeat 1871: 11)
<of cliopade> (L *exclamauit*; f. 96va15; Mark 1.23)	<of-cliopade> (Skeat 1871: 13)
<of eode> (L *exiuit*; f. 96vb2; Mark 1.26)	<of-eode> (Skeat 1871: 13)
<i(n) geonga ł i(n) cuma> (L *introire*; f. 97va14; Mark 1.45)	<i(n)geonga ł i(n)cuma> (Skeat 1871: 15)

8.3 Suffixes

Li.	Skeat
<sæcerd had> (L *sacerdotio*; f. 139vb10; Luke 1.8)	<sæcerd-had> (Skeat 1874: 15)
<hoga scipe> (L *prudentiam*; f. 140rb6; Luke 1.17)	<hoga-scipe> (Skeat 1874: 17)

As has been mentioned earlier, Skeat's tendency to normalize hides the variation found in the manuscript. For instance on f. 142ra19 (Luke 1.59) <ge ceigde>, the preterit of *gecigan* 'to call', appears with the prefix separated from the stem, whereas on f. 142ra23 (Luke 1.60) we find the past participle <geceiged> with the prefix attached to the verb. However, in Skeat's edition both forms are hyphenated: <ge-ceigde> (Skeat 1874: 25) and <ge-ceiged> (Skeat 1874: 25).

40 In Skeat's edition prefixes are usually attached to the stem (sometimes by means of a hyphen), although they appear spaced in the manuscript.

7 Expansion of abbreviations and runic letters

Abbreviations are not always expanded consistently. The abbreviation <vvt'>(L *autem*; e.g. f. 213va3; John 1.44) is usually expanded as <uut(edlice)> (Skeat 1878: 21). However, there are cases in which Skeat expands <vvt'> as <uut(edlico)> (e.g. f. 211vb9; John 1.12; Skeat 1878: 15) or as <uut(udlico)> (e.g. ff. 213ra14, 213rb3, 213rb5, and 213rb17; John 1.38, 1.39, 1.40, and 1.42; Skeat 1878: 19–20).

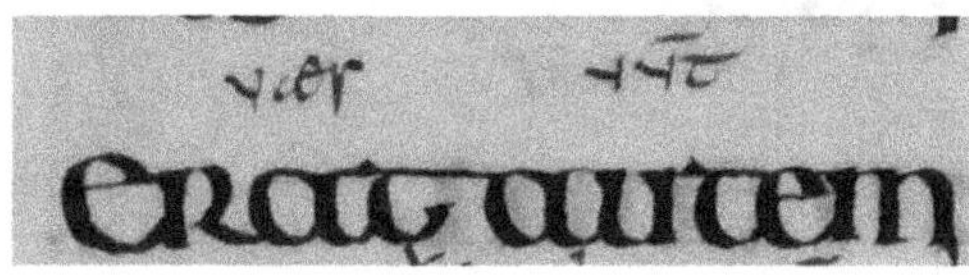

Figure 13. <vvt'> (f. 213va3 ; John 1.44)

Another example is <doas ł virc'> (L *facis*; f. 215rb8; John 3.2). Skeat expands <virc'> to <virc(as)> (<doas ł virc(as)>, Skeat 1878: 27). While it is true that the ending for the second person singular in Li. is generally -*s*, there are occasional instances of the -*ð* ending in this context. In the excerpt of Li. corresponding to John's Gospel there are three instances of verbal -*ð* in second-person singular contexts: <ðv gelef**eð**>, glossing L *credis* (f. 213vb10; John 1.50; Skeat 1878: 21); <avecc**eð**>, glossing L *excitabis* (f. 214vb21; John 2.20; Skeat 1878: 25); and <ðv gegiv**að**>, glossing L *poposceris* (f. 237rb6; John 11.22; Skeat 1878: 107). Therefore, although it seems logical to assume that the abbreviated form <virc'> was most probably intended to represent <vircas>, there is no way that we can be sure that the suffix would have been -*as*.

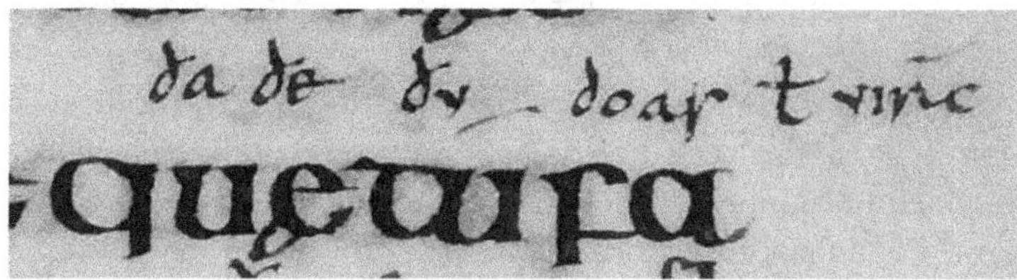

Figure 14. <doas ł virc'> (f. 215rb8; John 3.2)

The Li. glossator occasionally employs runic letters which are not always reproduced in Skeat's transcription. For instance, in the manuscript the M-rune is sometimes used as an abbreviation symbol for OE *mann*/*monn*. It is usually represented with dots at both sides (cp. Ross et al. 1960: 16–17). For instance, on f. 215ra19 (John 2.25) the M-rune in <ænig `·ᛗ·´>, which is expuncted and placed over the line, is expanded as *monn* (Skeat 1878: 27). A further analysis of the use of the runes in Li. would add to our knowledge of the function of runes in Anglo-Saxon manuscripts.

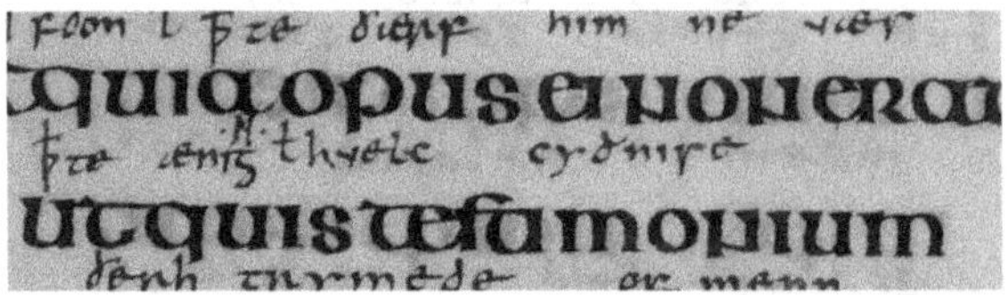

Figure 15. <ænig `·ᛗ·´> (f. 215ra19; John 2.25)

8 A note on merographs

The Li. glossator has the habit of writing abbreviated forms without any indication that they are abbreviated. Thus, for OE *fæder*, we find the forms <faed', fad', fae'> in which the abbreviated forms are indicated by the symbol ('), but also <faede, fade, fae> without any indication that the form has been abbreviated (Ross 1960: 37). The use of lexical merographs (called 'truncated' forms by Ross 1960: 39) may be an attempt on the part of the scribe to save time and also space and effort in the case of frequent lexical items, whose meaning and grammatical function could be easily retrieved from the context, as in the case of OE *fæder*.[41] Nevertheless, in some cases (when the inflection is not provided), it is harder to determine whether it is a case of the scribe rendering only the root form as a help for the reader of the Latin term or an instance of zero inflection, possibly due to syncretism. Ross (1960: 37) gives as an example "on wuord ðæs dom érn" (L *in atrium praetorii*; f. 127va3; Mark 15.16), which Skeat (1871: 125) transcribes as <wuord ðæs dom-érn>. In this case there is no indication that the inflection/-*s* ending is to be added to "dom-érn" (there is no abbreviation symbol). As the genitive singular in -*s* is almost categorically preserved in the 'strong' nominal declension in Li. (Ross 1960: 37), it may be safe to conclude that this is prob-

41 For frequency of use of syntactical or lexical merographs in Old English glosses see Gretsch 1999). The use of those glosses, which provide only part of the Old English *interpretamentum* of the Latin lemma, could be dependent on the prospective readership, whether novices or more advanced students (Gretsch 1999: 134–135). See also Gretsch (1999 : 134 n. 9) and Kornexl (1993: ccxx–xxi).

ably a lexical merograph. Nevertheless, in other cases the frequent absence of inflectional endings in the dative singular of the strong declension may reflect real morphological syncretism. In Li. the endingless form of the nominative and accusative singular is also very frequent for the dative singular, especially (but not exclusively) in monosyllabic nouns such as OE *dæg*, *gast*, *god*, *hus*, *lond* and *word*, where the zero ending is found side by side with *-e*: *dæge*, *gaste*, *gode*, *huse*, *londe* and *worde*.[42] In any case, as Skeat generally expands merographs, return to the facsimile of the original manuscript is required to account for the frequency in the use of these abbreviated forms in Li.[43] A detailed study of these endingless forms in the facsimile of the manuscript is required before it can be determined whether they represent merographs, providing roots (instead of full forms) as aids for the translation of the Latin original, or reflect a real process of change in process (accusative/dative syncretism; see Fernández Cuesta and Rodríguez Ledesma, forthcoming).

9 Conclusions

No clear distinction can be made between expunctation (dotting) and other diacritics (superscript and subscript letters), since in most cases forms which are found expuncted in Li. are documented in the gloss without dotting, as they are also in other Old English texts. In most cases expuncted forms appear to indicate orthographical/phonological variation rather than corrections and this variation may be evidence of linguistic change in progress. By omitting or normalizing variant forms Skeat deprives readers of potentially valuable information on linguistic variation in the text.

The use of diacritics may also reflect Aldred's attempts to be precise, which is also expressed at other linguistic levels in the gloss. At the morphosyntactic level, variation in Li. has been shown to be orderly by Cole (2014), who demon-

42 The dative singular in *-e* is called "rudimentary dative" by Ross (1960: 38 n. 8). In etymologically neuter nouns such as OE *word* and *lond*, the uninflected form is clearly dominant, even when glossing L dative/ablative and following prepositions such as OE *from* and *of*, which take the dative in standard Old English. However, in other nouns such as masculine *a*-stem OE *dæg*, the inflected form is more frequent and is found even when glossing a Latin nominative form. A detailed analysis is required to determine the variables that condition the presence and absence of the dative ending in *-e*, and the extent to which the Latin forms (the gender of the Latin noun for instance) may have influenced the choice of inflection.

43 Rodríguez Ledesma (this volume: p. 214) has also discovered examples of poor editorial practice and inconsistencies as regards the rendering of merographs in Skeat's edition.

strates that *-ð/-s* variation in the present indicative is governed by subject and adjacency effects. At the lexical level there is also variation in Aldred's habit of multiple glossing, which shows his determination to be precise and at the same time copious, and to enrich his gloss (see Bolze's and Pons-Sanz's papers in this volume). The fact that there is variation at other linguistic levels further supports the argument that use of diacritics may reflect alternative forms and that they are not necessarily corrections. It would be unreasonable to expect Aldred to be maximalist in deploying triple glosses and minimalist at the level of spelling. What is more, in Middle English manuscripts from many traditions subscript, superscript or marginal letters do not very often indicate corrections, but are better interpreted as insertions of elements omitted accidentally in the course of writing (Roger Lass, personal communication).

The research carried out for this article also indicates that Aldred's gloss reflects his scholarly interests (Robinson 1973: 466), although, as pointed out by Jolly (this volume: p. 371), the glossator surely had in mind other audiences apart from God and St. Cuthbert, as he also laboured for the good of his community.[44] The Lindisfarne gloss shows a great effort to render the Latin text appropriately into the vernacular, which could not yet be compared to the Latin original but was beginning to be explored as a valid vehicle to render the sacred words of the Gospel. It also achieves a high level of subtlety in the translation and interpretation of the text (double and multiple glossing, including empty slots to which the scribe presumably intended to return), as also shown in Aldred's marginalia, which can be interpreted as an attempt to clarify and even adapt the Gospel text to the needs of his community (see Cavill, this volume).

As regards Skeat's edition, I have tried to show that it is insufficient for the purpose of close linguistic analysis. According to Lass (2004: 22), editions containing any of the following seven traits are blighted for the purpose of linguistic analysis:

---

44 Cp. Robinson (1973: 466): "But few would suggest that the elaborate and scholarly gloss to the Lindisfarne Gospels or the highly finished interlineation of the Vespasian Psalter could have been designed for use in the classroom; the nature of the glosses as well as the physical character of the codices would render this quite preposterous. Some of the Psalter glosses – among them that of the Lambeth Psalter, which contains syntactical as well as lexical notations – are too learned in content even to be considered service books; as Sisam has pointed out, they are books for study".

1	Any emendation, even of what appear to be patent errors[45]	X
2	Any modernization, including the replacement of *thorn*, *eth*, *yogh* and *wynn* by modern equivalents	X
3	Capitalization practice different from that of the source	X
4	Alteration of MS punctuation, whether by modernization of the original or punctuation of unpointed text	X
5	Any alteration of scribal word-division or lineation, including the printing of apparent verse texts written as a continuous prose in verse form	X
6	Any attempt to reconstruct a 'lost original' or 'archetype' from a multi-source tradition, or to produce a 'best text'; in other words any multi-sourced or conflate reading text, such as the standard editions of Chaucer or Shakespeare	N/A
7	Any form of 'normalization', e.g. regularizing variable spellings of a given lexeme or grammatical form, or dialect translation	X

Of the seven sins defined by Lass, Skeat's edition is guilty of all except number six, which is not applicable in his case. The moral is that the edition should be used with caution and always in conjunction with the facsimile of the gloss. I also hope to have shown that some of the questions that can be asked of the text in the twenty-first century are much more subtle than would ever have occurred to Skeat. Despite his great achievements as a philologist, Skeat appears to have confused variation with correction. His attitudes to language are also revealed in his work as an editor. Our task is to be aware of these problems and return to the original manuscript as if to an archaeological site excavated decades ago with outmoded methods and equipment. The site fortunately is undisturbed and awaiting the treatment it deserves.[46]

45 It could be thought that this criterion is rather extreme. Nevertheless, apparent errors have been found later not to be such (see Laing 2007).

46 The research for the present article has profited from a grant of the Spanish Ministry of Science and Technology, the National Programme for Scientific Research Development and Technological Innovation, and the European Regional Development Fund (HUM2007-62926/FILO). Some of the results of this article were presented at the Conference of Historical Language and Literacy in the North Sea Area (HLLNSA 2009) in Stavanger (Norway). I wish to thank the scholars present for their comments and suggestions. I also wish to express my gratitude to Susan Irvine, Christopher Langmuir, Sara Pons-Sanz and two anonymous reviewers for insightful comments and suggestions on earlier drafts of this article. Naturally, all the errors and inaccuracies are my own.

Appendix to section 4.2.

The Li. scribal practice of writing superscript letters

	Li	Skeat
1.	<hre`o´ƿnisses> (L *pænitentiæ*; f. 95va11; Mark 1.4)	<hreownisses> (Skeat 1871: 9)
2.	<ƿiðerwo/earde> (L *satana*; f. 96ra12; Mark 1.13)	<wiðerwearde> (Skeat 1871: 11)
3.	<uute/odlice> (L *incipit*; f. 29r; Matthew 1.18)	<uutodlice> (Skeat 1887: 27)
4.	<r`o´ecels> (L *incensum*; f. 139vb15; Luke 1.9)	<roecels> (Skeat 1874: 17)
5.	<hiorde/a> (L *pastores*; f. 143vb12; Luke 2.1)	<hiorda> (Skeat 1874: 31)
6.	<beby`c´gendo> (L *uendentes*; f. 214va11; John 2.14)	<bebycgendo> (Skeat 1878: 25)
7.	<eft gemyn`d´go> (L *recordati*; f. 215ra2; John 2.22)	<eft gemyndgo> (Skeat 1878: 27)
8.	<ƿ`o´epende> (L *ploratus*; f. 31ra23; Matthew 2.18)	<woepende> (Skeat 1887: 33)
9.	<cn`a´ehtes> (L *pueri*; f. 31rb13; Matthew 2.20)	<cnaehtes> (Skeat 1887: 35)
10.	<toge`h´nealacede> (L *adpropinquauit*; f. 31va14; Matthew 3.2)	<to-ge(h)nealacede> (Skeat 1887: 35)
11.	<Iu´i`h> (L *uos*; f. 32ra4; Matthew 3.9)	<iuih> (Skeat 1887: 37)
12.	<to ƿorð/ianne> (L *adorare*; f. 30ra15; Matthew 2.2)	<to worðianne> (Skeat 1887: 31)
13.	<gefraign/ade> (L *sciscitabatur*; f. 30rb1; Matthew 2.4)	<gefraignade> (Skeat 1887: 31)
14.	<diac`o´nes> (L *leuitas*; f. 212rb1; John 1.19)	<diacones> (Skeat 1878: 15)
15.	<iohan`n´es> (L *iohanna*; f. 213rb19; John 1.42)	<iohannes (Skeat 1878: 21)
16.	<ful`g´vg`i´a> (L *baptizo*; f. 212va5; John 1.26)	<fulgugia> (Skeat 1878: 17)
17.	<icsæg/o> (L *dixero*; f. 215vb8; John 3.12)	<ic sægo> (Skeat 1878: 29)
18.	<næni`g´monn> (L *nemo*; f. 215vb10; John 3.13)	<nænig monn> (Skeat 1878: 29)
19.	<ƿ`o´el gelicade> (L *complacui*; f. 32va19; Matthew 3.17)	<woel gelicade> (Skeat 1887: 39)
20.	<geƿ/hyn/cgerde> (L *esuriit*; f. 32vb3; Matthew 4.2)	<gehyncgerde> (Skeat 1887: 39)
21.	<g`e´nom> (L *assumpsit*; f. 32vb15; Matthew 4.8)	<genom> (Skeat 1887: 41)
22.	<d\o/ƿl> (L *diabolus*; f. 33rb2; Matthew 4.11)	<diowl> (Skeat 1887: 41)
23.	<gbyes hli`f´giendr> (f. 34rb4 margin; Matthew 5.5)	<g[e]byes hlifgiendr[a]> (Skeat 1887: 45)
24.	<si`b´sume> (L *pacifici*; f. 34rb21; Matthew 5.9)	<sibsume> (Skeat 1887: 45)
25.	<lurr`n´e> (L *uestrum*; f. 34vb15; Matthew 5.16)	<lurrne> (Skeat 1887: 47)

	Li	Skeat
26.	<lu´i`h> (L *uos*; f. 36va11; Matthew 5.44)	<luih> (Skeat 1887: 51)
27.	<lu`e´re> (L *uestra*; f. 34va13; Matthew 5.12)	<luere> (Skeat 1887: 45)
28.	<oð`e´ra> (L *altera*; f. 36rb13; Matthew 5.39)	<oðera> (Skeat 1887: 51)
29.	<sv`u´opa> (L *flagellum*; f. 214va16 ; John 2.15)	<su(u)opa> (Skeat 1878: 25)
30.	<v`u´ritte> (L *scributuræ*; f. 215ra4; John 2.22)	<u(u)ritte> (Skeat 1878: 27)
31.	<hu/u> (L *qualis*; f. 140vb18; Luke 1.29)	<hu(u)> (Skeat 1874: 19)
32.	<gefreo`u´ad> (L *liberati*; f. 142vb9; Luke 1.74)	<gefreo(u)ad> (Skeat 1874: 27)
33.	<gefvlg`u´ade> (L *baptizabat*; f. 216rb12; John 3.22)	<gefulg(u)ade> (Skeat 1878: 31)
34.	<`h´eono> (L *ecce*; f. 216va8; John 3.26)	<(h)eono> (Skeat 1878: 31)
35.	<s`u´ona > (L *filium*; f. 31ra5; Matthew 2.15)	<s(u)ona> (Skeat 1887: 33)
36.	<fe`u´ortig> (L *quadraginta*; f. 32vb1; Matthew 4.2)	<fe(u)ortig> (Skeat 1887: 39)
37.	<on`d´sóc> (L *negauit*; f. 212rb5; John 1.20)	<ondsóc> (Skeat 1878: 15)

Part III: **Glossing Practice**

Christine Bolze

Multiple Glosses with Present Tense Forms of OE *beon* 'to be' in Aldred's Gloss to the Lindisfarne Gospels

Abstract: The Old English verb *beon* 'to be' consists of two semantically distinct present tense paradigms. This paper considers multiple glosses of present tense forms of OE *beon* in Aldred's gloss to the Lindisfarne Gospels. The analysis suggests that the order of the multiple glosses follows a certain pattern and that they are used for certain semantic purposes: they reflect Aldred's endeavour to convey the grammatical properties of a Latin form and the semantics of its context as precisely as possible into Old English.

1 Introduction

The Old English verb *beon* 'to be' (henceforth 'OE *beon*') consists of a partially twofold paradigm. Table 1 shows this for late Old Northumbrian, the northern Old English dialect, in which the gloss to the Lindisfarne Gospels (London, British Library, Cotton Nero D.iv) is preserved:

		Present Indicative		Present Subjunctive	
		s-root	*b-root*	*s-root*	*b-root*
sg.	1	am	biom		
	2	arð	bist	sie/se	(bia, bie)
	3	is	bið		
pl.	1	sint/	biðon/-un		
	2	sindun/-on	bioðon/-un	sie/se	–
	3	aron/-un	biað		
Infinitive: wosa, (bian)					

The paradigm of OE *beon* is a combination of several Proto-Indo-European roots: _*bhuh_^{2}- 'to grow, become', _*h_^{1}_es_- 'to exist, be', and _*h_^{2}_wes_- 'to stay' (Jasanoff 2003; Orel 2003). In the present indicative, there are two complete paradigms, one of which is produced by the _*b_-root. For the present subjunctive, Table 1 shows that there are no regular *b*-forms in the extant Northumbrian data. The two forms "bia" and "bie" occur once and are regarded as subjunctives (Brunner

1965: 354; Campbell 1959: 350); they have thus been given within brackets. This is different in West Saxon, where the subjunctive *b*-forms "beo" and "beon" form a separate paradigm (Brunner 1965: 354). The twofold structure of OE *beon* cannot be observed in the past tense; here the verb shows a single paradigm developed from **h²wes-* in all the attested Old English dialects.

Previous studies on the twofold paradigm of OE *beon* have shown that the *b*-forms, in particular those in the indicative, frequently have a future implication (Jost 1909; Kilpiö 1993; Wischer 2010; Bolze 2013). The sentence in (1) provides an example of Aldred's gloss to the Lindisfarne Gospels:

(1) Luke 1.15

L	***erit*** [3 sg. fut. ind. act.] *enim magnus coram domino et uinum et sicera non bibet et spiritu sancto* ***replebitur*** [3 sg. fut. ind. pass.] *athuc ex utero matris suę*
Trans.	'For **he will be** great before the Lord, and he will not drink wine and mead, and **he will be filled** of the Holy Spirit yet from his mother's womb'[1]
LkGl (Li) 1.15	**bið** forðon micel befora drihtno ⁊ win ⁊ bear ne drinceð & gaaste halge **gefylled bið** ða gett wæs in inna moderes his.[2]

Since the *b*-forms in (1) correspond to the Latin future tense forms *erit* and *replebitur* they can be described as indicators of futurity. In fact, 327 (57.46 %) of the 569 *b*-forms in the Lindisfarne Gospels render a Latin verb that is unambiguously inflected for the future tense.

It has furthermore been suggested that the indicative *b*-forms can occur in certain aspectual references: e.g. in durative, iterative, and generic implications (*Dictionary of Old English*, hereafter *DOE*: s.v. *beon*). Schumacher (2007), Lutz (2009), and Hogg and Fulk (2011) refer to a possible habitual implication of the *b*-forms. In a previous study (Bolze 2013), I have shown that these additionally ascribed references of the *b*-paradigm can be observed in the Lindisfarne Gospels, the late West Saxon Gospels (Cambridge, Corpus Christi College, MS 140) and the Rushworth Gospels (Oxford, Bodleian Library, MS Auct. D.ii.19). Nevertheless, an implied future reference of these *b*-forms could in most cases not be excluded. Of particular interest is Aldred's use of multiple glosses consisting of two or more inflected present tense forms of OE *beon*. One can distinguish between several types:

1 The translations into PDE here and henceforth in this article refer to the Latin and are my own.

2 The Latin text of the Lindisfarne Gospels, the Old English gloss and the abbreviations used to refer to it follow the *Dictionary of Old English Web Corpus* (hereafter *DOEC*).

1. multiple glosses of present indicative forms of OE *beon*
(a) two or more forms from the same indicative paradigm (e.g. "sind ł aron", "bið ł bið")
   (b) at least one form from each of the two indicative paradigms (e.g. "bið ł is")
2. multiple glosses of present indicative and subjunctive forms of OE *beon*
   (a) an indicative *b*-form coupled with a subjunctive *s*-form (e.g. "bið ł sie")
   (b) an indicative non-*b*-form coupled with a subjunctive *s*-form (e.g. "is ł sie")
3. multiple glosses of present subjunctive forms of OE *beon*.

Previous research discusses multiple glosses in the Lindisfarne Gospels in general, i.e. without focussing on forms of OE *beon* (cp. Ross and Squires 1980; Pons-Sanz 2004; Kotake 2006a; see also Pons-Sanz, this volume). Nagucka (1997) is to my knowledge the only one who comments on a double gloss of a present indicative *b*- and non-*b*-form of OE *beon*. With reference to Matthew 11.5, where L *leprosi mundantur* is rendered with OE "licðrouras geclaensad aron ł biðon", she remarks that examples of that sort "show Aldred's uncertainty, or perhaps, just the opposite, his certainty about the lack of glossal substitutes in Old English for overtly marked categories in Latin morphological forms" (Nagucka 1997: 192). In the following, I shall discuss the semantics and order of multiple glosses coupling two or more present tense forms of OE *beon* in Aldred's gloss to the Lindisfarne Gospels. I will examine to what Latin forms they correspond and argue that Aldred does not use them haphazardly.

2 Multiple glosses of present indicative forms of OE *beon*

2.1 Multiple glosses of *b*-forms

There are 12 multiple glosses consisting of two or more *b*-forms in Lindisfarne. They almost always refer to Latin verbs inflected for the future tense, mostly in the passive voice: nine of the 12 multiple glosses translate a Latin future tense form; seven of those nine are in the passive. This confirms the assumed preference for *b*-forms to indicate a future sense. The gloss to Matthew 12.25 illustrates a triple gloss of *b*-forms functioning as passive auxiliaries:

(2) Matthew 12.25

L	*omne regnum diuisum contra se* **desolabitur** [3 sg. fut. pass.]
Trans.	'Every kingdom divided against itself **will belaid waste**'
MtGl (Li) 12.25	eghuelc ric todæled bið wið him **forleten bið ł gewoested bið ł tosliten bið.**

In (2) the *b*-auxiliary *bið* occurs with the past participles of three different Old English verbs: *forlaetan* 'to lose, leave behind', *gewoestan* 'to desolate, destroy, lay waste', and *toslitan* 'to tear apart, break, separate'. Aldred is most probably sure about the tense of the Latin verb, i.e. he intends to convey the future tense of L *desolabitur* by using *b*-forms as auxiliaries. This suggests that the cause of the *b*-triplet is his effort to reflect the semantics of the Latin verb as correctly as possible in Old English by employing three different participles. The second option, "gewoested bið", is the most accurate translation of the Latin form, whereas the first and the third options might rather reflect Aldred's interpretation of the context. In particular the first translation, "forleten bið", is unusual. He normally uses OE *forlaetan* to render L *relinquere* 'to leave behind' and *dimittere* 'to dismiss, to abandon' (cp. Pons-Sanz, this volume). Yet, the three participles are adequate in this context and indicate that Aldred does not simply produce one-to-one literal translations of the Latin lemmata, but that he aims to convey the semantics of the Latin forms as correctly as possible in his gloss.

2.2 Multiple glosses of non-*b*-forms

Multiple glosses consisting of two or more non-*b*-forms predominantly refer to Latin forms in the present active, mostly in the present indicative. There are 23 multiple glosses with at least two non-*b*-forms in the Lindisfarne Gospels, and 16 of them translate a present indicative active form of L *esse* 'to be'. There are various types of such multiple glosses. Doublets between present indicative non-*b*-forms frequently reflect Aldred's effort to produce more idiomatic expressions in English:

(3) Mark 3.33

L	*et respondens eis ait* ***quae est*** [3 sg. pres. ind. act.] *mater mea et fratres mei*
Trans.	'And he answers them saying, "**Who are** my mother and my brothers?"'
MkGl (Li) 3.33	⁊ onsuarade him cwoeð **huæt ðiu is ł huæt ða sint** moder min ⁊ brodro min.

The first option of the double gloss in (3) reflects the Latin word order and is thus a literal gloss, whilst the second option takes into account that not one but two subjects follow the verb, which is likely to have prompted the addition of the *s*-plural "sint". Thus, the first option in a multiple gloss is usually literal, and the second one indicates a more idiomatic use in English. This can also be observed in (4):

(4) John 18.25

L	*negauit ille et dixit* ***non sum*** [1 sg. pres. ind. act.]
Trans.	'He denied it and said, **"I am not"**'
JnGl (Li) 18.25	onsoc he ⁊ cuoeð **ne am ł nam ic.**

The alternation "ne am ł nam ic" reflects the common use of contracted negation in order to avoid the trisyllabic "ne am ic" in English (cp. for example Miller 2010: I, ch. 9; van Bergen 2008).

Non-*b*-doublets can furthermore reveal Aldred's knowledge of synonymous forms within the non-*b*-paradigm, in particular in the plural. Table 1 above illustrates that Aldred had the choice between mono- and disyllabic *s*-forms and "aron" in the plural. In the Lindisfarne gloss, one can observe doublets of *s*- and *r*-forms, and of mono- and disyllabic *s*-forms. The latter type is infrequent: there are only two occurrences of doublets between mono- and disyllabic *s*-forms (cp. LkGl (Li) 14.28 and MkGl (Li) 14.36). Multiple glosses of *s*- and *r*-plurals are more frequent: there are seven doublets of that sort. The *r*-plurals are an Anglian phenomenon. Brunner (1965: 354) claims that the *s*-plurals are preferred in the 3 pl., whereas the *r*-forms are preferred in the 1 pl. and 2 pl. Table 2 illustrates the distribution of *s*- and *r*-plurals in the Lindisfarne Gospels and shows that Brunner's statement is only partly correct:

Table 2. Share of "sind(on)"/"sint" and "aron" in the 1, 2, 3 pl. in the Lindisfarne Gloss

1 pl.		Total: 12	
	s-form		8 (66.66 %)
	r-form		4 (33.33 %)
2 pl.		Total: 52	
	s-form		16 (30.77 %)
	r-form		36 (69.23 %)
3 pl.		Total: 188	
	s-form		155 (82.45 %)
	r-form		33 (17.55 %)

The figures indicate that Aldred most frequently decides on “aron” in the 2 pl., whilst he prefers “sind(on)”/“sint” in the 3 pl. This agrees with Kolbe’s (1912: 101) data; he notices that *r*-forms mainly occur in the 2 pl. A clear preference for “aron” in the 1 pl., as suggested by Brunner, cannot be observed; however, their distribution is more frequent in the 1 pl. than in the 3 pl. The predominance of 2 pl. “aron” has most probably been triggered by 2 sg. “arð”. Holmqvist (1922) demonstrates that OE 2 sg. *-s* spread to 2 pl., and subsequently to 3 pl. Berndt (1956) and Stein (1986) verify this observation. Stein (1986: 640) argues that the percentage of 2 pl. *-s* in the Lindisfarne Gospels and the Durham Ritual is 66 %, which is very close to my figures for 2 pl. “aron”. This strongly supports the generalization from 2 sg. to 2 pl.

Double glosses incorporating *s*- and *r*-forms mostly occur in the 3 pl.; in the 2 pl. they can be observed twice. The subsequent examples demonstrate an *s*-/*r*-doublet in the 3 pl. and in the 2 pl., respectively:

(5) Matthew 10.30

L	*uestri autem et capilli capitis omnes* ***numerati sunt*** [3 pl. perf. ind. pass.]
Trans.	‘But even the hairs of your head **are** all **numbered**’
MtGl (Li) 10.30	iweres soðlice ⁊ hera heafdes alle **getalad aron ł sint**

(6) Matthew 5.14

L	*uos* ***estis*** [2 pl. pres. ind. act.] *lux mundi*
Trans.	‘You **are** the light of the world’
MtGl (Li) 5.14	gie **aron ł sint** leht middangeardes.

In the double glosses in (5) and (6) “aron” occurs first, which demonstrates a regular pattern: apart from one instance (cp. LkGl (Li) 13.23), the *r*-forms always appear first when they appear in doublets with *s*-forms. This suggests that Aldred tends to provide the Anglian and perhaps more common form in Northumbrian first. Furthermore, the doublets illustrate an increasingly irregular use of the *r*- and *s*-plurals; “aron” in (5) might be an indicator for the spread of *r*-forms to the 3 pl. Earlier studies noted an irregular use of nominal and verbal endings in the Lindisfarne gloss, which have been described as a breakdown of the Old English inflectional system, and hence as a development towards Middle English (cp. Lea 1894; Füchsel 1901; Foley 1903; Kellum 1906). Therefore, doublets of *r*- and *s*-plurals can be regarded as reflections of the claimed progressive linguistic stage of the Northumbrian gloss in the Lindisfarne Gospels.

2.3 Multiple glosses of *b*- and non-*b*-forms

As pointed out in the introduction, 57.46 % of the *b*-forms in the Lindisfarne Gospels are used to translate a Latin verb inflected for the future tense. Hence, they can be regarded as indicators of futurity in Old English. By contrast, 987 (77.04 %) of the 1281 non-*b*-forms refer to a Latin verb in the present tense. This distribution of the *b*- and non-*b*-forms confirms the proposed time references of the two indicative paradigms.

Interestingly, Aldred occasionally employs multiple glosses of *b*- and non-*b*-forms. There are twenty-eight multiple glosses of *b*- and non-*b*-forms in the Lindisfarne Gospels. They predominantly refer to Latin verbs in the present tense: twenty-two of the *b*- and non-*b*-doublets translate a Latin verb in the present indicative active. Interestingly, they occur in semantically similar sentences:

(7) John 12.26

L	*si quis mihi ministrat me sequatur et ubi* ***sum*** [1 sg. pres. ind. act.] *ego illic et minister meus erit*
Trans.	'If anyone serves me, he follows me, and where **I am**, there will be my minister'
JnGl (Li) 12.26	gif hua me embehtes ł geheres mec gesoeca ⁊ suahuer **ic am ł ic beom** ðer ęc hera ł ðegn min bið

(8) John 17.24

L	*pater quos dedisti mihi uolo ut ubi* ***ego sum*** [1 sg. pres. ind. act.] *et illi sint mecum*
Trans.	'Father, those whom you have given me, I want that where **I am** they are with me'
JnGl (Li) 17.24	faeder ða ðu gesaldes me ic uillo þætte ðer **ic beom ł am** ⁊ hia ł ða sie mið mec.

Since the Latin sentences in (7) and (8) show the 1 sg. pres. ind. act. *sum* 'I am', the expected Old English equivalent would be "am"). The addition of a *b*-form might indicate an inferred reference to the future. In (7) the latter is strengthened by the occurrence of L *erit* at the end of the sentence and its translation with a *b*-form in the gloss. Furthermore, both verses are attested with future tense forms of L *esse* 'to be' in the *Afra*, i.e. the "African" version of the *Vetus Latina* (Jülicher et al. 1970): the sentence in (7) shows 1 sg. fut. ind. act. *ero*, and the sentence in (8) shows 1 sg. fut. perf. ind. act. *fuero* instead of 1 sg. pres. ind. act. *sum*. According to Ross (1981), it is probable that Aldred had access to further Latin versions of the Gospels (see also Kotake, this volume). The doublets in (7) and (8) might support the assumption that Aldred used various Latin Gospel versions in the course of glossing Lindisfarne. Alternatively, the sentences could be interpreted as habitual statements, which might have triggered the *b*-forms (cp. Hogg and Fulk 2011: 309).

There are further doublets of *b*- and non-*b*-forms in which a possible aspectual reference could have prompted the addition of the *b*-form. In (9), for instance, one may interpret the sentence as a possible durative reference:

(9) Luke 5.34

L	*quibus ipse ait numquid potestis filios sponsi dum cum illis* ***est*** [3 sg. pres. ind. act.] *sponsus facere ieiunare*
Trans.	'To whom he said: "Can you make sons of the bridegroom fast while/as long as the bridegroom **is** with them?"'
LkGl (Li) 5.34	ðæm he cuoeð ahne mago gie suno brydgumes *ða huil* mið him **is ł bið** se brydguma wyrca gefæsta.

Kilpiö (1993; cp. *DOE*: s.v. *beon*) argues that indicative *b*-forms are preferred to non-*b*-forms in statements with a durative quality. In (9) OE "ða huil" 'while' might be an indicator for durativity and could thus have triggered the addition of the *b*-form. The doublet hence suggests that Aldred first translated L *est* with "is", and then added "bið" to express an implied durative reading. This is, however, extremely rare: it is the only example in the Lindisfarne gloss in which a possible durative implication of a sentence might have resulted in a doublet of a non-*b*- and a *b*-form.[3]

Furthermore, there are *b*- and non-*b*-doublets having a gnomic or general reference:

(10) John 3.29

L	*qui habet sponsam sponsus* ***est*** [3 sg. pres. ind. act.]
Trans.	'The one who has the bride **is** the bridegroom'
JnGl (Li) 3.29	seðe hæfes ða brydo brydguma **is ł bið.**

The sentence in (10) describes something gnomic, i.e. an eternal truth, which Mitchell and Robinson (2012: 102) consider to be a trigger for indicative *b*-forms. As is the case in (9), one would expect L *est* to be rendered with the non-*b*-form "is" only. It might be therefore that the gnomic implication of the sentence prompted the addition of the *b*-form as a second option. Nevertheless, there is

3 The verse occurs again in Matthew 9.15, and MtGl (Li) 9.15 includes the same doublet.

also an implied future indication: gnomic statements naturally refer to something that is true now and remains true in the future. In any case, the addition of the *b*-form suggests that Aldred intends to emphasize that a non-*b*-form alone is insufficient in this context.

Overall, the examples in this section illustrate a tendency concerning the order of multiple glosses: apart from the doublet in (8), Aldred renders the Latin present tense form first using a non-*b*-form, whereas a *b*-form is provided as a second option. Thus, the first form in these doublets is literal, reflecting the grammatical properties of the Latin verb. The second form is semantic and represents Aldred's interpretation of the context. This order can be observed in the majority of *b*- and non-*b*-doublets translating a Latin present tense form in Lindisfarne: in 64 % of all instances, Aldred employs the non-*b*-form first. One can thus assume that he is aware of the semantic differences between the two present tense paradigms of OE *beon* and makes use of them in multiple glosses. This finding is in keeping with Kotake's (2006a), who observes that the first gloss in Lindisfarne generally reflects the grammatical properties of the Latin equivalent best. It is also in line with Nagucka's (1997) work. She states that "the glosses in the *Lindisfarne Gospels* are not one-to-one mechanical renderings, but rather conscious, occasionally very careful 'interpretive translations'" (Nagucka 1997: 180). The following analysis of multiple glosses with subjunctive forms of OE *beon* verifies this presumption.

3 Multiple glosses of present indicative and subjunctive forms of OE *beon*

3.1 Multiple glosses of indicative *b*-forms and subjunctive *s*-forms

There are 22 doublets incorporating an indicative *b*-form and a subjunctive *s*-form in the Lindisfarne gloss. In 45.45 % of all instances they refer to an unambiguous Latin future tense form, and in the majority of cases the *b*-form is given as the first alternative. This is in line with the ordering preferences in the multiple glosses discussed above, in which the first option reflects the tense and mood of the Latin form best. The sentence in (11) provides an example.

(11) Matthew 23.11

L	*qui maior est uestrum* ***erit*** [3 sg. fut. ind. act.] *minister uester*
Trans.	'He who is greatest of you **will be** your servant'
MtGl (Li) 23.11	seðe heist ł maas is iuer **bið ł sie** embihtmonn iuer

Bolze (2013) explains that Aldred occasionally uses doublets of indicative *b*- and subjunctive *s*-forms to express a future reference in combination with an implied wish, the latter being a trigger for the subjunctive mood in Old English (cp. Mitchell 1967: 146). Table 1 above shows that there was no separate subjunctive *b*-paradigm in Northumbrian. Thus, Aldred obviously employs *b*- and *s*-doublets instead: in (11) he presumably uses the *b*-indicative to render the future tense of the Latin verb and the *s*-subjunctive to convey an implicit wish.

The non-existence of appropriate Northumbrian forms of OE *beon* to render the Latin is also likely to have produced *b*- and *s*-doublets translating the formally ambiguous Latin form *fuerit* 's/he will/may have been', which can denote a future perfect indicative active or a perfect subjunctive active:

(12) Mark 14.9

L	*ubicumque* ***praedicatum fuerit*** [past part. + 3 sg. fut. perf. ind. act. / perf. subj. act.] *euangelium istud in uniuersum mundo et quod fecit haec narrabitur in memoriam eius*
Trans.	'Wherever the Gospel **is proclaimed** in the whole world, what she has done will be told in memory of her'
MkGl (Li) 14.9	suahuer **geboden sie ł bið** godspell ðis in allum middangearde ⁊ þæt dyde ðios asægd bið on gemynd hire.

It is likely that this doublet reflects the ambiguity of the Latin form, i.e. it conveys its possible future tense and also its possible subjunctive mood. This is a further example illustrating that Aldred makes an effort to render the Latin as correctly as possible into Old English.

3.2 Multiple glosses of indicative non-*b*-forms and subjunctive *s*-forms

Doublets of indicative non-*b*-forms and subjunctive *s*-forms are infrequent in the Lindisfarne Gospels; there are only three occurrences. (13) offers an example.

(13) Matthew 6.8

L	*nolite ergo assimilari eis scit enim pater uester quibus opus* ***sit*** [3 sg. pres. subj. act.] *uobis antequam petatis eum*
Trans.	'Thus do not be like them, for your Father knows what **is** necessary for you before you ask him'
MtGl (Li) 6.8	nallas ge ðonne wosa gelic him wat forðon fader iurre of ðæm ðearf **sie ł is** iuh aer ðon gie bidde hine.

The double gloss refers to the Latin present subjunctive form *sit*, and Aldred gives the Old English subjunctive "sie" first, which supports our preceding observations: the first item in Aldred's multiple glosses with OE *beon* generally reflects the grammatical properties of the Latin correspondent best. He provides the indicative non-*b*-form as a second alternative, which most probably indicates his effort to find a more suitable translation in Old English or to express a modal nuance. Hence, as we noted in some of the previous examples, Aldred adds a further form of OE *beon* that, according to his interpretation, fits the context better. This strengthens the thesis that his doublets not only reflect the grammatical information of their Latin equivalent, but also the semantic environment in which they occur. For an analysis of the two *b*-forms "bia" and "bie" occurring in Table 1, see Bolze (2013: 229), where I argue that they may be indicative rather than subjunctive forms.

4 Conclusion

The use of multiple glosses consisting of present tense forms of OE *beon* in the Lindisfarne Gospels demonstrates that Aldred was a good and careful glossator. The examples discussed in this paper illustrate that the doublets do not reflect any uncertainty as to which form he should use; they rather indicate that Aldred employed them for a certain reason. In multiple glosses of two or more indicative *b*-forms, the *b*-forms mostly occur with auxiliary function and are used with the participles of various Old English verbs in order to reflect the semantics of a Latin form and its context as accurately as possible. Doublets of indicative non-*b*-forms show Aldred's endeavour to provide more idiomatic Old English translations. The doublets of *s*- and *r*-plurals could moreover be interpreted as reflections of the claimed linguistic progressiveness of the Northumbrian language preserved in the Lindisfarne gloss.

The doublets with indicative *b*- and non-*b*-forms have proved to be of particular interest. The examples suggest that Aldred employed them to stress certain semantic connotations of a sentence. He frequently used them to refer to various time references and occasionally to indicate an aspectual reference. Thus, these doublets confirm the assumed semantic distinction between the two present indicative paradigms: *b*-forms in particular are preferred to make references to the future.

Furthermore, Aldred's multiple glosses reveal an ordering preference: in doublets consisting of forms of OE *beon* from different paradigms, the first option tends to reflect the grammatical properties of the equivalent Latin verb as correctly as possible, whereas the second option reflects his understanding of the context. Doublets consisting of forms of OE *beon* from the same paradigm can be observed with plural non-*b*-forms; in these cases the *r*-forms usually occur first and the *s*-forms afterwards. Concerning the multiple glosses with subjunctive forms of OE *beon*, the analysis illustrates that Aldred employed multiple glosses pairing a subjunctive *s*-form and an indicative non-*b*-form to indicate modal nuances of the Latin form in its context.

Overall, the multiple glosses of present tense forms of OE *beon* in the Lindisfarne Gospels reveal Aldred's endeavour to translate the grammatical properties of the Latin form *and* the context in which it occurs into Old English. In that respect, the findings in this paper confirm that the gloss in Lindisfarne is no mere one-to-one translation of the Latin. It demonstrates Aldred's attempt to enrich his gloss with forms of OE *beon* reflecting his own interpretation of the contents.

Sara M. Pons-Sanz

A Study of Aldred's Multiple Glosses to the Lindisfarne Gospels

Abstract: Aldred, the glossator of the Lindisfarne Gospels, presents himself as carefully interpreting the Latin lemmata in front of him, in terms of both their internal structure and meaning. His work includes a very high number of multiple glosses, which often attempt to clarify the polysemous character of a lemma or to provide additional information. This paper explores the multiple glosses including different lexemes which Aldred added to lexical lemmata in Mark's Gospel in an attempt to establish whether there is any correlation between Aldred's ordering practices and the frequency with which he used the interpretamenta to render those lemmata. The results of the study show some preference for placing the interpretamentum which most commonly translates the Latin lemma in first position, although Aldred's practice is not fully consistent.

1 Introduction

Aldred's Old English interlinear glosses to the Latin text of the Lindisfarne Gospels (London, British Library, MS Cotton Nero D.iv) have attracted significant attention from scholars interested in the history of the English language, not only in connection with what they can tell us about late Old Northumbrian,[1] but also because of the features in their morphosyntax and lexis that associate them with much later texts, particularly texts from the transition from the Old to the early Middle English period.[2] Aldred's glossing practices and techniques have also been scrutinized in order to gain a better understanding of issues as varied as his scholarly background or some of the possible purposes of the glosses.[3] Amongst Aldred's glossing preferences one has often caught the attention

1 For up-to-date work on the dialectal features of the glosses, see Fernández Cuesta and Rodríguez Ledesma (2007), and Fernández Cuesta et al. (2008).

2 For recent studies on the morphosyntax of the glosses, see for instance, Millar (2000), where the glosses are a very significant part of the data under analysis; and Cole (2014), which focuses on the origins of the so-called Northern Subject Rule. On the Norse-derived terms recorded in the glosses, see Pons-Sanz (2000, 2004 and 2013).

3 Boyd (1975a: 4–5, 8–10) points out that Aldred seems to have been particularly concerned with celibacy and simony. Brown (2003: 98–101) hypothesizes that, albeit a northerner, Aldred might have been educated south of the Humber, in the intellectual circles associated with the Benedic-

of those studying his work: his clear propensity to use multiple interpretamenta to render a single Latin lemma. This feature of his work becomes particularly obvious when his glosses are compared with those by Owun to the Rushworth or MacRegol Gospels (Oxford, Bodleian Library, MS Auct. D.ii.19), because the two sets of glosses are closely connected:[4] Ross and Squires (1980: 494–495) count 543 double glosses in the section of the Rushworth Gospels glossed by Owun (i.e. Ru^2), as opposed to 1,987 in the equivalent section of the Lindisfarne Gospels (or 1,846, if we exclude the double glosses recorded in the Lindisfarne contexts corresponding to lacunae in Ru^2).[5] On a number of occasions Aldred included even triple and quadruple glosses (Ross and Squires 1980: 490 count 106 and eight, respectively, in his work on the Lindisfarne Gospels and the Durham Collectar, Durham, Cathedral Library, MS A.iv.19).[6]

Aldred's multiple glosses vary greatly in the information they provide. While many of them simply present orthographic or grammatical alternatives (in terms of gender, case, simple vs. inflected infinitive, tense, mood, etc.), others include the use of synonyms or near-synonyms, or the juxtaposition of an interpretamentum which directly corresponds to the Latin lemma and another one which interprets it in the light of its context. For instance, in MkGl (Li) 5.41 L *puella* is rendered as "dohter ł mægden"; OE *mægden* 'girl, maiden' is the term that normally translates the Latin lemma, while OE *dohtor* 'daughter' is included because the girl referred to is the daughter of the head of the synagogue, who has been introduced in MkGl (Li) 5.35 (see below, category B, under L *puella*, in the Appendix).[7]

tine Reform; accordingly, his entering the community of St. Cuthbert might have had not only a spiritual purpose but also wider religious, social and even political aims, his use of English next to the Latin sacred text possibly hinting, as Brown indicates, at an attempt to support the 'Englishness' of the north in the face of contemporary Scandinavian activities. See, however, Rusche's paper (this volume).

4 On the basis of the clear similarities between the two sets of glosses, scholars have traditionally accepted the hypothesis that Owun copied his glosses directly from Aldred's. However, this suggestion has been belied by Kotake's recent work; see his 2008a and 2008b articles, and his paper in this volume.

5 On the relationship between the multiple glosses in Lindisfarne and Ru^2, see also Pons-Sanz (2004).

6 Aldred's enthusiasm for multiple glosses is not without parallels, though; for instance, Gretsch (1999: 49 n. 25) counts 1,400 double glosses, more than 60 triple glosses and three quadruple glosses in the Lambeth Psalter.

7 The meanings of Old English terms are given in accordance with the *Dictionary of Old English* (hereafter *DOE*) for the terms starting in any letter from *A* to *G*, and with Clark Hall (1960) for the others. The title abbreviations and editions of the Old English texts mentioned in this paper are those employed by the *Dictionary of Old English Web Corpus* (hereafter *DOEC*). On the classification of Aldred's multiple glosses, see also Ross (1933b: 108).

While the use of such an impressive number of multiple glosses points towards Aldred's interest in linguistic issues, scholars are still unsure about how best to explain their presence in narrower terms.[8] It is probably the case that there is more than one factor at work for his use of multiple glosses including different lexemes:

1. *Uncertainty*: it may be that Aldred was not sure about which Old English term best renders a Latin lemma, but this is not a very convincing explanation (certainly not for all cases) because very often a lemma that in some places receives a multiple gloss is on other occasions translated by a single Old English interpretamentum.
2. *Multiple sources*: Aldred's multiple glosses might reflect the fact that he was working with different sources, which provided him with various alternatives for a single lemma. The possibility that he had access to Latin versions of the Gospels other than the text recorded in the Lindisfarne manuscript has long been argued for and accepted (see Ross 1981; and Kotake, this volume; see also *DOE*: s.v. *bebēodan*, sense C.2, on the use of OE *bebeodan* 'to command' as the interpretamentum for L *comminari* 'to threaten, menace' in MkGl (Li) 1.25).[9]

   There are also various pieces of evidence suggesting that the Old English glosses are unlikely to be attributable to Aldred alone:
   (a) It would be unusual for a glossator not to rely on other sources. As Stanton (2002: 12) points out, the transmission of glosses normally brings together tradition, in the form of a received body of existing glosses, and innovation, as a result of the glossator's individual choices.
   (b) The analysis of Aldred's hand has shown that it includes a wide range of letter-forms and styles, which might reflect, at least partially, that he was copying from various exemplars (see Ker 1943; Brown 2003: 100; and Brookes's and Cole's papers in this volume).
   (c) The glosses exhibit very significant linguistic variation in terms of phonology, spelling and morphosyntax which cannot be simply attributed to the fact that glossing the Lindisfarne Gospels is likely to have taken Aldred years rather than months. This is the topic of Cole's paper (this volume) and readers wanting to know more about this are directed there.

8 His interest in lexical matters is also manifested in his careful rendering of the structure of the Latin lemmata, to such an extent that, at times, we could characterize his gloss as matching the Latin text morpheme by morpheme rather than just word by word (see Rusche's and Lendinara's papers in this volume).

9 The meanings of Latin terms follow those provided by Lewis and Short (1879).

(d) Kotake (2012) has shown that Aldred changes his lexical practices in MtGl (Li) 26–28, a passage which shares many affinities with Farman's glosses to this section of the Rushworth Gospels (i.e. Ru^1). Given that Farman's lexical practices when rendering particular terms here do not change in comparison with the rest of his work on the Rushworth Gospels,[10] Kotake indicates that the traditional view that Farman was influenced by Aldred's work when glossing this section of Matthew's Gospel needs to be revised. If anything, the extant evidence argues in favour of the opposite direction of influence. Yet, Kotake is careful not to suggest a direct relation between the texts, as it may be that the two glossators resorted to a now-lost exemplar.

Yet, while it looks highly likely that Aldred had access to other Old English texts when doing his work, there is also evidence to suggest that Aldred did not slavishly follow an exemplar, but composed some of the glosses on his own as he went along (a practice fully in keeping with the interplay between tradition and innovation that Stanton refers to). For instance, in f. 174r the two syllables of L *quinque* 'five' are split between the third and fourth lines of the left column; Aldred initially glossed L *quin-* as OE "ðaðe", probably having taken it for the contracted negative relative pronoun L *quin* 'who not, but that' (L *qui* + *no*/*ne*), but he probably realized his mistake, as this form has been erased and OE *fifo* 'five' has been written on top of L *quin-* instead (see Ker 1957: 216).

3. *Clarity*: in the case of multiple glosses which include an interpretation (e.g. the glosses for L *puella* in MkGl (Li) 5.41 discussed above, p. 302), the main issue at work seems to have been an attempt to help understand particular Latin passages.
4. *Lexicological and lexicographic concerns*: with some of his multiple glosses Aldred may have been trying to produce "some sort of *Roget's Thesaurus* for Old English", as Gretsch (1999: 50) puts it in connection with the gloss to the Lambeth Psalter.[11]
5. *Stylistic reasons*: Stanton (2002: 52–53) hypothesizes that on some occasions (e.g. when the Latin lemma is translated by various terms which alliterate)

10 For instance, Kotake (2012: 15) notes that Aldred renders L *respondere* 'to answer' consistently with OE *andwyrdan* up to MtGl (Li) 25.45, using OE *andswarian* only once (as the second interpretamentum in a double gloss; see MtGl (Li) 25.37). However, OE *andswarian* appears in the ten contexts where L *respondere* is recorded in MtGl (Li) 26–28, on two occasions with OE *andwyrdan* as an alternative (MtGl (Li) 26.23 and 27.12; cp. below, category A, under L *respondere*, in the Appendix). Farman, on the other hand, uses both verbs throughout Matthew's Gospel, without any clear change in lexical preferences.

11 See also Kuhn (1947: 168) and Kotake (2006b).

the multiple glosses might have been intended as stylistic models for poetry and prose. The influence of glossography on Old English literary language is suggested, for instance, by the fact that Byrhtferth relied very heavily in his *Enchiridion* on English interpretamenta recorded in the glosses to Aldhelm's *Prosa de virginitate* (see Stanton 2002: 48). Even if the glosses did not generally set stylistic trends, we can assume that they were affected by collocations that were fairly common: for instance, L *fidem* (cp. L *fides* 'faith, belief') in MkArgGl (Li) 4 is rendered as "lufo ł geleafo" and the union of these alliterating terms (viz. OE *lufu* 'love' and *geleafa* 'belief') is fairly common in Old English texts (see below, category B, under L *fides*, in the Appendix).[12] We find it, for instance, in a near-contemporary text of the glosses, viz. one of the Blickling homilies (late tenth century): "forðon þe nan wyrhta ne mæg god weorc wyrcean for Gode buton lufon ⁊ geleafan" (HomU20 (BlHom10) 71–73; 'For no worker may perform good works before God without love and belief', as translated by Morris 1874: 110). We should not forget either that Old English writers were familiar with the use of hendiadys and amplification by means of synonyms as stylistic techniques (cp. Gretsch 1999: 50–51 and n. 28). However, such stylistic concerns have not always been accepted by scholars as significant factors in the work of glossators; for instance, Kuhn (1947: 168) argues that "considerations of clarity and accuracy, rather than any striving after rhetorical elegance, motivated the work of the glossators".[13]

2 The present study

2.1 Aims of the study

While the large number of multiple glosses in Aldred's work has long been acknowledged, there have not been many attempts to establish whether Aldred followed any particular patterns when ordering the interpretamenta in such

12 On established word pairs in medieval English literature (frequently linked by phonetic devices such as alliteration, rhyme or assonance), see further Koskenniemi (1968).

13 Another reason for the existence of multiple glosses might be that they are the work of different glossators. For instance, that is the case of the Vespasian Psalter, where most of the second glosses were added in the eleventh century to bring the original ninth-century gloss in line with the D-type gloss for each lemma (see Campbell 1967: 90–92). Yet, as far as the Lindisfarne Gospels are concerned, this is not likely to be an explanation for the multiple glosses because palaeographic evidence suggests that there was a single glossator (see Ross et al. 1960: 20; and Cole's and Brookes's papers in this volume).

glosses. As far as I am aware, this issue has only been dealt with in a handful of studies:

1. In an article focusing on Anglo-Scandinavian contact and its effects on the English language, Hines (1991: 410–411) mentioned in passing that "[a]lternative glosses placed in second place are unlikely to be words that should be less familiar to the reader [...] if anything, they should be more familiar, ensuring that the meaning is not missed or mistaken".
2. Hines made that comment in the context of Aldred's use of various Norse-derived terms in multiple glosses, an issue that I researched further in an article aiming to interpret Aldred's and Owun's Norse-derived terms from a sociolinguistic perspective in the light of their dialectal origins (Pons-Sanz 2004). The findings of my article have been problematized by Hogg's (2004) warning against the traditional interpretation of Aldred's language as representative of Northern Northumbrian and Owun's as exemplifying Southern Northumbrian, given that we do not know where the glossators came from and (in Owun's case) worked, and that some of the linguistic differences between the glosses might indicate spelling practices rather than phonological variation. Yet, the relevant findings for our present purposes still stand. The article records the following figures for John's Gospel:
   (a) on 308 occasions (approx. 53%), Owun's glosses correspond only to the first interpretamentum in a multiple Aldredian gloss;
   (b) on 109 occasions (approx. 19%), Owun's glosses correspond only to the second interpretamentum in a multiple Aldredian gloss;
   (c) on 111 occasions (approx. 19%), Owun's glosses correspond to Aldred's multiple glosses in terms of lexical choices and order;
   (d) on 11 occasions (approx. 2%), Owun's glosses correspond to Aldred's multiple glosses in terms of lexical choices, but present a different order for the interpretamenta;
   (e) on 39 occasions (approx. 7%), Owun's lexical choices differ from Aldred's (Pons-Sanz 2004: 185).

   If Owun and Aldred had access to the same or very similar multiple glosses (as it seems likely), these percentages would suggest that Owun found the first interpretamentum to be the most appropriate and the one that would be most helpful for his audience. Thus, this could be taken to imply (*pace* Hines) that the first rather than the second interpretamentum was the more familiar one.
3. In an article that is specifically devoted to ordering issues, Kotake (2006a) has explored some of the grammatical double glosses that Aldred used to translate Latin verbs. He has shown that Aldred tends to provide first what he calls "literal translations", i.e. translations that are morphologically closer to

the Latin lemma (e.g. a simple, i.e. non-periphrastic, verbal form to render the Latin imperfect and future, or a form in the subjunctive mood), and afterwards translations that differ from the lemma from a morphological perspective but which are possibly more idiomatic (e.g. the use of a periphrastic form with OE *beon* in the past + a present participle to translate the Latin imperfect, or a verbal phrase with OE *willan*, *sculan* or *magan* to translate future and subjunctive forms). This would indicate that, as far as some grammatical glosses are concerned, Hines's assumption might be correct in the sense that the second gloss would be "more familiar, ensuring that the meaning is not missed or mistaken".

The present paper aims to remedy, at least partially, the scarcity of studies on Aldred's ordering principles, particularly in connection with lexical rather than grammatical multiple glosses. If some consistency were to be found in Aldred's practice, the findings could be used to shed some light on various lexical issues. For instance, the Lindisfarne glosses exhibit a very high use of non-technical Norse-derived loans, unparalleled in (near-)contemporary texts (except for Ru^2). This seems to point towards the close interaction between speakers of Old English and Old Norse and, perhaps, towards language shift by Old Norse speakers, as these loans might be the result of imposition rather than borrowing.[14] Van Coetsem (1988: 3) distinguishes between the two mechanisms as follows:

> If the recipient language speaker is the agent, as in the case of an English speaker using French words while speaking English, the transfer of material [...] from the source language to the recipient language is *borrowing* (*recipient language agentivity*). If, on the other hand, the source language speaker is the agent, as in the case of a French speaker using his French articulatory habits while speaking English, the transfer of material from the source language to the recipient language is *imposition* (*source language agentivity*).

Given that many of Aldred's Norse-derived terms appear in multiple glosses,[15] the findings of this study might help us to evaluate the level of integration of

---

14 On the somewhat special character of the Norse-derived terms recorded in the Aldredian glosses and their use in multiple glosses, see Pons-Sanz (2013: 253–257).

15 For instance, in MkGl (Li) 14.15 we find a double gloss for L *stratum*: "song ł bedd", where the first interpretamentum should be associated with OIc *sæng*, *sæing* 'bed' and OEN *sæng*, *siæng*, *siang* id. (see below, category C.2, under L *stratus*, in the Appendix); the interpretamenta indicate that the Latin term has been misunderstood and has been interpreted, not as a form of the past participle of L *sternere* 'to prepare, spread', but as the related noun meaning 'bed'. See as well MkGl (Li) 15.11, where L *concitare* 'to rouse, excite' receives a double gloss with OE *geeggian* (cp. OIc *eggja* 'to egg on, incite') and *geweccan* (see below, category C.2, under L *concitare*, in the Appendix); and MkGl (Li) 10.44 and 10.47, where L *servus* 'slave, servant' is rendered as OE *þræl* (cp.

the loans in the glosses and could therefore lead to a better understanding of the lexical effects of Anglo-Scandinavian linguistic contact. The difficulty lies, of course, in establishing whose language the glosses reflect: Aldred's, his sources' or a mixture. Even though it seems almost undeniable that Aldred must have relied on other materials when carrying out his work, we should also bear in mind that his *modus operandi* shows sufficient sophistication for us to rule out the idea that he was merely a scribe slavishly following his sources. Like Owun, he had some control with regard to the terms he included in the gloss and the order in which they were presented. Therefore, it seems difficult to believe that his idiolect is not somehow represented by the lexical choices in the glosses.

2.2 Data collection

In order to carry out the present study on Aldred's ordering preferences, the following decisions have been made:

1. Given that Kotake (2006a) has already done some work on the ordering principles of double grammatical glosses and that there is no other equivalent work for the lexical glosses, this study focuses on multiple lexical glosses, from two perspectives:[16]
   (a) it only examines cases where the glosses include different lexemes (except for the use of different forms of OE *beon-wesan*, which is the topic of Bolze's 2012 doctoral dissertation and her paper in this volume);
   (b) it focuses on interpretamenta for Latin lexical words, not grammatical terms such as prepositions or conjunctions.
2. The multiple glosses are those recorded in Mark's Gospel, including the preliminary material in the Lindisfarne Gospels (the *Argumentum* and *Capitula Lectionum*).[17] The selection of this particular Gospel responds to its controversial position in other linguistic studies: while Brunner (1947–1948) found clear spelling discrepancies between the glosses to Matthew's and Mark's Gospels up to MkGl (Li) 5.40 on the one hand, and those to the remainder of the Lindisfarne Gospels on the other, Cole's (2014 and this volume) findings on verbal morphosyntax do not support a clear-cut division between the

OIc *þræll* 'slave') and *esne* (see below, category C.3, under L *servus*, in the Appendix). See also Ross and Squires (1980: 491) and above, p. 306.

16 'Incomplete' multiple glosses, i.e. glosses where ł (L *vel* 'or') is added but it is not followed by any interpretamentum, have not been considered in this study.

17 The preliminary texts are abbreviated as MkArgGl (Li) and MkHeadGl (Li), respectively, in the *DOEC*.

initial chapters and the rest of Mark's Gospel. It was hoped that the present study might offer some additional information on the association of the glosses.

3. The study is based on Skeat's (1871–1887) edition of the Gospels, which is fully searchable in the *DOEC*; however, because of the inaccuracies of the edition (see Fernández Cuesta, this volume), an online reproduction of the Lindisfarne manuscript has also been accessed to check Skeat's readings and interpretations (see n. 6 in the Introduction). In his edition, Skeat consistently follows the order provided by Aldred for the interpretamenta in a multiple gloss wholly located directly above the Latin lemma, and, in those cases where the interpretamenta are not next to each other because one of them appears in the side margin, above or below, he gives as the first option the term that is directly above its lemma.[18]
   Thus, Mark's Gospel has initially been examined in order to identify the multiple glosses, and the Latin lemmata that receive multiple glosses have subsequently been searched in the Gospel using the *DOEC* in order to see how they are rendered on other occasions. As one might expect, there are some cases where a polysemous Latin lemma receives different interpretamenta according to the specific meaning in a context: for instance, when L *dimittere* means 'to let go, release, send forth', it is commonly translated by OE *forlætan* (this is the only interpretamentum in 15 out the 18 attestations of the Latin verb with this meaning); however, when it means 'to forgive', it is most frequently translated by OE *forgiefan* (this is the only interpretamentum in seven out the nine attestations of the Latin verb with this meaning; see below, categories B and C.3, under L *dimittere*, in the Appendix).[19] Accordingly, the searches in the *DOEC* have not been carried out mechanically, but the meaning of the terms has also been checked against the *Douay-Rheims Bible*.
4. Even though in order to have as many instances of the Latin lemmata as possible it might have been tempting to include in the searches not only the specific Latin lexemes that receive one or more multiple glosses but also other members of their word-field, this course of action has not been taken because it is not always the case that members of the same word-field receive com-

18 See, for instance, f. 90v, where "sceortum", one of the interpretamenta for L *breuia* (cp. L *brevis* 'short'; MkArgGl (Li) 13), is written in the left-hand-side margin; f. 122v, where "twigge", one of the interpretamenta for L *ramus* 'branch, twig' (MkGl (Li) 13.28), is written in the top margin above the Latin text and its gloss; and f. 100v, where "forleten biðon", one of the interpretamenta for L *dimittentur* (cp. L *dimittere* 'to forgive; to send out, send forth, release'; MkGl (Li) 3.28), is written below its lemma.

19 OE *forlætan* could also mean 'to forgive, pardon' (see *DOE*: s.v. *forlætan*, sense 22), but this is not the verb that Aldred favoured in Lindisfarne to express that meaning.

parable interpretamenta.[20] Sometimes the interpretamenta are simply different: for instance, L *invenire* 'to come upon, find, meet with' is rendered as OE *mittan* and *findan*, while L *venire* 'to come' is rendered as OE *cuman* (see below, category B, under L *invenire* and *venire*, in the Appendix). On other occasions members of the same word-field receive similar interpretamenta but their frequencies of use differ. That is the case, for instance, for various members of the L *ire* 'to go, travel' word-field (L *abire*, *ire*, *introire* and *praeterire*), which are translated in the main by OE *gan*, *gangan*, *feran* and *faran* (see below, the entries for these verbs in the different categories of the Appendix). The various members of an Old English word-field which render the same Latin intepretamentum are counted together, though. For instance, OE *gangan* and *fromgangan* as interpretamenta of L *abire* are counted together because the distinction between such forms is more appropriate for a paper concerned with the glosses from a morphological rather than a lexical perspective.

5. In the Appendix the multiple glosses have been classified into specific categories on the basis of the relationship between each of the interpretamenta that render the Latin lemma. Thus, for instance, L *abire* is associated with both category A ('cases where the first interpretamentum in a multiple gloss is the term that translates the Latin lemma most frequently in the Gospel') and category B ('cases where the first interpretamentum in a multiple gloss is not the term that renders the Latin lemma most frequently in the Gospel') because in one of the multiple glosses, viz. MkGl (Li) 1.35, OE *feran*, which translates the Latin verb on its own on four occasions, is followed by OE *faran*, which is only given as the equivalent for the Latin verb in that context (category A), while in the other multiple gloss, viz. MkGl (Li) 7.30, OE *feran* is followed by OE *gan*, which interprets the Latin verb on its own on seven occasions (category B).

2.3 Results

The process of data collection presented above has produced the following results. There are 261 pairs of words that appear in multiple glosses in Mark's Gospel. In 93 of those pairs (35.63%) the first interpretamentum is the term that is most commonly used to translate the Latin lemma, while in 59 of the pairs (22.60%) the more common interpretamentum to render the Latin lemma does

20 'Word-field' here is used as a synonym of 'word family', i.e. it refers to a group of words formed by terms that share the same root, including compounds where one of the roots is the term under analysis.

not appear in the first position. There is some uncertainty about the ordering patterns of 109 pairs (41.76%; see further the Appendix). The reasons for such uncertainty are varied:

1. As far as four pairs of interpretamenta are concerned, it is difficult to determine whether they should be included in category A or B because the members of each pair interpret the lemma on the same number of occasions and, when the interpretamenta appear in a multiple gloss, they always do so in the same order: e.g. L *traditio* 'tradition' is rendered as a multiple gloss with OE *selenes* and *setnes* in that order on two occasions (MkGl (Li) 7.3 and 7.5) and each of the interpretamenta translates the lemma on its own on two occasions in Mark's Gospel. It is therefore difficult to determine which one might have been Aldred's preferred term to translate the Latin lemma. It may be that such examples (category C.1 in the Appendix) represent common collocations, be it at a personal, dialectal or more general level. Indeed, it is interesting to note that some of the terms involved in such set glosses alliterate: viz. OE *selenes* and *setnes*, and OE *telga* and *twig*, which translate L *ramus* 'branch, twig'. The above suggestion, though, is difficult to substantiate: of the terms involved in such set glosses, only OE *telga* and *twig* are found in collocations outside the Lindisfarne Gospels (and Ru^2), but they appear in the reverse order (see Dan 503 and 514).[21] OE *telga* and *twig*, then, might have frequently occurred together but their order might not have been fully fixed.[22]
2. Eighty-three pairs present a slight variation of the pattern explained above: the interpretamenta only co-occur in one multiple gloss and, if they occur in a single gloss, their number of occurrences is the same (category C.2 in the Appendix). For instance, L *mendicare* 'to beg, ask alms' is recorded twice in Mark's Gospel: it is translated once by OE *gyrnan* (MkGl (Li) 10.46) and once by a double gloss with OE *gegiwian* and *beodan* (MkHeadGl (Li) 34).
3. Twenty-two pairs appear in multiple glosses without a clear ordering pattern (category C.3 in the Appendix); e.g. L *virtus* 'strength, vigour' is rendered on 12 occasions as a single gloss: ten times as OE *meaht* and twice as OE *mægen*; the two Old English terms gloss it together on two other occasions: in MkGl (Li) 9.1 OE *meaht* is the first interpretamentum, whereas that position is taken by OE *mægen* in MkGl (Li) 13.25.

21 Cp. MkGl (Li) 11.8, where the double gloss renders L *frons* 'leafy branch'. In the Arundel Psalter (PsGlJ (Oess) 79.12), OE *telgor* 'twig, branch', a member of the OE *telge* word-field, takes the first position in a similar double gloss.

22 On reversible word pairs in Old and Middle English, see further Koskenniemi (1968: 81–88).

These results indicate that Hines's (1991) aforementioned hypothesis (see above, p. 306) cannot be unconditionally accepted because, if anything, the trend to place the interpretamentum that most commonly renders a Latin lemma in first position (category A) is stronger than the opposite trend (category B). The preference for placing the most common interpretamentum in first position applies even in contexts where the Latin lemma has a rather specific meaning that might be better translated by an Old English term different from that which is most frequently used to translate it. For instance, OE *wif* is the most common interpretamentum for L *uxor* 'wife', but Aldred also renders the lemma as OE *laf* 'what is left, remnant; widow' on three occasions (viz. MkHeadGl (Li) 39, and MkGl (Li) 6.17 and 6.18) when it refers to the wife a dead man leaves behind; yet, even though that is the meaning of the lemma in MkGl (Li) 12.19, it is OE *wif* and not OE *laf* that appears in first position in a double gloss (see below, category A, under L *uxor*, in the Appendix). Similarly, L *civitas* 'city; citizenship, citizens united in a community' is always rendered as OE *ceaster*, either by itself or, on one occasion, as the first member in a multiple gloss, followed by OE *burhwaru*; in that context (MkGl (Li) 1.33), though, L *civitas* refers to the body politic, the citizens, and this is not a meaning commonly associated with OE *ceaster*, which refers to a place rather than its inhabitants, thus making OE *burhwaru* a better choice (the term translates L *civis* 'citizen' in LkGl (Li) 19.14; see below, category A, under L *civitas*, in the Appendix). Yet, as expected, Aldred's practice is not fully consistent: e.g. L *comederunt* (cp. L *comedere* 'to eat') in MkGl (Li) 4.4 is rendered as "fretton ł eton"; in this context, which refers to birds, OE *fretan* might have been a better choice to capture the nuances of the context because it commonly collocates with animals or monsters whereas OE *etan*, the most common interpretamentum for the Latin lemma, is used more widely (see below, category B, under L *comedere*, in the Appendix; see also *DOE*: s.vv. *etan* and *fretan*; cp. Kotake 2006b: 63–66). Similarly, although OE *ymbsellan*, the verb that translates L *circumdare* 'to surround, place around' most often in the Lindisfarne gloss,[23] is the only interpretamentum in MkGl (Li) 12.1, where it refers to a hedge placed around a vineyard, in MkGl (Li) 9.42 it follows OE *ymbbindan* in a reference to a millstone placed (or bound; cp. 'hanged' in the *Douay-Rheims Bible*) around someone's neck (see below, category B, under L *circumdare*, in the Appendix).

Thus, in general the results are not conclusive enough for them to be easily used in discussions about Aldred's lexicon of the sort mentioned above (see p. 307). Consistency, as is widely known amongst scholars who have studied Aldred's

23 The term is likely to be a loan-translation of the Latin verb, although it is not necessarily the case that Aldred (re-)coined it himself (see Waite 2014: 8).

works, was not his forte.[24] However, pessimism should not be the dominant tone arising from this study. Looking so closely at Aldred's lexical choices allows us to identify some of his practices, and to explain some of the cases where he seems to deviate from his usual practice of placing the most frequent Old English term (or word-field) that renders a Latin equivalent as the first interpretamentum in a multiple gloss:

1. The first interpretamentum in a multiple gloss tends to be formally and semantically closer to the Latin lemma, a trend that is in keeping with Kotake's (2006a) findings regarding Aldred's grammatical double glosses (see above, pp. 306–307). Here are some examples:
   (a) When the Latin lemma appears as well in a multiple gloss as a loanword, it tends to do so in first position: e.g. L *tunicis* (cp. L *tunica* 'under-garment, shirt, tunic') is rendered as "tunucum ł cyrtlum" in MkGl (Li) 6.9, even though OE *cyrtle* is the term that Aldred chooses most commonly to translate the Latin lemma (see below, category C.2, under L *tunica*, in the Appendix). Similarly, the OE *bringan* word-field is the most common choice to render L *adferre* 'to bring, carry' and *ferre* 'to bear, carry', but when the lemmata receive a double gloss in MkGl (Li) 1.32 and 2.3, respectively, a form of the similar-sounding OE *ferian* is placed in first position (see below, category B, under L *adferre* and *ferre*, in the Appendix).
   (b) On various occasions a Latin present participle acting as a *nomen agentis* is first glossed by a present participle and afterwards by a more idiomatic noun. For instance, in MkGl (Li) 4.3 L *seminans* (cp. L *seminare* 'to sow'), which should be translated here as 'the one who sows, sower', is rendered as "sawende ł sedere", where the first interpretamentum is the present participle of OE *sawan* and the second the agent noun OE *sædere* 'sower' (cp. OE *sædian*; see below, category A, under L *seminare*, in the Appendix).[25] Interestingly, Aldred does use the verb OE *sædian* in MtGl (Li) 13.3, but he does not seem to have been very fond of it (even though a member of its word-field, viz. OE *sæd*, is the term that most commonly translates L *semen* 'seed'), and OE *sawan* is the most common interpretamentum for L *seminare* instead. Thus, in this case we could say

24 On Aldred's inconsistencies when glossing the Lindisfarne Gospels, see, for instance, Nagucka (1997) and Kotake (2006a). Scholars have also noted very clear disparities between Aldred's glosses to the Lindisfarne Gospels and those which he added to the Durham Collectar. See, for instance, Ross (1970; 1978).

25 Cp. MkGl (Li) 4.26, where L *sementem* (cp. L *semens*) receives the same double gloss; Aldred probably mistook this term for the present participle (see below, category C.2, under L *semens*, in the Appendix).

that Aldred is doing nothing other than putting the term that he uses most commonly to render the Latin verb in the initial position, but the same cannot be said about the following example: in MkHeadGl (Li) 20 L *parentum* (cp. L *parens* 'parent, progenitor'), originally a present participle form of L *parire* 'to bring forth, bear', is rendered as "strionendra ł ældra", i.e. with a form of the present participle of OE *streonan* 'to beget, generate; gain, acquire' as the fist interpretamentum, even though OE *ealdor* is a much more common interpretamentum for the Latin lemma (see below, category B, under L *parens*, in the Appendix).

(c) L *videtur* 'it seems' (cp. L *videre* 'to see, consider, know') in MkGl (Li) 14.64 is translated first by another simple verbal form with that meaning, viz. a form of OE *þyncan* 'to seem, appear' (viz. "ðyncge"). OE *geseon* 'to see', the verb that normally renders the Latin lemma, appears in second position in a passive construction (viz. "is gesene"), reflecting the Latin passive voice (see below, category B, under L *videre*, in the Appendix). This example tallies with Kotake's (2006a) findings in two respects: Aldred's preference for placing simple forms first followed by periphrastic forms, and his tendency, when translating deponent verbs (i.e. verbs with a passive form but active meaning, which brings L *videtur* in this context close to them), to provide first an interpretamentum that renders the Latin meaning more precisely and then another which attempts to capture the passive form of the Latin lemma but which is either less natural or less appropriate from a semantic perspective.[26]

(d) When Aldred introduces a clarification or an interpretation of a Latin term based on the context, it does not tend to appear as the first member of a multiple gloss: see, for instance, MkGl (Li) 13.20, where L *caro* 'flesh' is rendered as "lichoma ł monn", OE *lichama* 'body' being the most common interpretamentum for the Latin lemma and OE *mann* 'person' having been introduced probably because the context refers as well to people who have been chosen to be saved (see below, category A, under L *caro*, in the Appendix).[27] Similarly, in MkGl (Li) 5.2, when glossing L *monumentum* 'sepulchre, tomb', Aldred gives first OE *byrgen*, its most common interpretamentum, and then OE *bend* 'bond, fetters', most likely as a reference to the fact that we are told at the beginning of Mark's

---

26 Notably, though, L *videtur* with the same meaning in MtGl (Li) 18.11 and 22.42, and in LkGl (Li) 10.36 is rendered first as "is gesene" and then as a form of OE *þyncan*.

27 The passage reads as follows in *Douay-Rheims* version of the Bible: "And unless the Lord had shortened the days, no flesh should be saved: but for the sake of the elect which he hath chosen, he hath shortened the days".

Gospel that the demon-possessed man that Christ encounters could not be restrained (cp. OE *fæstnung* 'fastening, confinement' as the second interpretamentum in MkGl (Li) 5.5; see below, category A, under L *monumentum*, in the Appendix; and *DOE*: s.vv. *bend*, sense I.a.iv, and *fæstnung*, sense 7). Yet, again, this is not always the case, an exception being, for instance, the aforementioned double gloss for L *puella* in MkGl (Li) 5.41 (see above, p. 302).

2. Although not clearly connected with ordering practices, it is interesting to notice that there are various cases where Aldred appears to have changed his lexical preferences. For instance, his glossing habits for L *accedere* 'to come near, approach' seem to change in MkGl (Li) 6: OE *cuman* and *neahlæcan*, in that order, render the term in MkGl (Li) 1.31 and 6.21, but from then onwards (MkGl (Li) 6.35, 10.2, 10.35, 11.27, 12.28, 14.45) the term is only glossed with the latter interpretamentum (see below, category B, under L *accedere*, in the Appendix). This is in line with what we see in the remainder of the Gospels: OE *neahlæcan* is clearly Aldred's preferred interpretamentum until MtGl (Li) 25 but, while it is still very prominent in MtGl (Li) 26–28, OE *cuman* gains significance there (see MtGl (Li) 26.7, 26.49, 26.60, 27.58). Interestingly, this change tallies with Kotake's (2012) findings concerning Aldred's lexical practices in these chapters (see above, p. 304). In Luke's and John's Gospels only OE *neahlæcan* translates the Latin verb.

   It is, of course, difficult to know whether changes in lexical preferences are attributable to the influence of various sources, or more simply to the fact that Aldred had various (near-)synonyms in his lexical repertoire and his preferences changed over time (cp. Kotake 2008b). A much more thorough analysis of his lexical choices is needed before any answer, however tentative, can be given in this respect, although it is worth pointing out that this study can neither support nor refute a suggestion for a change in Aldred's sources around MkGl (Li) 5.

3 Conclusion

This paper has explored the multiple glosses including different lexemes which Aldred used to render Latin lexical lemmata in Mark's Gospel in an attempt to establish whether there is any correlation between Aldred's ordering practices and the frequency with which he used the interpretamenta to translate those lemmata. The results of the study show some preference for placing the interpretamentum which most commonly renders the Latin lemma in first position, although Aldred's behaviour is not fully consistent. While the results might not allow us to make fully reliable inferences regarding the make-up of Aldred's lexicon on the basis of the position of a particular interpretamentum in a multiple gloss (either generally or specifically in terms of the Norse-derived terms recorded in the glosses), they do give us some insights into Aldred's ordering practices and lexical choices. In this respect, it is hoped that these findings may contribute to deepen our understanding of how Aldred carried out his work.[28]

28 I am very thankful to Julia Fernández Cuesta, Susan Irvine, Tadashi Kotake and James Rawson for their comments on various versions of this paper. I would also like to thank the Spanish Ministry of Science and Technology (project FFI2011-28272) for its financial support.

Appendix

Multiple lexical glosses in Mark's Gospel

The interpretamenta for each Latin lemma have been arranged in terms of frequency. When two or more terms have the same frequency, they have been arranged alphabetically. S + a number indicates the number of occurrences of the term in a single gloss; M + a number indicates the number of occurrences of the term in a multiple gloss. Only the relevant interpretamenta and contexts are given in each case. Unless otherwise stated, the contexts referred to belong to the section of the text that the *DOEC* abbreviates as MkGl (Li).

A. Cases where the first interpretamentum in a multiple gloss is the term that renders the Latin lemma most frequently in the Gospel

	Lemma	Interpretamenta	Relevant multiple gloss(es)
1.	*abire*	*feran* (S 4, M 2), *faran*[29] (S 0, M 1)	1.35
2.	*adhuc*	*get* (S 2, M 3), *geona* (S 1, M 2), *leng* (S 0, M 1)	14.63
3.	*adsumere*	*niman* (S 5, M 1), *onfon* (S 0, M 1)	16.19
4.	*aiere*	*cweþan* (S over 60, M 1), *soþ* (S 0, M 1)	11.31
5.	*amplius*	*forþor* (S 2, M 3), *mara* (S 0, M 1)	14.31
6.	*ascendere*	*(a)stigan* (S 15, M 1), *gan* (S 0, M 1)	4.7
7.	*aspicere*	*(ymb)sceawian* (S 0, M 2), *seon* (S 0, M 1)	13.1
8.	*calix*	*calic* (S 5, M 2), *copp* (S 0, M 1)	9.41
9.	*calix*	*calic* (S 5, M 2), *disc* (S 0, M 1)	7.4
10.	*candidus*	*hwit* (S 2, M 1), *lixian* (S 0, M 1)	9.3
11.	*capere*	*niman* (S 0, M 2), *tellan* (S 0, M 1)	12.13
12.	*caro*	*lichama* (S 7, M 1), *mann* (S 0, M 1)	13.20
13.	*cena*	*feorm* (S 2, M 1), *symbel* (S 0, M 1)	6.21
14.	*cessare*	*blinnan* (S 1, M 1), *restan* (S 0, M 1)	4.39
15.	*civitas*	*ceastre* (S 8, M 1), *burhwaru* (S 0, M 1)	1.33

29 On the relationship and overlap between OE *faran* and *feran*, see further Ogura (2002: 16–22).

A. (continued)

	Lemma	Interpretamenta	Relevant multiple gloss(es)
16.	*comminari* ('to command, charge, forbid')	*(be/for)beodan* (S 3, M 1), *stieran* (S 0, M 1)	8.30
17.	*comminari* ('to threaten, meanace, rebuke')	*stieran* (S 4, M 1), *(be/for)beodan* (S 0, M 1)	8.33
18.	*confestim*	*sona* (S 5, M 2), *hraþe* (S 0, M 1)	4.17
19.	*conquirere*	*(efne)frignan* (S 2, M 3), *secan* (S 1, M 2)	9.14, 12.28
20.	*conquirere*	*(efne)frignan* (S 2, M 3), *frasian* (S 0, M 1)	9.16
21.	*conspuere*	*(efne)spittan* (S 1, M 1), *gehorwian* (S 0, M 1)	14.65
22.	*conturbare*	*styrian* (S 0, M 2), *dedrefan* (S 0, M 1)	9.20
23.	*convocare*	*(efne)cigan* (S 5, M 1), *clipian* (S 0, M 1)	8.34
24.	*curare*	*geman* (S 5, M 2), *hælan* (S 0, M 1)	6.5
25.	*deprecari*	*biddan* (S 6, M 1), *geornian* (S 0, M 1)	1.40
26.	*descendere*	*(of/adun)stigan* (S 5, M 1), *cuman* (S 0, M 1)	3.22
27.	*dicere*	*cweþan* (S over 100, M 3), *secgan* (S 8, M 2)	7.36, 8.26
28.	*dicere*	*cweþan* (S over 100, M 3), *nemnan* (S 0, M 1)	15.7
29.	*diversus*	*ungelic* (S 0, M 2), *monigfeald* (S 0, M 1)	MkHeadGl (Li) 9
30.	*diversus*	*ungelic* (S 0, M 2), *beorht* (S 0, M 1), *fagung* (S 0, M 1)	MkHeadGl (Li) 42
31.	*donec*	*oþþæt* (S 3, M 3), *þa hwil* (S 0, M 1)	14.32
32.	*educere*	*(of)lædan* (S 2, M 1), *ateon* (S 0, M 1)	14.47
33.	*egredi*	*feran* (S 7, M 3), *faran* (S 4, M 3)	1.35, 8.27, 13.1
34.	*eicere*	*(for)drifan* (S 8, M 3), *afirran* (S 0, M 1)	1.34
35.	*emere*	*bycgan* (S 1, M 1), *ceapian* (S 0, M 1)	6.36
36.	*exoriri*	*arisan* (S 0, M 2), *upgan* (S 0, M 1)	4.6
37.	*generatio*	*cneores* (S 4, M 1), *þeod* (S 0, M 1)	8.12

A. (continued)

	Lemma	Interpretamenta	Relevant multiple gloss(es)
38.	*gens* ('nation')[30]	*cynn* (S 4, M 1), *hæþen* (S 0, M 1)	13.10
39.	*gustare*	*birgan* (S 1, M 1), *supan* (S 0, M 1)	MkHeadGl (Li) 27
40.	*hora*	*tid* (S 9, M 1), *hwil* (S 0, M 1)	13.32
41.	*iam*	*gea* (S 4, M 3), *hwæþere* (S 0, M 1)	15.44
42.	*ianua*	*duru* (S 2, M 1), *geat* (S 0, M 1)	1.33
43.	*ingredi*	*ingan* (S 1, M 2), *inferan* (S 0, M 1)	1.21
44.	*ingredi*	*ingan* (S 1, M 2), *ingangan* (S 0, M 1)	3.27
45.	*inquirere*	*cweþan* (S 1, M 1), *secgan* (S 0, M 1)	12.26
46.	*introire*	*(in)gangan* (S 0, M 5), *incuman* (S 0, M 1)	1.45
47.	*lignum*	*steng* (S 1, M 1), *treow* (S 0, M 1)	14.43
48.	*ire*	*gan* (S 6, M 2), *(for/from)gangan* (S 3, M 2)	1.38, 14.42
49.	*locus*	*stow* (S 5, M 1), *stede* (S 0, M 1)	1.35
50.	*lucerna*	*leoht(fæt)* (S 1, M 1), *þæcele* (S 0, M 1)	4.21
51.	*mane*	*arlice* (S 2, M 1), *on morgen* (S 0, M 1)	16.9
52.	*manifestare*	*(æt)eawan* (S 1, M 1), *mærsian* (S 0, M 1)	3.12
53.	*mittere*	*sendan* (S 34, M 1), *faran* (S 0, M 1)	4.37
54.	*mons*	*mor* (S 9, M 1), *dun* (S 0, M 1)	13.3
55.	*monumentum*	*byrgen* (S 8, M 2), *bend* (S 0, M 1)	5.2
56.	*monumentum*	*byrgen* (S 8, M 2), *fæstnung* (S 0, M 1)	5.5
57.	*omnis*	*æghwilc* (S 3, M 3), *ænig* (S 0, M 1)	13.20
58.	*oportere*	*sculan* (S 0, M 2), *becuman* (S 0, M 1)	14.31
59.	*pars*	*dæl* (S 1, M 1), *land* (S 0, M 1)	8.10
60	*percutere*	*(þurh)slean* (S 2, M 1), *hrinan* (S 0, M 1)	14.27
61.	*perdere*	*losian* (S 9, M 1), *fordon* (S 0, M 1)	9.22
62.	*peregre*	*feor* (S 1, M 1), *long wæg* (S 0, M 1)	13.34
63.	*petere*	*giwian* (S 7, M 1), *wilnian* (S 2, M 1)	6.22

30 On the glosses to L *gens*, see further Kotake (2006b).

A. (continued)

	Lemma	Interpretamenta	Relevant multiple gloss(es)
64.	*porcus*	*bearg* (S 4, M 1), *swin* (S 0, M 1)	5.11
65.	*potestas*	*meaht* (S 11, M 1), *onweald* (S 0, M 1)	13.34
66.	*praecedere*	*foregan* (S 1, M 1), *onforan gangan* (S 0, M 1)	10.32
67.	*praedicare*	(*fore*)*bodian* (S 15, M 2), *foresecgan* (S 0, M 2)	6.12, 13.10
68.	*procedere*	*feran* (S 0, M 2), *springan* (S 0, M 1)	1.28
69.	*procidere*	(*fore*)*feallan* (S 3, M 2), *hleotan* (S 0, M 2)	3.11, 5.22
70.	(*peregre*) *profici*	*feran* (S 1, M 3), *elþeodian* (S 0, M 1)	13.34
71.	*quantus*	*hu micel* (S 3, M 1), *swa*/*hu lenge* (S 1, M 1)	9.21
72.	*quidem*	*eac* (S 2, M 1), *soþlice* (S 0, M 1)	16.19
73.	*relinquere*	(*for*)*letan* (S 10, M 2), *læfan* (S 0, M 2)	12.19, 12.20
74.	*respondere*	(*ge*)*andwyrdan* (S 33, M 1), (*ge*)*andswarian* (S 8, M 1)	14.14
75.	*scandalizare*	*andspurnan* (S 8, M 1), *todrifan* (S 0, M 1)	14.27
76.	(*ne*)*scire*	*witan* (S 26, M 2), *cunnan* (S 0, M 2)	12.24, 14.71
77.	*semen*	*sæd* (S 4, M 2), *team* (S 0, M 2)	12.21, 12.22
78.	*seminare*	*sawan* (S 11, M 1), *sædere* (S 0, M 1)	4.3
79.	*sero*	*æfen*(*tid*) (S 2, M 2), *smolt*/*smyltnes* (S 0, M 2)	4.35, 6.47
80	*signum*	*beacen* (S 6, M 2), *tacn* (S 0, M 3)	MkHeadGl (Li) 24; 14.44, 16.19
81.	*sporta*	*cawl* (S 1, M 1), *mand* (S 0, M 1)	8.20
82.	*sufferre*	*niman* (S 2, M 1), *beran* (S 0, M 1)	8.19
83.	*transferre*	*oferferian* (S 1, M 1), *beleoran* (S 0, M 1)	14.36
84.	*synagoga*	*samnung* (S 9, M 1), *spræc* (S 0, M 1)	6.2
85.	*talis*	*þuslic* (S 3, M 1), *swilc* (S 0, M 1)	13.19
86.	*temptare*	*acunnian* (S 3, M 1), *costian* (S 0, M 1)	10.2
87.	*tempus*	*tid* (S 5, M 3), *hwil* (S 0, M 1)	2.19
88.	*tempus*	*tid* (S 5, M 3), *fyrst* (S 0, M 1)	9.21
89.	*tempus*	*tid* (S 5, M 3), *lif* (S 0, M 1)	10.30

A. (continued)

	Lemma	Interpretamenta	Relevant multiple gloss(es)
90.	*tollere*	*niman* (S 7, M 3), *beran* (S 0, M 2)	2.9, 2.11
91.	*uxor*	*wif* (S 8, M 1), *laf* (S 3, M 1)	12.19
92.	*vestimentum*	*wæd* (S 9, M 1), *hrægl* (S 3, M 1), *claþ* (S 0, M 1)	14.63
93.	*videre*	*geseon* (S over 70, M 2), *behealdan* (S 0, M 1)	13.9

B. Cases where the first interpretamentum in a multiple gloss is not the term that renders the Latin lemma most frequently in the Gospel

	Lemma	Interpretamenta	Relevant multiple gloss(es)
1.	*abire*	*gan* (S 7, M 1), *feran* (S 4, M 2)	7.30
2.	*accedere*	*neahlæcan* (S 6, M 2), *cuman* (S 0, M 2)	1.31, 6.21
3.	*adferre*	(*to*)*bringan* (S 8, M 1), *ferian* (S 0, M 1)	1.32
4.	*adprehendere*	*læcan* (S 4, M 1), *gegripan* (S 1, M 1)	7.33
5.	*amputare*	*ceorfan* (S 1, M 1), *snædan* (S 0, M 1)	14.47
6.	*aspicere*	(*ymb*)*sceawian* (S 0, M 2), *uplocian* (S 0, M 1)	8.24
7.	*brevia/breviter*	*sceort* (S 1, M 1), *lytel* (S 0, M 1)	MkArgGl (Li) 13
8.	*capere*	*niman* (S 0, M 2), *fon* (S 0, M 1)	2.2
9.	*circumdare*	*ymbsellan* (S 1, M 1), *ymbbindan* (S 0, M 1)	9.42
10.	*circumspicere*	*ymbsceawian* (S 3, M 1), *ymblocian* (S 2, M 1)	3.34
11.	*comedere*	*etan* (S 2, M 1), *fretan* (S 0, M 1)	4.4
12.	*complexari*	*frigian* (S 1, M 1), *clyppan* (S 0, M 1)	9.36
13.	*confestim*	*sona* (S 5, M 2), *recene* (S 0, M 1)	5.29
14.	*contemnere*	*niþerian* (S 1, M 1), *hinan* (S 0, M 1), *tellan* (S 0, M 1)	9.12
15.	*conturbare*	*styrian* (S 0, M 2), *unrotsian* (S 0, M 1)	6.50
16.	*convertere*	(*efne*)*cierran* (S 3, M 1), *hweorfan* (S 0, M 1)	4.12

B. (continued)

	Lemma	Interpretamenta	Relevant multiple gloss(es)
17.	*convincere*	*(efne)cierran* (S 1, M 1), *ofercuman* (S 0, M 1)	MkHeadGl (Li) 37
18.	*curare*	*geman* (S 5, M 1), *lacnian* (S 0, M 1)	1.34
19.	*deinde*	*æfterþon* (S 2, M 1), *soþe* (S 1, M 1)	4.17
20.	*difficilis*	*hefig* (S 1, M 1), *uneaþe* (S 0, M 1)	10.23
21.	*dimittere* ('to let go, release, send forth')	*forlætan* (S 15, M 1), *forgiefan* (S 2, M 1)	15.9
22.	*diripere*	*reafian* (S 1, M 1), *niman* (S 0, M 1)	3.27
23.	*dives*	*wlanc* (S 1, M 2), *welig* (S 0, M 2)	10.25, 12.41
24.	*docere*	*læran* (S 20, M 1), *tæcan* (S 0, M 1)	12.38
25.	*donec*	*oþþæt* (S 3, M 3), wiþ (S 0, M 2)	MkHeadGl (Li) 27; 6.10
26.	*exclamare*	*(of)clypian* (S 5, M 1), *ciegan* (S 0, M 1)	6.49
27.	*exoriri*	*arisan* (S 0, M 2), *upiernan* (S 0, M 1)	4.5
28.	*expirare*	*asweltan* (S 1, M 1), *gast agiefan* (S 0, M 1)	15.37
29.	*ferre*	*bringan* (S 1, M 1), *ferian* (S 0, M 1)	2.3
30.	*fides*	*geleafa* (S 7, M 1), *lufu* (S 0, M 1)	MkArgGl (Li) 4
31.	*fretum*	*luh* (S 3, M 1), *sweora* (S 0, M 1)	5.1
32.	*iam*	*witodlic* (S 3, M 1), *hwil* (S 0, M 1)	5.3
33.	*indigne*	*unweorþe* (S 1, M 1), *belgan* (S 0, M 1)	14.4
34.	*invenire*	*(on/in)findan* (S 5, M 1), *gemittan* (S 4, M 1)	7.30
35.	*lectio*	*ræde* (S 1, M 1), *lar* (S 0, M 1)	MkArgGl (Li) 2
36.	*minister*	*embehtmann* (S 3, M 1), *hera* (S 0, M 1)	10.43
37.	*multus*	*manig* (S 38, M 4), *micel* (S 3, M 1)	4.5
38.	*nihil*	*naht* (S 3, M 1), *æniht* (S 0, M 1)	15.5
39.	*novissime/ novissium*	*lætemest* (S 0, M 2), *æt ende* (S 0, M 1)	12.6

B. (continued)

	Lemma	Interpretamenta	Relevant multiple gloss(es)
40.	*novissime/ novissium*	*lætemest* (S 0, M 2), *æt neahste* (S 0, M 1)	16.14
41.	*oboedire*	*edmodigan* (S 1, M 1), *hieran* (S 0, M 1), *hyrsumian* (S 0, M 1)	4.41
42.	*parabola*	*bispell* (S 12, M 1), *bisen* (S 0, M 1)	4.34
43.	*parens*	*ealdor* (S 1, M 1), *streonend* (S 0, M 1)	MkHeadGl (Li) 20
44.	*praecipere*	*beodan* (S 8, M 1), *hatan* (S 6, M 1)	9.9
45.	*praeterire*	*bifaran* (S 1, M 1), *bigangan* (S 0, M 1)	15.21
46.	*procedere*	*feran* (S 0, M 2), *faran* (S 0, M 1)	14.35
47.	*proximus*	*neah* (S 5, M 1), *unfearr* (S 0, M 1)	13.29
48.	*puella*	*mægden* (S 9, M 1), *dohtor* (S 0, M 1)	5.41
49.	*sabbatum*	*sunnandæg* (S 6, M 1), *haligdæg* (S 1, M 1)	6.2
50.	*salutare*	*gretan* (S 2, M 1), *wilcumian* (S 0, M 1)	12.38
51.	*singulus*	*syndrig* (S 1, M 1), *an* (S 0, M 1)	MkArgGl (Li) 5
52.	*statim*	*sona* (S 22, M 1), *recen* (S 4, M 1)	9.20
53.	*summum*	*heah(nes)* (S 0, M 2), *brerd* (S 0, M 1)	13.27
54.	*summum*	*heah(nes)* (S 0, M 2), *hrof* (S 0, M 1)	13.27
55.	*turba*	*þreat* (S 22, M 1), *here* (S 1, M 1)	4.36
56.	*tollere*	*niman* (S 7, M 3), *lædan* (S 0, M 1)	6.8
57.	*venire*	*cuman* (S over 80, M 1), *mittan* (S 0, M 1)	11.13
58.	*vexare*	*beran* (S 1, M 1), *awælan* (S 1, M 1)	5.18
59.	*videre*	*geseon* (S over 70, M 2), *þyncan* (S 0, M 1)	14.64

C. Uncertain cases

C.1 Set order

	Lemma	Interpretamenta	Relevant multiple gloss(es)
1.	*accusare*	*tellan* (S 0, M 2), *niþerian* (S 0, M 2)	MkHeadGl (Li) 20; 3.2
2.	*modium*	*mitta* (S 0, M 2), *fæt* (S 0, M 2)	MkHeadGl (Li) 12; 4.21
3.	*ramus*	*telga* (S 0, M 2), *twig* (S 0, M 2)	4.32, 13.28
4.	*traditio*	*selenes* (S 2, M 2), *setnes* (S 2, M 2)	7.3, 7.5

C.2 Only one multiple gloss (with those terms)

	Lemma	Interpretamenta	Relevant multiple gloss(es)
1.	*abundare*	*manigfealdan* (S 0, M 1), *weaxan* (S 0, M 1)	12.44
2.	*adicere*	*geeacnian* (S 0, M 1), *sellan* (S 0, M 1)	4.24
3.	*adlidere*	*begitan* (S 0, M 1), *toslitan* (S 0, M 1)	9.18
4.	*aedificatio*	*geren* (S 0, M 1), *gleng* (S 0, M 1)	13.2
5.	*afficere*	*acwellan* (S 0, M 1), *fordon* (S 0, M 1)	13.12
6.	*amicere*	*gegearwian* (S 0, M 1), *ymbgyrdan* (S 0, M 1)	14.51
7.	*amputare*	*clænsian* (S 0, M 1), *tellan* (S 0, M 1)	MkArgGl (Li) 15
8.	*caecatus*	*blind* (S 0, M 1), *þeostrig* (S 0, M 1)	8.17
9.	*capitulum*	*forecwide* (S 0, M 1), *foremearcung* (S 0, M 1), *heafodweard* (S 0, M 1)	MkArgGl (Li) 1
10.	*colaphus*	*dynt* (S 0, M 1), *fyst* (S 0, M 1)	14.65
11.	*comminuere*	*forbrecan* (S 0, M 1), *toscænan* (S 0, M 1)	5.4
12.	*committere*	*efenesendan* (S 0, M 1), *geendian* (S 0, M 1)	10.11
13.	*concidere*	*feallan* (S 0, M 1), *þerscan* (S 0, M 1)	5.5
14.	*concitare*	*geeggian* (S 0, M 1), *geweccan* (S 0, M 1)	15.11

C.2 (continued)

	Lemma	Interpretamenta	Relevant multiple gloss(es)
15.	*dehinc*	*æfter þon* (S 0, M 1), *siþþa* (S 0, M 1)	MkArgGl (Li) 5
16.	*denuo*	*niwunga* (S 0, M 1), *sona* (S 0, M 1)	14.14
17.	*deorsum*	*geanþe* (S 0, M 1), *sundrig* (S 0, M 1)	11.46
18.	*destruere*	*tostregdan* (S 0, M 1), *towearpan* (S 0, M 1)	13.2
19.	(*dies*) *festus*	*bærlic* (S 0, M 1), (*dæg*) *halig* (S 0, M 1)	14.2
20.	*discumbere*	*hlinian* (S 0, M 1), *restan* (S 0, M 1)	2.15
21.	*disputare*	*flitan* (S 0, M 1), *tellan* (S 0, M 1)	9.34
22.	*disserere*	*secgan* (S 0, M 1), *tosceadan* (S 0, M 1), *trahtian* (S 0, M 1)	4.34
23.	*dissolvere*	*toslitan* (S 0, M 1), *undon* (S 0, M 1)	14.58
24.	*domare*	*healdan* (S 0, M 1), *temian* (S 0, M 1)	5.4
25.	*domicilium*	*hus* (S 0, M 1), *lytel by* (S 0, M 1)	5.3
26.	*eventura*	*gelimpan sculan* (S 0, M 1), *toweard* (S 0, M 1)	10.32
27.	*evertere*	*ofcierran* (S 0, M 1), *utdrifan* (S 0, M 1)	11.15
28.	*exaestuare*	*gedrugian* (S 0, M 1), *forbærnan* (S 0, M 1)	4.6
29.	*excutere*	*drygan* (S 0, M 1), *sceadan* (S 0, M 1)	6.11
30.	*exprobare*	*forcuman* (S 0, M 1), *fordrifan* (S 0, M 1)	16.14
31.	*exprobare*	*forcweþan* (S 0, M 1), *tælan* (S 0, M 1)	MkHeadGl (Li) 39
32.	*figuraliter*	*gastlice* (S 0, M 1), *magwlitlice* (S 0, M 1)	MkHeadGl (Li) 40
33.	*frons*	*telga* (S 0, M 1), *twig* (S 0, M 1)	11.8
34.	*galli cantus*	*hancred* (S 0, M 1), *uhttid* (S 0, M 1)	13.35
35.	*grandis*	*micel* (S 0, M 1), *swiþe* (S 0, M 1)	14.15
36.	*habitare*	*buan* (S 0, M 1), *wunian* (S 0, M 1)	4.32
37.	*harundo*	*gierd* (S 0, M 1), *hreod* (S 0, M 1)	15.19
38.	*holus*	*græs* (S 0, M 1), *wyrt* (S 0, M 1)	4.32

C.2 (continued)

	Lemma	Interpretamenta	Relevant multiple gloss(es)
39.	*imitare*	*gebysnian* (S 0, M 1), *gelician* (S 0, M 1)	MkHeadGl (Li) 32
40.	*immolare*	*agiefan* (S 0, M 1), *asecgan* (S 0, M 1)	14.12
41.	*impetus*	*ongean* (S 0, M 1), *ræs* (S 0, M 1)	5.13
42.	*ingemescere*	*gemænan* (S 0, M 1), *seofian* (S 0, M 1)	8.12
43.	*ingravatus*	*hefig* (S 0, M 1), *pislic* (S 0, M 1)	14.40
44.	*iniquis*	*unrihtwis* (S 0, M 1), *wohful* (S 0, M 1)	15.28
45.	*inquam* (defective)	*cweþan* (S 0, M 1), *secgan* (S 0, M 1)	12.26
46.	*inquirere*	*gefrignan* (S 0, M 1), *gesecan* (S 0, M 1)	MkArgGl (Li) 5
47.	*leprosus*	*hreof* (S 0, M 1), *licþrowere* (S 0, M 1)	MkHeadGl (Li) 5
48.	*locare*	*agiefan* (S 0, M 1), *gefæstan* (S 0, M 1)	12.1
49.	*ludere*	*bismerian* (S 0, M 1), *tælan* (S 0, M 1)	15.31
50.	*mendicare*	*beodan* (S 0, M 1), *gegiwian* (S 0, M 1)	MkHeadGl (Li) 34
51.	*mystice*	*deoplice* (S 0, M 1), *runlice* (S 0, M 1)	MkHeadGl (Li) 44
52.	*necessarius*	*behoflic* (S 0, M 1), *nydþearf* (S 0, M 1)	11.3
53.	*nudare*	*genacodian* (S 0, M 1), *unþeccan* (S 0, M 1)	2.4
54.	*numquid*	*ah* (S 1, M 1), *hwæþer* (S 1, M 1)	4.21
55.	*occaecatus*	*foreblind* (S 0, M 1), *foreþeostrian* (S 0, M 1)	6.52
56.	*opinio*	*mærsung* (S 0, M 1), *wena* (S 0, M 1)	13.7
57.	*oportere*	*beon riht(lic)* (S 1, M 1), *sculan* (S 0, M 2)	13.7
58.	*penuria*	*hienþ* (S 0, M 1), *unsped* (S 0, M 1)	12.44
59.	*pera*	*pohha* (S 0, M 1), *pusa* (S 0, M 1)	6.8
60.	*perfectio*	*endung* (S 0, M 1), *fyllnes* (S 0, M 1)	MkArgGl (Li) 3
61.	*petra*	*carr* (S 0, M 1), *stan* (S 0, M 1)	15.46
62.	*plectere*	*cursian* (S 0, M 1), *slean* (S 0, M 1)	15.17

C.2 (continued)

	Lemma	Interpretamenta	Relevant multiple gloss(es)
63.	*praesidens*	*heahgerefa* (S 0, M 1), *undercyning* (S 0, M 1)	13.9
64.	*primatus*	*ealdormann* (S 0, M 1), *forwost* (S 0, M 1)	MkHeadGl (Li) 2
65.	*procella*	*windræs* (S 0, M 1), *yst* (S 0, M 1)	4.37
66.	*propositio*	*foregearwian* (S 0, M 1), *temesian* (S 0, M 1)	2.26
67.	*retro*	*behindan* (S 0, M 1), *on bæce* (S 0, M 1)	8.33
68.	*rumor*	*mærsung* (S 0, M 1), *mærþu* (S 0, M 1)	1.28
69.	*sapientur*	*snotorlice* (S 0, M 1), *wislice* (S 0, M 1)	12.34
70.	*scindere*	*torendan* (S 0, M 1), *toslitan* (S 0, M 1)	14.63
71.	*secessus*	*feltun* (S 0, M 1), *utgeng* (S 0, M 1)	7.19
72.	*semens*	*sædere* (S 0, M 1), *sawan* (S 0, M 1)	4.26
73.	*semita*	*geong* (S 0, M 1), *stiga* (S 0, M 1)	1.3
74.	*sepe*	*oftest* (S 0, M 1), *simble/symle* (S 0, M 1)	5.4
75.	*splendentia*	*lixan* (S 0, M 1), *scinan* (S 0, M 1)	9.3
76.	*splendor*	*leoht* (S 0, M 1), *scinnes* (S 0, M 1)	13.24
77.	*sternere*	*brædan* (S 0, M 1), *lecgan* (S 0, M 1)	11.8
78.	*stratus*	*bedd* (S 0, M 1), *sang* (S 0, M 1)	14.15
79.	*sufficere*	*wel lician* (S 0, M 1), *wel magan* (S 0, M 1)	14.41
80.	*titulus*	*mearc* (S 0, M 1), *tacn* (S 0, M 1), *titul* (S 0, M 1)	15.26
81.	*tunica*	*cyrtle* (S 0, M 1), *tunece* (S 0, M 1)	6.9
82.	*undique*	*æghwanan* (S 0, M 1), *from halfe æghwilc* (S 0, M 1)	1.45
83.	*velare*	*gehydan* (S 0, M 1), *wrigan* (S 0, M 1)	14.65

C.3 Unclear order

	Lemma	Interpretamenta	Relevant multiple gloss(es)
1.	*adhuc*	*get* (S 2, M 3), *geona* (S 1, M 3)	8.17, 14.43, 14.63
2.	*amplius*	*forþor* (S 2, M 3), *leng* (S 1, M 2)	9.8, 15.5
3.	*cogitare*	*smeagan* (S 3, M 2), *þencan* (S 1, M 2)	1.6, 2.8
4.	*cognoscere*	*ongietan* (S 6, M 2), *cnawan* (S 0, M 2)	2.8, 6.38
5.	*condemnare*	*hinan* (S 0, M 2), *niþerian* (S 0, M 2)	14.64, 16.16
6.	*dimittere* ('to forgive')	*forgiefan* (S 7, M 3), *forlætan* (S 0, M 3)	2.7, 3.28, 11.25
7.	*effundere*	*agietan* (S 1, M 2), *todælan* (S 0, M 2)	14.3, 14.24
8.	*eiectare*	*(for)drifan* (S 8, M 3), *(for/to)weorpan* (S 6, M 2)	1.39, 7.26
9.	*facere*[31]	*don* (S 47, M 6), *wyrcan* (S 12, M 6)	1.3, 4.32, 6.21, 7.12, 7.13, 11.17
10.	*forte*	*eaþe* (S 0, M 2), *wenunga* (S 0, M 2)	11.13, 14.2
11.	*iam*	*gea* (S 4, M 3), *soþ(lice)* (S 2, M 2)	8.2, 12.34
12.	*interrogare*	*frignan/frægnian* (S 25, M 4), *ascian* (S 1, M 3)	8.5, 13.3, 15.2
13.	*introire*	*(in)gan* (S 19, M 4), *(in)gangan* (S 0, M 5)	5.12, 8.26, 10.23, 11.2
14.	*manducare*	*etan* (S 17, M 3), *brucan* (S 3, M 3)	6.37, 6.44, 14.14
15.	*multus*	*manig* (S 38, M 4), *felan* (S 2, M 3)	5.26, 6.34, 12.41
16.	*omnis*	*eall* (S 66, M 2), *æghwilc* (S 3, M 3)	9.15, 16.15
17.	*profici*	*feran* (S 1, M 2), *faran* (S 0, M 2)	12.1, 16.20
18.	*reus*	*scyldig* (S 0, M 2), *synnig* (S 0, M 2)	3.29, 14.64
19.	*sequi*	*(æfter)fylgan* (S 22, M 4), *secan* (S 0, M 4)	2.14, 8.34, 10.21, 10.28
20.	*servus*	*esne* (S 1, M 2), *þræl* (S 1, M 2)	10.44, 10.47
21.	*stupere*	*swigian* (S 1, M 2), *styltan* (S 0, M 2)	1.22, 6.51
22.	*virtus*	*meaht* (S 10, M 2), *mægen* (S 2, M 2)	9.1, 13.25

31 On the overlap of OE *don* and *wyrcan*, see further Kotake (2007).

Patrizia Lendinara

The 'Unglossed' Words of the Lindisfarne Glosses

Abstract: The Old English glosses to the Gospels in London, British Library, MS Cotton Nero D.iv represent one of the largest interlinear apparatuses to a single Latin text in the vernacular. However, about one thousand words of the Latin text are left unglossed both in the Gospels and the prefatory material. The largest number of omissions concern proper names (personal names, place-names and ethnonyms), but also words such as *camelus* or *ventilabrum* were left unglossed whether always or just sometimes. This paper investigates the number and the distribution of these unglossed terms as well as their nature.

The vernacular apparatus to the Gospels in London, British Library, MS Cotton Nero D.iv is famous for its double, triple and even quadruple glosses (see Pons-Sanz, this volume). A number of Latin words, however, were not glossed at all and the reasons for these omissions need to be investigated.

Generally speaking, three different types of glossing strategy can be seen at work: a Latin word might be glossed throughout with an Old English word (albeit with a degree of variation in spelling and also as regards the word selected), a word might bear more than one gloss and, finally, a word might be left unglossed altogether.[1] Puzzlingly, the words of the text which were left without a gloss and those which received multiple glosses often coincide. Moreover, with the exception of proper names, the words left unglossed have a limited number of occurrences.

A detailed investigation of the codex and an examination of the words that were left unglossed in the Lindisfarne Gospels seem to rule out the possibility of errors or shortcomings on the part of the glossator, at least in the majority of cases. Instead, the glossator's decision to leave certain words unglossed emerges as one of the most interesting strategies employed by Aldred in his interlinear gloss.

1 There are a few instances in which a Latin word is glossed with either the same or a different Latin word; see below, pp. 347–348 and 354. In JnGl (Li) 20.16 *rabboni* is glossed by *.i. bonus doctor*; in MtGl (Li) 18.14 *caelis* is glossed by *caelis*, the verse containing the familiar words of the *Pater noster*. The title abbreviations and editions of the Old English texts mentioned in this paper are those employed by the *Dictionary of Old English Web Corpus* (hereafter *DOEC*).

1 The Old English glosses

London, British Library, MS Cotton Nero D.iv, a well-known and rightly famous late seventh- or early eighth-century manuscript of the Gospels,[2] was provided with continuous interlinear glosses in Old English in the second half of the tenth century. The Latin text of MS Cotton Nero D.iv was written by one Eadfrith, who was also responsible for the iconographic apparatus of the manuscript (see Gameson 2001b). The continuous gloss was added, probably before 970, by Aldred.[3] Despite having had much research devoted to its linguistic features and to its relationship to the Latin text, the Lindisfarne gloss awaits a new edition as we are still dependent on Skeat's nineteenth-century edition (Skeat 1871–1887; see Fernández Cuesta, this volume).

MS Cotton Nero D.iv is a high-status Gospel book. The text of this elaborate display copy of the Gospels belongs to the Vulgate Italo-Northumbrian group, marked by the *siglum* Ny by Fischer (1988–1991). The use that this sumptuous manuscript, with its illustrations, decorative lettering, beautiful initials, and ornate display script, was put to is still far from certain. The vernacular interlinear glosses added by Aldred are also carefully inserted and provide a fine match for the beautifully laid-out Latin text.

The gloss did not spoil the outward appearance of the codex but rather enhanced its magnificence. Nor did the addition of the glosses alter the use of the manuscript, which was possibly kept with the altar equipment. The codex, which might have been used for reading at mass on major festivals (see Brown 1960: 42–43; Backhouse 1981: 22; and Lenker 1997: 387–389), was not used for instruction in Latin and was not a library book.

The purpose and function of the gloss are also uncertain. As with other interlinear glosses occurring in Anglo-Saxon manuscripts, these were to be read along with the Latin and could not be divorced from the text beneath. Analysis of the omission of glosses yields further proof of the ancillary character of interlinear glosses and highlights, should that be necessary, the difference between a gloss, even a continuous gloss, and a translation (but see Stanton 2002: 50–52).

Aldred did not confine his work on MS Cotton Nero D.iv to the glosses; he also added about seventy explanatory annotations to the manuscript (see Boyd 1975a). There is general agreement that Aldred alone was responsible for writing

2 See Ker (1957: no. 165), Gneuss and Lapidge (2014: no. 343), and Kendrick et al. (1956 and 1960) for a description and analysis of the codex, as well as the full facsimile.

3 For further discussion of the colophon at the end of John's Gospel on f. 259r, see Brown (2003: 102–103), Roberts (2006) and Brown (this volume).

the whole of the Lindisfarne gloss (see Ross et al. 1960: 20–21).[4] His 'scribal preferences' have been the object of several studies (see Brunner 1947–1948: 32–52; and van Bergen 2008: 275–312). Moreover, it has been remarked how his spelling changed over time and how the new spelling practices, in some cases, were maintained in his gloss to the Durham Collectar (see Ross 1970: 363–366).

On the other hand, it has been surmised that Aldred either employed a pre-existing manuscript accompanied by glosses (see Ross et al. 1960: 11) or made use of earlier material available in the form of either a glossed text or one or more versions of the Gospels in prose.[5] This would provide an answer to the doubts which have been raised on the authorship of the entire gloss. It is hard to imagine that Aldred had no draft of the glosses available to him when he added them so carefully to the manuscript. The balance of their layout and the scant evidence of hesitation bear witness to his use of a pre-existing gloss, which he may have drafted himself.

The nature of several omissions, which are far from random, also speaks in favour of a process of copying (which prompted the omission of glosses, both deliberate and otherwise) rather than of an impromptu rendering of the Latin. In a number of instances, when a place-name bears a gloss, Aldred copied the preposition *in* quite close to the place-name it referred to, and at times the preposition is actually affixed to it.[6] The possible copying from one text (the draft) to another (the Lindisfarne manuscript), progressing word by word, as well as phrase by phrase, produces, on the one hand, the copying of preposition plus noun as a single word, and, on the other, the omission of the preposition preceding the place-name in the original when the latter is left unglossed, as is the case in LkGl (Li) 4.27, where neither *in* nor *israhel* are glossed (f. 149v).[7]

4 Involvement of other hands in the gloss should not be entirely ruled out, though. See Cole (this volume) also on the authorship of the gloss.

5 The use of an Old English exemplar (which might also have been used by Farman) for the Passion text in Matthew 26–27 has been convincingly surmised by Kotake (2012: 14–19); see also Kotake (2009). A number of clues as regards the use of a translation of John's Gospel by Bede were put forward by Ross (1969: 482–494 and 1973: 519–521) and Elliott and Ross (1972: 49–72).

6 See, for example, "ingalilea" in MkGl (Li) 15.41 (f. 128v); "ongalilea" in LkGl (Li) 2.39 (f. 145r); "inhierusalem" in LkGl (Li) 2.42 (f. 145r); and "inhierusalem" in LkGl (Li) 2.45 (f. 145v).

7 The preposition *in* is left unglossed also when it precedes either personal names or common words which were not glossed by Aldred: see LiProlMt (Skeat) 10 and 12 (ff. 6v and 7r); MtArgGl (Li) 1 and 2 (f. 18v); MtHeadGl (Li) 6 (f. 19v); MtGl (Li) 2.5 (f. 30v), 4.13 (f. 33r), 9.9 (f. 42v), 17.22 (f. 62r), 21.8 (f. 68v), 27.6 (f. 85r); MkArgGl (Li) 5 (f. 90v); MkHeadGl (Li) 41 (f. 93v); MkGl (Li) 4.17 (f. 101v); LkHeadGl (Li) 84 (f. 136r); LkGl (Li) 2.34 (f. 144v), 4.27 (f. 149v), 11.15 (f. 168v), 11.18 (f. 168v), 12.28 (f. 172v), 17.4 (f. 182r) and 21.1 (f. 191v).

It is quite certain that Aldred made use of Latin manuscripts other than Lindisfarne.[8] Old English glosses that matched Latin readings drawn from a codex other than Lindisfarne would have been incorporated while the gloss was being drafted, not at the copying stage. In JnGl (Li) 4.26, *ego sum qui loquar tibi* ('I am he, who am speaking with thee') of the Latin text is glossed by "ðe ic spreco ðec mið"; "ðec mið" is the usual way in which Aldred glosses L *tecum*,[9] unlike other Old English interlinear glosses.[10] This means that the Latin text of John used by Aldred had the common variant reading *qui loquar tecum* (other attested variants are *qui loquor tecum* / *qui loquitur tecum*). The gloss "ðec mið" (as well as "mec mið" for L *mecum*, "usig mið" for L *nobiscum*, and "iowih mið" for L *vobiscum*) might be counted among the features of Aldred's idiolect.

Aldred followed the Latin text with great faithfulness. In a number of instances, when he encountered errors in the Latin text, he did not correct the mistake but glossed it by using the corresponding Old English word. For example, in MtGl (Li) 15.5 (f. 57r), *manus* (Vulgate *munus*) is glossed as "hond" (see Ross 1932a: 385–394 and 1933b: 110).[11] Also in the case of unique or rare readings of the Latin (different from the *textus receptus*) he followed faithfully the Latin text of the Lindisfarne Gospels. These features also prove that he drew up his draft copy of the glosses using the Lindisfarne Gospels as his main source and afterwards copied them into MS Cotton Nero D.iv at a steady pace which allowed no

8 See Ross (1932a: 392–394) and Kotake (this volume). For the manuscripts to which Aldred might have had access, see Ross (1981: 8–9). For a list of the Latin manuscripts of the Gospels in Chester-le-Street, see Verey (1989: 143–150). Some manuscripts might indeed have been lost.

9 See, only in John's Gospel, JnGl (Li) 3.26, 4.26, 9.37 and 21.3. For other glosses by Aldred, see HyGl 1 (Thomp-Lind) 11.3 and DurRitGl 1 (Thomp-Lind) 2.9. On the other hand, L *tibi* is regularly glossed by "ðe" by Aldred: e.g. JnGl (Li) 1.50, 2.4, 3.5, 3.7, 3.11, 4.10, 5.10, 5.12, 5.14, 6.30, 9.26, 9.26, 11.22, 11.40, 11.41, 13.38, 16.30, 18.30, 18.34, 19.11, 19.11 and 21.18; and on a few occasions by "to him" (e.g. JnGl (Li) 3.3) or "to ðe" (JnGl (Li) 4.10). Translations of the Latin text of the Bible rely on the *Douay-Rheims Bible*.

10 *Tecum* is often rendered as "mid þe"; see, for instance, ÆGram 108.8, Abbo 101.1; PsGlH (Campbell) 72.23; ArPrGl 1 (Holt-Campb) 17.74 and 40.46; and HyGl 2 (Milfull) 11.3.

11 A case like this needs special consideration and should be examined in the light of the Vulgate manuscripts available to Aldred. Aldred avoided making corrections to any reading which he knew to be wrong, especially when the Old English gloss available in his draft confirmed that reading. The contrary is also true: Aldred sometimes wrote the correct Old English rendering above a corrupt reading that mismatches it (e.g. *optimam patrem* [*recte partem*] is glossed as "gecoren dæl" in LkGl (Li) 10.42, f. 167v), and the manuscript features a number of corrections of both the Latin text and the Old English glosses (by either addition or deletion, by erasure or dotting either above or below the letters(s)). There are instances when the same hand adds a word missing from the text (usually at the end of line of the manuscript's column), apparently to provide a match for the Old English gloss written above: e.g. on f. 115v, the word *deus* (which is glossed above as "god") is added at the end of MkGl (Li) 10.18.

scope for second thoughts. The many incomplete double glosses bear witness to Aldred's intention to add a second gloss later.[12] Multiple glosses may differ in case, gender, word choice, and expand either the grammar or the vocabulary, but do not correct one another. In the prologue to the Gospels (LiEpis (Skeat) 3), for example, "ða salt wælla ł of saltwælla" ('the salt spring or of the salt spring') for *saliba* 'spittle' are both wrong.[13]

2 The Old English gloss to the Rushworth Gospels

The relationship between the Lindisfarne glosses and the interlinear glosses in Old English to the Rushworth Gospels has aroused much interest since Stevenson (1854–1865: I) printed this gloss in the apparatus of his edition of Lindisfarne. Oxford, Bodleian Library, MS Auct. D.2.19 was written at Birr, Ireland, around 800 (see Ker 1957: no. 292; Liuzza and Doane 1995: no. 206; and Gneuss and Lapidge 2014: no. 531), while its Old English gloss was added by Farman and Owun in the tenth century. The Latin text is different from that of Lindisfarne; it includes many Old Latin readings and does not belong to the same family of Vulgate manuscripts.[14] The codices were copied in two different scriptoria and were brought into physical contact in the second half of the tenth century. There is some agreement that the scriptorium where this contact took place was that of Chester-le-Street, but many aspects of the relationship between the two glosses' apparatuses are still far from being settled.

Farman is the author of the gloss in Mercian to Matthew's Gospel, and to some verses of Mark's Gospel (Mark 1–2.15) and John's Gospel (John 18.1–3) (Ru^1). According to Ross (1979: 194–198), Ru^1 should be divided into two parts: from the beginning to MtGl (Ru) 26.7, and the remainder of Ru^1, the latter having been influenced by Lindisfarne.[15] The part of MS Auct. D.2.19 glossed by Owun (Ru^2) in

12 Ross and Squires (1980: 490) write that there are 1147 double glosses in the Lindisfarne interlinear glosses and remark that "[t]he *raison d'être* of the incomplete glosses is obscure; did Aldred mean to return and fill them in?". For the typology of multiple glosses, see Kornexl (1993: ccxxii–ccxxiv).

13 The manuscript form *saliba* for L *saliva* is attested in Late antiquity; see Souter (1949: s.v. *salib-*) and Lendinara (2010: 168–169). OE *sealtwylle* used by Aldred in the double gloss rather renders L *salinae* 'saltworks, saltpits'.

14 The Latin text of Rushworth (Fischer's Hr) belongs to the "mixed Irish family of the Vulgate", with many Old Latin renderings. See also Glunz (1930: 14) and Kotake (this volume).

15 However, as far as MtGl (Ru) 26–27 is concerned, Kotake (2012) has detected a common textual tradition behind the two interlinear glosses.

Northumbrian also reflects the possible use of Lindisfarne as a source (see Lindelöf 1897, and 1901).

Ru[1] bears many unique features that are relatively rare in interlinear glosses (see Menner 1934: 25–26).[16] Farman's gloss is marked by considerable freedom of translation. The deviations from the Latin are numerous, especially as far as word order is concerned (although Farman's exemplar might have been an even freer translation which he intentionally corrected; see Kotake 2010). Farman's practice changed during the process of glossing and the gloss to Matthew is much more idiosyncratic than that to Mark. Moreover, a number of his Old English glosses are based on readings of a purer Vulgate (rather than on the readings of the Rushworth manuscript; see Schulte 1903).

The glosses written by Owun were significantly influenced by Aldred's gloss.[17] Owun makes a number of mistakes, which are occasionally due to a miscopying of Lindisfarne. He had a tendency to simplify Aldred's multiple glosses and also used a number of different words (some belonging to the same word family). His adherence to the Latin, as far as the word order is concerned, varies, and in general the Latin text of Rushworth tends to affect Owun's use of the Lindisfarne gloss.[18]

3 The unglossed words

The majority of the unglossed words in Lindisfarne are anthroponyms (e.g. *Maria*, *Martha*, *Pilatus*), toponyms (e.g. *Sidon*, *Tyrus*), and ethnonyms.[19] There are also cases of unglossed words that do not belong to these specific categories. These include words for festivals (*azyma* 'the Jewish feast of unleavened bread', *parasceve* 'the day of preparation, the day before the Sabbath'), offices (*tetrarcha* 'tetrarch'), buildings (*teloneum* 'toll booth, custom house'), animals (*camelus* 'camel', *scorpio* 'scorpion'), textiles (*sindon* 'shroud, cloth of fine linen'), and

16 According to Menner (1934: 21), Farman had another Latin text which was not necessarily accompanied by an Old English gloss.

17 See Ross (1981), and Bibire and Ross (1981). On the dependence of Ru[2] on Lindisfarne, see Kotake (2008a, 2008b, and this volume).

18 Part of the Lindisfarne vocabulary is examined and compared to the rest of the Old English corpus by Wenisch (1979). On the dialect of the gloss, see Schabram (1965: 61–62) and Hofstetter (1987: 479–485).

19 The question of unglossed words was briefly dealt with by Ross (1933b) and has been reexamined by Pons-Sanz (2001).

everyday objects mentioned in the Gospels (*clibanus* 'oven', *ventilabrum* 'winnowing shovel').[20]

Aldred tends to leave unglossed the words for which he would have used either a loanword or a transcription from Latin, thereby repeating almost verbatim the lemma. He probably deemed it irrelevant to offer a lexical substitution when this substitution would have been opaque and redundant. An unbroken set of glosses would have encumbered the layout of the manuscript, allowing space for the interlinear gloss, whereas it was the Latin text that mattered and was to be given prominence. According to this interpretation, the words left unglossed play the same role as either the abbreviated glosses or the so-called 'run-on' glosses. Aldred does not overburden the pages of the codex while providing the relevant information needed.

Omissions were not slips of the eye: in LkGl (Li) 12.28, as far as the gloss to *in clibanum* ('into the oven') is concerned, both *in* and *clibanum* were left unglossed (f. 172v). On the other hand, when proper names in a list were all left unglossed, Aldred took care to copy the abbreviation for the conjunction, "⁊", over each "et" of the Latin, possibly to keep a constant eye on his gloss and compel the reader to look at both lines. Only in a few instances did Aldred omit the gloss to words which had just been glossed. In this choice, Aldred's glossing technique is in direct opposition to the performance of a translation.[21]

A complete analysis of the manuscript confirmed that there is no codicological constraint whatsoever for the omission of the vernacular glosses.[22] As mentioned above, Aldred was quite conscientious in copying them. At the same time, he accomplished his task with a good deal of inventiveness, as the layout of the glosses shows. The glosses were also segmented and copied alongside the

---

20 As far as words such as these are concerned, Nagucka (1997: 196) explains the omission of a gloss as the result of its "semantic complexity or not immediate comprehensibility". Nagucka also attributes the omissions to the fact that "no English corresponding word was yet available". The latter reason is debatable.

21 By the same token, the substitution of a word by an Old English pronoun is very rare in the extant glossed texts, but we do have some examples in the Lindisfarne glosses: in LkGl (Li) 18.11 *pharisaeus* (which is the first word of the verse) is glossed by "se" ('that (one)'; f. 184v), while in LkGl (Li) 19.39 *quidam pharisaeorum* ('some of the Pharisees') is glossed by "sumo ðara" ('some of those/them'; f. 188r).

22 The only exceptions I can point out are the following: in f. 141v (LkGl (Li) 1.55) there is no space left over *abraham* (owing to the peculiar way the word is written at the end of the line, with *ra* copied above *hā* and the left limb of *r* extending to reach the baseline); in f. 142v (LkGl (Li) 1.72) the word *nostris* is added below the line (which is the last line of the first column), allowing no space for the gloss; in f. 235v (JnGl (Li) 9.40) *ei* is written below the line (which is the last of the second column), its letters being copied vertically and leaving no possible space for the gloss. On the availability of the manuscript online, see n. 6 in the Introduction.

vertical strokes of the large capitals (e.g. "cne/ure/suu/ ł cyn/nres/uu" at f. 19r) or widely spaced to match the width of the letters in the rubricated incipit and explicit of the Latin text.[23]

As far as the Lindisfarne manuscript is concerned, there is no interference between the capital letters and the glosses, which were adroitly combined. There are occasions when Aldred realized that there were errors and omissions in the Latin text, leading him to correct the Latin text and skilfully incorporate the corrections into the Old English gloss.[24] The gloss is written with great care but, at the same time, exhibits a remarkable degree of freedom. The glossator had much space to make use of, and, as far as the distance from the Latin line is concerned, he allowed himself some liberty when glossing the first line of each column. In these cases, the distance between the Old English gloss and the Latin text varies and is wider than in the following lines when the glossator was compelled to respect the distance between the lines of the Latin. In the case of double glosses, the second gloss is sometimes written over the first gloss, utilizing the upper margin of the folio (e.g. "grex : suner ł edo", 'herd of swine or herd', f. 42r). In a few cases, the lower margin is also used in the case of a double gloss to copy the second part of the gloss beginning with "ł" (e.g. JnGl (Li) 14.2, f. 243v). In Matthew's Gospel, there are a few instances where the gloss is written below the Latin in lines which are not the last ones of the column (e.g. ff. 36v and 54v).

Glosses were written starting from the beginning of the Latin word or were centred over the word beneath. In some cases, owing to the length of the vernacular words themselves (and/or the use of double and triple glosses), the last part of the gloss was copied to the right of the Latin text, either in the space between the two columns of the text, which are quite widely spaced, or in the right margin of the folio. The gloss regularly exceeds the length of its lemma when this is one of the *nomina sacra*; in all these cases the unabbreviated native word necessarily exceeds the abbreviated form of the Latin.

23 The ruling techniques of Anglo-Saxon manuscripts containing interlinearly glossed Latin texts have not yet been the object of an overall assessment. As far as Lindisfarne is concerned, Brown (2005: 117) remarks that the OE glosses were "inserted with care and sensitivity to the original layout [...], the generous ruling of which accommodated the minute minuscule glossing scripts". Whereas the Latin text is written between two ruled lines, there is no ruling for the glosses, which are also written in the margins and between the two columns of the text. The same can be said about the Rushworth Gospels and eight of the complete interlinear versions of the psalter, with the exception of the Winchcombe Psalter (Cambridge, University Library, MS Ff.1.23) and the Stowe Psalter (London, British Library, MS Stowe 2).

24 Ross et al. (1960: 21) suggest that "[t]here can be little doubt that these alterations were made *pari passu* with the writing of the Gloss, since they mostly exhibit exactly the same changes in the colour of the ink as does the Gloss itself".

In John's Gospel, the native gloss is usually centred above the Latin word; in cases of double glosses, the first gloss is followed by "ł", whereas the second gloss is copied in the right margin (or between the two columns). The last gloss of a line overspills into the folio margin and is often copied at some distance from the Latin word it glosses; in the majority of cases, this choice is not dictated by space restrictions. The second word of double glosses is also copied in the right margin when its lemma is not the last word of the line of the Latin text. In some instances (e.g. JnGl (Li) 15.13, f. 246r), a *signe de renvoi* is needed.

When writing a double gloss, Aldred begins the first element at the same height as the Latin word and is sometimes compelled, when the word occurs in the *a*-column of the folio, to split the double gloss and copy the latter part (either preceded or not by "ł") on the left margin of the text, hence inverting the two members of the doublet.

Examination of the palaeographical evidence did not provide any *de facto* reason for skipping a gloss (lack of space, overflowing Latin text, holes or creases in the folio). For example, proper names, the largest category of words to be left without a gloss, are left unglossed either at the beginning of a verse, at the end, or midway, despite there being always ample space for a gloss to be written above the Latin. Interestingly, at the beginning of Matthew 27.20, "*princeps autem* : ðe aldormonn" (f. 85v), Aldred already seems to know that *autem* will not bear a gloss (as is often the case with L *autem* in Lindisfarne, but also in other interlinear glosses in Old English) and allows himself a bit more space for the two glosses to *princeps* which extend interlinearly above the Latin.

3.1 Proper names

Among the categories of words frequently left unglossed, the highest percentage pertains to proper names (both personal names and place-names). According to Pons-Sanz's estimates, "approx. 22 %" of proper names "are left completely unglossed".[25] The highest number of omissions occur in Luke 3.24–38. These omissions are probably due to the similarity between the Latin form and its likely

25 Pons-Sanz (2001: 180) excludes from her reckoning the names *Iesus*, *Christus* and *Dominus*, which are never left unglossed in the Gospels (see below). The prefatory material features a few instances in which *Christus* is left unglossed. The proper names with a high percentage of instances where Aldred leaves them unglossed are those of the four Evangelists in the prefatory material to Matthew. The names *Johannes* (John the Baptist), *Maria*, and *Petrus* are frequently left unglossed. For further discussion of *Petrus*, see Lendinara (1999b: 53–55).

Old English rendering.[26] A comparison with other Old English texts confirms the circulation of these names and their relative stability. As far as the 78 % of personal names that do bear a gloss are concerned, Pons-Sanz (2001: 180) suggests that "8.2 % are glossed by a generic noun, and 1.44 % are rendered by a personal name and the generic noun together". In all the remaining cases, proper names are glossed by either the respective Latin form of the name, or by the Old English variant which is more similar to the Latin one. In a number of instances, Aldred does not follow the spelling of proper names in Lindisfarne, but that of other Latin manuscripts.[27] Personal names are frequently indicated by means of abbreviations, which are in part exclusive to the Lindisfarne glosses (see Ross 1943: 316–317).

The words *Iesus*, *Christus* and *Dominus* always bear a gloss.[28] They are consistently abbreviated in Latin with the standard combination of letters used in the text (see Traube 1907).[29] Just the reverse happens with the Old English glosses which are always spelled out. Moreover *Iesus* is constantly glossed by (*ðe/se*) *hælend*, *Christus* by *Crist*,[30] and *Dominus* by either *drihten* or *hælend*.

Ross (1933b: 108) judged the way in which Aldred glossed proper names highly successful, the more so because his gloss provided the reader with information about the meaning of particular names. However, the exegetical contribution of Aldred's glosses should not be overstated because the interpretations of Biblical proper names supplied in the place of the names themselves are usually commonplaces.[31] Also the Old English glosses provided for *Satanas*, *Belzebub*, and *Mammona* employ widespread interpretations: for instance, *Satanas* is regularly glossed by (*se/ðe*) *wiðerwearda* 'the adversary' (15x),[32] which is combined, in MtGl (Li) 12.26, with *wiðerbreca* 'adversary'; Aldred's choice has a counterpart,

26 Further evidence of this assertion occurs in MkGl (Li) 16.9 (*mariae magdalene*), where *mariae* is left unglossed and *magdalene* is glossed by "ðær magðalenesca" (f. 129v).

27 See, for example, "elizabeth" glossing *elisabet* in LkGl (Li) 1.5 and 1.13 (ff. 139v and 140r). For the spelling of proper names in relation to the Latin texts used by Aldred, see Ross (1958).

28 The few exceptions, as far as *Christus* is concerned, pertain to the prefatory material, the headings (5x) and JnGl (Li) 6.69, where the word is left without a gloss.

29 For the *nomina sacra*, their significance and possible origin, see Comfort (2005: 199–254) and Hurtado (2006).

30 There are two exceptions in John's Gospel: in JnGl (Li) 7.41 *christus* is glossed as "cynig" ('king'; f. 228r), and in JnGl (Li) 9.22 *christum* is glossed as "crist ł ðone cynig" ('Christ or the king'; f. 233r).

31 The same can be said, with a few exceptions, of the marginal comments by Aldred, which are examined by Boyd (1975a). For the sophisticated interest of Anglo-Saxon writers in proper names, see Robinson (1968).

32 The Lindisfarne and Rushworth glosses, when decontextualized, are quoted under the first form of the lemma in Clark Hall (1960).

among others, in the First Corpus Glossary: "*Satanan* : *adversarius*" (CorpGl 1 (Hessels) 285).

In a number of cases the gloss combines the proper name and the apposition which explains either degrees of kinship or the office or trade of the person in question. OE *witega* was used to typify the names of prophets,[33] and a generic noun such as *ðegn* either accompanies or substitutes the names of the disciples. See, for example:

Annas : Anna biscop 'Annas the high priest' (JnGl (Li) 18.24)
Caiaphae : Caifas ðæs aldormonnes 'Caiaphas the high officer' (JnGl (Li) 18.13)
Caiapha : Caifa biscope 'Caiaphas the high priest' (JnGl (Li) 18.28)
Racab : ðæm wife 'the wife' (MtGl (Li) 1.5)
Esaias : Esaias ðe uitga 'Isaias the prophet' (JnGl (Li) 12.39, 12.41)[34]
Herodes : se cynig 'the king' (LkGl (Li) 9.7, 9.9)[35]
Nicodemo : ðæm ðegne 'the noble' (e.g. JnHeadGl (Li) 6, 19)
Nicodemus : Nicodimus se aldormonn 'Nicodemus the high officer' (e.g. JnGl (Li) 3.4)
Nicodemus : se ðegn Nicodemus 'the noble Nicodemus' (JnGl (Li) 19.39)
Thomas : in ebreisc ðe embehtmonn 'in Hebrew the attendant' (JnGl (Li) 20.24)[36]
Thomas : ðe ðegn 'the disciple' (JnGl (Li) 21.2).

Slightly different is the case of *Barabbas*, which is twice rendered by *morsceaða* 'robber'. In Matthew's Gospel, *Barabbas* is left unglossed on five occasions (MtGl (Li) 27.16, 27.17, 27.20, 27.21, 27.26). In Mark's Gospel, *Barabbas* is glossed "barabbas" on its first occurrence (MkGl (Li) 15.7) and then, not long after in the text, twice with "ðone morsceaðe/morsceaðo" ('robber'; MkGl (Li) 15.11, 15.15). In Luke's and John's Gospels, *Barabbas* is glossed "barabbas" (LkGl (Li) 23.18, and JnGl (Li) 18.40). In the corresponding passages, the Rushworth Gospels feature different choices:[37] in MtGl (Ru) 27.16, 27.17, 27.20, MkGl (Ru) 15.11, LkGl (Ru) 23.18 and JnGl (Ru) 18.40, *Barabbas/Barrabas* is glossed "barabbas/barrabas"; in MtGl

---

33 In these instances, Aldred either models his glosses on the Biblical tags (e.g. *anna prophetissa* is glossed by "anna ðio uitga", 'Anna the prophetess', in LkGl (Li) 2.36, f. 145r) or substitutes the proper name with a generic gloss, using OE *witega*.

34 Esaias is accompanied by *propheta* (rendered by OE *witega*) in MtGl (Li) 3.3 and 4.14. In JnGl (Li) 1.23 *esaias propheta* is glossed by "witega". The proper name, not followed by the apposition in the Latin, is left unglossed in MtGl (Li) 15.7 and MkGl (Li) 7.6, where the verb *prophetare* occurs.

35 Out of a total of 29 occurences, *Herodes* is glossed (24x), unglossed (3x) and rendered by "se cynig" (2x). In this case the model is the Gospel phrase *Herodes rex*.

36 See MacGillivray (1902: 42–51) for the meaning of *ambihtmann* in the Lindisfarne and Rushworth glosses; see also Wenisch (1979: 131–132).

37 Relevant readings from the Rushworth Gospels will be quoted for the sake of comparison only in a few cases.

(Ru) 27.21, 27.26, and MkGl (Ru) 15.7 it is left unglossed.[38] Aldred's treatment of the name *Pilatus* (*Pontius Pilatus*) may be taken as representative of his glossing methods as far as proper names are concerned. *Pylatus* is recorded in the Gospels and the *capitula* (52x), and it is glossed as follows: "pylatus" (13x),[39] "geroefa" (5x), "gerefa" (1x), "groefa" (16x), "greofa" (1x), "ealdormann" (1x), unglossed (15x). In the first occurrence of the word, in MtGl (Li) 27.2, the proper name is left unglossed, but, in the same verse, Aldred anticipates his preferential use of *gerefa*,[40] introducing the word (an alternative to *undercyning*) as a gloss to L *praeses* (said of Pilate): *et tradiderunt pontio pilato praesidi* is rendered as "⁊ agefon ... ... ðæm undercynige ł geroefa" (MtGl (Li) 27.2). In this verse Aldred does not provide a gloss for *Pontius* either, refraining from using the adjective *pontisc*, which is employed in the corresponding verse of Rushworth and elsewhere in Old English texts.[41] His choice, at the very first occurrence of the proper name, which is also one of two cases where the name of Pilate is accompanied by his family name, shows that Aldred preferred to refer his readers to the Latin text rather than provide a redundant and possibly mistaken rendering.[42]

The omission of proper names is well attested in the Old English interlinear glosses, including the glosses to hymns and prayers. One of the Arundel prayers omits both the name of Elijah and Enoch and also the conjunction: *Recipe me sicut recepisti heliam et enoh in secreta beatae requiei habitacula* is rendered as "underfoh swa þu underfunge ... ... on digle eadigre reste eardungstowa" (ArPr 1 (Holt-Campb) 45.25). The same happens, for example, in *Ymnus ad matutinam* in Durham, Cathedral Library, MS B.iii.32: *hostis herodes impie, Christum venire quid times?* is rendered as "feond, *s. o.*, arlease crist cuman to hwi ondrædst þu" (HyGl 2 (Milfull) 45.1).

As far as proper names are concerned, Aldred employs a peculiar strategy in the *Prologus .X. canonum*, where a few proper names are not glossed by a more or

38 OE *morsceaða* occurs only in Lindisfarne and Rushworth, where it also glosses *latro* (7x): Mt (Li) 26.55, 27.38, 27.44; Mk (Li) 15.27; Lk (Li/Ru) 23.33, 23.39; Jn (Li) 18.40. See Wenisch (1979: 272, 325). In Mk (Li) 15.11 and Mk (Li/Ru) 15.15, *morsceaða* glosses *barabban*.

39 In the last three occurrences in Matthew the proper name is glossed as "pylatus", with a spelling that is also used in Rushworth and occurs for the first time in MtGl (Li) 27.2. The personal name is left unglossed on five occasions.

40 The high frequency of "groefa" in John's Gospel is striking. For further discussion of this form, see Pons-Sanz (2000: 108–109).

41 The *DOEC* records 14 occurrences, one of which in Rushworth (MtGl (Ru) 27.2) and two in the West Saxon Gospels (Mt (WSCp) 27.2 and Lk (WSCp) 3.1).

42 It is tempting to surmise that OE *pontisc* was invented on the basis of Pontus, the region in Asia Minor, afterwards a Roman province, rather than of the *Pontii*, a Roman *gens*, originally Samnites.

less Anglicized counterpart, but, rather, by the addition of "ceorles noma" placed above the proper name, see e.g. "*aquila* : ceorles noma" (LiEpis (Skeat) 8).[43] This glossarial strategy is abandoned by Aldred after the prologue and never used in the gloss to the Gospels, but can be compared to a similar kind of glosses which occur in the Salisbury Psalter. As in other interlinear glosses, proper names are often left unglossed in this psalter, but in several instances the glossator wrote "n" (and once "na"), standing for either OE *nama* or L *nomen*, over a proper name to point out the nature of the word beneath to his readers. For example, in the glosses to the psalter in Salisbury, Cathedral Library, MS 150 *zabulon* is glossed by "na" (PsGlK (Sisam) 67.28), and *nepthalim* by "n" (PsGlK (Sisam) 67.28), whereas *beniamin*, the first proper name of the verse, is left unglossed (PsGlK (Sisam) 67.28). In Psalm 79.3, *ephraim*, *beniamin* and *manasse* all bear the gloss "n" (PsGlK (Sisam) 79.3). This kind of glosses, which point out the grammatical nature of a word rather than providing an equivalent in Old English, might stem from teaching techniques employed to elucidate a Latin text. Moreover the example from Jerome's Prologue to Matthew's Gospel (see above) pertains to a proper name which could be misunderstood and taken for the substantive *aquila* 'eagle'.

3.2 Place-names and ethnonyms

The treatment of place-names is in some respects analogous to that of personal names,[44] although place-names tend to be glossed more often and the total number of their occurrences is much lower than that of personal names. For example, the word *nazareth* is left unglossed in MtGl (Li) 2.23 and LkGl (Li) 1.26; in MtGl (Li) 21.11, within the noun phrase *nazaret galilææe*, the place-name itself is left unglossed but *galilææe* is glossed as "geliornessa".[45] Otherwise this place-name is glossed as "natzareð" (MtGl (Li) 4.13), "nazareth" (MkGl (Li) 1.9, and LkGl (Li) 2.4, 2.39, 2.51, 4.16), and "natzareth" (JnGl (Li) 1.46, f. 213v). In two occurrences, the generic name *burg* 'town' is provided instead of the place-name: "ða burg" (MtHeadGl (Li) 8) and "ðær byrig" (JnGl (Li) 1.45). Ru[1] and Ru[2] do not

43 See also "*simmachus* : ceorles noma" (LiEpis (Skeat) 8), "*theodotion* : ceorles noma" (LiEpis (Skeat) 8), as well the supplementary gloss to *luciano et hesychio*, i.e. "lucianus ⁊ hesichio : twoe cearla noma" (LiEpis (Skeat) 11). Another similar gloss occurs in the Prologue to Matthew: "*cerinthi hebionis* : ceorles noma ceorles noma" (LiProlMt (Skeat) 12).

44 According to Pons-Sanz (2001: 5) "approximately 18 % of the place-names [...] have been left completely unglossed, whereas some gloss has been provided for the rest: either some form of the name (70.7 %), a generic noun instead of the proper name [...] (24.7 %) or both (4.5 %)".

45 OE *geleorednes* means 'departure, transmigration, death' and matches the interpretation of the Hebrew name, according to which *Galilea* means *transmigratio*.

feature the generic rendering *burg* except in MkGl (Ru) 1.9, and use the glosses "nazareþ", "nazaret", "nazareð", and "nazareth", omitting the gloss in LkGl (Ru) 1.26 and 2.4 (JnGl (Ru) 1.46 has a major omission at this point). Moreover, in LkGl (Ru) 2.39 *in civitatem suam nazareth* is glossed "in cæstre his nazarenes".

Aldred demonstrates his familiarity with a number of variant spellings of the place-names of the Gospels otherwise attested in Old English, and also with alternative names such as the Syriac reading *ramtha* for *Arimathia*. For example, *Arimathia* is left unglossed in MtGl (Li) 27.57, glossed by "arimathia" in MkGl (Li) 15.43 and LkGl (Li) 23.51, and by "arimaðia byrig ł ramattha" in JnGl (Li) 19.38. Rushworth has the form "arimaðia" in MtGl (Ru) 27.57, whereas the word is left unglossed in MkGl (Ru) 15.43. Besides *Nazareth* and *Arimathia*, town names occasionally left unglossed include *Bethlem*, *Capharnaum*, *Hierusalem/Hierosolyma*, *Tyrus*, *Sodom*, and *Sidon*.

The use of *burg* in addition to the place-name is quite frequent: e.g. "*bethania* : to ðær byrig" (LkGl (Li) 19.29); "*bethlehem iudeae* : ðær byrig" (MtGl (Li) 2.1); "*ad bethsaidam* : to ðær byrig" (MkGl (Li) 6.45);[46] "*in cana galilaeae* : in ðær byrig" (JnGl (Li) 2.11); "*capharnaum* : ða burug" (JnGl (Li) 2.12);[47] "*hiericho* : in ða burug" (MkGl (Li) 10.46); "*hierosolyma* : ða burug" (JnGl (Li) 2.13); "*in sareptha sidonæ* : in ðær byrig" (LkGl (Li) 4.26); "*in siloam* : in ðær byrig" (LkGl (Li) 13.4).[48]

Another feature of Aldred's glossing technique that stands out is his use of the phrase *þæt is* 'that is', which translates L *id est* and is frequently attested in the interpretamenta of glosses. Renderings include "*bethsaida* : ðæt is burug" (JnGl (Li) 5.2), "*capharnaum* : þæt is burg" (LkGl (Li) 10.15), and "*corazain* : þæt is burug" (LkGl (Li) 10.13). Aldred also makes some mistakes: *Decapolis*, which is the name of a group of ten cities on the eastern frontier of the Roman Empire, is glossed by *burg* 'town': "*decapolim* : of ðær byrig" (MtGl (Li) 4.25); "*decapoli* : in ðær byrig" (MkGl (Li) 5.20). Well known is the case of *in rama*, glossed by "in tuigga" (MtGl (Li) 2.18), where the place-name *Ramah* was evidently mistaken for *ramus* 'branch'.[49]

The same pattern applies to Aldred's renderings of the names of regions, such as *Galilaea* or *Idumea*: these are either left unglossed or glossed by words

---

46 See also "*bethsaida galilaeae* : bethsaida galilees byrig galilees" (JnGl (Li) 12.21).

47 In Lindisfarne, *Capharnaum* is hardly ever glossed by the respective proper name, which occurs only in MkGl (Li) 1.21 and 2.1 accompanied by *burg*, and in LkGl (Li) 4.31, where the Latin has *in capharnaum civitatem galileae*, which is glossed by "in capharnaum ceastra galilies". See also "*in capharnaum maritimam* : þæt is sæburug" (MtGl (Li) 4.13). OE *sæ-burg* 'seaport town' is a hapax legomenon.

48 But see "*in natatoria siloae quod interpretatur* : *in* ðær uele þæt is getractat ł" (JnGl (Li) 9.7); "*ad natatoriam siloae :* to ðæm pole ł" (JnGl (Li) 9.11).

49 Aldred's mistake was first pointed out by Ross (1932a: 391).

such as OE *mægð* 'province, country' (e.g. "*a iudaea in galilæam* : of iudea in ðær mægð" in JnGl (Li) 4.47),[50] *land* 'country', and *leod* 'nation'.

Naturally there is no way of knowing whether Aldred knew the exact meaning of the names of peoples recorded in the Gospels. The glosses, in these cases, feature a limited number of omissions and strive to clarify the meaning of these words by means of the above mentioned additions. For example, *samaritanus* 'Samaritan' is quite regularly glossed by *samaritanisc* (Boyd 1975a: 43; see also Boyd 1967: 26), but Luke's Gospel elucidates the meaning by using instead *leod* (LkGl (Li) 9.52; *leod* 'man' is also used as an alternative gloss in MtGl (Li) 10.5). LkGl (Li) 10.33 repeats "*samaritanus*", but provides the further interpretation "þæt is hæðinmonn" ('that is heathen man'), and in LkGl (Li) 17.16 "hæðin" ('heathen') is the only gloss to *samaritanus*. *Galilaeus* 'Galilean' is glossed by "galilesc" ('Galilean'),[51] but once Aldred combines Latin and Old English: "*galileus* ł galilesc" (MkGl (Li) 14.70). The adjective is also reinforced by *mann* 'man' in JnGl (Li) 4.45: "*galilaei* : ða galilesco menn".

3.3 The words left without a gloss

There are a number of words for which Aldred does not provide a gloss, either in all or in some occurrences of the word in question. In the latter instance, it is not possible to determine a clear pattern for these variations in his glossing technique, although a trend emerges moving from the Headings of the Gospels to the Gospels themselves and from Matthew's Gospel to John's. Aldred is apparently more confident in glossing the Gospels than the prefatory material and his confidence grows along the way with the minimum of unglossed words in John's Gospel.

The Latin lemmata (including prefaces and headings) that are left unglossed are in total 916:[52] 473 of these occur in Matthew's Gospel (137 of which in the prefatory material and the headings), 140 in Mark's Gospel (37 of which in the

50 Aldred uses *mægð*, not only for regions and districts, but also for towns and villages and unspecified place-names such as *Dalmanutha*, a place north of Tiberias where Jesus went by boat with his disciples; see "*dalmanutha* : ðære megða" in MkGl (Li) 8.10.

51 The Old English suffix *-isc* often appears as *-esc*: "galilesc" occurs seven times in the Lindisfarne gloss, including the two occurrences mentioned above.

52 When an entire phrase is left unglossed, I counted each word as one. A comparison of Skeat's edition with the reproductions of the manuscript showed only two mistakes, as far as the presence or not of the gloss is concerned: in MtGl (Li) 11.21 *tibi* bears the gloss "ðe" (f. 48r), which is not recorded in the edition (Skeat 1887: 93), whereas in JnGl (Li) 3.1 *nicodemus* is left unglossed (f. 215r), while Skeat (1887: 27) repeats *nicodemus* also in the gloss.

prefatory material and headings), 238 in Luke's Gospel (28 of which in the prefatory material and headings) and 65 in John's Gospel (18 of which in the prefatory material and headings).[53] More than half of the words left unglossed are personal names (494x), including surnames such as *scarioth*, said of Juda (2x), and by-names such as *baptista*, said of John (9x); there are 67 place-names left unglossed.

The omissions include a few phrases. Some of them, such as *dammulae hinnuloque cervorum* ('to a fallow deer and a young hart'; LiProlMt (Skeat) 7)[54] or *salvi facti sunt* ('were made whole'; MtGl (Li) 14.36)[55] were well known as they echoed other Biblical verses. Unglossed is also the Aramaic phrase occurring in two Gospels: *heli heli lema sabacthani* (MtGl (Li) 27.46) and *heloi heloi lama sabacthani* (MkGl (Li) 15.34).[56]

On a few occasions Aldred is understandably at a loss to provide an Old English gloss for a nonsense word or phrase produced by a corruption of the text, the more so when this happens in the headings, where he did not have the prop of the Biblical text. An example from Matthew's Gospel may suffice to illustrate this point: "*caro sine mendabiles* [read *caros inemendabiles*] : lichoma buta" (MtHeadGl (Li) 14). Aldred provides a proper Old English rendering for both *caro* ('flesh') and *sine* ('without'), which were both corrupt but yet extant Latin words, but then stops and leaves the nonce word *mendabiles* unglossed.

Only in a few instances does Aldred's decision to leave a word unglossed seem to be conditioned by the context; a few words of the Gospels were perceived as redundant as far as the meaning of the verse is concerned and not glossed, words such as *deliciis* (*qui in veste pretiosa sunt et deliciis*) 'they that are in costly apparel

53 The four remarkable instances when Aldred begins to gloss a Latin word and does not complete it are not included in this reckoning: *indisparabilis* ('the inseparable'), with "in" ('in') rendering *in-* (LkArgGl (Li), 6, f. 131v); *decemnas* ('ten pounds'), with "of" ('of') rendering *de-* (LkHeadGl (Li) 77, f. 135v); *supercilium* 'eyebrow', with "ofer" ('over') rendering *super-* (LkGl (Li) 4.29, f. 149v); and *decurio* ('decurion'), with "of" ('of') rendering *de-* (MkGl (Li) 15.43, f. 128v).

54 Only the last word and the conjunction *et* are glossed: "⁊ hearta"; see the Song of Solomon: *Similis est dilectus meus capreae hinuloque cervorum* ('my beloved is like a roe, or a young hart'; Canticle 2.9) and *Fuge dilecte mi et adsimilare capreae hinuloque cervorum super montes aromatum* ('flee away, O my beloved, and be like to the roe, and to the young hart upon the mountains of aromatical spices'; Canticle 8.14).

55 See *Mementote qualiter salvi facti sunt patres nostri in mari Rubro* ('remember in what manner our fathers were saved in the Red Sea'; 1 Maccabees 4.9) and *Ad te clamaverunt et salvi facti sunt* ('they cried to thee, and they were saved'; Psalms 21.6).

56 As far as other Aramaic phrases or words are concerned, Aldred provides some of them with an explanatory gloss identifying them as Hebrew: "*talitha cumi* : ðis is ebrisc word" (MkGl (Li) 5.41); "*gesemani* : ðæt is on ebrisc" (MkGl (Li) 14.32); *effetha* (MkGl (Li) 7.34), *golgotha* (MkGl (Li) 15.22) and *gabbatha* (JnGl (Li) 19.13) are left unglossed. In JnGl (Li) 19.17 *hebraice golgotha* is rendered by "ebresclice hefid-ponna styd".

and live delicately'; LkGl (Li) 7.25) or *die* (*septies in die* 'seven times in a day'; LkGl (Li) 17.4). The omission of conjunctions such as *autem* (10x) and adverbs such as *etiam* (1x) was quite common and these terms are regularly left untranslated in Old English interlinear glosses.

On the other hand, some words in the text which do not bear an interlinear gloss are apparently left unglossed simply as a result of a commonplace synthetic rendering in Old English: for example "*a longe* : fearra" (MkGl (Li) 11.3, LkGl (Li) 16.23, 17.12, 18.12), or "*ad invicem* : bituih" (LkGl (Li) 6.11), "*in invicem* : bituih" (JnGl (Li) 6.43); the same happens with negative contractions: e.g. "*non* [...] *erat* : næs" (JnGl (Li) 8.39).

Finally, there are words, a number of which will be examined below, that are not glossed for other reasons. Some of the unglossed words are loanwords from Greek that were absorbed into Christian Latin, largely through Biblical translations. Some of these were loanwords through Greek from Hebrew. They included a number of rare or difficult words and in some instances Aldred might have left them unglossed because he did not understand them.[57] Someone who knew his Latin as well as Aldred could not possibly have been in doubt as to the meaning of Latin words such as *centurio* or *sindon*, the more so because in the majority of cases a word is not left unglossed all the way through the interlinear gloss. Aldred undoubtedly had some difficulties with words such as *scenopegia*, while he seems to be aware of the manifold meanings of *sabbatum*.[58] Omissions might be due to a more complex cause, such as the wish to avoid making a mistake in identifying the exact meaning of a Latin word in the verse. This is the case, for example, of *gazophylacium* in MkGl (Li) 12.41 and MkGl (Li) 12.42, where Aldred prefers to repeat the Latin word in his gloss.

In what follows I will examine a number of the Latin words that Aldred leaves unglossed in the four Gospels and the Gospels' prefaces and *capitula*: *adulter, adulterus, altilia, azymus, camelus, cohors, corban, centurio, clibanus, cohors, colaphus, contubernium, corban, eunuchus, fullo, gazophylacium, hydropicus, locusta, parasceve, pharisaeus, proselytus, publicanus, scorpio, scenopegia, sindon, teloneum*, and *tetrarcha*.

Adulter, adulterus

In MtGl (Li) 16.4, in the phrase *generatio mala et adultera* ('a wicked and adulterous generation'), the adjective *adultera* is left unglossed. In the same phrase in MtGl (Li) 12.39, the

57 See (Ross 1933b: 108) for *altilia* and *fullo*.

58 See his several different renderings of L *sabbatum:* e.g. "*sabbatis* : on dagum" in LkGl (Li) 4.31; "*in sabbato* : in wico" in LkGl (Li) 18.12; "*sabbatum* : sunnadæg" in LkGl (Li) 23.54. On seven occasions *sabbatum* is left unglossed: MtGl (Li) 24.20, 28.1, 28.1; MkGl (Li) 1.21, 2.24; LkHeadGl (Li) 55; and LkHeadGl (Li) 58.

adjective is rendered by "arg" ('wretched'), which is possibly a better match for the adjective *mala*. Only in MkGl (Li) 8.38 does Aldred provide the gloss "derneleger" ('adulterous'; "*in generatione ista adultera et peccatrice* : in cneoreso ðas ðerne-leger ⁊ arg").[59] The restraint shown by Aldred is not shared by Farman who uses *forlegen* 'adulterer' in both MtGl (Ru) 12.39 and 16.4. With regard to MkGl (Ru) 8.38, Farman's word choice was conditioned by that of a previous verse (MkGl (Ru) 7.21) where Rushworth has *adultera* (and not *adulteria*), which is rendered as "dyrnegeligre", repeated in MkGl (Li) 8.38.[60]
Old English has various words for the substantivized form *adultera* 'adulteress, prostitute': *forlegnis*, *forlegis*, and *forleges*;[61] the words for the masculine counterpart, 'adulterer, whoremonger' are *wemmend*, *unrihthemere*, *fyrenhycga*, and *forliger* (also used of a woman),[62] but Aldred leaves *adulter* unglossed in MtHeadGl (Li) 15, showing, as in other instances, that he is more timid when glossing the *capitula* to the Gospels.

Altilia

Altilia (noun from the adjective *altilis* 'fattened animal'; applied to domestic animals) occurs only once in the Gospels, in MtGl (Li) 22.4, where it is left unglossed, possibly because Aldred did not feel confident about the meaning of the word. On the other hand, the gloss to the Durham Collectar provides a correct gloss of *altilia occisa* as "hehfaro gislægno" ('slaughtered heifers'; DurRitGl 1 (Thomp-Lind) 107.10, in the quotation of the same passage from Matthew). *Altilis* was often used (absolutely) of fattened birds, especially of poultry, and this meaning evidently affects the choices of both Farman, who glosses *altilia* with "foedelfuglas" ('fattened birds'; MtGl (Ru) 22.4), and the West Saxon Gospels, where "fugelas" ('birds') is used. That this was a widespread interpretation of the Gospel's phrase *tauri mei et altilia* ('my calves and fatlings'; Matthew 22.4) is confirmed by the Third Cleopatra Glossary, where the gloss "*Altilia* : fuglas" occurs in the Gospel of Matthew section of this glossary (ClGl 3 (Quinn), 209).

Azymus

Aldred clearly knew that *dies azymorum* and *azyma* referred to the Jewish feast of unleavened bread, as he gives it an appropriate rendering in MtGl (Li) 26.17, calling it "doege ðara ðorofra mæta" ('the day of unleavened food'). In LkGl (Li) 22.1 and 22.7 Aldred uses *dærst* 'leaven', which, as is evident from a double gloss in the Durham Collectar, he deemed to

59 See Wenisch (1979: 280 and 313) for the verb *dyrnlicgan* 'to fornicate', which is identified as an Anglian word, and for *dyrnlegere* 'licentiously' (LkGl (Li) 15.13). Although Aldred seems quite fond of this family of words in the Durham Collectar (see also "dernegileig'" for *fornicator* in DurRitGl 1(Thomp-Lind) 107.1; and "derne gilegerscip'" for *fornicationem* in DurRitGl 1(Thomp-Lind) 106.34), they also occur in Old English texts with different dialectal features, though they were evidently falling out of use in West Saxon. For "arg", see Ross (1932b: 451–452, and 1961: 258–260).

60 In MkGl (Ru) 8.38 we find "derne-geligru ⁊ arog-nisse" as the gloss for *adultera et peccatrice*, as if the text read *adulteria et peccati*.

61 Cp. *DOEC*; the Old English *Martyrologium* has three times the word *forligerwif*: Mart 5 (Kotzor) Aug 8 174.3, 174.8; and Mart 5 (Kotzor) Dec 13 262.18.

62 See the *DOEC* for the occurrences.

be synonymous with *ðeorf* 'unleavened'.[63] On the other hand, *azyma* is not glossed when in combination with *pascha* (*pascha et azyma* in MkGl (Li) 14.1), as Aldred is likely aware of the coincidence of the two feasts and their names (cp. *appropinquabat autem dies festus azymorum qui dicitur pascha*, 'now the feast of unleavened bread, which is called the pasch, was at hand'; Luke 22.1).

Camelus

The word *camelus* 'camel' is always glossed aside from Matthew 23.24 ("*Duces caeci excolantes culicem, camelum autem glutientes*", 'blind guides, who strain out a gnat, and swallow a camel'). In this case, both the gloss to *camelum* and the gloss to *glutientes* are omitted, betraying some uneasiness on Aldred's part in coping with the Biblical overstatement which singles out two animals, one very small and the other very large.[64] On the other hand, the heading to Matthew's Gospel, which summarizes the episode, contains the first occurrence of the loanword *camel*: "*de iuramento de camelo et culice* : of aðe of camele ðæm deare ⁊ of flege" ('of the oath of the camel and the gnat'; MtHeadGl (Li) 79). The word *camelus* is accompanied by "ðæm deare" ('the animal'). Later on, a marginal note, "se micla dear" ('the big animal'), is added alongside the verse of MkGl (Li) 10.25 (Boyd 1975a: 39–40), demonstrating how Aldred was aware of the possible difficulties inherent in the interpretation of the loanword *camel*. *Camel* is used in all the occurrences of *camelus* (MtGl (Li) 3.4 and 19.24, MkGl (Li) 1.6, and LkGl (Li) 18.25). Ru[1] uses *olbend* 'camel' twice (MtGl (Ru) 3.4 and 19.24), with the first occurrence of *camel* in MkGl (Li) 1.6; Ru[2] uses *camel* throughout. The choice of *camel* represents one of those instances in which I doubt whether it is correct to speak of a word occurring only in the Lindisfarne glosses (or both in the Lindisfarne and Rushworth glosses) as typical of the Northumbrian dialect.[65] I would rather speak of a lexical preference on the part of Aldred.[66] The occurrence of *camel* (MkGl (Li) 1.6) in Ru[1]

---

63 "*Fratres epulemur non in fermento ueteri neque in fermento malitiæ et nequitiæ sed in azymis sinceritatis et ueritatis* : bro' gihriordiga ve no in daerstum aldum ne æc in dærstvm yfelgiornisse ⁊ unwisnise ah on dærstum ł on ðearfum biluitnises ⁊ soðfæstnises" (DurRitGl 1 (Thomp-Lind) 25.9–11).

64 MtGl (Ru) 23.24 has the glosses "olbendu" and "glendrende".

65 As far as *camel* is concerned, see, among others, Jordan (1906: 81) and Wenisch (1979: 269, 325).

66 Besides frequently attested loanwords from Latin, the Lindisfarne glosses feature a number of rarer borrowings (some of which are examined here) and a few exclusive ones: *cursumbor* 'incense' (cp. ML *cozumber*) in MtGl (Li) 2.11; *palm* 'vine-sprout' (cp. L *palmes*) in JnHeadGl (Li) 37; *pinn* 'pen' (? L *penna, pinna*) in MtProlGl (Li), 2.18; *pis* 'heavy' (cp. L *pensus*) in MtGl (Li) 23.4 and LkGl (Li) 15.16; *plæce* 'open space, street' (cp. L *platea*; 5x, also in Rushworth and Durham Collectar); *plett* 'fold' (cp. L *plecta*) (3x); *postol* 'apostle' (cp. L *apostolus*) in LkArgGl (Li) 1 (and LkGl (Ru) 24.10); *titul* (cp. L *titulum*) in MkGl (Li) 15.26. Moreover, as for the majority of the words mentioned before, there are several instances in which Aldred employs a Latin loanword to gloss the corresponding Latin word of the Gospels. This is the case, for example, of *calic* 'chalice' glossing *calix* (22x); *carcern* 'prison' glossing *carcer* (18x) (on which see Wenisch 1979: 114–120); *palm, palma* 'palm, palm-tree' glossing *palma* in JnHeadGl (Li) 30 and JnGl (Li) 12.13; *papa* 'pope' glossing *papa* in LiEpis (Skeat), 23; *plantian* 'to plant' glossing *plantare* (2x); *port* 'door' (cp. L *porta*) glossing *porta* in MtGl (Li) 7.13 and 7.14; *purple* 'purple' glossing *purpureus* in JnGl (Li) 19.5; *portic*

adds weight to my argument. The Lindisfarne gloss was probably available to the glossators of Rushworth by the end of Matthew's Gospel, and, in MkGl (Li) 1.6, Farman follows Lindisfarne in his use of *camel*, whereas he had chosen *olbend* in the previous verses.

Centurio

The gloss to *centurio* 'centurion' is omitted once, in MtGl (Li) 27.54, where the word, occurring at the beginning of the verse, is misspelled as <centori>. The misspelling does not seem a good enough reason for Aldred not to provide a gloss for a word which he had already met in the same Gospel and for which he had also given an explanation. L *centurio* had been glossed twice (MtGl (Li) 8.5 and 15.44) with the loanword *centur*, which, in the first instance, was accompanied by an interpretation: "ðe centur þæt is hundraðes monna hlaferd" ('the centurion, that is the master of one hundred men').[67] In other verses (MtGl (Li) 8.8, 8.13, 15.39, 15.45; LkGl (Li) 7.2, 7.6 and 23.47) Aldred allows himself a degree of freedom and prefers the indigenous *ealdormann* 'high officer'.

Clibanus

The word *clibanus* 'oven, furnace' (a loanword from Greek) occurs not only in the Gospels but also in the psalter (Psalm 20.10). *Clibanus* receives a most interesting rendering when it first occurs in MtGl (Li) 6.30: "*si autem faenum agri quod hodie est et cras in clibanum mittitur* : gif uutedlice gers ł heg londes þæt todæg is ⁊ tomorgen in heofone bið gesended". In the corresponding verse in Luke the word is left unglossed. Farman uses the gloss "ofen" (MtGl (Ru) 6.30), as does Owun (LkGl (Ru) 12.28). As far as Aldred's use of "heofone" in his glosses to Matthew's Gospel is concerned, he might have miscopied a correct original. Aldred's choice of *heofon* 'heaven' could be prompted by the association of smoke rising in the air. He might even have tried his hand at a metaphorical reading. The awkwardness of his first choice of gloss possibly manifested itself when he got to Luke and hence he preferred to leave *clibanum* unglossed.

Cohors

Cohors occurs three times in the Gospels with reference to the train or retinue of the praetor in a province. Aldred does not gloss the word on one occasion (MkGl (Li) 15.16), whereas in JnGl (Li) 18.3 he offers an explanation of what a *cohors* was: "þæt monn-mægen ł ðegna uorud" ('that troop or throng of retainers'). The word is otherwise glossed as *þreat* ('crowd, troop'; MkGl (Li) 15.16), a word which also renders L *turba*.

Colaphus

As far as *colaphus* 'kick, blow with the fist' is concerned, the word is left unglossed in MtGl (Li) 26.67), whereas it is glossed as both *fyst* 'fist' and *dynt* 'blow' in MkGl (Li) 14.65. In this case, the omission may possibly be due to its redundancy (cp. *et colaphis eum caederunt* 'and buffeted him') in the verse in Matthew. In the same verse Ru[1] resorts to a pragmatic rendering and uses the word *hand* 'hand'.

'porch' glossing *porticus* in JnGl (Li) 10.23; *pytt* 'pit' glossing *puteus* (2x); *torr* 'tower' glossing *turris* (6x); *tunuc* 'tunic' glossing *tunica* (2x); *turtur* 'turtle-dove' glossing *turtur* in LkGl (Li) 2.24.

67 In fact, most centurions commanded from 60 to 80 men rather than the commonly assumed 100.

Contubernium

The lemma occurs in MkGl (Li) 6.39, where the crowd which follows Jesus and listens to his words is described as sitting down *secundum contubernia* ('by companies'). This specification was quite unnecessary to the understanding of the verse and was omitted in both the Lindisfarne and Rushworth glosses, as well as in the West Saxon translations of the Gospels, where no Old English counterpart is provided for the Latin word.[68]

The omission may also indicate that the word may have posed some difficulty, as is evident from its occurrence in the Bible section of the Third Cleopatra Glossary where it is spelled <contuberniam>.[69]

Corban

L *corban*, *corbam* (originally an Aramaic word meaning 'a consecrated gift') means 'gift, offering', as Mark's Gospel itself explains: *vos autem dicitis si dixerit homo patri aut matri corban quod est donum* ('but you say: If a man shall say to his father or mother, Corban (which is a gift)'; Mark 7.11). In this verse, it is evident how Aldred, possibly trying to avoid the use of a difficult (or rare) word (whether borrowed from Latin or coined for the occasion), uses "geafa" twice, both for *corban* and for *donum*. In MtGl (Li) 27.6, where *corban* refers to the offerings to the temple, he might have hesitated and have left the word initially unglossed. On the other hand, the addition of a marginal gloss "in temple" is indeed justified by the limited space available over *corban* and the large size of *b*. Moreover, *corbanan* is the last word of f. 84v.

Decurio

Owing to the Vulgate meaning of *decurio* and the context of the two Gospel verses,[70] Aldred apparently misinterpreted it as two words, *de* and *curio*, taking the latter for the name of a town. Whereas in MkGl (Li) 15.43 Aldred only offers a rendering for *de* (namely, "of"), in LkGl (Li) 23.50 *decurio* is glossed, following a common pattern for place-names, with "of ł ðær byrig". Ru[2] reproduces the aforementioned choices, but in the first instance omits the uncalled for preposition "of", which is retained in LkGl (Ru) 23.50. That Aldred was familiar with the most common meaning of *decurio* 'head or commander of a company of ten' is proven in the Durham Collectar: "*decanus super x vel decurio est* : tea mon' latwv of' teno oððe of megscire is" (DurRitGl 1 (Thomp-Lind) 193.10).[71]

---

68 Cp. "ðæt folc sæte ofer þæt grene hig" ('the people sit down upon the green grass'; Mk (WSCp) 6.39).

69 "*Contuberniam* : gadorwiste" (ClGl 3 (Quinn) 230). The same error is repeated in the First Cleopatra Glossary, which draws part of its lemmata mechanically from the above-mentioned glossary and repeats its Old English rendering (ClGl 1 (Stryker) 1171); see Lendinara (1999a: 32–35).

70 A *decurio* was a member of the senate of the municipia and the colonies. [*V*]*enit Ioseph ab Arimathia nobilis decurio* ('Joseph of Arimathea, a noble counsellor [...] came'; Mark 15.43); *ecce vir nomine Ioseph qui erat decurio vir bonus et iustus* ('behold there was a man named Joseph, who was a counsellor, a good and just man'; Luke 23.50).

71 OE *mægscir* is a hapax interpreted by Clark Hall (1960: s.v. *mægscir*) as 'division of a people containing the kinsmen of a particular family'.

Eunuchus

The word *eunuchus* occurs in Matthew 19.12 and in the headings to this Gospel. In Matthew 19.12, *eunuchus* occurs three times. The gloss provided by Aldred for the first occurrence, OE *cwenhierde*, is a hapax legomenon, probably a loan-translation of a Latin phrase such *custos virginum*.[72] The next occurrence of *eunuchus* is unglossed, the word being used with the same meaning as before; in the last occurrence in this verse, the allegorical sense of the word is conveyed by the choice of *unawemmed* 'unstained'.[73] The Lindisfarne glosses employ yet another word for *eunuchus* which is used in the headings to Matthew's Gospel: *hwasta* (MtHeadGl (Li) 64), whose etymology is debated but which also occurs in First Cleopatra Glossary: "*Molles* : fam, hwastas" (ClGl 1 (Stryker) 3951).[74]

Fullo

The only occurrence of *fullo* 'fuller' in MkGl (Li) 9.3 is left unglossed. Aldred did not resort to the loanword *fullere* (*wealcere* could also be used in Old English). The corresponding gloss in Rushworth, "afu",[75] is taken for a truncated form by Clark Hall (1960: s.v. *afulliend*).

Gazophylacium

The Late Latin word *gazophylacium* was borrowed from Gr. *γαζοφυλάκιον*. The *gazophylacium* (*gaio-*) was the strong box for holding offerings of treasure to the temple. There were several *gazophylacia* or treasuries in the hallway connected to the vestibule of the temple. In the Middle Ages, the word came to mean 'church treasury' or 'money-place' and had some circulation also in England. This is one of the cases in which a word referring to a specific Jewish practice is left unglossed twice in the *capitula* to the Gospels (MkHeadGl (Li) 41 and LkHeadGl (Li) 84). When Aldred gets to MkGl (Li) 12.41, he provides some information on what a *gazophylacium* was and speaks of a door in Jerusalem which is called "gazophilacium" ("ðæs dores ðe is sua genemned gazophilacium on hierusalem"),[76] apparently thinking of it as a room provided with a door.[77] In the two following instances (the second occurrence in MkGl (Li) 12.41 and 12.43) the Latin word is repeated in the gloss as well. The word is left unglossed again in LkGl (Li) 21.1, but receives a gloss in Latin, *divitiarum custodia*, in

---

72 The gloss could have been borrowed from the interpretation of a Biblical glossary, repeating the words of Esther 2.15: *Aegaeus eunuchus custos virginum* ('Egeus the eunuch, the keeper of the virgins').

73 See Jerome, *Comm. in Matheum* (Matthew 19.12): *Triplex genus est eunuchorum, duorum carnalium et tertii spiritalis* ('There are three kinds of eunuchs; two carnal and the third spiritual'; Hurst and Adriaen 1969: 168).

74 *Mollis* is a gloss equivalent to *eviratus* (Goetz 1888–1923: V, 223.15) and *effeminatus* (Goetz 1888–1923: IV, 119.5). On *hwasta*, see Jordan (1906: 85), where the word is listed among the Anglian words.

75 Ross (1982: 198) gives this definition of the gloss: "obscure; it is difficult to see how it can be a linguistic corruption of the Latin".

76 The word is glossed as "*gazophilacium*" also in LkGl (Ru) 21.1; in JnGl (Ru) 8.20 *gazophylacio* is rendered by "byrig".

77 None of the Fathers quoted by Boyd (1975a: 40–41) speaks explicitly of a door. Note also the generalness of the reference to Jerusalem.

JnGl (Li) 8.20.[78] It is remarkable that Aldred shuns all the possible Old English renderings such as *maðmhus*, *madmhus*, *welahord* or *feoh*, which are used to render *gazophylacium* in the contemporary Anglo-Saxon glossaries.[79] Aldred's prudence seems driven by his desire to avoid making a mistake: the West Saxon version of the Gospels confirms the difficulties surrounding the word, which is regularly – and intriguingly – mistaken for a *teloneum* and translated as *sceoppa* ('booth'; Lk (WSCp) 21.1), *tollsceamol* ('seat of custom'; Mk (WSCp) 12.41, 12.41 and 12,43), and *ceapsceamul* ('seat of custom'; Jo (WSCp) 8.20).

Hydropicus

L *hydropicus* is glossed with *unhal* 'sick' both in LkGl (Li) 14.2 and LkGl (Ru) 14.2, but in LkHeadGl (Li) 58 the word is left unglossed. It is remarkable that, in the other instances, Aldred resorts to a generic gloss and does not use OE *wæterseóc* 'dropsical', which is well-attested (Ælfric, Old English *Herbarium*, and glosses), along with the corresponding substantive *wæterseocnes* 'dropsy' (Old English *Herbarium* and *Medicina de quadrupedibus*).[80] The West Saxon Gospels employ *wæterseoc mann* (Lk (WSCp) 14.2), which is rarer but also attested in an anonymous homily (HomS 38 (ScraggVerc 20) 91A).

Locusta

Two verses containing the same material (MtGl (Li) 3.4 and MkGl (Li) 1.6) present us with the case where a word, *locusta* 'locust', is left unglossed on one occasion and is then glossed as *loppestre*. Ru[2] has the more common rendering of 'locust' as *gærshoppa* in MtGl (Ru) 3.4 (another widespread word for 'locust' is OE *gærstapa*), but in MkGl (Ru) 1.6 Owun follows Aldred's choice of *loppestre*, which is quite remarkable as it connects his glosses with the Biblical exegesis of Theodore of Canterbury (Bischoff and Lapidge 1994: 408, 520).[81]

Parasceve

L *parasceve* (a loanword from Gr. *παρασκευή*, lit. 'preparation') designates the day of preparation before the Jewish Sabbath or a feast of similar rank. The meaning of *parasceve* could not have been unknown to Aldred, but this is one of the cases in which Aldred both leaves a rare Latin word unglossed and provides different renderings for it throughout the Gospels. L *parasceve* is left unglossed once (MkGl (Li) 15.42); later on, in the same Gospel, Aldred

---

78 This is a common interpretation of *gazophylacium* (see e.g. Eucherius, *Instruct.* II.15; Wotke 1894), also found in all-Latin glossaries.

79 Cp. the Antwerp-London Glossary: "*Gazophilacium* : madmhus" (Porter 2011: no. 2075), "*Gazophilacium* : madmhus ł *Thesaurarium* goldhold ł *corbanan* ł *Donarium*" (Porter 2011: no. 2825); and the Third Cleopatra Glossary: "*Gazofilacium* : welahord, feoh" (ClGl 3 (Quinn) 294; an entry from Mark 12.41). The Antwerp-London Glossary is quoted from the recent edition by Porter (2011). For other instances of OE *madmhus*, *maðmhus* in the meaning of 'shrine in the Jewish Temple', including ÆGl 321.7, see the *DOEC*.

80 Cp, ÆLS (Sebastian) 144 and Med 1.1 (de Vriend) 10.16 for *wæterseoc*; and ÆCHom I, 5 221.132 and Lch I (Herb) 26.3 for *wæterseocnes*.

81 See the interpretation of Mark 1.6 in the second series of commentaries preserved in Milan, Biblioteca Ambrosiana, MS M.79 Sup.: *sunt locustae maris quas lopustran vocant; et sunt agrestes quas comedebat Iohannes* ('there are locusts of the sea which they call 'lobsters'; and locusts of the land, which is what John was eating'; Bischoff and Lapidge 1994: 408–409).

provides both a traditional gloss largely attested such as *foregearwung* 'preparation' (LkGl (Li) 23.54) and a more unusual one, *metes gearwung* 'preparation of food' (MtGl (Li) 27.62), which indicates that on that day of *parasceve* food was prepared for the following day's feast.[82] In John's Gospel, OE *foregearwung* 'preparation' is combined with *metes* 'of the food' and explained in both Old English and Latin in JnGl (Li) 19.14 ("metes foregearuung *i(d est) praeparatio cibi*"). In the two following instances in the same Gospel, Aldred felicitously concludes his lexical experimentation rendering *parasceve* with the compound *gearwungdæg*, lit. 'day of preparation' (JnGl (Li) 19.31 and 19.42), which is exclusive to the Lindisfarne gloss.

Pharisaeus

The Pharisees were members of a religious party or school of that name amongst the Jews at the time of Christ (see Finkelstein 1962, 1989: 229–277; Stemberger 1991). The word occurs numerous times in the Gospels, and even more so in Lindisfarne, owing to its occurrence in the headings to the Gospels (26x). The word usually occurs in the plural, referring to a group of people. With the exception of Matthew 23.26, the singular is used only in Luke, where Jesus is described dining on three occasions at the home of a Pharisee. The name of the Pharisees is often combined with that of other opponents of Jesus such as the scribes (15x).[83] In Matthew's and Mark's Gospels they are labelled as *hypocrites* (6x) and in that of Matthew they are condemned (Matthew 12.34); tirades against the Pharisees extend also to the scribes.

Notwithstanding the prevailing stereotypical views of this group and the negative connotations attached to this word, partly based on a widespread misreading of the New Testament, Aldred provides a number of personal and positive renderings and his glosses feature a wider variety of glosses than Ru²: *æcræftig* 'versed in law', *ælareow* 'a doctor of the law', *ealda* 'elder', *ealdor* 'civil or religious authority', *ealdormann* 'high religious officer' (the word is used to render a number of foreign titles), and *ealdwita* 'venerable man, sage'.[84] OE *ælareow* is employed in Luke and John, and is the most frequent rendering in the fourth Gospel. Indeed none of the words used by Aldred has negative connotations. *ælareow* and the above-recorded meanings of *ealda*, *ealdormann*, and *ealdwita* are exclusive to Lindisfarne and Ru². Both the substantivized use of *æcræftig* and the meaning 'versed in law' are exclusive to Aldred.

Pharisaeus occurs a total number of 116 times, including the Gospels' headings. The unglossed instances amount to 59, 18 of which occur in the headings. Once again, the *capitula* feature a high percentage of unglossed words, which is probably due to the technical nature of the headings, as this tends to restrain Aldred's lexical experimentation. Remarkably, Aldred never uses either the Latin word or its Old English adaptation in the glosses,[85]

82 This gloss has a counterpart in the First Corpus Glossary: "*Parasceuen* : *praeparatio cibi*" (CorpGl 1 (Hessels) 247).

83 In Lindisfarne, *scriba* is regularly glossed by *uðwita* ("uðwuta"); in Ru², *uðwita* occurs twice as a gloss for *pharisaeus*: "ælde uðwuta" in LkGl (Ru) 11.37 and "ðara uðwutuna" in LkGl (Ru) 14.1.

84 See the still useful remarks by MacGillivray (1902: 5–10).

85 On the contrary, Ru¹ employs only "faris(s)eus", with either Latin or Old English inflection (e.g. MtGl (Ru) 3.7 and 5.20). OE *ealda* with the meaning 'Pharisee' is used in MkGl (Ru) 2.16;

yielding further proof that the absence of a gloss, in cases such as these, was meant not to overburden the folios of the Lindisfarne Gospels.

Proselytus

A few glosses were skipped owing to Aldred's limited knowledge of the exact meaning of the Latin word. *Proselytus* is a loanword from Gr. *προσήλυτος*, which means 'foreign, come from abroad'. In Late Latin it came to mean 'one that has come over from heathenism to the Jewish religion' and it is with this meaning that it occurs in the Vulgate. In the Lindisfarne gloss, the word is left unglossed on two occasions, in the headings to MtHeadGl (Li) 79 and in MtGl (Li) 23.15. The term receives a brilliant rendering by Farman in MtGl (Ru) 23.15, where he uses "hæþne iudiscne" (lit. 'heathen Jewish', to be interpreted as 'a Jew that was a heathen'). In Anglo-Saxon glossaries the lemma, evidently drawn from Matthew 23.15, was given the meaning 'stranger' and glossed as either L *advena* (ClGl 3 (Quinn) 214) or OE *elðeodig* (CollGl 23 (Zupitza) 23; see Lendinara 1999a: 335 and 350).

Publicanus

The word *publicanus* 'publican' is left unglossed four times. In all the other instances (25x) it is glossed by *bærsynnig*. The word is reckoned among those exclusively Northumbrian; [86] in this case too I would prefer to speak of a word coined by Aldred. The Old English compound means lit. 'openly-sinful' and when used substantively 'an open or public sinner'; it is a loan-formation on the basis of *publicus peccator*.[87] This gloss is also used by Owun in LkGl (Ru) 3.12.[88] In Matthew's Gospel, Farman chooses *gafolgerefa* 'tax-gatherer' (a word exclusive to Ru[1], and devoid of negative connotations) and *æwiscfiren* 'shameless sinner' (< 'guilty of shameless sin'; MtGl (Ru) 21.31–32). This last word exploits the concept of a tax-gatherer as a public sinner, suggested by Gospel doublets such as *publicani et peccatores* ('publicans and sinners'; see Matthew 9.10, 9.11 and 11.9; Mark 2.15 and 2.16; and Luke 5.30, 7.34 and 15.1). Whereas in Luke 5.29 the word is redundant and the gloss may be left out, the reason for leaving the word unglossed in the other three occurrences must be sought in the fact that it either refers to Matthew (MtGl (Li) 10.3) or Zaccheus (LkHead (Li) 76 and LkGl (Li) 19.2). The former had left his trade to follow Jesus and the latter had been converted, hence the negative connotation of *bærsynnig* did not seem to be suitable in either case.

Scenopegia

Scenopegia 'feast of tabernacles' (Gr. *σκηνοπηγία*) is one of those words which are left unglossed in the headings to the Gospels (JnHeadGl (Li) 18). Here, Aldred does not enhance his rendering in JnGl (Li) 7.2, where *scenopegia* is glossed by "temples mæssa". OE *mæsse* also meant a 'festival of the church'. In the latter case he apparently confused the taber-

there is another occurrence of "fariseus" in JnGl (Ru) 18.3 and three occurrences of "phariseus" in Ru[2].

86 See Wenisch (1979: 268 and 325).

87 See Isidore, *Etymologiae* IX.iv.32 and X.227 (Lindsay 1911) for the connection of *publicanus* 'one who gathers public revenue' with *publicus* 'of or belonging to the people, public, common'.

88 The many corruptions (also due to the ambiguous and archaic spelling <ui> for <y> in Lindisfarne) of the word in the Rushworth glosses demonstrates that the term was copied from Aldred's work.

nacles 'tents, temporary dwelling places', where the Israelites dwelt in the desert, celebrated by the 'feast of the tabernacles' (*scenopegia*), with the Jewish tabernacle as a place of worship. Anglo-Saxon glossaries and glosses provide much more fitting interpretations: *getimberhalgung*, *getrimbra halgung*, lit. 'hallowing of the buildings', and *geteld wurþung* 'celebration of the tents' (e.g. "*Scenophegia* : getimbra halgung .ł geteld wurþung" in the Antwerp-London Class Glossary (Porter 2011: no. 73).

Scorpio

L *scorpio* 'scorpion' is once left unglossed (LkGl (Li) 10.19) and once glossed by repeating the Latin word (LkGl (Li) 11.12). The two instances are indicative of Aldred's technique, which tries to stay as close as possible to the Biblical text. In the first instance (*serpentes et scorpiones* 'snakes and scorpions'), the first word of the doublet is rendered as "nædre", which provides the required information and makes the repetition of *scorpio* in the gloss redundant. In the second instance where *scorpio* occurs alone, Aldred feels it necessary to provide a gloss, albeit in Latin, the more so given the obscurity of the verse. The plural form of the Latin word, *scorpiones*, is used (to refer to the animal) in Old English medical writings such as the Leechdoms and the Old English *Herbarium* (cp. Lch I (HerbHead) 148.3; Lch I (Herb) 2.9; and Med 1.1 (de Vriend) 5.15).

Sindon

Behind some of Aldred's choices – and not glossing a word is clearly a choice on the part of any glossator – it is possible to read his hesitation when faced with certain Biblical episodes. In the case of the word *sindon* 'shroud, cloth of fine linen', Aldred provides a gloss only in the instances where *sindon* denotes Jesus's burial shroud (MtGl (Li) 27.59, MkGl (Li) 15.46 and LkGl (Li) 23.53). On the other hand, in MkGl (Li) 14.51 and 14.52, where *sindon* refers to the cloth worn by Lazarus, Aldred does not provide a gloss. In MkGl (Li) 15.46 he twice employs *lin* 'linen', a word he had already used to specify the material of the *hrægl* 'cloth' in LkGl (Li) 23.53, where *sindone* is glossed by "linene hrægle".

Teloneum

It is hard to believe that Aldred was unable to find an Old English gloss for *teloneum* 'toll booth, custom house' and yet all the occurrences of this word except one are left unglossed (MtGl (Li) 9.9, MkHeadGl (Li) 7, MkGl (Li) 2.14, and LkGl (Li) 5.27). In LkHeadGl (Li) 18 (*mattheus de teloneo vocatur* 'Matthew is summoned from the toll booth'), the gloss repeats the Latin word. In this case, *teloneo* might have been taken for the place of origin of Matthew. The abbreviation "telo'" would favour this hypothesis, although, in this instance, we would expect the Old English preposition *from*. Only MkGl (Ru) 2.14 provides an Old English gloss: the compound "geafolmonunge", which is a hapax legomenon. As *gafol* means 'tribute, tax, duty' and *manung* 'place of toll', the compound word is tautological; nevertheless, it proves, once more, Farman's independence and his talent. Old English has a number of words for *teloneum*: the West Saxon Gospels have *ceapsceamol*, *tollsceamol*, and *ceapsetl*, which adroitly represent the 'toll booth' where Matthew was seated when he was summoned by

Jesus.[89] The Antwerp-London Class Glossary has the entry "*Teloneum* : tolsetl" (Porter 2011: no. 2921).[90]

Tetrarcha

The word *tetrarcha* 'tetrarch', which referred to a subordinate ruler of one fourth of a country (especially of Syria under the Romans), causes Aldred some difficulty. The first occurrences of the word are left unglossed (MtGl (Li) 14.1, LkGl (Li) 3.1, 3.1, 3.1 – a verse where all the proper names, as well as other words, are left unglossed – and 3.19). In the last occurrence (LkGl (Li) 9.7), L *tetrarcha*, which refers to Herodes, is rendered by means of a generic gloss, "se cynig". Farman repeats the word *tetrarcha* in his gloss (MtGl (Ru) 14.1). Both glossators betray their uneasiness in front of the late Latin loanword from Greek. Much later on, a writer such as Byrhtferth seems at ease with the word in his *Enchiridion*: "Se ðe þone feorðan dæl ah byð gecweden tetrarcha on Grecisc" ('whoever has the fourth part is called *tetrarcha* in Greek'; ByrM 1 (Baker/Lapidge), II.i.71–72), and there was also a corresponding Old English word in circulation, *fiþerrica* 'tetrarch', used by Ælfric.[91]

Ventilabrum

The word *ventilabrum* 'winnowing shovel' is one of the terms which would apparently not have been so hard to unravel for Aldred; yet it is left unglossed when it first occurs in MtGl (Li) 3.12. When the metaphor of the separation of the wheat from the chaff that will burn with unquenchable fire is repeated in LkGl (Li) 3.17, Aldred provides a double gloss for "*ventilabrum* : fonnæ ł windgefonnæ" ('fan or winnowing fan'). On the other hand, Farman has no hesitation in MtGl (Ru) 3.12 and employs *windscofl* 'fan' (lit. 'winnowing showel'), whereas Owun seems to follow Lindisfarne with his double gloss "fone ⁊ windfone" (LkGl (Ru) 3.17).

Behind many of the unglossed words which have been examined there is a careful glossator, well aware of the possible dangers of rendering incorrectly the Biblical text. Worthy of note are especially the cases in which Aldred begins by leaving the word unglossed (mainly in the *capitula* to the Gospel) and then tries out one or more different interpretamenta. The foregoing analysis of some of the words which were left unglossed by Aldred in either one or more of their occurrences in the Gospels and the prefatory material proves that each term deserves individual attention and is a case study *per se*. It is also possible to identify a consistent strategy of the glossator. Words such as *scenopegia*, to name a peculiar Jewish feast, show a glossator at work who possibly had in front of him a former

89 See Mt (WSCp) 9.9 ("tollsceamule"), Mk (WSCp) 2.14 ("cepsetle"), and Lk (WSCp) 5.27 ("ceapsceamule").

90 The Antwerp-London Class Glossary has another entry: "*Teloneum* : scipmanne myrtse ceping" (Porter 2011: no. 1329), whose interpretation is based on Isidore, *Etymologiae* XV.ii.45 (Lindsay 1911).

91 ÆCHom I, 26 388.17; ÆCHom I, 32 452.45 and 452.48; and ÆHomM 6 (Irv 1) 16.48. See also ChronC (O'Brien O'Keeffe) 12.1, and AldV 1 (Goossens) 1786 and AldV 13.1 (Nap) 1799.

gloss in the vernacular which did not look entirely accurate, and so he preferred not to provide an incorrect rendering.

There are differences throughout the Gospels as far as the number of omissions are concerned,[92] with Matthew's Gospel showing the largest percentage of unglossed words and John's Gospel the lowest percentage. Another difference worth noting regards the prefatory material, where Aldred seems to leave a number of words unglossed because he did not have the prop of the whole Biblical context and might not have had another vernacular gloss at hand.

4 Abbreviations and runes

Among the strategies employed by Aldred in order not to overburden his apparatus of glosses are a number of unusual abbreviations and other forms of shorthand, including the use of two runes.

In a number of instances Aldred strove to imitate the abbreviations of the names which had come to be known as *nomina sacra*, indicating proper names by means of an abbreviation, such as "isral'" for *Israhel* (JnGl (Li) 1.49).[93] In addition, he had the peculiar habit of abbreviating forms without any indication that they were abbreviated (e.g. "faede" = *fæder* in JnHeadGl (Li) 12).[94]

Worthy of notice is the system of abbreviations employed by Aldred in LkGl (Li) 3.24–38 (ff. 147v–148r), where each word of these Gospel verses is provided with a much abbreviated gloss, consisting mainly of one or two letters. Not only are proper names abbreviated, but so too are pronouns and verbs (*fuit* 'was' is abbreviated as "w'" (i.e. *was*) 74x), which are painstakingly glossed by means of an abbreviated form, mainly the initial(s) of the Old English gloss, with an eye to the aesthetics of the folios, rather than for the sake of comprehension of the Latin text. In this case, the abbreviations function as some sort of signpost for the words of the Latin text.

Remarkable too is what Ross (Ross 1937: 6; cp. Ross and Squires 1980: 490) has called the "short-hand" of the alternative forms. On several occasions Aldred's gloss provides two alternative forms, indicating the variant form by writing a letter or letters directly above the Old English word. Two different methods are employed: the superscript letter(s) may be written directly above one letter of the

92 See pp. 343–344 above for the estimate.

93 For a list of the abbreviations used by Aldred, see Ross (1943: 316–317).

94 Carpenter (1910: 10–37) has studied all the 'crude' or 'truncate' forms of the substantives in the gloss.

Old English gloss: for instance, in MtGl (Li) 8.26, *o* is written just above the *e* of “lytle” (f. 41v). The superscribed letter(s) may otherwise be written superscript between two letters of the Old English word: see, for instance, <oncne`o´w> in MtGl (Li) 13.51 (f. 54v).

Another kind of short-hand system employed by Aldred is the use of two runes.[95] Aldred employs the rune ᛞ and the rune ᛗ, whose names are quite common words, *dæg* ‘day’ and *mann* ‘man’, respectively. Aldred begins to use the rune ᛗ for the second part of the noun phrase *nænig mann* ‘nobody’ (rendering *nemo*)[96] in MkGl (Li) 9.39 (f. 114r) and continues to use this device, with a few breaks, until the end of John’s Gospel. The rune is also used as part of the noun phrases *ænig mann* (preceded by *ne*), which glosses *nemo*; *ænig mann* ‘any one’, which glosses *quisquam*; *sum mann* ‘someone’, which glosses *quidam*; and *ælc mann* ‘each one’, which glosses *omnis*. In LkGl (Li) 12.42 one of the double glosses for *dispensator* employs the rune ᛗ as part of a corrupted form of *scirmann* ‘steward’. The Old English glosses for *nemo*, as well as for *quisquam*, are always completely spelled out in Matthew’s Gospel and intermittently in Mark’s, Luke’s and John’s Gospels. The same happens with the rune ᛞ, which is used as part of the word *sunnangdæg* twice and for the first time when glossing Luke 23.56. All in all, the ᛞ rune occurs four times and the ᛗ rune 34 times in the Lindisfarne glosses.

The manuscript does not afford us with any apparent need for the use of runes. In all cases, there is plenty of space after the first member of the compound. On two occasions (JnGl (Li) 15.13 and 16.5) the use of the rune allows Aldred to end the gloss to the last word of the line in perfect alignment with the *o* of *nemo*. In JnGl (Li) 15.24 the rune ᛗ is written in the right margin of the folio.[97] The runes are, in the majority of cases, used within a compound word.[98] In his use of runes (i.e. of the rune names for which they stood), Aldred gets quite close to a systematic use.

---

95 See Derolez (1954: 401), who remarked that as “most rune-names were low-frequency words [...] they could hardly become a system of notae”.

96 *Nemo* is also glossed as “ne ænig” (MkGl (Li) 11.2).

97 In the Durham Collectar, as edited by Thompson and Lindelöf (1927), the ᛞ rune occurs 43 times and the ᛗ rune 13 times; in this gloss Aldred uses the ᛞ rune throughout for *dies*. Moreover the runes feature a greater degree of integration as Aldred adds the oblique case endings (*-es* or *-e*) after the rune. This also happens in LkGl (Li) 21.17 and JnGl (Li) 8.15.

98 The words *dæg* and *mann* are always spelled out, with the sole exception of LkGl (Li) 21.34, where ᛞ stands for *dæg*, and JnGl (Li) 9.16, where ᛗ stands for *mann*. There are many instances when Aldred does not employ the rune for phrases such as *nænig mann*, etc. See also Ross (1955: 516 and 1968: 12–13).

5 The omitted glosses of the Rushworth Gospels

A cursory comparison between the glosses which were omitted in Lindisfarne and the words left unglossed in Rushworth shows that omissions involve the same word categories: personal names, place-names, ethnonyms, infrequent words, including a number of loanwords, and conjunctions such as *autem* are frequently unglossed.

The methods followed by the glossators are not alike. While there is a correlation between the occasions on which words are left unglossed in Lindisfarne and Ru², which bears witness to the possible influence of the Lindisfarne gloss on Owun's gloss, there is no absolute correspondence either. In some instances Ru² provides a gloss to a proper name which was left unglossed in Lindisfarne; the same applies to other words, such as "ða pharis'" for *pharisaei* (MkGl (Ru) 3.6), with no corresponding gloss in Lindisfarne. The glosses with no counterpart in Lindisfarne have been judged independent insertions by Owun.

The difference between the two sets of glosses is much more evident as far as Farman's part is concerned, as he employs a glossing strategy which is at odds with that of Aldred, and this is also true with respect to the words which had been left without a gloss. A small list of examples drawn from the first verses of Matthew will suffice to prove that Farman did not shun the use of glosses which repeat the Latin, including the phrase "fariseas ⁊ saduceas" ('the Pharisees and the Sadducees'). In Rushworth *autem* is never left unglossed (being alternatively rendered by *soþlice*, *þa*, *þonne*, and *wutedlice*), and words such as *locusta*, *ventilabrum*, and *teloneum* receive a proper Old English gloss.

Matthew 2.6:	Li.: *israhel*; Ru.: "israhæl"
Matthew 2.23:	Li.: *nazareth*; Ru.: "nazareþ"
Matthew 3.1:	Li.: *iohannes*; Ru.: "iohannes"
Matthew 3.4:	Li.: *autem*; Ru.: "þanne"
Matthew 3.4:	Li.: *locustae*; Ru.: "græs-hoppa"
Matthew 3.7:	Li.: *pharisaeorum et sadducaeorum*; Ru. "farisea ⁊ saducea"
Matthew 3.12:	Li.: *ventilabrum*; Ru.: "windiuscoful"
Matthew 9.9:	Li. : *in teloneo*; Ru.: "æt gæflaes monunge"

The different – and independent – strategy of the Rushworth glosses (in this case of both Ru¹ and, although to a lesser extent, Ru²) is evident also in the use of abbreviations, which emerge as a kind of short-hand particularly cherished by Aldred.

6 Conclusions

In the past, the unglossed words of the Lindisfarne gloss have caused some embarrassment to those who, quite rightly, considered Aldred a conscientious glossator. Ross (1937: 5) was very critical in this respect and wrote on numerous occasions that Aldred was quite frequently unable to understand the Latin text.

The omissions examined in this paper do not support the hypothesis of shortcomings in either Latin or Biblical competence on Aldred's part. Also the possibility of an eye skip should be ruled out in the majority of cases. The unglossed Latin words should rather be viewed as part of his distinctive glossing practice, which, as far as personal names are concerned, resembles that employed in other interlinear glosses in Old English. In the Lindisfarne Gospels the largest number of omissions concern proper names (personal names, place-names and ethnonyms), the would-be gloss of which would scarcely have differed from the corresponding Latin word (e.g. "*Abraham* : Abraham"). Aldred does not want to cram the page and, I argue, a large share of the omissions can be likened to abbreviations, contractions and other forms of 'short-hand' employed by Aldred. Omissions of glosses with a commonplace rendering should be judged as an attempt to introduce a general economy within the page.

Continuous interlinear glosses have their own specific features, which are quite distinct from those of occasional glosses and to leave a word unglossed should not be seen as a shortcoming. Moreover, in the case of the interlinear glosses to the Lindisfarne Gospels, the gloss may have been conditioned by the prestigious status of the sacred text they accompany. In supplementing a Biblical text, the glosses lost their interpretative role and, by the same token, did not have a fully instrumental use. Unlike other interlinear glosses, the glosses to the Gospels were not meant to contribute to disseminating the text or explicating its meaning, as the text was well known and its meaning not to be altered. It was the Latin text which was to be highlighted and remembered, not its gloss. In such a context, a gloss avoiding the exacting literalism of a word-for-word rendering served to enhance the importance of the Latin text.

Karen Jolly

The Process of Glossing and Glossing as Process: Scholarship and Education in Durham, Cathedral Library, MS A.iv.19

Abstract: Aspects of Aldred's gloss to Durham, Cathedral Library, MS A.iv.19 shed light on his earlier gloss of the Lindisfarne Gospels. In particular, Aldred's focus on individual words suggests both a contemplative and a pedagogical function, particularly the element-by-element glosses and the alternative *vel* (ł) glosses. Care must be taken, therefore, with some of his word formations that may reflect a vocabulary exercise or Latin word analysis, rather than Northumbrian Old English. Examples from Aldred's interactions with Scribe B in the St. John poison prayer and from his glosses of encyclopedic materials demonstrate a primary interest in the bilingual conversation between Latin and Old English as a source of insight and instruction.

Understanding the nature of Aldred's contributions to Durham, Cathedral Library, MS A.iv.19 is vital to comprehending the Lindisfarne Gospels' gloss and Old English glossing as a whole, but his additions to Durham, MS A.iv.19 have not been fully studied enough to exploit the implications.[1] Durham, MS A.iv.19 is a scrappy little manuscript compared to the Lindisfarne Gospels, in more ways than one: it is a work book heavily marked by usage, not a treasured relic; it is a composite manuscript with multiple scribes adding material; and its constituent parts may have served multiple purposes over several decades from Chester-le-Street to Durham. The gloss to the Lindisfarne Gospels offers us the final product of a highly focused glossator who self-consciously records the completion of his assigned task in an unusually complex colophon. By contrast, the additions to Durham, MS A.iv.19 show us the process of textual compilation and glossing in a scribal community, remarked upon in a somewhat laconic colophon related only to one set of texts. In Durham, MS A.iv.19 we catch Aldred in the act of glossing and therefore learn much about his purposes and views of language.

1 I use Durham, MS A.iv.19 as a shortened label for this composite manuscript, rather than the misleading titles of Durham Ritual or Durham Collectar. All references to Durham, MS A.iv.19 additions use the numbering system in the critical edition in Jolly (2012), with quire number followed by text number; the folio numbers are those used in the facsimile (Brown 1969) with Quires IX and X re-sequenced.

1 Codicology and palaeography

As a composite manuscript with multiple scribes, Durham, MS A.iv.19 presents a number of codicological and palaeographic challenges, including the likelihood that the appended quires were in Aldred's time a collection of booklets only later bound with the collectar.[2] The original southern English collectar, penned by Scribe O and dated to the early tenth century, survives in eight quires, with at least one quire and more than 20 folios missing. After its acquisition by the community of St. Cuthbert at Chester-le-Street, Aldred glossed in Old English most, but not all, of the Latin texts. Quire VIII of the original collectar left several pages blank (ff. 61–65), into which Chester-le-Street scribes B, C, D, E, and F copied service book materials, with some glossing by Aldred (Brown 1969: 15–16; see also the Appendix). Appended to the manuscript are three more quires as presently numbered, with various materials added by Chester-le-Street and Durham scribes in the late tenth and early eleventh centuries. Quires IX and X form one booklet with connecting material, but are reversed in the binding and have been since before Humphrey Wanley cataloged the manuscript at the end of the seventeenth century; Quire IX has three bifolia plus an inserted half sheet, while Quire X is four singletons, of which the last, f. 76, has material that stands alone and could be placed elsewhere. The Quires IX–X booklet opens with Aldred's five glossed field prayers but primarily contains material copied by Scribe C unglossed by Aldred. Quire XI stands apart as a separate booklet dominated by texts and glosses in Aldred's hand. Although the first part of Quire XI includes service book material similar to the earlier quires, it changes after the colophon on f. 84r to encyclopedic materials. Moreover, as Jane Roberts notes in her paper in this volume, Quire XI's outer bifolium (ff. 77 and 88) contains separate work that could stand alone, leaving a more normal five-bifolia quire (ff. 78–87). Thus what survives in our hands as 'Durham, Cathedral Library, MS A.iv.19' may have been a loosely bound collection of booklets and independent folios at Chester-le-Street, only bound as one manuscript later. This is a very different manuscript project than the cohesive Lindisfarne Gospels, but for that reason quite enlightening.

Durham, MS A.iv.19's relationship to the Lindisfarne Gospels is problematic primarily in terms of dating Aldred's handiwork in both manuscripts and in determining his status. However long the gap between the Lindisfarne Gospels and Durham, MS A.iv.19, whether a few years or decades, Durham, MS A.iv.19's later linguistic evidence nonetheless sheds light on Aldred's entry work in the

2 For a full analysis of its codicology as disbound booklets, see Jolly (2012: 71–97 and 2013: 177–200); on booklets, see Hanna (1986) and Robinson (1978 and 1980).

Lindisfarne Gospels gloss. The most important feature of Durham, MS A.iv.19 in that respect is Aldred's preoccupation with word units, evident in 1) his element-by-element glossing of Latin morphemes producing in some cases calques; and 2) in his use of *vel* (ł) to offer more than one English translation of a Latin word. Indeed, these two strategies function together, the first offering a literal meaning that would enhance a student's understanding of the Latin word, and the second challenging himself or his readers to consider variable ways of thinking about a Latin concept. Durham, MS A.iv.19 is unique in that Aldred is glossing a great deal of service book material, prayers that ordinarily would not need glossing, and also because in it Aldred copied and glossed devotional and encyclopedic materials not found elsewhere, many with Irish antecedents. Analyzing these materials allows us a glimpse of bilingual glossing as a tool for reflection, communication, and instruction in the community of St. Cuthbert. The examples below reveal interactions between the glossator, the text, and possible pupils or readers that offer tantalizing evidence of the verbal environment of a religious community.

2 Aldred's logocentrism

Aldred loved words: he was preeminently and quite literally a philologist who strove to understand the variable meanings in words and found the bilingual interplay between Latin and Old English a rich and satisfying way to explore ideas. His 'logocentricity' had both literal and spiritual dimensions, most evident in the *Lit(er)a me pandat* verses attached to his colophon in the Lindisfarne Gospels:

> + *Lit(er)a me pandat sermonis fida ministra*
> 'letter me reveal of speech faithful servant' (literal trans.)
> *Omnes alme meos fratres voce salvta*
> 'all O kind one my brothers with voice greet' (literal trans.).

Translated loosely 'May the letter, faithful servant of speech, reveal me; salute all my brothers with your kindly voice', the verses express the glossator's sentiments toward his perceived audience. I take this as a challenge issued by Aldred to the reader, including us: unwrap this mystery. Moreover, the Lindisfarne Gospels' macaronic colophon sets up a four-fold, three-plus-one, pattern that is echoed in Aldred's linguistic exploits in Durham, MS A.iv.19, particularly the back part of Quire XI (ff. 85–88; Nees 2003: 333–377; Newton et al. 2013: 104-144; and Jolly 2012: 45–46).

Quire XI is very much Aldred's booklet, taken with him on his trip to Wessex with Bishop Ælfsige in 970 according to the colophon on f. 84r, where he notes the acquisition of the four Cuthbert collects recorded on that page (QXI.44–46; Jolly 2012: 60–70). The first portion of Quire XI, similar to the earlier quires, contains hymns, prayers, and psalms for the daily office, ending with the Cuthbert collects and Scribe E's later addition on f. 84, while the subsequent pages contain texts not directly related to services.

In this later section of the Quire XI booklet, Aldred wrote and glossed various lists, a kind of 'micropaedia', to use Kees Dekker's term (Dekker 2007: 279–315). There Aldred experiments with the *tres linguae sacrae* ('three sacred tongues') tradition, a form of philological exegesis (McNally 1958: 395–403). But he goes further and adds to the Hebrew, Greek, and Latin origins of titles and offices his own Northumbrian Old English. Just as he was the fourth maker of the Lindisfarne Gospels by adding his gloss, so his vernacular translation of the language lists shows him acting as the next generation of cultural go-between. For example, Aldred ended his explanation of ecclesiastical titles and their Biblical origins (QXI.51–52) with the phrase *id est antiqui plebi*(*u*?)*s* glossed "þæt is ða aldo folcum" ('that is, the old people'; f. 87vb15). In some ways this line epitomizes the task he set himself, to reveal by means of a gloss the ancient ways of thinking, to bring the Hebrew, Greek, and Latin patriarchs of the faith into contemporary Old English. As a consequence, understanding these vocabulary lists provides a key to understanding Aldred's glossing endeavor.

One curiously revealing moment occurs earlier in the encyclopedic section of Quire XI, in Aldred's gloss to the *notae juris* (QXI.48; Jolly 2012: 177–178). These abbreviations and expansions of juridical terms each receive an Old English equivalent in red, probably done in a second pass after the Latin was completed. As Aldred went back over the two-column text, he came to the abbreviation *q-s* (f. 86ra6). What apparently came first into his liturgical mind was the high frequency *quaesumus* 'we ask' or 'we pray', so he glossed it "we biddas", as he had done so many times before in the prayer texts. Then his eye must have traveled below to the Latin expansion he had written earlier for this abbreviation, *quasi* 'as if, just as, or like'. So he added the Old English equivalent of *quasi*, "suæ" (swæ) after "we biddas", without cancelling it, offering his pupils and readers two vocabulary words.

What does this incident tell us about Aldred's glossing project? First of all, he was looking at one word or even morpheme at a time, rather than whole phrases or lines, which is evident elsewhere in the manuscript in, for example, his habit of glossing every single word repeatedly, even *amen*, and yet also stopping his gloss mid-sentence at a page turn. Second, his purpose in creating and glossing the *notae juris*, as well as the other encyclopedic texts in this part of the manuscript, may have more to do with its value as a vocabulary exercise than strictly speaking as a guide for abbreviations or legal texts, since it does not appear that Aldred actually adopted any of the abbreviations from this list in his own Latin texts. This vocabulary exercise suggests a possible audience of Latin students for whom a translation of both words, *quasi* and *quaesumus*, would be useful. Whether these students were present as he glossed aloud to them, or only read the words later, is unknowable.

3 Master and pupil

However, one text in Durham, MS A.iv.19 does show us pupil and master interacting. A palaeographic analysis of Scribe B's copy of the John poison prayer, corrected and glossed by Aldred, reveals an intriguing pedagogical dialogue (Jolly 2012: 155–162). Aldred uses a Benedictine approach to reading and writing articulated in the *Regularis concordia*. The conversation between Aldred and Scribe B while they worked side-by-side may have ranged from pragmatic consideration of letter-forms to proper Latin pronunciation, from reptilian names to the meaning of evil.

The prayer against poison, derived from the apocryphal story of St. John, is a well-known and Irish favorite found also in late Anglo-Saxon medical texts (*Lacnunga* and *Bald's Leechbook*) and prayerbooks (*Cerne* and *Nunnaminster*), as well as the *Irish Liber Hymnorum* (Pettit 2001: II, 77–79). Scribe B's copy, his sole contribution, is in Quire VIII, in the first blank space after the end of the original collectar, although it was more than likely entered after later additions on subsequent pages (QVIII.1). Scribe B's work is not very competent in terms of orthography and Latin, so he may have been a novice, allowed this one opportunity to practise his craft. Aldred not only glossed the text, but corrected it in ways that indicate he was present while Scribe B worked, allowing Scribe B to effect changes in response to the master. In addition, some of the errors Scribe B committed suggest oral dictation as one possible mode of transmission, and indeed much of the vocabulary in this text is so difficult that it may have been chosen as purposely to test Scribe B's ability to record spoken Latin (Parkes 1997: 1–22 and 2008: 9; and Saenger 1997: 49). Following is a summary list of oddities indicating Scribe B's inexperience:

1. The opening letter *d* is overly thin for an enlarged initial because Scribe B attempted it with a narrow nib appropriate for the rest of his text, which nonetheless has a very uneven aspect.

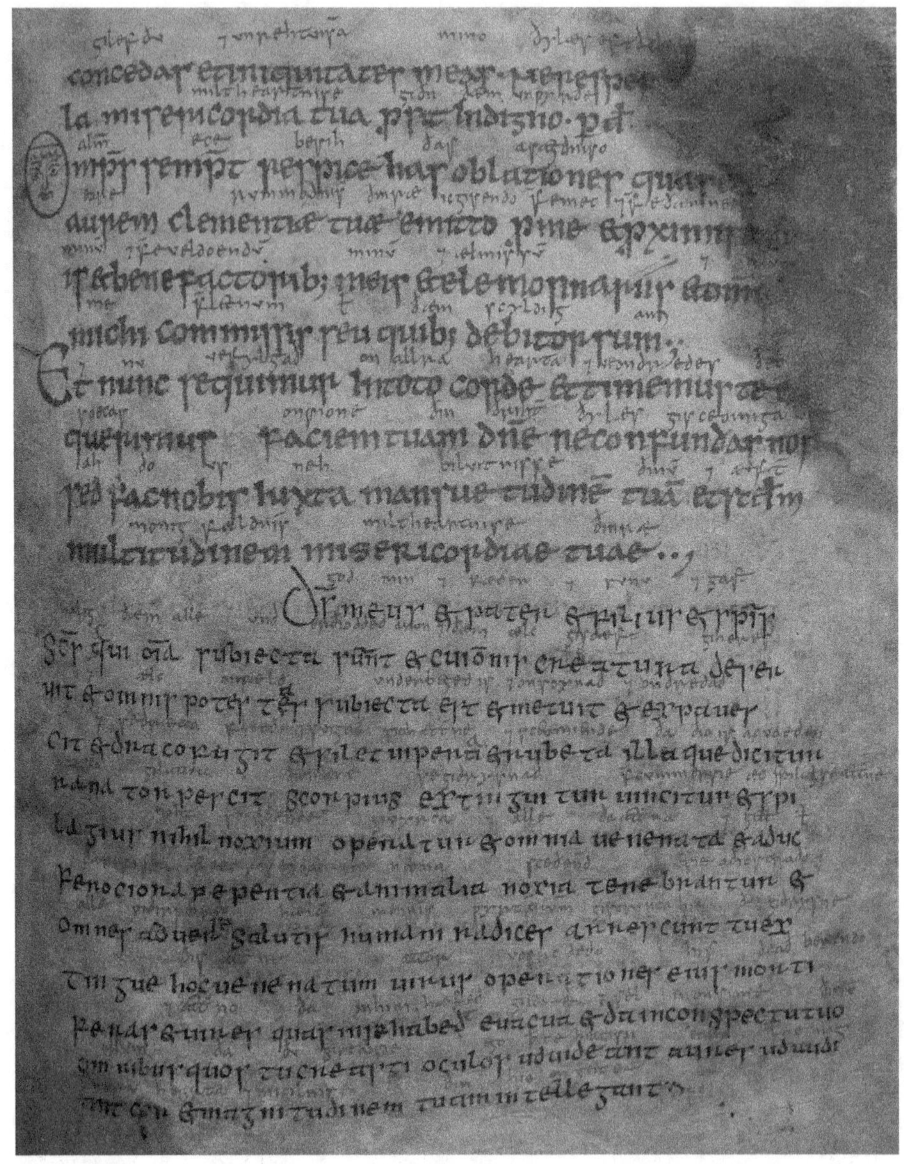

Figure 1. Durham, Cathedral Library, MS A.iv.19, f. 61r

2. In the first two lines (f. 61r11–12), Scribe B attempted abbreviations with macrons, but the results are non-standard: *spīs* for *spiritus* 'spirit', *ōia* for *omnia*, and *ōnis* for *omnis* 'all'. After that, he gave up abbreviating.

3. In his second line (f. 61r12), he wrote *qui* 'who' instead of *cui* 'whom', possibly an auditory error, but one that should have been corrected given the grammar of the phrase that follows, *cui omnia subiecta sunt* 'to whom all things are subject'. Aldred corrected it in the red ink of his glossing pen, but did not mark the anomalous abbreviation mark Scribe B put over *sunt*.
4. In the third line (f. 61r13), Scribe B changed *potestes*, putting a dot under the second *e* and adding an *a* above it to achieve *potestas* 'power'. Whether he caught this eye skip reduplicating error, or Aldred did, is unclear.
5. In the fourth line (f. 61r14), Aldred crossed out a letter *a* of Scribe B's and wrote a better one above it. Scribe B's letter *a* tended to be squarish, bordering on the appearance of a ligature *ti* (as in this case of *uipera* 'viper'), whereas Aldred's was a two-stroke Insular *a* with a curved bowl. In subsequent lines, Scribe B attempted to make some letters *a* like Aldred's, sometimes succeeding and other times forgetting, especially toward the end.
6. In the eighth line of his text (f. 61r18), Scribe B initially wrote a slurred word, *aduersalutis*, perhaps as he heard it. Then he corrected it, whether on his own or prompted by Aldred, adding the missing *-se* to form *aduerse salutis* 'adverse to health', e.g. 'unhealthy'.
7. In the last few lines, Scribe B misheard /d/ for /t/ in well-known Latin words: *habed* instead of *habet* 'has' (f. 61r20) and *ud* for *ut* 'that' (twice, f. 61r21). Aldred corrected all three with his red glossing ink.

Although these errors and corrections suggest a primary task of practising handwriting and spelling, Aldred's gloss also offered an opportunity to discuss the ideas in the text. In fact, he keeps glossing over to the next page of Scribe C's text for a few lines (QVIII.2; f. 61v1–10), as if he continued the lesson with Scribe B. One example there illustrating element-by-element glossing is *Redemptor* 'Redeemer', glossed "eftlesend" (f. 61v8), adding "eft" to emphasize *re-* 'again', although in other cases Aldred has glossed *redemptor* with simply *lesend* (from OE *lisan, lysan* 'to loose'). He may very well have been explaining the Latin morphemes to Scribe B, giving a literal rendering of *redemptor* as 're-leaser'.[3] Similarly he glossed *Auctor vitæ* 'Author of life' with "frumwyrhta lifes" ('first-wright of life'; f. 61v9), highlighting God as the original craftsman. He also varied the translation, glossing *subiecta* 'subjected' first as "underðiodded" ('join or attach under, subordinate'; f. 61r12) and then in the next line as "underbeged" ('bent

3 The West Saxon term for 'redeemer' is *alesend*; see also WS *liesan*, *lysan*, Angl. *lesan*. In addition to "eftlesend" here, Aldred also uses "onlesende" in QXI.54 (at f. 88vb3) to gloss the panther, allegorized as Christ the Redeemer: *Nemar id est christus iesus* ('panther, that is Christ Jesus') he glosses "onlesend þ' is crist se hæl'" ('redeemer, that is Christ the savior'). See Boyd (1975b: 51–55).

under'; f. 61r13). With this technique of glossing Latin morphemes, Aldred may have engaged Scribe B in a conversation of the text's spiritual import.

The prayer against poison Scribe B copied on the previous page provided an opportunity for Aldred to discuss word roots as well as Christian exorcism. The names of various reptiles not endemic in the British Isles may have been obscure even to Aldred, who could have known them only through classical sources like Pliny. For his pedagogical purposes, he chose literal renderings that allowed him to discuss Latin elements. For example, *rubeta*, identified in the text as *rana* 'frog', Aldred glossed with "sceomiende", evidently taking *rubeta* as the verb 'to redden' (f. 61r14). He again used a participle as a substantive to gloss *ferociora repentia* (f. 61r17) with "ða rifista feerræsenda". Although the noun *repentia* in this case is derived from the verb *reptio* 'creeping, crawling thing', i.e. a reptile, Aldred takes it as derived from *repens/repentinus* and offers a unique Old English compound: "fær", indicating 'sudden danger', and "ræsan" ('to rush violently'), a word he also used to gloss *impetu* in Luke 8.33 describing the herd of possessed pigs rushing over the cliff edge. Moreover, he also glossed *repentino* in Proverbs 3.25 with *id est diabolum*, indicating overall a sensitivity to the spiritual dimensions of *repens* as having demonic associations (Oxford, Bodleian Library, MS Bodley 819, f. 8r7). The choice of the St. John prayer against poison for this exercise perhaps indicates that Scribe B was at the lowly rung of exorcist and charged with learning prayers for cleansing sacramental utensils. Aldred may very well have used this text to engage Scribe B with the problem of evil-demonic, Viking, or otherwise.

This suggestive conversation between master and pupil is reminiscent of the learning environment encouraged by the Benedictine Rule and found in pedagogical dialogue literature. Monastic education in *lectio divina* 'divine reading' emphasizes meditative reading in relation to writing, as detailed by Malcolm Parkes and also explicated by Michelle Brown (Parkes 1991: 1–18 and 1997: 1–22; Brown 2011b: 30–32). We see Aldred instructing Scribe B in *lectio* or *rædan* 'reading', both in decoding letters and identifying morphological units, but also engaging in *emendatio*, correcting the text. Given the nature of the corrections and gloss, we also suspect that some *pronuntiatio* and *enarratio* or *areccan* 'stretching' or 'reaching' took place in an oral dialogue over the text on the page. Finally, one wonders if Aldred brought Scribe B to the stage of *iudicium* or *smeagan* 'to investigate, inquire, deliberate' in order to discern the *gastlic andgit* 'spiritual significance'. Aldred's conversation with Scribe B over the John poison prayer shows us a 'live' session of writing, reading, and pondering.

Similarly, the *Regularis concordia*, its compilation underway simultaneously with Aldred's work, connects mind and spirit, reading and prayer. The Rule urges them all to chant prayers aloud distinctly so that the mind, *mens* or *geþangc*, is in accord with the spirit, *spiritus* or *gast* (§ 8; Kornexl 1993: 10). During a quiet period the junior members are to read spiritual lessons while the senior members engage in divine *oratio*, implying that junior members need a book to guide prayer while the seniors do not (§ 25; Kornexl 1993: 44). An example of this practice occurs in a set of prayers for the hours that Aldred added in the first part of his Quire XI booklet. He left off glossing the psalm incipits for the hours and special times, but persisted in glossing the instructions, presumably because the Latin of the psalm was familiar to his audience, but the Latin instructions might prove difficult for some novices (QXI.43; Jolly 2012: 126–127). For example, the last psalm, the notoriously long Psalm 118, is recommended for 'practice': *Si exercere te uolueris in diuinis laudibus decanta* glossed "gif bigeonga ðec ðv wæll [...] on godcundum herenis' gesing" ('when you would want to practise singing divine praises'). One can almost imagine Aldred patiently explaining these meditative practices to his brothers. This suggests in turn that Aldred made his glossing habit the perfect tool for enhancing his community's prayer life.

4 Alternative reflections

In addition to element-by-element glossing, every *vel* (ɫ) in Aldred's gloss was an opportunity for reflection and instruction, perhaps even more so on the ones left 'empty' after the *vel*, which might have provided exactly that pause ("or ...") needed for reflection and discussion. As others have noted, Aldred's double glosses often include first a literal, often element-by-element, translation of the Latin, and second a more liberal Old English alternative, either of which might be neologisms found only in Aldred's glosses or involve seemingly odd or even 'wrong' translations (Ross 1979: 194–198; Ross and Squires 1980: 489–495; Pons-Sanz, this volume). But it is wise to remember we are missing the internal or external conversation that took place while he contemplated or explained what he was about. At the very least we should examine the manuscript context carefully rather than relying entirely on dictionary or thesaurus entries using older editions of the manuscript. For example, in the title to the field prayers (QIX.14), Aldred glossed Latin *creatura super messem p(ro) avib(us) in XIIII* [...] with "gescæft of 'hrippe f 'e fvglvm in feoverteno" ('creature over the fields for birds on fourteenth'; f. 66r1). Above "gescæft" is "ɫ halgung" ('blessing'), resulting in a dictionary entry identifying *halgung* as an Aldredian translation of *creatura*, although Aldred clearly understands and consistently glosses *creatura* with *gescæft* elsewhere (Jolly 2006: 104–105 and 2012: 61, 80, 144–146). The solution is in the manuscript, where in the upper left corner above the title Aldred has written an *xb'* for *christus benedictus* 'Christ blessing'. Thus the "ł halgung" is most likely a gloss to *benedictus*.[4]

The *vel* glosses, empty or not, may therefore tell us more about Aldred and his community than about Old English in general. Nonetheless, his process of thinking while glossing reveals a great deal about how bilinguality functioned in a religious community as a form of spiritual reflection. For example, in the tract *De octo pondera*, on the eight pounds of which Adam was made (QXI.49), Aldred's version of this Irish-rooted text includes speculations on the relationship between mind and spirit, evident in the last three items of Adam's composition, clouds, wind, and grace (Jolly 2012: 179–182). He identifies clouds (*nubis* / "uolcnes") with unstable thought (*instabilitas mentium*) but his gloss offered two alternatives for this mental instability (f. 86va1): "unstydfullnisse ł unstaðolfastnis' ðohta'". The first is a Northumbrianism unique to Aldred, "unstydfullnisse" seeming to indicate 'unsteadfast' or 'unsteady', but in other cases 'inconstant, indicating apostacy', while the second, "unstaðolfastnis'", is a more common Old English word for 'unstable'. Was he perhaps explaining the Latin to a mixed audience of Old English speakers, or just playing with the variants? With the pound of grace, *gratia* or *gefe*, he glossed the Latin explanation *sensus homini* with "ðoht ł [...] monnes" (f. 86va4–5), as if he were searching for an alternative word for sense than thought, since he had just used "ðohta'" two lines above to gloss *mentium*. Overall, he seems to be interested in exploring a range of words for human reflection, the very act in which he is engaged.

Meanwhile, the element of wind is addressed in two *Joca monachorum* style questions appended to the *De octo pondera* text (f. 86va5–16). The answer to the first question, 'tell me why the two breaths ("anhela") are not equal, whereby one is hot and the other is cold', purportedly explains inhaling and exhaling but with spiritual overtones: 'It is that the one is of fire and the other is of wind. And this signifies ("getacnað") that from these is made the spirit'.[5] This is continued with the answer to the second question, 'tell me whence the wind blows', identifying the angelic source: 'It is from the seraphim, hence it is said seraphim of the winds'. Similarly, the alphabet poem on the last page of Quire XI (on the separable outer bifolium) also suggests a conversation about the letter and the spirit

4 I should also like to add here an update to the incomplete title and parallels to Aldred's field prayers invoking the anomalous archangel Panchiel. In addition to the version in Vienna, Nationalbibliothek, MS Lat. 1888 (f. 6), another instance is found in a twelfth-century manuscript, Vatican City, Biblioteca Apostolica, MS Vat. Lat. 642, ff. 91v–94v, that does have the complete title, indicating the calendar reference is to XIII *luna* (Svenberg 1963: 36). My thanks to Richard Sowerby for bringing this manuscript to my attention.

5 Also an allusion to the Holy Spirit who appears as both wind and fire at Pentecost in Acts 1.

(QXI.54; f. 88va1–24, b1–21; Jolly 2012: 197–198). The poem moves from Creation to Last Judgment, with Christ woven throughout the Old Testament and Incarnate in the New. The crux of the poem occurs at the top of the b column (f. 88vb1): *Lumen id est uerum lumen*, glossed "leht þ' is soð leht ł" ('light, that is, true light'), is set amid Christological imagery reminiscent of *The Dream of the Rood* and the Ruthwell Cross.

Aldred's literalism here and elsewhere may seem pedantic at times, but clearly has a spiritual dimension that speaks to the heart of his religious community. These texts, and others in the encyclopedic additions of Quire XI, add to our picture of Aldred as a glossator. Aldred's word-for-word glosses, here and in the Lindisfarne Gospels, are not translations for Latin illiterate readers, they are guides for bilingual readers. We begin to see that glossing for him was a path to spiritual insight: bilinguality was a way of exploring the relationship between the local and the global, between Anglo-Saxon language and culture and that of the Roman Christian tradition. Aldred elevates the philologist to philosopher: the wordsmith is also a theologian.

5 Conclusions

What are the implications of these insights into Aldred's working life in Durham, MS A.iv.19 for those who study and use his gloss to understand the Lindisfarne Gospels as well as Old English language? First of all, Aldred's use of element-by-element glossing means that many of the unique compounds found only in his glosses, as for example in the Scribe B St. John prayer, may be calques, idiosyncratic 'Aldredisms' not necessarily representative of spoken or written Northumbrian Old English. Second, the glossing in Durham, MS A.iv.19, and therefore potentially in the Lindisfarne Gospels, may have been produced in conversation with an audience and intended thereafter for oral use in the community as they engaged in study and reflection of the texts, whether Gospels, prayers, poems, or tracts. Third, linguists should not rely exclusively on the dictionary extractions from the older editions of these texts, particularly when Aldred's is the only attested use of a term, but should go back to the manuscript to see the potentially oral or pedagogical context (Page 1992: 77–95). For this last task, I hope that placing the additions to Durham, MS A.iv.19 online will facilitate searching the text and inspire others to make bilingual Latin / Old English texts available electronically.[6]

Finally, the intense effort Aldred put into glossing both the Lindisfarne Gospels and Durham, MS A.iv.19 compels us to ask: why? The examples discussed in this paper suggest at least three purposes for his labor, intentionally interconnected: writing instruction, vocabulary study, and spiritual reflection. Because we are passive viewers of the final, written product, we often overlook the interactive, oral processes that took place while Aldred glossed, and the possibility that others might have been involved as auditors or interlocutors. Perhaps we need to let go of the notion of a silent scriptorium isolated from the schoolroom and begin to hear what might have taken place when scribes and readers interacted with a text in a group setting, particularly when that text is as consciously bilingual as Aldred's. The highly personal nature of Aldred's colophon in the Lindisfarne Gospels has contributed to the feeling of a solitary man laboring over his *opus Dei*, and yet that same colophon addresses his brothers as audience for that gloss. Even if he did work alone for much of the time while glossing, Aldred had specific audiences in mind besides God and St. Cuthbert.[7]

6 Now at the University of Hawai'i Scholar Space (<http://scholarspace.manoa.hawaii.edu/handle/10125/26967>). See also <http://www2.hawaii.edu/~kjolly>.

7 My thanks to Sara Pons-Sanz and Julia Fernández Cuesta for organizing the workshop on the Old English Gloss to the Lindisfarne Gospels at the University of Westminster, April 2012, and for allowing me to provide some later Chester-le-Street context from Durham, Cathedral Library, MS A.iv.19.

Appendix

	Durham, Cathedral Library, MS A.v.19 Additions: Codicological Map							
	Key:		**Ben**edictions; **Ora**tio; **Coll**ects; **Cap**itula	grey=discussed in essay; dark=stand alone bifolium	**Q# (Jolly 2012)**	***Scribe: A=Aldred; contemporary B, C, D, E, F; later M1, M2, M3. Gloss: Y=Yes; N=No; P=Partial***		
Quire	**foliation**		**type of material**	**folio #s**	**Q #**	**content**	**Scribe**	**Gloss**
VIII	6 bifolia	54–61r10				end of original collectar		
		61–65	**Additions:**		**QVIII**			
			Ben.	61r11–22	1	John poison cup	B	Y
			Ben.	61v1–62v18	2	Lections	C	P
			Ben.	62v18/–63v4	3	*lac et mel*, cross	C	N
			Ben.	63v5–64r8	4–7	grapes, bread, fruits, wells	D	N
			Orat.	64r9–17	8	generic (2)	E	N
			Hymn	64v1–16	9	Passiontide Hy 68	C	N
			Verses	64v17–65rb17	10	Tob., Jud., Macc., Min. proph.	F	N
			Hymn	65rb18–65v29	11–13	Easter Hy 55	C	N
IX	3 bifolia + 1 f.	66–72	**Additions:**		**QIX–X**	**booklet**		
			Ben.	66r1–67v5	14a–e	Field prayers (5)	A	Y
			Ben., Orat.	67v6–70r14	15–21	exorcism, prayers, memorials	C/M3	N
			Memorials	70r15–73r22	22–23	Memoria, Masses, Suffrages	C	N

Durham, Cathedral Library, MS A.v.19 Additions: Codicological Map								
	Key:		**Ben**edictions; **Orat**io; **Coll**ects; **Cap**itula	grey=discussed in essay; dark=stand alone bifolium	**Q# (Jolly 2012)**	***Scribe: A=Aldred; contemporary B, C, D, E, F; later M1, M2, M3. Gloss: Y=Yes; N=No; P=Partial***		
Quire	**foliation**		**type of material**	**folio #s**	**Q #**	**content**	**Scribe**	**Gloss**
X	4 folia	73–76						
			Mass/Suffrage	73r1–75v23	23 cont.	Masses, Suffrages	C	N
			Note	75v24–25	23M1	honoring Aldhun	M1	N
			Collects	76r1–26	24a–h	canonical hours (8)	C	N
			Verses	76v1–29	25	Kings, Wisdom, Job	F	N
XI	6 bifolia	77–88	**Additions:**		**QXI**			
			Hymn	77r1–77v18	26–31	Hy 7 –10, 72, 1	A	Y
			Pontifical?	77v19–25	32	Episcopal Benedictions	M2	N
			Cap., Coll.	78r1–79vb14	33–35	Prime	A	Y
			Cap., rubric	79vb15–80va11	36	Terce, Sext, None	A	Y
			Coll., Cap.	80va12–82rb11	37–39	Vespers	A	Y
			Hy, Cap., Coll.	82rb12–83rb10	40–41	Compline	A	Y
			Psalms	83rb11–84ra2	42–43	7 penitential, Prime–Vespers	A	Y/P
			Collects	84ra4–23, b1–18	44	Collects for Cuthbert (4)	A	N
			Note	84ra24–26, rb19–26	45–46	memorandum, colophon	A	N

	Durham, Cathedral Library, MS A.v.19 Additions: Codicological Map						
	Key:	**Ben**edictions; **Ora**tio; **Coll**ects; **Cap**itula	grey=discussed in essay; dark=stand alone bifolium	**Q# (Jolly 2012)**	***Scribe: A=Aldred; contemporary B, C, D, E, F; later M1, M2, M3. Gloss: Y=Yes; N=No; P=Partial***		
Quire	**foliation**	**type of material**	**folio #s**	**Q #**	**content**	**Scribe**	**Gloss**
		Verses	84v1–35	47	1st 4 Sundays in Advent	E	N
		Educ. Mem.	85ra1–86rb9	48	*notae juris*	A	Y
		Educ. Mem.	86rb10–86va16	49a–b	8 pounds of Adam & 2 Qs	A	Y
		Educ. Mem.	86va16–87ra10	50a–c	Titles and Offices	A	Y
		Educ. Mem.	87ra11–87va15	51	*De gradibus ęcclessię*	A	Y
		Educ. Mem.	87va16–b15	52	priesthood names	A	Y
			87vb16–35		blank		
		Educ. Mem.	88ra1–b24	53	apostles' burial places	A	Y
		Educ. Mem.	88va1–24, b1–21	54	alphabet of words	A	Y
		Educ. Mem.	88vb22–6, a25–6	55	Canon table	A	Y
binding	cut f. 89	Lectionary		56	8th cent. north. lectionary		

Tadashi Kotake

Did Owun Really Copy from the Lindisfarne Gospels? Reconsideration of His Source Manuscript(s)

Abstract: This paper considers the validity of the widespread premise that Owun, the second glossator of the Rushworth Gospels, copied his gloss (Ru^2) from Aldred's gloss to the Lindisfarne Gospels (Li.). Owun's glosses and corrections reflecting Latin readings found in neither of the two manuscripts are examined. Such readings, designated here as 'non R–Y readings', are collected and collated with variant readings extant in other Latin Gospels. The textual evidence presented in this survey indicates a more complex relationship between the two glosses than direct copying, and suggests that the answer to the question raised in the title of the paper should be "no". It is also pointed out that the 'non R–Y readings' introduced by Owun often agree with those in a specific textual family of the Latin Vulgate Gospels.

In order to achieve a fuller understanding of Aldred's gloss to the Lindisfarne Gospels (London, British Library, MS Cotton Nero D.iv), it is essential to scrutinize its relationship to the other extant Latin Gospel manuscript containing Old English continuous interlinear glosses, i.e. the Rushworth Gospels, also known as the MacRegol Gospels (Oxford, Bodleian Library, MS Auct. D.2.19).[1] The Rushworth Gospels was glossed by two glossators, Farman and Owun, as the colophons added to the manuscript reveal;[2] Farman undertook the glossing of all of

1 See *CLA* (II, no. 231), McGurk (1961: no. 33) and Gneuss and Lapidge (2014: no. 531) for the manuscript, and Ker (1957: no. 292) for the Old English glosses in particular. The Old English glosses to the Rushworth Gospels are printed in Skeat (1871–1887) without its own Latin text, which is presented only insufficiently in the appendices. A facsimile reproduction is published as part of the Anglo-Saxon Manuscripts in Microfiche Facsimile series; see Liuzza and Doane (1995). High-resolution images of the entire manuscript are available online at Bodleian Library's LUNA (see n. 6 in the Introduction), on which the observations presented in this paper are based.

2 Farman's colophon on f. 50v reads (see n. 8 below for the conventions used for transcription): "Far(man) p(res)b(yte)r þas boc þus gleosede dimittet ei d(omi)n(u)s omnia peccata sua si fieri po(test) ap(ud) d(eu)m:-" ('Farman the priest thus glossed this book; may the Lord forgive him all his sins, if it can be so with God.'). The translation follows Skeat (1878: xi), whose translation suggests that he reads, probably rightly, "dimittat" for "dimittet"; and Owun's on ff. 168v–169r "ðe min bruche gibidde fore owun ðe ðas boc gloesde. færmen ðæm preoste æt harawuda. | hæfe nu boc awritne bruca mið willa symle mið soðum gileofa sibb is eghwæm leofost:-" ('Let him who uses me pray for Owun, who glossed this book for Farman the priest at *harawuda*; take

Matthew, Mark 1.1–2.15 (up to "gereston ł hleonadun" 'rested or reclined' glossing *discumbebant* 'reclined at table') and John 18.1–18.3, and Owun the remainder. Comparative studies of the Old English glosses in the two manuscripts have shown that some portions of the Rushworth glosses bear similarities of varying degrees to Aldred's gloss to the Lindisfarne Gospels (hereafter Li.). In particular, Owun's gloss, called Rushworth 2 (Ru^2) as against Farman's Rushworth 1 (Ru^1), in its entirety resembles Li. so closely that one might assume Ru^2 to be a copy made directly from Li.[3] In fact, studies dealing with these glosses tend to rest on the premise that Owun copied his gloss from Li.[4] Yet, the notion of direct copying should not be taken for granted, as will be shown below, and the present paper will query this widespread premise by scrutinizing the evidence relating to Latin textual matters.

Of course, it must be admitted that the relationship of the two Old English glosses should be examined in the first place in respect of the glosses themselves, not Latin textual matters. Discussions of the phonology and morphology of Old English have paid due attention to Li. and Ru^2, identifying a considerable number of differences between them mostly relating to spellings which have been seen as Owun's dialectal adjustments made during the process of copying from Li.[5] Apart

now the book written (or 'glossed'?); use [it] with joy, always with true belief; peace is dearest to everyone.'). The translation is mine with reference to Skeat (1878: xi), and also to Cook (1898: lv), who regards the second part of Owun's colophon beginning "hæfe nu [...]" as "a poetic distich".

3 Ru^1 in Mark also bears close similarity to Li., which will be mentioned briefly later in this paper (see p. 393). Ross (1979) finds similarities between Li. and Ru^1 also in Matthew 26–28, but the nature and degree of agreement is different from that observed in Mark. See Kotake (2012) for a detailed discussion of the relationship between the two glosses in this section.

4 The notion of Owun's direct copying from Li. appears to derive from academic correspondence between W. W. Skeat, the editor of the Cambridge edition of the glosses (Skeat 1871–1887), and Sir James Murray. The former states in the first volume he edited that "Farman and Owun actually consulted the identical Lindisfarne MS. which we now possess" (Skeat 1871: xii-xiii). Murray (1875: 452), in developing Skeat's theories, summarily writes in his review of the edition that Skeat "is the first to point out with regard to (a great part of) the Rushworth gloss, that it is simply a copy of that of the Lindisfarne". Later, Skeat (1878: xii-xv) incorporates a large part of Murray's note (1875: 452–453), which is written based on the premise of direct copying, into the introduction to his edition of John's Gospel. Writing before these publications, however, George Waring, one of the editors of the Surtees Society edition of the glosses, assumes that the two glossators "drew from a common original" (Waring 1854–1865: IV, civ–cv). This possibility has been largely ignored by later studies, which tend to repeat Skeat and Murray's theory of direct copying, apart from some exceptions such as Ker (1957: no. 292), who leaves both possibilities open by stating that Ru^2 "is derived from the same source as" Li. and "may have been copied from" it.

5 For specific studies on the phonology and morphology of Ru^2, see Lindelöf (1901) and Ross (1977). For general works, see Campbell (1959), Brunner (1965), Hogg (1992a), and Hogg and Fulk (2011) among others.

from such discussions, however, Ru^2 has tended to be dismissed as a mere, and perhaps inferior, copy of Li. Although some recent studies have noted differences between Li. and Ru^2 in their vocabulary and syntax,[6] adding to the substantial list of their differences presented by Bibire and Ross (1981), the general assumption that Ru^2 is a copy made from Li. has not been challenged seriously, because the differences are not considered strong enough to disprove the premise. Yet, linguistic differences between the two glosses at least suggest the necessity of reconsidering their relationship, and the present study aims to show that evidence related to Latin textual matters, largely ignored by previous studies, can be useful in broadening the scope of this reconsideration.

The main reason why the present study proposes to investigate the evidence relating to Latin textual matters is the abundance of readings peculiar to the Rushworth Gospels. Its text, abbreviated as R according to the sigla used in Wordsworth and White's (1889–1898) edition of the Vulgate (WW), is usually assigned to the mixed Irish family of the Vulgate, and accordingly differs in many respects from the text of the Lindisfarne Gospels (Y), a purer Vulgate text assigned to the Italo-Northumbrian family.[7] Some Rushworthian readings are not, however, reflected in Owun's gloss, but instead his gloss often appears to follow purer Vulgate readings, as represented by the Lindisfarne Gospels. For example, in (1) Ru^2's "godes" 'of God' must be considered as reflecting a Latin reading differ-

6 For example, van Bergen (2008: 294–296) notes interesting differences between the two glosses as regards negative contractions. Kotake (2008a) compares the syntax of the two glosses; Kotake (2007: Appendix) and Kotake (2008b) deal with lexical differences shown by the synonymous word pairs *don/wyrcan* 'to do, work' and *andswarian/andwyrdan* 'to answer', respectively. These studies by the present author have shown that there are more differences between the two glosses in John than in the other two Gospels that Owun glossed.

7 See Liuzza (1994–2000: II, 1–26) for a convenient summary of the Latin Gospel texts available in Anglo-Saxon England, and Loewe (1969) for the medieval textual history of the Latin Vulgate. See also relevant chapters, especially those by Pierre-Maurice Bogaert and Dorothy Shepard, in Marsden and Matter (2012). No comprehensive survey of the Latin text of the Rushworth Gospels has been conducted, but see McGurk (1990), a textual survey of the Book of Kells (Dublin, Trinity College, MS 58), for a general account of the mixed Irish family of the Vulgate. Although there are sceptical views about the notion of 'Irish' readings, as expressed by Verey (1980), the point crucial for the present study is that R contains by far more non-Vulgate readings than Y, resulting in many textual disagreements between the two texts. This fact can be observed in a list presented in Fischer (2010: 132–136), which shows the degree to which each manuscript examined in Fischer (1988–1991) agrees with the Stuttgart Vulgate (Xz). R (Fischer's Hr) shows very low agreement, being the 415th highest of the 462 manuscripts examined (87.1% agreement), as against Y's (Ny) 90th (96.6%). I am grateful to Professor Patrick McGurk for drawing my attention to this reference.

ent from R, which wants *dei* 'of God', and Owun's direct copying from Li. would account for his use of "godes" in this particular example.

(1) Mark 4.11[8] (Y f. 101va13–15; R f. 57v21)

Y *uobis datum est scire misterium regni d(e)i illis autem qui foris sunt in parabolis omnia fiunt*

R *uobis datum est nosse mysterium regni illis autem qui foris sunt in parabulis omnia fiunt*

Li. iouh gesald is þ(æt) ge wita hernise rices godes ðæm uut(edlice) ða ðe uta sint in bispellum alle biðon

Ru² iow gisald is ðæt giwite rice **godes** ðæm ðonne ða ðe ute werun in bispellum alle bioðon

'To you it is given to know the mystery of the kingdom of God but to them that are without, all things are done in parables'.

Such an interpretation may further be reinforced by the fact that Owun sometimes corrects the Rushworth text to introduce readings agreeing with Y, as can be seen in (2):

(2) Luke 1.54 (Y f. 141vb20–22; R f. 88r2–3)

Y *suscepit israhel puerum suum memorari misericordię suę*

R *suscipit israhel puerum suum memorari misericordiae \suæ/*

Li. ondfeng isr(ae)l cnæht his þ(æt)te were gemyndgad miltheortnise his

Ru² onfeng israhelum cnæhte his þ(æt)te were gimyndgad mildheortnisse his

'He hath received Israel his servant, being mindful of his mercy'.

R in its original state wants *suæ* 'his', which is supplied in Owun's hand, and the resulting reading therefore agrees with Y. These examples apparently corroborate the theory of direct copying from the Lindisfarne manuscript. However, careful scrutiny of Owun's glosses and corrections yields the important fact that they contain traces of Latin readings not recorded in either the Lindisfarne or Rushworth manuscripts. Such readings are here called 'non R–Y readings'.

---

8 In citations, manuscript readings are reproduced. In both Latin texts and Old English glosses, abbreviations are expanded in round brackets, with the exception of ł (*vel* 'or') and ⁊ (*and* 'and') in the glosses. When the differences between Y and R are significant and relevant to the discussion, both readings are cited alongside. When they agree with each other, apart from insignificant spelling variations, only Y is cited. Insertions in the Latin text are indicated by \ /. Emphasis by bold face is editorial in order to indicate words or phrases relevant to the discussion. English translations are taken from the *Douay-Rheims Bible*.

The traces of non R–Y readings in Owun's portions have not gone entirely unnoticed, but, crucially, they have been examined only on the premise that his gloss is a copy made from the Lindisfarne Gospels. Thus, Bibire and Ross (1981: 114–115) classify such examples under the heading 'Owun's use of other manuscripts' – if his source was in fact the Lindisfarne Gospels itself, Owun must have introduced such non R–Y readings by using some other sources than Y. However, once the premise of direct copying is put aside, the existence of non R–Y readings may imply other possibilities, for example, that the two glosses stem from a common source, or that there were intervening copies between the two extant glosses through which non R–Y readings were introduced. In other words, the non R–Y readings may have been introduced into Owun's portions through textual transmission specific to his gloss.

The rest of this paper examines non R–Y readings found in Owun's glosses and corrections. A good starting point for this investigation is Bibire and Ross's list of examples suggesting Owun's use of other manuscripts. In re-examining their data, it is important to point out that their list fails to make a fundamental distinction between two different types of evidence, namely, between (1) Owun's corrections to the Latin text which introduce non R–Y readings and (2) Owun's Old English glosses reflecting non R–Y readings. The present study distinguishes these two types clearly, calling them Type 1 and Type 2, respectively. This distinction is important in several respects; for instance, Type 2 examples should not necessarily be taken as evidence for Owun's use of other Latin manuscripts, because they may have been copied from a now-lost Old English exemplar that reflected non R–Y readings, whereas Type 1 evidence will convey more accurate information about the Latin readings available to Owun. These two types of evidence will be considered separately below, and each non R–Y reading will be compared with WW's critical apparatus, in order to examine the distribution of the non R–Y readings in other Vulgate manuscripts.[9]

9 As to the distribution of these readings in other manuscripts, Bibire and Ross (1981: 115) emphasize the necessity of an investigation to ascertain whether the relevant non R–Y readings "can be attested in any of the Aldredian manuscripts". By this, they mean the manuscripts available at Chester-le-Street (or Durham) in Aldred's time. A list of such manuscripts compiled by Julian Brown is presented in Ross (1981: 7). It must be remembered, however, that these manuscripts have not been fully collated, and more importantly that the notion that Owun had access to the manuscripts Aldred could have used rests on the premise that Owun went to Chester-le-Street (or Durham) to copy his gloss from the Lindisfarne Gospels, a premise that requires further consideration. In the present study, therefore, comparisons will be made against the critical apparatus in WW, as mentioned. See Verey (1980: 60), for the advantage of using WW's apparatus, especially as a tool for an initial assessment of the Vulgate texts. When available and relevant to the discussion, data from Fischer (1988–1991) are reported in notes, which may point to the incomplete-

Type 1 examples are confined to insertions in the Latin text, because corrections to the Latin text can be securely attributed to Owun only when his handwriting is involved. Apart from the palaeographical dimension, identification of Type 1 examples is a more straightforward procedure than that of Type 2 examples. For this reason, the instances assigned to this type overlap with those identified by Bibire and Ross. A typical example is given in (3) below, where Latin *uero* 'indeed, however' is inserted in R by Owun, with its corresponding gloss "wutud" (presumably for *wutudlice* 'truly, however', but without any mark of abbreviation). However, Y does not have *uero*, and therefore Owun's use of the Lindisfarne Gospels does not account for this insertion. In contrast, several other Gospel manuscripts do have the Latin adverb:

(3) [1-1][10] Luke 2.15 (Y f. 143vb12–13; R f. 89v9)
Y *Pastores loquebantur ad inuicem*
R *pastores \uero/ loquebantur ad inuicem*
Li. ða hiorde`a´ gesprecon bituih[11]
Ru² ða hiordas wutud gisprecun bitwih him
'the shepherds said one to another'
pastores + uero: Ea, Eb, Jb, Jo, Jz.[12]

All the Type 1 examples are presented in Table 1, which shows that their distribution is uneven, with all of the instances found in Luke, even though corrections to the Latin text in general are found more evenly through the three Gospels that Owun glossed.[13] The list of Gospel manuscripts that contain these non R–Y readings is presented as Table 2, which will be analyzed in detail later in this paper.

ness of WW's apparatus in terms of the number of the manuscripts examined. However, because the examples with which we are concerned are found sporadically throughout the Gospels, it is impossible to rely solely on Fischer (1988–1991), which presents the collation of more than 450 manuscripts, but only for 16 selected extracts of the four Gospels.

10 The citation number in square brackets agrees with those used in Tables 1–3.

11 In the manuscript, *a* is written above *e* of "hiorde", with the latter being not cancelled. Skeat (1874: 31) reads "hiorda", but as cancellation is not marked, both readings should be noted. See Ross (1937: 6), who assumes that this type of superscript without cancelling the original should be read as "hiorde ł hiorda".

12 For the sigla used, which follow Fischer (1988–1991), see Appendix. A siglum followed by * indicates the manuscript's original reading that is later corrected. A siglum followed by ^{c} indicates a corrected reading in the manuscript.

13 There is one instance of possible relevance outside Luke. As cited by Bibire and Ross (1981: 15), in John 6.11, *et* is inserted in R by Owun (*similiter \et/ ex piscibus* 'in like manner also of the fishes'), which is also lacking in Y. Yet, the resulting reading is very common, shared with most of other manuscripts, and it is difficult to judge whether this insertion is Owun's spontaneous

It should be noted for the moment that they are shared most frequently with Eb (eight instances out of 11) and Jo (seven instances).

Table 1. List of the Type 1 non R–Y examples

Citation No.	Verse	Owun's insertion to R
1-1	Lk 2.15	*pastores* + *uero*/
1-2	Lk 3.23	*filius* +*e(ss)e*/
1-3	Lk 9.18	*discipuli* + *ei(us)*/
1-4	Lk 9.55	*conuersus* + *ie(su)s*/
1-5	Lk 9.58	*caput* + *suu(m)*/
1-6	Lk 16.31	*credent* + *ei*/
1-7	Lk 19.1	*perambulabat* + *in*/
1-8	Lk 19.44	*filios* + *tuos*/
1-9	Lk 19.45	*ingressus* + *ie(su)s*/
1-10	Lk 20.26	*responso eius* + *et*/
1-11	Lk 24.19	*dixerunt* + *ei*/

Table 2. List of the manuscripts sharing the Type 1 non R–Y readings

	Vulgate																	**OL MSS**
	Ai	**Be**	**Cv**	**Ea**	**Eb**	**Ge**	**Hd**	**Hq**	**Jb**	**Jo**	**Jx**	**Jz**	**Oh**	**Om**	**Ot**	**Pg**	**Tg**	
1-1				+	+				+	+		+						
1-2							+									+		+
1-3		+		+	+					+								+
1-4										+								+
1-5			+	+	+					+			+(1)	+	+		+	+

alteration or a reflection of a variant reading. For this reason, this example is excluded from our discussion.

Table 2. (continued)

	Vulgate																	OL MSS
	Ai	Be	Cv	Ea	Eb	Ge	Hd	Hq	Jb	Jo	Jx	Jz	Oh	Om	Ot	Pg	Tg	
1-6					+					+			+	+(C)				+
1-7							+											
1-8	+	+	+	+	+		+	+	+	+	+(*)	+			+		+	+
1-9					+						+(C)							
1-10					+													
1-11				+	+	+				+								+

NB + designates that the manuscript shares the particular reading. Due to limited space, individual Old Latin manuscripts are not listed; instead, 'OL MSS' is checked when at least one of Old Latin manuscripts shares the reading. Later manuscripts (i.e. those not used by Fischer as WW's W) and printed editions are not examined.
WW's conventions are followed: * [original reading in the main text, but later corrected]; C [correction by a hand not specifically identifiable]; (1) [correction by hand 1].

The analysis of Type 2 evidence involves a more complicated process. Liuzza (1994–2000: II, 26), writing on the Old English prose translation of the Gospels, summarizes the likely causes of complication: "accidental omissions, deliberate alterations, and additions for clarity undoubtedly arise spontaneously in the course of the long labour of translation". Although the process of interlinear glossing may allow fewer opportunities for such spontaneous alterations than that of translation, it is essential to understand the margin for a glossator's spontaneous alterations. Some such alterations may result in a reading that appears to be translated from a variant Latin reading. A simple example, where Ru^2 inserts a conjunction, will clarify this difficulty:

(4) Luke 22.46 (Y f. 195vb17–18; R f. 120r19–20)
Y=R *surgite orate ne intretis in temtatione(m)*
Li. arisað gebiddað þ(æt)te gie ne Inngeonga In costunc(ge) ł in gesuoenc(ge)

Ru^{2} arisað ⁊ gibiddað ðæt ge ne gæ in costunge
(cp. WSCp[14]: Arisað ⁊ biddað ge on costunge ne gan)
'arise, pray, lest you enter into temptation'
surgite + *et*: Be, Bt, Hd, Hq.

Bibire and Ross (1981: 114–115) cite four instances of the insertion of "⁊" 'and' as in the example, to which two more may be added,[15] but this kind of insertion might easily have been made spontaneously by a glossator. In fact, we find Owun inserting "⁊" spontaneously elsewhere (i.e. examples not supported by Latin variant readings), either through error or for the sake of semantic clarification. The former is found, for example, when the Latin text has the *-et* ending (e.g. "ineode ⁊" 'went into and' [Li. "ineode" 'went into'] for *introisset* 'went into' in Mark 9.28)[16] or *ex-* as prefix (e.g. "⁊ ofercliopade" 'and cried out' [Li. "ofercliop-pade" 'cried out'] for *exclamauit* 'cried out' in Luke 23.18).[17] As to semantic addition, it should be pointed out that "⁊" is sometimes inserted at the beginning of a verse (e.g. Luke 8.44, John 1.41, 9.27), which, though not supported by any Latin variant readings, might have functioned as a link between the verses. In addition to semantic factors, syntactic concerns appear to have made Owun occasionally insert "⁊". For example, he appears to avoid using two finite verbs within a clause, as can be observed in the following instance:

(5) Mark 12.8 (Y f. 119rb7–9; R f. 74r2–3)
Y *et apprehendentes* (*adprae-* R) *eum occiderunt et eiecerunt* (*eicierunt* R) *extra uineam*
Li. ⁊ gelahton hine ofslogon ⁊ gewurpon buta ðæm wingeard
Ru^{2} ⁊ gilahtun hine ⁊ ofslogun ⁊ giwurpun butu ðone wingeord
'And laying hold on him, they killed him, and cast him out of the vineyard'.

Here, as a result of translating a Latin participle (*adprehendentes* 'laying hold on, capturing') into a finite verb ("gilahtun" 'seized'), the clause would have had two finite verbs, had he not inserted "⁊" before "ofslogun" 'killed'.[18] This example

14 The text of the West Saxon Gospels (Cambridge, Corpus Christi College, MS 140) is taken from Skeat (1871–1887).

15 Mark 13.3 ("⁊ gifrugnun hine" 'and interrogated him' [Li. "geascadon ł frugnon hine" 'asked or interrogated him'] for *interrogabant eum* 'interrogated him') and Luke 9.60 ("gaa ⁊ sæge" 'go and tell' [Li. "gaa saeg" 'go, tell'] for *uade adnuntia* 'go, preach').

16 Similar examples are found for *faciet* in Luke 18.7 and for *dixisset* in John 20.20.

17 Similar examples are found for *exæstuauit* in Mark 4.6 and for *expetiuit* Luke 22.31.

18 Similar examples are found in Mark 9.27, 11.33 and 14.39.

brings us back to (4), which Bibire and Ross regard as evidence for Owun's use of other Latin manuscripts. There, too, "⁊" may have been added spontaneously by Owun in order to avoid the juxtaposition of two imperatives, presumably the very reason why multiple Latin manuscripts have *et* there.

What should be emphasized with regard to this brief account of inserted "⁊" is that all the examples listed by Bibire and Ross do not bear equal significance in our discussion; their value varies from one instance to another. Close analysis of Owun's glossing practice may reveal that some instances listed by them have actually little value, because his spontaneous alteration may account for a given example as fittingly as would his use of an exemplar. Here, although such a detailed analysis of his glossing practice cannot be presented fully, the examples highly susceptible to explanation as spontaneous alteration by Owun, such as the case of inserted "⁊", will be excluded from our discussion, and our focus will be on more significant instances which allow less room for spontaneous alteration.

For this reason, we consider here the following three groups of examples: (a) insertion of words (other than "⁊" 'and' and prepositions); (b) difference in word order; and (c) difference in wording. Two examples from the first group are cited below:

(6) [2a-1] Mark 3.4 (Y f. 99va3–6; R f. 56r9–10)
Y=R *licet sabbatis bene facere an male animam saluam facere an perdere*
Li. Is alefed hræstdagu(m) wel wyrce ł yfle ða sawele hal gedoa ł losiga
Ru² **gif** is alefed on ræstedagum wel wyrca ł yfle ða sawle hale gidoa ł loesiga
'Is it lawful to do good on the sabbath days, or to do evil? to save life, or to destroy?'
si licet (for *licet*): Jo, Jz*, Ot, Pg, Tg.

(7) [2a-9] Luke 10.4 (Y f. 165vb9–11; R f. 99r14–15)
Y=R *Nolite portare sacculum neq(ue) peram neq(ue) calciamenta*
Li. næallað gie gebeara seam ne posa ne sceoe
Ru² nallað **f(or)ðon** gibeara seom ne posa ne giscoe
'Carry neither purse, nor scrip, nor shoes'
Nolite + *ergo*: Ea, Jb, Jo, Jz, Ot, Tg.

In (6), Ru²'s "gif" 'if' must be regarded as reflecting a Latin reading different from R and Y, and in fact there are readings with *si* 'if' at the beginning of the sentence. Similarly, "f(or)ðon" 'therefore' in (7) is explicable if we refer to the Latin variant reading with *ergo* 'therefore', which is usually glossed with *forðon* in Owun's gloss.

Into the second group, 'difference in word order', fall the examples in which disagreement between Owun's gloss and the Latin text as regards word order can be explained by Latin variant readings. There are two instances where Owun inverts the Latin 'Verb (V) + Subject (S)' order to 'S + V' in the gloss, as in:

(8) [2b-1] Mark 14.9 (Y f. 123va12–13; R f. 78r4–5)
Y=R *et quod fecit haec narrabitur in memoria(m) eius*
Li. ⁊ þ(æt) dyde ðios asægd bið on gemynd hire
Ru² ⁊ þ(æt)te **ðios dyde** asægd bið on gimynd hire
'that also which she hath done, shall be told for a memorial of her'
haec fecit (for *fecit haec*): Jo, Ot.

It must be stressed that this instance and the one listed as 2b-2 (Luke 22.60) in Table 3 are the sole instances where Owun inverts the Latin 'V + S' order which is followed by Aldred, as I have shown elsewhere.[19] Another instance shows the same phenomenon for a different syntactic pattern, where Owun inverts the Latin 'Object (O) + V' to 'V + O' in the gloss:

(9) [2b-3] John 5.30 (Y f. 221va15–18; R f. 137v17)
Y *quia non quaero uoluntatem* (+ *eius* R) *meam sed uoluntatem eius qui me misit* (*missit* R)
Li. f(or)ðon ne soeco ic uillo min ah uillo his se ðe mec asende
Ru² forðon ne soeco ic willo his ł minne ah willo his se ðe **sendeð mec**
'because I seek not my own will, but the will of him that sent me'
misit me (for *me misit*): Ai, Be, Cv, Hd, Jb, Jj, Jm, Jo, Jz, Nd, Om, Ot, Pg, Sc, St, Tg.

Again, this example is the sole instance in which Owun inverts the Latin 'O + V' to 'V + O' in the gloss, whereas the corresponding gloss in Li. follows the Latin word order.[20] It is significant that, in the four instances assigned to this group, Latin variant readings account for the syntactic features that are identified as exceptional in Owun's syntax by the data presented in my earlier survey (Kotake 2008a).

19 Kotake (2008a: 69–70).

20 Kotake (2008a: 68). The other instance assigned to this group (2b-4 in John 12.45) involves the inversion of Latin 'V + O' to 'O +V', a pattern found only twice in Owun's gloss; see Kotake (2008a: 66–67).

From the third group, 'difference in wording', the following instance is interesting in considering the textual transmission that may underlie Owun's gloss:

(10) [2c-6] Luke 10.41 (Y f. 167vb15–17; R f. 100r8–9)

Y *martha martha* (*martha* only once in R) *sollicita es et turbaris circa plurima*

Li geornfull ł arð ⁊ ðu bist astyred ymb ða menigo

Ru[2] geornful is ⁊ ðu bist astyred **forðon** monige

'Martha, Martha, thou art careful, and art troubled about many things'

erga for *circa*: Be, Cv, Ea, Eb, Hd, Jb, Jj, Jx, Jz, Ot, St, with an Old Latin manuscript.

Owun's gloss "forðon" 'therefore' for *circa* 'about' appears to be a curious error, but reference to a variant reading accounts for the semantic discrepancy. Many manuscripts have *erga* 'in respect to' for *circa* (in fact WW adopts the former), which can easily be mistaken as *ergo* 'therefore', as actually attested by some Latin manuscripts.[21] Since *ergo* is usually glossed with *forðon* in Owun's gloss, it is highly likely that his seemingly unexpected use of "forðon" above *circa* reflects a variant reading with *erga*, which at some point in the textual transmission could have been mistaken as *ergo* and received the gloss "forðon".

Further examples of 'difference in wording' can be found in Owun's glosses to Latin *autem* 'but, however'. In translating *autem*, Owun mostly uses *ða* 'then', *ðonne* 'then', *wutodlice* 'truly, however' and less frequently *soðlice* 'truly, indeed' while *forðon* is used for *enim* and *ergo* (roughly synonymous 'therefore'). Amongst 574 instances where R originally reads *autem* (not counting instances involving corrections), *forðon* occurs only five times.[22] One of them (Luke 23.8) is explicable by referring to the corresponding sentence in the Lindisfarne Gospels, where Y reads *enim*, glossed with *forðon* by Aldred. However, in the examples listed as 2c-3 (Mark 13.8) and 2c-9 (John 9.31), where *autem* is glossed with *forðon* by Owun, his reliance on the Lindisfarne Gospels does not account for his use of *forðon*, because Y agrees with R there and *forðon* is not used by Aldred. Nevertheless, there are some other Latin manuscripts with *enim* for these two examples, which would account for Owun's use of *forðon*. Given that *forðon* is used to translate *autem* only very rarely (less than 1% of the total), and that most of the instances of

21 See Fischer (1988–1991: III, 299) for the manuscripts reading *ergo*, which is usually corrected promptly. Bibire and Ross (1981: 115) list this example, but print the variant reading as *ergo* mistakenly.

22 In collecting the data, the *Dictionary of Old English Web Corpus* (*DOEC*) is used with necessary corrections made by examining manuscript readings.

autem glossed with *forðon* by Owun are paralleled by variant readings of *enim* or *ergo*, it is fairly reasonable to assume that Owun's use of *forðon* in these examples is due to Latin variant readings found in manuscripts other than the Lindisfarne Gospels.[23]

Table 3. List of the manuscripts sharing the Type 2 non R–Y readings

		Vulgate																				OL MSS
		B-R	**Ai**	**Be**	**Bt**	**Cv**	**Ea**	**Eb**	**Hd**	**Jb**	**Jj**	**Jo**	**Jx**	**Jz**	**Oh**	**Om**	**Ot**	**Pg**	**Sc**	**St**	**Tg**	
2a-1	Mk 3.4	-										+		+(*)			+	+			+	
2a-2	Mk 7.2	*						+								+	+					
2a-3	Mk 13.20	*			+							+					+	+		+		
2a-4	Mk 14.43	-			+			+				+					+					
2a-5	Mk 15.15	*			+	+							+(*)	+							+(*)	
2a-6	Mk 15.40	*	+				+					+	+(*)	+	+		+	+			+	
2a-7	Lk 2.12	-						+		+		+	+(*)	+								
2a-8	Lk 9.3	*										+										
2a-9	Lk 10.4	-					+			+		+		+			+				+	
2a-10	Jn 13.29	-																				+
2b-1	Mk 14.9	-										+					+					
2b-2	Lk 22.60	*		+		+	+			+		+	+(*)	+							+	+
2b-3	Jn 5.30	-	+	+		+			+	+	+	+		+		+	+	+	+	+	+	
2b-4	Jn 12.45	-		+																		
2c-1	Mk 5.38	*										+					+					
2c-2	Mk 8.5	*										+(*)						+	+			
2c-3	Mk 13.8	-					+		+			+		+			+					+
2c-4	Mk 14.58	*			+		+								+(1)+							+

23 In Mark 10.32, both Li. and Ru[2] have *forðon* for *autem*. No variant readings are reported for this instance in either WW or Fischer (1988–1991: II).

Table 3. (continued)

		Vulgate																				**OL MSS**
		B-R	**Ai**	**Be**	**Bt**	**Cv**	**Ea**	**Eb**	**Hd**	**Jb**	**Jj**	**Jo**	**Jx**	**Jz**	**Oh**	**Om**	**Ot**	**Pg**	**Sc**	**St**	**Tg**	
2c-5	Lk 2.40	*			+				+(*)			+	+(*)									
2c-6	Lk 10.41	*		+		+	+	+	+	+	+		+	+			+			+		+
2c-7	Jn 5.24	*		+		+	+		+			+		+							+	+
2c-8	Jn 7.40	-	most of other MSS																			
2c-9	Jn 9.31	-		+								+					+					

NB B-R: * (listed in Bibire and Ross 1981); - (not listed);
Due to limited space, the manuscripts which share only one instance are omitted from the table.

These Type 2 examples, even when limited to the three groups, are found more frequently and distributed more widely in Owun's portions than Type 1 examples, as can be seen in Table 3. For the purposes of the present study, it is important to consider how these readings were introduced into Owun's gloss. It should be stressed that, if we accept the widespread premise of Owun's direct copying from the Lindisfarne Gospels, it becomes difficult to reconstruct his working procedures in relation to these examples. Since the Latin readings of the two manuscripts are identical in the relevant examples, there is no conceivable reason for Owun to introduce another reading, unless he was keenly concerned about textual variants and undertook careful collation in the course of glossing. Although it is not entirely implausible that he may have had access to a third manuscript, the general character of his gloss suggests that it is unlikely that he was such a careful collator, and it must be remembered that Owun does not correct the Latin when writing a gloss at odds with the main text. Of course, he sometimes corrects the Latin text, as we have seen in Type 1 examples, but his corrections are highly haphazard and far from consistent. Even obvious errors or corrupt readings are often left uncorrected, for example:

(11) Mark 6.9 (Y f. 105vb21–24; R f. 61v2–3)
Y *sed calciatos sandalis et ne induerentur duab(us) tunicis*
R *sed calciatos scandalis et ne induerentur duabus tonicis*
Li. ah gescoed mið ðuongum ⁊ ne gegearuad were mið tuæm tunucu(m) ł tuæm cyrtlum

Ru² ah giscoed mið ðwongum ⁊ ne gigeorwad were mið twæm tunucum
'But to be shod with sandals, and that they should not put on two coats'.

Here, the obvious error *scandalis* 'with stumbling blocks' for *sandalis* 'with sandals', which could have been easily corrected by cancelling *c*, is left uncorrected in R, and his gloss nevertheless translates the correct reading. In this and similar examples, it appears that Owun unconsciously introduces an expected reading as a gloss, without recognizing the defect in the Latin text he was glossing. As to Type 2 examples, it is also more reasonable to assume that Owun copied a gloss at odds with the Latin text without recognizing the difference than that he consciously introduced a reading not recorded in either the manuscript he was glossing or the source manuscript from which he was copying. If we hypothesize that the Type 2 examples are copied from Owun's exemplar, then that exemplar was certainly not the Lindisfarne Gospels; and this is the tentative conclusion of the present paper.

Before concluding, it is necessary to introduce yet another group of examples, which may be considered as counter evidence to the tentative conclusion. There are some examples, though smaller in number than the Type 1 and Type 2 examples presented so far, which reflect readings peculiar to the Lindisfarne Gospels. The most significant instance is cited below, where even Aldred's correction to Y, which results in a very rare reading, is reflected in Owun's gloss.

(12) John 20.15 (Y f. 256va18–19; R f. 166v16)
Y ***dic cito*** (corrected from *dicito* by Aldred) *mihi ubi posuisti eum*
R *dicito mihi ubi possuisti eum*
Li. cuæð **ræðe** me huer ðu gesettes hine
Ru² sæge **hræðe** me hwer ðu settes hine
'tell me where thou hast laid him'
dic cito (for *dicito*): not recorded in WW[24]

24 However, it is difficult to know whether Aldred made this correction spontaneously, or was affected by a reading familiar to him. Fischer's collation (1988–1991: IV, 493) identifies three manuscripts (Hh, Hs, Ht) which read *dic cito*, and its variation, *cito dic*, in Eh. It may be significant that all these manuscripts are Insular (though with diverse details), and it cannot be ruled out that such readings gained more currency in Anglo-Saxon England by the time of Aldred's glossing. It is beyond the scope of this survey to present the details of these manuscripts; see *CLA* entries Hh (II, no. 157), Hs (VII, no. 901), Ht (II, no. 267) and Eh (II, no. 138), and also Gneuss and Lapidge (2014) for Hh (no. 266) and Eh (no. 138).

Aldred corrects Y's original reading *dicito* 'tell' to *dic cito* 'tell quickly' by adding another *c*, and his gloss "cuæð ræðe" 'tell quickly' translates the corrected reading, taking *cito* as an adverb. Then, "ræðe" is taken into Owun's gloss as "hræðe", though he does not correct the Latin *dicito*.[25] Whether our tentative conclusion should be dismissed because of such examples is a matter of balancing the evidence, but what should be emphasized here is that even if we assume that Owun's direct source was not the Lindisfarne Gospels, there remains the good possibility that Owun's gloss is a descendant of Aldred's gloss with some intervening copies between them, and that the non R–Y readings were introduced to Owun's portions through these intervening copies.

Although the textual nature of such hypothetical intervening copies may hardly be retrievable from the patchy evidence we have, it is nevertheless interesting to examine the distribution of the non R–Y readings identified so far in Tables 2 and 3. The tables cannot, of course, hope to identify the very manuscript used by Owun, but we can examine them to see whether the distribution suggests any discernible tendency. From this perspective, it is interesting that the majority of the non R–Y readings of both types are shared by Jo, one of the two manuscripts labelled as the Gospels of St. Augustine (Oxford, Bodleian Library, MS Auct. D.2.14; *CLA*: II, no. 230). The text of Jo belongs to the mixed-Italian family of the Vulgate, yet another textual family current in Anglo-Saxon England.[26] The some-

25 Similar examples are found in Mark 12.38, where Ru[2] reads "tahte ł lærde" 'taught or instructed' for *dicebat* 'said', but the gloss agrees with Li. "tahte ł lærde" glossing *docebat* 'taught', a unique reading not found in the other manuscripts examined; in Luke 12.55, where Ru[2] reads "winde" 'wind' for R *aestus* 'heat', but the gloss agrees with Li. "wind" glossing Y *uentus* 'wind' (some variant readings [Na, Eb, Sc, St] have *uentus*, but most of other manuscripts agree with R); and in Luke 17.34, where Ru[2] reads "hrofe" 'roof' for R *lecto* 'bed', but the gloss agrees with Li. "hrofe" glossing Y *tecto* 'roof' (Na is the only manuscript other than Y with *tecto*).

26 For the history of this manuscript, see Marsden (1999) and Ganz (2001), and for bibliography Gneuss and Lapidge (2014: no. 529). Although the manuscripts with the texts classified to the mixed-Italian family tend to show closer affinities with southern England, the availability of such texts outside southern England, especially in Northumbria, has also been noticed; see Liuzza (1994–2000: II, 7–8) and Loewe (1969: 136–137). The exact Anglo-Saxon provenance of Jo is still in dispute; the two separate pieces of evidence, one for Lichfield in the eighth century and the other for Bury St. Edmunds in the eleventh, have been interpreted with varying degrees of credibility. See Doane (2002: 62) for a summary. The manuscript's Lichfield provenance is based on an inscription on f. 149v, written upside down, referring to St. Chad, a saint closely associated with Lichfield. Ganz (2001: 40–41), in a paper apparently not available to Doane (2002), presents a detailed analysis of this inscription and a sacramentary extract on f. 39v added by the same hand, and concludes that they were probably "made in the see of Lichfield". As to the Bury St. Edmunds provenance, Ganz (2001: 35 n. 3) notes that the booklist on the endleaf of the manuscript, on which this provenance is based, is "a later insertion" and that "there is no valid reason to suggest that this manuscript was ever at Bury".

what close affinity of the non R–Y readings with the textual family exemplified by Jo may be supported further by the fact that Type 1 examples are shared most frequently with Eb, Codex Bigotianus (Paris, Bibliothèque Nationale, MSS Lat. 281 + 298; *CLA*: V, no. 526), which "displays certain textual affinities with OX [i.e. Jo and Jx]".[27] In passing, it is also interesting to turn our attention to Farman's portion in Mark, in which the glossator is considered to have used the same source as used by Owun, which previous studies have identified with the Lindisfarne Gospels itself. Now that the present study has hypothesized that Owun's source was not the Lindisfarne Gospels, but an exemplar containing its non R–Y readings, it seems reasonable to expect to find similar indications of non R–Y readings also in Farman's portion in Mark. And indeed, despite the relative shortness of the section, we find a few traces of non R–Y readings in Farman's corrections to the Latin text, of which two are shared by Jo.[28] These pieces of evidence point to the likelihood that at least one of the hypothetical intervening copies must have contained a text more or less similar to Jo.

In fact, it would probably not be surprising if one of the hypothetical intervening copies contained a text similar to Jo, given, for example, that Jo itself was still in use in tenth-century Anglo-Saxon England, as some later additions to the manuscript indicate.[29] It is also interesting to note that the text of Jo, in its long history, was collated by an Insular hand which introduced readings like some found in the Book of Kells and the Rushworth Gospels.[30] This is not to say that there is a special connection between the Rushworth Gospels and the Oxford Gospels of St. Augustine (Jo) themselves, but we can observe, on the one hand, that Jo, a mixed-Italian family text, was once collated against a text similar to that of the Rushworth Gospels and, on the other, that Owun introduced, though probably unconsciously in many cases, readings shared by Jo into the Rushworth Gospels. Neither would it be surprising if a text aligned to the Italo-Northumbrian

27 Verey (1980: 69). Codex Bigotianus is a manuscript "of possible Kentish origin" (Gameson 1999: 347) or "perhaps" a product of "Worcester and its environs" (Brown 2012: 146). See also Gneuss and Lapidge (2014: no. 878).

28 Farman's corrections to Latin which agree with Jo are found in Mark 1.10 *sp(iritu)m \s(an) c(tu)m/* (*sp(iritu)m* Y; + *sanctum* Jo, Jz, Oh^{c}, Om); and in Mark 2.5 *peccata \tua/* (*peccata* Y; + *tua* Be, Eb, Hd, Hl, Jo, Pg).

29 There is a group of lectionary annotations mostly in Matthew, which are traditionally attributed to a tenth-century English hand (Chapman's Ob; see Chapman 1908: 192, 199–202). More recently, Ganz (2001: 41–43) identifies two hands for these additions. See also Glunz (1933: 304–305) and Lenker (1997: esp. 406–411), the latter of which offers a very detailed survey on pericope notes from Anglo-Saxon England.

30 These corrections were made by a hand that Ganz (2001: 36, 39) calls the "insular corrector", in whose script the same study finds Mercian palaeographical features.

family, to which Y belongs, was collated against a text similar to Jo. Indeed, for example, London, British Library, MS Royal 1.B.vii, whose main text is considered to be related to the Lindisfarne Gospels, shows traces of corrections that "bring [the main text] into line with the so-called mixed Italian textual recension".[31] If Aldred's gloss was copied into a manuscript containing such a mixed text with some care to accommodate the gloss to the main text, the resulting gloss might have been similar to Owun's exemplar we have hypothesized in this paper. These observations exemplify how complicated the textual history of the Latin Gospels in Anglo-Saxon England is, not only as regards the main text, but also in respect of later additions and corrections. Nevertheless, studies dealing with the Rushworth and Lindisfarne glosses have tended to present the two glossed manuscripts in a rather simplistic context, assuming that they were physically juxtaposed – but these two manuscripts are not exceptions to the complex history of Latin Gospel texts. The present study has identified some traces of the complicated textual history behind Owun's work, and such traces, which are hardly explicable if we rest on the widespread premise of his direct copying from the Lindisfarne Gospels, have led us to the tentative conclusion that the likely answer to the question "Did Owun really copy from the Lindisfarne Gospels?" is "no". This conclusion will remain tentative until the relationship of the two glosses can be examined in the light of further evidence, but it should be emphasized that such evidence must be sought by investigating these glosses in a wider context than direct copying between two manuscripts.[32]

31 Gameson (1994: 31). London, British Library, MS Royal 1.B.vii (Fischer's Nr; not collated by WW; Gneuss and Lapidge 2014: no. 445) is an eighth-century Latin Gospel manuscript, written "probably in Northumbria" (*CLA*: II, no. 213). According to Verey (1980: 69 and n. 26), the main text "is basically Italo-Northumbrian", but at the same time contains "a number of readings shared with O and X". In fact, some of the non R–Y readings identified by the present study agree with the main text of Nr, not the corrections (the folio number in brackets refers to Nr): 2c-4 (f. 75rb6), 2c-7 (f. 136ra13) and 2c-8 (f. 139vb3). There are some instances of the non R–Y readings that agree with the corrections in Nr: 1-6 (f. 114va20), 1-8 (f. 119ra3), 1-9 (f. 119ra7), 1-11 (f. 126va22), and 2a-8 (f. 101rb13). Besides, Farman's addition in Mark 1.10, mentioned in n. 28 above, agrees with the correction in Nr (f. 55rb16).

32 This survey is part of my postdoctoral research project "Editing the Rushworth Gospels on the basis of philological and historical research" supported by a Postdoctoral Fellowship for Research Abroad awarded by the Japan Society for the Promotion of Science. I am very grateful to Professor Jane Roberts for her comments and suggestions on a draft of this paper. I also would like to thank the anonymous reviewers of this paper for their important suggestions.

Appendix

Sigla of Latin Gospel manuscripts

Fischer	WW	MSS
Ai	I	Munich, Universitätsbibliothek, MS 2° 29
Be	E	London, British Library, MS Egerton 609
Bt	*gat*	Paris, Bibliothèque Nationale, MS Nouv. Acq. Lat. 1587
Cv	V	Rome, Biblioteca Vallicelliana, MS B.6
Ea	*aur*	Stockholm, Kungliga Biblioteket, MS A.135
Eb	B	Paris, Bibliothèque Nationale, MSS Lat. 281 + 298
Eh	–	Cambridge, University Library, MS Kk.1.24; + London, British Library, MS Cotton Tiberius B.v f. 26; + London, British Library, MS Sloane 1044 f. 2
Ge	(E+P)	Paris, Bibliothèque Nationale, MS Lat. 9389
Hd	D	Dublin, Trinity College, MS 52
Hh	–	Hereford, Cathedral Library, MS P.I.2
Hl	L	Lichfield, Cathedral Library, MS 1
Hq	Q	Dublin, Trinity College, MS 58
Hr	R	Oxford, Bodleian Library, MS Auct. D.2.19
Hs	–	St. Gall, Stiftsbibliothek, MS 51
Ht	–	Dublin, Royal Irish Academy, MS D.II.3 (foll.1–11)
Jb	(B+F)	London, British Library, MS Add. 5463
Jj	J	Cividale, Museo Archeologico, s.n.; + Prague, Clm 1; + Venice, S. Marco
Jo	O	Oxford, Bodleian Library, MS Auct. D.2.14
Jx	X	Cambridge, Corpus Christi College, MS 286
Jz	Z	London, British Library, MS Harley 1775
Na	A	Florence, Biblioteca Medicea-Laurenziana, Cat. Sala Studio 6
Nr	–	London, British Library, MS Royal 1.B.vii
Ny	Y	London, British Library, MS Cotton Nero D.iv
Oh	H	London, British Library, MS Add. 24142
Om	Θ	Paris, Bibliothèque Nationale, MS Lat. 9380
Ot	(M+T)	Tours, Bibliothèque Municipale, MS 22
Pg	G	Paris, Bibliothèque Nationale, MS Lat. 11553
Sc	C	Cava dei Tirreni, Biblioteca della Badia, MS 1 (14)
St	T	Madrid, Biblioteca Nacional, MS Vitr.13–1 (Tol. 2–1)
Tg	K	London, British Library, MS Add. 10546

References

Abraham, Werner. 1991. "Null Subjects: From Gothic, Old High German and Middle High German to Modern German – From Pro-Drop to Semi-Pro-Drop". *Groninger Arbeiten zur germanistischen Linguistik* 34: 1–28.

Alexander, J. J. G. 1978. *Insular Manuscripts, 6th to the 9th Century*. London: Miller.

Allen, Cynthia L. 1999. *Case Marking and Reanalysis: Grammatical Relations from Old to Early Middle English*. Oxford: Oxford University Press.

Anderson, John M. 1975. *The Grammar of Case: Towards a Localistic Theory*. Cambridge: Cambridge University Press.

Anlezark, Daniel (ed. and trans.). 2009. *The Old English Dialogues of Solomon and Saturn*. Anglo-Saxon Texts 7. Cambridge: Brewer.

d'Ardenne, S. R. T. O. (ed.). 1961 (for 1960). *Þe Liflade ant te Passiun of Seinte Iuliene*. Early English Text Society OS 248. Oxford: Oxford University Press.

d'Ardenne, S. R. T. O. and E. J. Dobson (eds.). 1985. *Seinte Katerine. Re-Edited from MS Bodley 34 and Other Manuscripts*. Early English Text Society SS 7. Oxford: Oxford University Press.

Antonsen, Elmer H. 2002. *Runes and Germanic Linguistics*. Berlin: Mouton de Gruyter.

Arngart, Olof S. 1981. "The Durham Proverbs". *Speculum* 56: 288–300.

Arnold, Thomas. (ed.). 1882. *Simeon of Durham: Symeonis Monachi Opera Omnia*. Volume I: *Historia Dunelmensis ecclesiae*. Rolls Series 75 (I). London: Longman.

Atkins, J. W. H. (ed.). 1922. *The Owl and the Nightingale: Edited with Introduction, Texts, Translation and Glossary*. Cambridge: Cambridge University Press.

Axel, Katrin. 2007. *Studies on Old High German Syntax: Left Sentence Periphery, Verb Placement and Verb-Second*. Amsterdam: Benjamins.

Backhouse, Janet. 1981. *The Lindisfarne Gospels*. Ithaca, NY: Cornell University Press/London: Phaidon.

Bale, Christian Emil. 1907. *The Syntax of the Genitive Case in the Lindisfarne Gospels*. Iowa Studies in Language and Literature 1. Iowa, IA: State University of Iowa Press.

Barton, John and John Muddiman (eds.). 2001. *The Oxford Bible Commentary*. Oxford: Oxford University Press.

Bately, Janet (ed.). 1980. *The Old English Orosius*. Early English Text Society SS 6. London: Oxford University Press.

Battiscombe, C. F. (ed.). 1956. *The Relics of Saint Cuthbert*. Oxford: Oxford University Press.

Bauer, Gero. 1963. "Über Vorkommen und Gebrauch von ae. *sin*". *Anglia* 81: 323–334.

Bech, Kristin. 2001. "Word Order Patterns in Old and Middle English: A Syntactic and Pragmatic Study". Unpubl. PhD dissertation, University of Bergen.

Behaghel, Otto and Burkhard Taeger. 1996. *Heliand und Genesis*. 10th ed. Halle: Niemeyer.

Benskin, Michael. 2011. "Present Indicative Plural Concord in Brittonic and Early English". *Transactions of the Philological Society* 109: 158–185.

Benveniste, Émile. 1946. "Structure des relations de personne dans le verbe". *Bulletin de la Société de Linguistique de Paris* 43: 1–12.

van Bergen, Linda. 2003. *Pronouns and Word Order in Old English with Particular Reference to the Indefinite Pronoun* Man. Outstanding Dissertations in Linguistics. New York: Routledge.

van Bergen, Linda. 2008. "Negative Contraction and Old English Dialects: Evidence from Glosses and Prose. Part I". *Neuphilologische Mitteilungen* 109: 275–312.

Berndt, Rolf. 1956. *Form und Funktion des Verbums im nördlichen Spätaltenglischen: Eine Untersuchung der grammatischen Formen und ihrer syntaktischen Beziehungsbedeutungen in der großen sprachlichen Umbruchsperiode*. Halle: Niemeyer.

Bibire, Paul and A. S. C. Ross. 1981. "The Differences between Lindisfarne and Rushworth Two". *Notes and Queries* 226: 98–116.

Billett, Jesse D. 2010. "The Divine Office and the Secular Clergy in Later Anglo-Saxon England". In: David Rollason, Conrad Leyser and Hannah Williams (eds.). *England and the Continent in the Tenth Century: Studies in Honour of Wilhelm Levison (1876–1947)*. Studies in the Early Middle Ages 37. Turnhout: Brepols. 429–471.

Bischoff, Bernhard and Michael Lapidge. 1994. *Biblical Commentaries from the Canterbury School of Theodore and Hadrian*. Cambridge Studies in Anglo-Saxon England 10. Cambridge: Cambridge University Press.

Blakeley, Leslie. 1948–1949. "Accusative-Dative Syncretism in the Lindisfarne Gospels". *English and Germanic Studies* 1: 6–31.

Blakeley, Lesley. 1949–1950. "The Lindisfarne s/ð Problem". *Studia Neophilologica* 22: 15–47.

Bolze, Christine. 2012. "Forms and Functions of the Verb 'to Be' in the Old English Gospels". Unpubl. PhD dissertation, University of Cambridge.

Bolze, Christine. 2013. "The Verb *to Be* in the West Saxon Gospels and the Lindisfarne Gospels". In: Gabriele Diewald, Leena Kahlas-Tarkka and Ilse Wischer (eds.). *Comparative Studies in Early Germanic Languages, with a Focus on Verbal Categories*. Studies in Language Companion Series 138. Amsterdam: Benjamins. 217–234.

Bond, E. A., E. M. Thompson and G. F. Warner (eds.). 1873–1883. *Facsimiles of Manuscripts and Inscriptions*. Series I. London: Palaeographical Society.

Bonner, Gerald. 1989. "St Cuthbert at Chester-le-Street". In: Gerald Bonner, David Rollason and Clare Stancliffe (eds.). *St Cuthbert, His Cult and His Community to A.D. 1200*. Woodbridge: Boydell. 387–395.

Bosworth, Joseph and T. Northcote Toller (eds.). 1882–1898. *An Anglo-Saxon Dictionary*. Oxford: Clarendon; Toller, T. Northcote (ed.). 1908–1921. *Supplement* to *An Anglo-Saxon Dictionary Based on the Manuscript Collections of the Late Joseph Bosworth*. Oxford: Clarendon.

Bouterwek, Karl W. (ed.). 1857. *Die vier Evangelien in alt-northumbrischer Sprache*. Gütersloh: Bertelsmann.

Bouterwek, Karl W. 1858. *Screadunga: Anglosaxonica Maximam Partem Inedita*. Elberfeldae: Lucas.

Bowden, John. 2005. "Kingdom of God". In: John Bowden (ed.). *Christianity: The Complete Guide*. London: Continuum. 690–691.

Boyd, W. J. P. 1967. "Aldrediana VII: Hebraica". *English Philological Studies* 10: 1–32.

Boyd, W. J. P. 1975a. *Aldred's Marginalia: Explanatory Comments in the Lindisfarne Gospels*. Exeter Medieval Texts and Studies 4. Exeter: University of Exeter Press.

Boyd, W. J. P. 1975b. "Aldrediana XXV: 'Ritual' Hebraica". *English Philological Studies* 14: 1–57.

Brinton, Laurel J. and Elizabeth Closs Traugott. 2005. *Lexicalization and Language Change*. Research Surveys in Linguistics Series. Cambridge: Cambridge University Press.

Brook, G. L. and R. F. Leslie (eds.). 1963–1972. *Laȝamon: Brut. Edited from British Museum MS Cotton Caligula A.ix and British Museum MS Cotton Otho C.xiii*. Early English Texts Society OS 250 and 277. Oxford: Oxford University Press.

Brown, Gerald Baldwin. 1903–1937. *The Arts in Early England*. 6 vols. London: Murray.

Brown, Michelle P. 1990. *A Guide to Western Historical Scripts from Antiquity to 1600*. London: British Library.

Brown, Michelle P. 1996. *The Book of Cerne: Prayer, Patronage and Power in Ninth-Century England*. London: British Library.

Brown, Michelle P. 2000. *"In the Beginning was the Word": Books and Faith in the Age of Bede*. The Jarrow Lecture, 2000. Newcastle-upon-Tyne: Bealls.

Brown, Michelle P. 2002–2003. *The Lindisfarne Gospels: Cotton MS Nero D.iv of the British Library London*. 2 vols. Lucern: Faksimile Verlag.

Brown, Michelle P. 2003. *The Lindisfarne Gospels: Society, Spirituality and the Scribe*. London: British Library/Toronto: University of Toronto Press.

Brown, Michelle P. 2005. "Building Babel: The Architecture of the Early Written Western Vernaculars". In: Anne J. Duggan, Joan Greatrex and Brenda Bolton (eds.). *Omnia Disce: Medieval Studies in Memory of Leonard Boyle, O.P.* Aldershot: Ashgate. 109–128.

Brown, Michelle P. (ed.). 2006. *In the Beginning: Bibles before the Year 1000*. Exhibition Catalogue, Freer Gallery of Art. Washington, DC: Smithsonian Institution.

Brown, Michelle P. 2007a. "The Barberini Gospels: Context and Intertextuality". In: Alastair Minnis and Jane Roberts (eds.). *Text, Image, Interpretation: Studies in Anglo-Saxon Literature and Its Insular Context in Honour of Éamonn Ó Carragáin*. Turnhout: Brepols. 89–116.

Brown, Michelle P. 2007b. "The Lichfield Angel and the Manuscript Context: Lichfield as a Centre of Insular Art". *Journal of the British Archaeological Association* 160: 8–19.

Brown, Michelle P. 2011a. *The Lindisfarne Gospels and the Early Medieval World*. London: British Library.

Brown, Michelle P. 2011b. *The Book and the Transformation of Britain, c. 550–1050: A Study in Written and Visual Literacy and Orality*. The Sandars Lectures in Bibliography, 2009. London: British Library.

Brown, Michelle P. 2012. "Writing in the Insular World". In: Richard Gameson (ed.). *The Cambridge History of the Book in Britain*. Volume I: *c. 400–1100*. Cambridge: Cambridge University Press. 121–166.

Brown, Michelle P. 2013. "Mercian Manuscripts: The Implications of the Staffordshire Hoard, Other Recent Discoveries, and the 'New Materiality'". In: Erik Kwakkel (ed.). *Writing in Context: Insular Manuscript Culture 500–1200*. Studies in Medieval and Renaissance Book Culture. Leiden: Leiden University Press. 23–64.

Brown, Michelle P. Forthcoming a. "Reading the Lindisfarne Gospels: Text, Image, Context".

Brown, Michelle P. Forthcoming b. "*Starcraeft* and the Interface between Faith and Science in Anglo-Saxon England, from Bede to Byrhtferth...and Beyond". In: Eric Lacey (ed.). *Starcraeft*.

Brown, T. J. 1960. "The Latin Text". In: Kendrick et al. (eds.). 1960. Book I. 31–58.

Brown, T. J. (ed.). 1969. *The Durham Ritual: A Southern English Collectar of the Tenth Century with Northumbrian Additions, Durham Cathedral Library A.IV.19*. Early English Manuscripts in Facsimile 16. Copenhagen: Rosenkilde & Bagger.

Brown, T. J. and R. L. S. Bruce-Mitford. 1960. "Origins and History". In: Kendrick et al. (eds.). 1960. Book I. 5–28.

Bruce-Mitford, R. L. S. 1960. "Decoration and Miniatures". In: Kendrick et al. (eds.). 1960. Book I. 108–260.

Brunner, Alice. 1947–1948. "A Note on the Distribution of the Variant Forms of the Lindisfarne Gospels". *English and Germanic Studies* 1: 32–52.

Brunner, Karl. 1965. *Altenglische Grammatik. Nach der angelsächsischen Grammatik von Eduard Sievers neu bearbeitet*. 3rd ed. Tübingen: Niemeyer.
Budny, M. O. 1985. "London, British Library, MS Royal 1.E.vi: The Anatomy of an Anglo-Saxon Bible Fragment". Unpubl. PhD dissertation, University of London.
Burns, A. 1969. "Holy Men on Islands in Pre-Christian Britain". *Glasgow Archaeological Journal* 1: 2–6.
Callaway, Morgan, Jr. 1918. *Studies in the Syntax of the Lindisfarne Gospels, with Appendices on Some Idioms in the Germanic Languages*. Baltimore: Hopkins.
Camacho, José and José Elías-Ulloa. 2010. "Null Subjects in Shipibo Switch-Reference Systems". In: José Camacho, Rodrigo Gutiérrez-Bravo and Liliana Sánchez (eds.). *Information Structure in Indigenous Languages of the Americas: Syntactic Approaches*. Berlin: Mouton de Gruyter. 65–85.
Campbell, Alistair. 1959. *Old English Grammar*. Oxford: Clarendon; repr. with corrections 1962.
Campbell, Alistair. 1967. "The Glosses". In: David H. Wright (ed.). *The Vespasian Psalter, British Museum, Cotton Vespasian A.I.* Early English Manuscripts in Facsimile 14. Copenhagen: Rosenkilde & Bagger. 81–92.
Campbell, Alistair. 1970. "Verse Influences in Old English Prose". In: James L. Rosier (ed.). *Philological Essays: Studies in Old and Middle English Language and Literature in Honour of Herbert Dean Merritt*. The Hague: Mouton. 93–98.
Carpenter, Henry C. A. 1910. *Die Deklination in der nordhumbrischen Evangelienübersetzung der Lindisfarner Handschrift*. Bonner Studien zur englischen Philologie 2. Bonn: Hanstein.
Cavill, Paul. 1999. *Maxims in Old English Poetry*. Cambridge: Brewer.
Cavill, Paul. 2012. "Maxims in the Making of a Homily: Formulaic Composition in Archbishop Wulfstan's Notes". In: Elise Louviot (ed.). *La Formule au Moyen Âge*. Atelier de Recherche sur les Textes Médiévaux 15. Turnhout: Brepols. 105–113.
Chadwick, D. E. 1934. "An Index Verborum to the Lindisfarne Gospels". Unpubl. MA dissertation, University of Leeds.
Chadwick, H. Munro and Nora K. Chadwick. 1932–1940. *The Growth of Literature*. 3 vols. Cambridge: Cambridge University Press.
Chapman, John. 1908. *Notes on the Early History of the Vulgate Gospels*. Oxford: Clarendon.
CLA = *Codices Latini Antiquiores: A Palaeographical Guide to Latin Manuscripts Prior to the Ninth Century*. Ed. E. A. Lowe. 1934–1971: 11 vols. plus supplement; 1972: Volume II: *Great Britain and Ireland*. 2nd ed. Oxford: Clarendon.
Clark, Cecily (ed.). 1970. *The Peterborough Chronicle, 1070–1154*. 2nd ed. Oxford: Oxford University Press.
Clark Hall, John R. 1960. *A Concise Anglo-Saxon Dictionary*. 4th ed., with a supplement by Herbert D. Meritt. Cambridge: Cambridge University Press.
Clemoes, Peter. 1995. *Interactions of Thought and Language in Old English Poetry*. Cambridge: Cambridge University Press.
Coates, R. 1997. "The Scriptorium of the Rushworth Gospels: A Bilingual Perspective". *Notes and Queries* 242: 453–458.
van Coetsem, Frans. 1988. *Loan Phonology and the Two Transfer Types in Language Contact*. Publications in Language Sciences 27. Dordrecht: Foris.
Cole, Marcelle. 2008. "What is the Northern Subject Rule? The Resilience of a Medieval Constraint in Tyneside English". *Journal of the Spanish Society for Medieval Language and Literature* 15: 91–114.

Cole, Marcelle. 2012a. "The Old English Origins of the Northern Subject Rule: Evidence from the Lindisfarne Gloss to the Gospels of John and Mark". In: Merja Stenroos, Martti Mäkinen and Inge Særheim (eds.). *Language Contact and Development around the North Sea*. Current Issues in Linguistic Theory 321. Amsterdam: Benjamins. 141–168.

Cole, Marcelle. 2012b. "Old Northumbrian Verbal Morphology in the Glosses to the Lindisfarne Gospels". Unpubl. PhD dissertation, Universidad de Sevilla.

Cole, Marcelle. 2014. *Old Northumbrian Verbal Morphosyntax and the (Northern) Subject Rule*. NOWELE Supplement Series 25. Amsterdam: Benjamins.

Colgrave, Bertram and R. A. B. Mynors (eds. and trans.). 1969. *Bede's Ecclesiastical History of the English People*. Oxford: Clarendon.

Comfort, Philip. 2005. *Encountering the Manuscripts: An Introduction to New Testament Paleography and Textual Criticism*. Nashville, TN: Broadman and Holman.

CoNE = *A Corpus of Narrative Etymologies from Proto-Old English to Early Middle English and Accompanying Corpus of Changes*. Roger Lass, Margaret Laing, Rhona Alcorn and Keith Williamson. Edinburgh: Version 1.1, 2013–, © The University of Edinburgh. (http://www.lel.ed.ac.uk/ihd/CoNE/CoNE.html).

Cook, Albert S. 1894. *A Glossary of the Old Northumbrian Gospels (Lindisfarne Gospels or Durham Book)*. Halle: Niemeyer.

Cook, Albert S. 1898. *Biblical Quotations in Old English Prose Writers*. London: Macmillan.

Corrêa, Alicia (ed.). 1992. *The Durham Collectar*. Henry Bradshaw Society 107. London/Rochester, NY: Boydell & Brewer.

Corrêa, Alicia. 1995. "Daily Office Books: Collectars and Breviaries". In: Richard W. Pfaff (ed.). *The Liturgical Books of Anglo-Saxon England*. Old English Newsletter Subsidia 23. Kalamazoo, MI: Medieval Institute Publications, Western Michigan University. 45–60.

Cox, Robert S. 1972. "The Old English Dicts of Cato". *Anglia* 90: 1–42.

Cramp, Rosemary. J. 1981. *The Hermitage and the Offshore Island*. Second Paul Johnstone Memorial Lecture, 1981. London: National Maritime Museum.

Cramp, Rosemary J. 1989. "The Artistic Influence of Lindisfarne within Northumbria". In: Gerald Bonner, David Rollason and Clare Stancliffe (eds.). *St Cuthbert, His Cult and His Community to A.D. 1200*. Woodbridge: Boydell. 220–221.

Craster, E. 1954. "The Patrimony of St Cuthbert". *English Historical Review* 69: 177–199.

Cross, James E. and Thomas D. Hill (eds.). 1982. *The* Prose Solomon and Saturn *and* Adrian and Ritheus. McMaster Old English Studies and Texts 1. Toronto: University of Toronto Press.

Cross, James E. and Jennifer Morrish Tunberg (eds.). 1993. *The Copenhagen Wulfstan Collection*. Early English Manuscripts in Facsimile 25. Copenhagen: Rosenkilde & Bagger.

Crowley, Joseph. 2000. "Anglicized Word Order in Old English Continuous Interlinear Glosses in British Library, Royal 2.A.XX". *Anglo-Saxon England* 29: 123–151.

Cubitt, Catherine. 1997. "The Tenth-Century Benedictine Reform in England". *Early Medieval Europe* 6: 77–94.

Curme, George O. 1912. "A History of English Relative Constructions". *Journal of English and Germanic Philology* 11: 10–29, 180–204, 355–380.

Curzan, Anne. 2003. *Gender Shifts in the History of English*. Cambridge: Cambridge University Press.

Dekker, Kees. 2007. "Anglo-Saxon Encyclopaedic Notes: Tradition and Function". In: Rolf H. Bremmer, Jr. and Kees Dekker (eds.). *Foundations of Learning: The Transfer of Encyclopaedic Knowledge in the Early Middle Ages*. Storehouses of Wholesome Learning I. Mediaevalia Groningana NS 9. Leuven: Peeters. 279–315.

Derolez, René. 1954. *Runica manuscripta: The English Tradition*. Brugge: De Tempel.

Di Sciacca, Claudia. 2007. "The Manuscript Tradition, Presentation, and Glossing of Isidore's *Synonyma* in Anglo-Saxon England: The Case of CCCC 448, Harley 110 and Cotton Tiberius A. iii". In: Rolf H. Bremmer, Jr. and Kees Dekker (eds.). *Foundations of Learning: The Transfer of Encyclopaedic Knowledge in the Early Middle Ages*. Storehouses of Wholesome Learning I. Mediaevalia Groningana NS 9. Leuven: Peeters. 95–124.

Di Sciacca, Claudia. 2011. "Glossing in Late Anglo-Saxon England: A Sample Study of the Glosses in Cambridge, Corpus Christi College 448 and London, British Library, Harley 110". In: Patrizia Lendinara, Loredana Lazzari, and Claudia Di Sciacca (eds.). *Rethinking and Recontextualizing Glosses: New Perspectives in the Study of Late Anglo-Saxon Glossography*. Fédération Internationale des Instituts d'Études Médiévales. Textes et Études du Moyen Âge 54. Turnhout: Brepols. 299–336.

Doane, A. N. (ed.). 2002. *Anglo-Saxon Manuscripts in Microfiche Facsimile*. Volume VII: *Anglo-Saxon Bibles and "The Book of Cerne"*. Tempe, AZ: Arizona Center for Medieval and Renaissance Studies.

DOE = *Dictionary of Old English in Electronic Form, A–G*. 2007. Ed. Antonette diPaolo Healey et al. Toronto: University of Toronto. <http://www.doe.utoronto.ca/>.

DOEC = *Dictionary of Old English Web Corpus*. 2007. Ed. Antonette diPaolo Healey et al. Toronto: University of Toronto. <http://www.doe.utoronto.ca/pages/pub/web-corpus.html>.

Douay-Rheims Bible = *The Holy Bible, Douay-Rheims Version, with Revisions and Footnotes by Bishop Richard Challoner, 1749–52*. 1899. Baltimore: John Murphy. <http://www.drbo.org>.

Dumville, David N. 1987. "English Square Minuscule Script: The Background and Earliest Phases". *Anglo-Saxon England* 16: 147–179.

Dumville, David N. 1992. *Liturgy and the Ecclesiastical History of Late Anglo-Saxon England: Four Studies*. Woodbridge: Boydell.

Dumville, David N. 1993. *English Caroline Script and Monastic History: Studies in Benedictinism, AD 950–1030*. Studies in Anglo-Saxon History 6. Woodbridge: Boydell.

Dumville, David N. 1994. "English Square Minuscule Script: The Mid-Century Phases". *Anglo-Saxon England* 23: 133–164.

Dumville, David N. 1999. *A Palaeographer's Review: The Insular System of Scripts in the Early Middle Ages*. Volume I. Suita: Kansai University Press.

Dunning, T. P. and A. J. Bliss (eds.). 1969. *The Wanderer*. London: Methuen.

Eggenberger, Jakob. 1961. *Das Subjektpronomen im Althochdeutschen: Ein syntaktischer Beitrag zur Frühgeschichte des deutschen Schrifttums*. Grabs: self-published.

Elliott, Constance O. and A. S. C. Ross. 1972. "Aldrediana XXIV: The Linguistic Peculiarities of the Gloss on St. John's Gospel". *English Philological Studies* 13: 49–72.

d'Evelyn, Charlotte and Anna J. Mill (eds.). 1956. *The South English Legendary: Edited from Corpus Christi Cambridge MS. 145 and British Museum MS. Harley 2277 with Variants from Bodley MS. Ashmole 43 and British Museum MS. Cotton Julius D.IX*. Volume I. Early English Texts Society OS 235. Oxford: Oxford University Press.

Exter, Otto. 1911. Beon *und* wesan *in Alfreds Übersetzung des Boethius, der Metra und der Soliloquien*. Kiel: Fienke.

Farmer, D. H. 1975. "The Progress of the Monastic Revival". In: David Parsons (ed.). *Tenth-Century Studies: Essays in Commemoration of the Millennium of the Council of Winchester and* Regularis concordia. London: Phillimore. 10–19.

Faulkner, Mark J. 2008. "The Uses of Anglo-Saxon Manuscripts c. 1066–1200". Unpubl. PhD dissertation, University of Oxford.
Fernández Cuesta, Julia. 2009. "On the Importance of Being Faithful: Diplomatic Transcriptions of Historical Texts for Contemporary E-Corpora". Unpubl. MS, University of Seville.
Fernández Cuesta, Julia. 2011. "The Northern Subject Rule in First-Person Singular Contexts in Early Modern English". *Folia Linguistica Historica* 32: 89–114.
Fernández Cuesta, Julia. Forthcoming. "Verbal Morphology in the Gloss to the Durham Ritual".
Fernández Cuesta, Julia and Mª Nieves Rodríguez Ledesma. 2001a. "Dialectología del inglés medieval: Nivel léxico y textos". In: Isabel de la Cruz Cabanillas and Francisco Javier Martín Arista (eds.). *Lingüística histórica inglesa*. Barcelona: Ariel. 510–572.
Fernández Cuesta, Julia and Mª Nieves Rodríguez Ledesma. 2001b. "Dialectología del inglés medieval: Niveles fonético-grafémico y morfológico". In: Isabel de la Cruz Cabanillas and Francisco Javier Martín Arista (eds.). *Lingüística histórica inglesa*. Barcelona: Ariel. 447–509.
Fernández Cuesta, Julia and Mª Nieves Rodríguez Ledesma. 2007. "From Old Northumbrian to Northern ME: Bridging the Divide". In: Gabriella Mazzon (ed.). *Studies in ME Forms and Meanings*. Studies in English Medieval Language and Literature 19. Frankfurt am Main: Lang. 117–132.
Fernández Cuesta, Julia and Mª Nieves Rodríguez Ledesma. Forthcoming. *A Linguistic History of Northern English*. New Approaches to English Historical Linguistics. Houndmills: Palgrave Macmillan.
Fernández Cuesta, Julia, Mª Nieves Rodríguez Ledesma and Inmaculada Senra Silva. 2008. "Towards a History of Northern English: Early and Late Northumbrian". *Studia Neophilologica* 80: 132–159.
Ferraresi, Gisella. 2005. *Word Order and Phrase Structure in Gothic*. Leuven: Peeters.
Fertig, David. 2000. "Null Subjects in Gothic". *American Journal of Germanic Linguistics & Literatures* 12: 3–21.
Feulner, Anna Helene. 2000. *Die griechischen Lehnwörter im Altenglischen*. Münchener Universitätsschriften: Texte und Untersuchungen zur Englischen Philologie 21. Frankfurt am Main: Lang.
Finkelstein, Louis. 1962. *The Pharisees: The Sociological Background of Their Faith*. 3rd ed., with suppl. Philadelphia, PA: The Jewish Publication Society of America.
Finkelstein, Louis. 1989. *The Cambridge History of Judaism*. 2 vols. Cambridge: Cambridge University Press.
Fischer, Bonifatius. 1988–1991. *Die lateinischen Evangelien bis zum 10. Jahrhundert*. 4 vols. Freiburg: Herder [Matthew (1988), Mark (1989), Luke (1990), John (1991)].
Fischer, Bonifatius. 2010. "Die lateinischen Evangelien bis zum 10. Jahrhundert: Zwei Untersuchungen zum Text". *Zeitschrift für die neutestamentliche Wissenschaft und die Kunde der älteren Kirche* 101: 119–144.
Fischer, Olga, Ans van Kemenade, Willem Koopman and Wim van der Wurff. 2000. *The Syntax of Early English*. Cambridge: Cambridge University Press.
Fisher, Ronald A. 1922. "On the Interpretation of $\chi 2$ from Contingency Tables, and the Calculation of P". *Journal of the Royal Statistical Society* 85: 87–94.
Fleming, Damian. 2004. "Eþel-weard: The First Scribe of the *Beowulf* MS". *Neuphilologische Mitteilungen* 105: 177–186.
Foley, Emily H. 1903. *The Language of the Northumbrian Gloss of Saint Matthew*. Volume I: *Phonology*. Yale Studies in English 14. New York, NY: Holt.

"Fontes Anglo-Saxonici: A Register of Written Sources Used by Anglo-Saxon Authors". Funded by the Arts and Humanities Research Board, 11 February 2002. <http://fontes.english.ox.ac.uk>.

Foot, Sarah. 2006. *Monastic Life in Anglo-Saxon England,* c. *600–900*. Cambridge: Cambridge University Press.

Foster, Meryl. 1994. "Custodians of St Cuthbert: The Durham Monks' View of Their Predecessors". In: David Rollason, Margaret Harvey and Michael Prestwich (eds.). *Anglo-Norman Durham 1093–1193*. Woodbridge: Boydell. 53–65.

Fowler, Joseph Thomas. 1898. *Extracts from the Account Rolls of the Abbey of Durham, from the Original MSS.* Volume II. Publications of the Surtees Society 100. Durham: Andrews & Co.

Füchsel, Hans. 1901. "Die Sprache der northumbrischen Interlinearversion zum Johannes-Evangelium". *Anglia* 24: 1–99.

Fulk, Robert D. 1992. *A History of Old English Meter*. Philadelphia, PA: University of Pennsylvania Press.

Fulk, Robert D. 2007. "Archaisms and Neologisms in the Language of Beowulf". In: Christopher M. Cain and Geoffrey Russom (eds.). *Studies in the History of the English Language*. Volume III: *Managing Chaos: Strategies for Identifying Change in English*. Berlin: Mouton de Gruyter. 267–287.

Fulk, Robert D. 2008. "Anglian Dialect Features in Old English Anonymous Homiletic Literature: A Survey, with Preliminary Findings". In: Susan Fitzmaurice and Donka Minkova (eds.). *Studies in the History of the English Language*. Volume IV: *Empirical and Analytical Advances in the Study of English Language Change*. Berlin: Mouton de Gruyter. 81–100.

Fulk, Robert D. 2012. "Anglian Features in Late West Saxon English". In: David Denison, Ricardo Bermúdez-Otero, Chris McCully and Emma Moore (eds.). *Analysing Older English*. Cambridge: Cambridge University Press. 63–74.

Gameson, Richard. 1994. "The Royal 1.B.vii Gospels and English Book Production in the Seventh and Eighth Centuries". In: Richard Gameson (ed.). *The Early Medieval Bible: Its Production, Decoration, and Use*. Cambridge: Cambridge University Press. 24–52.

Gameson, Richard. 1999. "The Earliest Books of Christian Kent". In: Richard Gameson (ed.). *St Augustine and the Conversion of England*. Stroud: Sutton. 313–373.

Gameson, Richard. 2001a. *The Scribe Speaks? Colophons in Early English Manuscripts*. H. M. Chadwick Memorial Lectures 12. Cambridge: Department of Anglo-Saxon, Norse and Celtic, University of Cambridge.

Gameson, Richard. 2001b. "Why Did Eadfrith Write the Lindisfarne Gospels?" In: Richard Gameson and Henrietta Leyser (eds.). *Belief and Culture in the Middle Ages*. Oxford: Oxford University Press. 45–58.

Gameson, Richard. (ed.). 2001–2002. *The Codex Aureus: An Eighth-Century Gospel Book, Stockholm, Kungliga Bibliothek, A. 135*. 2 vols. Early English Manuscripts in Facsimile 28 and 29. Copenhagen: Rosenkilde & Bagger.

Gameson, Richard. 2010. *Manuscript Treasures of Durham Cathedral*. London: Third Millennium.

Gameson, Richard. 2012. "From Vindolanda to Domesday: The Book in Britain from the Romans to the Normans". In: Richard Gameson (ed.). *The Cambridge History of the Book in Britain*. Volume I: *c. 400–1100*. Cambridge: Cambridge University Press. 1–9.

Gameson, Richard. 2013. *From Holy Island to Durham: The Contexts and Meanings of the Lindisfarne Gospels*. London: Third Millennium.

Ganz, David. 2001. "The Annotations in Oxford, Bodleian Library, Auct. D.II.14". In: Richard Gameson and Henrietta Leyser (eds.). *Belief and Culture in the Middle Ages: Studies Presented to Henry Mayr-Harting*. Oxford: Oxford University Press. 35–44.

Ganz, David. 2012. "Latin Script in England: Square Minuscule". In: Richard Gameson (ed.). *The Cambridge History of the Book in Britain*. Volume I: *c. 400–1100*. Cambridge: Cambridge University Press. 188–196.

García García, Luisa. 2000. "Tendencia a la simplificación morfológica en inglés antiguo". In: Pere Gallardo and Enric Llurda (eds.). *Proceedings of the 22nd International Conference of AEDEAN*. Lleida: Edicions de la Universitat de Lleida. 53–58.

García García, Luisa. 2005. *Germanische Kausativbildung: Die deverbalen* jan-*Verben im Gotischen*. Göttingen: Vandenhoeck & Ruprecht.

García García, Luisa. 2012a. "Morphological Causatives in Old English: The Quest for a Vanishing Formation". *Transactions of the Philological Society* 110: 122–148.

García García, Luisa. 2012b. "Old English *jan*-Causatives: Between Grammar and Lexicon". In: Javier Martín Arista, Roberto Torre Alonso, Andrés Canga Alonso and Inmaculada Medina Barco (eds.). *Convergent Approaches on Mediaeval English Language and Literature*. Newcastle: Cambridge Scholars. 13–28.

García García, Luisa. 2013. "Lexicalization and Morphological Simplification in Old English *jan*-Causatives: Some Open Questions". *Sprachwissenschaft* 38: 245–264.

van Gelderen, Elly. 2000. *A History of English Reflexive Pronouns: Person,* Self, *and Interpretability*. Amsterdam: Benjamins.

van Gelderen, Elly. 2011. *The Linguistic Cycle: Language Change and the Language Faculty*. Oxford: Oxford University Press.

Gelling, Margaret and Ann Cole. 2000. *The Landscape of Place-Names*. Stamford: Tyas.

Gilbert, J. E. P. 1990. "The Lindisfarne Gospels: How Many Artists?". *Durham University Journal* 51: 153–160.

Glunz, H. H. 1930. *Britannien und Bibeltext: Der Vulgatatext der Evangelien in seinem Verhältnis zur irisch-angelsächsischen Kultur des Frühmittelalters*. Kölner anglistische Arbeiten 12. Leipzig: Tauchnitz.

Glunz, H. H. 1933. *History of the Vulgate in England from Alcuin to Roger Bacon: Being an Inquiry into the Text of Some English Manuscripts of the Vulgate Gospels*. Cambridge: Cambridge University Press.

Gneuss, Helmut. 1955. *Lehnbildungen und Lehnbedeutungen im Altenglischen*. Berlin: Schmidt.

Gneuss, Helmut. 1998. "Old English Texts and Modern Readers: Notes on Editing and Textual Criticism". In: Peter S. Baker and Nicholas Howe (eds.). *Words and Works: Studies in Medieval English Language and Literature in Honour of Fred C. Robinson*. Toronto: University of Toronto Press. 127–141.

Gneuss, Helmut and Michael Lapidge. 2014. *Anglo-Saxon Manuscripts: A Bibliographical Handlist of Manuscripts and Manuscript Fragments Written or Owned in England up to 1100*. Toronto Anglo-Saxon Series 15. Toronto: University of Toronto Press.

Goetz, Georg. 1888–1923. *Corpus glossariorum latinorum a Gustavo Loewe inchoatum*. 7 vols. Leipzig: Teubner.

Goossens, Louis (ed.). 1974. *The Old English Glosses of MS Brussels, Royal Library, 1650 (Aldhelm's* De laudibus virginitatis*)*. Brussels: Paleis der Academiën.

Gordon, Ida L. (ed.). 1979. *The Seafarer*. Old and Middle English Texts. Manchester: Manchester University Press.

Greenfield, Stanley B. and Richard Evert. 1975. "*Maxims II*: Gnome and Poem". In: Lewis E. Nicholson and Dolores Warwick Frese (eds.). *Anglo-Saxon Poetry: Essays in Appreciation for John C. McGalliard*. Notre Dame, IN: University of Notre Dame Press. 337–354.

Gretsch, Mechthild. 1999. *The Intellectual Foundations of the English Benedictine Reform*. Cambridge Studies in Anglo-Saxon England 25. Cambridge: Cambridge University Press.

Gwara, Scott (ed.). 2001. *Aldhelmi Malmesbiriensis Prosa de virginitate cum glossa latina atque anglosaxonica*. 2 vols. Corpus Christianorum Series Latina 124 and 124A. Turnhout: Brepols.

de Haas, Nynke. 2008. "The Origins of the Northern Subject Rule". In: Marina Dossena, Richard Dury and Maurizio Gotti (eds.). *English Historical Linguistics 2006*. Volume III: *Geo-Historical Variation in English*. Amsterdam: Benjamins. 111–130.

de Haas, Nynke. 2011. "Morphosyntactic Variation in Northern English: The Northern Subject Rule, Its Origins and Early History". Unpubl. PhD dissertation, Radboud University Nijmegen.

Håkansson, David. 2008. "Syntaktisk variation och förändring: En studie av subjektslösa satser i fornsvenska". Unpubl. PhD dissertation, University of Lund.

Hanna, Ralph. 1986. "Booklets in Medieval Manuscripts: Further Considerations". *Studies in Bibliography* 39: 100–111.

Hansen, Elaine Tuttle. 1988. *The Solomon Complex: Reading Wisdom in Old English Poetry*. McMaster Old English Studies and Texts 5. Toronto: University of Toronto Press.

Haspelmath, Martin. 1993. "More on the Typology of Inchoative/Causative Verb Alternations". In: Bernard Comrie and Maria Polinsky (eds.). *Causatives and Transitivity*. Amsterdam: Benjamins. 87–120.

Haspelmath, Martin and Thomas Müller-Bardey. 2000. "Valency Change". In: Geert Booij, Christian Lehmann and Joachim Mugdan (eds.). *Morphologie: Ein internationales Handbuch zur Flexion und Wortbildung (Morphology: An International Handbook on Inflection and Word-Formation)*. Volume II. Handbücher zur Sprach- und Kommunikationswissenschaft 17. Berlin: De Gruyter. 1130–1145.

Heidermanns, Frank. 1993. *Etymologisches Wörterbuch der germanischen Primäradjektive*. Studia Linguistica Germanica 33. Berlin: De Gruyter.

Hermodsson, Lars. 1952. "Reflexive und intransitive Verba im älteren Westgermanischen". Unpubl. PhD dissertation, University of Uppsala.

Herold, Curtis Paul 1968. *The Morphology of King Alfred's Translation of the 'Orosius'*. The Hague: Mouton.

Hessels, John Henry. 1906. *A Late Eighth-Century Latin-Anglo-Saxon Glossary Preserved in the Library of the Leiden University (MS Voss. Qo. Lat. no. 69)*. Cambridge: Cambridge University Press.

Hill, Betty. 1989. "Seven Old English Glosses to the Lindisfarne Gospels". *Notes and Queries* 234: 148–150.

Hill, Joyce. 2012. "Wulfsige of Sherborne's Reforming Text". In: Alexander R. Rumble (ed.). *Leaders of the Anglo-Saxon Church from Bede to Stigand*. Woodbridge: Boydell. 147–163.

Hiltunen, Risto. 1983. *The Decline of the Prefixes and the Beginnings of the English Phrasal Verb: The Evidence from Some Old and Middle English Texts*. Annales Universitatis Truknensis 160. Turku: Turun Yliopisto.

Hines, John. 1991. "Scandinavian English: A Creole in Context". In: P. Sture Ureland and George Broderick (eds.). *Language Contact in the British Isles: Proceedings of the Eighth*

International Symposium on Language Contact in Europe, Douglas, Isle of Man, 1988. Linguistische Arbeiten 238. Tübingen: Niemeyer. 403–427.
Hofstetter, Walter. 1987. *Winchester und der spätaltenglische Sprachgebrauch.* Texte und Untersuchungen zur englischen Philologie 14. München: Fink.
Hogg, Richard M. 1992a. *A Grammar of Old English.* Volume I: *Phonology.* Oxford: Blackwell.
Hogg, Richard M. 1992b. "Phonology and Morphology". In: Richard M. Hogg (ed.). *The Cambridge History of the English Language.* Vol. 1: *The Beginnings to 1066.* Cambridge: Cambridge University Press. 67–167.
Hogg, Richard M. 2004. "North Northumbrian and South Northumbrian: Geographical Statement?". In: Marina Dossena and Roger Lass (eds.). *Methods and Data in English Historical Dialectology.* Linguistic Insights: Studies in Language and Communication 16. Bern: Lang. 241–255.
Hogg, Richard M. and R. D. Fulk. 2011. *A Grammar of Old English.* Volume II: *Morphology.* Oxford/Chichester: Wiley-Blackwell.
Holmberg, Anders. 2010. "Null Subject Parameters". In: Theresa Biberauer, Anders Holmberg, Ian Roberts and Michelle Sheehan (eds.). *Parametric Variation: Null Subjects in Minimalist Theory.* Cambridge: Cambridge University Press. 88–124.
Holmberg, Anders and Ian Roberts. 2010. "Introduction: Parameters in Minimalist Theory". In: Theresa Biberauer, Anders Holmberg, Ian Roberts and Michelle Sheehan (eds.). *Parametric Variation: Null Subjects in Minimalist Theory.* Cambridge: Cambridge University Press. 1–57.
Holmqvist, Erik. 1922. *On the History of the English Present Inflections, Particularly* -th *and* -s. Heidelberg: Winter.
Holthausen, Ferdinand (ed.). 1888. *Vices and Virtues.* Early English Texts Society OS 89. London: Trübner.
Holthausen, Ferdinand (ed.). 1934. *Altenglisches etymologisches Wörterbuch.* Germanische Bibliothek (Series 4) 7. Heidelberg: Winter.
Horobin, Simon. 2013. *Does Spelling Matter?* Oxford: Oxford University Press.
Householder, Fred W. 1981. *Syntax of Apollonius Dyscolus.* Amsterdam: Benjamins.
Howe, Nicholas. 1985. *The Old English Catalogue Poems.* Anglistica 23. Copenhagen: Rosenkilde & Bagger.
Huang, Yan. 2000. *Anaphora: A Cross-Linguistic Study.* Oxford: Oxford University Press.
Hulk, Aafke and Ans van Kemenade. 1995. "V2, Pro-Drop, Functional Projections and Language Change". In: Adrian Battye and Ian Roberts (eds.). *Clause Structure and Language Change.* Oxford: Oxford University Press. 227–256.
Hurst, David and Marc Adriaen (eds.). 1969. *S. Hieronymi Presbyteri Commentariorum in Matheum Libri IV.* Corpus Christianorum Series Latina 77. Turnhout: Brepols.
Hurtado, Larry. 2006. *Earliest Christian Artifacts: Manuscripts and Christian Origins.* Grand Rapids, MI: Eerdmans.
Ingham, Richard. 2006. "On Two Negative Concord Dialects in Early English". *Language Variation and Change* 18: 241–266.
Jasanoff, Jay H. 2003. *Hittite and the Indo-European Verb.* Oxford: Oxford University Press.
Johnson, Daniel E. 2009. "Getting Off the GoldVarb Standard: Introducing Rbrul for Mixed Effects Variable Rule Analysis". *Language and Linguistics Compass* 3: 359–383.
Johnson South, Ted (ed. and trans.). 2002. *Historia de Sancto Cuthberto: A History of Saint Cuthbert and a Record of His Patrimony.* Anglo-Saxon Texts 2. Cambridge: Brewer.

Jolly, Karen Louise. 2006. "Prayers from the Field: Practical Protection and Demonic Defense in Anglo-Saxon England". *Traditio* 61: 95–147.

Jolly, Karen Louise. 2012. *The Community of St. Cuthbert in the Late Tenth Century: The Chester-le-Street Additions to Durham Cathedral Library A.IV.19*. Columbus, OH: Ohio State University Press.

Jolly, Karen Louise. 2013. "Dismembering and Reconstructing MS Durham, Cathedral Library, A.IV.19". In: Jonathan Wilcox (ed.). *Scraped, Stroked, and Bound: Materially Engaged Readings of Medieval Manuscripts*. Utrecht: Brepols. 177–200.

Jones, Charles. 1967a. "The Functional Motivation of Linguistic Change". *English Studies* 48: 97–111.

Jones, Charles. 1967b. "The Grammatical Category of Gender in Early Middle English". *English Studies* 48: 289–305.

Jones, Charles. 1983. "Determiners and Case-Marking in Middle English: A Localist Approach". *Lingua* 59: 331–343.

Jones, Charles. 1987. *Grammatical Gender in English 950–1250*. London: Croom Helm.

Jordan, Richard. 1906. *Eigentümlichkeiten des anglischen Wortschatzes: Eine wortgeographische Untersuchung mit etymologischen Anmerkungen*. Anglistische Forschungen 17. Heidelberg: Winter.

Jost, Karl. 1909. Beon *und* wesan*: Eine syntaktische Untersuchung*. Anglistische Forschungen 26. Heidelberg: Winter.

Jülicher, Adolf (ed.). 1938–1963. *Itala: Das neue Testament in altlateinischer Überlieferung. Nach den Handschriften*. 4 vols. Berlin: De Gruyter.

Jülicher, Adolf, Walter Matzkow and Kurt Aland (eds.). 1970. *Itala: Das Neue Testament in altlateinscher Überlieferung. Nach den Handschriften*. 2nd rev. ed. Berlin: De Gruyter.

Keefer, Sarah L. 2007. "Use of Manuscript Space for Design, Text and Image in Liturgical Books Owned by the Community of St Cuthbert". In: Sarah Larratt Keefer and Rolf H. Bremmer, Jr. (eds.). *Signs on the Edge: Space, Text and Margin in Medieval Manuscripts*. Paris: Peeters. 85–115.

Keller, Wolfgang. 1925. "Keltisches im englischen Verbum". In: *Anglica: Untersuchungen zur englischen Philologie; Alois Brandl zum siebzigsten Geburtstage überreicht*. Volume I: *Sprache und Kulturgeschichte*. Palaestra Untersuchungen zur europäischen Literatur 147. Leipzig: Mayer & Müller. 55–66.

Kellum, Margaret. D. 1906. *The Language of the Northumbrian Gloss to the Gospel of St. Luke*. Yale Studies in English 30. New York, NY: Holt.

Kemble, John M. and Charles Hardwick. 1858. *The Gospel according to Saint Matthew in Anglo-Saxon and Northumbrian Versions Synoptically Arranged*. Cambridge: Cambridge University Press.

van Kemenade, Ans. 1987. *Syntactic Case and Morphological Case in the History of English*. Dordrecht: Foris.

van Kemenade, Ans. 2009. "Discourse Relations and Word Order Change". In: Roland Hinterhölzl and Svetlana Petrova (eds.). *Information Structure and Language Change*. Berlin: Mouton de Gruyter. 91–120.

van Kemenade, Ans and Bettelou Los. 2006. "Discourse Adverbs and Clausal Syntax in Old and Middle English". In: Ans van Kemenade and Bettelou Los (eds.). *The Handbook of the History of English*. London: Blackwell. 224–248.

Kendrick, T. D., T. J. Brown, R. L. S. Bruce-Mitford, H. Roosen-Runge, A. S. C. Ross, E. G. Stanley and A. E. A. Werner (eds.). 1956. *Evangeliorum Quattuor Codex Lindisfarnensis, Musei*

Britannici Codex Nero D.IV. Volume I: *Totius codicis similitudo folii 1–259*. Olten/Lausanne: Graf.

Kendrick, T. D., T. J. Brown, R. L. S. Bruce-Mitford, H. Roosen-Runge, A. S. C. Ross, E. G. Stanley and A. E. A. Werner (eds.). 1960. *Evangeliorum Quattuor Codex Lindisfarnensis, Musei Britannici Codex Nero D.IV*. Volume II: *Commentariorum libri duo, quorum unus de textu evangeliorum latino et codicis ornatione, alter de glossa anglo-saxonica*. Olten/Lausanne: Graf.

Ker, N. R. 1943. "Aldred the Scribe". *Essays and Studies by Members of the English Association* 28: 7–12; repr. in: Andrew George Watson (ed.). 1985. *Books, Collectors and Libraries: Studies in the Medieval Heritage*. London: Hambledon. 3–8.

Ker, N. R. 1957. *Catalogue of Manuscripts Containing Anglo-Saxon*. Oxford: Clarendon; repr. with supplement 1990.

Ker, N. R. (ed.). 1963. *The Owl and the Nightingale. Reproduced in Facsimile from the Surviving Manuscripts Jesus College Oxford 29 and British Museum Cotton Caligula A.ix*. Early English Text Society OS 248. Oxford: Oxford University Press.

Ker, N. R. 1971. "The Handwriting of Archbishop Wulfstan". In: Peter Clemoes and Kathleen Hughes (eds.). *England before the Conquest: Studies in Primary Sources Presented to Dorothy Whitelock*. Cambridge: Cambridge University Press. 315–331; repr. in: Andrew George Watson (ed.). 1985. *Books, Collectors and Libraries: Studies in the Medieval Heritage*. London: Hambledon. 9–26.

Ker, N. R. 1976. "A Supplement to *Catalogue of Manuscripts Containing Anglo-Saxon*". *Anglo-Saxon England* 5: 121–131.

Keynes, Simon. 1985. "King Athelstan's Books". In: Michael Lapidge and Helmut Gneuss (eds.). *Learning and Literature in Anglo-Saxon England: Studies Presented to Peter Clemoes on the Occasion of His Sixty-Fifth Birthday*. Cambridge: Cambridge University Press. 143–201.

Keynes, Simon. 2014. "Appendix II: Archbishops and Bishops". In: Michael Lapidge, John Blair, Simon Keynes and Donald Scragg (eds.). *The Wiley Blackwell Encyclopedia of Anglo-Saxon England*. 2nd ed. Chichester: Wiley-Blackwell. 539-566.

Kilpiö, Matti. 1989. *Passive Constructions in Old English Translations from Latin: With Special Reference to the OE Bede and the Pastoral Care*. Mémoires de la Société Néo Philologique à Helsingfors 49. Helsinki: Société Néophilologique.

Kilpiö, Matti. 1993. "Syntactic and Semantic Properties of the Present Indicative Forms of the Verb *to Be* in Old English". In: Matti Rissanen, Merja Kytö and Minna Palander-Collin (eds.). *Early English in the Computer Age: Explorations through the Helsinki Corpus*. Topics in English Linguistics 11. Berlin: Mouton de Gruyter. 97–116.

Kilpiö, Matti. 1997. "On the Forms and Functions of the Verb *Be* from Old to Modern English". In: Matti Rissanen, Merja Kytö and Kirsi Heikkonen (eds.). *English in Transition: Corpus-Based Studies in Linguistic Variation and Genre Styles*. Topics in English Linguistics 23. Berlin/New York: Mouton de Gruyter. 87–120.

Kimmens, Andrew C. (ed.). 1979. *The Stowe Psalter*. Toronto: Published in association with the Centre for Medieval Studies, University of Toronto, by University of Toronto Press.

Kitson, Peter. 2002. "Topography, Dialect, and the Relation of Old English Psalter Glosses (I)". *English Studies* 83: 474–503.

Kolbe, Theodor. 1912. *Die Konjugation der Lindisfarner Evangelien: Ein Beitrag zur altenglischen Grammatik*. Bonner Studien zur englischen Philologie 5. Bonn: Hanstein.

Korhammer, Michael. 1980. "Mittelalterliche Konstruktionshilfen und altenglische Wortstellung". *Scriptorium* 34: 18–58.

Kornexl, Lucia (ed.). 1993. *Die* Regularis Concordia *und ihre altenglische Interlinearversion*. Münchener Universitätsschriften: Texte und Untersuchungen zur Englischen Philologie 17. München: Fink.

Koskenniemi, Inna. 1968. *Repetitive Word Pairs in Old and Middle English Prose: Expressions of the Type* Whole and Sound *and* Answered and Said, *and Other Parallel Constructions*. Annales Universitatis Turkuensis B.107. Turku: Turun Yliopisto.

Kotake, Tadashi. 2006a. "Aldred's Multiple Glosses: Is the Order Significant?". In: Michiko Ogura (ed.). *Textual and Contextual Studies in Medieval English*. Studies in English Medieval Language and Literature 13. Frankfurt am Main: Lang. 35–50.

Kotake, Tadashi. 2006b. "Aldred's Multiple Glosses to Latin *Gens*: One of His Intentions in Giving Multiple Glosses". *English Literature* (Waseda University) 19: 58–73.

Kotake, Tadashi. 2007. "*Don* in Old English Translations of the Gospels: A Syntactic and Semantic Analysis through Comparison with *Wyrcan*". In: Michiko Ogura (ed.). *Language Contact: Examined from Viewpoints of Language Teaching, Comparative Linguistics and Historical Linguistics*. Chiba: Graduate School of Humanities and Social Studies, Chiba University. 68–89.

Kotake, Tadashi. 2008a. "Differences in Element Order between *Lindisfarne* and *Rushworth Two*". In: Masachiyo Amano, Michiko Ogura and Masayuki Ohkado (eds.). *Historical Englishes in Varieties of Texts and Contexts: The Global COE Programme, International Conference 2007*. Studies in English Medieval Language and Literature 22. Frankfurt am Main: Lang. 63–77.

Kotake, Tadashi. 2008b. "Notes on the Relationship between Lindisfarne and Rushworth Two: A Lexical Analysis of *andswarian* and *andwyrdan*". *The Round Table* (Keio University) 22: 31–44.

Kotake, Tadashi. 2009. "The Trail of a Glossator's Activities: A Textual and Contextual Study of Farman's Activities in the Rushworth Gospels". Unpubl. PhD dissertation, Keio University.

Kotake, Tadashi. 2010. "Farman's Changing Syntax: A Linguistic and Palaeographical Survey". In: Osamu Imahayashi, Yoshiyuki Nakao and Michiko Ogura (eds.). *Aspects of the History of English Language and Literature: Selected Papers Read at SHELL 2009, Hiroshima*. Studies in English Medieval Language and Literature 25. Frankfurt am Main: Lang: 239–256.

Kotake, Tadashi. 2012. "Lindisfarne and Rushworth One Reconsidered". *Notes and Queries* 257: 14–19.

Kotake, Tadashi. 2013. "Gospel Glosses in Context: With Special Reference to Old English Scratched Glosses in London, BL, Additional 40000". In: Michio Hosaka, Michiko Ogura, Hironori Suzuki and Akinobu Tani (eds.). *Phases of the History of English: Selection of Papers Read at SHELL 2012*. Studies in English Medieval Language and Literature 42. Frankfurt am Main: Lang. 111–125.

Krapp, George Philip and Elliott van Kirk Dobbie (eds.). 1936. *The Exeter Book*. The Anglo-Saxon Poetic Records: A Collective Edition 3. New York, NY: Columbia University Press.

Kroch, Anthony. 1989. "Reflexes of Grammar in Patterns of Change". *Language Variation and Change* 1: 99–244.

Kroch, Anthony and Ann Taylor. 1997. "Verb Movement in Old and Middle English: Dialect Variation and Language Contact". In: Ans van Kemenade and Nigel Vincent (eds.). *Parameters of Morphosyntactic Change*. Cambridge: Cambridge University Press. 297–325.

Kuhn, Sherman M. 1947. "Synonyms in the Old English Bede". *Journal of English and Germanic Philology* 46: 168–176.

Labov, William. 2006. *The Social Stratification of English in New York City*. 2nd ed. Cambridge: Cambridge University Press.
Labov, William. 1994. *Principles of Linguistic Change*. Volume I: *Internal Factors*. Oxford: Blackwell.
Laing, Margaret. 1993. *Catalogue of Sources for a Linguistic Atlas of Early Medieval English*. Cambridge: Brewer.
Laing, Margaret. 2007. "*The Owl and the Nightingale*: Five New Readings and Further Notes". *Neuphilologische Mitteilungen* 108: 445–477.
Lapidge, Michael. 1982. "The Study of Latin Texts in Late Anglo-Saxon England: The Evidence of Latin Glosses". In: Nicholas Brooks (ed.). *Latin and the Vernacular Languages in Early Medieval Britain*. Leicester: Leicester University Press. 94–140.
Larrington, Carolyne. 1993. *A Store of Common Sense: Gnomic Theme and Style in Old Icelandic and Old English Wisdom Poetry*. Oxford: Clarendon.
Lass, Roger. 1997. *Historical Linguistics and Language Change*. Cambridge: Cambridge University Press.
Lass, Roger. 2004. "Ut custodiant litteras: Editions, Corpora and Witnesshood". In: Marina Dossena and Roger Lass (eds.). *Methods and Data in English Historical Dialectology*. Linguistic Insights 16. Bern: Lang. 21–48.
Lawrence-Mathers, Anne. 2003. *Manuscripts in Northumbria in the Eleventh and Twelfth Centuries*. Woodbridge: Brewer.
Lea, Elisabeth Mary. 1894. "The Language of the Northumbrian Gloss to the Gospel of St. Mark". *Anglia* 16: 62–206.
Lendinara, Patrizia. 1992. "Glosses and Glossaries: The Glossator's Choice". In: René Derolez (ed.). *Anglo-Saxon Glossography: Papers Read at the International Conference, Brussels, 8 and 9 September 1986*. Brussels: Koninklijke Academie voor Wetenschappen, Letteren en Schone Kunsten van België. 207–243.
Lendinara, Patrizia. 1997. "The Kentish Laws". In: John Hines (ed.). *The Anglo-Saxons from the Migration Period to the Eighth Century: An Ethnographic Perspective*. Rochester, NY: Boydell. 211–243.
Lendinara, Patrizia. 1999a. "Il glossario del ms. Oxford, Bodleian Library, Bodley 163". In: Patrizia Lendinara. *Anglo-Saxon Glosses and Glossaries*. Rev. repr. Variorum Collected Studies Series 622. Aldershot: Ashgate. 329–355; originally printed in: *Romanobarbarica* 10 (1988-1989): 485–516.
Lendinara, Patrizia. 1999b. "Glosses and Glossaries: The Glossator's Choice". In: Patrizia Lendinara. *Anglo-Saxon Glosses and Glossaries*. Rev. repr. Variorum Collected Studies Series 622. Aldershot: Ashgate. 27–70; originally printed in: René Derolez (ed.). 1992. *Anglo-Saxon Glossography: Papers Read at the International Conference Brussels 8 and 9 September 1986*. Brussels: Koninklijke Academie voor Wetenschappen, Letteren en Schone Kunsten van België. 207–243.
Lendinara, Patrizia. 2010. "Una omissione ex homoeoteleuto nei Vangeli di Lindisfarne". In: Corrado Bologna, Mira Mocan and Paolo Vaciago (eds.). *'Percepta rependere dona': Miscellanea di filologia e linguistica in onore di Anna Maria Luiselli Fadda*. Florence: Olschki. 163–175.
Lenker, Ursula. 1997. *Die westsächsische Evangelienversion und die Perikopenordnungen im angelsächsischen England*. Münchener Universitätsschriften: Texte und Untersuchungen zur Englischen Philologie 20. Munich: Fink.

Lewis, Charlton T. and Charles Short (eds.). 1879. *A Latin Dictionary Founded on Andrew's Edition of Freund's Latin Dictionary*. Oxford: Clarendon.

Lindelöf, Uno. 1897. *Glossar zur altnorthumbrischen Evangelienübersetzung in der Rushworth-Handschrift (die sogenannte Glosse Rushworth 2)*. Acta Societatis Scientiarum Fennicae XXII, 5. Helsingfors: ex Officina typographica Societatis litterariae Fennicae.

Lindelöf, Uno. 1901. *Die südnorthumbrische Mundart des 10. Jahrhunderts: Die Sprache der sog. Glosse Rushworth 2*. Bonn: Hanstein.

Lindsay, W. M. (ed.). 1911. *Isidori Hispalensis Episcopi Etymologiarum sive originum, libri XX*. 2 vols. Oxford Classical Texts. Oxford: Clarendon.

Lindsay, W. M. (ed.). 1921. *The Corpus Glossary*. Cambridge: Cambridge University Press.

Lindsay, W. M. 1922. *Palaeographia latina*. Part I. St Andrews University Publications 14. London: Oxford University Press.

Lindsay, W. M. (ed.) 1959. *The Old English Prudentius Glosses at Boulogne-sur-Mer*. Stanford; CA: Stanford University Press.

Liuzza, R. M. (ed.). 1994–2000. *The Old English Version of the Gospels*. 2 vols. Early English Text Society OS 304, 314. Oxford: Oxford University Press.

Liuzza, R. M. and A. N. Doane (eds.). 1995. *Anglo-Saxon Manuscripts in Microfiche Facsimile*. Volume III: *Anglo-Saxon Gospels*. Medieval & Renaissance Texts & Studies 144. Binghamton, NY: Medieval & Renaissance Texts & Studies.

Loewe, Raphael. 1969. "The Medieval History of the Latin Vulgate". In: Geoffrey W. H. Lampe (ed.). *The Cambridge History of the Bible*. Vol. II. Cambridge: Cambridge University Press. 102–154.

Lowe, E. A. 1928. "More Facts about Our Oldest Latin Manuscripts". *The Classical Quarterly* 22: 43–62; repr. in: Ludwig Bieler (ed.). 1972. *Palaeographical Papers, 1907–1965*. Volume I. Oxford: Clarendon. 251–274.

Lowe, E. A., see *CLA*.

Lutz, Angelika. 2009. "Celtic Influence on Old English and West Germanic". *English Language and Linguistics* 13: 227–249.

MacGillivray, Hugh S. 1902. *The Influence of Christianity on the Vocabulary of Old English*. Halle an der Saale: Niemeyer.

Marsden, Richard. 1999. "The Gospels of St Augustine". In: Richard Gameson (ed.). *St Augustine and the Conversion of England*. Stroud: Sutton. 285–312.

Marsden, Richard and E. Ann Matter (eds.). 2012. *The New Cambridge History of the Bible*. Volume II: *From 600 to 1450*. Cambridge: Cambridge University Press.

Martín Arista, Javier. 2012. "The Old English Prefix *ge-*: A Panchronic Reappraisal". *Australian Journal of Linguistics* 32: 411–433.

McAlister, R. A. S. 1913. "The Colophon in the Lindisfarne Gospels". In: E. C. Quiggin (ed.). *Essays and Studies Presented to Sir William Ridgeway*. Cambridge: Cambridge University Press. 299–305.

McGurk, Patrick. 1961. *Latin Gospel Books from A.D. 400 to A.D. 800*. Paris/Brussels: Éditions Érasme.

McGurk, Patrick. 1990. "The Gospel Text". In: Peter Fox (ed.). *The Book of Kells: MS 58, Trinity College Library, Dublin*. Luzern: Faksimile-Verlag. 59–152.

McIntosh, Angus. 1989. "Present Indicative Plural Forms in the Later Middle English of the North Midlands". In: Angus McIntosh and Margaret Laing (eds.). *Middle English Dialectology: Essays on Some Principles and Problems*. Aberdeen: Aberdeen University Press. 116–122.

McNally, Robert E. 1958. "The 'Tres Linguae Sacrae' in Early Irish Bible Exegesis". *Theological Studies* 19: 395–403.

Meaney, Audrey L. 1984. "Variant Versions of Old English Medical Remedies and the Compilation of Bald's *Leechbook*". *Anglo-Saxon England* 13: 235–268.

Meehan, Bernard. 1998. "Notes on the Preliminary Texts and Continuations to Symeon of Durham's *Libellus de exordio*". In: David Rollason (ed.). *Symeon of Durham: Historian of Durham and the North*. Stamford: Tyas. 128–137.

Menner, Robert J. 1934. "*Farman Vindicatus*: The Linguistic Value of Rushworth I". *Anglia* 58: 1–27.

Mertens-Fonck, Paule. 1960. *A Glossary of the Vespasian Psalter and Hymns (Brit. Mus. Ms. Cotton Vespasian A 1), with a Latin-Mercian Index*. Volume I: *The Verb*. Paris: Société d'Édition "Les Belles Lettres".

Miles, George. 1898. *The Bishops of Lindisfarne, Hexham, Chester-le-Street, and Durham, A.D. 635–1020*. London: Gardner, Darton & Co.

Milfull, Inge B. 1996. *The Hymns of the Anglo-Saxon Church*. Cambridge Studies in Anglo-Saxon England 17. Cambridge: Cambridge University Press.

Millar, Robert McColl. 2000. *System Collapse, System Rebirth: The Demonstrative Systems of English 900–1350 and the Birth of the Definite Article*. Oxford/Bern: Lang.

Millar, Robert McColl. 2012. *English Historical Sociolinguistics*. Edinburgh: Edinburgh University Press.

Miller, D. Gary. 2010. *Language Change and Linguistic Theory*. 2 vols. Oxford: Oxford University Press.

Miller, D. Gary. 2012. *External Influences on English: From Its Beginnings to the Renaissance*. Oxford: Oxford University Press.

Miller, Thomas (ed.). 1890–1898. *The Old English Version of Bede's Ecclesiastical History of the English People*. 4 vols. Early English Text Society OS 95, 96, 110, 111. London: Trübner.

Mitchell, Bruce. 1967. "An Old English Syntactical Reverie". *Neuphilologische Mitteilungen* 68: 139–149.

Mitchell, Bruce. 1985. *Old English Syntax*. 2 vols. Oxford: Clarendon.

Mitchell, Bruce and Fred C. Robinson. 2012. *A Guide to Old English*. 8th ed. Oxford: Wiley-Blackwell.

Montgomery, Michael. 1994. "The Evolution of Verb Concord in Scots". In: Alexander Fenton and Donald McDonald (eds.). *Studies in Scots and Gaelic: Proceedings of the Third International Conference on the Languages of Scotland*. Edinburgh: Canongate. 81–95.

Morrell, Minnie C. 1965. *A Manual of Old English Biblical Materials*. Knoxville, TN: University of Tennessee Press.

Morris, Richard (ed.). 1872. *An Old English Miscellany, Containing a Bestiary, Kentish Sermons, Proverbs of Alfred, Religious Poems of the Thirteenth Century*. Early English Texts Society OS 49. London: Trübner.

Morris, Richard (ed. and trans.). 1874. *The Blickling Homilies of the 10th Century*. Part I. Early English Text Society OS 58. London: Trübner.

Mossé, Ferdinand. 1956. *Manuel de la langue gotique*. 2nd ed. Paris: Aubier.

Muir, Bernard (ed.). 1994. *The Exeter Anthology of Old English Poetry: An Edition of Exeter Dean and Chapter MS 3501*. 2 vols. Exeter: University of Exeter Press.

Murray, James A. H. 1875. "The Anglo-Saxon Gospels". *The Athenæum* April 3: 451–453.

Mynors, R. A. B. 1939. *Durham Cathedral Manuscripts to the End of the Twelfth Century: Ten Plates in Colour and Forty-Seven in Monochrome*. Oxford: Oxford University Press.

Mustanoja, Tauno F. 1960. *A Middle English Syntax*. Helsinki: Société Néophilologique.
Nagucka, Ruta. 1997. "Glossal Translation in the Lindisfarne Gospel according to Saint Matthew". In: Jacek Fisiak (ed.). *Festschrift for Roger Lass on His Sixtieth Birthday. Studia Anglica Posnaniensia* 31: 179–201.
Napier, Arthur S. (ed.). 1900. *Old English Glosses, Chiefly Unpublished*. Oxford: Clarendon.
Nees, L. 2003. "Reading Aldred's Colophon for the Lindisfarne Gospels". *Speculum* 78: 333–377.
Nelson, Marie. 1981. "'Is' and 'Ought' in the Exeter Book Maxims". *Southern Folklore Quarterly* 45: 109–121.
Nevalainen, Terttu and Helena Raumolin-Brunberg. 2003. *Historical Linguistics: Language Change in Tudor and Stuart England*. Longman Linguistics Library. London: Pearson Education.
Newton, Francis L., Francis L. Newton, Jr. and Christopher R. J. Scheirer. 2013. "Domiciling the Evangelists in Anglo-Saxon England: A Fresh Reading of Aldred's Colophon in the 'Lindisfarne Gospels'". *Anglo-Saxon England* 41: 101–144.
ODNB = *Oxford Dictionary of National Biography*. May 2008. Online. Ed. David Cannadine. Oxford: Oxford University Press. <http://www.oxforddnb.com>.
OED = *The Oxford English Dictionary*. 2000–. 3rd ed. online. Oxford: Oxford University Press. <http://www.oed.com/>.
Ogura, Michiko. 2002. *Verbs of Motion in Medieval English*. Cambridge: Brewer.
Ogura, Michiko. 2006. "Element Order Varies: Samples from Old English Psalter Glosses". In: Michiko Ogura (ed.). *Textual and Contextual Studies in Medieval English*. Frankfurt am Main. Lang: 105–126.
Okasha, Elisabeth. 1971. *Hand-List of Anglo-Saxon Non-Runic Inscriptions*. Cambridge: Cambridge University Press.
Oliphant, Robert T. (ed.). 1966. *The Harley Latin-Old English Glossary*. Paris: Mouton & Co.
Orel, Vladimir. 2003. *A Handbook of Germanic Etymology*. Leiden: Brill.
O'Sullivan, William. 1994. "The Palaeographical Background to the Book of Kells". In: Felicity O'Mahony (ed.). *The Book of Kells*. Aldershot: Scolar. 175–182.
Page, Raymond I. 1992. "On the Feasibility of a Corpus of Anglo-Saxon Glosses: The View from the Library". In: Rene Derolez (ed.). *Anglo-Saxon Glossography: Papers Read at the International Conference Held in the Koninklijke Academie voor Wetenschappen, Letteren en Schone Kunsten van België, Brussels, 8 and 9 September 1986*. Brussels: Belgian Academy of Science. 77–95.
Page, Raymond I. 1999. *An Introduction to English Runes*. Woodbridge: Boydell & Brewer.
Palmatier, R. A. 1969. *A Descriptive Syntax of the Ormulum*. The Hague: Mouton.
Parkes, Malcolm B. 1991. *Scribes, Scripts and Readers: Studies in the Communication, Presentation and Dissemination of Medieval Texts*. London: Hambledon.
Parkes, Malcolm B. 1997. "*Rædan, Areccan, Smeagan*: How the Anglo-Saxons Read". *Anglo-Saxon England* 26: 1–22.
Parkes, Malcolm B. 2008. *Their Hands before Our Eyes: A Closer Look at Scribes*. Aldershot: Ashgate.
Pettit, Edward (ed. and trans.). 2001. *Anglo-Saxon Remedies, Charms, and Prayers from British Library MS Harley 585: The Lacnunga*. 2 vols. Lewiston, NY: Mellen.
Pfaff, Richard W. (ed.). 1995. *The Liturgical Books of Anglo-Saxon England*. Old English Newsletter Subsidia 23. Kalamazoo, MI: Medieval Institute Publications, Western Michigan University.

Pfaff, Richard W. 2012. "Liturgical Books". In: Richard Gameson (ed.). *The Cambridge History of the Book in Britain*. Volume I: *c. 400–1100*. Cambridge: Cambridge University Press. 449–459.
Pheifer, Joseph D. (ed.). 1974. *Old English Glosses in the Épinal-Erfurt Glossary*. Oxford: Clarendon.
Pietsch, Lukas. 2005. "'Some Do and Some Doesn't': Verbal Concord Variation in the North of the British Isles". In: Berd Kortmann, Tanya Herrmann, Lukas Pietsch and Susanne Wagner (eds.). *A Comparative Grammar of British English Dialects: Agreement, Gender, Relative Clauses*. Berlin: Mouton de Gruyter. 125–209.
Pintzuk, Susan and Leendert Plug. 2001. *The York-Helsinki Parsed Corpus of Old English Poetry*. Department of Linguistics, University of York. <http://www-users.york.ac.uk/~lang18/pcorpus.html>.
Plummer, Charles (ed.). 1892–99. *Two of the Saxon Chronicles Parallel: With Supplementary Extracts from the Others*. 2 vols. Oxford: Clarendon.
Pogatscher, Alois. 1901. "Unausgedrücktes Subjekt im Altenglischen". *Anglia* 23: 261–301.
Polanyi, Michael. 1956. *Personal Knowledge: Towards a Post-Critical Philosophy*. London: Routledge/Kegan Paul.
Pons-Sanz, Sara M. 2000. *Analysis of the Scandinavian Loanwords in the Aldredian Glosses to the Lindisfarne Gospel*. Studies in English Language and Linguistics: Monographs 9. Valencia: Department of English and German Philology, University of Valencia.
Pons-Sanz, Sara M. 2001. "Aldredian Glosses to Proper Names in the *Lindisfarne Gospels*". *Anglia* 119: 173–192.
Pons-Sanz, Sara M. 2004. "A Sociolinguistic Approach to the Norse-Derived Words in the Glosses to the Lindisfarne and Rushworth Gospels". In: Christian J. Kay, Carole A. Hough and Irené Wotherspoon (eds.). *New Perspectives on English Historical Linguistics: Selected Papers from 12 ICEHL, Glasgow, 21–26 August 2002*. Volume II: *Lexis and Transmission*. Current Issues in Linguistic Theory 252. Amsterdam: Benjamins. 177–192.
Pons-Sanz, Sara M. 2013. *The Lexical Effects of Anglo-Scandinavian Linguistic Contact on Old English*. Studies in the Early Middle Ages 1. Turnhout: Brepols.
Porter, David W. (ed.). 2011. *The Antwerp-London Glossaries: The Latin and Latin-Old English Vocabularies from Antwerp, Museum Plantin-Moretus 16.2, London, British Library Add. 32246*. Volume I: *Texts and Indexes*. Publications of the Dictionary of Old English 8. Toronto: Pontifical Institute of Mediaeval Studies.
Pulsiano, Phillip (ed.). 2001. *Old English Glossed Psalters*. Volume I: *Psalms 1–50*. Toronto Old English Series 11. Toronto: University of Toronto Press.
Ramat, Paolo. 1992. "Thoughts on Degrammaticalization". *Linguistics* 30: 549–560.
Rapp, C. 2007. "Holy Texts, Holy Men, and Holy Scribes: Aspects of Scriptural Holiness in Late Antiquity". In: William E. Klingshirn and Linda Safran (eds.). *The Early Christian Book*. Washington, DC: Catholic University of America Press. 194–222.
Roberts, Jane. 2005. *A Guide to Scripts Used in English Writings up to 1500*. London: British Library.
Roberts, Jane. 2006. "Aldred Signs Off from Glossing the Lindisfarne Gospels". In: Alexander R. Rumble (ed.). *Writing and Texts in Anglo-Saxon England*. Publications of the Manchester Centre for Anglo-Saxon Studies 5. Woodbridge: Boydell & Brewer. 28–43.
Roberts, Jane. 2011. "Some Psalter Glosses in Their Immediate Context". In: Leo Carruthers, Raeleen Chai-Elsholz and Tatjana Silec (eds.). *Palimpsests and the Literary Imagination of Medieval England: Collected Essays*. New York, NY: Palgrave Macmillan. 61–78.

Roberts, Jane, Christian Kay and Lynne Grundy. 1995. *A Thesaurus of Old English*. 2 vols. King's College London Medieval Studies 11. London: King's College, Centre for Late Antique and Medieval Studies.

Robinson, Fred C. 1968. "The Significance of Names in Old English Literature". *Anglia* 86: 14–58.

Robinson, Fred C. 1973. "Syntactical Glosses in Latin Manuscripts of Anglo-Saxon Provenance". *Speculum* 48: 443–475.

Robinson, P. R. 1978. "Self-Contained Units in Composite Manuscripts of the Anglo-Saxon Period". *Anglo-Saxon England* 7: 231–238.

Robinson, P. R. 1980. "The 'Booklet': A Self-Contained Unit in Composite Manuscripts". In: A. Gruys and J. P. Gumbert (eds.). *Codicologica*. Volume III: *Essais typologique*. Litterae Textuales. Leiden: Brill. 46–69.

Rodríguez Ledesma, Mª Nieves. 2013. "The Northern Subject Rule in First Person Singular Contexts in Fourteenth-Fifteenth-Century Scots". *Folia Linguistica Historica* 34: 149–172.

Rollason, David. 1989. "St Cuthbert and Wessex: The Evidence of Cambridge, Corpus Christi College MS 183". In: Gerald Bonner, David Rollason, Clare Stancliffe (eds.). *St Cuthbert, His Cult and His Community to A.D. 1200*. Woodbridge: Boydell. 413–424.

Rollason, David. 1992. "Symeon of Durham and the Community of Durham in the Eleventh Century". In: Carola Hicks (ed.). *England in the Eleventh Century: Proceedings of the 1990 Harlaxton Symposium*. Stamford: Watkins. 183–198.

Rollason, David. (ed. and trans.). 2000. *Symeon of Durham: Libellus de exordio atque procursu istius, hoc est Dunelmensis ecclesie*. Oxford: Clarendon.

Rosenthal, Jane E. 2011. "The Image in the Arenberg Gospels of Christ Beginning to Be 'What He Was Not'". In: Colum Hourihane (ed.). *Insular and Anglo-Saxon Art and Thought in the Early Medieval Period*. The Index of Christian Art: Occasional Papers 13. Princeton, NJ: Dept. of Art and Archaeology, Princeton University. 229–246.

Ross, Alan S. C. 1932a. "The Errors in the Old English Gloss to the Lindisfarne Gospels". *Review of English Studies* 8: 385–394.

Ross, Alan S. C. 1932b. "Notes on Some Words in the *Lindisfarne Gospels*". *The Modern Language Review* 27: 451–453.

Ross, Alan S. C. 1933a. "Northumbrian *forwost*". *Acta Philologica Scandinavica* 8: 146–149.

Ross, Alan S. C. 1933b. "Notes on the Method of Glossing Employed in the Lindisfarne Gospels". *Transactions of the Philological Society*: 108–119.

Ross, Alan S. C. 1934. "The Origins of the *s*-Endings of the Present-Indicative in English". *Journal of English and Germanic Philology* 33: 68–73.

Ross, Alan S. C. 1936. "Sex and Gender in the Lindisfarne Gospels". *Journal of English and Germanic Philology* 35: 321–330.

Ross, Alan S. C. 1937. *Studies in the Accidence of the Lindisfarne Gospels*. Leeds School of English Language Texts and Monographs 2. Leeds: University of Leeds.

Ross, Alan S. C. 1940. "Four Examples of Norse Influence in the Old English Gloss to the Lindisfarne Gospels". *Transactions of the Philological Society* 39: 39–52.

Ross, Alan S. C. 1943. "Prolegomena to an Edition of the Old English Gloss to the *Lindisfarne Gospels*". *Journal of English and Germanic Philology* 42: 309–321.

Ross, Alan S. C. 1955. "*Runica manuscripta: The English Tradition* by R. Derolez". *Modern Language Review* 50: 516.

Ross, Alan S. C. 1958. "On the 'Text' of the Anglo-Saxon Gloss to the Lindisfarne Gospels". *Journal of Theological Studies* 9: 38–52.

Ross, Alan S. C. 1960. "Standard Paradigms". In: Kendrick et al. (eds.). 1960. Book II. 37–42.

Ross, Alan S. C. 1961. "Aldrediana II: Observations upon Certain Words of the Lindisfarne Gloss". *Zeitschrift für vergleichende Sprachforschung auf dem Gebiete der indogermanischen Sprachen* 77: 258–295.

Ross, Alan S. C. 1968. "Aldrediana XVII: Ritual Supplement". *English Philological Studies* 11: 1–43.

Ross, Alan S. C. 1969. "A Connection between Bede and the Anglo-Saxon Gloss to the Lindisfarne Gospels". *Journal of Theological Studies* 20: 482–494.

Ross, Alan S. C. 1970. "Conservatism in the Anglo-Saxon Gloss to the Durham Ritual". *Notes and Queries* 215: 363–366.

Ross, Alan S. C. 1973. "Supplementary Note to 'A Connection between Bede and the Anglo-Saxon Gloss to the Lindisfarne Gospels?'". *The Journal of Theological Studies* 24: 519–521.

Ross, Alan S. C. 1977. "Notes on the Accidence of Ru^2". *Neuphilologische Mitteilungen* 78: 300–308.

Ross, Alan S. C. 1978. "A Point of Comparison between Aldred's Two Glosses". *Notes and Queries* 223: 197–199.

Ross, Alan S. C. 1979. "Lindisfarne and Rushworth One". *Notes and Queries* 224: 194–198.

Ross, Alan S. C. 1981. "The Use of Other Latin Manuscripts by the Glossators of the Lindisfarne and Rushworth Gospels". *Notes and Queries* 226: 6–11.

Ross, Alan S. C. 1982. "Rare Words in Old Northumbrian". *Notes and Queries* 227: 196–198.

Ross, Alan S. C. and Ann Squires. 1980. "The Multiple, Altered and Alternative Glosses of the Lindisfarne and Rushworth Gospels and the Durham Ritual". *Notes and Queries* 225: 489–495.

Ross, Alan S. C. and E. G. Stanley. 1960. "Index Verborum Glossematicus". In: Kendrick et al. (eds.). 1960. Book II. 45–176.

Ross, Alan S. C. and E. G. Stanley. 1969. "Glossary to Aldred's Gloss". In: T. J. Brown (ed.). *The Durham Ritual: A Southern English Collectar of the Tenth Century with Northumbrian Additions, Durham Cathedral Library A.IV.19.* Early English Manuscripts in Facsimile 16. Copenhagen: Rosenkilde & Bagger. 53–92.

Ross, Alan S. C., E. G. Stanley, and T. J. Brown. 1960. "Some Observations on the Gloss and the Glossator". In: Kendrick et al. (eds.). 1960. Book II. 5–33.

Rumble, Alexander R. 2009. "The Construction and Writing of Anglo-Saxon Manuscripts". In: Gale R. Owen-Crocker (ed.). *Working with Anglo-Saxon Manuscripts*. Exeter: University of Exeter Press. 29–59.

Rusche, Philip G. 1994. "Dry-Point Glosses to Aldhelm's *De laudibus virginitatis* in Beinecke 401". *Anglo-Saxon England* 23: 195–213.

Rusche, Philip G. (ed.). 1996. "The Cleopatra Glossaries". Unpubl. PhD dissertation, Yale University.

Rusche, Philip G. 2005. "Isidore's *Etymologiae* and the Canterbury Aldhelm Scholia". *Journal of English and Germanic Philology* 104: 437–456.

Rusche, Philip G. Forthcoming. *Aldhelmi Malmesbiriensis Carmen de virginitate cum glossa latina atque anglosaxonica.*

Rushforth, Rebecca. 2012. "English Caroline Minuscule". In: Richard Gameson (ed.). *The Cambridge History of the Book in Britain*. Volume I: *c. 400–1100*. Cambridge: Cambridge University Press. 197–210.

Rusten, Kristian A. 2013. "Empty Referential Subjects in Old English Prose: A Quantitative Analysis". *English Studies* 94: 970–992.

Rusten, Kristian A. 2015. "A Quantitative Study of Empty Referential Subjects in Old English Prose and Poetry". *Transactions of the Philological Society* 113: 53–75.

Saenger, Paul. 1997. *Space between Words: The Origins of Silent Reading*. Figurae: Reading Medieval Culture. Stanford, CA: Stanford University Press.

Samuels, M. L. 1989a. "Some Applications of Middle English Dialectology". In: Margaret Laing (ed.). *Middle English Dialectology: Papers on Some Principles and Problems by Angus McIntosh, M. L. Samuels and Margaret Laing*. Aberdeen: Aberdeen University Press. 64–80.

Samuels, M. L. 1989b. "Chaucerian Final *-e*". In: Jeremy J. Smith (ed.). *The English of Chaucer and His Contemporaries: Papers by M. L. Samuels and J. J. Smith*. Aberdeen: Aberdeen University Press.7–12.

Sankoff, Gillian. 2006. "Age: Apparent Time and Real Time". In: Keith Brown (ed.). *Encyclopedia of Language and Linguistics*. Volume I: *A–Bil*. 2nd ed. Amsterdam: Elsevier. 110–116.

Sawyer, Peter H. 1968. *Anglo-Saxon Charters: An Annotated List and Bibliography*. London: Royal Historical Society.

Schabram, Hans. 1965. *Superbia: Studien zum altenglischen Wortschatz*. Volume I: *Die dialektale und zeitliche Verbreitung des Wortguts*. Munich: Fink.

Schulte, Ernst. 1903. *Untersuchung der Beziehung der altenglischen Matthäusglosse im Rushworth-Manuskript zu dem lateinischen Text der Handschrift*. Bonn: Georgi.

Schumacher, Stefan. 2007. "Die Deutschen und die Nachbarstämme: Lexikalische und strukturelle Sprachkontaktphänomene entlang der keltisch-germanischen Übergangszone". In: Hans Hablitzel and David Stifter (eds.), unter redaktioneller Mitarbeit von Hannes Tauber. *Johann Kaspar Zeuß im kultur- und sprachwissenschaftlichen Kontext (19. bis 21. Jahrhundert), Kronach 21.7.–23.7.2006*. Keltische Forschungen 2. Wien: Praesens. 167–207.

Scragg, Donald G. 1970. "Initial *h* in Old English". *Anglia* 88: 165–196.

Seebold, Elmar. 1970. *Vergleichendes und etymologisches Wörterbuch der germanischen starken Verben*. Den Haag: Mouton & Co.

Seebold, Elmar. 1974. "Die ae. Entsprechungen von Lat. *sapiens* und *prudens*: Eine Untersuchung über die mundartliche Gliederung der ae. Literatur". *Anglia* 92: 291–333.

Shippey, T. A. 1976. *Poems of Wisdom and Learning in Old English*. Cambridge: Brewer.

Simpson, Luisella. 1989. "The King Alfred/St Cuthbert Episode in the *Historia de sancto Cuthberto*: Its Significance for Mid-Tenth-Century English History". In: Gerald Bonner, David Rollason, Clare Stancliffe (eds.). *St Cuthbert, His Cult and His Community to A.D. 1200*. Woodbridge: Boydell. 397–411.

Sisam, Kenneth. 2004. "Skeat, Walter William (1835–1912)". In: *Oxford Dictionary of National Biography*. Rev. by Charlotte Brewer. <http://dx.doi.org/10.1093/ref:odnb/36116>.

Skeat, Walter W. (ed.). 1871–1887. *The Holy Gospels in Anglo-Saxon, Northumbrian, and Old Mercian Versions*. 4 vols. Cambridge: Cambridge University Press [Mark (1871), Luke (1874), John (1878), Matthew (1887)].

Smith, A. H. 1956. *English Place-Name Elements*. 2 vols. English Place-Name Society 25, 26. Cambridge: Cambridge University Press.

Smith, A. H. (ed.). 1978. *Three Northumbrian Poems*. Exeter: Short Run/London: Methuen.

Smith, Jeremy. 2000. "Standard Language in Early Middle English?" In: Irma Taavitsainen, Terttu Nevalainen, Päivi Pahta and Matti Rissanen (eds.). *Placing Middle English in Context*. Berlin: Mouton de Gruyter. 125–141.

Souter, Alexander. 1949. *A Glossary of Later Latin to 600 A.D.* Oxford: Clarendon.

South, T. Johnson (ed.). 2002. *Historia de sancto Cuthberto: A History of St Cuthbert and a Record of His Patrimony*. Anglo-Saxon Texts 3. Cambridge: Brewer.

Sparks, Nicholas A. 2013. "An Insular Fragment of Bede's *Historia Ecclesiastica*". *Anglo-Saxon England* 42: 27–50.

Stanley, E. G. (ed.). 1960. *The Owl and the Nightingale*. London: Nelson.

Stanley, E. G. 1981. "The Date of *Beowulf*: Some Doubts and No Conclusions". In: Colin Chase (ed.). *The Dating of Beowulf*. Toronto Old English Series 6. Toronto: University of Toronto Press. 197–212; repr. in: E. G. Stanley. 1987. *A Collection of Papers with Emphasis on Old English Literature*. Publications of the Dictionary of Old English 3. Toronto: Pontifical Institute of Mediaeval Studies. 384–399.

Stanton, Robert. 2002. *The Culture of Translation in Anglo-Saxon England*. Woodbridge: Boydell & Brewer.

Stefanowitsch, Anatol and Stefan T. Gries. 2003. "Collostructions: Investigating the Interaction of Words and Constructions". *International Journal of Corpus Linguistics* 8: 209–243.

Stein, Dieter. 1986. "Old English Northumbrian Verb Inflection Revisited". In: Dieter Kastovsky and Aleksander Szwedek (eds.). *Linguistics across Historical and Geographical Boundaries; in Honour of Jacek Fisiak on the Occasion of His Fiftieth Birthday*. Volume I: *Linguistic Theory and Historical Linguistics*. Trends in Linguistics: Studies and Monographs 32. Berlin: Mouton de Gruyter. 637–650.

Stemberger, Günter. 1991. *Pharisäer, Sadduzäer, Essener*. Stuttgarter Bibelstudien 144. Stuttgart: Verlag Katholisches Bibelwerk.

Stevenson, Joseph, see Stevenson and Waring. 1854–1865.

Stevenson, Joseph (vol. 1) and George Waring (vols. 2–4). 1854–1865. *The Lindisfarne and Rushworth Gospels*. 4 vols. Publications of the Surtees Society 28, 39, 43, 48. Durham: Andrews.

Stevenson, William Henry 1912. "Yorkshire Surveys and Other Eleventh-Century Documents in the York Gospels". *The English Historical Review* 27: 1–25.

Stolz, Walther. 1908. *Der Vokalismus der betonten Silben in der altnordhumbrischen Interlinearversion der Lindisfarner Evangelien*. Part I: *Die ältesten Lautveränderungen*. Bonn: Georgi.

Stork, Nancy Porter. 1990. *Through a Gloss Darkly: Aldhelm's Riddles in the British Library MS Royal 12.C.xxiii*. Toronto: Pontifical Institute of Mediaeval Studies.

Suárez Gómez, Cristina. 2009. "On the Syntactic Differences between OE dialects: Evidence from the *Gospels*". *English Language and Linguistics* 13: 57–75.

Svenberg, Emmanuel. 1963. *Lunaria et zodiologica latina*. Studia graeca et latina Gothoburgensia 16. Stockholm: Almqvist & Wiksell.

Sweet, Henry (ed.). 1978. *A Second Anglo-Saxon Reader: Archaic and Dialectal*. 2nd ed. rev. by T. F. Hoad. Oxford: Clarendon.

Tamoto, Kenichi (ed.). 2013. The Macregol Gospels *or* The Rushworth Gospels*: Edition of the Latin Text with the Old English Interlinear Gloss Transcribed from Oxford Bodleian Library, MS Auctarium D. 2. 19*. Amsterdam: Benjamins.

Taylor, Ann. 2008. "Contact Effects of Translation: Distinguishing Two Types of Influence in Old English". *Language Variation and Change* 20: 341–365.

Taylor, Ann, Anthony Warner, Susan Pintzuk and Frank Beths. 2003. *The York-Toronto-Helsinki Parsed Corpus of Old English Prose (YCOE)*. Department of Linguistics, University of York. <http://www-users.york.ac.uk/~lang22/YcoeHome1.htm>.

Temple, E. 1976. *Anglo-Saxon Manuscripts*. London: Miller.

Thomason, Sarah G. and Terrence Kaufman. 1988. *Language Contact, Creolization, and Genetic Linguistics*. Berkeley, CA: University of California Press.

Thompson, E. M., see Bond, Thompson and Warner (eds.). 1873–1883.

Thompson, A. Hamilton and Uno Lindelöf (eds.). 1927. *Rituale Ecclesiae Dunelmensis: The Durham Collectar. A New and Revised Edition of the Latin Text with the Interlinear Anglo-Saxon Version*. Publications of the Surtees Society 140. Durham: Andrews.

Thomson, Rodney L. 1961. "Aldrediana V: Celtica". *English and Germanic Studies* 7: 20–36.

Toon, Thomas E. 1992. "Old English Dialects". In: Richard M. Hogg (ed.). *The Cambridge History of the English Language*. Volume I: *The Beginnings to 1066*. Cambridge: Cambridge University Press. 409–451.

Traube, Ludwig. 1907. *Nomina sacra: Versuch einer Geschichte der christlichen Kürzung*. Munich: Beck.

Travis, Catherine E. 2007. "Genre Effects on Subject Expression in Spanish: Priming in Narrative and Conversation". *Language Variation and Change* 19: 101–135.

Vainikka, Anne and Yonata Levy. 1999. "Empty Subjects in Finnish and Hebrew". *Natural Language and Linguistic Theory* 17: 613–671.

Verey, Christopher D. 1980. "Notes on the Gospel Text". In: Christopher D. Verey, T. Julian Brown and Elizabeth Coatsworth (eds.). *The Durham Gospels, Together with Fragments of a Gospel Book in Uncial, Durham, Cathedral Library, MS A.II.17*. Early English Manuscripts in Facsimile 20. Copenhagen: Rosenkilde & Bagger. 68–76.

Verey, Christopher D. 1989. "The Gospel Texts at Lindisfarne at the Time of St Cuthbert". In: Gerald Bonner, David Rollason, Clare Stancliffe (eds.). *St Cuthbert, His Cult and His Community to A.D. 1200*. Woodbridge: Boydell. 143–150.

Waite, Greg. 2014. "Translation Style, Lexical Systems, Dialect Vocabulary, and the Manuscript Transcription of the Old English Bede". *Medium Ævum* 83: 1–48.

Walkden, George. 2013. "Null subjects in Old English". *Language Variation and Change* 25: 155–178.

Walkden, George. 2014. *Syntactic Reconstruction and Proto-Germanic*. Oxford: Oxford University Press.

Waring, George, see Stevenson and Waring. 1854–1865.

Warner, G. F., see Bond, Thompson and Warner (eds.). 1873–1883.

Wallenberg, Joel, Anton Karl Ingason, Einar Freyr Sigurðsson and Eiríkur Rögnvaldsson. 2011. *Icelandic Parsed Historical Corpus (IcePaHC)*. Department of Linguistics, University of Iceland. <http://www.linguist.is/icelandic_treebank>.

Weinrich, William C. (trans. and ed.). 2011. *Ancient Christian Texts: Latin Commentaries on Revelation*. Downers Grove, IL: InterVarsity.

Wenisch, Franz. 1979. *Spezifisch anglisches Wortgut in den nordhumbrischen Interlinear-glossierungen des Lukasevangeliums*. Anglistische Forschungen 132. Heidelberg: Winter.

Wieland, Gernot. 1983. *The Latin Glosses on Arator and Prudentius in Cambridge University Library MS Gg.5.35*. Toronto: Pontifical Institute of Mediaeval Studies.

Wiesenekker, Evert. 1991. *Word be Worde, Andgit of Andgite: Translation Performance in the Old English Interlinear Glosses of the Vespasian, Regius and Lambeth Psalters*. Huizen: Bout & Zn.

Wischer, Ilse. 2010. "On the Use of *beon* and *wesan* in Old English". In: Ursula Lenker, Judith Huber and Robert Mailhammer (eds.). *English Historical Linguistics 2008: Selected Papers from the Fifteenth International Conference on English Historical Linguistics (ICEHL 15), Munich, 24–30 August 2008*. Volume I: *The History of English Verbal and Nominal Constructions*. Current Issues in Linguistic Theory 314. Amsterdam: Benjamins. 217–235.

Wojtyś, Anna. 2008. *Past Participle Marking in Mediaeval English*. Warsaw Studies in English Historical Linguistics 3. Warsaw: Institute of English Studies, University of Warsaw.

Wolfe, Don Marion (ed.). 1959. *Complete Prose Works of John Milton*. Volume II: *1643–1648*. New Haven, CT: Yale University Press.

Wordsworth, John and Henry Julian White (eds.). 1889–1898. *Nouum testamentum domini nostri Iesu Christi latine: Secundum editionem Sancti Hieronymi*. Part I: *Quattuor euangelia*. Oxford: Clarendon.

Wotke, Karl. 1894. *Sancti Eucherii Lugdunensis Opera Omnia*. Part I: *Formulae spiritalis intelligentiae*. Corpus Scriptorum Ecclesiasticorum Latinorum 31. Vienna and Prague: Tempsky/ Leipzig: Freitag.

Index

The abbreviation 'n' after a page number indicates that the item appears only in a footnote; when the item is also present in the main body of the text, only the page number is given. For the sake of consistency, when a manuscript is referred to by its general name (e.g. Rushworth, MacRegol or Birr Gospels) and shelfmark (e.g. Oxford, Bodleian Library, MS Auct. D.2.19), it can be found under its shelfmark.

www.ingramcontent.com/pod-product-compliance
Lightning Source LLC
Chambersburg PA
CBHW061341300426
44116CB00011B/1941
9783110635294